A Hundred Years of Republican Turkey

A HUNDRED YEARS OF REPUBLICAN TURKEY

A History in a Hundred Fragments

Edited by

Alp Yenen and Erik-Jan Zürcher

LEIDEN UNIVERSITY PRESS

Cover design: Andre Klijsen
Cover illustration: © Hans Theunissen, Ankara 2014.
Lay-out: Crius Group

ISBN 978 90 8728 410 7
e-ISBN 978 94 0060 455 1 (e-PDF)
https://doi.org//10.24415/9789087284107
NUR 686

Table of Contents

Fragments from a Century:
A History of Republican Turkey, 1923–2023

Alp Yenen
Erik-Jan Zürcher

29 October 2023 marks the centennial of the Republic of Turkey. The Republic, which emerged in 1923 as the successor of the defeated and partitioned Ottoman Empire after 600 years of existence across three continents, was the outcome of a process of nation-state formation that was triumphant for some and traumatic for others. As the longest-lasting secular republican regime in a region that is uniquely positioned between Europe and the Middle East, Turkey has remained the focus of international attention as a consequence of the hopes and fears it raises in the hearts and minds of contemporary observers.

In its hundred years of existence, Republican Turkey has undergone multiple political and social transformations. The post-Ottoman founding of Turkey under the auspices of the single-party regime of the Republican People's Party (*Cumhuriyet Halk Partisi*, CHP) in the interwar years was shaped by authoritarian efforts at nation-building through cultural reforms and modernisation projects that radically constructed a new revolutionary ethos commonly known as Kemalism and from which arose a personality cult surrounding President Mustafa Kemal Atatürk (1881–1938). At the end of the Second World War, Turkey's political system changed from a dictatorship to a democracy over a period of five years. The tumultuous decades of the Cold War opened the way for a more democratic and culturally diverse field in state-society relations, but rapid socio-economic developments and ideological radicalisation resulted in political instability, which in turn legitimised Turkey's endemic military tutelage over civilian-democratic affairs. Post-Cold War Turkey suffered from corruption and intensified identity politics that fanned the flames of a debilitating violent conflict between the state and Kurdish insurgents. The brief moment of political opening as well as economic growth that was attained under the Justice and Development Party (*Adalet ve Kalkınma Partisi*, AKP) in the 2000s, a period of time when a number of laws that bolstered citizens' rights were passed, ultimately proved to be a false promise. The AKP regime's impressive expansion of state services and infrastructure in terms of scale and scope prioritised quantity over quality, ultimately changing the face of Turkey. Contemporary Turkey is now afflicted by multiple problems that have arisen as a result of the authoritarianism, populism, economic mismanagement, and misled and misleading foreign policies that have been brought into being during the two decades of AKP rule.

This volume, the first of its kind, offers an exploration of a hundred years of Republican history through a hundred "fragments" in which scholars who are experts in their fields introduce and discuss historical sources related to a wide range of issues including politics, economics, society, culture, gender, and the arts. In doing so, this book not only delves into a truly multifaceted history of the country, but also allows readers to encounter the bygone voices and images of a past that is both captivating and critical for understanding Turkey's today and tomorrow.

A Fascination with Turkey: The Founding of the Republic

Proclaimed a century ago, the Republic of Turkey was the last of the new nation-states to appear on the map of Europe after the great continental empires had imploded in the aftermath of the First World War. At the same time, it was the first independent state to emerge from the ruins of the Ottoman Empire in the Middle East and the only country whose borders were, for the most part, not drawn or dictated by the European powers of the day.[1]

Even before the proclamation of the Republic on 29 October 1923, Turkey had acquired an exceptional reputation in both Europe and throughout the Muslim world. On the one hand, as a result of its victorious War of Independence (1919–1922), Turkey was the only country that had been defeated in the First World War to repudiate the vindictive terms of peace that had been imposed by the victorious Entente powers through the Treaty of Sèvres. Muslims, as well as the citizens of many oppressed nations in Asia and Africa, championed Mustafa Kemal Pasha and the Turkish National Struggle as the spearhead of a global anticolonial struggle.[2] By way of the Treaty of Lausanne, the international community recognised Turkey's independence and national borders and defined its minority regime that recognised only non-Muslim communities as such, for the most part in line with the demands made by the Turkish delegates.[3] On the other hand, when the Grand National Assembly of Turkey took the radical step of abolishing the monarchy—the six-hundred-year-old Ottoman sultanate—in

[1] For the period of chaos that erupted in the aftermath of the First World War, see Robert Gerwarth, *The Vanquished: Why the First World War Failed to End 1917–1923* (New York: Farrar, Straus and Giroux, 2016). Stanford J. Shaw's *From Empire to Republic: The Turkish War of National Liberation 1918–1923 – A Documentary Study*, 5 vols. (Ankara: Türk Tarih Kurumu Yayınları, 2000) provides a great deal of detail but largely reflects the views of the Turkish General Staff. For a new critical history of the Turkish War of Independence, see Ryan Gingeras, *Last Days of the Ottoman Empire, 1918–1922* (London: Allen Lane, 2022), and for an overview of the rise and fall of Muslim republics in the aftermath of the First World War, see Stefan Reichmuth, "Der Erste Weltkrieg und die muslimischen Republiken der Nachkriegszeit," *Geschichte und Gesellschaft* 40 (2014): 184–213.

[2] A global history of the Turkish War of Independence has yet to be written. For a transnational account of Turkish diplomacy during the War of Independence, see Carolin Liebisch-Gümüş and Alp Yenen, "Petitions, Propaganda, and Plots: Transnational Dynamics of Diplomacy During the Turkish War of Independence," *Journal of Balkan and Near Eastern Studies* 25, no. 2 (2023): 185–206. For vignettes of mutual expressions of solidarity with the Turkish National Struggle across Asia and Africa, see Hadiye Yılmaz, *Kurtuluş Savaşımız ve Asya-Afrika'nın Uyanışı Hâkimiyeti Milliye Yazılarıyla* (İstanbul: Kaynak Yayınları, 2007); Bilal N. Şimşir, *Doğunun Kahramanı Atatürk* (Ankara: Bilgi Yayınevi, 1999); and Orhan Koloğlu, *Gazi'nin Çağında İslam Dünyası* (İstanbul: Boyut Yayıncılık, 1994).

[3] For a comprehensive history of the Treaty of Lausanne, see the numerous blog posts and podcasts created by a wide range of scholars on The Lausanne Project's website: https://thelausanneproject.com/

November of 1922, Turkey became the only republican regime in the Balkans and Middle East at the time. Since then, the republican form of government has remained in place, which may make it easy to overlook the revolutionary nature of the abolition of the monarchy in 1922 and the proclamation of the Republic of Turkey a year later, whereas a century ago, that transition was quite a sensation in world politics. Even more controversial was the abolishment of the Ottoman caliphate in March 1924, five months after the proclamation of the Republic, which led to the disappointment of many of Mustafa Kemal's admirers across the Muslim world.[4]

It should come as no wonder then that the international public was intrigued by the entirely novel phenomenon of how a people, and a country, that had been perceived as "backward" and "Oriental" could successfully defend itself and then transform its system of governance into that of a "modern" republic. This international fascination with Turkey only increased when, in the following decade, the republican regime, utilising its flexible doctrine of Kemalism, made clear its intentions to Europeanise Turkey's institutions, legal system, and culture.[5] As Turkey underwent a series of transformations in the 1920s and 1930s, it sparked interest among the numerous facets of European public opinion. For communists, as well as for leftists in general, it was the first nation to successfully resist Western imperialism and implement a planned economy.[6] For liberals, particularly in France, the introduction of laicism held great appeal.[7] As for the right, particularly in Germany, the spectacle of a "*völkisch*" and militarist nation-state led by a strong leader who pushed through revisions of the peace treaties that had been imposed upon his country was a source of inspiration.[8]

[4] Cemil Aydın, *The Idea of the Muslim World: A Global Intellectual History* (Cambridge: Harvard University Press, 2017), 127–32.

[5] For a thorough overview of the transnational appeal of Kemalism in the interwar years, see Nathalie Clayer, Fabio Giomi, and Emmanuel Szurek, "Transnationalising Kemalism: A Refractive Relationship," in *Kemalism: Transnational Politics in the Post-Ottoman World*, eds. Nathalie Clayer, Fabio Giomi and Emmanuel Szurek (London: I.B. Tauris, 2019), 1–37. For more on the transnational appeal and international affairs of Kemalist Turkey in the Middle East, see Amit Bein, *Kemalist Turkey and the Middle East: International Relations in the Interwar Period* (Cambridge: Cambridge University Press, 2017). For a comparative history of Kemalism in relation to Italian Fascism and Russian Bolshevism, see Stefan Plaggenborg, *Ordnung und Gewalt: Kemalismus – Faschismus – Sozialismus* (Berlin: Walter de Gruyter, 2012).

[6] Vahram Ter-Matevosyan, "Turkish Transformation and the Soviet Union: Navigating Through the Soviet Historiography on Kemalism," *Middle Eastern Studies* 53, no. 2 (2017): 281–96.

[7] Remzi Çağatay Çakırlar, "Radikal Faktör: Tek Parti ve Kemalizm'in Oluşum Sürecinde Radikal Parti Etkileşimleri," in *Tek Parti Dönemini Yeniden Düşünmek: Devlet, Toplum ve Siyaset*, eds. Sevgi Adak and Alexandros Lamprou (İstanbul: Tarih Vakfı Yurt Yayınları, 2022), 287–322; Pınar Dost-Niyego, *Le Bon Dictateur: L'image de Mustafa Kemal Atatürk en France (1923-1938)* (İstanbul: Libra Yayınevi, 2014).

[8] Stefan Ihrig, *Atatürk in the Nazi Imagination* (Cambridge: The Belknap Press of Harvard University Press, 2014); Sabine Mangold-Will, *Begrenzte Freundschaft: Deutschland und die Türkei, 1918–1933* (Göttingen: Wallstein Verlag, 2013).

What Was New About the Republic? Continuity and Change after the Empire

The extent to which the "new Turkey" that emerged from the post-war chaos can truly be defined as a "new" state is, of course, open to debate. The fact that the new Turkey was now led by representatives who derived their legitimacy solely from reference to the "national will" and that power was exercised (de facto since 1920, de jure from 1923) through a revolutionary parliament established in the provincial capital of Angora/Ankara in the heart of Anatolia rather than wielded by the Sultan-Caliph in the great multicultural metropolis of Constantinople/İstanbul—a capital city for 1,600 years—was certainly a novelty. Ankara, the sizable Christian communities of which had largely perished during the war years, would be reconstructed to embody the new Turkish and Republican ethos of Turkey.[9]

Despite all of its radical breaks with the past, however, the new Turkey under the Kemalist single-party regime of the CHP was a continuation of the "Young Turk" Committee of Union and Progress (*İttihad ve Terakki Cemiyeti*, CUP) that had ruled over the Ottoman Empire as a single-party government from its seizure of power in a coup d'état in 1913 until its military defeat in 1918.[10] The War of Independence was initiated as part of the CUP's wartime contingency plans for a post-war resistance movement of which Mustafa Kemal, a former CUP member, ultimately took over leadership, and soon afterwards he ousted CUP loyalists while co-opting other Unionist cadres.[11] As such, the armed struggle against the imposition of the Treaty of Sèvres was in fact won by the remnants of the regular Ottoman army under the command of Unionist officers who had acquired experience in the Balkan Wars and the First World War. The Republic of Turkey thus inherited far more from the Ottoman Empire than any of the other successor states that came into being in the Balkans and the Middle East,[12] as the new regime in Ankara maintained the central, provincial, and local bureaucracy

---

[9] Alev Çınar, "State Building as an Urban Experience: The Making of Ankara," in *Power and Architecture: The Construction of Capitals and the Politics of Space*, ed. Michael Minkenberg (New York: Berghahn Books, 2014), 227–60.

[10] For more on the nature of the CUP's single-party regime, see Erik-Jan Zürcher, "Young Turk Governance in the Ottoman Empire During the First World War," *Middle Eastern Studies* 55, no. 6 (2019): 897–913 and Erol Ülker, "İttihatçı Tek-Parti Rejimi Kurulurken Hizipler, Seçimler, Boykot," *Mülkiye Dergisi* 45, no. 4 (2021): 940–62. For the single-party regime under Atatürk, see Ryan Gingeras, *Eternal Dawn: Turkey in the Age of Ataturk* (Oxford: Oxford University Press, 2019).

[11] For more on the continuity and competition between the Unionists and Kemalists during the War of Independence, see Erik-Jan Zürcher, *The Unionist Factor: The Rôle of the Committee of Union and Progress in the Turkish National Movement 1905–1926* (Leiden: Brill, 1984); Emel Akal, *Milli Mücadelenin Başlangıcında Mustafa Kemal, İttihat Terakki ve Bolşevizm*, revised and extended edition (İstanbul: İletişim, 2012); and Alp Yenen, "Elusive Forces in Illusive Eyes: British Officialdom's Perception of the Anatolian Resistance Movement," *Middle Eastern Studies* 54, no. 5 (2018): 788–810.

[12] For a preliminary overview that deserves an updated revisiting, see Ergun Özbudun, "The Continuing Ottoman Legacy and the State Tradition in the Middle East," in *Imperial Legacy: The Ottoman Imprint on the Balkans and the Middle East*, ed. Carl L. Brown (New York: Columbia University Press, 1996), 133–57. For Ottoman continuities in the Arab Middle East, including the role played by Ottoman-Arab military officers in post-war insurgencies and governments, see Michael Provence, *The Last Ottoman Generation and the Making of the Modern Middle East* (Cambridge: Cambridge University Press, 2017).

of the empire as well as its legislation and military.[13] As a consequence, the new republic also inherited its political elite from the empire. While the Ottoman dynasty was exiled and expatriated, the leading cadres of the new regime consisted of former members of the CUP who would continue to govern all the way up until the 1960 coup d'état, when the third and last Unionist president of the Republic, seventy-seven-year-old Celal Bayar (1883–1986), was removed from office. Given that situation, the novelty of the regime was limited to its radical and republican reforms, but the process of nation-state formation nonetheless rested on the legacy of the Young Turks.[14]

The territorial contours of the "new Turkey" were also partly a consequence of the earlier policies of the "Young Turkey" of the 1910s. The new national borders were redrawn after a decade-long series of wars that lasted from 1912 to 1922.[15] Even if the CUP regime had never relinquished its commitment to Ottoman imperialism and Muslim nationalism in favour of the creation of a Turkish nation-state in Anatolia, as is often wrongly assumed, many Unionists (and later-day Kemalists) were refugees from the Balkan provinces who had adopted the idea of Anatolia as the new national homeland of Turkish Muslims after the loss of the empire's European territories in 1913 and irreversibly so after parting with its Arab provinces in the armistice of 1918.[16] Turkey's new territorial shape was not unfamiliar, as Western cartographers had long referred to the Ottoman provinces, especially those in Anatolia, as "Turkey in Asia," as opposed to the Balkan provinces, which were called "Turkey in Europe". But after the Treaty of Lausanne, in the minds of the Turkish leadership there was no room for Kurdistan and Armenia on the map of Anatolia. However, in contrast to the claims that have long been asserted in Turkish and Arab nationalist and European colonialist narratives, the separation of Turkey from its Arab provinces was not a forgone conclusion but a consequence of the post-war struggles in which France and Britain were able to suppress the uprisings of Arab and Kurdish insurgents in Syria and Iraq who stood in solidarity with the Turkish national forces in Anatolia as well as the Turkish nationalists' defeat of the (largely Armenian) French occupying forces in Cilicia.[17] These new borders cut straight across landscapes through which

---

[13] For a schematic survey, see Erik-Jan Zürcher, "The Ottoman Legacy of the Kemalist Republic," in *The Young Turk Legacy and Nation Building: From the Ottoman Empire to Atatürk's Turkey* (London: I.B. Tauris, 2010), 136–50.

[14] For an examination of various aspects of this issue, see the essays in Erik-Jan Zürcher, *The Young Turk Legacy and Nation Building: From the Ottoman Empire to Atatürk's Turkey* (London: I.B. Tauris, 2010).

[15] Alexander E. Balistreri, "Revisiting *Milli*: Borders and the Making of the Turkish Nation State," in *Regimes of Mobility: Borders and State Formation in the Middle East, 1918–1946*, eds. Jordi Tejel and Ramazan H. Öztan (Edinburgh: Edinburgh University Press, 2021), 29–58.

[16] Erik-Jan Zürcher, "How Europeans Adopted Anatolia and Created Turkey," *European Review* 13, no. 3 (2005): 379–94. For a critical intervention that examines the teleology of Turkey's nation-state formation in the general historiography, see Ramazan H. Öztan, "Point of No Return? Prospects of Empire After the Ottoman Defeat in the Balkan Wars (1912–1913)," *International Journal of Middle East Studies* 50, no. 1 (2018): 65–84.

[17] Hasan Kayalı, *Imperial Resilience: The Great War's End, Ottoman Longevity, and Incidental Nations* (Oakland: University of California Press, 2021); Alp Yenen, "Envisioning Turco-Arab Co-Existence Between Empire and Nationalism," *Die Welt des Islams* 61, no. 1 (2021): 72–112; Ü. Gülsüm Polat, *Türk-Arap İliskileri: Eski Eyaletler*

people and goods had travelled unhindered for centuries and continued to do so until Ankara and its neighbours were able to enforce stricter border regimes.[18]

In socioeconomic and demographic terms, during its final decade the empire had also changed to the point of almost becoming unrecognisable. This was again primarily due to the demographic violence that erupted during the ten years of continuous warfare between 1912 and 1922. Because the Ottoman conscript army had recruited primarily from the peasant population of Anatolia, that populace had been decimated, not only through battlefield casualties, but also because of cholera and typhus epidemics.[19] The problem of depopulation had been further exacerbated by the mass killings of Armenians in 1915–1916. The survivors of the genocide now largely lived in French Syria, Soviet Armenia, or farther abroad as part of a worldwide diaspora,[20] and their return to Turkey was rendered practically impossible. By the time of the proclamation of the Republic in 1923, the majority of the Greek Orthodox inhabitants of western Anatolia and the Marmara region had either fled, been driven out, or been killed. The military reconquest of western Anatolia by the Turkish national forces had led to widespread atrocities on both sides and panic among the Greek Orthodox populace, many of whom sought sanctuary in Greece.[21] The "population exchange" of 1923–1925, which in reality was a process of reciprocal deportations, led to the departure of Orthodox Greeks from central Anatolia and the Pontic region in exchange for some 400,000 Muslims from what was then northern Greece.[22] The fact that the exchanged populations were identified as Greeks and Turks not because their mother tongues were Greek or Turkish but on the basis of whether they were Christian or Muslim underscored the cryptic logic of Muslim nationalism in the founding of the Turkish nation-state (as well as, of course, the dual nature of Hellenic-Orthodox

---

Yeni Komşulara Dönüşürken (1914–1923) (İstanbul: Kronik, 2019); Vahe Tachjian, *La France en Cilicie et en Haute-Mésopotamie: Aux confins de la Turquie, de la Syrie et de l'Irak (1919–1933)* (Paris: Karthala, 2004).

[18] For an overview of the scholarship on the making of post-Ottoman borders, see Jordi Tejel and Ramazan H. Öztan, eds., *Regimes of Mobility: Borders and State Formation in the Middle East, 1918–1946* (Edinburgh: Edinburgh University Press, 2021).

[19] Erik-Jan Zürcher, "The Ottoman Conscription System, 1844–1914," *International Review of Social History* 43, no. 3 (1998): 437–49; Mehmet Beşikçi, *The Ottoman Mobilization of Manpower in the First World War: Between Voluntarism and Resistance* (Leiden: Brill, 2012); Yiğit Akın, *When the War Came Home: The Ottomans' Great War and the Devastation of an Empire* (Stanford: Stanford University Press, 2018).

[20] Ronald Grigor Suny, Fatma Müge Göçek, and Norman M. Naimark, eds., *A Question of Genocide: Armenians and Turks at the End of the Ottoman Empire* (Oxford: Oxford University Press, 2011).

[21] Emre Erol, *Ottoman Decline in Western Anatolia: Turkey's Belle Epoque and the Transition to a Modern Nation State* (London: I.B. Tauris, 2015); Ryan Gingeras, *Sorrowful Shores: Violence, Ethnicity, and the End of the Ottoman Empire, 1912–1923* (Oxford: Oxford University Press, 2009).

[22] Aslı Iğsız, *Humanism in Ruins: Entangled Legacies of the Greek-Turkish Population Exchange* (Stanford: Stanford University Press, 2018); Ellinor Morack, *The Dowry of the State? The Politics of Abandoned Property and the Population Exchange in Turkey, 1921–1945* (Bamberg: University of Bamberg Press, 2017); Emine Yeşim Bedlek, *Imagined Communities in Greece and Turkey: Trauma and the Population Exchanges under Atatürk* (London: I.B. Tauris, 2016); Renee Hirschon, *Crossing the Aegean: An Appraisal of the 1923 Compulsory Population Exchange Between Greece and Turkey* (New York: Berghahn Books, 2003).

nationalism in Greece).[23] Because the Greeks had held a dominant position in the urban trade and service sectors, and the Armenians dominated the fields of artisanal crafts and services, the demographic change brought with it an enormous reduction in the skilled labour available to the new republic.[24] Early republican Anatolia (as well as eastern Thrace, the only remaining part of Turkey in Europe besides İstanbul) was thus very different from the same area in late Ottoman times; it was more rural and had fewer skilled labourers, in addition to being impoverished and emptied out. Many of its towns and villages were in ruins. Large parts of major towns and cities like Ankara, Manisa, and İzmir had been burnt down. The emptiness of the country was something that nearly all foreign visitors in the 1920s remarked upon, to such an extent that estimates of the population varied between a mere five to ten million. The results of the first republican census, which was carried out in 1927, showed that in fact Turkey had a population of approximately 13.5 million, which came as a positive surprise.[25]

There are also less tangible, but nevertheless important, ideological elements of continuity between the empire and the republic that continue to be relevant down to the present day.[26] Michael Meeker aptly speaks of a "Nation of Empire".[27] There is a strong culture of state nationalism and *"raison d'état"* as a transcendent value across the political spectrum,[28] as well as an implicit identification of the secular state as the guardian of Hanafi-Sunni Islam[29] and a strong emphasis on the militarist character of the Turkish culture of masculinity.[30] Last but not least, it could be said that there are twin—yet contradictory—historical imperial legacies. On the one hand, there is a general sense of pride in an imperial past in which the Ottomans were one of the benevolent superpowers of the day and ruled as a Turkish empire over three

[23] Y. Doğan Çetinkaya, "Mübadele: Müslüman Milliyetçiliğinin Tescili," *Toplumsal Tarih*, no. 349 (January 2023): 2–7; Erik-Jan Zürcher, "Young Turks, Ottoman Muslims and Turkish Nationalists: Identity Politics 1908–38," in *The Young Turk Legacy and Nation Building: From the Ottoman Empire to Atatürk's Turkey* (London: I.B. Tauris, 2010), 213–35.

[24] Roger Owen and Şevket Pamuk, *A History of Middle East Economies in the Twentieth Century* (London: I.B. Tauris, 1998), 11.

[25] William M. Hale, *The Political and Economic Development of Modern Turkey* (London: Croom Helm, 1981), 18.

[26] For studies on Ottoman continuities in the ideological outlook of the Turkish Republic, see Erik-Jan Zürcher, "Ottoman Sources of Kemalist Thought," in *Late Ottoman Society: The Intellectual Legacy*, ed. Elisabeth Özdalga (London: RoutledgeCurzon, 2005), 14–27; M. Şükrü Hanioğlu, "Garbcılar: Their Attitudes Toward Religion and Their Impact on the Official Ideology of the Turkish Republic," *Studia Islamica*, no. 86 (1997): 133–58; Selim Deringil, "The Ottoman Origins of Kemalist Nationalism: Namık Kemal to Mustafa Kemal," *European History Quarterly* 23, no. 2 (1993): 165–91; Paul Dumont, "The Origins of Kemalist Ideology," in *Atatürk and the Modernization of Turkey*, ed. Jacob M. Landau (Boulder: Westview Press, 1984), 25–44.

[27] Michael E. Meeker, *A Nation of Empire: The Ottoman Legacy of Turkish Modernity* (Berkeley: University of California Press, 2002).

[28] Tanıl Bora, "Nationalist Discourses in Turkey," *The South Atlantic Quarterly* 102, no. 2-3 (2003): 433–51.

[29] Ceren Lord, *Religious Politics in Turkey: From the Birth of the Republic to the AKP* (Cambridge: Cambridge University Press, 2018).

[30] Ayşe Gül Altınay, *The Myth of the Military Nation: Militarism, Gender, and Education in Turkey* (New York: Palgrave Macmillan, 2004).

continents.[31] On the other hand, there is a collective memory of traumatic foreign encroachment, internal rebellions, and territorial losses that ultimately put the continued existence of the state itself in jeopardy—a fate that, in the eyes of many Turkish nationalists even today, could potentially befall the state once again.[32]

A comparison of the incarnation of the state that came into being a century ago with the Turkey of today immediately reveals that the country has undergone a series of dramatic transformations. The Turkey of 1923, comprised of 13 million people who were predominantly rural, illiterate, destitute, and afflicted by poor health, is quite different from the Turkey of today, which has a largely urban, literate population of 85 million and is now a middle-income country (even if there is a very high degree of inequality). Public works have turned Turkey into a country that is integrated to an extent that would have been unimaginable in 1923, not to mention fifty years ago. The combined effect of these transformations essentially makes the centenary of the Republic seem to come across as a success story. The citizens of Turkey today are incomparably wealthier and healthier than their forebears were in 1923, or even fifty years ago, and Turkey is also the most successful post-Ottoman state in the Middle East. It is logical, therefore, that the centenary of the republic would be commemorated and even celebrated. At the same time, however, the Turkish Republic was not only the beneficiary of the violent unmixing of the peoples of Anatolia as the Ottoman Empire collapsed, but it has unapologetically continued with the violent oppression of ethnic-religious minorities and political dissidents ever since.[33]

Neither a Celebration nor a Condemnation: Thinking Critically about the Republic's Centenary

Turkey today is, in many ways, a vastly better country than it was in 1923, but it continues to have immense problems with its political system, implementation of the rule of law, human rights, and polarisation along ideological and cultural lines. So, how does this book fit into

---

[31] Unlike clichés which claim that the Kemalist regime enforced a type of amnesia intended to erase its imperial past, recent studies demonstrate that the Ottoman Empire, with all its glory and gloom, was enthusiastically but selectively internalised by various political factions in the shaping of Republican Turkey's political ethos. Erdem Sönmez, "A Past to Be Forgotten? Writing Ottoman History in Early Republican Turkey," *British Journal of Middle Eastern Studies* 48, no. 4 (2021): 753–69; Halil Akkurt, *Türkiye Solunda Osmanlı Toplum Yapısı Tartışmaları: 1960–1980* (Ankara: İmge Kitabevi Yayınları, 2020); Nicholas Danforth, "The Ottoman Empire from 1923 to Today: In Search of a Usable Past," *Mediterranean Quarterly* 27, no. 2 (2016): 5–27; Nicholas Danforth, "Multi-Purpose Empire: Ottoman History in Republican Turkey," *Middle Eastern Studies* 50, no. 4 (2014): 655–78.

[32] This is commonly referred to as Sèvres Syndrome or a Sèvres Complex. Feroz Ahmad, *Turkey: The Quest for Identity* (Oxford: Oneworld, 2003), 163; Fatma Müge Göçek, "Why Is There Still a Sèvres Syndrome? An Analysis of Turkey's Uneasy Association with the West," in *The Transformation of Turkey: Redefining State and Society from the Ottoman Empire to the Modern Era* (London: I.B. Tauris, 2011), 98–184.

[33] For an insightful local history of the violence that plagued eastern Anatolia, see Uğur Ümit Üngör, *The Making of Modern Turkey: Nation and State in Eastern Anatolia, 1913–50* (Oxford: Oxford University Press, 2011). The history of violence in Turkey is also surveyed in Stephan Astourian and Raymond Kévorkian, eds., *Collective and State Violence in Turkey: The Construction of a National Identity from Empire to Nation-State* (New York: Berghahn, 2020).

that picture? It is neither a celebration nor a condemnation of the Republic of Turkey in its centennial. While it seems to us that the centenary offers a superb opportunity to pause and reflect on the resilience of Republican Turkey, we are fully aware of the fact that the history of Turkey has had both bright and dark pages.

Looking back at Turkey's century-old history, we should resist the temptation to slip into "Turkish exceptionalism" in explaining Turkey's prospects and problems.[34] Many of the changes that Turkey has experienced were not unique to Turkey but rather were part and parcel of global trends, including post-imperial nation-state formation after 1918, the Great Depression of 1929–1939, and the global order of the Cold War after 1945, as well as the emergence of neoliberalism, neoconservatism, and postmodernist identity politics after 1989. At the same time, many of these changes have been expressed in Turkey in a very specific way. Any story of nation-building is also a story of exclusion, expulsion, assimilation, and suppression. But that, of course, is no excuse. It is not necessary to journey to the dark side of the moon, as Maurus Reinkowski noted, to discover that Turkey too had its fair share of violent episodes during the course of its nation-building process.[35] While Turkey's transition to a multi-party system was part of a second global wave of democratisation after the Second World War, which was celebrated by modernist Orientalists like Bernard Lewis as an exception in the Muslim world, Turkey's democratic trajectory left much to be desired given the realities of pervasive military tutelage and human rights abuses.[36] Like elsewhere across the world, industrialisation, mass migration, large-scale tourism, globalisation, and the building of a welfare state followed by its demise under neoliberalism have shaped Turkish society and the economy. All of these developments created opportunities for a few at the expense of large-scale human suffering and enabled the social mobility of different groups at different times but without necessarily creating a more pluralist society.

Turkey entered 2023 in the grips of a severe humanitarian, financial, and political crisis, governed, as it has been, for the previous two decades by a democratically elected but increasingly populist-authoritarian regime that has openly rejected some of the foundational principles of the Republic. All the same, hundreds of events and projects are being planned, among them a number of commemorative publications devoted to the centennial of the Republic of Turkey. When compared to the celebrations that took place on the occasion of the fiftieth anniversary of the Republic in 1973 and the hundredth anniversary of Mustafa Kemal Atatürk's birthday in 1981, it immediately becomes apparent how much has changed. In both 1973 and 1981, Turkey was under the sway of the repressive repercussions of the military interventions that took place in 1971 and 1980, respectively. All the publications that were linked to those celebrations bore the mark of the official state discourse (and also literally

---

[34] Lerna K. Yanık, "The Making of Turkish Exceptionalism: The West, the Rest and Unreconciled Issues from the Past," *Turkish Studies* (online-first 2022): 1–18. https://doi.org/10.1080/14683849.2022.2159816

[35] Maurus Reinkowski, *Geschichte der Türkei: Von Atatürk bis zur Gegenwart* (München: C.H. Beck, 2021), 162.

[36] Bernard Lewis, "Why Turkey Is the Only Muslim Democracy," *Middle East Quarterly* (March 1994): 41–49. For a critique of Turkey's democratisation in the post-Cold War era, see Kerem Öktem, *Turkey Since 1989: Angry Nation* (London: Zed Books, 2011).

in the sense that they shared a single logo).[37] While Turkey is going through dark days once again and has suffered as a result of an attempted coup d'état in 2016 and subsequent political purges and repression, the imposition of such a uniform vision of commemoration would be impossible today. In spite of repeated attempts by the AKP regime to violently suppress dissident voices and unabashedly promote its Islamist-populist outlook, a vibrant civil society continues to exist and publicly challenge state doctrine in its various forms. The state is no longer an ideological hegemon in Turkey, even if it still is a political behemoth.

So how can we celebrate the centennial of the Republic of Turkey while also honouring those who have been marginalised and mistreated throughout its history? How can we laud Turkey's democratic political institutions without pardoning their undemocratic record? How can we appreciate Turkey's development and progress while at the same time decrying the despair and disparities it has simultaneously created? Although we are not interested in offering up a middle ground for the purposes of establishing a rapport between these contradictions, we argue that these critical questions should be part of the commemoration of the centenary of the Republic of Turkey in 2023 without necessarily discrediting it altogether either.

What We Offer: A Fragmented Illustration of Historical Complexity

This book is certainly not another history of "modern Turkey". There are several textbooks that cover that subject for university students and interested readers, including Erik-Jan Zürcher's now thirty-year-old *Turkey: A Modern History*, the fourth revised edition of which came out in 2017.[38] As an edited volume, the current book is also unlike other academic handbooks that

---

[37] Some exceptions include the highly recommendable collection of articles in Ali Kazancıgil and Ergun Özbudun, eds., *Atatürk: Founder of a Modern State* (London: Hurst, 1981) and Jacob M. Landau, ed., *Atatürk and the Modernization of Turkey* (Boulder: Westview, 1984).

[38] Histories of "modern" Turkey are generally defined by their coverage of both (late) Ottoman and Republican history in a single volume. The most detailed political history in English is still Erik-Jan Zürcher, *Turkey: A Modern History*, 1993, 4th ed. (London: I.B. Tauris, 2017), which also offers many critical perspectives on the official historiography. Although considerably outdated, Bernard Lewis' *The Emergence of Modern Turkey*, 1961, 3rd ed. (New York: Oxford University Press, 2002) remains a classic that every serious student of modern Turkey should read, especially for its (rather Western-centric) treatment of the history of culture and ideas. While rich in detail, Carter Vaughn Findley's *Turkey, Islam, Nationalism and Modernity: A History 1789–2007* (New Haven: Yale University Press, 2010), Sina Akşin's *Turkey, from Empire to Revolutionary Republic: The Emergence of the Turkish Nation from 1789 to the Present*, trans. Dexter H. Mursaloğlu (New York: New York University Press, 2007), and Feroz Ahmad's *The Making of Modern Turkey* (London: Routledge, 1993) adopt secular-modernist narratives that are close to Kemalist historiography. In French, Hamit Bozarslan's *Histoire de la Turquie: de l'empire à nos jours* (Paris: Tallandier, 2013) and in German, Reinkowski's *Geschichte der Türkei* (2021) are a good alternative for critical approaches. Then there is the odd format that covers the history of the Turks from premodern Turkestan to modern Turkey, the most notable examples of which are Klaus Kreiser and Christoph K. Neumann, *Kleine Geschichte der Türkei* (Stuttgart: Reclam, 2003) and Carter Vaughn Findley, *The Turks in World History* (New York: Oxford University Press, 2005).

FRAGMENTS FROM A CENTURY: A HISTORY OF REPUBLICAN TURKEY, 1923–2023

offer state-of-the-art surveys on certain key themes concerning Turkey.[39] Our aim was not to craft a cohesive narrative or a complete survey, but rather to embrace the unconnected and incomplete nature of vignettes of historical records.

What we have tried to do in this book can perhaps best be described as a fragmented illustration of historical complexity. We call the short chapters of our book "fragments" because each of them offers a glimpse into the workings of a partial historical reality that is part of a larger whole that could not have been illustrated in its entirety and diversity by any other means. Together with a group of colleagues, we collected one hundred such fragments that deal with political, social, cultural, and economic moments that have, in one way or another, been significant in the shaping of Turkey as we know it today.

It should be noted, however, that while our book offers up one hundred historical fragments, beginning in 1923 and ending in 2023, not every year is represented by a fragment of its own. The method we used to structure the fragments consisted of dividing those hundred years into ten decades. For each decade, we collected ten fragments that we thought represent developments that are significant for particular moments in history. In building a thematic collection of a hundred fragments covering ten decades, we consciously tried to strike a balance between the familiar and the fringe, combining major events with curious instances. Of course, we realise that this decade-based structure is, to a certain extent, an artificial device and that the fragments included here can neither represent all the major trends and transformations of a particular decade nor fully capture the scope of large processes that took place over periods of time lasting longer than ten years. Consequently, it is impossible for such a collection to claim to be complete. Nevertheless, we are confident that readers will grasp the "spirit" of each decade through our selection and be able to trace the developmental traits of certain issues across several fragments over the course of multiple decades.

By way of a uniform format, each fragment in our book introduces and then discusses a fragmentary piece of a historical artifact, such as a law, speech, essay, letter, newspaper article, poem, song, memoir, photograph, poster, map, diagram, and so on. These historical

---

[39] For comprehensive collected volumes on modern Turkey that still offer excellent thematic surveys despite being slightly outdated in some chapters, see Reşat Kasaba, ed., *The Cambridge History of Turkey, Volume 4: Turkey in the Modern World* (Cambridge: Cambridge University Press, 2008) and Celia Kerslake, Kerem Öktem, and Philip Robins, eds., *Turkey's Engagement with Modernity: Conflict and Change in the Twentieth Century* (Basingstoke: Palgrave Macmillan, 2010). In recent years, Routledge Publishing House published a number of handbooks about Turkey that may not offer much in the way of detailed content coverage due to their short chapter format but still provide a very useful service by concisely surveying the state of research in various fields and on a variety of themes. Metin Heper and Sabri Sayari, eds., *The Routledge Handbook of Modern Turkey* (London: Routledge, 2012); Alpaslan Özerdem and Matthew Whiting, eds., *The Routledge Handbook of Turkish Politics* (London: Routledge, 2019); Joost Jongerden, ed., *The Routledge Handbook on Contemporary Turkey* (London: Routledge, 2021); Didem Havlioğlu and Zeynep Uysal, eds., *The Routledge Handbook on Turkish Literature* (London: Routledge, 2023). Similarly useful is Güneş Murat Tezcür, ed. *The Oxford Handbook of Turkish Politics* (New York: Oxford University Press, 2022). Although not as complete as could be in these times of online encyclopaedias, students of modern Turkish history may also benefit from the concise information provided in Metin Heper, Duygu Öztürk-Tunçel, and Nur Bilge Criss, eds., *Historical Dictionary of Turkey*, 4th ed. (Lanham: Rowman & Littlefield, 2018).

excerpts, objects, and snapshots will enable our readers to encounter a wide variety of voices and images from Republican Turkey's past. We have tried to ensure that our selection of historical fragments is balanced by including a combination of central, top-down, and elite perspectives with peripheral, bottom-up, and subaltern viewpoints. Moreover, our contributors have striven to embed the historical fragments in their due contexts in order to illustrate the political and social developments that shaped their cultural production. Thanks to their format, each fragment constitutes a stand-alone entry, so readers do not have to read the hundred fragments chronologically from cover to cover. Each fragment yields surprising insights into as well as original takes on Republican Turkey's history, sociology, and culture. Ideally, these fragments will not only impart knowledge about the various topics and decades they cover, but also give readers a "feel" for Turkey's complex realities.

Due to the very nature of these small fragments of primary sources, at a glance our book may resemble those documentary sourcebooks that are commonly used in university courses to give students the opportunity to read and analyse primary sources in translation.[40] To date, no such sourcebook has been published in English that is solely devoted to the history of the Republic of Turkey.[41] As such, our book fills that gap, as it was designed for use in university courses, and lecturers are invited to share these historical fragments with their students so they can hold discussions about various aspects of Turkey's politics, society, culture, and economy on the basis of primary sources. However, the concept of our book also goes beyond being a sourcebook that merely offers an unannotated collection of historical records, as our fragments combine the presentation of historical sources with expert commentary. So, in addition to allowing the sources to speak for themselves, we have given our contributors ample space to introduce, describe, interpret, and explain the meaning and relevance of these fragmented historical sources. In that way, we hope that our book will also find a place in the

[40] There are numerous sourcebooks that cover the history of the Middle East, including Turkey, such as Camron Michael Amin, Benjamin Fortna, and Elizabeth Brown Frierson, eds., *The Modern Middle East: A Sourcebook for History* (Oxford: Oxford University Press, 2006); Julia Clancy-Smith and Charles Smith, eds., *The Modern Middle East and North Africa: A History in Documents* (Oxford: Oxford University Press, 2013); John Felton, ed., *The Contemporary Middle East: A Documentary History* (Washington DC: QC Press, 2008); Marvin E. Gettleman and Stuart Schaar, eds., *The Middle East and Islamic World Reader* (New York: Grove, 2003); J.C. Hurewitz, ed., *The Middle East and North Africa in World Politics: A Documentary Record*, 2nd revised and enlarged ed., 2 vols. (New Haven: Yale University Press, 1979); Kemal H. Karpat, ed., *Political and Social Thought in the Contemporary Middle East*, revised and enlarged edition (New York: Praeger, 1982); Akram Fouad Khater, ed., *Sources in the History of the Modern Middle East* (Boston: Cengage Learning, 2010).

[41] Credit must be given to Hülya Adak, Erika Glassen, and Sabine Adatepe, eds., *Hundert Jahre Türkei: Zeitzeugen Erzählen* (Zürich: Unionsverlag, 2010), which is an anthology of excerpts from literature and memoirs from the late Ottoman Empire to the twenty-first century. For sourcebooks and readers that cover specific aspects of Turkey's history and sociology, see Şirin Tekeli, *Women in Modern Turkish Society: A Reader* (London: Zed Books, 1995) and Esra Özyürek, Gaye Özpınar, and Emrah Altındiş, eds., *Authoritarianism and Resistance in Turkey: Conversations on Democratic and Social Challenges* (Cham: Springer, 2019). There are, of course, anthologies of literary works, such as Talat S. Halman and Jayne L. Warner, eds., *An Anthology of Modern Turkish Drama*, 2 vols. (Syracuse: Syracuse University Press, 2008) and Kemal Silay, ed., *An Anthology of Turkish Literature* (Bloomington: Indiana University Turkish Studies, 1996), just to name a few.

private libraries of avid readers who want to learn more about Turkey's history on their own through the guiding narrative of scholars of Turkish Studies.

A Collective Effort in Times of Crisis: Turkish Studies at a Critical Juncture

In order to realise this ambitious project, we involved a large circle of specialists working on Turkey—not all of them historians by any means, but they all have a strong historical interest in the country. The authors are from a variety of countries (though there is a large Turkish contingent), have backgrounds in various disciplines in the social sciences and humanities, and are from different generations. What this means is that the collection not only offers a survey of a wide range of aspects of Turkey's development in the last hundred years, but also an overview—or perhaps it would be better to say a snapshot—of the landscape of Turkish Studies today, which is a very lively and diverse field.

Turkish Studies, as an academic discipline, has dual roots. On the one hand, in what used to be called Turcology at European universities, which essentially was a branch of Oriental Studies, the work of scholars was devoted to the history and philology of Turkic peoples from antiquity to the present.[42] On the other hand, in Area Studies, a field that developed primarily in the United States from the Cold War onwards, scholars of Turkish Studies began to focus more on the implicitly policy-relevant aspects of historical and social-scientific research on Turkey.[43] In the last four decades or so, these two traditions have increasingly merged and Turkish Studies has developed into an interdisciplinary field that brings together international scholars of history, cultural studies, and the social sciences who study modern Turkey utilising a variety of theoretical and methodological approaches as well as transnational and comparative perspectives which have reduced the isolation of the field to a great extent.[44]

[42] Emmanuel Szurek, "Épistémologie de la turcologie," *European Journal of Turkish Studies* 24 (2017): https://doi.org/10.4000/ejts.5524; Hans Theunissen, "Turks in Nederland," in *Nederland in Turkije – Turkije in Nederland*, ed. Jan Schmidt (Leiden: Leiden University Press, 2012), 92–117; Christoph Herzog, "Notes on the Development of Turkish and Oriental Studies in the German Speaking Lands," *Türkiye Araştırmaları Literatür Dergisi* 8, no. 15 (2010): 7–76.

[43] Nathan J. Citino, "The Ottoman Legacy in Cold War Modernization," *International Journal of Middle East Studies* 40, no. 4 (2008): 579–97; Cangül Örnek, "From Analysis to Policy: Turkish Studies in the 1950s and the Diplomacy of Ideas," *Middle Eastern Studies* 48, no. 6 (2012): 941–59; İlker Aytürk, "The Flagship Institution of Cold War Turcology," *European Journal of Turkish Studies*, no. 24 (2017): https://doi.org/10.4000/ejts.5517. For a comparative study of the politics of Cold War Turkey, see Begüm Adalet, *Hotels and Highways: The Construction of Modernization Theory in Cold War Turkey* (Stanford: Stanford University Press, 2018). For the history of Area Studies in the US during the Cold War, see Zachary Lockman, *Field Notes: The Making of Middle East Studies in the United States* (Stanford: Stanford University Press, 2020); Zachary Lockman, *Contending Visions of the Middle East: The History and Politics of Orientalism* (Cambridge: Cambridge University Press, 2004), 100–48.

[44] On the advancement of Turkish Studies, see Marie Bossaert and Emmanuel Szurek, eds., "Transturcologiques: Une histoire transnationale des études turques / Transturkology: A Transnational History of Turkish Studies," special issue of *European Journal of Turkish Studies* 24 (2017), https://journals.openedition.org/ejts/5370; Erik-Jan Zürcher, "Monologue to Conversation: Comparative Approaches in Turkish Historiography," *Journal of Turkish Studies* 15, no. 4 (2014): 589–99; Howard Eissenstat, "Children of Özal: The New Face of Turkish Studies," *Journal of*

As part of a diverse epistemic community, the contributors to our book mostly utilise critical approaches in Turkish Studies, as we commonly question and deconstruct the official, national, and popular narratives related to Turkey. For that reason, our book also allows for glimpses into the current research trends and paradigmatic transformations of critical approaches in Turkish Studies.

Currently, Turkish Studies is going through a critical juncture of its own making. Pioneering works of critical scholarship emerged in the 1980s and 1990s as a reaction to the brutal military intervention of 1980 and the Kemalist discourse of military tutelage.[45] Quite a few of the scholars who took a critical approach lost their jobs at universities under the military junta, which led directly to the (re-)formation of alternative publication venues such as the publishing house İletişim (1983), the Tarih Vakfı (1991), which is a historical association, and critical journals such as *Tarih ve Toplum* (1984–2003, 2005–2014, 2021–) and *Birikim* (1975–1980, 1989–). Retrospectively referred to as "post-Kemalist" scholarship, such critical studies have brilliantly deconstructed some of the foundational myths in the field and bravely pointed out some of the "original sins" of the Republic of Turkey that continue to plague Turkish politics. In the face of the growing challenges posed by Islamist and Kurdish identity politics, Kemalism did indeed go through a crisis after the 1990s.[46] Kemalism had developed into a threefold cult of Western modernity, Turkish sovereignty, and Atatürk's personality. In the 2000s, a more activist-based version of this post-Kemalist critique became more and more mainstream in Turkey's public discourses—as well as in international Turkish Studies. Scholars and opinion-leaders increasingly upheld the idea that the cure for Turkey's problems resulting from its Kemalist establishment could only arise from a takeover by the antagonising forces of liberal Islamism.[47] Hence, in the immediate aftermath of the 9/11 attacks, major

the Ottoman and Turkish Studies Association 1, nos. 1–2 (2014): 23–35; Sinan Ciddi and Paul T. Levin, eds., "Turkish Studies from an Interdisciplinary Perspective," special issue of *Turkish Studies* 15, no. 4 (2014); Robert Zens, "Turkish Historiography in the United States," *Türkiye Araştırmaları Literatür Dergisi* 8, no. 15 (2010): 149–77; Donald Quataert and Sabri Sayarı, eds., *Turkish Studies in the United States* (Bloomington: Indiana University Ottoman and Modern Turkish Studies Publications, 2003).

[45] For the establishment of a new academic consensus in Turkish Studies in the aftermath of the 1980 coup, see Metin Heper and Ahmet Evin, eds., *State, Democracy, and the Military: Turkey in the 1980s* (Berlin: De Gruyter, 1988) and Irvin Cemil Schick and Ertuğrul Ahmet Tonak, *Turkey in Transition: New Perspectives* (Oxford: Oxford University Press, 1987).

[46] Key features of the crisis of Kemalism are summarised in Şerif Mardin, "Some Notes on Normative Conflict in Turkey," in *The Limits of Social Cohesion: Conflict and Mediation in Particularist Societies*, ed. Peter Berger (Boulder: Westview Press, 1998), 207–31. For the identity crisis of Kemalism, see also Sibel Bozdoğan and Reşat Kasaba, eds., *Rethinking Modernity and National Identity in Turkey* (Seattle: University of Washington Press, 1997); Hans-Lukas Kieser, ed., *Turkey Beyond Nationalism: Towards Post-Nationalist Identities* (London: I.B. Tauris, 2006); Ayşe Kadıoğlu and E. Fuat Keyman, eds., *Symbiotic Antagonisms: Competing Nationalisms in Turkey* (Salt Lake City: University of Utah Press, 2011).

[47] Most prominently critiqued in İlker Aytürk, "Post-Post-Kemalism: In Search for a New Paradigm," trans. Kevin Cole, *European Journal of Turkish Studies* (forthcoming), originally published as İlker Aytürk, "Post-Post-Kemalizm: Yeni Bir Paradigmayı Beklerken," *Birikim*, no. 319 (November 2015): 34–48. For his responses to his critics, see İlker Aytürk, "Bir Defa Daha Post-Post-Kemalizm: Eleştiriler, Cevaplar, Düşünceler," *Birikim*, nos. 374–375

international publications in the 2000s celebrated the AKP and its particular brand of "moderate Islamism" as the harbinger of the democratisation, liberalisation, and pluralisation of Turkey. The hype was real, since the promises were backed up by deeds. The AKP government energetically curbed the regressive influence of the old Kemalist-secular establishment in the military, bureaucracy, industry, and media. The end of the military tutelage of the political system in Turkey was realised through the passing of a huge number of laws (261 within the first year) that strengthened the roles of elected officials and of civil society. However, the subtle but growing authoritarianism of the AKP regime became undeniable as late as the Gezi Protests of 2013.[48] This unmasking of the uglier sides of the regime rendered a great number of more recent works by Turkey experts suddenly obsolete as they had not only failed to foresee these authoritarian developments but also uncritically reproduced the AKP's own myths and vigorously denied any wrongdoing on the behalf of the AKP despite evidence to the contrary.[49] The complete unmaking of Turkey's political institutions in the last decade, including a transition to an all-powerful presidential system, and the utterly incomprehensible scale of human rights abuses and shameless corruption scandals garnered the attention and energy of most Turkey experts.[50] While the changes that Turkey has undergone in recent decades might perhaps inspire a need for new syntheses and new interpretations of Republican history, the risk remains that Turkish historiography is once again being written retrospectively on the basis of contemporary political contentions.

By publishing this collected volume of one hundred fragments, we highlight some of the new approaches that emerged after this critical juncture. First, while remaining firmly critical, we offer new and more nuanced interpretations of the Kemalist single-party regime and its repressive policies.[51] Second, unlike the mainstream post-Kemalist scholarship of the 2000s, we offer new critical studies of the Islamist and right-wing movements that arose in the Cold War and post-Cold War eras. Third, acknowledging that critical studies on identity

(June–July, 2020): 101–19. See also the multidisciplinary contributions in İlker Aytürk and Berk Esen, eds., *Post-Post-Kemalism: Türkiye Çalışmalarında Yeni Arayışlar* (İstanbul: İletişim Yayınları, 2022). How the Turkish liberal-left and their global partners embellished the rise of Islamism is discussed in Cangül Örnek and Funda Hülagü, "Idiocy or Ideological Fallacy?: An Attempt to Interpret the Fatal Amour Between the Left Liberal Intelligentsia and the Islamists in Turkey," (2018), https://www.academia.edu/42911424/Idiocy_or_ideological_fallacy_An_Attempt_to_Interpret_the_Fatal_Amour_Between_the_Left_Liberal_Intelligentsia_and_the_Islamists_in_Turkey

[48] For an early warning that went beyond voicing neo-Kemalist discontent, see Yunus Sözen, "Turkey Between Tutelary Democracy and Electoral Authoritarianism," *Private View*, no. 13 (2008): 78–84. https://www.academia.edu/43163465/Turkey_between_tutelary_democracy_and_electoral_authoritarianism

[49] Claire Berlinski. "Guilty Men: How Democracies Die," *The American Interest*, 24 April 2017, https://www.the-american-interest.com/2017/04/24/guilty-men/. For a confession and explanation of such fallacies in the political sciences, see Paul Kubicek, "Faulty Assumptions About Democratization in Turkey," *Middle East Critique* 29, no. 3 (2020): 245–57.

[50] For a recent overview of these issues, see Yeşim Arat and Şevket Pamuk, *Turkey Between Democracy and Authoritarianism* (Cambridge: Cambridge University Press, 2019).

[51] For a collection of state-of-the-art research on the Kemalist single-party regime with which we share many contributors, see Sevgi Adak and Alexandros Lamprou, eds., *Tek Parti Dönemini Yeniden Düşünmek: Devlet, Toplum ve Siyaset* (İstanbul: Tarih Vakfı Yayınları, 2022).

and minority politics have made some of the most crucial contributions to Turkish Studies in recent decades, we prominently featured such approaches in our volume too, most notably regarding the Kurdish conflict and women's rights. The unconventional structure of the book also made it possible for us to overcome some of the weaknesses of the current state of research in Turkish Studies. For one thing, our decision to start off the chronology with the year 1923 went decidedly against the grain of most historical surveys of modern Turkey that—for good reason—devote much attention to the late-Ottoman origins of the Republic of Turkey. Since we have acknowledged these continuities from empire to republic in this introduction, the remainder of the book will offer a reading of the decades of Republican history in their more momentary temporality. Moreover, by giving each decade equal weight and space, we have countered some of the imbalances and bridged some of the gaps in the current state of research in Turkish Studies. Our book thus avoids the typical overemphasis on the early decades of the Republic marked by the Kemalist single-party state, which feature prominently in the works of both Kemalist and post-Kemalist historians as the "singular" formative period in Republican history. The decade-based structure forced us to give understudied periods, especially that of the Cold War, due attention. Furthermore, our book avoids slipping into the presentism and historical myopia that is common among social scientists working in Turkish Studies who tend to magnify the contemporary political struggles that have occurred in the last two decades of the AKP's rule as the ultimate trajectory of history. Instead, our fragments demonstrate the existence of numerous alternative routes and moments that subdue teleological expectations.[52]

***

Last but not least, the mobilisation of such a broad array of expert knowledge would not have been possible without the enthusiastic cooperation of our colleagues, which, we are happy to say, was offered in abundance. We would like to thank our colleagues and PhD candidates in the Turkish Studies programme at Leiden University's Institute for Area Studies (LIAS), in alphabetical order: Onur Ada, Petra de Bruijn, Remzi Çağatay Çakırlar, Uğur Derin, Bilgen Erdem, Ömer Koçyiğit, Gözde Kırcıoğlu, Nicholas Kontovas, Nicole van Os, Deniz Tat, Hans Theunissen, and Didem Yerli, for their input in the design of the style and format of the book's fragments.[53] In addition, we are immensely grateful to the international circle of friends and colleagues associated with Leiden's Turkish Studies programme for making this book possible with their imaginative ideas and contributions. Many of the contributors also volunteered to peer-review the contributions to guarantee the quality of the content, for which we are

[52] For more on such alternative approaches, see Erik-Jan Zürcher, "Turning Points and Missed Opportunities in the Modern History of Turkey: Where Could Things Have Gone Differently?" in *The Young Turk Legacy and Nation Building: From the Ottoman Empire to Atatürk's Turkey* (London: I.B. Tauris, 2010), 285–95.

[53] The idea for this book was inspired by the format of the online teaching materials prepared as a retirement gift for Erik-Jan Zürcher from the chair of the Turkish Studies in August 2018. https://www.universiteitleiden.nl/en/humanities/institute-for-area-studies/turkish-studies/courses

greatly thankful. We would also like to thank Didem Yerli and Uğur Derin, who provided invaluable assistance in launching the project and keeping up with correspondences and editorial procedures, especially during the COVID-19 pandemic, and Mark David Wyers, who is himself a historian as well as a professional editor and translator, for providing a final review and copy-editing the manuscript. This book project benefitted from the Leiden Faculty of Humanity's Faculty Impact Fund and also from a LIAS publication grant, for which we are grateful, as we are to Saskia Gieling and her colleagues at Leiden University Press for their enthusiasm in including such a large project among their offerings.

It was the German Romantics of the Jena Circle at the turn of the nineteenth century who popularised the format of the fragment as a short stylistic genre of writing in philology and philosophy. "What are these fragments? What is it that gives them such great value? To which power of spirit do they particularly belong?" asked Friedrich Schlegel (1772–1829) in a treatise he wrote in 1804 about the work of Gotthold Ephraim Lessing (1729–1781). "If we do not look to each fragment cowardly [*sic*], but the mass and the spirit of the whole, we may boldly say: the spirit that rules them is wit."[54] We trust our readers' "wit" as the formative principle of these one hundred fragments in understanding the historical complexity of Republican Turkey as it has unfolded in the last hundred years. While acknowledging that the whole is greater than the sum of the parts, we have also trusted in the "wit" of our colleagues in the organic shaping of the composition and variety of the fragments presented here, which we hope will give a sense of the spirit of the whole in understanding Turkey's history in its centenary.

---

[54] Quoted from the English translation in Tanehisa Otabe, "Friedrich Schlegel and the Idea of Fragment: A Contribution to Romantic Aesthetics," *Aesthetics*, no. 13 (2009): 64. See also Andreas Käuser, "Theorie und Fragment: Zur Theorie, Geschichte und Poetik kleiner Prosaformate," in *Kulturen des Kleinen: Mikroformate in Literatur, Kunst und Medien*, eds. Claudia Öhlschläger, Sabiene Autsch, and Leonie Süwolto (Leiden: Brill, 2014), 41–55.

1923–1932

1
A Lasting Legacy:
The Proclamation of the Republic

Alp Yenen

The proclamation of the Republic by the Grand National Assembly of Turkey (*Türkiye Büyük Millet Meclisi*) on 29 October 1923 marks one of the most important dates in modern Turkish history, known by heart by all school children and designated a public holiday commemorated with official celebrations since its tenth anniversary in 1933. The proclamation signalled the end of the transitional period of the "National Struggle" (*Millî Mücadele*) in Turkey's official historiography from the Ottoman Empire to the Republic of Turkey.

The proclamation of the Republic was, however, neither determined nor rendered self-evident by earlier developments in the National Struggle; rather, it was contingent on the global crisis of empire and the decade of war through which the Ottoman Empire had fought. After the Armistice of Mudros took effect in November 1918, bringing an end to the First World War in the Middle East, the Ottoman government in İstanbul found itself caught up in a crisis of legitimacy as it faced occupation and partition by a bloc of Allied powers comprised of Britain, France, Italy, and Greece. Before the leaders of the "Young Turk" Committee of Union and Progress (*İttihat ve Terakki Fırkası*, CUP), who were largely responsible for the Ottoman defeat in the war, went into hiding at the onset of the armistice, they had already laid the groundwork for a continuation of the armed struggle against the Allied occupation through a network of resistance cells and rogue officers. This "Unionist" resistance and subversion of the military demobilisation led to an increase in the violence and lawlessness plaguing Anatolia, especially in contested intercommunal territories, thereby destabilising Allied control. Under the leadership of Mustafa Kemal Pasha (Atatürk, 1881–1938), the initial resistance movement was transformed into a conventional war during what came to be known as the War of Independence (*İstiklâl Harbi*), which concluded in a victory for the Turkish resistance with the signing of the Armistice of Mudanya with the Allied powers in October of 1922.

During the National Struggle, republicanism was neither a policy per se nor a popular discourse. Nevertheless, notions of national sovereignty (commonly referred to as *saltanat-ı milliye* or *hakimiyet-i milliye*) had gained wide popularity and currency in the debates carried out by the Grand National Assembly in Ankara, which was founded on 23 April 1920 as a revolutionary parliament with legislative and executive powers outside of Allied-controlled territories. While the personal subservience of Sultan Mehmed VI Vahideddin (1861–1926) to the Allied occupation in İstanbul and his opposition to the National Forces (*kuvva-yı milliye*) marred the reputation of the Ottoman sultanate, Muslim nationalism and transnational

Islamic solidarity increased the status of the symbolic power of the Ottoman caliphate in Anatolia and the wider Muslim world. This led the Ankara government to separate the office of the caliphate from the Ottoman sultanate and abolish the latter on 1 November 1922 (which was celebrated thereafter as a public holiday of "national sovereignty" until 1935, when it was combined with the celebrations of 23 April). However, the abolition of the sultanate and Vahideddin's exile did not resolve the ongoing constitutional ambiguity between the Grand National Assembly in the newly declared capital city of Ankara and the Ottoman caliphate in İstanbul, which was taken over by another Ottoman successor, Abdülmecid Efendi (1868–1944). This ambiguous status was a matter of concern for Mustafa Kemal at a time when the sovereignty of Turkey was on the cusp of being established at the Lausanne Conference.

The Lausanne Conference also coincided with the emergence of political opposition in Ankara. During the negotiations at Lausanne, Foreign Minister İsmet Pasha (İnönü, 1884–1973) opted to follow the instructions of Mustafa Kemal, who was the president of the Assembly, and not those of Prime Minister Hüseyin Rauf (Orbay, 1881–1964). Out of protest, Rauf resigned on 4 August 1923. After Mustafa Kemal's ally Ali Fethi (Okyar, 1880–1943) was elected prime minister, an oppositional group emerged among the deputies. Mustafa Kemal established a commission of experts to draft a proposal for the founding of the country as a republic, but there was some opposition among the deputies, since, as they argued, it would grant too many powers to Mustafa Kemal. When Rauf, as the opposition's candidate, was elected deputy president of the Assembly on October 25, Mustafa Kemal created a crisis in the cabinet by calling on Fethi and his cabinet to resign. In the evening of 28 October, he revealed to his close friends, "Tomorrow we will proclaim the Republic." Indeed, the proposal for the proclamation of the Republic was first discussed in a closed morning session held by the People's Party and then accepted "unanimously" by the Grand National Assembly—although it remains doubtful whether there was a clear two-thirds majority since the votes were not officially counted.

*The Proclamation of the Republic**

First Article: Sovereignty belongs unconditionally to the Nation. The form of the administration is based on the fact that the people will administer their destiny in person and in deeds. The State of Turkey's form of government is a republic.

Second Article: The State of Turkey's religion is the religion of Islam. Its official language is Turkish.

Third Article: The State of Turkey is administered by the Grand National Assembly of Turkey. The Assembly administers the government's division of administrative affairs through executive ministers.

* Translated from the original Turkish document in Murat Bardakçı, "94. Yıldönümünde İlk Defa Yayınlanıyor: İşte, Cumhuriyet'in Kuruluş Belgeleri," *HaberTürk*, 29 October 2017. https://www.haberturk.com/yazarlar/murat-bardakci/1691337-94-yildonumunde-ilk-defa-yayinlaniyor-iste-cumhuriyetin-kurulus-belgeleri

Fourth Article: Turkey's President of the Republic is elected by a plenum of the Grand National Assembly of Turkey from among its deputies during the legislative period. The term of office of the presidency continues until a new President of the Republic is elected. It is permissible to be re-elected.

Fifth Article: Turkey's President of the Republic is the head of state. He presides over the Assembly and the cabinet of ministers as he deems necessary within that capacity.

Article Six: The Prime Minister is elected by the President of the Republic from among the deputies of the Assembly. After the other ministers are elected by the Prime Minister from among the deputies of the Assembly, they are collectively presented for the approval of the Assembly by the President of the Republic. If the Assembly is not currently holding sessions, the matter of approval will be postponed until the [next] session of the Assembly is held.

29 October 1923

***

In content, the proclamation of the Republic was not a foundational document, but rather a series of amendments to the Law on the Fundamental Order (*Teşkilât-ı Esasiye Kanunu*) consisting of twenty-three articles which was passed by the Grand National Assembly two years earlier on 10 January 1921. This "first constitution" of 1921, as it was later labelled, had already declared national sovereignty and the legislative and executive mandate of the Grand National Assembly, but the proclamation of Republic redefined the form of the government and the character of the state. In terms of the form of the state, the new Republic resembled the Third Republic in France and also drew upon the Ottoman tradition of constitutional monarchy. As in France, the president was elected by the Assembly, though only a single chamber existed (the parliamentary sessions of the People's Party more or less comprised an exclusive second chamber, though it consisted of the same members), and the president nominated a prime minister who then appointed an executive cabinet of ministers to be approved by the parliament. Like the Ottoman sultan, the president was the head of the state, but he enjoyed the liberty of being able to lead parliamentary sessions or cabinet meetings whenever he pleased.

After the proclamation of the Republic, Mustafa Kemal was elected as the first president and his loyal companion İsmet was appointed as the first prime minister of the Republic of Turkey. The leaders of the opposition, who were absent from Ankara at the time, were surprised by the issuance of these decisions and publicly criticised the move, stating that such a radical regime change as calling the country a "republic" did not necessarily make it democratic. In doing so, they either remained loyal to the principles of Ottoman constitutionalism laid out in 1908 or proposed a more democratic transition—that is, if they did not simply oppose Mustafa Kemal's growing powers. Despite the continued existence of a Young Turk zeitgeist in Republican Turkey, the proclamation of the Republic entailed a clear departure from the Ottomanist and imperialist notions embedded within the Young Turk political framework.

Continuing and consolidating certain aspects of identity politics that had been in place since the Young Turks came to power, the proclamation openly declared that the Turkish state's religion was Islam and its official language was Turkish. In 1928, the declaration that Islam was the state religion was removed from the constitution, but Sunni-Islamic beliefs have remained an underlying feature of Turkish nationalism ever since. In the proclamation of the Republic, there was no mention of the office of the caliphate in İstanbul, but later, on 3 March 1924, the caliphate was abolished. All of the members of the House of Osman were exiled and prohibited from returning to Turkey (until 1952 for female members and 1974 for male members). On 20 April 1924, the Grand National Assembly approved a new and more comprehensive constitution which was replaced only in 1961, ending the "first republic" of Turkey.

***

From a global perspective, the proclamation of the Republic of Turkey was not a singular event. The popularity of notions of national sovereignty was related to the Wilsonian and Leninist campaigns of national self-determination in international politics. As such, the Republic of Turkey was one of the last to do so in a global wave of proclamations of independent republics during the crisis of empires after the end of the First World War. Although other short-lived experiments with republics had taken place in the Muslim world, such as the various Muslim republics that were declared during the Russian civil war and the proclamations of the Tripoli Republic in Libya and the Rif Republic in Morocco, all of which predated the founding of the Turkish Republic, Turkey remains the longest-lasting uninterrupted republican regime in the Muslim world. Despite multiple instances of resistance to and rebellions against the Ankara regime in the interwar years, no popular movements arose with the aim of reinstating the Ottoman monarchy or abandoning the republican system.

Considering its fundamental importance, the history of the proclamation of the Republic received relatively little attention in the official historiography, which uncritically depicted the Republic as the ultimate outcome of the secret agenda and singular agency of Mustafa Kemal Atatürk starting with the National Struggle in 1919. Hence, in the Kemalist logic, the proclamation of the Republic is considered a necessary, inevitable step in the natural evolution of a modern state and society away from the cultural backwardness and Oriental despotism of the Ottoman Empire. Nevertheless, such singular and teleological narratives have been subjected to their fair share of revisions and corrections in past decades, which point out the roles played by the collective action of elites, Ottoman institutional and intellectual legacies, historical contingencies, and the undemocratic measures put forward by Mustafa Kemal during his rise to power. Despite a growing sense of nostalgia for the imperial Ottoman past as well as increasing criticism, particularly since the 1990s, of the processes that went into the formation of the Kemalist nation-state, republicanism—in its various interpretations—remains a major feature of contemporary Turkish political culture. The idea of the Republic unifies in a unique way the three core tenets of Kemalism: a commitment to Atatürk's personality, Turkey's national sovereignty, and Turkey's path to modernity.

Select Bibliography

Alpkaya, Faruk. *Türkiye Cumhuriyeti'nin Kuruluşu (1923–1924)*. İstanbul: İletişim Yayınları, 1998.

Gingeras, Ryan. *Eternal Dawn: Turkey in the Age of Atatürk*. Oxford: Oxford University Press, 2019.

Hanioğlu, M. Şükrü. *Atatürk: An Intellectual Biography*. Princeton: Princeton University Press, 2011.

Morack, Ellinor. "Ottoman Parliamentary Procedure in the Chamber of Deputies (Meclis-i Mebusan) and the Great National Assembly of Turkey (Türkiye Büyük Millet Meclisi), 1876–1923." In *Planting Parliaments in Eurasia, 1850–1950: Concepts, Practices, and Mythologies*, edited by Ivan Sablin and Egas Moniz Bandeira, 220–55. New York: Routledge, 2021.

Özbudun, Ergun. *The Constitutional System of Turkey: 1876 to the Present*. New York: Palgrave Macmillan, 2011.

Toprak, Zafer. *Atatürk: Kurucu Felsefenin Evrimi*. İstanbul: Türkiye İş Bankası Kültür Yayınları, 2020.

2

Anxious Inquiries:
The League of Nations on the Population Exchange

Gözde Kırcıoğlu

Negotiations that were carried out in Lausanne following the Greco-Turkish War of 1919–1922 resulted in the Convention Concerning the Exchange of Greek and Turkish Populations, which was signed on 30 January 1923. The convention set forth the terms of the forced migration of Muslim and Greek-Orthodox (*Rum*) populations between Turkey and Greece, excluding Muslims in Western Thrace and Greeks in İstanbul, and retrospectively included those who had fled their homelands after 18 October 1912, which marked the beginning of the First Balkan War.

Following the outbreak of the Balkan Wars, the Greek inhabitants of Ottoman territories in Thrace and Anatolia started fleeing to Greece and other countries such as Russia and the United States. In 1913 and 1914, the *Teşkilat-ı Mahsusa* (Special Organisation), which was a clandestine paramilitary force established by elements in the Ottoman Army and the Committee of Union and Progress (*İttihad ve Terakki Cemiyeti*, CUP), launched a brutal campaign of persecution and intimidation in Eastern Thrace and along the Aegean coast of Anatolia. A large segment of the Rum population fled or was killed, their assets seized. Within weeks after the Treaty of Constantinople was signed between the Ottoman Empire and the Kingdom of Bulgaria, on 29 September 1913, which stipulated a population exchange, a similar exchange covering a geographically limited area was proposed by Eleftherios Venizelos (1864–1936) and agreed upon between Greece and the Ottoman Empire, but it came to a halt when World War I broke out.

By November 1922, when the Greek and the Turkish delegates arrived in Lausanne, an estimated five-sixths of the Orthodox Greeks of eastern Thrace and Anatolia had already fled their homelands, and it seems the aim of the diplomats was to frame that *de facto* situation in legal terms. Following the Greco-Turkish War, all of the parties involved were of the opinion that a compulsory population exchange was an essential prerequisite for peace. The Turkish delegation also intended to sign an exchange agreement that would include Armenians, but the absence of Armenian representatives and the Allies' insistence on an Armenian homeland prevented İsmet Paşa (İnönü, 1884–1973) from pushing forward with that demand.

The convention stipulated the terms not only for an exchange of populations, but also the allocation of properties to compensate for the financial losses that had been incurred. Accordingly, exchangees would be granted properties of equal value and of a similar nature to what they had left behind. However, the process of indemnification envisioned at the negotiations in Lausanne proved to be unrealistic. For most of the migrants who had fled their homes, it had been impossible to take any belongings with them, such as furniture or documentation indicating the valuation and liquidation of exchangeable assets. In the end, questions concerning the rules governing appraisals, the exchangeability of applicants, and verification of property rights were relegated to a mixed commission, but the problems that arose were never resolved in a manner that benefitted the exchangees. The commission spent eighteen months overseeing the transfer of populations, but over the course of the next nine years it failed to fulfill its task of ensuring that compensation was granted to the exchangees as was intended in the Lausanne Convention. The Agreement of Athens of 1926 and the Ankara Agreement of 1930 first diminished and then completely did away with the property rights that had been granted under the Treaty of Lausanne, and ultimately the resolution of issues concerning ownership fell to the respective states. Some argue that the desire to secure high valuation rates as a means of making the other state pay larger sums of money conflicted domestically with detailed appraisals that resulted in refugees laying claim to high property values. Additionally, after properties were transferred to their new owners, there was little desire on the behalf of the respective states to carry out appraisals, and it has been established that in 1924 both governments had started selling off the properties of Rum and Muslim exchangees. In short, Greece does not seem to have wanted its refugee settlement project disturbed, for the purposes of which previously Muslim-owned lands seized in Macedonia were being used, and in Turkey, seizures of Greek property had long been underway, having gotten started back in 1913.

Between 1915 and 1922, laws passed by the CUP and the Ankara government allowed for the seizure of "abandoned properties". These two laws legislated the confiscation of Armenian and Greek properties, placing the government in the position of custodian of those assets, ostensibly with the aim of distributing them or providing the owners with compensation upon their return. Such distribution, however, was neither regulated nor did it actually occur. The return of Armenians and Greeks was subsequently banned by domestic laws and the Treaty of Lausanne, and the law of 1915 remained in effect until 1986 (with the exception of the years 1920–1922).

Many people were concerned about their families and, anxious about the outcomes of the treaty, sent letters to the authorities in Turkey, Greece, and Geneva. Eudock K. Egypt (Missirloghlou) sent such a letter to the League of Nations. He was a Rum who had migrated to the US, possibly after 1913, where he was employed as a dishwasher at a Jewish restaurant in Brooklyn. Having read a news story in the *New York Times* about the convention for the population exchange, Eudock sent a letter requesting compensation for his property in Ankara and the resettlement of his mother and sister, as well as her three children, in Crete.

*Letter to the President of the League of Nations from Eudock K. Egypt, Brooklyn, NY**

League of Nations Registry   Grabel's Restaurant,

9 April 1923   Care of Julius Grabel,

27659   1830 Pitkin Avenue

March 26, 1923   Brooklyn N.Y.

                                                                          U.S. America

President of the League of Nations,

Geneva Switzerland

Dear Sir,

I read in the "New York Times" that a committee consisting of one neutral, one Greek and one Turk will be formed by which a Greek leaving a house in Turkey will get another house in exchange when he reaches Greece, or words in that effect. My mother, 65 years old and my sister, 40 years old are both widows and dependent upon me for support. When my father died, he did not leave any money, but he left one house in Angora Turkey, worth 100 gold Turkish liras approximately in 1913, one vineyard worth 40 gold Turkish liras in 1913 and another vineyard in Angora worth about 9 Turkish gold liras (pounds) in 1913.

Please send my present letter to the chairman of the above committee formed to look after the houses of the refugees, so that he and his associates may try that my mother and sister may get justice when they reach Greece by getting another house in Greece. My sister's address is:

Mrs. Maria Vasileou Shikiaroghlou, house of Mr. Khariton Missirloghlou, Imam Youssouf mahlessi [ward] Angora Turkey.

My mother's name is: Mrs. Kharieleia Khariton Missirloghlou ["Missir" in Turkish means Egypt], and she is living together with my sister.

I received a letter from my people in Angora wherein they wrote me that they will stay a little longer in Angora and they get out to go to Greece. If the committee created to look after the real estate of the refugees pays attention to my case and by its efforts my people get a house in exchange in Greece, I will donate nine dollars to the three members of the committee three dollars to each member.

My people will get out of Turkey either in April or in May 1923.

* Cited per the original document in the League of Nations Archives, R1686/41/27659.

I am a dishwasher in a Jewish restaurant, earning 12 dollars a week and three meals, or else if I were making more money I would give more to the members of the committee herein before mentioned.

My sister has three minor children.

I translated the present letter into French, as best I could, and am enclosing the translation herewith.

My people are Greeks born in Turkey.

Thankfully yours

P.s. – I wish my mother and sister to go the city of Hania on the island of Crete, Greece, if they wish to go there. To whom must my sister apply to leave her house recorded?

***

Eudock K. Egypt received a reply to his letter which stated that the treaty had not yet been ratified, nor had a mixed commission been formed (ratification would take another four months). He was told to apply directly to the commission at a later date after it was assembled and the application process was put into place. It is unclear how the commission processed the case of Mr Egypt, but his letter was submitted in September of 1923. These communications are indicative of the anxieties that the treaty caused and how little agency the people who were directly affected by the choices made in Lausanne actually had.

***

After the Greco-Turkish War, the governments of Turkey, Greece, and the Allied states forced people to leave their homes and then failed to compensate them properly for their material losses. Although attempts were made to compensate in both countries, the promise of the Lausanne Convention for individual and full compensation was not fulfilled. Moreover, the international agreements that were signed between 1923 and 1930 were not fully implemented in Turkey. While the Ankara Agreement of 1930 stated that ownership of properties would be transferred to the government, in practice such transfers had already occurred when virtual "custodianship" was introduced by parliament in Ankara on the basis of the law concerning abandoned properties that was enacted in 1922. Perhaps the most significant point that has been raised in recent studies is the claim that the history of the Greek-Turkish population exchange cannot be taken up separately from the experiences of Anatolian Armenians. Both the Unionist and Kemalist regimes used the so-called "abandoned properties" (*emval-i met-ruke*) of both Armenians and Greeks as a source of revenue, and Turkey's national economy was largely built upon repurposing such properties.

Since the early 2000s, there has been an increase in the number of studies about the economic policies of the Unionist and Republican leadership with regard to the properties of minorities, partly as the result of the opening of some archival materials concerning Armenians. However, fears that Armenians and Greeks will stake out claims to compensation for lost properties are still very much alive and present among the Turkish public. Even though existing international agreements would make it impossible to assert such claims for the properties of the Greek exchangees, the archives in Ankara that contain documents concerning the Greek-Turkish property exchange of 1923 remain closed to research.

Select Bibliography

Akçam, Taner, and Ümit Kurt. *The Spirit of the Laws: The Plunder of Wealth in the Armenian Genocide*. New York: Berghahn, 2015.

Erol, Emre. *The Ottoman Crisis in Western Anatolia: Turkey's Belle Epoque and the Transition to a Modern Nation State*. London: I.B. Tauris, 2016.

Morack, Ellinor. *The Dowry of the State? The Politics of Abandoned Property and the Population Exchange in Turkey, 1921–1945*. Bamberg: University of Bamberg Press, 2017.

Üngör, Uğur Ü., and Mehmet Polatel. *Confiscation and Destruction: The Young Turk Seizure of Armenian Property*. London: Continuum International, 2011.

Yıldırım, Onur. *Diplomacy and Displacement: Reconsidering the Turco-Greek Exchange of Populations, 1922–1934*. New York: Routledge, 2012.

3

Echoes of Modernity:
Nazım Hikmet's "Machinisation" of Turkish Poetry

Petra de Bruijn

While in Anatolia a new republic was being born, the young poet Nazım Hikmet (Ran, 1902–1963) was studying Marxism-Leninism, French, and Russian at the Communist University for the Workers of the East in Moscow. After discovering how difficult it was for a schoolteacher to impart Mustafa Kemal's modernist secular ideas to the generally traditional Islamic-minded inhabitants of central Anatolia, he had travelled by train to Moscow, passing through a countryside that had been devastated by the Russian civil war.

The shocking impressions of that journey inspired Nazım to write a new kind of poetry. In Batum on his way to Moscow, he encountered a kind of poetry that was unlike anything he had ever seen before, most likely the work of Vladimir Mayakovsky (1893–1930). He did not know Russian at the time, but he was inspired by the poetry's form. In Moscow, Nazım Hikmet met with Mayakovsky and even shared the stage with him at several poetry readings (in those days, poetry was often recited at public events). Although Nazım claimed that he first read Mayakovsky's poetry in the 1940s, he could not deny that there were formal similarities with his own work.

Cultural life in Moscow in the early years of the Soviet Union was fragmented. Nazım associated himself with the constructivist journal *LEF* of the Left Front of the Arts (*Levy Front Iskusstv*). Literary constructivists, who were the revolutionary successors of the futurists, argued that literature had to be composed in harmony with modern technology and modern principles of organisation. They asserted that literature should depict reality and be free to use collage techniques, drawing from prose, statistics, business language, and citations from documents.

Nazım Hikmet stayed in Moscow during the years 1922 to 1924. His grasp of Russian at the time was good enough to allow him to become involved in the Russian experimental theatre scene. More so than by poets, he was impressed by the innovative work of theatre producer Vsevolod Emilyevich Meyerhold (1874–1940), who incorporated circus acting into his plays. The poems Nazım wrote in those years were performed in Turkish and some were translated and published in literary magazines.

Backed by his experience of those new forms of art, Nazım returned to İstanbul in 1924. He garnered acclaim with his poetry as well as articles on Marxism published in *Aydınlık*, the periodical of the Communist Party of Turkey (*Türkiye Komünist Partisi*, TKP), and he became involved with the more radical *Orak-Çekiç* (Hammer and Sickle). After the Kurdish rebellion of 1925, which gave Mustafa Kemal the pretext to suppress communist voices as well as others, Nazım was sentenced to fifteen years of imprisonment. Granted amnesty in 1926, he stayed briefly in Moscow from 1926 to 1928, at which time the TKP asked him to establish a publishing venue for the production of party literature. Differences of opinion, however, led him to be expelled from the party in 1932. Nevertheless, he remained dedicated to communist ideals.

"Makinalaşmak"*

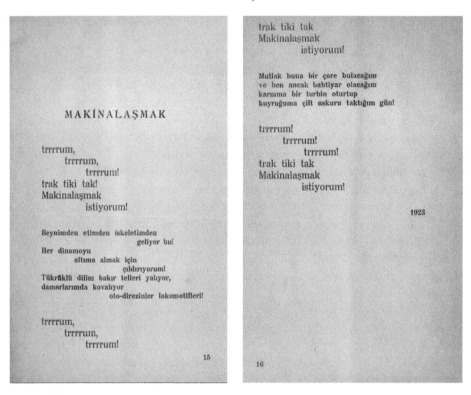

MAKİNALAŞMAK

trrrrum,
    trrrrum,
        trrrrum!
trak tiki tak!
Makinalaşmak
      istiyorum!

Beynimden etimden iskeletimden
           geliyor bu!
Her dinamoyu
    altıma almak için
        çıldırıyorum!
Tükrüklü dilim bakır telleri yalıyor,
damarlarımda kovalıyor
        oto-direzinler lokomotifleri!

trrrrum,
    trrrrum,
        trrrrum!

15

trak tiki tak
Makinalaşmak
      istiyorum!

Mutlak buna bir çare bulacağım
ve ben ancak bahtiyar olacağım
karnıma bir turbin oturtup
kuyruğuma çift uskuru taktığım gün!

trrrrum!
    trrrrum!
        trrrrum!
trak tiki tak
Makinalaşmak
      istiyorum!

1923

16

---

* Nazım Hikmet, *835 Satır* (İstanbul: Mualim Ahmet Halit Kitaphanesi, 1929), 15–16. University of Toronto, Robarts collection: https://archive.org/details/835iesekizyzotoonzuoft/page/14/mode/2up

To Machinise

trrrum,
    trrrum,
        trrrrum!
trak tiki tak!
To become an engine
        is what I want!

From my brain, my flesh and my bones
                    this comes!
To attach each dynamo
      under me
            makes me go out of my mind!
My tongue with saliva licks the copper threads
in my veins the lorries
      chase the locomotives!

trrrum,
    trrrum,
        trrrrum!
trak tiki tak!
To become an engine
        is what I want!

I will certainly find a solution for it
and I will only be happy
on the day I place a turbine in my belly
and attach a screw-propeller to my tail!

trrrum,
    trrrum,
        trrrrum!
trak tiki tak!
To become an engine
        is what I want!

1923

***

Nazım Hikmet wrote "Makinalaşmak" (To Machinise) in 1923 in Moscow. Written in the vein of the constructivists, the poem invites the audience to embrace mechanisation to such an extent that they become engines themselves.

"Makinalaşmak" was first published in 1928 in Baku in *Güneşi İçenlerin Türküsü* (The Song of Those Who Drink the Sun) in Ottoman script. The version analysed here was included in *835 Satır* (835 lines), which was published in Latin script by Ahmet Halit in İstanbul. The layout of the poem emphasises the content. The title is set in the largest font, followed by the refrain in a slightly smaller font, and the rest of the text is set in the smallest font. The refrain consists of the onomatopoetic sound of a starting engine together with the exclamations of a first-person narrator who states that he wants to become an engine. As that is the essential message of the poem, it is foregrounded. The fact that a larger font is used for the refrain could be read to indicate that the performer of the poem should read that part more loudly and in a more theatrical manner.

The lines of the poem take on the appearance of waves in a staircase form that highlights the meaning they carry. In the refrain, the *trrrrum*s emanate from one another. The way that the second and third *trrrrum*s are indented successively under the first *trrrrum* is suggestive of the sound of a starting engine, and after the third *trrrrum*, the engine starts. The idea of a starting engine is reinforced by the alliteration of the consonant "r" in the word *trrrrum*.

Nazım placed the second line of the second sentence of the refrain under the second "m" of the verb *makinalaşmak*, which incorporates the Turkish grammatical suffix indicating the infinitive form of the verb. In this way, the desire to become an engine emerges through that very action. Conforming to the constructivist manifesto, the poet thus appears to call on the proletariat to internalise mechanisation.

The first stanza after the refrain, again in staircase form, works in a similar manner. By placing *"geliyor bu"* ("this comes") under the words for brain, flesh, and bones, the words actually do emanate from those very elements. The same principle applies to the second and third sentences of the stanza. The placement of the part of the sentence which indicates that a dynamo has to be placed underneath the narrator further adds to its meaning. The way that the verb *"çıldırıyorum"* ("I am going out of my mind") emerges from the sentence above emphasises the causal effect of the element that is indeed making him go out of his mind. In the next sentence, only the third and last lines are indented, and as the objects of the sentence, lorries and locomotives, are actually under the verb *"kovalıyor"* ("chasing"), the words are physically chased by the verb. Moreover, the use of the present continuous tense reinforces the feeling of becoming a machine, making it even more pronounced by emphasising the continuity of the effort involved.

The last stanza before the last refrain does not utilise the staircase form. Due to this lack of indentation, the text becomes compact, as though something is speeding up. It is as if the urge to become an engine has reached its most intense stage. The form of this stanza resembles traditional poetry. The first two lines rhyme with each other and even employ a meter; the *hece* (syllable count) meter is 4+6 = 10, with a caesura after the first four syllables. In terms of content, both lines contain the most important parts at the end. The rhyme and meter highlight the fact that the narrator will only become happy when he finds a solution. In the next two lines, in free verse, an innovative solution is presented.

Makinalaşmak does not contain metaphors or comparisons. However, the poem as a whole, through a realistic description of someone who becomes an engine, comes to constitute a metaphor of the need for mechanisation in order to establish a happy modern future.

***

Nazım Hikmet's break with existing forms of Ottoman/Turkish poetry was radical. While some Turkish poets began experimenting with metre, rhyme, and content in the second half of the nineteenth century, none of them had used free verse and the actual layout of the text on the page to contribute to the meanings of poetry.

The collection in which the poem was first printed in Turkey received a strongly positive response from literary critics. The well-known female writer Halide Edip Adıvar even paid tribute to the poem in her play *Maske ve Ruh* (Masks and Spirits), in which she uses a slightly adapted version of the work as a song for schoolchildren. When the play was published in 1937, Nazım Hikmet was being heavily persecuted. Although early Republican Turkey was fiercely anti-communist, Kemalist Turkey had nonetheless taken steps towards modernisation and industrialisation in collaboration with the Soviet Union. And while both Nazım Hikmet and Mustafa Kemal Atatürk shared the idea that Turkey had to adapt to modern times, Nazım's conceptualisation of change ultimately did not mesh with that of Mustafa Kemal.

Select Bibliography

Adıvar, Halide Edib. *Kenan Çobanları, Maske ve Ruh.* İstanbul: Atlas Kitabevi, 1982. (First published in the newspaper *Yedigün* in 1937).

Aydemir, Aydın. *Nazım: Çocukluğu, Gençliği, Cezaevi Yılları.* 2nd edition. İstanbul: Cem Yayınları, 1979.

Ermolaev, Herman. *Soviet Literary Theories 1917-1934: The Genesis of Socialist Realism.* Berkely and Los Angeles: University of California Press, 1963.

Göksu, Saime and Edward Timms. *Romantic Communist: The Life and Work of Nazım Hikmet.* London: Hurst, 1999.

Hikmet, Nazım. *835 Satır.* İstanbul: Mualim Ahmet Halit Kitaphanesi, 1929.

4

"Foreigners with their Fake Turkish and Muslim Masks": A Public Debate about *Dönmes*

Didem Yerli

The Treaty of Lausanne (1923), which dealt with the exchange of Greek and Turkish popu-lations, mainly involved the simultaneous expulsions of the minority Greek-Orthodox and Turkish-Muslim populaces of Turkey and Greece, respectively. The issue of individuals with non-matching ethnic and religious backgrounds as well as undefined crypto-faith practition-ers came to the fore as a puzzling matter for both governments. Following the agreement, more than 350,000 Muslims were deported to Turkey, predominantly from northern Greece. The uprooted Muslim population also included non-Turkish Muslim groups such as Greek Muslims, Muslim Roma, Macedonian Muslims, Megleno-Romanian Muslims, certain Albanian Muslims (also known as Chams), and crypto-Jews (known as Salonican Sabbatians or *Dönme*). Despite their willingness to stay, the Salonican Sabbatians, who were publicly considered Muslims, were also swept into the population exchange.

Salonica was a former Ottoman port city which had been home to a large population of Sephardic Jews since their expulsion from the Iberian Peninsula in 1492. Salonican Sabbatians were also Sephardic Jews, but they had publicly converted to Islam in the seventeenth century following in the footsteps of Sabbatai Zevi, who had claimed to be the Jewish messiah but was persecuted by the Sultan and so chose to convert to Islam as a means of being acquitted of the charge of engaging in sedition. Up until the twentieth century, the sincerity of their conversion and their secret religious practices were not a subject of concern for the Ottoman authorities. Conversion to Islam in the Ottoman Empire involved a combination of different motivations and was welcomed in many aspects by the authorities. Following his sudden death, the followers of Sabbatei Zevi split into three sub-sects: *Yakubi*, who mainly held administrative positions and were few in number; *Kapancı*, who were involved in large-scale trading; and *Karakaş*, who led relatively secluded lives as they were involved in small-scale commercial activities. In the nineteenth century, the Sabbatians became prominent traders in Salonica and established themselves within the global commerce network. They developed close ties with European cities, and, as a consequence, their lifestyles quickly changed in line with the modern standards of the time. Some contributed financially to the Salonica branch of the Committee of Union and Progress, though very few continued to be involved in politics after the revolution of 1908. Contrary to popular conspiracy theories, crypto-Jews were never the secret driver of the Young Turk movement. In fact, the Sabbatians' identity and their secret practices began to be a matter of concern for Turkish Muslims following the revolution. In 1912 during the First Balkan War, Ottoman Salonica surrendered to Greece. As true supporters of Ottomanism, the Salonican Sabbatians were faced with the challenge of adjusting economically and politically to life in the Greek nation-state and its national identity. A similar challenge soon arose in İstanbul as well, which officially became a part of the Turkish nation-state in 1923.

The population exchange of 1924 was struck upon as a means of satisfying the will of the two states to achieve their goal of establishing homogeneous nations. The burden of relocating the populations was already quite heavy from a humanitarian perspective. Within the scope of that endeavour, the issue of non-Turkish yet Muslim communities such as the Sabbatians became the subject of knotty public debates and piqued people's curiosity given the secluded lives they led. Ironically, the public debate about the Sabbatians was largely prompted by a letter of proclamation sent to the Grand National Assembly of Turkey and delivered in person to Mustafa Kemal by a Salonican Sabbatian. The letter was first published by Yunus Nadi (Abalıoğlu, 1879–1945) on 1 January 1924 in the newspaper *Yenigün* (*New Day*).

Karakaşzade Rüştü Efendi's Open Letter*

The people who will protect and support you on this sacred path of being both materially and spirit-ually homogeneous are your fellows, who are also your true nation. Because of this fact, you embraced the principle and notion of nationality. You had refused the Albanians and Arabs [a place] within the borders of your nation despite the fact that they are Muslims. You are completely right in rejecting them. Those are the principles that save the union and the prosperity of the nation and the fatherland. For this reason, our fathers conveyed the materiality and spirituality of the nation to certain people. Among those people there might be traitors, but they cannot affect the fatherland's true people, the citizens. It is the government's main responsibility and duty to identify these traitors and drive them outside the nation's borders the moment they demonstrate their truth and reveal themselves!

First and foremost, the community of Salonican *Dönme* should be thoroughly investigated. The Dönme, who have three sub-groups—the *Yakubi*, *Karakaş*, and *Kapancı*—are originally Jews and have no relation to Islam spiritually or conscientiously! They have been deceiving the population by wearing varicoloured clothes in public. By being interposed within Turkish society with their various forms of fake behaviour, clothing, and hypocrisy, they made a fortune. They became a fatal and terminal cause for the country by capturing the great and essential commercial and economical centres. To that end, while the Turks in Macedonia are being exchanged, the issue of the Dönme should be cleared up. In that way, social and economic growth can be protected from danger, and it can be empowered and organised!

---

* Translated from the original Turkish letter published in *Akşam* on 4 January 1924.

I address you with all my sincerity,

Great Assembly of Turkey and its honourable members,

What do you think about these Dönme? Are you going to exchange them? Or are you going to allow these foreigners with their fake Turkish and Muslim masks to reside and get wealthier in the economical centres of the country such as İstanbul, İzmir, and Bursa?

***

The letter was conveyed during the process of planning out the population exchange while the majority of Sabbatians were still residing in Salonica. Public knowledge about the community was limited before the publication of the letter in newspapers. Karakaşzade Mehmet Rüştü (1880–1926), the author of the letter, was a graduate of the Feyziye School (a Sabbatian educational institution in Salonica) and a trader of textile goods who owned stores in Salonica, İstanbul, and Berlin. According to his letter, the Salonican Sabbatians were living a secret life and had been deceiving the Ottomans for centuries. His ostensible aim with sending the letter was to alert the authorities and the public about "the true identity" of the community. After its publication in *Yenigün*, the letter appeared in several other daily newspapers, and debates about the secluded community were ongoing. Rüştü's motivation for sending such a letter constituted a contradictory situation in and of itself. Although he stated that he longed for a radical change within the community and full integration into the Turkish identity, he also informed the Grand National Assembly that Turkey should not allow a wealthy non-Turkish community of intermarriage practitioners to settle and grow even wealthier in their homeland. For Rüştü, the Sabbatians were religiously and ethnically Jewish and thus not a match or eligible for Turkish citizenship. Rüştü's open letter was clearly an unusual expression of racial nationalism.

Several interpretations can be offered up to explain Rüştü's motivation for making this unconventional statement. By looking at the period in which he sent the letter, it could be argued that he was trying to avoid becoming a part of the population exchange, as had been the case with Muslim Albanians, the exchange of whom was rejected outright by the Turkish government. Indeed, at the time, by revealing that they were actually Jewish, many Sabbatian families pushed to obtain Greek citizenship so they could go on living in Salonica. Nonetheless, their revelation was immediately rejected by the rabbi of Athens. On January 4, Necmettin (Sadak, 1890–1953) published the complete version of the letter in the newspaper *Akşam*. According to the article, a similar letter had been sent to the Greek government but the Sabbatian community's request for citizenship was refused by Greek officials, who considered the Sabbatians to be even more dangerous than the Turks. Several articles dealing with the issue appeared in daily newspapers within a couple of weeks. Rüştü's reasons for writing the letter were interpreted as being a consequence of financial disagreements he had with the community, which eventually led to him being excluded. Some even claimed that he may have been paid by the Turkish government to reveal the community's perplexing identity.

Rüştü's attack was indeed a reflection of the burgeoning racial nationalism that had been advocated by certain Turkish figures since the revolution of 1908. His statement prompted others to rephrase their animosity towards non-Turkish Muslim groups who were included in an "erroneous" population exchange policy. Hüseyin Cahit (Yalçın, 1875–1957), a journalist and politician, published an article in the newspaper *Tanin* on 5 January arguing that the nation was above culture and cultural differences, so *Selanik'liler* (people from Salonica), Albanians, and Arabs could be part of the Turkish nation as well. Ten days after the first publication of Rüştü's letter, an anonymous front-page article titled "A Mysterious Page of History" ("*Tarihin Esrarengiz bir Sahifesi*") appeared in the newspaper *Vatan*, the first in a series of articles that continued for almost two weeks (11–17 and 19–22 January). Through the series, the issue of *Selanik'liler* was brought to light by way of calls for an understanding of civic nationhood based on a social contract which citizens would pledge to uphold without reference to race or culture. The anonymous writer was in fact a *Yakubi* named Ahmet Emin (Yalman, 1888–1972), a sociologist with a doctoral degree from Columbia University and a graduate of the Feyziye School like Rüştü. Ahmet Emin condemned Ottoman notions of tolerance and pluralism which, he argued, should be replaced by state control and homogeneity. Hence, for Ahmet Emin, the Sabbatian community was a result of a "medieval" system that had existed for several generations but was disappearing through intermarriage. He contended that, in the new society, identity should be defined and imposed by the state, and since the Sabbatians were just a "backward" sectarian Sufi order, not secret practitioners of Judaism, they should be buried in the "medieval" past together with other offshoots of Islam. Ahmet Emin, in point of fact, was not completely objecting to Rüştü's claims but providing a reinterpretation of the obscure situation while rejecting the existence of a mysterious secluded community and economic lobbying. Additionally, Ahmet Emin addressed what he referred to as "crucial" differences between the sub-sects by pointing out the *Karakaş* and their reclusive lifestyle.

***

In the years that followed, further accounts were published about the mysterious customs of the Salonican Sabbatians. The axis of the discussion, however, was no longer their race or whether they were fit for Turkish citizenship. Rather, public distrust focused on their distinct incompatible identity as non-Turkish Muslims and their so-called secret beliefs. Meanwhile, in 1928 the issue of secularism (*laiklik*) was introduced through an amendment to the constitution of 1924. Unlike other definitions of secularism, Turkish *laiklik* implied state control over religion instead of the separation of religious institutions and the state. Yet, for the majority of the population, Islam was an undeniable symbolic component of Turkish identity. That conflict was surely not unique to Turkey. In many nation-states, national identity has often become dependent on religion. Paradoxically, within the framework of that model, the state's stance was defined as being neutral with regard to all religions. If that were the case, then why were the Sabbatians still a problem for Turkish identity?

In his letter, Rüştü proposed the adoption of a unifying identity that would do away with the existence of "parasitical" communities and initially he asked Mustafa Kemal and the Grand National Assembly to take measures accordingly. An article published in the newspaper *Vakit* on 7 January 1924 claimed that the Grand National Assembly held a closed session on the matter, one outcome of which may have been a directive to start recording the origins of Salonicans the moment they arrived in Turkey. However, the first official action taken against the Sabbatians (which also officially acknowledged their existence) took place in 1942 when the Wealth Tax was introduced. The tax, in essence, was implemented with the aim of disrupting the financially advantageous position of non-Muslim minorities and guiding capital towards the newly emerging Turkish-Muslim bourgeoisie. Like many Greeks, Jews, and Armenians, the Sabbatians were also subject to additional taxes although they were lower in comparison.

In the second half of the twentieth century, whether they slowly vanished through inter-marriage or not, the Sabbatians became less of a concern for the public as the debates about them lost their political significance in the now more firmly established nation-state of Turkey. In the last twenty years, two popular books about conspiracy theories have come out, claiming to have solved the mystery of the secret identity of the ruling and wealthy elite of Turkey—as the argument goes, they are Sabbatians. Since then, the Turkish popular imagination has again been haunted by the idea of ghostly Jews masquerading as Muslim-Turkish elites, but bearing a different political significance.

Select Bibliography

Baer, Marc David. *The Dönme: Jewish Converts, Muslim Revolutionaries and Secular Turks.* Stanford: Stanford University Press, 2010.
Bali, Rıfat N. *A Scapegoat for All Seasons: The Dönmes or Crypto-Jews of Turkey.* İstanbul: Isis Press, 2008.
Şişman, Cengiz. *The Burden of Silence: Sabbatai Sevi and the Evolution of the Ottoman-Turkish Dönmes.* Oxford: Oxford University Press, 2015.

5
"Stricken by Illness":
Political Plagues of the New Capital

Onur Ada

On 13 November 1924, Ahmet Emin (Yalman, 1888–1972), the editor of the İstanbul-based newspaper *Vatan*, announced to readers that Prime Minister İsmet (İnönü, 1884–1973) and his political opponent Rauf (Orbay, 1881–1964) were suffering from malaria, as a result of which they would be unable to perform their official duties for an uncertain period of time. İsmet's cabinet had secured a vote of confidence just a few days earlier on 8 November in a session that he was unable to attend due to his illness. Although Rauf was leading the opposition within the People's Party (*Halk Fırkası*, PP), he could not join the naysayers, as his colleague Refet (Bele, 1881–1963) stated in his defence against those deputies who were particularly critical of Rauf's views.

İsmet and Rauf had been at loggerheads for years in the course of numerous heated debates on sensitive issues involving allegations of corruption and the type of regime that should be installed. While the leading faction associated with President Mustafa Kemal (Atatürk, 1881–1938) and İsmet had recently advocated for and succeeded in achieving the abolition of the sultanate and caliphate, in the eyes of Rauf and his colleagues, who also considered themselves "devotees of the Republic," the question of whether the regime was democratic or authoritarian in nature was a pressing matter. In November 1924, the latter was about to finalise preparations for the establishment of an opposition party, the Progressive Republican Party (*Terakkiperver Cumhuriyet Fırkası*, PRP). It was a notable coincidence that these two political rivals, İsmet and Rauf, fell ill at roughly the same time, just as tensions between them were at their peak.

This political confrontation took place primarily in Ankara, which had been the de facto capital of the National Forces during the War of Independence, and slightly more than a year had passed since it was officially designated the new capital in October 1923. A number of politicians, bureaucrats, and middle-class professionals, many of whom had left İstanbul to live and work in Ankara, were dissatisfied because of the rapid spread of epidemics, poor working conditions, and the lack of social life and opportunities for leisure in the town.

*Two Beloved Political Figures Stricken by Illness**

Telegrams sent from Ankara report that İsmet Pasha and Rauf Bey have fallen gravely ill. We cannot imagine a Turk who would not be deeply saddened by this news. Both İsmet Pasha and Rauf Bey stand among those outstanding cherished figures who have made history throughout their lives. But yes, they are human beings just like us. Anyone can fall prey to any kind of affliction. Three factors appear to have played a role in them falling ill, which we would like to evaluate here one by one.

The first one is Ankara and its environs. It is a terrible act of recklessness to gather together these great men who represent such irreplaceable national capital and have them live in a malaria-infested area. If Ankara is to remain the seat of government in this country, the swamps must be drained immediately. In terms of protective health measures, today's Ankara is worse off than any primitive place untouched by the hand of civilised men.

The second point concerns the lifestyle of Ankara's residents. Many of us work like the most advanced Westerners today, but our endeavours leave us exhausted because we do not know their working methods. The tasks we complete after toiling away for many hours per day could be done much more quickly with an organised system of work. Moreover, we live in the most primitive conditions, even though we work like Westerners. The only means of pleasure and relaxation we can imagine in Ankara is drinking [akşamcılık], which is nothing but a new way of wasting energy.

The third factor is that an intense, gloomy sense of hatred and rage dominates our public life. This atmosphere, which is so full of enmity, devours our health and willpower like a monster. It turns brothers who need to be thinking about the various needs and shortcomings of the country into enemies instead of encouraging them to work together for the common good of the fatherland. We are no different than two camps that seek out conflict in the presence of an enemy. It is difficult to find anyone who regularly deals with governmental agencies and political life but has not been tainted. The people who carry out the most important services for this country are subjected to insults within a few years. Their services are seen through the flip side of binoculars, as so many people compete with each other to zoom in and view their mistakes as if through a microscope.

***

During the War of Independence, the National Forces not only fought against their military adversaries but also had to deal with epidemics, which radically increased the mortality rate, and this legacy of the First World War persisted well after the founding of the Republic. The ruling elite, predominantly comprised of military officers, declared war on epidemics, particularly malaria, which by 1924 had become more prevalent than ever. The response of

* Translated from the original Turkish in Ahmet Emin (Yalman), "İki Aziz Hasta," *Vatan* (İstanbul), 13 November 1924.

the authorities was based on a series of recommendations drawn up by a malaria commission. As part of its plan of action, the government sought to institute a variety of measures, including the supply of medication (mainly quinine) largely to the peasants, the launching of information campaigns about preventative measures, the draining of swamps, and the training of health officials.

The authorities were aware that malaria could be lethal, but it was thought that the disease was confined to certain parts of Anatolia, and they did not realise that a new strand of malaria was spreading throughout the country. Moreover, the epidemic was particularly detrimental to the peasants, who were largely ill-informed about the affliction and were already suffering from poor nutrition. As such, the notion that malaria was a rural disease and that it was necessary to enlighten the peasantry to eradicate it was internalised and disseminated during the single-party period. Efforts to protect public health were carried out in the manner of military campaigns involving not only state agencies and civil society organisations but also the military itself. The decision to involve the military was based on the conviction that it represented the strongest and most disciplined state department. All those assumptions, however, contrasted sharply with the reality on the ground. Firstly, the type of malaria that was spreading was a new strand that had been brought back by Ottoman troops returning home from battlefields and prisoner camps in distant places such as North Africa and Siberia. This strand, known as tropical malaria, was much more lethal than the local variations found in Anatolia. Secondly, it affected the population at large, not just the peasants—although they did constitute the largest segment of society—and people from all walks of life had been infected, including leading military commanders such as Mustafa Kemal, İsmet, Rauf, and Kazım (Karabekir, 1882–1948), who now represented the new political elite. As indicated by statistics, the military was hit particularly hard, which should come as no surprise since peasants constituted the primary fighting force. It seems that this led the authorities to frame malaria as an issue of national security. Ironically, the military officers who were involved in the spread of the disease were expected to take their place on the "front lines" of the malaria "campaign" side by side with health officials.

In his column, Ahmet Emin depicted Ankara as a desolate, malaria-infested town. His harsh criticism was by no means the exception and can be seen as illustrative of a sentiment common among its new inhabitants. For the ruling elite, most of whom had moved there from the most urbanised areas of the Ottoman Empire, such as İstanbul, the Balkans, and the Aegean region, Ankara proved to be a difficult place to live and work. This rural Anatolian town, the outlying areas of which were largely agrarian, had little to offer in terms of the entertainment they had enjoyed back home, and the new residents had difficulty fulfilling even their most basic needs, such as housing and medical care. Given these circumstances, many turned to the consumption of alcohol, which Ahmet Emin described as "a waste of energy." Ironically, the law on the prohibition of alcoholic beverages, which had been in force since September 1920, was repealed in April 1924, not long before the publication of his piece.

In the early 1920s, Ankara was surrounded by swamps and marshes, the ideal breeding ground for mosquitos, which was likely why Ahmet Emin drew attention to the town's environs to account for İsmet and Rauf's illness, and it offered little in the way of social life, which, according to Ahmet Emin, undermined the health and morale of prominent figures, resulting in bitter rivalries and an increase in the potential for loss of life. For the Kemalist government, anti-malaria campaigns represented much more than ordinary measures aimed at eradicating the disease: not only was the ruling elite concerned about the well-being of the population, their own lives were at risk too. Moreover, the expectation was that Ankara would be the embodiment of Kemalist ideals of modern urban spaces in practice, which itself represented a challenge to prove that science could overcome the difficulties posed by nature and the lack of knowledge among the populace. In line with Enlightenment notions of development, the ruling elite believed that they could equip society with the scientific knowledge and skills needed to combat and overcome diseases. That was seen as crucial, especially because the population, which was estimated to be between 10-14 million people, was considered dangerously small given Turkey's geographical size, so malaria had to be conquered to ensure the growth of a robust, healthy society.

***

The early years of the Republic of Turkey witnessed political confrontations that centred around issues ranging from the type of regime to be installed and economic policy to epidemics and life in the new capital. The PRP only managed to survive the fierce state of competition with the ruling PP until June 1925, and after its closure, an authoritarian single-party regime that restricted the press and, to a large extent, shut down public debates became firmly established. İsmet strengthened his powerbase in the regime, thereby securing his position as one of the country's most powerful political figures. Even though he occasionally became embroiled in power struggles with Mustafa Kemal, Fethi (Okyar, 1880–1943), and Celal (Bayar, 1883–1986), the intensity of political tensions decreased dramatically.

Ankara was not only the setting of many of the political rivalries of the early 1920s, but it was also the subject of fierce debates about whether it was a suitable place to establish the seat of government. Nonetheless, despite widespread opposition, Ankara remained the capital of the Turkish Republic. In line with the regime's urban planning goals, this small town was transformed to suit the interests and expectations of its inhabitants, and during the single-party period, it came to represent the hallmark of a modern, national lifestyle bolstered by events such as republican balls, festivals, and concerts.

The widespread impacts of the malaria epidemic on Ankara's entire population, including the ruling elite, detracted from the image of the town as a modern capital—an image that the regime so fervently sought to disseminate. While the single-party government repeatedly claimed to have prevailed over malaria, due to a lack of resources and medication, it was unable to eradicate the disease. Only after the Second World War did Turkey make substantial progress in the struggle against malaria, and that was primarily because of the development of the pesticide DDT and the allocation of large sums of money acquired through the Marshall Plan and the World Health Organisation (WHO). In short, technological developments and foreign aid appear to have played a decisive role in bringing malaria under control by 1950, as did an increase in know-how and expertise. However, malaria resurfaced in the late 1970s, and since then, it has remained a pressing issue in some parts of the country.

Select Bibliography

Evered, Kyle T., and Emine Ö. Evered. "Governing Population, Public Health, and Malaria in the Early Turkish Republic." *Journal of Historical Geography* 37, no. 4 (2011): 470–82.

Yalman, Ahmet Emin. *Yakın Tarihte Gördüklerim ve Geçirdiklerim (1922–1971)*. 2 vols. İstanbul: Pera Turizm ve Ticaret A.Ş., 1997.

Yanıkdağ, Yücel. *Healing the Nation: Prisoners of War, Medicine and Nationalism in Turkey, 1914–1939*. Edinburgh: Edinburgh University Press, 2013.

Zürcher, Erik-Jan. *Political Opposition in the Early Turkish Republic: The Progressive Republican Party, 1924–1925*. Leiden: Brill, 1991.

6

"Empowered to Prohibit":
The Law on the Maintenance of Order

Erik-Jan Zürcher

The Law on the Maintenance of Order (*Takrir-i Sükûn Kanunu*), which was passed by the Grand National Assembly on 4 March 1925, was a product of the insecurity of the republican regime established a year and a half earlier. The political leadership of the young republic felt that it was under threat from both the inside and the outside.

The threat from the inside was posed by the political opposition that had emerged in November 1924 in the form of the Progressive Republican Party (*Terakkiperver Cumhuriyet Fırkası*). The party was officially founded when a number of parliamentary representatives broke away from the People's Party (*Halk Fırkası*), which had been established by President Mustafa Kemal Pasha (Atatürk, 1881–1938) in 1923, but it was actually the crystallisation of two oppositional currents that had slowly been building for almost three years following the victory of the Turkish nationalists in the "National Struggle" (*Millî Mücadele*) after the First World War.

One current consisted of the remaining leaders of the Committee of Union and Progress (CUP), which had brought about the constitutional revolution of 1908 and governed the country as a single-party dictatorship from 1913 to 1918. During the struggle for independence, these prominent Unionists had supported the nationalist leadership, but after victory was achieved, they assumed it was only natural for them to reclaim their position in Turkish politics. In April 1923 they convened in İstanbul, drew up a political program for a revived CUP, and proposed to Mustafa Kemal that he become their leader—a proposal he rejected out of hand. Although a few former Unionists entered the Grand National Assembly in the elections of the summer of 1923, they were very conscious of the crucial role that the Unionist organisation had played in the national resistance movement and therefore they felt that they had been unjustly rejected by the leadership in Ankara.

The other current was comprised of Mustafa Kemal's former comrades in arms—the military and political leaders of the national resistance movement. After the victory of 1922, they had been increasingly marginalised by Mustafa Kemal. They were not involved in the founding of the People's Party in September 1923 or the drafting of the election manifesto, the "Nine Principles," in April 1923, nor were they consulted about the decision to proclaim the Republic on 29 October. Their spokesman, Hüseyin Rauf (Orbay, 1881–1964), was fiercely attacked when he expressed critical ideas on the subject during newspaper interviews. The decision by the Grand National Assembly in March 1924 to abolish the caliphate alarmed this group of former leaders because they saw in the caliph a necessary counterweight to the increasingly authoritarian tendencies of President Mustafa Kemal.

During the summer, this group, which included most of the top-ranking generals in Turkey, held informal consultations. When the president found out about their gatherings, he forced them to make a decision: either stay in the army and renounce their seats in the Grand National Assembly (which they had been given on the basis of their record as leaders in the National Struggle from 1919 to 1922) or opt for a role in politics and resign from their posts. In October, they resigned their commands. A fortnight later they founded a new party, in which some leading erstwhile Unionists, including former Finance Minister Mehmed Cavid Bey (1875–1926) and former Mamuret el-Aziz Governor Sabıt Bey (Sağıroğlu, 1882–1960), also played a prominent role.

The Progressive Republican Party only managed to draw in about thirty parliamentarians, or approximately twenty per cent of the Grand National Assembly, but the Ankara leadership was well aware of both the nationwide prestige of the former military leaders, these "pashas," and of the vast organisational network of the former CUP. Such a combination had the potential to be quite powerful, which partially explains why the leadership felt that it was internally under threat.

Moreover, in February 1925, an external threat arose—external, that is, to the political leadership of the Republic. The first reports of a widespread insurrection among Kurdish tribes to the north of Diyarbekir (Diyarbakır after 1937) started reaching the capital. The insurrection was led by a dervish sheikh (in Turkish, şeyh), Said of Palu, and its rallying cries included a call for the rejection of the "godless" Republic, the reestablishment of sharia (in Turkish, şeriat—Islamic canon law), and the reinstatement of the caliphate. At the same time, however, preparations for the rebellion had been underway for over a year under the leadership of a secret organisation called the Azadî (Kurdish for "Freedom") which was comprised of Kurdish officers who had served in the Ottoman army. It thus became clear that the rebels sought not only Kurdish independence, but also Islamic restoration.

For the young Republic, those developments represented a grave threat to its very existence. Kurdish independence had been included as an option in the terms of the Treaty of Sèvres set forth in 1920 but not in the Treaty of Lausanne signed in 1923 which replaced it, so there was a great deal of frustration brought on by unfulfilled expectations among Kurdish nationalists. Further exacerbating the issue was the fact that Turkey and the United Kingdom were engaged at the time in a dispute over the future of the—largely Kurdish—former Ottoman province of Mosul. Turkey rejected British claims that it should be included in the Kingdom of Iraq, largely on the grounds that Turks and Kurds had historically been united. Clearly, the eruption of a Kurdish rebellion against the new Republic of Turkey was quite damaging to that claim.

Drawing on the support of the majority in the Grand National Assembly, Mustafa Kemal reacted swiftly. He replaced Prime Minister Fethi (Okyar, 1880–1943), who was recognised as a political liberal with a distaste for extra-legal means, with İsmet (İnönü, 1884–1973), a former military officer known for his loyalty to the president. The next day he had the assembly adopt the Law on the Maintenance of Order, which, despite its brevity, had far-reaching consequences.

The Law on the Maintenance of Order*

Article 1

The government is hereby empowered to prohibit on its own initiative and by administrative measure (subject to the approval of the president) all organisations, provocations, exhortations, initiatives, and publications which disrupt social structures, law and order, and security, and incite reactionism and subversion. The government may hand over the perpetrators of any such acts to an Independence Tribunal.

Article 2

This law shall be in force for a period of two years starting from the date of its promulgation.

Article 3

The cabinet is entrusted with the implementation of this law.

***

Since the law covered such broad categories, it clearly granted the government almost unlimited powers, which it would not hesitate to use. New Independence Tribunals (*İstiklâl Mahkemeleri*), revolutionary courts where the accused had no representation and no right of appeal, were instituted the very same day. In the short run, they were used against elements of the press that had been critical of the republican government in the previous two years. These included most of the large İstanbul-based newspapers (*Tevhid-i Efkâr, Son Telgraf, İstiklâl,* and *Sebilürreşad*), the socialist organs *Orak-Çekiç* and *Aydınlık,* as well as the CUP-linked *Tanin,* in addition to provincial publications such as *Sayha* and *Toksöz* in Adana and *İstikbâl* in Trabzon. The Progressive Republican Party had strongly supported the suppression of the Kurdish rebellion but opposed the Law on the Maintenance of Order on the grounds that it was too broad. And they were right: on 5 May 1925, the Ankara Independence Tribunal demanded the closure of the PRP and a month later the party was closed down, in spite of its support for the state's policies in the east of the country.

These, however, were only the short-term effects. In June-July 1926, during show-trials in Izmir and Ankara, an Independence Tribunal convicted the former leaders of the CUP and some leading members of the PRP on rather spurious grounds that they had been planning to assassinate the president.

---

* Translated from the original Turkish in *T.B.M.M. Zabıt Ceridesi*, vol. 15, 4 March 1925, 131, http://www5.tbmm. gov.tr/tutanaklar/TUTANAK/TBMM/d02/c015/tbmm02015069.pdf.

The law was extended for another two years in March 1927 and only allowed to lapse in 1929. As a result, the government and its tribunals exercised unrestricted powers to suppress any and all forms of criticism and opposition precisely during the period 1925 to 1929, during which many of the Kemalist regime's most renowned reforms were carried out: the closure of dervish orders in September 1925; the clothing reform (and introduction of the hat as compulsory headgear for officials) in November 1925; the introduction of a civil code of law derived from the Swiss code in 1926; the conversion to Europe's system of time, calendars, and measurements in 1926; the proclamation of Sunday as the day of rest; and, the famed alphabet reform of 1928. All of these reforms were enacted when the Law on the Maintenance of Order was in effect and allowed for unrestricted authoritarianism. In the historiography of the early Republic, these reforms loom very large indeed, but the role played by the Law on the Maintenance of Order is generally overlooked.

Select Bibliography

Olson, Robert. *The Emergence of Kurdish Nationalism and the Sheikh Said Rebellion, 1880–1970.* Austin: University of Texas Press, 1989.

Tunçay, Mete. *Türkiye Cumhuriyetinde Tek Parti Yönetiminin Kurulması 1923–1930.* Ankara: Yurt Yayınları, 1981.

Zürcher, Erik-Jan. *Political Opposition in the Early Turkish Republic: The Progressive Republican Party, 1924–1925.* Leiden: Brill, 1991.

7
"The Congregation of Civilisation": Mustafa Kemal Pasha's Speech in Kastamonu

Remzi Çağatay Çakırlar

On 30 August 1925, Mustafa Kemal Pasha (Atatürk, 1881–1938) gave a speech in the northern Anatolian city of Kastamonu which was of particular significance in terms of its content and context. By that time, efforts to implement reforms had been underway for more than a year, resulting in the abolition of the Ottoman Caliphate, the unification of primary and secondary schools for boys and girls and their administration by the Ministry of Education, and lastly the abolition of the Ministry of Pious Foundations (*Evkaf Vekâleti*) and the office of the Chief Mufti (*Şeyhülislam*). The latter two bodies, however, were replaced by the Directorate-General for Pious Foundations (*Evkaf Umum Müdürlüğü*) and the Directorate of Religious Affairs (*Diyanet İşleri Reisliği*). Moreover, both offices were brought under the control and supervision of the office of the prime ministry.

The Kastamonu speech was delivered five months after the Sheikh Said Rebellion, which erupted in eastern Anatolia in February of 1925, and the proclamation of the Law on the Maintenance of Order in March of the same year, which gave extraordinary powers to the Republican People's Party government of İsmet (İnönü, 1884–1974). Although the rebellion bore an element of Kurdish dissidence, official emphasis was placed on the assertion that it had been a religious reactionary (*irticai*) insurrection. Mustafa Kemal's visit to Kastamonu was in that sense symbolic and of great importance. The city was not only an essential transit point connecting Ankara to the Black Sea, its population had also loyally supported the national resistance movement from the very beginning. The local newspaper *Açıksöz* (Straightforward) played a significant role by conveying Mustafa Kemal's messages throughout Anatolia. In contrast to other places in north-western Anatolia which, under the direction of the sultan's government in İstanbul, had witnessed small- and large-scale rebellions against the Grand National Assembly in Ankara during the National Struggle, Kastamonu had remained loyal. Moreover, when the Ottoman Sheik-ul-Islam Dürrîzâde Abdullah Efendi (1867–1923) signed five fatwas against the National Forces (*Kuvâ-yi Milliye*) and condemned Mustafa Kemal to death for opposing the Sultan Caliph and his government in İstanbul, the religious scholars who signed the counter-fatwa of Rıfat Bey (Börekçi, 1860–1941), the Mufti of Ankara and the first president of the Directorate of Religious Affairs, for the most part hailed from Kastamonu. As a result, the city's scholars contributed to the religious legitimisation of the cause of the National Struggle in opposition to the Allied occupation and the İstanbul government.

Following the proclamation of the Republic in 1923, Kastamonu was to play yet another symbolic role in the modernisation projects of Mustafa Kemal, who was then the first president of the Republic. Earlier in 1925, Mustafa Kemal had received an invitation from two groups of delegates from the city, whose residents wanted to hold an audience with him. Mustafa Kemal saw the trip as an opportunity to introduce his most recent reform to the conservative Anatolian populace: the wearing of the Western-style hat (*şapka*) to replace the fez, which had been commonly worn by men in the nineteenth century. On August 27 at the İnebolu branch of the Turkish Hearths (*Türk Ocakları*), he delivered a well-known speech in which he presented the hat reform to the public. On 30 August, he delivered another speech, excerpts of which are given below, at the Republican People's Party's city headquarters.

Excerpts from Mustafa Kemal's Speech in Kastamonu[*]

Gentlemen!

The most outstanding aspect of my observations is that the genuine people of this beautiful region are possessed of such a very enlightened, and very capacious and sublime, mentality. [...] I think that those foolish people who strive to paralyze our steps towards renovation by claiming and offering up quite the opposite of this fact, while adjudicating, rely on their own defective knowledge, rotten logic, and deficient minds.

If those miserable egoists, had, instead of doing such things, consulted the common sentiments of the people, thereby receiving insights and inspiration from them, they would not have fallen into those vile errors which have left them today in that shameful position. However, acknowledging the great significance of common sense through the superiority of the mind, rationale, and merit would not serve the purposes of dishonest scholars. My friends, no one has the right to suspect that our nation has acquired a sturdy consciousness after the great work of action and events whose hero was (the nation) itself. Consciousness always leads to progress and renovation.

Since retreat has such an unacceptable character, the people of the Republic of Turkey will continue to stride towards progress and renovation with great steps; the choice to go backwards or halt cannot be considered [an option] unless one loses that consciousness. Over the centuries, those malicious efforts that were exerted, except at times, to put the nation to sleep, could never succeed in paralyzing the nation's consciousness. [...]

True revolutionaries are those who know how to penetrate the spirit and conscience of the people whom they want to direct towards progress and renovation. [...]

[*] Translated from the original Turkish first published in *Hakimiyet-i Milliye*, 1 September 1925, available in transliteration in *Atatürk'ün Söylev ve Demeçleri*, vol. II, ed. Nimet Arsan, 3rd ed. (Ankara: Türk İnkilap Tarihi Enstitüsü Yayımları, 1981), 213-17.

Gentlemen!

The aim of the revolutions that we carried out and are carrying out today is to convey the people of the Republic of Turkey to a thoroughly contemporary and, in all its meaning and framing, civilised social community. These are the actual principles of our revolutions. It is imperative to smash any mentalities that cannot accept this reality. Those who have such a mentality have been the ones who corroded and numbed the mind of this nation thus far. In any case, the existing superstitions of the intellect will be totally eradicated. If they are not removed, it will be impossible to bring the light of truth to the mind. Begging for help from shrines and dead and false saints is shameful for a civilised society. What could be the aim of existing congregations for their followers aside from carrying them to the prosperity of material and moral life? Today, given the complete extent of science and knowledge in the illuminated face of civilisation, I do not accept the existence of, within the civilised community of Turkey, primitive people who seek material and moral prosperity through the guidance of this or that sheikh.

Gentlemen and nation!

You should know that the Republic of Turkey cannot be a country of sheikhs, dervishes, and followers and members [of congregations]. The straightest and most truthful congregation is the congregation of civilisation. [...] The government of our republic has a Directorate of Religious Affairs. There we can find officials such as muftis, preachers, and imams who have their place at this office and who are on active duty. The merit of excellence of knowledge of those individuals in charge is evident. However, in this sense, I also see a lot of people who are not in charge but continue to dress as they used to. I have come across, among people such as these, very ignorant and even illiterate individuals. In some places, such ignorant people in particular attempt to conduct the affairs of others while pretending to be their representatives. In a manner, they seek to hinder [our] direct connection with the people. I would like to ask of people such as them: From where and whom do they assume such authority and titles? [...]

Just like any other nation, we too have our own national attire; however, unquestionably that attire is not what we are wearing. As a matter of fact, only a few of us know what our national attire is. For instance, in a crowd, I see someone. [There is] a fez on his head and a green turban on top of the fez; [he is wearing] a shirt and a jacket like mine over his shirt, but I cannot even see what [he is wearing] under that. Now, what kind of attire is that? Would a civilised human being wear just anything and thus make himself a laughingstock in the face of the whole world? The entire nation, and state officials as well, will correct their attire. [...]

Friends,

The Turkish nation has proven itself to be, after so many incidents, a reformist and revolutionary nation. It is not that in previous periods before these final years that our nation did not tread the path of renovation, nor did it not go through social revolutions. However, the proper outcomes are nowhere to be seen. Have you ever inquired why? In my opinion, the reason is that those attempts did not target the roots, the foundation [of the problem]. Let me explain this clearly. A social community consists of two kinds of human beings, namely men and women. Is it possible for us to advance one part of that corpus and put up with the other and have the entire corpus achieve progress? Is it possible for one half to rise into the sky while the other half of the community is chained to the ground? [...].

***

This speech embodied manifold characteristics of the early republican single-party period and its emerging Kemalist ideology. First, it signalled the social turn taking place in reforms and revolutions by clearly showing that Mustafa Kemal and the leadership around him not only sought to transform state institutions and laws, but also the behaviour, attire, habits, and outlooks of the people. Thus, the Kastamonu speech can be read as a commentary indicating that republican Turkey was ready to proceed further and adopt what was considered contemporary, which, in one aspect, was Western forms of attire. Moreover, Mustafa Kemal underscored the notion that a break had occurred with Ottoman reformers of the past, claiming that they had neglected the roots of the country's problems, which leads to his second point: the role of woman in society. Mustafa Kemal argued that previous attempts to implement reforms had failed and did not endure because they solely targeted half of society, namely men, and neglected women.

Another notable aspect of the speech is that it represents an open challenge to anyone who would oppose the new regime's political authority and cultural hegemony. Mustafa Kemal did not hide his intention to clear aside any and all obstacles that could stand in his way as he set about instituting reforms and bringing about modernisation. By openly proclaiming that it was necessary to quash troublemakers, he was signalling those showdowns that were likely to take place between himself and any potential opponents or resistance to his reforms. Mustafa Kemal was not only targeting political dissidents, but also the traditional forces and institutions in society that used religion to dominate people's minds. He openly set his sights on such opposition figures, referring to them as "false scholars" and "self-proclaimed representatives of the people". A few months after the speech, the government closed down dervish lodges and religious brotherhoods. Moreover, the speech is an important piece of testimony showing that Mustafa Kemal and the republican leadership did not just counter such self-appointed authorities with representative figures and bodies such as deputies, parliament, and the government, but also with state officials employed with the Directorate of Religious Affairs such as imams, muftis, and preachers.

Mustafa Kemal's choice of words in his speech is also notable, as it echoes the scientistic and positivistic vocabulary of the Young Turks and Kemalists with regard to the issues of modernity, society, science, and morals, and that can be seen in the way he employed terms such as "progress," "renovation," "civilisation," "civilised," "contemporary," "reason," "knowledge," "science," "consciousness," "mind," "logic," "sentiment," "moral," "spiritual power," "inspiration," and "conscience". Mustafa Kemal often spoke of both personal and national conscience in relation to values, virtues, and a moral compass that enables individuals and societies to distinguish between good and evil and guides them in their decision-making and actions. Moreover, the speech is indicative of Mustafa Kemal's knowledge about crowd psychology.

***

Mustafa Kemal's speech connected his efforts towards modernisation with an international audience, which was considered to be representative of modern civilisation. Europe in the post-Great War period of reconciliation bore witness to increasingly anticlerical, laic, and secular politics, as can be seen in the examples of the Soviet Union and the French Third Republic under the Left Cartel Government (1924–1925). With regard to reforms targeting family and attire, Mustafa Kemal did not hide his concerns about the negative reputation Turkey had acquired as a result of woman's position in society and their traditional forms of clothing. Thus, the reforms mentioned in the Kastamonu speech also had the aim of altering republican Turkey's image abroad.

Select Bibliography

Azak, Umut. *Islam and Secularism in Turkey: Kemalism, Religion and the Nation State*. London: I.B. Tauris, 2010.

Gawrych, W. George. *The Young Atatürk: From Ottoman Soldier to Statesman of Turkey*. London: I.B. Tauris, 2013.

Hanioğlu, M. Şükrü. *Atatürk: An Intellectual Biography*. Princeton: Princeton University Press, 2014.

Toprak, Zafer. *Türkiye'de Popülizm (1908–1923)*. İstanbul: Doğan Kitap, 2013.

Zürcher, Erik-Jan. *Political Opposition in the Early Turkish Republic: The Progressive Republican Party, 1924-1925*. Leiden: Brill, 1991.

8
A Step Forward, a Step Back:
Women' Rights and the Civil Code of 1926

Nicole A.N.M. van Os

Even almost a century after the Civil Code of 1926 entered into force, supporters of the legacy of Mustafa Kemal Atatürk (1881–1938) still celebrate its anniversary every year as a historical milestone in the process of the secularisation and modernisation of Turkish society that took place under his leadership.

When the first efforts to develop and codify a system of civil law were undertaken towards the end of the period of reforms known as the *Tanzimat* between 1867 and 1876, family law was excluded, and jurisdiction over issues regarding marriage, divorce, and inheritance remained with the religious authorities of the various ethno-religious communities living in the Ottoman Empire. Only in 1917 during the First World War was Ottoman family law codified for the first time. A committee appointed by the Unionist government drafted a Decree on Family Law which was limited to the regulation of marriage and divorce; the overall aim of promulgating the decree was to achieve legal unity by divesting the religious authorities of the various eth-no-religious communities of their jurisdiction over such matters. While the Decree on Family Law was largely based on Islamic law, it also included separate chapters for non-Muslims. After a heated debate in the Ottoman parliament, the decree was referred to the Council of Justice so that it could advise MPs on the issue, but that advice never materialised. After the war, which ended with the defeat of the Ottomans and the collapse of the Unionist government, the decree was repealed by the highest religious authority, the Sheikh ul-Islam, who at the time was also the acting Grand Vizier (Prime Minister) of the İstanbul government. By making that decision, the government, which at the time was under the control of British occupying forces in İstanbul, was pandering to the fierce opposition that had been voiced by the conservative religious authorities of the various ethno-religious communities, who were happy to see their jurisdiction restored. Although the oppositional government established in Ankara in 1920 had issued a decree stating that it would not recognise any of the rulings made by the government under occupation in İstanbul, it accepted the cancellation of the decree and, for a short period, left the jurisdiction of family affairs to the religious authorities once again.

In 1923, the Ankara government appointed a Civil Code Commission, which was tasked with drawing up a new code. The stipulations of the resulting code, however, prioritised religious regulations over the principles of a modern state and as such was quite similar to the Decree on Family Law of 1917. Since the new code did not correspond with Mustafa Kemal's vision of modernity, in 1925 a new commission was assembled and assigned the responsibility of translating, examining, and annotating the Swiss Civil Code of 1907, which was one of the most recently drafted and implemented civil codes in Europe. The Swiss code was not only new, the simplicity and clarity of the text made it preferable to the other civil codes in force in Europe at the time. The work of the commission resulted in the Turkish Civil Code, which was passed by Parliament on 17 February 1926 and published in the Official Gazette on 4 April of the same year, eventually taking effect six months later on 4 October.

The Civil Code of 1926 consisted of four books, the second of which included articles 82 to 438 dealing with family law. The articles quoted below were drawn from that book, with the exception of the last one, article 439, which is in book three on the law of inheritance.

The Civil Code of 1926

[...]

Article 21 – The domicile of the husband shall be deemed the domicile of his wife; the domicile of the mother and the father shall be deemed that of the children under their authority; and the location of the court shall be that of anyone who has been placed under its guardianship.

The wife of a man whose domicile is undetermined or a woman who is permitted to live separately from her husband may be assigned a separate domicile.

[...]

Article 93 – Anyone who wants to re-marry must prove that his or her previous marriage has been terminated through death, divorce, or a ruling of full nullity.

Article 112 – Under the following circumstances a marriage may be deemed null and void:

1 – If either the wife or husband is married at the time of the marriage ceremony. [...]

Article 152 – The husband is the head of the [family] unit. The choice of the home is his [responsibility], as is the maintenance of his wife and their children.

Article 153 – [...] The wife shall assist and advise her husband to the greatest extent possible with regard to achieving shared happiness. The wife shall look after the home.

Article 154 – The husband represents the [family] unit. The husband is personally responsible for all savings, regardless of the [system of] administration of property to which the husband and wife have agreed.

[...]

Article 159 – Regardless of the [system of] administration of property that the husband and wife have agreed upon, the wife can [only] be engaged in a job or vocation with the explicit or implicit permission

* Translated from the original Turkish in *Türk Kanunu Medenisi*, no. 743. https://www.tbmm.gov.tr/tutanaklar/ KANUNLAR_KARARLAR/kanuntbmmc004/kanuntbmmc004/kanuntbmmc00400743.pdf

1923–1932

of the husband. That permission can also be granted by a judge if the wife has been refused that right by her husband and if she can prove that being engaged in the job or vocation is beneficial for the union [of the husband and wife] or for the family as a whole.

[...]

Article 439 – The nearest heirs of a deceased person are his or her progeny. All children shall receive an equal share of any inheritance.

***

The reason why some Kemalist feminists still celebrate the adoption of the Turkish Civil Code is that, in their argument, it created greater equality between husbands and wives than had been the case before. Although this is certainly true in some regards, a close reading of the Code demonstrates that in essence it was still quite patriarchal.

With the promulgation of the new Civil Code, greater equality was indeed created through the abolition of polygyny, by means of which (Muslim) men had been able, per the terms of Sharia law, to marry up to four women (arts. 93 and 112). Women also obtained the right to demand a divorce (art. 134), a right which, according to Muslim law, had been the sole prerogative of men. Moreover, under the new code women were to receive shares of any inheritance that were equal to those of their male siblings, which stood in contrast to Muslim law, under the terms of which women only received half of the amount their male siblings inherited (art. 439).

As the code was based on the Swiss Civil Code of 1907 and therefore propagated aspects of the patriarchal systems that permeated contemporaneous European civil codes, men were still deemed to be responsible for maintaining the family, while women were expected to "look after the home," as had also been the case under Muslim family law (arts. 152 and 153).

One of the most strikingly negative aspects of the new code resulting from its patriarchal character was that according to its terms, women were stripped of their legal agency when they got married. According to the Muslim legal traditions that prevailed until the introduction of the Turkish Civil Code of 1926, marriage did not change women's legal capacity, which meant that married women not only had the right to independent ownership of property, they could also manage and dispose of their properties as they so desired. In other words, they could freely trade, buy, or sell any and all goods, and, as such, they were personally responsible for managing their own finances. The Civil Code of 1926, however, changed the status quo; the husband was now not only the head of the marital unit, he was also its sole official representative (arts. 152 and 154). Moreover, he had the right to manage the savings of the marital unit regardless of whether they belonged to him or his wife (art. 154). In addition, a woman had to obtain the permission of her husband if she wanted to take up paid employment (art. 159).

While the lived effects of these latter changes have yet to be exhaustively researched, it is possible to say that the abolition of polygyny did not just have positive outcomes. Polygamous liaisons continued to exist after the Civil Code of 1926 went into effect, but the fact that they lacked lawful status had potentially dire implications for second wives (in most cases) and their children, as there were no legal guarantees in place to protect their rights.

***

In terms of its secularisation of family law, the Civil Code of 1926 can be regarded a step towards the modernisation, or Westernisation, of Turkish society as envisioned by Mustafa Kemal Atatürk. In particular, the symbolic value of women's emancipation in this context should not be underestimated, and it can be regarded as one more step towards, for example, the enfranchisement of women in the 1930s.

Over the years, some elements of the Turkish Civil Code were amended. For instance, the Constitutional Court ruled in 1990 that women no longer had to obtain permission from their husbands to take up employment. Despite some of its shortcomings, the code ultimately remained in effect for more than 75 years until 1 January 2002, when it was replaced by a completely revised civil code of law.

Select Bibliography

Özsu. Umut. "'Receiving' the Swiss Civil Code: Translating Authority in Early Republican Turkey." *International Journal of Law in Context* 6, no. 1 (2010): 63–89.

Örücü, Esin. "A Legal System Based on Translation: The Turkish Experience." *Journal of Civil Law Studies* 6, no. 2 (2013): 445–73.

van Os, Nicole A.N.M. "Polygamy Before and After the Introduction of the Swiss Civil Code in Turkey." In *The State and the Subaltern: Modernization, Society and the State in Turkey and Iran*, edited by Touraj Atabaki, 179–198. London: I.B. Tauris, 2007.

9
"Citizen, Speak Turkish!":
A Jewish Appeal for Turkification

Deniz Tat

It had been less than five years since the proclamation of the Republic of Turkey when the student union of İstanbul University's Faculty of Law launched a campaign called "Citizen, speak Turkish!" In the new nation-state of Turkey, which was founded in place of a collapsed multinational empire, one of the founding pillars of nation-building was a common language, such that citizenship was equated with being a fluent speaker of the Turkish language. However, there were in fact native speakers of other languages who may or may not have had knowledge of Turkish. As of 1927, non-Muslim citizens, such as Armenians, Greeks, and Jews, who spoke their own respective languages, constituted 2.5% of the entire population. Because only non-Muslim members of society in Turkey were granted minority status per the terms of the Treaty of Lausanne (1923), Kurdish citizens, who outnumbered the other non-Turkish-speaking groups by a large margin, were excluded from minority status assignation and, since they were Muslim, they were simply considered "Turks." Posters calling for people to only speak Turkish were hung up all around İstanbul, especially in neighbourhoods like Eminönü, Balat, Beyoğlu, and the Princes' Islands, which were all largely inhabited by non-Muslim communities. More than a quarter of the population of İstanbul at the time spoke a language other than Turkish as their first language.

Within the scope of the "Citizen, Speak Turkish!" campaign, the student union of İstanbul University's Faculty of Law formed a special committee. Together with the Turkish Hearths (*Türk Ocağı*), which has been a civil society organisation dedicated to the promotion of Turkish language and culture since 1912, they formed a commission to encourage the "proper" teaching of Turkish at schools across the country, asked the press to provide assistance for their campaign, and secured the support of not only the Municipality of İstanbul but also the Ministry of Education.

The general political atmosphere and the specific call made by the student union in İstanbul paralleled state policies. Just a few months later, the Latin script was adopted on November 1, 1928, and a year after that Arabic and Persian were removed from the school curriculum as foreign languages. The campaign was soon met with approval in other cities with sizable non-Muslim populations such as İzmir and Edirne. Once the press began supporting the campaign, its impacts became much more pronounced in everyday life, leading to frequent verbal and even physical attacks on people who spoke languages other than Turkish in public. The people who came under attack were the non-Muslim speakers of languages such as Armenian, Greek, and Ladino (Judeo-Español). Reports of attacks on Muslim citizens speaking languages other than Turkish were rare. As such violent attacks started getting out of control, Yunus Nadi (Abalıoğlu, 1879–1945) and Falih Rıfkı (Atay, 1894–1971) wrote articles in the newspapers *Cumhuriyet* and *Milliyet*, respectively, calling for restraint and explaining that the shift in language usage would only occur in the long term.

The campaign primarily targeted Armenians, Greeks, and Jews. But there was one important difference: while Armenians spoke Armenian and the Greeks Greek, the majority of Jews spoke Judeo-Español, a variety of Spanish, the language of the greater society they had once been part of, not Hebrew. Since Jewish elites at the time agreed that Hebrew was the native language of Jews, the Jewish community was accused by the general public of being ungrateful, as they were speaking the language of the people who had expelled them from Spain, as well as French, the *lingua franca* of the Mediterranean bourgeoisie, but not the language of the people who had welcomed them into their homeland in the first place.

The campaign was not only supported by Turkish-speaking citizens and leaders who identified as Turkish, but also certain intellectuals from minority groups who themselves were in favour of an assimilationist process of nation-building in Turkey. Of those, Moiz Kohen, who later adopted the name Munis Tekinalp (1883–1961), and Avram Galanti (Bodrumlu, 1873–1961) were prominent Jewish intellectuals. They advocated the Turkification of minority groups and supported the "Citizen, Speak Turkish!" campaign. They also played active roles in the founding of various societies, such as the National Culture Association (*Millî Hars Birliği*), aim of which was to facilitate Turkification and promote Turkish culture. For those who believed in the civic nationalism of Kemalism, citizenship necessitated being a fluent speaker of Turkish.

Avram Galanti, who supported the Turkification of Jews in Turkey, wrote a short book that was published mere months after the launch of the "Citizen, Speak Turkish!" campaign. Although he was a strong advocate of the campaign, he was certainly uncomfortable with the social unrest it created. After all, it was unreasonable, he argued, to expect the members of non-Muslim communities to switch to Turkish overnight. As the title of the book suggests, it was an open response to the aftermath of the campaign.

Citizen, Speak Turkish! – Or the Problem of Popularising Turkish*

What should be done for Turkification?

In addition to language, history, and geography courses, which until now have been delivered in Turkish, the Republic of Turkey, having now reviewed its national education policy from a scientific

* Translated from the original Turkish in Avram Galanti, *Vatandaş Türkçe konuş! – Yahut Türkçenin Ta'mîmi Meselesi: Tarihî, İçtimaî, Siyasî Tedkik* (İstanbul: Hüsn-i Tabîat Matbaası, 1928), 65–67. Also published in modern Turkish transliteration in Avram Galanti, *Vatandaş Türkçe Konuş!*, ed. Ömer Türkoğlu (Ankara: Kebikeç Yayınları, 2000), 46–47.

perspective and become determined to Turkify the minorities, has stipulated that school subjects such as citizenship education, science, and nature analysis be delivered in Turkish as well. While this order has been enforced, the right to demand that minorities become Turkified is the incontestable right of the government.

Rather than banning home languages, as mentioned above, in order to bolster [the speaking of] Turkish at home, the only <u>solution is an education [system] in which all instruction is conducted in Turkish</u> [emphasis in the original]. Therefore, this element must be given greater emphasis. In order to achieve complete success in this affair, it is necessary to observe the following points.

1. The government itself must carry out the policy of Turkification with authoritative leadership.
2. The government must provide a maximum of accommodation for those constituents that it seeks to Turkify, open formal schools in areas that are densely populated by minority groups, and appoint competent teachers to minority schools.
3. Since language is a "skill" that provides sustenance just like other "competencies," people who undergo Turkification must be provided with facilities in this matter.

Foreign countries as well as foreign schools that have sought or currently seek to popularise their own languages have achieved favourable results by following the same points, as validated by the following examples:

1. The United States of America offers free English evening courses to foreign immigrants who move there and presents [them with] the American flag in the first lesson in order to endear them to America, and also articulates [particular] words to inspire fondness for it.
2. A number of countries allocate extra funds to maintain the schools they have opened abroad for the purpose of popularising their languages.
3. In order to recruit students, some foreign school administrations provide support for them. The people who graduate from some of these schools find jobs and make a living thanks to the recommendations and help of their schools.

Provided that action is taken within the scope of the points herein, together with consideration of the three stages mentioned above, that is, if the Turkification process is left to the powers of nature, half a century later in a city like İstanbul where a number of languages are spoken—apart from the languages foreigners would speak to one another—<u>the main societal language that will dominate will be Turkish</u> [emphasis in the original]. This is not a rare phenomenon unique to İstanbul, but, without a doubt, [it is] a general law of sociology in terms of language. The countries that have acted within the realm of the same law have achieved the same results. The Jews of Bulgaria and Serbia are about to say goodbye to Judeo-Español thanks to the authoritative leadership of the Bulgarian and Serbian governments. The new generation speaks Bulgarian and Serbian.

Turkish has reaped its first benefits in this regard. Until fifty or sixty years ago, people who were known as Thessaloniki *Dönme* used to speak Judeo-Español at home. However, since the number of Turkish schools started to increase—that is, once their children attended Turkish schools and then graduated—Turkish slowly effaced Judeo-Español from the home environment and replaced it. Today, Thessaloniki Dönmes, excluding the very old ones, do not speak Judeo-Español. If the mainstream education is delivered in Turkish at minority schools, the Turkification of minorities will turn out to be a very natural process, and half a century later, the statement "Citizen, Speak Turkish!" will explicitly characterize the prevailing status of Turkish in the history of the Turkish language.

***

The section cited above is from the conclusion of the book, which consists of five chapters as a whole. In the first chapter, which serves as an introduction, Galanti summarises three natural stages of the popularisation of languages: (i) *devre-i asliyye:* the "original state of affairs" when a language has not yet replaced another language in the home environment; (ii) *devre-i nâkıle:* the "transitional stage" when a generation of speakers adopts a new language through schooling; (iii) *devre-i müstakbele:* the final "anticipated stage" when this new language is transmitted to the next generation in the home environment. In chapters two, three, and four, Galanti introduces a historical perspective to the language preferences of the Greek, Armenian, and Jewish communities of Turkey, respectively. He especially focuses on the latter, starting from the forced migration of the Jews from Spain in 1492. In the fifth and final chapter, Galanti provides examples of countries that adopted languages other than their own, such as that of the ancient Egyptians as well as nations which attempted to popularise their own languages such as ancient Rome. He then provides a summary of the language policies of the various non-Muslim communities of the Ottoman Empire since the *Tanzimat* reforms (1839). Lastly, he raises the question, "What should be done to bring about Turkification?"

Galanti's book aims to explain the reasons why the Jewish community of Turkey had not switched to speaking Turkish as of 1928 and to provide a scientific explanation as to why the language shift will take time. It thus seeks to both explain the historical reasons why the Jews did not speak Turkish and exhorts them to switch to Turkish as soon as possible. Galanti also urges the government to take an active role in language policies and highlights the crucial role of schooling in successful processes of language shifts. He strongly recommends that all education at minority schools be delivered in Turkish so that Turkish will become the dominant communal language of minority groups. Galanti had a point: all around the world, schooling has proven to be a key factor in the success or failure of attempts to impose a particular language on speakers of other languages.

***

The "Citizen, speak Turkish!" campaign only lasted for a few months but its immediate effects on the lives of the masses lasted at least until the mid-1940s. By that time, Turkish had become more widespread among the members of non-Muslim communities, especially the younger generations, whose dominant language became Turkish while their respective mother tongues were restricted to the domain of the home. Whether this language shift was a direct result of the campaign is arguable, but without a doubt it unequivocally affected the lives of hundreds of thousands of people and left lasting emotional scars as well. The linguistic Turkification movement and its slogan had started to lapse by the end of the Second World War and the beginning of the multi-party system in Turkey, but to date language has remained at the heart of debates concerning citizenship.

Select Bibliography

Aslan, Senem. "'Citizen, Speak Turkish!': A Nation in the Making." *Nationalism and Ethnic Politics* 13, no. 2 (2007): 245–72.

Bali, Rıfat N. "'Vatandaş Türkçe Konuş!' Veya Bir Ulus-Devletin Kuruluşunda Dil Birliğinin Gerçekleşmesi Çabaları." Foreword to Galanti, Avram, *Vatandaş Türkçe Konuş!* edited by Ömer Türkoğlu. Ankara: Kebikeç Yayınları, 2000.

Bali, Rıfat N. *Cumhuriyet Yıllarında Türkiye Yahudileri: Bir Türkleştirme Serüveni (1923–1945).* İstanbul: İletişim Yayınları, 2000.

İçduygu, Ahmet, Şule Toktaş, and B. Ali Soner. "The Politics of Population in a Nation-Building Process: Emigration of Non-Muslims from Turkey." *Ethnic and Racial Studies* 31, no. 2 (2008): 358–89.

Toktaş, Şule. "Citizenship and Minorities: A Historical Overview of Turkey's Jewish Minority." *Journal of Historical Sociology* 18, no. 4 (2005): 394–429.

10

An Unusual Letter, an Unusual Opposition: The Free Republican Party

Uğur Derin

With the closure of the Progressive Republican Party (*Terakkiperver Cumhuriyet Fırkası*) in June 1925, Turkey became a single-party state. Now that opposition on multiple fronts had been suppressed, by way of the powers accorded to him through the Law on Maintenance of Order, President Mustafa Kemal (Atatürk, 1881–1938) embarked on an ambitious program of reforms. Within a few years, the country underwent drastic changes in various fields, including legal reforms, regulations on attire, and the adoption of foreign systems of measurements, as well as the reconfiguration of the calendar and introduction of the Latin alphabet. These reforms were intended to modernise Turkey and bring it closer to the West. By 1930, most Western observers celebrated Atatürk as a champion of modernisation and praised the reforms that were being introduced in Turkey, even though the country's government was still understood to be a kind of Oriental dictatorship.

By the summer of 1930, there was a great deal of discontent, both in society at large and also among the elites, not only because of the impacts of the Great Depression of 1929 and Kurdish insurgencies in the eastern cities, but also because of a lack of public discussions, which was reflected in how deputies boycotted parliamentary sessions by way of silent protests. Various reasons can be attributed to the emergence of a new opposition party at the time and the justifications for taking such action. In popular politics, it was argued that an opposition party would offer a venue for disgruntled elites and the public to channel their reactions within the constitutional system. Within the ranks of the Republican People's Party (*Cumhuriyet Halk Fırkası/Partisi*, CHF/CHP), it would counterbalance the growing influence of Prime Minister İsmet Pasha (İnönü, 1884–1973) and show him that he was not indispensable. Internationally, and especially with regard to the Western world, it would present Turkey in a more democratic light, which is something that Turkish leaders have always placed great value upon. Anecdotal evidence, such as the negative reactions that Turkish deputies received from their European counterparts when they travelled abroad, or statements made by the American ambassador at the time in Ankara, Joseph Grew, suggest that both Mustafa Kemal and Turkish deputies were well aware of the country's undemocratic image abroad. Upon deciding that a loyal opposition party was in fact needed, Mustafa Kemal approached his long-time friend and former political partner Ali Fethi (Okyar, 1880–1943), who had been ousted as prime minister and replaced by İsmet Pasha in 1925 and who had just returned from Paris where he was serving as Turkey's ambassador. It was decided that having Fethi

Bey, who had strong relations with the international financial world, establish the opposition party could possibly improve Turkey's image, which in turn could help financially shore up the country at a time when its economy was facing collapse. Knowing that he could not openly oppose Mustafa Kemal, Fethi nonetheless expressed his concerns, stating that he feared being accused of treason in the future, and he refused the offer at first. However, Mustafa Kemal managed to convince him to go along with the plan after declaring his impartiality, which Fethi had requested him to do. Mustafa Kemal asked Fethi to write an open letter stating his intention to form a second party, which resulted in the letter presented below. Sent out on 9 August 1930, it was published in various newspapers in subsequent days.

Fethi Okyar's Letter to President Mustafa Kemal Pasha[*]

Dear Mr. President,

In the five-year period that I have been in Paris, in addition to following and analysing the situation of our country from the outside, I also spent some time in the country during my leave of absence. I carried out thorough analyses based on my observations. I hereby ask that I may present my judgement and the ideas I have developed if you could indulge me. A sense of distress that is striking at first sight and felt generally is the fiscal and economic crisis our country is going through. As a matter of fact, in terms of the prices of basic goods, the collapse of the world market has caused more or less a state of stagnation in the economic activities of virtually every country.

Yet I reckon that, other than these general reasons, what has caused the economic depression to be felt in our country to an even greater extent compared to other places is the fiscal and economic policy that the government has been following for more than five years.

The government has engaged in expenses that are at odds with our fiscal power and are unproductive for today's generation. To cover those expenses, taxes have been levied which are beyond the means of the people. As internal skills and our products were not properly incentivised, our exports have suffered.

Most of the sacrifices the government has chosen to undertake have been spent on extremely heavy interest rates and the rest on foreign imports, which therefore involves buying foreign currencies.

No substantial precautions were taken until our national currency showed signs that roused concern. I do not wish to make my case longer by adding to these matters certain deficiencies concerning the distribution of justice as well as domestic and foreign policies.

---

[*] Translated from the original Turkish in Cemil Koçak, *Belgerlerle İktidar ve Serbest Cumhuriyet Fırkası* (İstanbul: İletişim Yayınları, 2006), 699.

In short, despite the praiseworthy work of our villagers and the commendable efforts made by all strata of society to elevate our country during the time of peace in which our country has been free from all manner of capitulations since the Lausanne treaty, the resulting situation, I think, is far from satisfactory. I could not refrain even for a moment from asking myself how such a result emerged, given the doubtless efforts and good intentions of government dignitaries, whom I hold in high esteem. The only answer I can think of is that the Grand National Assembly consists of only one party. The truth is that, as a result of party members eschewing criticisms from their own cabinet, free discussion in the national assembly has decreased and the government has been left unaccountable.

Your excellency the President, you have defended this country against great enemy attacks the likes of which have never been seen. You have recorded a victory that is so resplendent in our history.

You have provided independence and liberty, which the children of this country had so far never experienced. You abolished the ramshackle establishment that prevented our country from walking the path of civilisation, and you founded the republic. By this merit you deserve eternal gratitude from this country and admiration and appreciation from the world in general.

I could never doubt that, to eternalise the Turkish republic, his excellency more than anyone else is in favour of establishing a system that is based on free discussions. Contrary to a one-party system, the government will be held accountable concerning national matters, and problems will be solved through open and free discussions. It is my sacred desire as an admirer of the republic for these efforts to take place. Hence, by means of a separate party that is fully and genuinely republican and by all means secular, but critical of the many fiscal and economic and internal and foreign issues of the Republican People's Party, I wish to embark on the quest of taking up a political struggle.

Apart from being the head of state, since his excellency is also the general director of the Republican People's Party—of which I have so far been a member—I feel the need to know how this desire of mine will be received in the eyes of the state.

I am expecting the reply of the state. Expressing my heart-felt love and deepest respect, Sir.

Fethi

***

Although the letter does give the impression that Fethi had indeed observed Turkey from abroad, identified certain problems, and sought to explain in his letter his ideas for solving those problems, that only partially reflects the truth. We know from various memoirs and diaries that the letter and the party program were drawn up together with President Mustafa Kemal, Prime Minister İsmet, and the would-be founder of the party, Fethi. Moreover, as late as April 1930, three months before Fethi's letter was published in newspapers, Mustafa

Kemal had already mentioned to his close circles that he was considering the possibility of an opposition party being founded. Therefore, it was clearly not Fethi who sought to establish an opposition party, but Mustafa Kemal who tasked him with the mission. Moreover, numerous memoirs and diaries also confirm that although there were no legal barriers, it was simply not possible to form an opposition party in a bottom-up manner within the authoritarian atmosphere that prevailed at the time, and that some figures from the circle of Mustafa Kemal (including Fethi) were instead in favour of founding an oppositional group within the Republican People's Party.

The main concerns addressed in the letter are economic (the words "fiscal" and "economic" appear multiple times), which is in line with the major impact the Great Depression had on Turkey. The government, including Mustafa Kemal himself, was aware at the time that discontent was sweeping across the country, not only because of a series of unpopular reforms that had been implemented, but also because of economic and financial grievances. Although the government's policies were blamed for those economic woes, the fact that the letter carefully avoided mentioning any specific names makes it clear that they did not want to run the risk of antagonising İsmet.

Following Mustafa Kemal's reply to Fethi a few days later, which also took the form of an open letter in which he stated that he had long cherished a system of governance in which ideas could be freely discussed in parliament, the Free Republican Party (*Serbest Cumhuriyet Fırkası, SCF*) was formally established on 12 August 1930. Soon enough, the party came under a great deal of attacks and intimidation, mostly carried out by the pro-government media. Although they were wide-ranging, the most typical critiques targeted the new party's deputies—all of whom, until recently, had been deputies of the CHP—by associating them with the Greeks, and accusing the party not only of harbouring communists and religious reactionaries, but also of being a front for traitorous agents. Nevertheless, the Free Republican Party roused unprecedented enthusiasm in the country. Weighed down by economic grievances and subjected to public censorship, the masses welcomed Fethi like a saviour. His rallies attracted huge crowds and thousands of people registered to be members of his party. The large-scale allure of the Free Republican Party became tangible during the local elections that were held in September 1930. Despite its lack of preparations, immense pressure from the government, and obvious election fraud, the party still managed to win in approximately thirty municipalities. Meanwhile, the circle of Mustafa Kemal, fearing that things were getting out of control, asked him to state his allegiance to the CHP, which he did, also in the form of a letter published in the newspapers. During the ensuing discussions that took place in parliament about how the elections had been held, tensions rose, and concerned that opposition to the government might turn into opposition to Mustafa Kemal, Fethi decided to close down his party on 16 November 1930, the petition for which was again drawn up in consultation with Mustafa Kemal. The party was closed down in less than 100 days.

***

In Turkish historiography, the Free Republican Party is predominantly referred to as a case of "guided opposition" (*güdümlü muhalefet*). Mustafa Kemal oversaw the whole process including deciding its fourteen members, some of whom joined the new party against their own will and went back to their own party later. The letter presented above, when not taken at face value, makes it clear that, although the party had garnered a large amount of support, it was not an opposition party in the true sense of the word.

The story of the Free Republican Party is important, both in terms of its place within the Kemalist modernisation project and how opposition movements are often regarded in Turkey. In the Kemalist literature, the Free Republican Party emerges as part of a conscious experiment with democracy that was aborted for fear of instigating populist tumult and instability. According to this narrative, Mustafa Kemal, who sought to secure the establishment of a democratic system of governance in the long run, made a sincere attempt to achieve pluralism, but the party was flooded by religious reactionaries and dissenters to the regime, proving that such a move was premature. In 1946, after the establishment of the Democrat Party, İsmet Pasha stated that the transition to a multi-party system had long been the will of Atatürk. Although that narrative has been taken up in a number of critical revisionist accounts in the last few decades, it is still frequently invoked to depict Turkey's single-party regime as part of a smooth transition to democracy.

The story of the Free Republican Party is also revealing in terms of portrayals of the opposition, both in the Kemalist literature and in Turkey in general. It demonstrates how, both in the past and today, governments and leaders in Turkey often pay lip service to democratic pluralism but prefer to exercise control over it, thereby preventing it from flourishing.

Select Bibliography

Emrence, Cem. *Serbest Cumhuriyet Fırkası: 99 Günlük Muhalefet*. 3rd edition. İstanbul: İletişim Yayınları, 2018.

Koçak, Cemil. *Belgelerle İktidar ve Serbest Cumhuriyet Fırkası*. 2nd edition. İstanbul: İletişim Yayınları, 2014.

Okyar, Osman and Mehmet Seyitdanlıoğlu. *Atatürk, Okyar ve Çok Partili Türkiye: Fethi Okyar'ın Anıları*. 3rd edition. İstanbul: Türkiye İş Bankası Kültür Yayınları, 2006.

Tunçay, Mete. *Türkiye Cumhuriyeti'nde Tek-Parti Yönetimi'nin Kurulması (1923–1931)*. 6th edition. İstanbul: Tarih Vakfı Yurt Yayınları, 2012.

Weiker, Walter F. *Political Tutelage and Democracy in Turkey: The Free Party and Its Aftermath*. Leiden: Brill, 1975.

1933–1942

11

Geography of a Nation in the Making:
The Settlement Law of 1934

Çiğdem Oğuz

The Settlement Law of 1934, which remained in effect until 2006, was the main regulation concerning immigration to and settlement in the Republic of Turkey. It laid down the legal stipulations regarding the immigration of Muslims from former Ottoman territories as well as from other countries, such as the USSR, into Turkey starting in the years following the establishment of the Turkish Republic. The Turkish state sought to address both domestic and international concerns through the introduction of a detailed new settlement law. Accordingly, for the sake of creating a homogenous population for a culturally, linguistically and ethnically united nation-state, the government promoted an open-door immigration policy for former Ottoman Muslims abroad in a bid to revive underpopulated areas in Anatolia. In support of the nationalistic agenda of the Turkish government, the law aimed at achieving broad-spectrum demographical engineering while settling migrants in specific areas.

Law No: 2510 İskan Kanunu (Settlement Law)*

Article 1 – The Ministry of the Interior is tasked with regulating settlement and the demographic structure in Turkey on the basis of connections to Turkish culture in line with a plan drawn up by the Council of Ministers.

Article 2 – Turkey shall be divided into three zones in accordance with a map to be prepared by the Ministry of the Interior upon the approval of the Council of Ministers.
Zone no. 1 includes places which are desirable for settlement by people who have direct connections to Turkish culture.
Zone no. 2 is reserved for the transfer and settlement of people who are to be assimilated into Turkish culture.
Zone no. 3 includes places that are to be evacuated and where settlement is prohibited for reasons related to space, health, the economy, culture, politics, the military and security.

---

* Translated from the Turkish original in *TBMM Zabıt Ceridesi* IV. Dönem Vol. 23 65. İnikat; *Resmi Gazete*, No. 2733, 21 June 1934.

Article 3 – People who belong to the Turkish race, whether settled or nomads, and individuals or tribes with direct connections to Turkish culture who intend to migrate collectively or individually for the purposes of settlement in Turkey shall be accepted into [Turkey] upon the decision of the Ministry of the Interior on the basis of the conditions determined by this law. They are to be called refugees. The Council of Ministers shall determine who has direct connections to Turkish culture. [...]

Article 4 – A. People not deemed to have direct connections to Turkish culture; B. Anarchists; C. Spies; Ç. Nomadic Roma people; D. People who have previously been deported shall not be accepted as refugees in Turkey.
People who have contagious diseases are to be sent to public hospitals to be treated free of charge.

[...]

Article 7 – A. Refugees and immigrants belonging to the Turkish race who declare that they will not demand any settlement aid from the government are free to settle anywhere they choose. Those who demand settlement aid are obliged to settle where the government permits. B. Those who do not belong to the Turkish race (whether they request aid or not) are obliged to settle and live where the government permits. Those who abandon the place where they settled will be sent back to their settlement. If they repeat [this offense], they will be denaturalised upon the decision of the Council of Ministers.

[...]

Article 9 – The Ministry of the Interior is vested with the power to settle and disperse nomadic Roma people with Turkish citizenship and other nomads who do not have direct connections to Turkish culture in zones where Turkish culture is dominant, and to resettle people suspected of spying away from the borders and to deport Roma people with foreign citizenship and nomads who do not have direct connections to Turkish culture.

Article 10 – A. The law does not recognise tribes as legal entities. [...]
B. Tribal properties are to be confiscated by the state. These properties will be distributed to refugees, migrants, nomads, resettled people, and peasants without land or with small landholdings. [...]

Article 11 – A. People whose mother tongue is not Turkish are not allowed to establish workers' and artisans' communities or form new villages and neighbourhoods [...].
B. The Ministry of the Interior is vested with the power to take necessary measures concerning people who do not have direct connections to Turkish culture or who have direct connections to Turkish culture but speak a language other than Turkish [...]. These measures include settling them in a dispersed manner and denaturalisation.
C. In cities and towns the total number of foreigners cannot exceed 10 per cent of the entire population and they cannot establish separate neighbourhoods.

[...]

***

The Settlement Law contains 52 articles which are separated into eight sections. The first part of the law concerns the procedures to be followed for refugees and immigrants. The second part of the law concerns domestic policies related to resettlement, culture, and administration. The third part defines the resettlement of people in different zones on the basis of the criteria of having direct connections to Turkish culture. The concept "connections to Turkish culture" was based on Ziya Gökalp's notion of *hars*, which refers to Islam and the Turkish language as well as the common values of Ottoman Muslims. The law considered being a Muslim as the minimum requirement for the category of people with non-Turkish ethnic and linguistic affiliations yet could be assimilated into Turkishness through settlement. The fourth part is about the liquidation of abandoned properties and property rights on new lands after settlement. Within one year people who left had to sell all their properties; if they did not do so, the state would liquidate them. Settled refugees, immigrants, and people settled in zone no. 1 were obliged to remain in the locales to which they were assigned for ten years. The fifth part concerns exemptions from certain taxes on settlers' goods and military service regulations for refugees. The sixth part is about the financial regulations of settlement zones. For example, in no. 1 zones, settlers would be allocated free land, while in no. 2 zones they had to start paying for the land after eight years and the full sum was to be paid within twenty years. The remaining parts are about the logistics of land distribution, assigned commissions, and the duties of local authorities.

The Settlement Law was a response not only to the pressing problem of migration flows into Turkey and interwar territorial disputes, but also to Kurdish opposition, as the regulation also sought to settle nomads (including Roma people), tribes, and "insurgent elements" such as Kurdish tribal groups. Kurdish opposition to the newly established Turkish state started as early as 1925 with the Sheikh Said revolt and continued with other uprisings. With the Settlement Law of 1934, the government hoped to restore its authority in Kurdish regions by dispersing Kurdish tribes to other Anatolian cities while settling Muslim/Turkish immigrants of Balkan and Caucasian origin in their place.

***

Settlement and immigration were key to the making of the Turkish nation-state. Starting in the early years of the Republic, the Turkish government enacted a series of laws regarding settlement. The late Ottoman demographic policy of forced migration and settlement provided a formative background for the Republic's drive to homogenise the population; however, the version of settlement enacted in the 1930s emphasised "Turkish culture" as a dominant element in the pursuit of this policy in an unprecedented way. The law discussed here constituted the most detailed program drawn up to that end. While the literature has often emphasised the role of Turkish nationalism and the assimilation of the Kurds in analyses of the law, recent studies have considered the transnational context and the interwar mobility of people across eastern Europe in terms of push and pull factors that led to the Muslim exodus from the Balkans. The presence of the British in Iraq and the French in Syria along the country's southern borders, Bulgarian irredentism along the border in eastern Thrace, and the threat posed by fascist Italy in the Mediterranean constituted important factors in the drafting of the law, as the aim was to prevent land disputes and foreign interference through regimes of minority rights. Feudal ties in Kurdish regions were targeted as a consequence of their support for nationalist projects in French Syria and British Iraq. However, due to the existence of more pressing concerns related to Bulgaria and Italy, the settlement law was efficiently applied in Western Turkey and Thrace to settle the Balkan Muslims in a way to deter any land disputes based on population ratios. In the Eastern cities, also due to geographical and structural difficulties, its implementation remained rather limited.

The Settlement Law remained in effect until 2006 and was only replaced by another one for the sake of compliance with European Union accession regulations. Notably, in the course of drafting the new version, the notions of connections to Turkish culture (*Türk kültürü*) and race (*Türk soyu*) were taken under deliberation as parameters for facilitated access to Turkish citizenship and immigration rights. While in 1934 the Ministry of the Interior was vested with the power to determine who belonged in that category, by means of new amendments to the 2006 law passed in 2018, the president of the Turkish Republic alone has the power to decide who is a member of the Turkish race and culture. The new version, just like the old one, represents a response to the pressing problem of migration flows into Turkey as much as more recent concerns regarding borders, security, and ambitious new construction projects undertaken by the Turkish government which have changed demographic and socioeconomic structures in certain parts of the country.

Select Bibliography

Kirişçi, Kemal. "Disaggregating Turkish Citizenship and Immigration Practices." *Middle Eastern Studies* 36, no. 3 (2000): 1–22.

Öztan, Ramazan Hakkı. "Settlement Law of 1934: Turkish Nationalism in the Age of Revisionism." *Journal of Migration History* 6, no. 1 (2020): 82–103.

Ülker, Erol. "Assimilation, Security and Geographical Nationalization in Interwar Turkey: The Settlement Law of 1934." *European Journal of Turkish Studies* 7 (2008). https://journals.openedition.org/ejts/2123

12

A Glimpse into Policies on Spirits:
Alcohol Percentages in *Rakı* Production

Emre Erol

The consumption of alcohol has become a significant topic of study with regard to the history of the Middle East. Turkey stands out as a unique case in this respect, as it is situated in a geography where the consumption and production of spirits, wine, and beer has a long and complicated history ranging from pre-modern times to the present day. The presence of large non-Muslim populations in the Ottoman Empire who were allowed to produce and consume alcohol, *meyhane* (tavern) culture, the consumption of alcohol by ruling elites (since the beginning of the empire but especially after the introduction of modernising reforms in the Tanzimat era), and a relative indifference to household practices of consumption, which stands in contrast to more rigid forms of social pressure in public spaces, all combined to create a complex situation in which alcohol was frequently consumed (especially by male elites and their courtiers as well as by ordinary Muslims throughout history) but also forbidden at times on religious and legal grounds.

In more recent history, the consumption and production of alcohol was banned from 1920 until 1926 during the years of the National Struggle and the subsequent period of state forma-tion. The law on prohibition was passed with a parliamentary vote that first resulted in a tie and was only resolved with a ruling in favour of prohibition on the basis of motivations that are still a matter of scholarly debate. It has been argued that the ban was likely introduced due to the necessity of discipline during the war, the portrayal of the National Struggle as being led by Saviours of Islam (*Halâskârân-ı İslâm*), and economic nationalism that targeted the predominantly non-Muslim owners of alcohol-producing enterprises. It is also worth noting that this was one of the first laws passed in the newly established parliament, which testifies to the significance of the issue at the time. The ban did not last long, however, and it was repealed in 1926.

Within that context, the establishment of the Republic of Turkey truly represents a turn-ing point in the history of the production and consumption of spirits in the region. Three dynamics stand out as the main drivers of change in this regard: new economic policies, an emphasis on the secular nature of the state, and the Westernising tendencies of the Kemalist regime. However, Kemalist Turkey's policies set it apart from other predominantly Muslim countries such as Iran, which was known in the past for its strong culture of wine production and consumption but underwent periods of prohibition in the modern era, especially after the Islamic Revolution. In Turkey, a law introduced by the new Republic in 1926 allowed Muslims to consume and produce alcohol. The establishment of state monopolies, one of which produced and sold spirits, resulted in one of the highest sources of tax revenue in the country and triggered state investments with the aim of fostering the development of a national industry of alcohol production. Soon enough, *rakı*—the Turkish iteration of an old Eastern Mediterranean culinary legacy that is similar to Greek ouzo, Levantine araq, and Balkan rakija, which are strong spirits usually made from twice-distilled grapes and flavoured with anise—was refashioned as the "national drink" of modern and secular Turks.

The excerpt below, which dates from 1934, offers a rare glimpse into the internal discussions among early Republican-era bureaucrats about alcohol production and consumption. It not only sheds light onto the past, but also presents an opportunity to frame current discussions about the history of alcohol in Turkey.

Decreasing the Percentage of Alcohol in Rakı Production*

To the Honourable Prime Ministry [led by İsmet İnönü (1884–1973)],

The issue of lowering the percentage of alcohol in rakı production following the orders of your honourable sir has been investigated and various samples of the Directorate of the Monopoly's rakı production have been analysed. It has been understood based on our inquiry that it is indeed possible to lower the percentage of alcohol in rakı production to 45 per cent [from the previous 50 per cent] and this result has been communicated to the Ministry of Customs and Monopolies. In response, based on the report attached to this correspondence and delivered by the General Directorate of the Monopolies, it has been communicated to us that lowering the percentage of alcohol would affect tax revenues, and this would be highly undesirable. I present the issue for the evaluation of your honourable sir.

Minister of Health and Social Welfare

Refik [Saydam (1881–1942)]

[*The remainder of the correspondence consists of a detailed report submitted by the General Directorate of the Monopolies in favour of preserving the status quo. The following are excerpts that comprise an overview of the significant sections of the correspondence.*]

[...] Based on the reasons presented below, [it was found that] decreasing the maximum percentage of alcohol in rakı production and capping it at 45 per cent would cause many problems in practice. In addition, it would also stir up discontent among the people and consequently our tax revenue would be adversely affected. [...]

* These excerpts are translated from the original correspondences in Turkish that are archived in the Republican Archives (*Devlet Arşivleri Başkanlığı Cumhuriyet Arşivi*). The file of the correspondences is titled "Rakılarda alkol derecesinin indirilmesi," which is used as the title of the excerpts provided here. The Republican Archives, Location Number: 182-254-12, File: 211 (27.08.1934).

[...] The truth is that our rakı variant with 50 per cent alcohol can absorb the highest amount of aniseed oil and rakı of that taste is highly desired by the people. As a matter of fact, there are considerable numbers of people who complain that even the taste of anise in our strongest 50 per cent product is not strong enough. As a result, if we were asked to cap the percentage of alcohol at 45 per cent, that would make it necessary to use less aniseed in our production and that would naturally be detrimental for demand for our high-end product [which is currently rakı with 50 per cent alcohol].

[...] In fact, due to the Great Depression a considerable segment of consumers of grape-based rakı [the industry standard] started preferring fig-based rakı [a cheap substitute for the standard] due to its lower cost, albeit temporarily, and as of the year 1927 [and later in 1931 and 1933] fig-based rakı outsold grape-based rakı. Our directorate, in the face of these recent developments, was considering putting a cap on the volume of fig-based rakı by making 50 centilitre bottles the largest size available [to promote the sales of our grape-based rakı and to mitigate our losses in tax revenue since fig-based rakı does not produce as much revenue].

[...] Based on the arguments presented above, our Directorate is fully convinced that lowering the highest percentage of alcohol in rakı to 45 per cent will upset the balance [of supply and demand] between the various types of rakı production [the norm being *Fevkalade* at 50 per cent, *Aliyülalâ* at 47 per cent, *Alâ* at 45 per cent, and *Birinci* at 40 per cent] and [that would] trigger adverse consequences. Also, in essence, it is customary for rakı to be consumed with water in our country [referring to the usual practice of half a glass of rakı being topped up with water] and that effectively decreases the percentage of alcohol to somewhere between 20-25 per cent. Therefore, we kindly ask for your honourable sir's permission to maintain 50 per cent as the highest standard, as has heretofore been the case.

***

The document quoted above consists of a correspondence between three bodies of government: the prime ministry, the equivalent of the ministry of health, and the directorate overseeing state monopolies at the time, which would later be privatised in successive steps between 1983 and 2002. The folder of the original file consists of two separate documents comprising four pages in total. The first document is a missive addressing then-prime minister İnönü and the second document presents the highly detailed report of the General Directorate of Monopolies. The report explains the status quo and goes on to present two separate scenarios to the ministry of health for the capping of the maximum level of alcohol at 45 per cent. It is strongly opposed to the proposal, which seems to have initially been handed down by the prime ministry, and defends the status quo. Three arguments are repeatedly presented in the report, namely the issues of tax revenue, consumer demand, and health hazards. The economic argument is more or less ubiquitous, followed far less frequently by an emphasis on consumer demand, and only at the end of the report do there appear very indirect references to the matter of health hazards, which are brushed aside by pointing out that it is customary to drink rakı with water. But one could ask, why is any of this significant?

This primary source is a true reflection of the Zeitgeist that shaped the affective disposition of Republican-era bureaucrats in the 1930s in the sense that it is indicative of almost every aspect of how state monopolies were governed during the economically troublesome times of the Great Depression era. The correspondence was clearly initiated by the prime ministry on the grounds of concerns about public health with regard to the consumption of spirits containing high levels of alcohol. While that may not be surprising since alcohol was banned between 1920 and 1926, the fact remains that once the Kemalist regime established a firm grip on power and thwarted the existential problems it faced during the war years, the ban was lifted and both the consumption and production of alcohol by Muslims were promoted. Moreover, the regime's self-portrayal as leading the Saviours of Islam was now being contrasted with reforms and legislation that emphasised what was then perceived to be the contemporary norms of civilised nations. In the 1930s, prohibition in the US (1920–1933) influenced perceptions and policy-making about alcohol around the world, and there was an increase in global public awareness about the ill effects of alcohol consumption. However, in the case of Turkey none of those issues seem to have sufficed to outweigh economic pragmatism and necessity. State monopolies had existed since the times of the Ottoman Empire and the new Republic of Turkey attempted to give them a new shape and structure. The monopolies had two functions in the Republic: economic gain and political clout. The economic functions were directly related to generating considerable tax revenues and financing the repayment of the country's international debt to European creditors which had been inherited from the Ottoman Empire. The numerous political functions included, above all, the expansion of the state's bureaucratic apparatus, increasing the economic presence of the state in the economy, especially in the era of the Great Depression, and a drive to "nationalise" an industry that had previously been dominated by non-Muslims and foreign nationals.

The set of documents under discussion here about the percentage of alcohol in rakı production testifies to the economic and political significance of state monopolies, particularly the monopoly that governed the production of spirits. This claim is substantiated by the nuanced, detailed, and rationalised discussion of the various detrimental consequences that cutting the percentage of alcohol in rakı could have on the industries and agricultural economy linked to the production of spirits. The existence of these monopolies thus clearly reflected the role of the state as a principal economic actor in 1930s Turkey. Needless to say, this particular set of correspondences is also invaluable for scholars who are interested in statist economics, culinary culture, and the history of alcoholic beverages in the Middle East.

***

Although the documents examined here do not indicate what decisions were ultimately reached, a brief overview of the Official Gazette of the Republic of Turkey (*Resmi Gazete*) and the parliamentarian minutes of the Grand National Assembly of Turkey for the years following these correspondences indicate that the proposal to lower the percentage of alcohol in rakı production was discarded and 50 per cent remained in place as a high-end product standard until the monopolies were disbanded and even afterwards.

Beyond its significance as a "national drink," rakı has also retained its place as a political and cultural symbol. That was evident in the years of the early republic, as well as in the 1950s and perhaps even more so since 2002, starting with the long political tenure of the Justice and Development Party (*Adalet ve Kalkınma Partisi*, AKP). Each decade in modern Turkey's history has brought with it a new set of reasons why alcohol consumption has remained a major issue economically, politically, and culturally. Today, it appears to be an extremely prominent "line of demarcation" in identity politics within the realm of the secular-religious binary, perhaps even as strong a "sign" of political belonging as the headscarf was in the last three decades.

The production and consumption of alcohol has been a contested issue since the establishment of the Republic of Turkey in 1923, but the documents presented here are even more relevant today than they would have been in the 1980s when the monopolies were being privatised. The AKP government has been attempting to refashion the hegemonic nationalist narrative by placing more emphasis on Islam and being a Muslim Turk as a primary marker of identity. The AKP's populist strongman Recep Tayyip Erdoğan (1954–) is known for his polemics when it comes to the issue of alcohol consumption. He has often employed a discourse that is at times derogatory in his remarks about the culture of alcohol consumption, and his criticisms have also targeted Atatürk (1881–1938) and İnönü's drinking habits, which have prompted strong public reactions. Erdoğan's rhetoric paints a picture in which alcohol consumption was forcefully promoted by the early Republican regime against the will of the people. Moreover, he has also made the assertion that *ayran*, a yogurt-based traditional non-alcoholic beverage, is the true "national drink of the Turk." Like those of many contemporary populists, the discourses he invokes about the past are selective and misleading. His penchant for promoting ayran over rakı in his nationalist rhetoric seems to play into the ongoing state of social polarisation and the culture wars that have been stoked between different segments of society that adhere to supposedly "opposing ways" of life and national identity in Turkey. History tells us that alcohol was consumed before and during the early Republican era, and it was and still is a significant source of state revenue. Downplaying the central role of economic concerns and the role of not only bureaucratic pragmatism but also the necessities and realities of Turkey in the 1930s would make it appear that identity politics were the primary drivers shaping state policies, which would be quite misleading. Indeed, examining how the past is remembered may very well be a useful means of diagnosing how the present is shaped.

Select Bibliography

Anadol, Çağatay, Zat Erdir, and Fügen Basmacı, et al. *Rakı Ansiklopedisi.* İstanbul: Overteam Yayınları, 2010.

Evered, Emine Ö., and Evered, Kyle T. "A Geopolitics of Drinking: Debating the Place of Alcohol in Early Republican Turkey." *Political Geography* 50, no. 1 (2016): 48–60.

Evered, Emine Ö., and Evered, Kyle T. "From *Rakı* to *Ayran*: Regulating the Place and Practice of Drinking in Turkey." *Space and Polity* 20, no. 1 (2016): 39–58.

Gölçek, Şeyda Güdek, and Ali Gökhan Gölçek. "Erken Cumhuriyet Dönemi Tekel Uygulamaları: 1920-1950 Döneminde Tuz, İspirto ve İspirtolu İçkiler ile Kibrit." *Cumhuriyet Tarihi Araştırmaları Dergisi* 15/30 (Fall 2019): 253–88.

Matthee, Rudi. "Alcohol in the Islamic Middle East: Ambivalence and Ambiguity." *Past & Present* 222, issue supplement 9 (2014): 100–25.

13
Defining Kemalism:
The Program of the CHP
in an Age of Ideologies

Remzi Çağatay Çakırlar

The Republican People's Party (*Cumhuriyet Halk Partisi*, CHP) was founded in 1923. Despite the establishment of the short-lived Progressive Republican Party (*Terakkiperver Cumhuriyet Fırkası*, TPCF) and Free Republican Party (*Serbest Cumhuriyet Fırkası*, SCF), the CHP ruled the country unopposed until 1946. One of the most established definitions of the CHP's political ideals was constructed over time and associated with a set of ideas known as the "Six Arrows." In the party's statute set forth in 1927, the CHP defined itself as a "republican," "populist," and "nationalist party" and promoted the separation of political and religious affairs. Four years later, the party reiterated the same principles in its program, officially referring the ideal of the separation of political and religious matters as "*laiklik*," which was derived from the French term "*laïcité.*" In addition, by 1931 the CHP's program had come to be represented through six ideals: republicanism (*cumhuriyetçilik*), secularism (*laiklik*), nationalism (*milliyetçilik*), populism (*halkçılık*), statism (*devletçilik*), and revolutionarism (*inkılâpçılık*). Recep Peker (1889–1950), the secretary general of the CHP at the time, explained in a party program speech he gave in May 1935 what each ideal meant. Peker's speech is important not only because it explains each notion in detail, but also because it demonstrates the relationship between the state, party, and society in Turkey at the time. Moreover, it also provides significant clues about the ideological positioning of the single-party regime within the context of interwar Europe and beyond. Those six principles were later incorporated into the Turkish constitution in 1937, thereby officially becoming the underlying ideological framework of the Republic of Turkey.

Recep Peker's Declaration of the Republican People's Party Program*

My friends, the most striking and outstanding feature of the new [party] program is that the existence of the Republican People's Party, which has been working together with the state from the very beginning in the New Turkey, is coming closer together through the existence of the state.

---

* Translated from the original Turkish in "Genel Sekreter Recep Peker'in Program Açıklaması (1935)," in *C.H.P Genel Sekreteri R. Peker'in Söylevleri* (Ankara: Ulus Basımevi, 1935), 124–38.

The main principles of the party—republicanism, nationalism, populism, revolutionarism, statism, and secularism—became the principles of the new Turkish state after the new program was approved.

[...]

Friends, let's say nationalism remained a party principle and is not included in the law of the state or in the principles of the state. This would not be right, correct, or in accordance with the sanction of the existence of the state and its main ideas and needs.

[Consider the statement] "Turkey will be republican but it may not be nationalist," meaning that Turkey's mind and door could be open to transnational currents. Who would believe the accuracy of such an idea? Just as the existence of a non-republican Turkey is unimaginable, the path of a republican but non-nationalist Turkey leading towards glory and honour and at the same time towards a future full of challenges would be doomed to remain weak and flawed. A non-republican but nationalist Turkey is as irrational an idea as a republican but non-nationalist Turkey. Our principle of nationalism is as crucial and supreme for guarantees of our progressive existence as for the security of our future life.

In terms of geography, Turkey is in such a position in the world that all kinds of winds pass over us from all directions, from the north, from the south, from the east, and from the west. This geographical exposure of our country to all kinds of winds is the same in terms of ideas and political propaganda. Anarchist, Marxist, Fascist, Caliphist, and internationalist propaganda, as well as much of the other similar kinds of propaganda, always passes over us. In the face of all these poisonous currents, one feeding the other, Turkey can only protect itself by holding to a firm belief in nationalism. In order to protect the people of Turkey against these tendencies, the lock of nationalism, which until now has been considered one of the main characteristics of the party, will become the property of the state so it can tightly close the door of Turkey.

[...]

We are populists [halkçıyız]. Our [form of] populism is as we understand it. In numerous other places, there are many parties [taking up] the cause of populism [halkçılık] with names like popular [popular] or populist [populist]. But an important quality of our populism is that it is not a mere cliché like theirs. When we shake the hand of every citizen as a citizen and work together with him, we see in him qualities worthy of respect and recognise every citizen as a human being of equal dignity, and we recognise the mass of citizens who do not claim privileges as commoners and populists.

[...]

In Turkey, there is no class, gradation, or privilege.
There are no ideas about regional privilege, nor the privilege of lordships, aghas, families or communities. In Turkey, the value [of a person] can only arise only through superior knowledge, capacity,

and work. On the one hand, we leave no room for workers to act forcefully to disrupt the harmony of national work by relying on the power of numbers and party strength; on the other hand, we leave no room for the owners of big businesses and capital holders to violate the rights of workers by relying on the power of money and wealth. Therefore, a mentality that eradicates the mentality of class struggle, hegemony, and privilege will complete the mentality of this country. However, being populist in the sense we desire and understand it is what raises nationalism to its cleanest and purest level.

[...]

I find it unnecessary to speak of secularism and revolutionarism because lacking those two concepts would mean the collapse of two of the pillars of the new state from their very basis. If we say that everything is complete and that our order has been established and if we conclude that we have made enough progress, not only do we endanger our future, we also endanger the yields of the revolutions that we have hitherto carried out. Such a form of comprehension would detract from that holy excitement which is mother to the entire idea of revolutions. That would entail nothing other than setting the pace of progress, returning to a dark path, and swimming against the currents of vitality and humanity.

[...]

The feudal state failed, and the liberal states that replaced it are collapsing all over the world as a result of their own internal decay. Various types of states are being established in their place. Friends, the collapse of liberal states following the feudal state has brought about the era of the birth of the national state. The national state is not an arbitrary regime. It does not entail a distributive administration with a voice issuing forth from every head. The national state as we understand it entails the private initiative of everyone in an orderly administration. Some people say, "The liberal state is collapsing; the class state is coming to take its place." We say "no" [to such notions]. We are convinced that the class state, which will be established in place of the liberal state, will eventually find the right path and will achieve success only by taking the path of the national state.

[...]

Friends, in the new party program, we explain the definition of statism clearly. In line with the definition in the old program, we used to say that "private initiative is free; the state too is free to do whatever it wishes in terms of economic initiatives." Partisan liberals on the right side, without quoting our second assertion, say, "The state cannot interfere with my business. It can neither hold me to account nor control me. It can neither ask me about the nature of the work I will do, nor the first substance I will use, nor the price I will ask from consumers, nor the rights of the workers I use."

On the other hand, a red Marxist would say that the state will do everything and nothing will be left to private initiative. The truth is neither like this, nor like that. The new program clarifies this point. The genuine meaning of our statism is that private enterprise is free but in every economic enterprise, for the common good, the state maintains its constructive rights and authority. The state will build and control the industry that it itself encourages and guards.

[...]

Friends, Switzerland has a referendum system. People gather and vote for the law. Of course, this procedure, which suits the conditions of Switzerland, cannot be applied in France. Today, according to our own conditions, we are in the position of holding elections with one more degree.

Democracy is not a revelation, nor is it a verse. It is a spirit, a sense, and a meaning. If work is carried out after being filtered through reason and is adapted to the needs of the environment, it will be beneficial and take root. You cannot plant an orange tree on Mount Zigana. We are not one of those who say, "They did things this way in so and so nation or in so and so place, so let us do the same." In the affairs of the nation, instead of imitation and outward admiration, we find ways that are suitable for life [so as] to be correct.

***

Firstly, Peker's speech not only underscores an ideological and historical reality, it also shows that the party ideology had a geostrategic dimension. The principles of the CHP program were drafted during a period that was affected by regional and global changes. Benito Mussolini (1883–1945) and the Italian Fascists had held power in Italy for more than a decade and were pursuing colonial efforts to revive the Roman Empire by expanding into the Mediterranean, and they were about to launch an aggressive war against Ethiopia. Indeed, Fascism was just off the coast of Turkey as a result of Italy's colonisation of the Dodecanese islands. At the same time, on the Black Sea coast there was the Soviet reality, the centre of international communism, which survived the Great Depression with its statist economic policies. Another important change was the rise to power of Adolf Hitler (1889–1945) and the National Socialist regime in Germany. Other political forces surrounding Turkey included the British and French mandates established in its southern neighbourhood such as in Iraq, Syria, and Palestine. That geostrategic dimension becomes all the more evident when Peker talked about an ideal of "nationalism" that would close Turkey's "mind and door" to "transnational currents," many of which were characterised as "poisonous."

Secondly, the CHP program speech of 1935 contributes to our understanding of the debates on the party's relationship with democracy. The question of the CHP's attitude towards democracy and whether single-party Turkey was in fact a dictatorship has been debated in Turkey for a very long time, even since the 1930s when Peker made his speech. The single-party regime itself vehemently rejected accusations that it was a dictatorship. Their argument was that under the CHP, the Republic based its regime on the "unconditional sovereignty" of the "people" and that it retained the formal image of parliamentary democracy throughout the single-party era. At the same time, following the promulgation of the Law on the Maintenance of Order (*Takrir-i Sükûn Kanunu*) in 1925, the regime developed strong authoritarian tendencies that were supported by a cult of leadership around Mustafa Kemal Atatürk (1881–1938) and in many ways by a militarised society. Peker's speech is important in terms of how it exemplified the party's stance on democracy, a stance that has never been univocal. In short, while Peker saw democracy as a relative issue, he did not seem to prioritise the establishment of a democratic regime but rather the implementation of a modernisation project based on the themes of republicanism, nationalism, and a unique adaptation of secularism.

In order to justify his views, Peker resorted to comparative analysis and referred to the specific historical trajectories of democratic countries in Europe. Challenging notions of a monolithic image of the West, he pointed out the political differences among Western democracies. According to Peker, while Switzerland was a direct democracy, France was not because the two countries had different characteristics, institutions, and historical trajectories. Stating that an advanced European country like France was lagging behind Switzerland in terms of democratic standards and democratic maturity, Peker seems to have been implying that such relativism left ample room for Turkey's leaders, who did not see democracy as a pressing matter, to decide on their own about issues of democracy or the lack thereof.

However, no matter how vague such a stance towards democracy may have been, Peker's speech offers some clues about how Turkey, ruled as it was by the CHP, was on the same level with other authoritarian regimes and dictatorships of the period. Peker's criticisms of political liberalism and liberal democracy were similar to the common arguments employed by European dictators when they railed against liberal democracies at the time. Just as was done under European dictatorships, Peker made the assertion that political liberalism and liberal democracies were outdated. Economically, the inability of Western democracies to cope with the world economic crisis seemed to undermine their credibility as role models, while the Soviet Union and Fascist Italy seemed to have dealt with the crisis much more effectively. However, Peker also rejected classist and Marxist ideologies which claimed to invalidate liberal democratic regimes and emerged as an alternative on the ideological map of Europe. Peker argued that the continuation of nation-states was the best option available and concluded his analysis with a rationalisation of "nationalism" as one of the six ideals of the party and the state.

***

By the second half of the 1930s, under the single-party rule of the CHP, the Republic of Turkey would come to be known abroad as Kemalist Turkey, and at the same time Europe would witness a proliferation of enthusiastic literature about the "new Turkey." Peker's speech was originally given in Turkish, but it was later translated into French and sent out to various embassies. In that respect, the speech clearly illustrates the paradox of the single-party regime in the sense that it created an ideological repertoire that was aimed at both branding the regime internationally and keeping the country free of "poisonous currents." Peker's proposal to put the party in charge of the country's administration with a supra-parliamentary status seems to have been inspired by fascist models. Although Atatürk rejected the proposal, a declaration was made a year later which stated that the Republic was a single-party state, which was clearly in line with other authoritarian models in Europe.

Select Bibliography

Clayer, Nathalie, Fabio Giomi, and Emmanuel Szurek. "Introduction: Transnationalising Kemalism: A Refractive Relationship." In *Kemalism: The Transnational Making of Kemalism in the Post-Ottoman Space*, edited by Nathalie Clayer, Fabio Giomi and Emmanuel Szurek, 1–38. London: I.B. Tauris, 2018.

Mango, Andrew. *Atatürk*. London: John Murray, 1999.

Plaggenborg, Stefan. *Ordnung und Gewalt: Kemalismus, Faschismus, Sozialismus*. München: Oldenburg Verlag, 2012.

Zürcher, Erik-Jan, "Institution Building in the Kemalist Republic: The Role of the People's Party." In *Men of Order: Authoritarian Modernization under Atatürk and Reza Shah*, edited by Erik-Jan Zürcher and Touraj Atabaki, 98–112. London: I.B. Tauris, 2004.

14

Language, Nation, and their Enemies: Linguistic Nationalism

Emmanuel Szurek

The language reform is arguably one of the most enduring legacies of Turkey's single-party era. After the Romanisation of the script (1928–1930), the reforms continued with the purging of Arabic and Persian lexical and syntactical components of Ottoman Turkish under the guidance of the Turkish Language Institute (*Türk Dili Tetkik Cemiyeti*, later the *Türk Dil Kurumu*), which held its renowned first congress (*kurultay*) in İstanbul from 26 September to 5 October in 1932. "Modern" Turkish was principally introduced into society through schools and newspapers. In order to reach a wider audience in a country where four out of five citizens were illiterate, the party created the People's Houses (*Halkevleri*), which were its official "cultural organisations". From 1934 to 1949, every year on 26 September—the anniversary of the first *kurultay*—citizens were summoned to the local *Halkevi*, which could be found all around the country, to attend what were called "Language Festivals".

The Language Festivals included plays, musical performances, games, and, principally, public lectures. Under the distant supervision of the Language Institute in Ankara, local notables, teachers, and civil officers pontificated to "the people" about the "Language Revolution". The cause for "pure Turkish" hence became a central part of the vulgate of the "Turkish Revolution". In addition, starting in the early 1930s it became commonplace in the nationalist canon to celebrate Turkish in its original purity as the greatest, the most beautiful, and one of the oldest languages. This self-glorifying discourse reached its apogee with the Sun Language Theory (1935), which attributed the birth of language to a superior prehistoric race originating in Central Asia called *Alpine brachycephalic Turks* and made Turkish the origin of all of mankind's languages.

However, being distant from Ankara sometimes allowed for concerns that were seemingly unrelated to come to the surface at these Language Festivals. What follows is an excerpt from a speech that was given in Urfa in southeast Anatolia during the Language Festival that was held on 26 September in 1936. The region of southeast Turkey is predominantly inhabited by ethnic non-Turks, particularly Kurds and Arabs, and at the time of the festival it was still haunted by the mass killings that had occurred during the First World War when the local Armenians were exterminated, deported, or forcefully Islamised. The speaker, a twenty-five-year-old named Ratıp Akdeniz, had no personal involvement in those events. The son of a religious man, he was born and raised in Lefkoşa (Cyprus), a former province of the Ottoman Empire and a British colony since 1858. After moving to Turkey, he became one of the first graduates of the Gazi Institute for Education, a prestigious teacher's college founded in Ankara in 1926. He was then appointed to a post in Urfa as a junior high school teacher of Turkish literature. He is likely to have considered himself a "missionary of the Republic".

About the Language Revolution*

To have a strong sense of our identity, that is, of our Turkishness, we need a language that is pure Turkish before anything else. Our drowsy ancestors failed to foresee this for many centuries. While Europe was arming itself with national sentiment, we fell asleep with the idea that "within the *umma*, the idea of a nation is a sin". While they [the Europeans] progressed, we persisted in our dream. One day the nations within the Ottoman Empire woke up too, like those in Europe. And still, we did not touch the issue of nationality within the ummah. Then, they [the nations within the ummah] struck us. They made Europe strike us. Still, we could not even prick their chest with a needle. Today, we have discarded the nations within the ummah. Who is paying for their sins? The removal from our country of the nations that wanted to strike us was a sin for us, but for our livelihood it was a blessing. Today, a pure Turkish air blows in their place.

My fellow compatriots, today too there are nations that are taking root in our language. Each and every one of those nations that obstruct the independence of our Turkish language are not only our enemies, seeking to weaken our identity, they are also driving like nails into our children's skulls, killing them because those fresh brains can simply not absorb them. Just like we drove those nations away from our bosom, we shall drive them away from our language. Just like it is hard to think of a family where the mother and father are Turkish, the daughter is French, the son is Italian, and the grandson is Greek, we find it bizarre that there are still foreign nations existing within the family of the Turkish language.

[As for] those foreign nations that lived within Turkish intellectual life for over nine centuries, may they never forget that in Republican Turkey, unlike what happened in the Ottoman Empire, one does not simply lie around. The Republic exposed and drove away each and every enemy of the Turk, and it still does so. Before the eyes of civilisation, it [the Republic] puts each and every one of them to death.

My friends! Our language is such that all the languages of the world stem from it. The Turkish language is the fundament of all languages. We proclaim that French, Arabic, and Russian took their roots from the Turkish language, and if this surprises anyone among you, I would like to remind them that, on this very matter, there was a gathering of linguists a month ago in İstanbul who confessed this truth and those foreign scholars stated the same thing in their own parlance. [In the past] our own brainless heads did not acknowledge the value of our language, a language which was born on the wide steppes of Central Asia that brought culture to a worldwide civilisation. So for centuries they embraced

* Translation of the original Turkish typescript of a speech entitled "About the Language Revolution" by Ratıp Akdeniz, 26 September 1936. Box 1170, folder 111, number 1. Archives of the Political Parties (490-1-0-0). Devlet Arşivleri Başkanlığı Cumhuriyet Arşivi, Ankara.

foreign influences without realising that one day it would be poisoned by those snakes that they held warm on their chests, resulting in the devastation of the thousand-year-old Turkish culture like it was nothing. As for our generation, when we wanted to read a book, we could not understand anything in the midst of all of the dark mirages of those foreign words. So, this language never could create the slightest movement in our brains. Who knows among the thousands of Turkish achievements how many millions of Turkish children had their tongues confined like ours, how many had their brains paralysed like ours.

***

It is impossible to know how many people actually attended this public lecture. But photographs of other Language Festivals show several dozen individuals in attendance, mostly school children and male adults, whereas official reports often refer to audiences of "hundreds" of participants.

In his lecture, Akdeniz takes up a number of classical tropes of the Turkist discourse, which proceeds by identifying a national self as much as anything by constructing significant "others". A first banal feature is the evolutionist dichotomy between "them," the Europeans, who had been running ahead on the path to nationhood, and "us," the Muslims, lagging behind because nationalism was perceived as posing a threat of division (*fitna*) within the Muslim world, the *umma*. Then comes the Republican distinction between "them," the Ottomans—"our drowsy ancestors" who dozed in the Islamic refusal of nationhood for centuries—as opposed to "us" modern Turks who were now awakened to nationhood. The notion of Europeans "striking us" can be read as a reference to imperialism (of which Akdeniz had direct experience in Cyprus).

In addition to these temporal (Ottomans vs. Turks) and civilisational (Europeans vs. Muslims) patterns of othering and self-identification, there is a third opposition, the interpretation of which is less evident: "we" Turks, who long remained truthful to Islamic tenets, against "them," "the nations [that existed] inside the umma" which had to be "discarded" because they were the accomplices and minions of imperialist Europe. But to whom does this "them" refer?

They could be the non-Turkish Muslims of the Ottoman Empire who were once an integral part of the ummah, the Muslim nation; namely, Albanians (who "abandoned" the Empire in 1912), Arabs (who "betrayed" the Ottomans in 1916), and Kurds, who had been resisting the Republic since it was founded. However, those who were "removed from our country" or "driven away from our bosom" are most likely Christians, specifically Armenians. They were the community that was customarily accused of colluding with foreign powers, even before they were "discarded". Akdeniz refers to this "removal" as both a "sin" and a "blessing for our lives". The use of such religious terminology could be interpreted as acknowledgement of a collective sense of guilt for what is now referred to as the genocide of a people. But, as we shall see, it can also be read as a justification for that crime, as it is those "others" who are made responsible, by way of their own "sins," for what happened to them.

Then comes the question of what Akdeniz's speech is actually about. In the excerpt presented here, cleansing the nation and purifying the language are presented as two inseparable operations. To be sure, discussing the presence of numerous Arabic and Persian words in the Ottoman-Turkish lexicon as indicating a state of "linguistic occupation" or "linguistic imperialism" is a banal metaphor of the Turkish-Republican metalinguistic discourse. In *Principles of Turkism* (1923), for instance, Ziya Gökalp (1876–1924), the chief ideologue of the Ottoman Committee of Union and Progress and a major intellectual at the time of the founding of the new regime, draws those "foreign" words or constructions into the realm of "linguistic capitulations" that prolonged, in the realm of "culture," the financial and juridical privileges that had been imposed by Europeans on the Empire and which were ultimately abolished with the Treaty of Lausanne (1923). Likewise, calling the language reform a fight for cultural "independence" implies that the lexical purge was a continuation of the War of Independence (1919–1922). By placing the purification of the language and the ethnic cleansing of the nation on the same level, Akdeniz perpetuates the same line of thinking. He does, however, make the analogy deeper and more explicit.

At this point language and the nation become completely conflated. Thus, making proto-Turkish, in its original purity, the *Ursprache* of mankind amounts to making the original Turks a superior race, as was notoriously claimed at the third *Kurultay* of Language that was held in İstanbul in August 1936. Conversely, non-Turkic words are equated with "those foreign nations that lived within Turkish intellectual life for over nine centuries". Such a system of dating presumably points to the eleventh century, when the Turks embraced Islam and started to use Arabic and Persian words. Still, those repudiated words are also compared with individuals who, in the Ottoman Empire, used to simply "lie around". This latter expression could be a reference to the abovementioned "drowsy" Ottomans, which Republican leaders vilified for having lived off the Turks for centuries. And yet it is also reminiscent of a common xenophobic narrative that targeted non-Muslims as "parasites" as well as internal "foreigners". Saying they had been such for "nine centuries"—that is, since the arrival of the Turks in Anatolia—makes them paradoxical foreigners indeed, considering that it was Christians who were the autochthonous inhabitants of Asia Minor long before the Turks arrived.

Lastly, the speech justifies violence, both past and future. "Foreign" words are deemed to be the symptoms of an existential threat to the nation, as they are pictured like vicious animals ("snakes") or weapons ("nails") used to disable the bodies (skulls perforated, brains paralyzed, tongues confined) of the most fragile elements of society—children—thereby "killing" them and "devastating" Turkish culture. In the face of such tremendous peril, only unyielding severity can suffice as a response, to which all things foreign—words *and* people— are to be subjected. Thus, the junior high school teacher not only supports the eradication of non-Turkic words, following the guidelines sent from Ankara by the Turkish Language Institute, he also articulates a series of threatening statements against flesh-and-bone people that can be construed as going beyond the framework of the Language Festivals.

Indeed, far from euphemising the genocidal practices that made Turkey possible, Akdeniz acknowledges "the Republic" as the political and moral heiress of this extreme violence.

Moreover, he even calls for its perpetuation—"before the eyes of civilisation"—if necessary. And yet those threats remain once again tainted with ambiguity, as the targets are not named. Certainly, they need to be considered within the context of the suppression of the Kurdish revolts that were taking place in southeast Anatolia, and they must have also resonated with Urfa's local social and sociolinguistic landscape through their designation of all the non-Turkish speakers in the province as potential "enemies".

***

The history of the language reform has generally been written from a top-down perspective, principally in terms of it being a "success" or a "catastrophe," and the question of language has thus been treated separately from other major issues that were involved in the creation of Turkey as a nation. The above-quoted excerpts mark an exception both to such an analytical perspective and the hundreds of speeches that were made on the occasion of the Language Festivals, numerous copies of which have been kept in the archives in Ankara. This text demonstrates that in southeastern Anatolia, from the perspective of the local elite, there were not necessarily clear-cut lines between different policies of social engineering (here ethnic, there linguistic), between different categories of "enemies" (former Ottoman elites, non-Turkish Muslims, non-Muslims), and lastly between different patterns of physical and symbolic violence (the Armenian Genocide, the suppression of Kurdish revolts and identity), all of which we often think of as being disparate. The general confusion, or conscious ambiguity, that runs through Akdeniz's speech thus reflects the overwhelming presence of state violence in southeastern Turkey in the 1930s. But it also questions, in turn, the extent to which the "Language Revolution" itself was inhabited, albeit in discrete and latent forms, by the same impetus.

Select Bibliography

Aytürk, İlker. "Turkish Linguists Against the West: The Origins of Linguistic Nationalism in Atatürk's Turkey." *Middle Eastern Studies* 40, no. 6 (2004): 1–25.

Lewis, Geoffrey. *The Turkish Language Reform: A Catastrophic Success.* Oxford: Oxford University Press, 1999.

Suciyan, Talin. *The Armenians in Modern Turkey: Post-Genocide Society, Politics and History.* London: I.B. Tauris, 2016.

Szurek, Emmanuel. "Dil Bayramı. Une lecture somatique de la fête politique dans la Turquie du Parti unique." In *Penser, agir et vivre dans l'Empire ottoman et en Turquie. Études réunies pour François Georgeon*, edited by Nathalie Clayer and Erdal Kaynar, 497–523. Leuven: Peeters, 2013.

Üngör, Uğur Ümit. *The Making of Modern Turkey: Nation and State in Eastern Anatolia, 1913–1950.* Oxford: Oxford University Press, 2011.

Yıldırım, Yüksel. "10 Kasım 1938: Büyük Kaybın Urfa İline Yansıması." *Çağdaş Türkiye Tarihi Araştırmaları Dergisi* XVIII, no. 36 (2018): 163–92.

15
"Treacherous and Insidious": Turkey's Southern Border

Ramazan Hakkı Öztan

Even though the Turkish-Syrian border was a product of the partitioning of the Ottoman Empire after the First World War, its exact shape was determined by the contours of armed struggles that took place between the local resistance led by Mustafa Kemal in Ankara and the Allied Powers that sought to dictate the terms of the ensuing peace treaty by force. While Ankara was engaged in cutthroat conventional warfare against the Greek invasion of western Anatolia, its struggle against the French and Armenian forces in the south largely took the form of irregular fighting which, together with local mobilisation, managed to further check French advances in the south. Ankara's successes on the battlefield resulted in initial diplomatic talks that were held in London in February and March of 1921, when the Turkish and French agreed that the Turkish-Syrian border would parallel the tracks of the Baghdad railroad. Although this agreement was ultimately not ratified by Ankara, it foreshadowed what was to come. The Ankara Agreement, concluded on 20 October 1921, set the Turkish-Syrian border, largely along the lines of what had already been decided a number of months earlier. Yet, in the upcoming years the demarcation of the border was a contentious affair to say the least, since new political opportunities brought to the fore renewed discussions about what constituted national borders as defined by the National Pact of 1920. The following newspaper article from 1937 focuses on one such context that captures Turkey's continued anxieties over its border with Syria in the interwar period.

The Southern Border is a Treacherous and Insidious Border[*]

Our southern border is just like the broken window of an otherwise orderly house. Whenever things quiet down here and the streets become deserted, the servant girls sneak out and welcome in their foreign lovers who carry on their backs Aleppine silk cloth, Japanese textiles, cigarette papers, flintstones, and salt... Even loads of sugar were popular at one point. Once the vagrants sell their goods and stuff their pockets with cash, they take off across the border.

In terms of Turkey's peace of mind, security, and economy, the southern border constitutes an important national cause, one that we have to settle sooner or later.

[*] Translated from the original Turkish in Mümtaz Faik, "Cenup Hududu Hain, Sinsi bir Huduttur," *Tan*, 1 January 1937.

I have seen many borders in my life, such as the Polish-Russian, German-Polish, and Bulgarian-Turkish borders... I have even seen a bizarre border that cut across a house, one part of which was left in Holland, the other in Belgium. Yet, I cannot help but admit that I have never come across a border that is as odd as Turkey's southern border.

Here, the border consists solely of an imaginary line marked by piles of stones erected at regular intervals. Yet, these border stones cut into two a topography that features the same soil and vegetation, and a geography inhabited by the same people. Both sides are Turkish, but the French, seeking to create an artificial barrier, had inserted between the two sides sizeable communities that have anti-Turkish leanings, while also scattering a handful of Arabs in their midst.

You see, people even plant thorn bushes to separate their vineyards from those of their neighbours, but when it comes to Turkey's southern border, no such urgency to create separation exists in any form. Out here, there are many vineyards and olive groves, in which it is impossible to point out where exactly this unnecessary country of Syria starts. That's how fictitious Syria is around here.

Since half of the vineyards remain in Syria and the other half are in Turkey, it is no exaggeration to claim that smuggling does not require human labour around here. Under favourable conditions, for example when the southern winds pick up pace, it might even be possible for cigarette papers and silk textiles, if placed carefully on one side of a path, to just fly over across the border. That being the case, the border patrols, always on guard and alert, do their best to prevent such trespasses and serve as human border walls, as they at times halt flying bullets with their bodies.

No matter what we do though, this is an insidious border, and a mysterious and a treacherous one as well. After all, the south has nights as dark as tar pits, and vast deserts that, as if they had absorbed the sun, continue to dazzle humans. My dear readers, from now on we will delve into the curious depths of these tar pits and mingle with the people who navigate the deserts as deftly as desert lizards.

***

Thus starts a series of articles authored by Mümtaz Faik Fenik (1905–1974), a young journalist (and later a deputy for the Democrat Party) who, over the course of the first three months of 1937, shared his observations about the Turkish-Syrian border with the national readership of *Tan*, a popular Turkish daily with leftist credentials. His column titled "On the Southern Border" was context-specific, however, as it spoke to the evolving crisis over the sanjak of Alexandretta at the time. The Ankara Agreement of 1921 had included a clause (article 7) that foresaw the establishment of "a special administrative regime" in the district of Alexandretta, as it was home to sizeable Turkish-speaking communities. During the peace negotiations held in Lausanne, the Turkish delegation argued for the necessity of including the sanjak in Turkey but was forced to compromise in the end. In the years that followed, Ankara continued to make overtures to the French for the protection of the rights of those Turkish-speaking communities.

Only in 1936 did a real opportunity present itself for Ankara as French and Syrian nationalists had launched negotiations for Syrian independence, resulting in a confrontation with Ankara, which did not agree to have Alexandretta become part of an independent Syria. The Turkish side quickly brought the case to the League of Nations, which it had joined only a few years earlier in 1932, arguing that the inhabitants of the sanjak of Alexandretta spoke Turkish. As such, the Turkish authorities constructed their claims over the district by emphasising language as the predominant marker of national identity. That line of argument was not only common in irredentist discourses of the time, it also aligned well with the position of the League of Nations vis-à-vis nationalism as the organising principle of modern territoriality.

Ankara's diplomatic efforts abroad coincided with the discursive positions prevalent at home, where Turkish nationalists referred to Alexandretta as "Hatay," a toponym that alleg-edly dated back to the times of the Hittites, an ancient Anatolian civilisation to which Turks could be traced, according to the state's official historical narrative. As such, Mümtaz Faik's column was a typical example of an officially sanctioned press campaign in the high Kemalist era, seeking as it did to create and disseminate a particular discourse on a popular level. Mümtaz Faik's emphasis on the primacy of Turkish along the border zone and French intrigues aiming to ethnically jumble up and dilute the region are a clear illustration not of only the strong anti-French sentiment that prevailed at the time, but also point to the arguments that Ankara presented in Geneva regarding its claims over Hatay. Taken altogether, these efforts ultimately bore fruit when the Republic of Hatay was established in 1938, which was then annexed by Turkey in less than a year following a staged referendum in a deal that ostensibly demonstrated French goodwill towards Ankara on the eve of the Second World War.

While Mümtaz Faik's articles are illustrative of a specific moment when Turkish national newspapers solicited contributions from journalists about mounting tensions between Turkey and Syria, his reporting from the border zone also sheds light on some of Ankara's economic anxieties, which had persisted since the creation of the Turkish-Syrian border back in 1921. Largely following the tracks of a railroad and an old Roman route instead of more typical markers of borders, such as rivers or mountain chains, the Turkish-Syrian border was often framed as artificial and unnatural by Turkish and Syrian officials alike as a way of advancing their own territorial claims—a position to which Mümtaz Faik did not fail to allude, either. Yet, this does not mean that choosing a railway as the path of a border was inconsequential. A project devised to connect rather than divide, the Baghdad railroad traversed flat and at times densely-populated agricultural landscapes, which explain Mümtaz Faik's passing references to vineyards and olive groves that were divided into two by the Turkish-Syrian border. As such, the demarcation of the border not only created very practical problems on a daily basis for those who inhabited the region, it also introduced a wide range of challenges for state authorities on both sides of the border, as they were concerned about the flows and crossings of people that were so characteristic of the region.

The border reflected at its very heart the painful changes that take place when a formerly connected imperial economy is divided into two. As early as the spring of 1921, the prospects of a border crossing just north of Aleppo, an Ottoman city that until then had served as the hub of commerce for the region and beyond, created a backlash among merchants who profited from Aleppo's connections to southern Anatolia. Tariff negotiations between Turkey and France, which went on for years, took place against that backdrop. When the Great Depression of 1929 struck, shaking up the global economy, it also had a direct impact along the Turkish-Syrian border, transforming it into a hub of illicit trade where smugglers exchanged commodities supplied by global chains such as Japanese textiles as well as local goods like Aleppine silk. Mümtaz Faik's references to these circuits and his caricaturised view of the people involved in smuggling operations fit well with the otherwise immediate context of ongoing interstate political rivalries.

***

In the 1920s and 1930s, Turkey's border with Syria became a crucial point of reference in the context of broader public debates surrounding the themes of national security and economic independence. The "artificiality" of the Turkish-Syrian border, a point that was so distinctly emphasised in Mümtaz Faik's account, reflected less of a rupture than continuity in Ankara's discursive positions and policy orientation. Moreover, highlighting the necessity of revising such "unnatural" borders was certainly not peculiar to the Middle East. In fact, Turkey's southern border reflected the complex relationships that all former "master" nations had with their former territories, relationships that had become particularly strained in the charged political climate leading up to the Second World War. What took place along Ankara's southern border was therefore part of a larger trend coming to the fore in Europe, where irredentist aspirations and identity politics had become the currency with which neighbouring powers began to compete with one another. As such, the developments that took place along the Turkish-Syrian border were not peripheral and local, but rather quite central to the making of regional political and economic realities. Today this is perhaps stating the obvious, but as the aftermath of the Syrian Civil War of 2011 has demonstrated time and time again, the issue of borders, and who or what crosses them and why, can steer politics in unpredictable ways and with far-reaching repercussions.

Select Bibliography

Altuğ, Seda, and Benjamin Thomas White. "Frontières et pouvoir d'état: La frontière turco-syrienne dans les années 1920 et 1930." *Vingtième Siècle: Revue d'histoire* 103, no. 3 (2009): 91–104.

Bein, Amit. *Kemalist Turkey and the Middle East: International Relations in the Interwar Period.* Cambridge: Cambridge University Press, 2017.

Öztan, Ramazan Hakkı. "The Great Depression and the Making of Turkish-Syrian Border, 1921– 1939." *International Journal of Middle East Studies* 52, no. 2 (2020): 311–26.

Shields, Sarah D. *Fezzes in the River: Identity Politics and European Diplomacy in the Middle East on the Eve of World War II.* Oxford: Oxford University Press, 2011.

Tejel, Jordi. "States of Rumors: Politics of Information along the Turkish-Syrian Border, 1925–1945." *Journal of Borderlands Studies* 37, no. 1 (2022): 95–113.

16

Modernising Attire, Modernising the Nation: Reflections of Kemalist Clothing Reforms

Sevgi Adak

In March of 1935, Lilo Linke (1906–1963), a German writer and reporter, started a year-long journey across Turkey. Traveling from İstanbul to several provinces in Anatolia, Linke described a rapidly changing country, the story of which she told in her book *Allah Dethroned: A Journey Through Modern Turkey*. *Allah Dethroned* was one among several other books published on Turkey in interwar Europe, attesting to Western interest in and fascination with the transformation of Turkey under the new republican regime established in 1923. Linke's narrative was illustrated in the book with photographs documenting the transformations she had observed. Among the images she used was a propaganda poster created by the country's ruling (and only) political party, the Republican People's Party (*Cumhuriyet Halk Fırkası*, CHF), in the 1930s. She had seen the poster in a classroom at a primary school she visited in Malatya, a province in eastern Turkey. It seems that the poster was sent to provinces to be displayed in school buildings, and most likely in other state offices as well, by the Ministry of the Interior. The poster, which is similar to other political propaganda materials of the time, aimed at promoting the "new ways" that the republican regime had introduced through rigorous efforts targeting cultural modernisation. Among the key components of this cultural modernisation were clothing reforms, which aimed at both "modernising" and regulating dress norms in the public sphere, as clothing was seen as one of the most powerful means of displaying the new national identity the republican regime aspired to create. Kemalist clothing reforms, however, did not take a single form. The state opted for various methods and strategies to initiate the desired changes in clothing. While certain garments, such as the Ottoman fez, were banned by law, intervening in the clothing practices of ordinary citizens through legislation was indeed a less preferable option. For the most part, the new republic sought to achieve the goal of reforming citizens' attire by way of propaganda, given the limited capacity of the state and scant resources in the predominantly rural and economically strained Turkey of the interwar period. Posters put out by the CHF and other visual materials, while rare, were thus used to promote regime ideals and bolster state-led reforms.

Republican People's Party Poster: "Revolution in Clothing and Marriage"

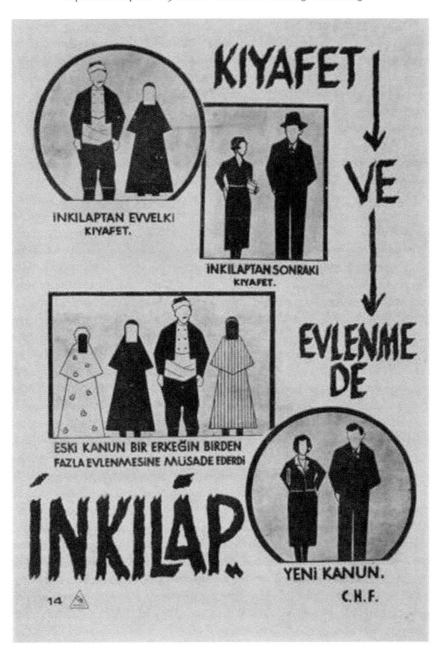

* Published in Lilo Linke, *Allah Dethroned: A Journey Through Modern Turkey* (London: Constable & Co Ltd, 1937), 215.

The CHF poster presented above, captioned "Kıyafet ve Evlenmede İnkılâp" (Revolution in Clothing and Marriage), emphasises the radical character of the transformation in the way people—supposedly, that is—dressed and the type of marriage allowed under the new laws and regulations that were put into effect by the Kemalist regime. Juxtaposing the "new" norms of clothing and marriage with the "old" ways of the Ottoman past, a comparison that Kemalist discourse deployed frequently to mark the historical rupture it wanted to represent, the poster is most likely a reference to the adoption of a secular Civil Code in 1926. The new code outlawed polygamy, which is depicted in the poster via the image of a traditionally dressed man with three wives, all of whom are fully veiled. The "modern" marriage that the new code envisioned was the monogamous union of a heterosexual couple, as can be seen in the image in the circle in the bottom right corner of the poster. The adoption of a fully secular Civil Code was indeed quite revolutionary at the time, and Turkey was the only predominantly Muslim country to do so.

The poster also reflects, however, the ruling party's view that a revolution had occurred in clothing as well. As can be seen in the poster, the "old" style of clothing, shown via the image in the circle in the top left corner of the poster and captioned "clothing before the revolution," was essentially symbolised by traditional male attire consisting of baggy trousers and traditional headgear, and the black *çarşaf*, a full body covering common among women as the primary type of outdoor attire, combined with the *peçe*, or face veil. Next to that image is a depiction of "clothing after the revolution," as the caption reads, which is portrayed through an image of a woman and a man dressed in European-style clothing, most clearly symbolised by the adoption of the European hat by men as well as the casting off the *çarşaf* and the *peçe* for women. Traditional male headgear, such as the Ottoman fez, was banned by law in 1925, only two years after the establishment of the republic. The European-style hat was promoted as the new form of headgear for Turkish men, and it was compulsory for state officials and members of parliament to wear such hats. That was indeed the only piece of legislation in interwar Turkey that directly intervened in ordinary people's clothing. Changes in women's clothing and other aspects of male attire came about neither in the form of legislation nor as governmental decrees but rather local political endeavours. Local campaigns, mainly initiated by municipalities, sought to ban the use of the *peçe* and the *çarşaf*, and in a handful of provinces efforts were made to proscribe the baggy trousers that men wore. Anti-veiling campaigns, which had their peak in the mid-1930s at the height of Kemalist efforts to enact cultural modernisation, remained largely local and were essentially shaped by the specific dynamics of each province. Although they became a country-wide phenomenon, these local anti-veiling campaigns lacked the force of law and hence in practice resulted in an uneven, less radical change in clothing styles in early Republican Turkey than the word "revolution" would suggest. As such, it is telling that the CHF poster would nevertheless refer to a "revolution" in clothing, as the use of such a term illustrates the preferences of the regime and the ideals it envisioned rather than what actually took place in practice. It demonstrates that European-style attire and the unveiling of women were set up as an ideal that remained a yardstick in all subsequent debates about clothing and women's veiling in Turkey in the decades that followed.

***

The state regulation of clothing in Turkey during the single-party era did not adhere to a singular approach, and contrary to what is often assumed, legislation aimed at directly banning certain garments was indeed limited. For the most part, the Kemalist regime turned to propaganda to discourage the use of certain types of attire, especially the *peçe* and the *çarşaf* for women, and it promoted those styles of clothing it considered to be modern and national. Using posters for propaganda, however, does not seem to have been very common; aside from a few images in newspapers and journals that were primarily accessible by the literate segments of society, there is limited evidence of visual images being used to drive forward the "revolutions" initiated by the state. It is this rarity that makes the CHF poster presented above so significant, as it is one of the few surviving official illustrations of how the political regime of the time understood the shift in clothing styles that interventions were intended to achieve. It is important to note, however, that the poster, as in the case of many other visual materials used for propaganda at the time, reflects an ideal rather than what actually occurred in practice. In other words, while a clothing revolution did take place in early Republican Turkey—in the sense that various attempts were made to modernise how ordinary people dressed—that should not be taken to mean that all citizens adopted the European-style attire envisioned in the poster. Such visualisations of Kemalist ideals should always be cross-read with different kinds of historical sources (e.g., newspapers, archival materials, and memoirs) as it is important to analyze not just the top-down, elite visions of reforms, but the processes of implementation that went into them and the various ways in which those reforms were negotiated, domesticated, and resisted by social actors in practice.

Select Bibliography

Adak, Sevgi. *Anti-Veiling Campaigns in Turkey: State, Society and Gender in the Early Republic.* London: I.B. Tauris, 2022.

Baker, Patricia. "The Fez in Turkey: A Symbol of Modernization?" *Costume* 20 (1986): 72–85.

Libal, Kathryn. "From Face Veil to Cloche Hat: The Backward Ottoman versus New Turkish Woman in Urban Public Discourse." In *Anti-Veiling Campaigns in the Muslim World: Gender, Modernism and the Politics of Dress*, edited by Stephanie Cronin, 39–58. London: Routledge, 2014.

Norton, John. "Faith and Fashion in Turkey." In *Languages of Dress in the Middle East*, edited by Nancy Lindisfarne-Tapper and Bruce Ingham, 149–77. London: Curzon Press, 1997.

Yılmaz, Hale. *Becoming Turkish: Nationalist Reforms and Cultural Negotiations in Early Republican Turkey, 1923–1945.* Syracuse: Syracuse University Press, 2013.

17
Mapping Nomadism:
The Construction of the Nation-State

Reşat Kasaba

The widespread existence of pastoral nomadism in and around Anatolia had a long history and was related, in part, to the geographic characteristics and climate of the region. Ranges of mountains and valleys are interspersed across Anatolia, creating a setting where sedentary and mobile communities lived in proximity. Peasants and nomads interacted, their activities overlapped, and they depended on one another for survival. Far from being a marginal mode of living, nomadism was in fact an integral part of the Anatolian economy for centuries. Throughout history, nomads used their unique position in the rural economy as a form of leverage to advance their interests and to resist the policies of sedentarisation that empires and states, including the Ottoman Empire and its successors throughout the Middle East, sought to implement.

It was not, however, only the economic role they played or their ability to resist the centralising policies of the Ottoman Empire that enabled nomadic tribes to survive into the twentieth century. Like other empires in world history, the Ottomans extended their authority through the mediation of tribal chiefs, sedentary and nomadic alike. This led to the integration of tribes into the administration of the Ottoman Empire, which accorded their chiefs the added prestige and power of being affiliated with the imperial state. The Ottomans continued this policy of co-opting tribes even after they embarked on a program of reforms and centralisation in the nineteenth century, when they were laying the foundations of a modern state. First Abdülhamid II and then the Young Turk governments took the additional step of organising and arming certain Kurdish tribes in the east as part of their campaign to pacify the countryside and carry out massacres of Armenians in 1894–1896, as well as the Armenian Genocide in 1915.

Tribal groups, which were spread throughout Anatolia, predominantly supported the nationalist struggle, as a result of which they remained an integral part of the social fabric in the new Republic, as can be seen in "Directions of Nomadism," which is a map that depicts the movement of nomadic tribes in Turkey in the late 1920s and 1930s. The map, which was prepared by the Republic's Ministry of the Interior, was included among the ministry's publications, and it also appears in the book *La Turquie: Passé et Présent* by Marcel Clerget (1900–1984), who was the Director of the French Institute in Ankara and a teacher at the Galatasaray Lycée in İstanbul. The map "Directions of Nomadism" shows how the republican state created graphic representations of nomadism and how such maps featured in the construction of the new state in the early decades of the twentieth century.

CARTE V. — LES DIRECTIONS DU NOMADISME. (Échelle : 1 : 12 000 000).

1, Quartiers d'hiver; 2, Pâturages d'été; 3, Voies commerciales du trafic de bétail. — (D'après les Services du Ministère de l'Intérieur.)

***

The dots in "Directions of Nomadism" show the wintering grounds of nomadic tribes, while short arrows indicate their migratory routes. The longer arrows, including those that crossed the country's southern and eastern borders, trace the trade routes along which tribes sold their livestock. There are more than a hundred seasonal migration routes indicated on the map, making it clear that in the early republican era, nomadism continued to be pervasive across all of Turkey and even crossed into neighbouring countries. With its demarcation of provinces and provincial centres, the map demonstrates that the new state was being established in a geography that was largely unsettled; as the government set about creating institutions and implementing state policies, social relations and structures remained in flux and the country's borders were porous. The map also indicates that the routes that were used to smuggle livestock, weapons, and other merchandise across the southern border—pathways which in the meantime had been declared illegal—were in fact a continuation of trade and

* Translated from the original Turkish in Marcel Clerget, *La Turquie: Passé et Présent* (Paris: Librarie Armand Colin, 1947 [1937]). The version of the map reproduced here is from Clerget's book, which has six other maps and plans, all of which reference the Ministry of the Interior and provide details about geographical features as well as patterns of settlement and social interaction in Anatolia. Clerget used these maps and the accompanying information to explain the role that the physical environment played in shaping Turkey's "recent transformation". I would like to thank Canan Bolel for her help with some of the research that went into this article.

migration routes that had existed for centuries but now crisscrossed the newly established border between Turkey and the French mandate of Syria.

The patterns of mobility that are depicted on the map suggest that pastoral nomadism remained an integral part of Turkey's local commerce and agriculture well into the twentieth century. At the same time, the partially armed tribes that had become intertwined with pastoral nomadism in the eastern and south-eastern parts of the country in the late nineteenth and early twentieth centuries became a major security problem for the republican state in the 1920s and 1930s. In particular, as a consequence of their distinct histories and strong allegiance to their tribal chiefs, religious communities, and cultural identities, Kurds posed a formidable challenge to the government's project of creating a centralised state and a homogenous nation. Known for having been loyal subjects of the Ottoman Sultan-Caliph, Kurds now found themselves excluded from the international and national deliberations that shaped the post-Ottoman political space. The new republican state was keen to reimagine the Anatolian peninsula as a Muslim-Turkish homeland, which, in the eyes of the government, required the suppression and forceful assimilation of Kurds. The geographical characteristics of Anatolia, however, provided an ideal environment for continued nomadism and made it quite difficult for the Turkish state to establish its authority, especially in the mountainous terrain in the eastern regions. Starting immediately after the establishment of the Republic and continuing into the 1930s, a series of Kurdish rebellions broke out, including the Sheikh Said, Mt. Ararat and Dersim revolts, which severely tested the viability of the new nation-state.

The Turkish state responded to Kurdish resistance with uncompromising ferocity, and a large swathe of the country's eastern regions was placed under martial law. Of the eighteen military operations launched by Turkey between 1924 and 1938, all but one took place in Kurdistan. Tens of thousands of Kurds were forcefully relocated to other parts of the country, thousands of tribal leaders and members were tried and executed, and an unknown number of villages and settlements were razed. The Turkish military conducted aerial bombings around the town of Dersim, which was the site of a particularly strong resistance movement in 1938. The entire population of Dersim and its environs were exiled to the west, the region was renamed Tunceli, and people from other parts of Turkey were settled there.

One of the tactics employed by the Turkish state to counter Kurdish insurgencies was to block the migratory routes of tribes to prevent them from moving to their summer pastures; moreover, the state confiscated their livestock and drove them away from their homes. Targeting tribal chiefs was seen as an especially effective means of quelling Kurdish uprisings because their removal along with their families was often detrimental to the continued existence of tribal communities. Along with these operations against tribes in the east, the state engaged in a sustained campaign of disarmament that extended well into the late 1930s.

The Turkish state's anti-Kurdish campaigns were carried out within the context of two comprehensive laws that were implemented in 1926 and 1934 with the aim of regulating the sedentarisation of tribes and the settlement of refugees in Turkey. Both of these laws had the clear purpose of building up and strengthening "the Turkish race" as the defining axis of the new nation. As such, while policies of sedentarisation targeted all nomadic groups, only the

Kurds were subjected to unyielding pressure to change their modes of living. The pastoralism of other groups such as Türkmen Yörüks was absorbed into the ongoing construction of a new Turkish society and even celebrated as an aspect of Turkey's cultural diversity and richness.

The persecution of Kurds and the building of the new nation-state were carried out on the basis of extensive information the government had been collecting about the Anatolian countryside. The practice of gathering information for the purposes of understanding, pacifying, and ultimately engineering the social and ethnic makeup of Anatolia had started in Ottoman times and gained momentum during the Young Turk era. In addition to perpetuating the Ottoman system of registration as well as other practices it had inherited, the republican state conducted its own census for the first time in 1927. The somewhat incomplete data collected in the 1927 census was buttressed by granular information that was collected by four inspectors general who functioned as all-powerful supra-governors overseeing groups of provinces across the country. The government commissioned special reports from these representatives and used them as the basis for setting up new institutions and reinforcing old ones to realise its military, political, and cultural imperatives. It is inconceivable that the new state could have created maps such as the one presented here, targeted specific tribal leaders and their families, interrupted the migratory routes of individual tribes, and crafted meticulously designed policies without having access to a vast reservoir of information.

***

The ways that the new republic dealt with Kurdish and other nomadic tribes fits with the high-modernist model of development that became conspicuous in many parts of the world in the 1920s and 1930s. In those years, Turkey became one of several states that conceived of society as a project and deployed its wide-ranging powers to shape it according to an ideologically modelled vision of modernity and civilisation that regarded nomadism and tribalism as being antithetical to its ideals. Maps, diagrams, and plans were a significant part of the creation and implementation of Turkey's modernist project in the interwar years. They made it possible for the government to render in sharp relief those issues it considered to be important, which in turn facilitated the execution of precise interventions. Such policies were implemented under conditions that allowed for no societal participation or protests, and they appeared to be successful, at least in the short run.

Through its centralised bureaucracy, one of the aims of which was to homogenise society, the republican state was far more successful than its imperial predecessor in controlling, if not completely sedentarising, nomadic tribes. The waves of rural-urban migration that started in the 1950s—and have continued ever since—fundamentally altered social structures and relations in Turkey's countryside, undermining tribal power in Anatolia.

However, the use of tribal solidarity for political purposes, especially in the case of Kurdish resistance movements, did not remain suppressed for long. Especially since the early 1980s, tribal identities have been marshalled once again in intra-Kurdish politics, as well as in the Kurdish struggle against the Turkish state. Aside from Kurdish groups, other nomadic tribes have also continued to have a presence in Turkey. While their economic role may have been diminished and they may have lost some of their leverage, such tribes periodically emerge as key players in the region's politics. A recent example of this occurred when Turkey attempted to link up with certain Turcoman tribes in northern Syria as part of its incursion into the region in 2020.

The map "Directions of Nomadism" reflects the early republican state's desire to get a clear and comprehensive perspective on the countryside of the newly founded nation, and such meticulous renderings provided the basis for the implementation of policies that sought to create an orderly and pacified country. However, the interventions carried out by the Turkish state never worked out exactly how they were envisaged. In addition to provoking resistance, they also resulted in compromises with tribes and other rural elements of society, which allowed nomadism to remain a part of Turkey's countryside social structure for much longer than had been imagined by the nation's modernising elites.

Select Bibliography

Bozarslan, Hamit. "Kurds and the Turkish State." In *The Cambridge History of Turkey.* Volume 4, *Turkey in the Modern World*, edited by Reşat Kasaba, 333–56. Cambridge: Cambridge University Press, 2008.

Bozdoğan, Sibel. *Modernism and Nation Building: Turkish Architectural Culture in the Early Republic*. Seattle: University of Washington Press, 2001.

Kasaba, Reşat. *A Moveable Empire: Ottoman Nomads, Migrants, and Refugees*. Seattle: University of Washington Press, 2009.

Khoury, Philip, and Joseph Kostiner, eds. *Tribes and State Formation in the Middle East*. Berkeley: University of California Press, 1990.

Scott, James. *Seeing Like a State: How Certain Schemes to Improve the Human Condition Have Failed*. New Haven: Yale University Press, 1998.

18

"The Lament of Laç Valley": Mourned Memory of the Dersim Massacre

Uğur Ümit Üngör

Under the authoritarian and Turkish-nationalist rule of Kemalism, one case of mass violence against Kurds and Alevis stands out for its genocidal nature: the Dersim genocide of 1938. The massacres, deportations, kidnappings, dispossessions, and material destruction carried out that year was a response to the region's resistance to Kemalist nation-building. The Resettlement Law of 1934 and a year later the promulgation of the "Tunceli Law," which consolidated Republican authority and efforts targeting Turkification in the Dersim region, were countered with sabotage and resistance by an alliance of tribes in Dersim. The government's counterinsurgency operations were exceptionally brutal, barely distinguishing between combatants and civilians; the army torched villages and executed thousands of unarmed civilians, carrying out mass killings using methods that paralleled those utilised in the Armenian genocide of 1915 under the rule of the Committee of Union and Progress. Upon invading a village, troops would routinely disarm the villagers, strip them of their belongings, and collectively tie them up by their hands with ropes. They were then taken to trenches and cliffs, where they were executed with machine guns. Another method was to pack the villagers into haylofts and sheds and set fire to the buildings, burning them alive. Precise data is lacking, but it is estimated that approximately 15,000 civilians were killed. Many of the killings were part of routine operations conducted per the dictates of standard orders: comb through the villages, gather up the inhabitants, take them to a deserted area outside of the settlement, and execute them. Moreover, the impunity granted to the troops accorded them fiats to take the initiative and carry out discretionary violence against civilians. While figures for the destruction cannot be definitively verified without access to the archives of the Turkish military and security apparatus, the oral tradition of the Dersim people offers unique insights into how they experienced the violence. "The Lament of Laç Valley" is one of Dersim's most famous oral laments (Zazaki: *şüare* or *kılam*) concerning the massacres of 1938.

*Hewa Derê Laçî**

Ah what a state
Our state is dire
They sent the army against us
It surrounded us, leaving no way out
Just come to Laç Valley
Full of dust and smoke
Just come to Laç Valley
In it echo laments and requiems
May God put out the hearth of the tribes
Nobody even tells us, "May God save them"
Let the tribes delude themselves
After the army is finished with us
It will do to us like [it did to] the Armenians
Now the army will kill us
It won't leave a single one of you alive
Qemerê Hesen was shot in front of the cave
Look at my hero, my lion
Hesê Kal is fighting hard
He is returning with rifles on his back
And if you're asking about Hemê Civê Kej
He rivals a battalion, an army
İvisê Sey Kali is on Pilhatun Hill
He is fighting and singing at the same time
The army commander is on Anabar Hill
He is looking with his binoculars saying
"Let me listen to İvis,
What is İvis saying to us?"
İvis says
"Tyrant, you have set three battalions on us
This time I will fight your army, God willing
I won't leave a single soldier alive,"
İvis is passing in front of Laç Valley
Today the Pêter front is slogging on
When the steel bullet struck my İvis
Red blood dripped from his body
When the steel bullet struck my hero

* Translated from the original Zazaki in Mesut Özcan, *Öyküleriyle Dersim Ağıtları – 1* (Ankara: Kalan, 2002), 100-104. For a rendering by Sılo Qız, see: www.youtube.com/watch?v=nOXoq7lOG8g (last accessed 20 November 2021).

Then the soldiers entered the valley

"My love, there is nobody

To bring this dark news to your parents"

Today this tyrant gives us no respite

It cast the world into fire for us

My İvis struggles in front of Laç Valley

Just come to Laç Valley

The sun froze in the sky

God knows we fought well

We avenged our ancestors

To die on these mountains

Is a pleasure and a sultanate for us

Whoever died with us on these mountains

In the hereafter will be placed in heaven

Whoever died with us on these mountains

On Imam Hüseyin's path will be placed in heaven

***

The lament "Derê Laçi" is one of hundreds of laments that comprise the oral tradition of the Dersim region. It tells of the clashes between the Turkish army and the people of Dersim, especially the Haydaran and Demenan tribes, who were besieged in Laç Valley in the summer of 1938. The fighters of these two tribes held out for a short period before the Turkish army broke through and committed a massacre that went beyond the two tribes. The lament was composed by Weliyê Wuşenê Yimami (1889–1958) of the Kureşan tribe, an eyewitness to the clashes and survivor of the massacres. The lament was transmitted and performed by various singers who changed the lyrics over time and created different versions. The best-known rendition may be the one by Sılo Qız (1915–2019), whose official name was Süleyman Doğan; the version presented above corresponds to his rendition, which was recorded on several occasions by oral historians. Most of the lyrics are fairly straightforward and descriptive, following the local lore of social banditry, heroisation, and martyrdom, but two lines are noteworthy. Firstly, the line "Let the tribes delude themselves" is a reference to the Dersim tribes who chose to remain neutral in the conflict. The composer here predicts that regardless of their neutrality, their end too will be bloody (and indeed it was). Secondly, the composer mentions the fate of the Armenians, which indicates that the people of Dersim were acutely aware of what had happened to the Armenians just two decades earlier. As such, "The Lament of Laç Valley" is not only a testimony to the genocide of 1938, but also to the broader history of mass violence in modern Turkey.

***

The destruction of Dersim in 1938 and beyond represents the bloodiest episode of mass violence against civilians in the entire history of the Republic of Turkey, even when compared to the other massacres that took place. The state's comprehensive, ideologically-sanctioned policy of annihilation not only led to the destruction of Dersim's livelihood physically, but also culturally, and it can be seen as a cornerstone of the Turkish nation-building process in the Kurdish provinces. The relevance of "The Lament of Laç Valley" is threefold. First is its empirical detail; without this lament, the four protagonists it mentions by name, the four locations it pinpoints, and the course of events it describes would have remained relatively unknown. Our only recourse would have been the official Kemalist narrative of the "cleansing" of "banditry" and "reactionism". Second is its provenance; in "successful" genocides such as the 1940 Katyn massacre or the 1965 Indonesian genocide, i.e.. genocides in which the perpetrating regime remains in power, the voices of the victims remain suppressed and underrepresented. The topographical renaming of the province (from Dersim to Tunceli), including the Turkification of village names, contributed to such an imposed silence. However, "The Lament of Laç Valley" pierced that silence long before the Dersim genocide became the subject of public discussions from the mid-2000s onwards. Third is how the lament bears transgenerational cultural relevance; it has sensitised broader segments of Kurdish society to the genocide of 1938 and as such has mobilised the younger generations of Dersim to take political action in the name of justice and recognition.

Select Bibliography

Kieser, Hans-Lukas. "Dersim Massacre, 1937–1938." *Online Encyclopedia of Mass Violence*, 2011. https://www.sciencespo.fr/mass-violence-war-massacre-resistance/en/document/dersim-massacre-1937-1938.html

Schulz-Goldstein, Esther. *Die Sonne blieb stehen, Band 2: Der Genozid in Dêsim 1937/38*. Neckenmarkt: Novum Pro, 2013.

Türkyılmaz, Yektan. "'Die Sonne gefror am Himmel': Von den Schwierigkeiten der Genozidforschung unter den Bedingungen der Verleugnungsideologie." *Werkstattgeschichte* 81 (2021): 129–44.

Watts, Nicole. "Relocating Dersim: Turkish State-Building and Kurdish Resistance, 1931–1938." *New Perspectives on Turkey* 23 (2000): 5–30.

Wiener Jahrbuch für Kurdische Studien 6 (2017). Special issue, "Dêrsim 1938: Genocide, Displacement and Repercussions: Eighty Years Later."

19
Nationalisation of the Banking System: The Increase in General Deposits

Y. Doğan Çetinkaya

The creation of the Turkish nation-state and the Islamisation and Turkification of Anatolia in the early twentieth century had various aspects. Besides demographics, the economy was one of the main fields that underwent a process of nationalisation. Like many other issues, the nationalisation of the economy had its roots in the last decades of the Ottoman Empire. The elimination of the native non-Muslim population and the eviction of foreign residents was a significant chapter of this transformation. On the one hand, it was the state, the political elite, and political organisations that played decisive roles in this process, which is why it was a political project. However, it was also a social process that was impacted by a variety of social actors and their mobilisation. As a whole, such policies were referred to within the scope of the National Economy (*Milli İktisat*). The National Economy had its own particular history which had different phases and took shape on various levels. On the one hand, immediately after the 1908 Revolution it was more or less an Ottomanist project favouring the development of the economy in terms of all its various elements, including the country's religious and ethnic communities. In the course of the Second Constitutional Period (1908–1918), however, particularly after the Balkan Wars of 1912–1913, the National Economy became an economic slogan and influenced policies targeting the Islamisation and Turkification of the empire. Therefore, despite the existing literature's treatment of the National Economy predominantly as an intellectual current or political project, it was also a social movement with a social base, and it had been transformed from an abstract notion into a social reality within a rather short period of time.

Within that context, Muslim/Turkish merchants, who represented one of the main social bases of National Economic policies, founded local and national banks that played crucial roles in the economic and political life of the empire in the first quarter of the twentieth century. The Muslim merchant class not only supported social movements such as boycotts against non-Muslims, published periodical journals defending a national economy such as the *Journal of Public Trade* (*Ticaret-i Umumiyye Mecmuası*), and created voluntary associations like the Society of Entrepreneurs (*Cemiyet-i Müteşebbise*) and the Society of National Industrialists (*Milli Fabrikacılar Cemiyeti*), it also established national banks, including the Bank of Konya (*Konya Bankası*) in 1909. The place of these kinds of national and local banks in the economy as institutions involved in what was then known as an Economic Holy War (*İktisadi Cihad*) or Economic Warfare (*İktisadi Harb*) increased up through the founding of the Republic.

That era was referred to as the National Banking Period. In 1923, there were thirteen foreign and nineteen national and local banks in Turkey. Most of the national banks were small and local, operating in Anatolian towns only having one or just a few branches. By the onset of the Great Depression in 1929, twenty-eight banks were operating in Turkey, and some of the larger national banks were established in this period of time, including the most prominent bank in Turkey's fiscal history, *Türkiye İş Bankası*, which was founded in 1924. Like many others involved in international markets, some of those banks had to shut down as a consequence of the Great Depression. While some scholars have attributed those closures to the minor roles those banks played in the market, local and national banks were far from being weak in comparison to the foreign banks operating at the time. For instance, the profits of *Selanik Bankası*, one of the most prominent foreign banks in Turkey, were 416,101 TL and 463,135 TL in 1928 and 1929, respectively, whereas those figures stood at 129,630 TL and 124,904 TL for *Aksaray Halk İktisat Bankası* and 119,714 TL and 150,964 TL for *Adapazarı Türk Ticaret Bankası*, two local banks. In 1929, while there were six foreign banks that reported losses for those years and seven foreign banks (excluding the *Selanik* and *Osmanlı* banks) recorded a total profit of 323,000 TL, the profits of *Türkiye İş Bankası* stood at 1,707,119 TL. Those figures are indicative of the rise and prominence of national and local (that is to say, Turkish) banks in the Turkish financial system at the end of 1920s, and the 1930s marked a period in which they enjoyed complete dominance. The charts presented below were drawn from a report issued by the Public Directorate of Statistics, which in the early 1930s was relegated to the Prime Ministry, and they show the amounts of general deposits and deposits made at national and foreign banks for a period of six years in the 1930s.

*Distribution of General Deposits Made at National and Foreign Banks by Year**

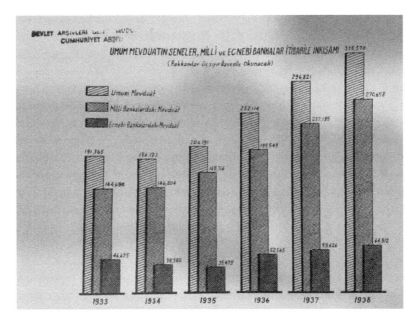

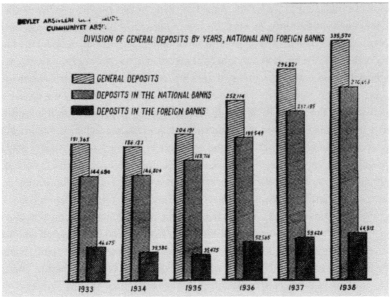

* Graphic presented by the Public Directorate of Statistics to Prime Minister Dr Refik Saydam. The graphic is from a statistical report archived in the Republican Archives (*Devlet Arşivleri Başkanlığı Cumhuriyet Arşivi*: BCA 30-1-0-0/95-595-2).

***

The promulgation of the Deposit Protection Law of 1933 and the Bank Law of 1936 were significant developments for that period. The Public Directorate of Statistics, which was institutionally reorganised in 1930, started to compile information about national and foreign banks in 1933 within the framework of a regulatory act put into place in 1933. The charts presented here indicate the progress of general deposits made at all banks operating in Turkey between 1933 and 1939. As is made apparent by the figures given, the amounts of money deposited at national banks were much higher than those made at foreign banks. Moreover, the difference in the rates of increase is also notable, as there was a sharp contrast between the Ottoman and republican eras in terms of banking practices. In the Ottoman Empire, foreign banks had largely dominated the financial sector, although the National Economy movement and new policies started to change the status quo in the last decade of the empire, and Islamisation and the Turkification of the economy marked a distinct phase in the second decade of the Turkish Republic.

***

The transformation that occurred was an outcome of the creation of the Turkish nation-state, which marked a complete transformation in various regards. As such, other aspects of the process of nationalisation, including demographic engineering and the nationalisation of the masses, were impacted as well. One important issue in this regard was the share and size of national banks at the time. By 1933, *Türkiye İş Bankası*, which had been established nine years earlier, was receiving the greatest amount of deposits, as indicated by the fact that 30 per cent of the deposits made at national banks were made at *Türkiye İş Bankası*, not at public banks owned by the state. Much of the current literature, which often attributes the process of founding the nation-state entirely to the agency of the political elite and the state, has tended to underestimate the fact that *Türkiye İş Bankası* was a private bank in the fullest sense of the term. In capitalist societies, however, the state and the market, or the political elite and the upper social classes, are not separated or isolated from each other. That is why the close relationships that were established between the administrators of *Türkiye İş Bankası* and the state elite did not contradict the former's status as a private company but rather confirmed how, in the twentieth century, the connection between the state and capitalist classes is an almost universal state of affairs. Within that context, the National Economy was also a project that incorporated the hegemony of the ruling class with a social base, behind which operated the social mobilisation of members of various social classes such as merchants, businessmen, shop owners, employees, and workers who made deposits at national banks. Therefore, the dominance of Turkish banks in the financial system at the time and the success of policies of Turkification should be seen as being related to the needs of those social classes. Furthermore, the rise of practices of statism all around the world in those years was not an outcome of anti-market sentiment, as the charts above indicate; rather, they were a manifestation of the needs of the dominant social classes.

Select Bibliography

Çetinkaya, Y. Doğan. *The Young Turks and the Boycott Movement: Nationalism, Protest and the Working Classes in the Formation of Modern Turkey*. London: I.B. Tauris, 2013.

Kazgan, Haydar, and Toktamış Ateş. *Financial History from the Ottoman Empire to the Present*. İstanbul: İstanbul Stock Exchange, 1999.

Tahsin, Hamit, and Remzi Saka. *Sermaye Hareketi*. İstanbul: Amedi Matbaası, 1930.

Tezel, Yahya S. *Cumhuriyet Döneminin İktisadi Tarihi (1923–1950)*. İstanbul: Türkiye İş Bankası Yayınları, 2015.

Toprak, Zafer. *Türkiye'de Milli İktisat 1908–1918*. İstanbul: Türkiye İş Bankası Kültür Yayınları, 2019.

20

Steering the Economy: Turkey in the Second World War

Alexander E. Balistreri

For the Turkish government, the Second World War played out as an increasingly haz-ard-laden juggling act of international and domestic obligations. While Ankara maintained neutrality at the international level, domestically it also had to navigate between the interests of producers, who were compelled to work at their limits for the needs of the state, and consumers, who were plagued by the skyrocketing cost of living. The war upended the normal balance between these groups in multiple ways. First, Turkey had to support a large standing army. Military planners foresaw a need for mobile ground forces on the order of 1.3 million men, or thirty per cent of the conscription-age male population. The development of such an army—eight times the size of Turkey's peacetime army—effectively turned hundreds of thousands of Turkey's normally productive individuals into consumers of grain, textiles, animal products, fuel, and construction materials. The war also disrupted the balance of trade. Imports plummeted to half of pre-war levels within a year, hindering access to raw materials and supplementary goods needed for domestic production. Exports, however, were a different story. The price of agricultural products shot up during the war, leading to sizable profits for the merchants who controlled the trade in such goods. For people who earned their keep with salaries, meanwhile, rising prices became a scourge. The cost of living in Turkey increased more than fourfold during the war, as real wages earned by industrial workers declined by half.

Turkey was, of course, not alone in dealing with such problems. In the years leading up to the war, both democratic and fascist states around Europe granted their governments new wide-ranging powers to intervene in their economies by regulating prices, requisitioning private property, punishing profiteering, and compelling men and women to work in the war industry. The Turkish government was comparatively late in launching similar economic measures. Only in late 1939 after the war began did the government review draft laws on "economic defence" and "economic protection". After concerns were raised suggesting that the proposed laws jeopardised constitutional guarantees of private property and freedom of commerce, a revised draft quickly emerged. Now called the "National Protection Law" (*Millî Korunma Kanunu*), the proposal contained 72 articles which detailed a wide array of economic measures, added strategies to limit profiteering and firmed up the prosecution of economic crimes. The National Protection Law was approved by the Grand National Assembly, despite some questioning on the part of individual deputies, on 18 January 1940.

National Protection Law, No. 3780*

1. During a state of exception, the Council of Ministers shall be assigned duties and authorities [...] with the purpose of strengthening the State apparatus from the perspective of economics and national defence. The following are to be deemed states of exception:

a. Complete or partial mobilisation.

b. The possibility that the State may go to war.

c. A state of war among foreign States which is also of concern to the Turkish Republic.

2. Should a state of exception be declared, the Council of Ministers [...] may immediately begin implementing this law and must declare this situation publicly and report to the Turkish Grand National Assembly.

3. The government shall decide when states of exception come to an end [...]

[...]

8. The government has the authority to request production plans from industrial and mining establishments or to dictate a plan [...] directly to such establishments. It may, for this purpose, determine the volume, amount, variety, sort, and type of production for industrial and mining establishments, in consideration of the needs of the state of exception and the ability of the establishment to shoulder this burden.

9. In order to increase the production of industrial and mining establishments or the amount of work at other places of employment to a level that can satisfy the needs set forth in this law, the government shall secure the necessary labourers and experts. For this purpose, paid compulsory labour may be imposed on citizens.

10. Labourers, technicians, engineers, experts, and other employees at industrial and mining establishments or other places of employment are forbidden from leaving the establishments or places where they are employed without an acceptable justification and without giving prior notice. [...]

11. The government may purchase manufactured products or production from industrial and mining establishments at the normal cost of production plus a fixed percentage of profits. The handing over of these goods to the government is obligatory.

[...]

14. To prevent materials and supplementary materials from accumulating in particular hands, thus placing stress on the needs of the people or of national defence, the government may confiscate [such

---

* Translated from the original Turkish in *T.C. Resmî Gazete* 4417 (26 January 1940): 13213–13216.

materials] in exchange for their actual value and allocate them, without earning a profit, to establishments which need them.

[...]

19. While this law is in force and in cases where an increase of work is needed at industrial and mining establishments or other places of employment, daily working hours may be extended by up to three hours [...]. It is not necessary to carry out the standing provisions of Article 50 of the Labour Law [prohibiting night-time employment] with regard to children and women in industrial establishments and other places of employment. The law on weekends shall not be applied on matters related to the aims of this law; however, this provision shall not infringe on the right of a labourer to one day off per week.

[...]

21. When necessary, the government may determine and limit the amount of consumption of indispensable materials that are needed for the people and for national defence.

[...]

30. During the period in which this law is implemented, the rental prices of real estate in cities and towns or places with landings, harbours, or train stations may not exceed the rental prices fixed during the year prior to the enactment of this law. [...]

31. The government shall fix maximum prices, sorts, types, and attributes for materials it deems necessary within the country. To ensure that this aim is fulfilled, it is obligatory to submit all types of information and show all documents to the government. [...].

32. The following acts are prohibited: raising the prices of commodities without a legitimate reason; refusing to sell available goods; concealing goods under the pretence that they are not available; removing goods in any way with the intent of selling them at a higher price; disposing of goods by means of collusion; failing to clear goods through customs without a reasonable cause; purchasing more goods than is necessary; accumulating such goods; colluding on prices to the detriment of the producer or the consumer; [...] carrying out propaganda for any of these purposes; or artificially raising prices by other means.

[...]

59. Any person who commits any of the acts of profiteering or exploitation outlined in Articles 32 and 35 of this law shall be punished, in accordance with the severity of the act they have committed, with a monetary fine ranging between 500 and 5,000 lira [approximately USD 13,600 and 136,000 in 2023] and with temporary exile for a period ranging between two and five years; their goods shall also be confiscated. [...]

***

Going beyond the Turkish constitution's strict provisions on "martial law," the National Protection Law (NPL) granted the government unilateral authority to decide when a "state of exception" existed and when it would end. Indeed, a state of exception was duly declared in February 1940 and it was only annulled twenty years later in September 1960 (the law itself was never explicitly repealed). During this state of exception, the government enjoyed a wide range of prerogatives to intervene in the economy as it saw fit. The government could, for example, kick-start industry by imposing mandatory production plans, compelling citizens to work, and relaxing labour protections for women and children. It could also "purchase" industrial and agricultural products at low prices, create stocks for such products, and distribute them as deemed necessary. Furthermore, it could fix rents, limit exports and imports, and set punishments for hoarding and profiteering. Other sections of the law were related to the establishment of a bureaucratic and judicial apparatuses to oversee the implementation of such measures.

The true nature of the NPL would become clear as the government, over the course of subsequent decades, made hundreds of decisions about exactly how to implement the law. Those decisions centred around three main priorities: requisitioning goods and setting prices so that urban dwellers (and bureaucrats in particular) would be cushioned from the effects of the rising cost of living; increasing the productivity of the mines in Zonguldak and of textile and armament factories; and combatting profiteering and rampant corruption in rationing. Measures could be as sweeping as the government takeover of all privately owned shipping or the introduction of bread rationing in 1942; or they could be as fine-tuned as a prohibition on the use of wheat flour in *börek* and cakes.

As lawmakers observed how such decisions affected the economy, they frequently returned to the text of the law to amend it. The vast majority of the articles in the NPL were modified while the law was in force, with the articles presented here being among the most mutable. In general, the government sought to clarify or expand its authority by means of those changes so it could intervene in certain aspects of the economy. The limits on child labour in Article 19, for example, were further loosened. Article 21 was expanded so that the government could limit the consumption of certain goods while prohibiting the consumption, production, and sale of particular products as well. The government also found that the punishments it had set for economic crimes did not have a sufficiently deterrent effect. In 1944, an amendment to the law stipulated that some of the crimes listed in Article 32 would be punishable by death.

***

The NPL was the most significant of several statist policies that were drafted in Turkey during the Second World War. Yet despite the unprecedented nature of the authority it granted, the Turkish government was inconsistent in its application of the law during the war. The government's provisioning policy is illustrative of such vacillations. In order to provide provisions for the swelling ranks of the army and state employees, Prime Minister Refik Saydam (1881–1942) sought to acquire as much grain as possible at a low cost and vastly expand the bureaucratic apparatus in charge of overseeing its distribution at state-imposed prices. The country's rural population was particularly disadvantaged by this approach. Saydam's successor, Şükrü Saraçoğlu (1886–1953), however, adopted a radically different strategy which was aimed at appeasing agricultural and commercial interests. Saraçoğlu's government limited the ability of the government to requisition grain, raised the prices used to compensate for such requisitions, and allowed for increased sales, even exports, of grain at market prices. Saraçoğlu's policy led to runaway inflation and an untenable rise in government expenditures; moreover, it resulted in some merchants making extraordinary profits. The notorious Wealth Tax (*Varlık Vergisi*) emerged out of an attempt to both finance new state policies and take a cut of merchants' profits. The tax proved to not only be unpopular but also insufficient (let alone discriminatory). In 1944 the government thus imposed a sweeping ten per cent tax on agricultural production, which was the country's first major direct agricultural tax since the days of the Ottoman Empire and a major burden on peasant households that engaged in small-scale farming. At an institutional level, two bodies that were established under the auspices of the NPL remain in operation today: the Petrol Ofisi (established in 1941) and the Meat and Fish Institution (*Et ve Balık Kurumu*, established in 1952, later renamed the Meat and Milk Institution in 2013).

More broadly, the NPL and the way it was implemented affected the direction of post-war Turkish politics and society. The mismanagement of the wartime economy exposed the inadequacy of infrastructure development and state formation during the period of single-party rule. Under the wartime Saydam government, criticism was directed at the *ad hoc* organisation of a plethora of new institutions and restrictions on free trade. Under the Saraçoğlu government, weak enforcement of the law and the ineffectiveness of sanctions became major targets of criticism. In both cases, the government was unable to satisfy one of the central aims of the NPL—the prevention of hoarding and profiteering—because of widespread corruption among bureaucrats, even in its own ranks. Wartime economic measures also sharpened the edges between social classes in Turkey. The rural majority in particular—both landowners who profited significantly from the wartime measures and peasants who did not—no longer saw their interests as being adequately represented by the ruling Republican People's Party.

Select Bibliography

Aydemir, Şevket Süreyya. *İkinci Adam (1938-1950) 2. Cilt*. İstanbul: Remzi Kitabevi, 1968.

Koçak, Cemil. *Türkiye'de Milli Şef Dönemi, 2. Cilt (1938-1945)*. İstanbul: İletişim Yayınları, 1996 [1986].

Pamuk, Şevket. "War, State Economic Policies, and Resistance by Agricultural Producers in Turkey, 1939–1945." In *Peasants and Politics in the Modern Middle East*, edited by Farhad Kazemi and John Waterbury, 125–42. Miami: Florida International University Press, 1991.

Parslow, Joakim. "Theories of Exceptional Executive Powers in Turkey, 1933–1945." *New Perspectives on Turkey* 55 (2016): 29–54.

Tekeli, İlhan, and Selim İlkin. *İkinci Dünya Savaşı Türkiyesi, 2. Cilt: İktisadî Politikaları ve Uygulamalarıyla*. İstanbul: İletişim Yayınları, 2014.

1943–1952

21

A Precarious Offer:
The Dodecanese Islands and Turkish Neutrality in the Second World War

Onur İşçi

After four years of maintaining a stance of neutrality during the Second World War, Turkey was under mounting pressure from the West to take sides with the Allies. News of the Soviet victory in Stalingrad arrived 48 hours after a crucial meeting was held in Adana between Winston Churchill (1874–1965) and İsmet İnönü (1884–1973) on 31 January 1943. Churchill tried to sway the Turkish president, discussing terms for Turkey's active contribution to the Allied war effort, but his efforts were in vain. The Adana Conference and the ensuing Soviet triumph on the Volga marked a downswing in Turkey's relations with the Allies. As Turkey continued to put off entering the war, British Foreign Secretary Anthony Eden made his government's dissatisfaction yet more explicit. On several occasions, Eden coupled Turkey's name with Spain and Portugal as neutral countries, implying that Ankara was engaging in tacit connivance with the Axis powers. In September of 1943, Eden once again urged the Turkish authorities to change their position so they could ultimately join peace talks as an ally that had engaged in the war effort, implying that if they continued to hold to a stance of neutrality, Turkey would be unable to do so when talks were eventually held.

The timing of Eden's final warning was hardly coincidental. After Benito Mussolini's arrest and the subsequent Armistice of Cassibile, which was signed with Italy on 8 September 1943, Turkey's active participation in the war became more than a necessity. Ever since the Casablanca Conference, which was held in January of 1943, Churchill had been entertaining scenarios to retake Europe through amphibious and airborne landings on the Nazi-occupied Dodecanese Islands, which are located in the south-eastern Aegean Sea. That plan, in fact, constituted the crux of his negotiations with İnönü in Adana a fortnight after the Casablanca gathering. With Mussolini's arrest, the Dodecanese Campaign finally seemed possible, but İnönü's heel-dragging presented an annoying predicament.

Nazi Germany was acutely aware of the impending Allied campaign a few miles off the Turkish coast in the Aegean Sea and of Britain's attempts to coerce Turkey into taking part in the venture. In order to impede Allied operations following Italy's capitulation, Adolf Hitler personally ordered the Gran Sasso Raid, rescued Mussolini on 12 September and placed him at the helm of the puppet Italian Social Republic on 23 September. Two days later, Nazi Germany's ambassador in Ankara, Franz von Papen, sent instructions to the Nazi Intelligence Chief asking him to inquire whether the Turkish government would be interested in acquiring the Dodecanese. By way of offering such a precariously situated territorial reward, Nazi Germany clearly sought to counter-balance Britain's efforts and entice the Turkish government into taking a more benevolent neutral stance towards the Reich.

The Nazi proposal to repatriate the Dodecanese Islands to Turkey in September of 1943 was part of a broader scheme that had been in the planning stages since at least 1941. When Hitler ordered the Wehrmacht to invade the Soviet Union, State Secretary Ernst von Weizsäcker decided to seize the moment and communicated to Foreign Minister Joachim von Ribbentrop possible ways to cultivate pro-Axis sentiment amongst members of İnönü's close circles. In a detailed memorandum dated August 1941, von Ribbentrop passed von Weizsäcker's sugges-tions on to Ambassador Franz von Papen in Ankara, telling him that winning Turkey over to Nazi Germany's side as a non-belligerent state in the manner desired would be feasible only if the Nazis could interest İnönü in the acquisition of new territories, which included redrawing borders in Thrace, offering the Dodecanese, and presenting further acquisitions in the Caucasus at Moscow's expense. However, Franz von Papen was doubtful. He thought that it would not be in Germany's best interests to negotiate with the Turks about territorial rewards, at least not until after Russia had been definitively beaten in the autumn of 1941; he was of the opinion that, for the time being, they should simply try to promote and sustain Turkey's supposedly hitherto dormant imperialist tendencies. German records demonstrate that an intriguing dynamic existed in the dispute between Foreign Minister von Ribbentrop and Ambassador von Papen. Ultimately, however, for two years the Wehrmacht had been unable to defeat the Red Army and in the end the Nazis had to shelve the Dodecanese plan. When the scheme resurfaced in September 1943, it was in the context of Nazi Germany grasp-ing at straws, as the Allied forces were advancing on all fronts.

That was not the first time İnönü had found himself dealing with the issue of the Dodecanese Islands. Twenty years prior to the precarious Nazi offer, in 1923 İnönü had led the Ankara delegation at the Lausanne Conference, where he renounced Turkish claims to the islands. The Ottoman Empire had surrendered the Dodecanese to the Kingdom of Italy after the Italo-Turkish War of 1911–12 and Turkey officially recognised that concession at Lausanne when İnönü signed off on it. The Dodecanese have long played a crucial role in Aegean security and it was a difficult decision for İnönü to concede the islands at the Lausanne Conference, but at the time there were more pressing items on the agenda such as, for instance, international recognition of Turkey's full sovereignty. Two decades after Lausanne, at a critical moment in the war, İnönü was once again faced with the question of the Dodecanese Islands. The following correspondence should be read against that backdrop.

*Correspondence between Prime Minister Şükrü Saraçoğlu and President İsmet İnönü**

[25 September 1943, from Prime Minister Şükrü Saraçoğlu to President İsmet İnönü]

1. The Nazi intelligence chief in Ankara asked for a meeting and communicated the following conversation to Naci Perkel which I [Şükrü Saraçoğlu] summarise in my next point.

2. Our ambassador, Franz von Papen, told me [the Nazi intelligence chief] the following: "I received a telegram from the chief of staff, who instructed me to inquire whether the Turks would be willing to accept an offer to repatriate the Aegean islands and to report back. As I was certain that the Turkish government would refuse to accept the islands under the circumstances, in my response I advised against the extension of such an offer. But I also asked if I should move forward in spite of my observation. I am confident that in a few days Berlin will give orders to extend the offer regardless. Go and speak with Naci Perkel, and relay his response immediately."

3. My instructions to Naci Perkel are included in the point below.

4. Please receive the Nazi intelligence chief this evening and tell him the following: "After giving your offer thorough consideration, if we were to convey it to [İsmet İnönü] as is, I imagine he would demand clarification on a number of issues associated with repatriation and I feel the need to discuss them in advance. These issues include, but are not limited to: What intentions do the Germans have in offering those islands? What does the term 'islands' exactly entail? Are there any strings attached to this offer? Who will be in charge of the Germans stationed on the islands? Will the German arms on the islands be placed under Turkey's control? Will Turkey have the liberty to exercise full control of the islands after their transfer? Will we have, for instance, the ability to re-transfer the islands to the British government?" I told Naci Perkel to come back with his response.

5. I would like to express my deepest commitment and await your instructions on this matter.

[26 September 1943, President İsmet İnönü to Prime Minister Şükrü Saraçoğlu]

You are absolutely right. We can take the islands only if they come with no strings attached. We cannot risk a conflict with either the British or the Greeks over this issue. Greetings from Kars.

* Translated from the Turkish original in the Prime Ministry Republican Archive (*Başbakanlık Cumhuriyet Arşivleri*) 030.01.00/40.240.19.

If taken out of context, the Nazi scheme to repatriate the Dodecanese back to Turkey could have been misconstrued as a Turkish-German alliance given the soaring levels of trade between the two states. Nevertheless, as the Saraçoğlu-İnönü cables demonstrate, Turkey's neutrality in the Second World War was not determined by revisionist post-war dreams. Despite Berlin's attempts to further inculcate the idea of a Turkish *Lebensraum* in the Aegean, von Papen refrained from language that could be misconstrued as a military alliance, since Nazi Germany's primary objective was to guarantee Turkey's friendly neutrality. Far from being susceptible to Hitler's fuelling of irredentism, in fact Turkey was vexed by the presence of Axis soldiers across the Thracian border and in the Dodecanese. Undergirding Ankara's diplomacy during the Second World War was a desire to maintain relations with both Britain and the Third Reich as a means of checking Soviet aggression. When Hitler launched Operation Barbarossa, fears of the Soviet Union were so strong that Ankara hoped for a Nazi victory over the Soviet Union, provided that Britain would then able to check the Third Reich, which encircled Turkey via Romania, Bulgaria, Greece and the Aegean Sea.

This was an unusual case of phased thinking, and it did not take long for Nazi Germany to realise that the prospect of becoming embroiled in a prolonged war was a nightmarish scenario for the Turks. For some members of Hitler's entourage, it seemed possible that Turkey would appeal to Germany to help defend itself against a Russian attack, just as it had done in the previous World War. But, unlike Nazi Foreign Minister Joachim von Ribbentrop, for instance, the Third Reich's ambassador in Ankara, Franz von Papen, knew that Turkey was not wavering between Germany and England like a shopper at a bazaar waiting to see with whom it would be better to make a deal. It was clear to von Papen that Turkey was a silent ally of Great Britain and that the Turks inconspicuously hoped the UK would emerge triumphant from the war. But von Papen was equally aware that the mere existence of an Anglo-Russian alliance was clearly displeasing to Turkey and that a Soviet victory would eclipse all other considerations. From that point onwards, Germany did everything in its capacity to orchestrate anti-Soviet propaganda, while at the same time offering unrealistic territorial rewards, such as the Dodecanese Islands, to lure the Turkish government into taking a more benevolent position.

As the document cited above indicates, the tone and content of Franz von Papen's instructions to the Nazi intelligence chief in Ankara reflect deep reservations about his government's decisions. In August of 1941, the Dodecanese loomed large in Nazi machinations to extricate Turkey from its continued dilemma of whether to engage in an alliance or mere friendship with the Third Reich. In September 1943, however, von Papen seemed even more certain that the Turkish leadership would rebuff such a proposal, and, in fact, President İnönü would go on to mention it to the British simply to curry favour with them. Turkish Prime Minister Saraçoğlu's instructions to Naci Perkel (1889-1969), who presided over the Turkish National Intelligence Agency until 1953, confirm von Papen's suspicions.

Ultimately, Turkey refused to accept the Dodecanese, knowing all too well that it might jeopardise their neutrality, which was already being questioned by Great Britain. In fact, Saraçoğlu was quite explicit in his instructions to Naci Perkel when he stated that Ankara would be willing to accept the islands only if the offer came with no strings attached. To that end, they wanted to know whether the islands could be retransferred immediately to Great Britain if they took control of them.

Despite their geostrategic position in the Aegean, İnönü twice made concessions regarding the Dodecanese. Those unpopular decisions were later condemned by Turkish nationalists and various right-wing political leaders who ironically tried to portray him as a friend of Adolf Hitler or Benito Mussolini. Perhaps even more ironically, İnönü's harshest critics at the time were mostly pan-Turkists and Nazi sympathisers who piqued the CIA's interest during the Cold War, as they were seen as potential operatives who could be used against the Soviet Union.

Select Bibliography

Deringil, Selim. *Turkish Foreign Policy During the Second World War: An Active   Neutrality.* Cambridge: Cambridge University Press, 1989.

İşçi, Onur. *Turkey and the Soviet Union during World War II: Diplomacy, Discord and International Relations.* London: I.B. Tauris, 2020.

Pekesen, Berna. *Zwischen Sympathie und Eigennutz: NS-Propaganda und die türkische Presse im Zweiten Weltkrieg.* Berlin: Lit-Verlag, 2014.

22

"I am a Victim of the Capital Tax": The Voices of İstanbul Greeks

Alexandros Lamprou

The Capital Tax (*Varlık Vergisi*) was an extraordinary levy introduced by the Turkish government in December 1942. Officially, the aim was to tax the wealth amassed during the war years and thus ease the budgetary pressure caused by the mobilisation and maintenance of a huge army of conscripts. Turkey did not enter the Second World War, but maintained a position of armed neutrality.

Notwithstanding the official reasons for the imposition of the tax and although the Capital Tax Law made no reference to Muslims or non-Muslim citizens, it quickly became clear that the levy targeted the non-Muslims of Turkey, i.e., the Armenian, Greek, and Jewish communities of the country. From its inception to its implementation, one of the foremost aims of the Capital Tax was to overtax non-Muslims. Thus, the Capital Tax should not be understood solely within the context of the Second World War. In essence, it was a continuation of earlier policies implemented by the Turkish state to "Turkify" the economy, commerce, and job market, thereby supplanting the non-Muslim bourgeoisie with a Muslim middle class of merchants and entrepreneurs.

Although the tax law itself did not discriminate between Muslims and non-Muslims, in practice Muslims were taxed at relatively low levels or not at all, while thousands of non-Muslims and foreign subjects were asked to pay exorbitant amounts in the form of the Capital Tax. The Capital Tax Law stated that anyone who was taxed could not appeal the decision. They had to pay the amount due in full within a fortnight, and if they were unable to do so, their movable and immovable property could be confiscated by the state and auctioned off. Starting in January 1943, the tax offices in İstanbul began auctioning off merchandise, furniture, clothing, shops, and, in several cases, the houses of non-Muslims, often at very low prices. The Capital Tax Law also stipulated that the property of close family members of the taxpayer (parents, spouses, and offspring) could also be auctioned if the levy was not paid in full. Although they were fully aware of the complete unlawfulness of this stipulation and of the Capital Tax law in general, legislators happily accepted it, as it was understood that the targets of the tax were the non-Muslims of Turkey. The task of carrying out tax assessments was left to local committees, which consisted solely of Muslim Turks. In essence, implementation of the Capital Tax led to a significant transfer of property from non-Muslims to Muslims and state-owned institutions, and likely contributed to the emigration of many non-Muslims in the immediate post-war period.

The Capital Tax Law also stipulated that the state could arrest and subject to forced labour anyone who did not pay their taxes in full. In the end, the state arrested and, according to the accounts of the İstanbul Tax Director, sent around 1,400 non-Muslim males to a forced labour camp in Aşkale, which is in the eastern part of Turkey. They were forced to stay there under brutal conditions until August 1943, when the Turkish government transferred the remaining inmates to Sivrihisar in the province of Eskişehir. They were then released in December 1943, in part due to the intervention of foreign governments. There was not a single Muslim among those who were exiled to the east, twenty-one of whom died as a result of disease and lack of proper medical care.

The excerpts below are translations of parts of petitions sent to the Social Assistance and Relief Committee of the Association of İstanbul Greek Citizens (Σύνδεσμος Ελλήνων Πολιτών Ιστανμπούλ, Επιτροπή Κοινωνικής Προνοίας και Περιθάλψεως). Most of the petitioners requested financial assistance or help in finding a job. The small amount of monthly monetary assistance provided—in November 1943 it was thirty Turkish Lira—was granted through the Committee by the Greek Consular authority in İstanbul, which also funded a number of soup kitchens at Greek Orthodox churches and communal buildings for students and the poor, as well as for victims of the Capital Tax.

Petitions of Greek Orthodox "Victims" of the Capital Tax Sent to the Greek Consulate in İstanbul*

"I am a victim of the Capital Tax. Unable to pay the 6,000 Turkish Lira tax, I was expelled from my small tobacco shop and on the same day all of my property ... was confiscated and auctioned. [...] I was sent to Aşkale. I will skip a description of the life of torment there and restrain myself to describing my current depraved situation. I am exhausted, sick, unprotected, alone with no job, and bedridden." C. A., 15 December 1943.

"...until last year I was a merchant ... in İstanbul. [...] I was unable to pay the 18,000 Lira Capital Tax and all my merchandise, my house, all my mobile property, even my underwear was confiscated and auctioned. I was even body-searched and the 500 Lira I had on me were also confiscated. And yet, as the tax amount could not be paid, I was exiled to Aşkale with the third group [on 23 February 1943] and for the next ten months I managed to survive only with the assistance of several compassionate fellows. After my return here, I am in complete destitution, temporarily sheltered by my friend." G.F., c. December 1943.

"I fell victim to the Capital Tax. My husband B.I., who, due to our financial situation, was unable to pay a single penny of the 9,000 Lira Capital Tax, is now in Sivrihisar. The property of our grocery store, valued at 200-250 Lira, was auctioned by the government, leaving us in dire poverty. With the assistance of neighbours, I endured our destitute situation for six months, looking after our three children.

* Translated from the original Greek petitions in the Greek State Archives (GAK), Archive of the Middle East, Folder 1553.

One is suffering from tuberculosis and, although exempted from military service, cannot work. I have no hope of help from my friends and relatives anymore, as they are also in the same terrible financial state. Faced with this hopeless situation, I was obliged to resort to the assistance of your Association [Association of İstanbul Greek Citizens], which I see as the only possible deliverance from starvation and death for four souls subject to undeserving suffering." E. I., 25 October 1943.

"I am fifty-six years old, a Turkish citizen by marriage, and locked in a constant struggle to sustain my family of seven on the small daily wages of my eighteen-year-old son, who was working as a clerk. My eldest son has been conscripted for the last three years and my daughter is a worker at a knitting factory. My working son has now been conscripted and taxed with a 500 Lira Capital Tax. Two months before the announcement of the Capital Tax, my husband K.M., in order to obtain a small daily wage ... rented a small room at a Han in Tahtakale. He was registered ... as a carton-box manufacturer and was taxed with a 4,500 Lira Capital Tax. He was then arrested and sent to Sivrihisar to pay his tax through forced labour, although he cannot even walk for an hour. I am also obliged to look after my brother A.S., a Greek subject, who is paralysed and cannot work, and has nobody else except me." A.M., 13 September 1943.

"I am imploring you for some help. Seven months ago my husband was sent abruptly and completely unjustly to Aşkale. Although he is a worker, a steelworker, they registered him as a merchant and taxed him 45,000 Lira. As this amount could not be paid, they immediately sent him away after confiscating and auctioning his shop and house. I was left completely destitute with two children, one six years old and the other just twenty days old. I was obliged to take shelter at my mother's home, who is also poor." A.M., 6 September 1943.

"Five months ago our father P.V. had his shop auctioned off and then he was sent to Aşkale. My mother died six months ago. There are five of us, all orphans abandoned with no support. Our situation is completely tragic. We even lack our everyday bread. We are five children, the older is sixteen, the younger is three years old. [...] The situation of our father is also tragic. Many times he has asked for our [financial] help, which we are unable to send because we cannot even feed ourselves." 6 September 1943.

***

While the Capital Tax Law itself made no reference to the religion of the taxpayers, in the implementation of the law, the Turkish state intentionally discriminated against non-Muslims, taxing them much more than the others, confiscating their and their families' property, and eventually exiling 1.400 of them to labour camps. The declared purpose of the law was to tax war profits, and initially it targeted the propertied and wealthy, such as rentiers, merchants, businessmen, shop owners, and people involved in the liberal professions. Yet in another act of discrimination in the implementation of the law, the government started to tax low-income earners, but only non-Muslims. In this way, the Capital Tax not only affected the propertied classes (mostly non-Muslims), but exclusively targeted non-Muslims among the low-income segments of society. The inclusion of non-Muslim artisans, street vendors, and clerks was an attempt to facilitate their removal from the job market during the war years so that the Muslims among the masses of unemployed city dwellers could take their place. In that sense, it was based on the same rationale as Law no. 2007 implemented in 1932, which forbade foreign subjects from engaging in many professions and whose impact was equally devastating for thousands of non-Muslims. The rationale was the "Turkification" of the economy and society through the impoverishment and emigration of the country's non-Muslim population. From the Greek Orthodox community alone thousands had to emigrate due to unemployment in the 1930s, and many more were to follow the same path after the end of the war.

This class and ethnic bias in the implementation of the Capital Tax is evident in the background of the majority of those who petitioned the Greek consulate for assistance in 1943. Most of them were small shopkeepers, artisans, and workers. And yet, from a list of forty families that received a small monthly allowance from the Greek consulate, half were taxed between 1,500 and 6,000 Lira, still a huge amount of money. To give an indication of the value of those amounts, one of the İstanbul Greeks who petitioned the Greek Association for help, a 75-year-old whose initials were P.N., had to sell his small house for 1,500 in order to pay the 2.000 Lira Capital Tax he owed. Another petitioner, T.A., whose husband was in Aşkale, was paying 17 Lira rent and her son's salary was 8 Lira per week. This makes it clear that even poor non-Muslims were hard-hit by the Capital Tax.

***

The petitions presented here were sent by social actors not frequently studied in the literature. Most studies of the Capital Tax examine the issue within the context of Turkish nationalism and the anti-minority policies of the Turkish state. As such, they take up the conception, implementation, and consequences of the Capital Tax from the perspective of the state, the Turkish press, and nationalist elites. In contrast, the excerpts of the petitions quoted above offer an "inside story" concerning the on-the-ground realities surrounding the implementation of the tax, presenting a picture of the hardships suffered by the victims of the Capital Tax among the Greek Orthodox community in İstanbul. Moreover, they offer a gendered perspective on the implementation of the law, which is generally lacking in the literature as it tends to primarily be based on sources produced by men, such as textual materials put out by the press and state authorities. As the taxpayers were almost exclusively male and the state only sent non-Muslim males to forced labour camps, the majority of the petitioners and recipients of assistance were their wives or children, who had been left behind with little or no means to survive. In their petitions, they presented their side of the events, describing in some detail the everyday effects of the Capital Tax on their lives and the lives of their families, as well as the community at large. The petitions also shed light on the processes of impoverishment affecting members of the Greek Orthodox community from various social strata. Among the impoverished petitioners were the wives and sisters of workers and small shopkeepers, but there were also more affluent individuals who appear to be fearful of losing their social status because they applied for assistance, as was the case with the two sisters of an exiled merchant who wrote, "...due to our social position ... we cannot ask for help elsewhere [and are] confident of your discretion" (C.A., no date, probably the end of 1943).

These petitions constitute a significant contribution to the existing body of sources on the Capital Tax, which were predominantly produced in Turkish by (male) state authorities. In that sense, the petitions presented above offer a nuanced understanding of the implementation of the tax and more generally of the policies of "Turkification" that the Turkish state had been implementing since the First World War. The Capital Tax has been associated with earlier and later instances of discrimination and violence against non-Muslims throughout the history of modern Turkey. In the historiography of Turkey, the study of the event from the perspective of the receiving end, i.e., the victims of the Capital Tax, has only attracted attention in the past ten to fifteen years. The petitions of those affected by the tax serve not only as a reminder of the relevance of ego-documents that can assist with new and alternative paths in the study of similar events, but also specifically point to the ruthless character of the nation-building process in Turkey.

Select Bibliography

Akar, Rıdvan. *Aşkale Yolcuları: Varlık Vergisi ve Çalışma Kampları.* İstanbul: Belge, 1999.
Aktar, Ayhan. "'Tax Me to the End of my Life!' Anatomy of an Anti-minority Tax Legislation (1942–3)." In *State-nationalisms in the Ottoman Empire, Greece and Turkey: Orthodox and Muslims, 1830-1945*, edited by Benjamin C. Fortna, Stefanos Katsikas, Dimitris Kamouzis, and Paraskevas Konortas, 188–220. London: Routledge, 2012.
Aktar, Ayhan. *Varlık Vergisi ve Türkleştirme Politikaları.* İstanbul: İletişim, 2000.
Alexandris, Alexis. *Greek Minority of İstanbul and Greek-Turkish Relations.* Athens: Centre for Asia Minor Studies, 1992.
Bali, Rıfat. *The "Varlık Vergisi" Affair: A Study of Its Legacy; Selected Documents.* İstanbul: ISIS, 2005.
Ökte, Faik. *The Tragedy of the Turkish Capital Tax.* Translated by Geoffrey Cox. Kent: Croom Helm, 1987.

23
"Enlightening" the Turkish Countryside: The Village Institutes

Sacit Yarımoğlu

For the young Republic of Turkey, educating the rural population was extremely important because the overwhelming majority of the populace lived in the countryside. Education was crucial not only because there was a need to increase the productivity of peasants and farmers, but also to consolidate the legitimacy of the new political regime by winning the hearts and minds of the people. At the time, the "people" of course meant the peasants. In the early 1930s, the intellectuals of the new regime were encouraged to "go to the people," and institutions such as People's Houses (*Halk Evleri*), which were associated with the single-party regime of the Republican People's Party (*Cumhuriyet Halk Partisi*, CHP), were perceived as a means of achieving that goal. More remarkable was the idea of establishing Village Institutes (*Köy Enstitüleri*), which were on the agenda of the Republic's political elites from the mid-1930s onwards. Radically different in approach from the purely intellectual and romantic aspirations that underpinned the People's Houses and the romanticism of many of the intellectual endeavours of the time, Village Institutes, which were established in rural Turkey, aimed to educate rural children by training a generation of teachers who themselves were from peasant families and were aware of the realities of rural life. In so doing, the teachers could stay in their villages rather than trying to find employment in cities. It was thought that such an approach would thus prevent peasants from moving to urban areas, which was in accordance with the so-called "peasantist" ideology of the time (*köycülük*), a doctrine that perceived urbanisation and industrialisation as serious threats to the social and political order.

The Village Institute project was developed by a well-known teacher, İsmail Hakkı Tonguç (1893–1960), a Balkan refugee who was inspired by the agrarian ideologies he had witnessed in the Balkans. Thanks to his efforts, which were supported by the influential Minister of Education, Hasan Ali Yücel (1897-1961), the Village Institutes were officially founded in 1940, although preparations for their establishment had been underway since 1935. As indicated in the following excerpt from an article that was written by Tonguç, one of the most important contributions of the institutes to the Turkish education system was thought to be the introduction of the principle of "learning by doing." The idea was to devise an educational system of "enlightenment" centred on the concept of "work" rather than abstract knowledge:

The Principles of Education and Training at Our Village Institutes*

[...] Village Institutes, which spread across the country from Kars to Edirne, take in students from all kinds of villages. The teachers and primary education inspectors who go to villages to select the students explain to the parents of the children at length the aims and nature of the Institutes and the rights that those who study there will obtain. Nevertheless, a considerable number of realistic fathers do not want to send off their children without seeing the Institutes first. They make their final decision after seeing the Institutes in their region or after talking to a number of the children studying there. After that, caravans of children dressed in all kinds of clothes, [their minds filled] with different thoughts and imaginings, most of them wanting to become master craftsmen of some sort and thus escape from the harsh [conditions of] working life in the villages, begin to flow towards the Village Institutes. Those who arrive are cleaned up and those who bring with them illnesses that can be cured quickly and with a little care are treated. The meeting squares of the Institutes and the paths between the buildings are filled with peasant children who, at the age of thirteen or fourteen, are dressed in the clothes of adults and have learned their poses as well as ways of speaking, walking, and sitting. It takes a few months for the children to get used to the Institutes. [...]

As soon as a student sets foot in an Institute, they begin to take up a variety of different activities on a very large scale. The children who are involved in these activities, which are divided into many branches such as lectures, agricultural and artistic work, construction, and animal care, are easily separated in a short period of time from those who will have the right to stay at the Institutes. The ones who remain begin to undergo training. The devoted teachers start to teach them how to clean, how to eat, how to respect and love their friends and teachers, how not to damage Institute property, how to protect state property, how to take good care of animals and vehicles, how to be hardworking, how to do all kinds of work with love, how to be kind-hearted, and how to play various games in their free time, starting with the alphabet. It is hard for the children to abandon ingrained habits. The work of the first few months even leads some teachers who do not know village children to fall into despair. Then, all of a sudden, most of the students make astonishing progress. Most of them blossom into mature children whose fruit ripens quickly after flowering. After that, there begin to appear at the Institute a group of people who can be trusted in every way. Before long, they take all the work of the Institute into their own hands. They attend classes and begin to do all kinds of work for the Institute. Upon seeing these groups of hardworking, skilful, and successful students, the other children cannot remain in a stagnant state on the sidelines without joining them, and they take part too. The Institutes take on their true identity after that point. [...]

[...] The tens of thousands of young people who will emerge from the Institutes will tomorrow begin to be dispersed throughout the country, even to the most isolated villages. They will take millions of citizens into their hands and get to work on them. Through them, these values will be appropriated by

* Translated from the original Turkish in İsmail H. Tonguç, "Köy Enstitülerimizde Eğitim ve Öğretim İlkeleri," *Ankara Üniversitesi Dil ve Tarih-Coğrafya Fakültesi Dergisi* 1, no. 5 (1943): 137–147.

the nation. By way of this human capital they will create, a new nation will be born, alive and vibrant, the one we long for. The dough kneaded at the Village Institutes is being kneaded for that very purpose.

***

The idea was that by using the "learning-by-doing" principle, the students at the Institutes would be able to learn on the job and be immersed in the nature of the work by practicing it. That's because, according to Tonguç, methodologically speaking, abstract knowledge acquired from written sources is not likely to be permanent. Practical education, on the other hand, was thought to be a requirement of modernity. By increasing the level of education in villages in this way, the aim was to both catch up to the level of development of European civilisation and contribute to the development of democracy in Turkey. Thus, through a transformation in the countryside, good reliable citizens of the nation-state would be created, the majority of whom would consist of peasants, and as such they would be the backbone of ideological support for the existing political regime of the time. After all, for the purposes of nation-building, the single-party regime also expected something else from the Institutes: the dismantling of feudal structures in the countryside. In other words, the regime sought to limit the political and cultural power of the landowning class, which traditionally had been a strong component of the power bloc in the late Ottoman Empire and in early Republican Turkey. However, subsequent research has shown that this expectation was never truly fulfilled.

In the fourteen-year period between their establishment and closure, the years 1946 and 1950 constitute two important turning points for the Village Institutes. Due to the emergence of political competition with the transition to a multi-party system in 1945, President İsmet İnönü (1884–1973) increasingly resorted to pragmatic policies which he thought would favour him in the coming elections. To the surprise of many, he tried to discredit the Village Institutes, for which he had previously served as a benefactor. It seems that İnönü himself wanted to use and abuse anti-communist hysteria with the aim of pre-empting his opponents' use of that issue as a weapon against himself. At the same time, he gave in to conservative critiques of the Institutes that were based on the fact that girls studied at them together with boys in a co-educational system. He therefore did nothing at all to prevent the conservative assault that was launched against the Institutes. İnönü even went so far as to appoint Reşat Şemşettin Sirer (1903–1953), an extreme nationalist and conservative, as Minister of National Education in 1946, knowing that he was a harsh critic of the Institutes. The new minister's first act was to remove Tonguç from the post of director general of primary education, to which he had been appointed in 1940. Soon after, the existing functions of the Institutes were changed in 1947 and 1948 through new legislation. Accordingly, the teaching equipment needed for the implementation of the "learning by doing" method was taken from the Institutes. While implementing these and similar policies, the new minister also received the full support of the Democrat Party (*Demokrat Parti*, DP), the new opposition party at the time.

Under Hasan Tahsin Banguoğlu (1904–1989), who became Minister of National Education in June 1948, policies aimed at eroding the functioning of the Institutes continued. Through

Law no. 5541 enacted in 1949, the policy of only accepting students from villages was abandoned. From then on, 25 per cent of primary school students from surrounding towns would also be admitted to the Institutes. Another change was that religion lessons were introduced into the curriculum of primary schools in the late 1940s. Consequently, between 1946 and 1950, the Institutes were eroded both by the nationalist conservative political elites within the ruling CHP through the connivance of İnönü and also by the new opposition party, the DP. A second breaking point took place in 1950 with the coming to power of the DP, which had used the Institutes as a scapegoat to attack the CHP. The Institutes were eventually closed down through Law no. 6234, which was enacted by the DP on 27 January 1954, and they were subsequently transformed into teacher training schools. Thus, the story of the Village Institutes came to an end. Nonetheless, they had taken their place on the stage of history as an institution that trained more than 17,000 teachers who would later play an important role in the intellectual life of Turkey.

***

There is no doubt that the Village Institutes represented one of the most interesting and original educational experiments carried out in the early Republican era. Still, for both their supporters and opponents, then and now, they were apparently much more than an educational undertaking, as indicated by the fact that they are still the focal point of ongoing controversies. The right-wing conservatives of the era harshly criticised the Institutes for their emphasis on "enlightenment" and the secular values embodied in their day-to-day practises. Notably, the Turkish conservative right never stopped in their condemnations of the Institutes, which have been continuing from the mid-1940s to the present. In fact, despite the original expectations of the ruling elite and the critiques of right- and left-wing politicians and intellectuals, the Institutes succeeded in cultivating a vigorous generation of teachers in Turkey who played a considerable role in Turkish left-wing secular politics for decades to come. Moreover, as evidenced in the excerpt above, there is no doubt that the hopes, synergy, devotion, missionary and visionary sensitivity, and, above all, enthusiasm of the teachers and students who took part in that novel experience were perhaps second to none in modern Turkish history.

Select Bibliography

Karaömerlioğlu, M. Asım. "The Village Institutes Experience in Turkey." *British Journal of Middle Eastern Studies* 25, no. 1 (1998): 47–73.

Kirby, Fay. *Türkiye'de Köy Enstitüleri*. Translated by Niyazi Berkes. İstanbul: Tarihçi Kitabevi, 2010.

Özsoy, Seçkin. "A Utopian Educator from Turkey: Ismail Hakki Tonguç (1893–1960)." *Journal for Critical Education Policy Studies* 7, no. 2 (2009): 249–78.

Tonguç, İsmail Hakkı. *Canlandırılacak Köy*. Second ed. İstanbul: Türkiye İş Bankası Kültür Yayınları, 2020.

Türkoğlu, Pakize. *Tonguç ve Enstitüleri*. İstanbul: Yapı Kredi Yayınları, 1997.

24

Inspecting the East:
The CHP Secretary General's Views
on the Kurdish Provinces

Senem Aslan

Eastern and south-eastern Anatolia are mountainous regions with harsh climates, which has long made it difficult for the central authorities to access and control them. Even as late as the early 1940s, the Republican People's Party (*Cumhuriyet Halk Partisi, CHP*) had yet to establish branches in the area. Moreover, these regions are also ethnically and religiously mixed, which hampered the Republican project of creating a homogenous nation. Kurdish rebellions led the single-party government (1923–1950) to rule the region through Inspectorates General (*Umumi Müfettişlikler*), which were granted state of emergency powers over all administrative and military institutions from 1928 until the end of the 1940s. The state suppressed the rebellions and pacified the region but fell short in terms of transforming it in line with the government's ambitious project of modernisation and Turkification.

Memduh Şevket Esendal (1883–1952), the secretary general of the CHP and a member of parliament, travelled to the eastern provinces in the fall of 1942. Not only was he a politician and bureaucrat, Esendal was also a prominent Turkish novelist and short-story writer. Among the places he visited were Elazığ, Tunceli (Dersim), Muş, Bingöl, Genç, Van, Bitlis, Siirt, Batman, Diyarbakır, Mardin, Harran, Urfa, Suruç, Gaziantep, Maraş, and Malatya. While his primary aim was to assess the feasibility of establishing local party branches in these regions, Esendal was particularly interested in Tunceli, where Kurds of the Alevi faith constituted the majority of the local population. Alevis, about one-fifth of whom are Kurdish, are a heterodox community with Shi'i roots. Today, Alevis are estimated to comprise between 15 to 20 per cent of Turkey's population. Dersim, with its distinctive ethno-religious makeup, history of strong regional autonomy, and difficult terrain, presented a challenge to the regime in terms of its efforts to establish central control over the area. Kurdish tribes launched a rebellion in Dersim in 1937, and the region remained the focus of highly repressive counterinsurgency operations until 1938.

Report of Memduh Şevket Esendal Regarding His Travels Through the Eastern Provinces*

It can be said that the cleaning up of Tunceli and the building of roads, bridges, and barracks have left a deep impact on these people. However, that impact will clearly not save them from believing in a mystical religion called Alevism, [nor help them] change and improve their lives. [...]

Some claim that the people who follow the Alevi sect in our country are of Turkish origin. Although I do not know what kind of evidence and documentation this claim is based on, it seems to me that it is true, and I believe it. The people whose origins are Kurdish belong to the Shafi'i school in our country and to the Sunni sect in Iran. In this respect, the majority of the population of Tunceli can be considered and thought of as Turks. (6)

It is my opinion that the people of Tunceli and the Alevis in Hatay will be Turkified more quickly than the others. More challenging than their Turkification, however, is the difficulty of introducing our people to their innate Turkishness and explaining it to them. Once I wanted to place an Alevi boy named Mehmet, whom I knew to be a Turk, in a military school. I had asked the Honourable Field Marshal [Fevzi Çakmak, 1876– 1950] to do so, and the Field Marshal gave the order. Although the inspector who was in charge of such matters could not directly disobey the Field Marshal, he told the boy, "This year's registration period is over, so I will accept you next year,' and brushed him off. [...] I think that this man still believes that he did a service to his country by refusing this boy [admission to the school}. In these men's minds, the words Alevi, Kurdish, and *Kızılbaş* [a historical pejorative term used for Alevis] more or less mean the same thing. (6-7)

It is my supposition that even prominent members of our society in Adana and Hatay are doing their utmost to drive away the Alevis, saying that they are filthy, despite the fact that the Alevis would like to develop closer relations with us. (7)

I believe that our party and People's Houses [community centres established by the single-party regime to spread the state's ideals to the masses] should remain vigilant and help eradicate these false ideas. (7)

A fourth stratum of people in Elazığ consists of the General Inspectorate's consultants and officials, as well as the governors and officials of Tunceli province and Elazığ with whom I had contact. Although it would not be right to judge people at first sight, I trust my experience and intuitions and hence believe that I am not misled. These people are ancien régime types who do nothing but try to kill time, are indifferent about whether their job is done well or not, and lack hope about their country's future. Among them I have not encountered a single one who is fierce and passionate [about doing the work of the state]. (11)

* Translated from the original Turkish in Memduh Şevket Esendal, *Doğu İllerine Yaptığı Gezinin Raporu*, 14 June 1945, T.C. Başbakanlık Devlet Arşivleri, BCA 490.01-571.2274.1. The excerpts appear on pages 6, 7, 11, 84, and 85 of the report.

The reason why these places are unable to support the party's organisation is likely related to the scarcity of people who can speak Turkish, notably as one goes from the cities to the districts, townships, and villages, rather than a shortage of people who are literate. (84)

In this respect, these provinces stand out as if they were stitched onto our country, not only in appearance but also in reality. (84)

In the city centres of our eastern provinces, there are people who speak Turkish at home. Nevertheless, because the [people living in the] surrounding areas do not speak Turkish, the market languages of these provinces are Kurdish or Arabic. (84)

As such, it would be more appropriate to open People's Houses, as cultural establishments, before opening party institutions, and ask them to engage in work to spread [the Turkish] language and information. (84-85)

During my tour, I repeatedly requested that language teaching be spread at every eastern People's House I visited. [...] It is clear that the activities of the People's Houses will have an effect on the people, and they can teach [the Turkish] language to children and young people at their locations. However, the payoff we will obtain will not be significant enough given the scale of the job we would like to undertake. (85)

[...] As a language, Kurdish is no different than Persian. [In fact], it is a corrupt, hybrid dialect of Persian. When this language is taught, it becomes Persian, and no one can assimilate the Kurds more easily than the Persians thanks to their language. The Turks living in Iran are also Turks, and population exchanges have been carried out before. (85)

The people who live in areas adjacent to Iraqi or Syrian territories are either Arabs or Arab-like people of mixed race who are descended from the ancient Semitic nations. It would not be wrong to assert that they would live more comfortably in Iraq and Syria. (85)

***

Esendal's report demonstrates the struggles that the regime faced in determining who could be assimilated and brought into the fold of Turkishness and what kinds of policies would bring about Turkification most efficiently. In his report, while Esendal's tone oscillates between optimism and pessimism, the latter predominates. According to Esendal, in theory people could become Turkified by learning Turkish. Like some other Turkish nationalists at the time, he believed that the Alevi Kurds in Tunceli were of Turkish origin, and thus the Alevi-Kurds of Tunceli could be integrated into the Turkish state more easily than other minority groups. Nonetheless, he also called attention to the challenges that made Turkification an unrealistic goal. For instance, as he argued, there were too many people who spoke languages other than Turkish. He asserted that in the city centres, the language of the markets was Kurdish or Arabic, and he lamented that there were not enough schools or People's Houses (*Halkevleri*) to teach the Turkish language to such a large populace. He complained about the bureaucracy, saying that it was incompetent, old-fashioned, and sluggish, and he criticised state officials for being solely concerned with their own interests and looking forward only to the day when they would leave the region. Esendal stated that they lacked dedication to the state's transformative project and hence were incapable of working towards its goals with passion and a sense of self-sacrifice. He even found members of the upper cadres, like governors and inspectors general, to be cynical, narrow-minded, and bereft of culture.

Esendal further argued that before expanding the party's organisation into the region, it would be better to open People's Houses as a means of disseminating the Turkish language to the local people. He based his claim on the contention that language barriers would make expansion of the party and broadening its base unfeasible. He was aware, however, that teaching Turkish through the People's Houses would take time, which is why, in the conclusion of his report, Esendal contemplated whether a population exchange between Turkey and Iran or between Turkey, Iraq, and Syria would be a more effective solution to creating homogeneity than assimilation. Indirectly he pointed to the precedent of the Greek Orthodox-Muslim population exchange of 1923, as a result of which at least 400,000 Muslims were forced to move to Turkey from Greece and 1.2 million Orthodox Greeks from Turkey were settled in Greece. It should be noted, however, that in those times, Esendal's proposal of a population exchange would neither have been unique nor deemed to be unreasonable. Immediately after the Second World War, the great powers approved of population exchanges as a permanent means of securing the stability of nation-states and even thought of them as a way to ensure that minorities would not suffer from discrimination. Esendal believed that it would be easier for the Kurds to integrate into society in Iran and that the Arabs were better suited for life in Iraq and Syria, and once more he expressed his pessimism about the capacity of the bureaucracy to successfully undertake such a project of ethnic engineering, commenting on the failures of the resettlement administration (*İskan Umum Müdürlüğü*). The Resettlement Law of 1934 sought to assimilate the Kurds by dispersing them among Turkish speakers as well as uprooting influential Kurdish tribal and sectarian leaders from their homelands and confiscating their property. Enforcement of the law was poorly coordinated, however, and it had numerous unanticipated consequences; ultimately, it failed to achieve its aims of weakening tribal structures, transferring land from landowners to the peasants, and assimilating the Kurds.

***

Esendal's report reveals the ambiguities and challenges the Republican elite faced in their attempts to govern and transform the Kurdish regions of the country and hints at why the state was unable to achieve its goals. While the report suggests that the state did secure stability and order in the region by military means, that did not necessarily lead to greater state control nor drive forward social transformations. The state's reliance on coercion through militarisation can be seen as evidence that it did not have the necessary infrastructural means nor the human capital to expand its authority. Such dependency on coercion also stemmed from the colonialist mindset of the Republican regime, which considered the populace of the region to be backward, inferior, and disloyal to the state.

Ever since the founding of the Republic, the state has had a fraught relationship with its ethnolinguistic and religious minorities. Its rigid and coercive attitude towards the Kurds has contributed to the consolidation of the nationalist Kurdish movement and the Kurdish conflict continues to be one of the most serious problems the Turkish Republic faces today. The relationship between Alevis and the state has also become more contentious. Starting in the 1990s, Alevi groups became increasingly mobilised and more vocal in their demands for equal rights. Reading Esendal's report more than seven decades after it was written raises the question of why the state's approaches to its minorities have largely remained coercive, even though such policies have repeatedly exacerbated tensions over time.

Select Bibliography

Aslan, Senem. "Everyday Forms of State Power and the Kurds in the Early Turkish Republic." *International Journal of Middle East Studies* 43, no. 1 (2011): 75-93.

Belge, Ceren. "State Building and the Limits of Legibility: Kinship Networks and Kurdish Resistance in Turkey." *International Journal of Middle East Studies* 43, no. 1 (2011): 95-114.

Dressler, Markus. "Physical and Epistemic Violence Against Alevis in Modern Turkey." In *Collective and State Violence in Turkey: The Construction of a National Identity from Empire to Nation-State*, edited by Stephan H. Astourian and Raymond H. Kevorkian, 347-71. New York, Oxford: Berghahn, 2021.

Önen, Nizam. "Bir Tek Parti Dönemi Politikacısının Gözünden Cumhuriyet'in Doğu Meselesi: CHP Genel Sekreteri Memduh Şevket Esendal'ın Doğu Gezisi." *Tarih ve Toplum* 12 (Bahar 2011): 153-98.

25
Planting the Seeds of Multiparty Politics: Memorandum of the Four

Alexander E. Balistreri

In the mid-1920s, the Republic of Turkey was administered under a single-party system that increasingly left politicians with little to no room to engage in public political debates. By the 1930s, foreign policy decisions were made by the president and foreign minister alone. While domestic policy decisions could be shaped by the government and the Parliamentary Group of the Republican People's Party (*Cumhuriyet Halk Partisi*, CHP), they still required the approval and guidance of the president. In spite of the central role it theoretically played in the Turkish constitution, the Grand National Assembly of Turkey remained a legislature in name only. By the mid-1940s, its members had long become used to rubber-stamping government proposals as a mere formality.

In the first half of 1945, which witnessed the defeat of the fascist powers and Turkey's entry into the United Nations, there was an increase in calls for democratisation in Turkey. Signs of open dissatisfaction surfaced in the speeches that deputies made at a session of the CHP Parliamentary Group in April, including one given by Fuat Köprülü (1880–1966), a well-known historian and the representative of Kars in the Grand National Assembly. In May, President İsmet İnönü (1884–1973) signalled in an address to the Turkish youth that as the need for wartime measures dissipated, the principles of democracy—represented by popular will and Parliament—would play an ever-larger role in Turkish political life. That same month, there was a sudden outburst of opposition in the Grand National Assembly over days of discussions regarding plans for land redistribution. Adnan Menderes (1899–1961), who was a landowner, and Refik Koraltan (1889–1974) were among the proposal's most vocal opponents. They criticised not only the content of the law, which would allow the government to expropriate the properties of large landowners, but also the way in which the government had attempted to impose its own version of the law when it was being drafted. Opposition to other measures spread as well. Now joined by Celâl Bayar (1883–1986) and other representatives, Köprülü, Menderes, and Koraltan voted against the government's yearly budget proposal and opposed the government in a subsequent vote of confidence. On 7 June 1945, Bayar, Koraltan, Köprülü, and Menderes submitted a pro-democracy memorandum addressed to the chairmanship of the CHP Parliamentary Group, an office that was shared by President İnönü and Prime Minister Şükrü Saraçoğlu (1886–1953). This "Memorandum of the Four" (*Dörtlü Takrir*), as it came to be known, was discussed in a heated seven-hour session of the Parliamentary Group five days later on 12 June.

*Memorandum of the Four**

To the Esteemed Chairmanship of the CHP Parliamentary Group:

Democracy has been the most fundamental principle of the Turkish Republic and of the Republican People's Party since their very establishment. There cannot be any doubt that the vast majority of the citizens who make up this country and in particular the vast majority of the members of our party believe in the principles of democracy; nor can there be any doubt of their conviction that the Turkish nation can only achieve [improved] welfare and prosperity by carrying out these principles to their fullest. With this conviction in mind, we consider it our duty to present to our party's Parliamentary Group our recommendations for measures we deem necessary for the realisation of this aim, one that is held so dearly by the nation.

The Turkish Republic was born out of our sacred War of Liberation, a war bound to the everlasting name of Atatürk. This Republic created the Law of Fundamental Organisation [*Teşkilat-ı Esasiye Kanunu*]—perhaps the most democratic Constitution in the world—and, in so doing, enabled [the realisation of] both individual liberties and national oversight in the broadest manner possible.

In the years following 1925, we know that some restrictions were imposed on political liberties in order to protect the country from a handful of pernicious institutions left over from the Middle Ages and to defeat reactionism [*irtica*]. Yet the Turkish Republican State remained ever faithful to the democratic spirit of the Law of Fundamental Organisation, while the Founder of the Republic, Atatürk the Great, never once in his life departed from his ideal of helping it attain a democratic form in its entirety. [...]

The emergence of the Second World War and the constant state of jeopardy in which our country found itself because of the threat of war [spilling over its borders] naturally meant that political liberties were restricted yet again, a further move away from the democratic spirit of the Law on Fundamental Organisation. While we recognise that the formation of an independent group within the Republican People's Party represented an attempt to better ensure national oversight and to ameliorate the harm brought about by a single-party style of rule, we have also noted that the artificialness of its formation prevented it from achieving any positive results.

In this day and age, at a time when the forces of liberty and democracy have achieved complete victory around the world and when respect for democratic liberties is soon to be ensured by international agreements, there can be no doubt whatsoever that in our country, too, the entire nation—from the president down to its humblest member—nurtures the same democratic principles. [...]

---

* Translated from the Turkish original in Cemil Koçak, *Türkiye'de İki Partili Siyâsî Sistemin Kuruluş Yılları (1945–1950)*, Cilt 1: İkinci Parti (İstanbul: İletişim Yayınları, 2010), 314–16.

And so we have been inspired, on the one hand, by the political maturity brought about by such positive developments in our domestic sphere and, on the other, by the general state of the civilized world today, to believe that the time has come to reinvigorate our political life and institutions with the democratic spirit that predominated as early as our first Law of Fundamental Organisation. Our ideas about how to bring this about as quickly as possible can be summarised as follows:

1. Take measures to reinvigorate parliamentary oversight—which, simultaneously, is one of the most natural consequences of and foundations for national sovereignty—so that it exists in complete accordance with the spirit of the Constitution and not only on paper.

2. Find ways for citizens to make use of the political rights and liberties that were guaranteed to them as early as [the promulgation of] our first Law of Fundamental Organisation.

3. Completely reorganise all party functions so that they are in full compliance with the basic principles outlined above. [...]

***

The Memorandum of the Four seems to have presented its demands for democratisation in a limited and essentially conservative way; its authors called for reforms from within the CHP and the restoration of the true force of the existing constitution as indicated in the 1924 Law of Fundamental Organisation (*Teşkilât-ı Esasiye Kanunu*). Those demands, however, were to have far-reaching implications. For the four dissidents, two features of the constitution were particularly important: parliamentary oversight and basic freedoms. With regard to parliamentary oversight, the constitution stated that the Grand National Assembly could "supervise and dismiss the government at any time" (Article 7). Indeed, the legislature's supervisory role had given rise to a major question: how could deputies effectively exercise oversight under a single-party regime? The notion of "national oversight" (*millî murakabe*), highlighted several times in the Memorandum of the Four, echoed the CHP's own election slogans of 1939, which had featured references to the term. In line with those promises, that year the ruling CHP established an "independent group" (*müstakil grup*) consisting of 21 members from within the party. That group would be allowed to speak and vote during legislative sessions without being bound to the decisions of the party's Parliamentary Group. The Memorandum's call for "measures to reinvigorate parliamentary oversight" implied allowing institutions operating beyond the scope of the supposedly "independent" but actually "artificial" and obedient faction to speak up.

The second feature of the constitution which the four deputies highlighted was its guarantee of political rights and freedoms. Indeed, the constitution counted freedom of speech and the freedom to form associations, including political parties, as being among the many "natural rights of Turks" (Article 70). According to the Memorandum, previous restrictions on such rights, including the closures of the Progressive Republican Party (*Terakkiperver Cumhuriyet*

Fırkası) in 1925 and the Liberal Republican Party (Serbest Cumhuriyet Fırkası) in 1930, may have been justified on the grounds that the threat of counterrevolution (irtica) was becoming an increasingly pressing matter. However, as the Memorandum emphasises, the people had now attained a state of political maturity that made it possible for a democratic initiative to come to the fore. The Memorandum did not go so far as to call for the establishment of an opposition party and it confined itself to making demands for fundamental internal party reforms. Nevertheless, the references to the shortcomings of internal party opposition and to previous attempts to establish opposition parties indicate that some of the signatories might have been prepared to take more "radical" steps. In fact, the Memorandum was submitted during the same week in early June 1945 when many Turkish newspapers were speculating on the establishment of a second party, even correctly guessing its future name. Some within the CHP suspected that the signatories had already made up their minds about founding an opposition party and that they were using the Memorandum as an "excuse" to do so. There is widespread agreement today, however, that the signatories of the Memorandum of the Four did not have explicit plans to form a second party at the time of its submission.

***

After the Memorandum was discussed by the CHP Parliamentary Group, its signatories' proposals concerning the reformation of structures within the CHP were rejected by all the other party members in attendance. İnönü went so far as to suggest that the signatories should leave the party if they wished to express such criticism (a comment that underlines a dearth of intra-party democratic culture in Turkey that continues to this day). The vehemence with which the party leadership attacked the Memorandum and its authors soured Turkish politics in the months that followed. Persistent as they were in their public opposition, Köprülü, Menderes, and later Koraltan were expelled from the CHP in the fall of 1945; in an act of protest, Bayar resigned from the Grand National Assembly in September and then in December he resigned from the CHP as well. Seeing that it would be impossible to engage in opposition from within the CHP, the drafters of the Memorandum decided to establish a new party, which they registered on 7 January 1946 as the Democrat Party (Demokrat Parti, DP). With Menderes as Prime Minister and Bayar appointed President, the DP would go on to dominate Turkish politics in the 1950s.

The Memorandum stands as one of the most forceful expressions of a democratising tendency in both Turkey's domestic and foreign policies in the mid-1940s. For instance, notwithstanding the CHP leadership's vocal opposition to the Memorandum when it was submitted, the government decided to make it easier to establish viable alternative political parties. In December of 1945, the Ministry of the Interior proposed amendments to the Law of Assembly (Cemiyetler Kanunu) which would allow citizens to establish political parties without the explicit approval of the Ministry; these amendments were subsequently approved in June of the following year. That same month, the Grand National Assembly approved a shift from indirect to direct elections for representatives (Milletvekilleri Seçimi Kanunu).

Meanwhile in the field of foreign politics, Turkey signed the Charter of the United Nations in August of 1945. As Menderes pointed out during parliamentary debates about ratification of the Charter, promising to uphold its calls for "fundamental freedoms" would require eliminating anti-democratic elements in the Turkish political system. Although politics in Turkey in the second half of the 1940s were still far from being democratic, in July of 1947 President İnönü promised to remain impartial in terms of his relations with the CHP and the DP, personally vouching for the legitimacy of the opposition party. Thus, the Memorandum of the Four signalled the impasse that single-party rule had reached, and it has been interpreted as the driving force behind the transition to multiparty politics that took place in Turkey after the Second World War.

Select Bibliography

Karpat, Kemal H. *Turkey's Politics: The Transition to a Multi-Party System*. Princeton, NJ: Princeton University Press, 1959.

Koçak, Cemil. *Türkiye'de İki Partili Siyâsî Sistemin Kuruluş Yılları (1945–1950)*. Vol. 1, *İkinci Parti*. İstanbul: İletişim Yayınları, 2010.

Toker, Metin. *Tek Partiden Çok Partiye*. İstanbul: Milliyet Yayınları, 1970.

Vanderlippe, John M. *The Politics of Turkish Democracy: İsmet İnönü and the Formation of the Multi-Party System, 1938–1950*. Albany, NY: State University of New York Press, 2005.

26

The Future of an Ancient Capital: Henri Prost's Master Plan for İstanbul

F. Cânâ Bilsel

The proclamation of Ankara as the capital of the Republic of Turkey on 13 October 1923 was driven by a strategic and symbolic decision. The relocation of the capital, that manifested the Republican regime's determination to break with its Ottoman past, deprived İstanbul from its title of capital city of an empire. In the years following the founding of the Republic, public funds were largely channelled towards constructing the nation's new capital. However, in 1933, just a few years after a city planning competition was held for Ankara, internationally renowned city planners were invited to devise ideas for the redevelopment of İstanbul. For the young Republic, modernising the historic and most populated city was as imperative as the construction of the new capital.

Alfred Agache (1875–1959) and Henri Prost (1874–1959) from France and Hermann Ehlgoetz (1880–1943) from Germany were personally invited by way of an official letter dated 26 February 1933 and signed by the governor-mayor of İstanbul, Muhittin Üstündağ (1884–1953). However, Prost was forced to decline the invitation because he was already occupied with planning the Paris Region, and he recommended that Jacques Lambert (1884–1960) take his place. Agache, Lambert, and Ehlgoetz submitted their master plan proposals and reports towards the end of 1933. All three planners foresaw that İstanbul would develop as a port and industrial centre in the future. Ehlgoetz's project was selected by the jury, as it was found to be more applicable and more respectful of the character of the historic city. However, the Municipality of İstanbul did not sign any contract with him and continued to search for another city planner. In 1934, Henri Prost was invited to Turkey once again, firstly to study the planning of the Yalova Thermal Station, where the summer residence of President Atatürk (1881–1938) was located. A few months later, he received an offer from the governor-mayor of İstanbul to serve as a consultant for the planning of İstanbul.

Henri Prost was a pioneering architect-urbanist who contributed greatly to the development of the discipline of town planning in France. Besides participating in the activities of "urban and rural hygiene" in the Sixth Section of the *Musée Social*, he was invited by Maréchal Lyautey to Morocco, where he worked on the planning of several cities under the French protectorate from 1914 to 1922. He was appointed chief planner of Paris in 1932 and conducted the planning works of the Paris metropolitan region until 1936. Prost was engaged in the planning of İstanbul within the capacity of consultant to the municipality's Directorate of Public Works from 1936 to 1951. His planning activities in İstanbul comprised a wide range of studies that extended from a master plan for the European side of İstanbul (1937), a master plan for the Asian side of the city (1939) and planning for the shores of the Bosporus (1936–1948) to numerous urban design projects for squares and the construction of new avenues, parks, and promenades. In October 1937, he completed the master plan for the European side of İstanbul, which consisted of two distinct plans of 1/5,000 scale that focused on Old İstanbul and the area of Galata-Pera (Beyoğlu). Prost emphasised in his reports that he developed his plans for İstanbul around three principal issues: transportation (*la circulation*), hygiene (*l'hygiène*), and aesthetics (*l'esthétique*). In September 1947, he gave a speech titled *"Les Transformations d'Istanbul"* at the Académie des Beaux-Arts in Paris, in which he explained his approach to the planning of İstanbul. Segments of that speech are presented below.

The Transformation of İstanbul*

[...] The Republic of Turkey has been founded. Ankara, which is located in the centre of Anatolia, has become the capital of the Government. İstanbul, now deprived of its role as the great Capital of a large Empire, has become the principal harbour of the new Turkey.

Social reforms have come one after the other. There is no official religion anymore. The Government waived the suzerainty that the Sultan had exercised over the World of Muslims (from India to the frontier of Morocco). [...] The Turkish language has been subjected to profound reforms, the old script has been outlawed, and the Latin alphabet has been adopted. [...] Lastly, the final reform has had incalculable consequences: ATATÜRK removed the women's veil, and wearing the veil is now rigorously banned.

This last reform has had considerable repercussions on the urbanisation of İstanbul. Turkish women no longer want the old-style houses with their barred windows. Some of them have demanded apartments in collective buildings with elevators, central heating, and a hot water supply in every season, while others have requested sumptuous villas with large gardens on the shores of the Marmara or Bosporus.

This is the reason why the relatively well-off inhabitants have left Old İstanbul for the new neighbourhoods close to the European neighbourhoods of Pera or the newly established residential areas along the shores of the Asian side and even the islands. However, [...] business activities have become more intense than ever before in the old commercial quarters of Old İstanbul, in Galata, along the banks of the Golden Horn, and in the old bazaars, which are now in the process of being modernised.

[...] The commercial centres have not changed their locations, so all the old inhabitants are constrained to come to work in Old İstanbul, between Galata Bridge and the Bazaar, and along the two sides of the

---

* Translated from the original French in *"Les Transformations d'Istanbul,"* a presentation given by Henri Prost, who was a member of the Institut de France, at the Académie des Beaux-Arts on 17 September 1947.

Golden Horn. The result is an unimaginable congestion of means of transportation: trams, buses, taxis, and steamboats from the Bosporus and Asian side as well as the Islands all converge around Galata Bridge. This bridge is truly a Central Station for all means of urban transport and [represents] a unique case in the planning of cities.

URBANISM

The modernisation of İstanbul can be compared to a chirurgical operation of the most delicate nature. It is not about creating a New City on virgin land, but rather directing an Ancient Capital in the process of undergoing a complete social change towards a Future, through which the mechanisms and probably the redistribution of wealth will transform the conditions of existence.

This City thrives with incredible activity. Constructing the main axes of circulation without harming commercial and industrial development and without stopping the construction of new settlements is an imperious economic and social necessity; however, conserving and PROTECTING the INCOMPARABLE LANDSCAPE, which is dominated by glorious EDIFICES, is another necessity as imperious as the former. [...]

PRINCIPLES OF THE MASTER PLAN

Two main circulation roads will [serve as the] spine for the agglomerations of Pera and İstanbul, which are but one single city. These two arteries of capital importance will originate from TAKSİM Square [...] at the junction of the old and new neighbourhoods. They will connect this square to both GALATA BRIDGE and ATATÜRK BRIDGE.

The first one will extend beyond Galata Bridge through Old İstanbul to BAYAZID Square and the UNIVERSITY, after serving the Grand BAZAAR. The second artery, extending beyond Atatürk Bridge, will connect the shores of the Golden Horn to those of the Marmara, where a large residential neighbourhood will be created.

Taksim Square in Pera was transformed in order to provide an opening for the two main circulation arteries that were projected. This square is also the beginning of a LARGE PROMENADE measuring a length of approximately 1,500 meters that overlooks a PARK of around thirty hectares on the slope towards the Bosporus and opening onto a marvellous panorama. The PROMENADE is nearing completion and planting in the whole Park will be completed in Spring 1948. [...] PARK No. 2 constitutes the RECREATIONAL CENTRE of the new neighbourhoods on the European shores of the Bosporus. [...]

Photograph of a physical model showing Henri Prost's İstanbul Master Plan as revised in 1943
(Académie d'architecture/Cité de l'architecture et du patrimoine/Archives d'architecture du XXe siècle).

***

Prost's descriptions reveal the principal motivation behind the new city plan for İstanbul: namely, the modernisation of the city, a goal which was determined by the socio-political circumstances of the time in Turkey. The planned changes encompassed both a structural transformation targeting transportation infrastructure and the creation of green spaces, along with the transformation of the existing urban fabric. In his speech, Prost underlined that İstanbul was undergoing societal changes that had gathered momentum through the reforms of Atatürk, and women in particular played a significant role in that transformation. Several neighbourhoods that had been destroyed by fires in Old İstanbul largely remained vacant, which was one of the main reasons why the well-to-do groups left the old city for the new settlements towards north at the European side and towards East at the Asian side, a process that had already started in the late Ottoman period. However, as the planner pointed out, the city's central business district maintained its vitality and continued to develop around the district of Eminönü. In spite of the fact that the overall population of İstanbul had decreased, the city continued to expand because of new development in the peripheries, which caused transportation problems due to daily commuting.

Prost praised the "incomparable landscape of İstanbul" and paid close attention to the conservation of the city's historic monuments and unique silhouette through the planning decisions and regulations he introduced. On the other hand, he concluded in his report of 1937 that the Master Plan of İstanbul had to be an "urban concentration plan" (*"Plan de Concentration"*) in order to consolidate the centre of the city, instead of an "urban extension plan" (*"Plan d'Extension"*). According to him, the historical core of the city would continue to be the centre of the agglomeration in the future, just as it had been in the past. For this reason, Prost focused on the necessity of reorganising the historical urban fabric of the city. In his speech, he legitimised this by the ongoing social change and women's aspiration for living in modern houses with better conditions in particular. The high-standing residential quarter that he proposed to create along the Marmara shore would replace the old neighbourhoods where mostly middle and low-income groups from different ethnicities lived. In other words, the planner proposed an urban transformation that would bring along gentrification in this part of the city. Fortunately, his proposal for these historic neighbourhoods could not be implemented, however the entire old city would be subject to over densification through a piecemeal yet continuous reconstruction of the built environment, due to an unprecedented population increase in the following decades.

Prost's Master Plan for the European Side of İstanbul restructured the city around "a spine" that would connect the newly developing residential areas around Taksim in the north to the old city and the central business district. To that end, the opening of Atatürk Boulevard was an urban operation of primary importance. He aimed at facilitating urban transportation by introducing an *"auto-route* system" that would provide uninterrupted automobile transportation in the city, traversing the centre from one end to the other. Those roads would cross hills and valleys by way of tunnels and viaducts.

Henri Prost ascribed particular importance to developing green areas and public open spaces in İstanbul. His Master Plan included two large parks, one in Old İstanbul and the other in the new areas of development to the north. Park No. 1 was to extend from Aksaray to the Byzantine land walls, following Bayrampaşa Creek. The creation of an Archaeological Park, which he conceived of as an open-air museum that would run from Sarayburnu to the south of Sultanahmet, was a significant project that combined archaeology and recreation.

In his Master Plan of Galata and Pera, Prost allocated the area of the valley between Maçka, Harbiye, and Dolmabahçe to Park No. 2, which he foresaw as a large recreation area and the "lungs" of new residential neighbourhoods. In continuity with his design for the park, from 1939 to 1943 he developed plans for İnönü Esplanade (originally referred to as *İnönü Gezgisi* and later *Taksim Gezisi*) in place of the Taksim Barracks. Dolmabahçe Stadium, a Sports and Exhibition Hall, and the Harbiye Open-air Amphitheatre were added to the plans for Park No. 2. Prost introduced a variety of public open spaces—*espaces libres*—including parks, esplanades, public squares, and sports areas, both in the existing city and in new areas of development, to nurture new forms of sociability as well as a healthy environment.

***

Henri Prost had a good working relationship with Dr Lütfi Kırdar (1889–1961), who was the governor-mayor of İstanbul from 1938 to 1949. In 1943, he prepared a Decennial Plan (1943–1953) in which he proposed a series of operations that would be undertaken in line with his revised master plan. In spite of the economic hardships brought on by the war, some of his proposals were in fact implemented in this period. The main transportation artery connecting Taksim to Yenikapı was opened with the completion of Atatürk Boulevard and Dr Refik Saydam Avenue. Eminönü Square was reconfigured and İnönü Esplanade (today *Taksim Gezisi*) was constructed according to Henri Prost's designs in 1942–1943. Park No. 2, which consisted of a large urban park of 30 hectares, was opened to the public together with the Harbiye Open-air Amphitheatre (*Harbiye Açık Hava Tiyatrosu*) and the Palace of Sports and Exhibitions (today *Lütfi Kırdar Spor ve Sergi Sarayı*) in 1947 and 1949, respectively.

The planner's relationship with the municipal authorities changed after 1949, and Prost left his position in January 1951. Following a period of transition and revisions to Prost's plans by a commission, large-scale urban operations were undertaken in İstanbul by Prime Minister Adnan Menderes (1899–1961) in 1957. Although these undertakings seemed to have drawn inspiration from Prost's Master Plan, unfortunately they lacked the sensibility of the urbanist's detailed urban design studies. They were implemented without taking the measures needed to relocate residents before work commenced, measures which Henri Prost had insisted on repeatedly in his reports.

Select Bibliography

Académie d'Architecture. *L'Œuvre de Henri Prost, Architecture et Urbanisme*. Paris: L'Académie d'Architecture, 1960.

Akpınar, İpek Yada. "The Making of a Modern Pay-ı Taht in İstanbul: Menderes' Executions After Prost's Plan." In *From an Imperial Capital to the Modern City of the Republic: Henri Prost's Planning of İstanbul (1936–1951)*, edited by Bilsel, F. Cânâ, and Pierre Pinon, 167–211. İstanbul: İstanbul Research Institute, 2010.

Bilsel, Cânâ. "Remodeling the Imperial Capital in the Early Republican Era: The Representation of History in Henri Prost's Planning of İstanbul." In *Power and Culture: Identity, Ideology, Representation*, edited by Jonathan Osmond and Ausma Cimdina, 95–115. Pisa: Pisa University Press, 2007.

Bilsel, F. Cânâ, and Pierre Pinon. *From an Imperial Capital to the Modern City of the Republic: Henri Prost's Planning of İstanbul (1936–1951)*. İstanbul: İstanbul Research Institute, 2010.

27

"What Is to Be Done?":
The Legacy of Leftist Minority Artists in Turkey

Nicholas Kontovas

In the bleak Siberian winter of 1949, poet, painter, songwriter, and folklorist Xasani Xelimişi penned his best-known poem, "Oh Son, What Shall We Do!" Here in exile far from his native village on the northeastern coast of Turkey, Xelimişi wrote this time not in Turkish or Russian, but in his native language: Laz.

Spoken by anywhere from an estimated 45,000 to 500,000 people, Laz is closely related to the Megrelian language of western Georgia and more distantly related to Georgian itself. Laz has been spoken on the eastern coast of the Black Sea around Rize for millennia, a region known in Ottoman times as Lazistan. Yet despite its long history, Laz did not have an extensive written literature until the early twentieth century. Furthermore, due in large part to hostility towards the public use of minority languages in Turkey at the time, most of its early written literature was composed by a group of émigrés living in the Soviet Union. Xasani Xelimişi (a.k.a. Hasan Helimişi, Xelimişi Xasani, or Hasan Cuhadaroğlu) was one of those émigrés.

Born in 1907 in the eastern Black Sea town of Orta Hopa (Xopa in Laz) in the Ottoman Sancak of Lazistan near Turkey's current border with Georgia, Xelimişi was the only son of a shoemaker. From a young age, he displayed a talent for painting and songwriting, as well as a passion for the traditional Laz way of life. Armed with the latest in recording equipment, he travelled the region collecting examples of Laz oral literature. It was during his nomadic youth that Xelimişi met with members of the invading Russian army, from whom he became familiar with Marxism.

Though the details of what led to his self-imposed exile remain unknown, Xelimişi's affiliation with local communist organisations prompted several arrests and short periods of imprisonment in Turkey. Convinced that the newly formed Soviet Union would provide greater opportunities and appreciation for his particularly Laz brand of art, Xelimişi migrated first to Batumi and then to Leningrad sometime during the early 1930s. He would spend the rest of his life in various regions within the USSR.

Though he was able to promote his language and culture there, Xelimişi's life in the Soviet Union was anything but easy. In addition to losing his leg in a train accident early on in his travels, the USSR's renewed paranoia surrounding the security of its Georgian border after the Second World War led to increasingly harsh policies aimed at assimilating the Laz and other minorities into the local Georgian population. As with many of his comrades, Xelimişi was imprisoned several times, first locally and then from 1949–1953 in the Vasyugan swamps of south-central Siberia along with his Georgian-speaking wife and children. Though the death of Stalin enabled his return to Georgia, Xelimişi found fewer friends there than when he had left. Unable to maintain gainful employment, Xelimişi was turned away first from the house of his in-laws in Tbilisi, then from that of his cousins in Abkhazia. In a paradoxical turn of events, Xelimişi was recognised for his talents in language only when he was appointed as a teacher of Turkish at Tbilisi State University. Even then, after a year of unpaid wages Xelimişi retreated entirely from academic life and returned to his father's profession of shoemaking. He never stopped composing or collecting literature in his native language, however, and he died in 1976 in the Laz village of Sarpi on the Georgian-Turkish border, surrounded by a dedicated group of his pupils.

"Oh Son, What Shall We Do!" is one of a number of poems which have come down to us in Xelimişi's own voice on cassettes recorded shortly before his death. Interspersed with these are personal reflections which provide us with unique insights into his life and art. Understood in these contexts, Xelimişi's poem becomes a poignant remark on the often precarious relationship between politics and artistic expression, and the impact this has had on the legacy of the minority language artist as an individual throughout Turkish history.

"Oh Son, What Shall We Do!"*

Write poems if you want to, sing songs if you want
Work hard if you want to, or sleep if you want
Either way, it's all just one big lie they tell you
Doesn't matter a damn, son, so what'll we do?

I don't know what to do; my luck's down on the floor
And who knows what they want me to be anymore
Only I know what it is I've been through
So who can I count on, son, what can I do?

Everybody has worth in the right place and time,
But who am I kidding? I'm not worth a dime!
Who can I count on, what am I to who?
And whose door can I run to, son, tell me now, who?

When everyone's scared of their own shadow, too,
And real human beings are vanishingly few
Everything that you do's for a morsel or two
And I'm not a rich man, son, so what can I do?

* Translated from the original Laz in Xasani Helimişi, "Mu Ƥat E Sǩiri," in *Mu Ƥat E Sǩiri*, ed. İsmail Bucaǩlişi (İstanbul: Lazika Yayın Kollektifi, 2015), 53–54.

One day you'll search each nook and cranny for me
And keep writing my words down, from A down to Z
Only then will you all know me like I knew you
But you won't find me, son, no matter what you do!

So when I've lost all of the teeth from my head
And the blood's all dried up in my corpse, cold and dead
You'll look down at my head where dwarf elder grew
And remember me, son – but then what will you do?

***

On the surface, the first four stanzas of the poem seem to be a simple reflection on the inescapable misery of Xelimişi's present circumstances. Yet in the final two stanzas, the poet shifts his gaze to the future. The use of the second person plural—"Only then will *you all* know me"—makes it clear that the son he is addressing is in fact a metonym for the next generation. Xelimişi's genuine misfortune notwithstanding, the image of the long-suffering poet unappreciated in their own time would have been a familiar didactic device to Xelimişi and his audience. Having grown up in the Ottoman Empire, Xelimişi had been exposed to copious examples of classical Arabic, Persian, and Turkish poetry, which makes frequent use of *fahriye* (rhetorical boasting) and *şekva* (rhetorical complaint) combined in just the same manner. While contemporary Turkish leftist poets, such as Nâzım Hikmet Ran (1902–1963), often chose freer structures to consciously distance their works from earlier idioms, Xelimişi blends classical forms and imagery with those from the Laz oral tradition. "Oh Son, What Shall We Do!" is written, for example, in dactylic tetrameter, with a relatively simple rhyming scheme and structural parallelism, reminiscent of traditional folk quatrains.

Xelimişi's work is not, however, devoid of contemporary influence. He remained a dedicated Leninist until his death, and the title of the poem, repeated in a slightly modified way at the end of each verse, is inspired by Lenin's famous pamphlet, *What Is to Be Done?* Though paradoxical given the poem's pessimistic view of the Soviet world in which he lived, Xelimişi exhorts his son to consider what the hardships of his life might mean for him much in the same way as Lenin's pamphlet expounds upon the need for the masses to interpret their struggles within the framework of the revolution. At their core, both works are a call to action which crucially implore the reader keep in mind a "bigger picture". In Xelimişi's work, however, this is a bigger picture in which the landscape of past traditions is not entirely erased.

Viewed in this light, "Oh Son, What Shall We Do!" is as much a contemplation of personal misery as a didactic poem which asks the reader to reinterpret the poet's individual suffering as part of a greater legacy. Yet, apart from the mention of "my words" in the fourth stanza, the poem is noticeably vague on the matter of what this legacy is. For that, we must turn to another of Xelimişi's poems: "To the Hopans," which he prefaces in his recordings by saying,

"My whole philosophy is in this poem." Here, the poet addresses the people of his homeland who question the purpose of his arduous existence in exile:

> To the Hopans I sing in Laz alone [...]
> For so much I have suffered for the Laz [...]
> And so I sing to all the Laz in Laz
> with every breath I breathe, I sing in Laz,
> and so long as I sing my heart goes on!

From this we understand not only that Xelimişi remained in exile because of the relative freedom it provided him to express his Laz identity, but that the Laz language is central to that identity. Here, the classical trope of the underappreciated poet gains new meaning: the "words" whose worth will not be recognised until it is too late refer not only to the meanings of his poems, but to the language itself.

Xelimişi's work frequently betrays a preoccupation with themes inextricably linked to the Laz homeland, and his use of language reveals this. The dwarf elder shrub (Laz *inçiri*) mentioned in the last stanza has no single-word translation in Turkish, but it is ubiquitous along the eastern Black Sea coast where it is traditionally thought to grow above gravesites. In locating his son's reckoning with his faded memory in such a setting, Xelimişi envisions his suffering as nourishing the soul of his homeland—both in its soil and in the fertile minds of its next generation.

***

The image of the son frantically writing and rewriting his father's language after his death becomes all the more poignant when one understands the resistance which the Laz face in preserving their language. While Laz was more vital in Xelimişi's time than it is now, its decline in popularity in subsequent decades is a result of the hostility which regional languages other than Turkish faced in the early years of the Republic. After the Constitution of 1924 made Turkish the official language, a campaign popularly known as "Citizen, Speak Turkish!" prompted the passage of a series of laws restricting the use of regional minority languages in public. From 1930 onwards, there was effectively no locally mass-produced minority literature outside of Greek, Ladino, and Armenian periodicals, which were circulated largely within İstanbul.

The particular precarity of Laz in early twentieth century Turkey owed much to the history of Turkish-Russian relations. Already in the latter decades of the Ottoman Empire, a certain Faik Efendi, about whose life little is known, had developed a writing system for Laz—an act for which he was imprisoned and his publications destroyed. It is likely that the Ottoman administration perceived Faik's act as a step in the development of a national consciousness which, under the wrong circumstances, might prompt a movement for the annexation of Lazistan by the encroaching Russian Empire. With the October Revolution of 1917, anti-Russian sentiment gave way to the first "Red Scare," and fears of Russian territorial incursion became intermingled with anti-Communist rhetoric from the increasingly powerful Turkish right. Censorship laws made the importation of literature from abroad difficult regardless of the language; however, because of its association with Communism, Laz émigré literature was effectively completely inaccessible. A 1930 presidential decree bearing the signature of Mustafa Kemal Atatürk (1881–1938) himself attests to this, specifically banning the importation of the periodical *Red Star*, which was published in Sokhumi by Xelimişi's fellow Laz language activist Iskender Žitaşi (1904–1938; also spelled Ts'itaşi/Tzitaşi/Chitaşi).

As draconian policies targeting the use of minority languages in Turkey continued, minority artists continued to flee the country, seeking refuge in the USSR. Over time, this led to a situation wherein the overwhelming majority of art widely available in languages such as Laz or Kurmanji Kurdish was effectively leftist art. This is by no means a reflection of the political leanings of most members of linguistic minority groups within Turkey who, as with the broader Turkish population, ascribe to a wide variety of social and political beliefs. Yet over time it became increasingly impossible to keep "foreign" art from reaching the Turkish market, and as the USSR slowly opened up to communication with the outside world, the influence of leftist minority language art in Turkey became more noticeable. Rightist elements within Turkey were aware of this and in 1983 they enacted Law no. 2932 banning publications or broadcasts in any language other than Turkish. As if to will into being the very disappearance of languages like Laz, against which Xelimişi fought, it stated, "The mother tongue of all Turkish citizens is Turkish."

The law was revoked in 1991 and Laz literature now runs the gamut from Marxist philosophy to Qur'anic translations and textbooks for official use in Laz elective courses at public schools. Be that as it may, the link between minority languages in Turkey and socialism has continued, both in reality and as an element in the discourse discouraging the public use of minority languages. Younger Laz artists, such as the late singer Kâzım Koyuncu (1971–2005), continue to be drawn to leftist political movements for the greater freedom of expression they promise, even if this often proves a political liability. Yet, though Xelimişi may be remembered as part of a by-gone era of Communist émigrés, the quality of "Oh Son, What Shall We Do!" that renders it so relatable for minority language speakers is not its Leninist framing, but the poet's exasperated resignation expressed as the hope that their suffering may help future generations remember the legacy which they have been taught to forget.

Select Bibliography

Andrews, Peter Alfred, ed. *Ethnic Groups in the Republic of Turkey*. Wiesbaden: Dr. Ludwig Reichert Verlag, 1989.

Helimişi, Xasani. "Mu Ṗat E Sḱiri." In *Mu Ṗat E Sḱiri*, edited by İsmail Bucaḱlişi, 53–54. İstanbul: Lazika Yayın Kollektifi, 2015.

Kutscher, Silvia. "The Language of the Laz in Turkey: Contact-induced Change or Gradual Language Loss?" *Turkic Languages* 12 (2008): 82–102.

Marr, Nikolai. "Iz poezdki v Tureckij Lazestan." *Mélanges asiatiques tirés du Bulletin de l'Académie Impériale des sciences de St.-Pétersbourg* 19 (1910): 283–332.

Solomon, Thomas. "Who Are the Laz? Cultural Identity and the Musical Public Sphere on the Turkish Black Sea Coast." *The World of Music* 6, no. 2 (2017): 83–113.

28

The Language of Religion:
The Reversion of the *Ezan* from Turkish to Arabic

Ömer Koçyiğit

There was a period in Turkey's history lasting from 1932 to 1950 during which the Muslim call to prayer—the *ezan* (or in Arabic, *adhan*)—was recited in Turkish instead of Arabic, the language of the Qur'an and Islamic worship. The "Turkification" policies of the Kemalist regime, which were defended in the name of modernisation, secularism, and nationalism, resulted in the passing of numerous laws, one of which concerned the *ezan*, one of the most significant aspects of Muslim communal life as the voice of Islam. Initially, many elite members of the young Republic of Turkey perceived the shift of the recitation of the *ezan* from Arabic to Turkish as a revolutionary step, and the law was strictly implemented. While many people were punished for violating the administrative order concerning the Turkish *ezan* after 1932, and also on the basis of Article 526 of the Penal Code in 1941, those who recited the *ezan* and *kamet* (second call to prayer) in Arabic began to be sentenced to up to three months in prison or punished with a small fine. However, practices of Turkification pertaining to religion were not limited to the call to prayer, as indicated by the fact that the Friday *hutbe* (sermon) and also the *tekbir* (from the Arabic phrase *Allahu akbar*, meaning God is great) were also rendered in Turkish, and the state issued an order stating that the text of the Qur'an, along with a book of commentary and hadiths, would be translated into Turkish as well.

The first *ezan* in Turkish was recited at Fatih Mosque in İstanbul on 30 January 1932. By July of the same year, the Directorate of Religious Affairs (*Diyanet İşleri Başkanlığı*, hereafter Diyanet) had sent the official Turkish translation of the call to prayer to every mosque in the country. However, some members of the Diyanet tried to protect Islamic practices of worship from policies of Turkification. For instance, when a request was made for a report about prayers being conducted in Turkish, Ahmed Hamdi Akseki (1887–1951), who was a member of the consultation committee of the Diyanet at the time, penned a pamphlet entitled *Namaz ve Kuran* (*Prayer and the Qur'an*) in which he asserted that reciting Turkish translations of the Qur'an during ritual prayers was absolutely unacceptable.

The recitation of the *ezan* in Turkish also became a point of contention for the general public, as can be seen in various memoirs. Some people expressed their disapproval, while others directly opted to protest the policy, as was seen in the Bursa Incident of 1933. In particular, members of the Tijaniyya Sufi order, the origins of which can be traced to North Africa, rallied under the leadership of Kemal Pilavoğlu (1906–1977) and publicly protested the new law by loudly reciting the *ezan* and chanting *tekbir*s in Arabic around 1946 to 1950. As a result, they were sentenced to imprisonment per the terms of the law. Aside from the people who suffered the consequences of breaking the law, many journalists and even statesmen criticised the policy, especially after the transition to a multi-party system in 1945.

However, opposition to the Turkish *ezan* became more palpable towards the 1950s. Thousands of people, for instance, had gathered for the funeral prayers of Marshal Fevzi Çakmak (1876–1950) on 12 April in 1950 at Eyüp Sultan Mosque, and many of them chanted *tekbir*s in Arabic. Ultimately, the funeral became a protest gathering, and some people were arrested for violating the law banning the recitation of the Arabic *tekbir*. One month later on 14 May, general elections were held, resulting in a victory for the Democrat Party (DP). One of the first actions undertaken by the new DP government concerned the Turkish *ezan*, and proposals were made to ensure its abolition before the month of Ramadan that year. As a result of a motion made by the DP, the abolition of the Turkish *ezan* was passed by Parliament on 16 June 1950. Following that decision, two statesmen, Refet Ülgen (1888–1964), a former deputy of the Republican People's Party (*Cumhuriyet Halk Partisi*, CHP), and Ahmed Hamdi Akseki, the head of the Diyanet mentioned above, wrote letters about the issue.

*Two Letters Concerning the Reversion of the Ezan from Turkish to Arabic**

The First Letter:

To the Attention of the Supreme Authority!

The recital of the *ezan* in [Arabic] has not resulted in positive effects among enlightened persons. It represents a setback. A particular supreme personage, who had been a dear friend of Atatürk's, should have prevented this from occurring.

As you know, closing the dervish lodges was a precautionary measure, but the recital of the *ezan* in Turkish was a revolution, a revolution carried out by Atatürk. Wouldn't it be reactionary, that is to say, *irtica* [fundamentalist reaction], to change it back to Arabic?

There is no such thing as a "language of religion" on earth and such a thing cannot exist. The expression "language of religion" is itself very commonplace and ignorant.

In summary, I would like to state that the recital of the *ezan* in [Arabic] is not a good move in favour of the democrats.

---

* Translated from the original Turkish documents in the Republican Archives (BCA) of the Directorate of State Archives. See BCA, 30.1.0.0 (Başbakanlık Özel Kalem Müdürlüğü): 41.242.2; BCA, 51.0.0.0 (Diyanet İşleri Reisliği): 4.31.3.

It has caused many who are filled with love and respect to worry, and it has made them feel discouraged and even turn away. I hereby present this missive with my deepest respects.

Refet Ülgen
Former deputy of Urfa
16 June 1950

The Second Letter:

To the offices of the Mufti,

It is a scientific and religious truth that the *ezan* and the *kamet* are not just notifications, but declarations and announcements concerning prayer times by means of special words that were approved of by the Prophet. That is proved by the Qur'an and the Sunnah.

Since "particular words" are elements of the *ezan* and a prerequisite for its correctness, if terms other than those particular words are used, it cannot be deemed legitimate, even in the case of the most accurate translation.

The fact that the abolition of the prohibition of reciting the *ezan* in its original form, which is pure religious worship—in other words, the Grand National Assembly's overturning of the ban on the recital of the *ezan* and *kamet* in the "language of religion"—brought great relief to the citizenry and gladdened their hearts. That has been demonstrated by letters sent from various parts of the country.

Upon the notification hereby made in this context, on the basis of information procured about the situation in your city/district, it has been deemed necessary to indicate from what day and time it was put into practice, whether there are muezzins who do not know how to read the *ezan* in their own way and in the "language of religion," and if there are such [persons] what measures have been taken in this regard.

Ahmed Hamdi Akseki
Head of Religious Affairs
23 June 1950

***

These two letters, which present two very different views, were penned following the declaration of the abolition of the Turkish *ezan*. Refet Ülgen, the former deputy, wrote the first letter in İstanbul and sent it to Ankara. It would appear that he hurriedly wrote the letter on the day that Parliament abolished the law (16 June), as there are some mistakes in the letter; for example, the word "Turkish" was used instead of the word "Arabic" (those errors were corrected in the translation of the letter presented above by means of brackets). In his letter, Ülgen, who was a deputy in Parliament when the law about the Turkish *ezan* was passed, made it clear that he was addressing Celal Bayar (1883–1986), who was president at the time, not Prime Minister Adnan Menderes (1899–1961), by way of his reminder about Bayar's friendship with Mustafa Kemal Atatürk (1881–1938). In doing so, he was directly requesting the authorities to back down on their decision. Notably, in his letter Ülgen made reference to the disappointment felt by "enlightened people" who were followers of the revolutions carried out by Atatürk.

While refuting the phrase "language of religion," Ülgen stressed the issue of returning to Arabic. "Language of religion" (*din dili*) was a common description used in those days, as those who critiqued the Turkish call to prayer highlighted the importance of the original form of the *ezan*, asserting it must be recited in the language of Islam. Like-minded people also tended to avoid using the word "Arabic" when rejecting the Turkish *ezan*. Some figures, such as Ömer Rıza Doğrul (1893–1952), explicitly stated that the language of the *ezan* was not Arabic per se, but rather the language of Islam. On 5 June 1950, newly elected Prime Minister Menderes himself used the phrase "language of religion" in an interview with the newspaper *Zafer*. Menderes stated that insisting on the Turkish *ezan* went against freedom of conscience and resulted in a strange contradiction with prayers made in the "language of religion" at mosques. In this regard, Ülgen's rejection and denigration of the term should be examined within the context of the arguments that were being put forward in that period.

The second letter represents a circular that was to be sent to muftis in Turkey, but the author's inclusion of a description about how the decision to abolish the prohibition on reciting the Arabic *ezan* "gladdened" the hearts of the people is striking. Ahmed Hamdi Akseki, who had already played a role in policies of Turkification targeting religious matters in the early Republican era, now openly expressed his opinions about the reversion of the *ezan* to Arabic. In his letter, he seems to be making an urgent call to have the language of the *ezan* changed back to the "language of religion". In doing so, he stresses the fallaciousness of translating the original form of the *ezan* and states that the "particular words" (*elfaz-ı mahsusa*) of the *ezan* came from the Prophet. Moreover, Akseki asserts that "people from various parts of the country" were pleased by Parliament's decision. In a similar manner, newspapers of the time also cited examples of such satisfaction being expressed in different cities and ran news stories about how the decision was greeted with a positive response. Unlike Ülgen, who based his arguments on the tenets of Kemalism, Akseki avoided mentioning Atatürk, as did others who refuted the policy by separating the implementation of the law concerning the Turkish *ezan* from Kemalist reforms and interpreting Atatürk's "real intentions" about the call to prayer from a different viewpoint. In contrast, Akseki based his views on what he perceived to be the wishes of the general public.

***

The two letters presented here, both of which were written by members of the elite of early Republican Turkey, provide a useful summary of the split that existed between secular Kemalists and conservative nationalists in Turkey. However, the abolition of the Turkish *ezan* was widely accepted in the country, and despite some rather individual proposals that were made during the military coups that took place in subsequent decades, the *ezan* has been recited in its original form—in Arabic—since June of 1950.

Nonetheless, the reversion of the *ezan* from Turkish to Arabic should not be taken up as a victory scored by conservatives/Islamists over secularists/Kemalists in the management of the state. Rather, it might be more useful to bear in mind that many of those who ultimately favoured the reversion of the *ezan* had played a significant role in state affairs in the period of time when the law concerning the Turkish *ezan* had been passed and they had approved of the decision, whether enthusiastically or not. It is also worthy of note that the law was repealed not only on the basis of votes cast by the deputies of the DP, but also those of the CHP, in good grace or otherwise. Given that situation, the issue should also be evaluated in light of public opinion. In that sense, emphasis should be placed on the fact that Ülgen expressed his dissatisfaction with the decision to repeal the law on behalf of the "enlightened" segment of society by stressing the importance of Kemalist reforms. Akseki, on the other hand, defended the "righteousness" of the decision by citing the positive responses of the country's citizenry. Ultimately, the reversion of the *ezan* from Turkish to Arabic came about as a consequence of the transition to a multi-party system, which made it essential to heed public opinion and consider the religious sensibilities of the people. As such, the case of the Turkish *ezan* is yet another example of how the demands of the periphery were becoming increasingly important for the centre within the context of the global-historical developments that were occurring in the Cold War era.

Select Bibliography

Azak, Umut. *Islam and Secularism in Turkey: Kemalism, Religion and the Nation State.* London: I.B. Tauris, 2010.

Kara, İsmail, and Rabia K. Gündoğdu. *Diyanet İşleri Başkanı Ahmet Hamdi Akseki: Hayatı, Mücadelesi ve Eserleri.* Vol. 1. Ankara: Diyanet İşleri Başkanlığı Yayınları, 2019.

Danforth, Nicholas L. *The Remaking of Republican Turkey: Memory and Modernity Since the Fall of the Ottoman Empire.* Cambridge: Cambridge University Press, 2021.

Zürcher, Erik-Jan. *The Young Turk Legacy and Nation Building: From the Ottoman Empire to Atatürk's Turkey.* London: I.B. Tauris, 2010.

29
"The Sincerest Feeling of all the Peace-Loving Turkish People": Pacifism and the Korean War

Nadav Solomonovich

The Korean War started on 25 June 1950 when thousands of troops from the Democratic People's Republic of Korea (North Korea) crossed the thirty-eighth parallel and invaded the Republic of Korea (South Korea). The United Nations Security Council, led by the United States, passed Resolution 83, calling on UN members to assist South Korea. As a result, sixteen countries sent infantry brigades or battalions to Korea. On 25 July, a month after the outbreak of the war and after consulting US representatives, the Turkish cabinet, the Turkish Chief of Staff, and the president of the Republic, Celal Bayar, met in Ankara. At the end of the meeting, they announced that Turkey would send an armed unit consisting of 4,500 soldiers to Korea to fight as part of the UN forces. Although it was denied by Turkish politicians at the time, the decision was aimed at improving Turkey's chances of being accepted into NATO. Between 1950 and the signing of the armistice in 1953, about 14,936 Turkish soldiers participated in the war as part of three rotating brigades; 721 of them fell in battle, and 2,147 were injured. While the Turkish public largely supported the war effort, there were some who publicly objected to it and were persecuted as a result. The "Peace-Lovers Association" (*Barış Severler Cemiyeti*), which had been established in İstanbul just a few weeks earlier under the leadership of former Ankara University professor Behice Boran (1910–1987), sent a telegram to the Turkish Parliament expressing its disapproval of the decision to take part in the war, but ultimately joined the ranks of those whose oppositional voices were silenced in those years.

*Telegram from the Turkish Peace-Lovers Association to the Presidency of the Grand National Assembly**

Immediately after American senator Mr. Cain contacted state officials, the Council of Ministers decided to send an armed force of 4,500 troops to Korea, causing both excitement and sadness among the public. Although the government stated that this decision was made to fulfil commitments made to the United Nations, it goes against both the Turkish Constitution and the United Nations Constitution, because Article 43 of the United Nations Constitution stipulates the existence of certain special agreements made

---

* Translated from the original Turkish in Behice Boran and Adnan Cemgil, "Türk Barışseverler Cemiyetinin B.M.M. Başkanlığına Çektiği Telegraf," *Barış*, 1 August 1950, 11.

in advance concerning the armed intervention of countries included in the council in any conflict. However, there is no special agreement on this issue between the Turkish nation and the United Nations. Moreover, in accordance with the aforementioned article of the United Nations constitution, these special agreements are made by signatory states. Each of them must be ratified in line with the procedures of the constitution. It seems that, let alone sending armed forces, the government has to obtain the approval of the Turkish Grand National Assembly for any agreement it might make in this regard.

With the decision to send ground troops to Korea, the Turkish government decided to declare war, although this was not explicitly stated. However, since the authority to declare war in accordance with the Turkish constitution rests exclusively with the Turkish Grand National Assembly, the government has exceeded its authority in making this decision, which is extremely dangerous for the future and security of the country and does not comply with the provisions of the constitution.

The Turkish Peace-Lovers Association, holding to the belief that it expresses the sincerest feeling of all the peace-loving Turkish people at the moment, wishes that instead of actually participating in the armed conflict in Korea in this way, Turkey would try to stop the war and save world peace from danger through peaceful initiatives like those of the Indian government. Our association conveys its deep respect and hope that your esteemed office will invite the Turkish Grand National Assembly to a special meeting so that the government's decision, which runs contrary to our national interests and the United Nations Constitution, will be cancelled as soon as possible.

President   General Secretary
Dr Behice Boran   Adnan Cemgil

***

The Peace-Lovers Association was the main organisation in Turkey that objected to the country's participation in the war. Immediately after the decision was announced by the government, the association sent the above telegram to the Grand National Assembly and on 28 July protested the decision, distributing a pamphlet that addressed the Turkish public in an effort to gain support for their position in opposition to the war. While the telegram focused on legal concerns as to why the decision was unconstitutional, the pamphlet addressed the public's emotions. It accused the government of placing "Turkish children" under the command of General MacArthur in Korea for the sake of "American interests," suggesting that the decision might provoke some of Turkey's neighbours (there was a fear of retaliation by Soviet satellite states such as Bulgaria), and even speculated that the Korean War might lead to the outbreak of a Third World War. The association thus called on Parliament to cancel the decision and adopt a more peaceful solution, such as following in the footsteps of Jawaharlal Nehru, the prime minister of India.

The government was quick to retaliate. Given that Boran had already been a member of Turkey's banned Communist Party for some time and that the Peace-Lovers Association was closely aligned with Moscow's policies, Adnan Menderes (1899–1961), the prime minister, used the press to accuse the organisation of having international roots and a hidden agenda. Similarly, Foreign Minister Fuad Köprülü (1890–1966) attacked the association with accusations, saying that it was disseminating Communist propaganda. On 29 July, a day after their demonstration, the president of the organisation, Behice Boran, the general secretary, Adnan Cemgil (1909–2001), and Vahdettin Barut, a lawyer who served on the organisation's executive board, were arrested along with Cemal Anıl, the owner of the printing house, for disseminating "a publication aimed at harming national interests and weakening national strength". The organisation was banned and on 30 December 1950, its leaders, including Boran and leftist high school teacher Adnan Cemgil, were sentenced to jail for three years and nine months. Other members were sentenced to shorter periods of imprisonment, while the owner of the printing house was acquitted. The authorities harassed members of the organisation even after the trial had ended and an appeal had been submitted. The organisation's members were eventually released after spending fifteen months in prison. However, that was not the only instance in which the state tried to silence opposition to the war. In August 1950, a number of satirical magazines based in İstanbul, Ankara, and İzmir were closed down because they published articles and cartoons that were critical of the troop deployment in Korea. In December 1950, when Turkish troops were already fighting in Korea, the Grand National Assembly—in which the Democrat Party held a large majority—approved the decision that had been made in July.

However, ratification of the decision did not increase the DP's tolerance of criticism. When two MPs from the Republican People's Party (*Cumhuriyet Halk Partisi*, CHP) criticised Turkey's involvement in the war in 1951, official complaints were submitted to parliament by none other than Prime Minister Menderes and the minister of justice. However, both were acquitted by a special subcommittee of the constitutional committee and justice commission.

***

On 18 February 1952, Turkey was officially accepted into NATO. The decision to send troops to Korea and join the war had thus achieved its purpose. After her release from prison, Boran remained an influential figure among left-wing circles and later supported the Soviet invasion of Czechoslovakia, thus leading to a split in the Workers Party of Turkey (*Türkiye İşçi Partisi*, TKP). While the Korean War was met with surprisingly little public resistance in the West, the Peace-Lovers Association was not the only such group to oppose the war. The pro-Communist Women's International Democratic Federation, established in Paris in 1945, voiced its objections to the war and also sent a commission to "investigate war atrocities in Korea". The Peace-Lovers Association was not the last group to be subjected to state persecution by the Turkish state after publicly calling on it to adopt a more peaceful stance in the case of armed conflicts. The Turkish Peace Association (*Barış Derneği*), which was founded in İstanbul in April 1977 and called for Turkey's withdrawal from NATO as well as for nuclear disarmament, was closed down after the coup of 1980. In 1982, its leading members were accused of being pro-Soviet agents aiming to destabilise Turkey, and they were subsequently put on trial. The founders and directors of the association were released at the end of the same year, and they were acquitted after a trial that lasted until 1991. On 11 January 2016, 1,128 academicians in Turkey and abroad signed a petition calling on the Turkish authorities to cease state violence in the mainly Kurdish-populated areas of the country, which were under curfew and an extended state of emergency. In what seems like a move from the Democrat Party's playbook, President Recep Tayyip Erdoğan (1954–) immediately reacted by accusing the signatories of treason and terrorist propaganda. He subsequently demanded that public prosecutors launch an investigation. However, by October 2019, more than three hundred Peace Petition signatories had reportedly been acquitted. Nevertheless, supporting peace, it seems, remains a dangerous business in Turkey to this day.

Select Bibliography

Brockett, Gavin D. "The Legend of 'The Turk' in Korea: Popular Perceptions of the Korean War and Their Importance to a Turkish National Identity." *War & Society* 22, no. 2 (2004): 109–42.

Selek, Pınar. *Barışamadık*. İstanbul: İthaki Yayınları, 2004.

Solomonovich, Nadav. *The Korean War in Turkish Culture and Society*. Cham: Palgrave-Macmillan, 2021.

Tuğtan, Mehmet Ali, ed. *Kore Savaşı: Uzak Savaşın Askerleri*. İstanbul: İstanbul Bilgi Üniversitesi Yayınları, 2013.

30
Beekeeping, Agriculture, and Democracy: The Debate over Cold War Modernity

Nicholas Danforth

Turkey's transition to a multi-party democracy at the outset of the Cold War coincided with its embrace of the United States as a new ally, culminating with NATO membership in 1952. These two changes reconfigured ongoing Turkish debates about the nature of modernity in ways that continue to reverberate today. American academics and statesmen were eager to promote a distinctly liberal vision of modernity while constantly recalibrating it to align with American interests. Their Turkish counterparts, in turn, used the US as both a model and a foil to advance their own agendas. Thus, a shared conviction in the fundamental relationship between democracy, technology, and material prosperity led to heated disagreements over what that meant in practice.

During the 1950s, the question of modernity touched on all aspects of society, from running a government to combatting a bee infestation. The following transcript, which is from a Voice of America radio broadcast, sought to convince Turkish farmers to take advantage of new technical programs being offered by Ankara and Washington.

*Agricultural Talks**

Chief: "What has happened to you, Mr. Ahmet? Your face and eyes are swollen?

Ahmet: Don't ask, Chief, those bees are killing me! I am aching all over....

Chief: Have you ever applied to the Agricultural Center for help?

Ahmet: Five years ago I called the Agricultural Center to talk about this problem...

Chief: Did you do what he told you to?... The important point is you can't do this alone. All of the bee farmers must fight this thing together.

* "Agricultural Talks," 11 June, 1952. Voice of America Daily Broadcast Content Reports and Script Translations, 1950–1955. Box 44, Record Group 306, National Archives and Records Administration.

Ahmet: Our neighbors, Recep, Omeri, Satilmi and many others did not believe in [following the Agricultural Center's advice]. "This is what we have learned from our fathers," they said...

Chief: [But now] most of the bee-farmers in your village have children who have been to school. Do you know that last year we opened a course on bee-culture?

Ahmet: Last year I went to my son's wedding in Eskishehir and I couldn't take the course.

Chief: Never mind. There will be courses on bee-culture this year too. They will teach you about scientific bee-culture and how to extract honey and what to do about the enemies of bees. You will benefit from these courses if you take them.

Ahmet: This time I hope nothing will prevent me. I want very much to take these courses, really.

Chief: You see, Mr. Ahmet, as the number of educated people grows and the number of bee-farmers who take these courses increases, the number of scientific bee farmers will grow in proportion. Then these hornets won't have a chance. Meanwhile, you do what the farm expert told you.... The Agricultural center will help all of you in this task.

Ahmet: You gave me courage, Chief. I feel as if I can forget the pain caused by the hornets' stinging.

***

The Truman Plan of 1947 marked the beginning of a massive influx of American military, technical, and financial assistance into Turkey. American policymakers believed that by modernising all aspects of Turkish society, from the armed forces to the agricultural economy, they could help the country better resist Soviet designs. To aid such efforts, in Turkey and elsewhere social scientists worked to integrate their understanding of cultural and technological transformation into a broader "modernisation theory," often using Turkey as a field site for their research. Meanwhile, US diplomats strived to inculcate a new, more "modern" mindset among Turkish citizens to speed up the country's progress—while also making its citizens better appreciate America's value as an ally.

In that context, American radio broadcasts like the Voice of America skit quoted above consistently sought to demonstrate the value of American technical expertise in improving the lives of ordinary Turkish villagers. Other programs that aired on Voice of America during this period included "Turkey Attends the American Classroom," which featured the profiles of Turkish exchange students in the US, and "Here are the Answers," which tackled listener's questions such as, "When was nylon invented and who invented it?"; "How long will the Cold War last?"; "Will it be possible to form a world nation?"; "Is there a remedy against snoring"; and, "How can a 17-year-old man become a woman?" From beehives to the battlefield to the basketball court, "American propaganda" (and that was the term Americans themselves used) stressed that there was a modern way of doing things and America could teach it.

After 1950, this approach initially seemed to fit quite well with the ambitions of Turkey's newly-elected Democrat Party (*Demokrat Parti*). The party sought to convince Turkish voters that by means of tractors, roads, and dams, they would modernise rural Turkey and deliver the material prosperity that had been promised but never delivered by the Kemalist regime. Moreover, they emphasised that democracy itself would ensure the realisation of such progress. In their speeches, Adnan Menderes and his fellow party members told villagers that while the previous government had ignored them, that would no longer be possible. After "twenty-seven years" of "no one listening to our voices nor hearing our local needs," Menderes told an audience in Kocaeli on 12 September 1952, "we now have a state that listens to our troubles, that offers us all kinds of aid." In a free country, he explained to another audience in Bolu in December 1952, if his party had not delivered, "Your criticism would have burned us like flames from the mouth of an oven."

***

In theory, the model was elegant. The Menderes government and its American partners would offer the Turkish people modernity and be rewarded with their political and geopolitical loyalty. Initially, everything seemed to be going as planned. The post-war Turkish economy experienced substantial growth. New "scientific" agricultural techniques boosted crop yields across Anatolia, while the mass media, in the form of new newspapers and magazines, blossomed. Yet the limits of this model were quick to emerge. New technologies like tractors tore away the topsoil, leading recently expanded crops like wheat to fail. Farmers who had put their faith in scientific agriculture found themselves struggling, and some began to use the country's American-funded roads to migrate to the cities. For American observers, the dams that Menderes was fond of opening with much fanfare started to seem less like evidence of his modern spirit and more like signs of irresponsible populism. When constituents began to voice complaints of their own, Menderes found the flames to be a little too hot, and he began arresting his critics.

Indeed, Americans' abstract commitment to democratic modernity could prove malleable in its application. While it subsequently became an article of faith that Washington had pressured the Republican People's Party (*Cumhuriyet Halk Partisi*, CHP) to hold free elections in 1950, US archives reveal no evidence of such pressure. And as the Menderes government became increasingly authoritarian during the course of the 1950s, diplomats found ways to convince themselves that those setbacks were understandable, even unavoidable, in a society making a rapid transition from tradition to modernity. So long as Menderes remained a loyal ally, even concerns about his "exploitation of religion" were readily dismissed as being "in line with worldwide trends."

Inevitably, Menderes's opponents had their own ideas about modernity. As a young journalist, future Prime Minister Bülent Ecevit (1925-2006) participated in a four-month internship with a newspaper in Winston Salem, North Carolina. He charmed his hosts, but failed to draw all the conclusions that his State Department sponsors had hoped he would arrive at. Upon returning to Turkey to carry on with his regular newspaper column, Ecevit criticised the Democrat Party for failing to live up to the democratic principles he observed in America—but at the same time he also criticised the US for violating those very principles by supporting the party regardless of its failings. Nonetheless, Ecevit remained confident that as Turkish society became more modern, the values that his party had once sought to force upon the population would eventually be embraced by voters of their own accord. In an article he wrote for the newspaper *Ulus* on 5 May 1954, Ecevit argued that "[i]n Turkey, every person who learns to read and write...is a new hope for the CHP and a new threat to the Democratic Party.... In the single-party era, the Six Arrows were imposed on the people. In the multi-party era, the Six Arrows must originate from the people!"

When Menderes was toppled by a military coup in 1960, some American observers again recalibrated their understanding of modernity accordingly. As a result of American aid, the military, for many, had become the most modernised and modernising segment of Turkish society. Evaluating the coup for the Brookings Institution, political scientist Walter Weiker concluded by saying that although the United States "cannot look with benign approval on military usurpation of power...[t]he questions whether and to what extent the United States might encourage continuation of military or one-party governments...are extremely difficult ones."

Viewed from today, the legacy of early Cold War debates on modernity continues to reverberate in Turkish politics. Even as the US remains a consistent reference point in articulating visions of social and technological progress, its motives, particularly as they relate to Turkey, are now viewed with a deep and almost universal suspicion. Yet the conviction articulated by politicians and voters during this period concerning how modernity is inextricably linked to competitive electoral democracy has proven to be remarkably enduring in the face of past and present challenges.

Select Bibliography

Adalet, Begüm. *Hotels and Highways: The Construction of Modernization Theory in Cold War Turkey*. Stanford: Stanford University Press, 2018.

Athanassopoulou, Ekavi. *Turkey-Anglo-American Security Interests, 1945–1952: The First Enlargement of NATO*. London: Frank Cass, 1999.

Aydemir, Şevket Süreyya. *Menderes'in Dramı*. İstanbul: Yükselen Matbaası, 1969.

Danforth, Nicholas. *The Remaking of Republican Turkey: Memory and Modernity Since the Fall of the Ottoman Empire*. London: Cambridge University Press, 2021.

Gilman, Nils. *Mandarins of the Future: Modernization Theory in Cold War America*. Baltimore: Johns Hopkins University Press, 2003.

Gürel, Perin. *The Limits of Westernization: A Cultural History of America in Turkey*. New York: Columbia University Press, 2017.

1953–1962

31
"Male Beauty Kings":
Gender, Biopolitics, and Pageantry
in the Annals of İstanbul

Müge Özoğlu

While physical training had become a popular pastime by the end of the nineteenth century, the rhetoric of creating a healthy and robust nation consolidated team sports and gymnastics in the early years of the Republic of Turkey. Training and disciplining the body was an essential mission of the state, in part to invert the Ottoman Empire's reputation as the "Sick Man of Europe" during the years of the single-party regime (1923–1950), and body politics was a significant concern as it related to the prosperity of the nation. In the 1930s, eugenics gained in popularity and facilitated the regulation of the human body in the recently established nation-state. The Physical Education Law (*Beden Terbiyesi Kanunu*) was introduced in 1938, aiming to increase the physical activities of citizens. Of course, regulation of the human body through sports was not unique to the Republic of Turkey in the early twentieth century. From Scandinavian countries like Denmark in the 1910s to Germany in the 1920s and Eastern Bloc countries in the 1950s, gymnastics played an important role in nationalist projects.

As early as 1926, Robust Child Competitions (*Gürbüz Çocuk Yarışmaları*) started to be organised to foster the progeniture of healthy generations. The importance of the human body and the physical training thereof brought about a novel understanding of beauty and aesthetics, as beauty was often equated with healthy corporality. In addition to sports competitions and gymnastics, beauty contests were organised as well. The first beauty contests for women were organised between 1929 and 1932, but they came to a halt by the 1950s. Still, newly emergent political and medical discourses surrounding the human body continued to resound in the 1950s and eventually beauty contests for women resumed. The 1950s was also the decade in which male body beauty contests started to be held. The men who participated in these contests displayed their muscular, trained bodies, which represented an ideal of male corporal beauty as configured by the Turkish nation-state in terms of being healthy and robust.

Sources on these male body beauty contests are few and far between. Nevertheless, like many other often unremembered historical events that occurred in İstanbul, the contests were included in the *İstanbul Ansiklopedisi* (*Encyclopaedia of İstanbul*), a unique collection of works produced by Reşad Ekrem Koçu (1905–1975), an intriguing historian and writer. The encyclopaedia contains a wide array of captivating content covering various historical periods in Ottoman and more recent Turkish history. In addition to entries on İstanbul's architecture and urban structure, Koçu provided an abundance of niche information and fascinating details about the city concerning a broad range of issues including murders, fires, and thefts as well as interesting figures such as bath attendants, roughnecks, dancers, and the young street traders of the city. The entry on male body beauty contests appears in volume ten of the *İstanbul Ansiklopedisi*. Like several other entries in which the author's particular interest in beautiful boys and young men resonates, Koçu did not miss the opportunity to include male body beauty contests in the encyclopaedia either. The following is an excerpt from the entry on those contests.

Male Body Beauty Contests*

[Male body beauty] contests, which have a quite long history in Europe and America, were held among young men whose muscular bodies were cultured via various gymnastic activities and apparatuses, and the private gymnastic houses organising these contests had numberless illustrated periodicals such as "Muscle Power," "Muscle Builder," "Modern Phyrique" [*sic*], "Adonis," "Body Beautiful," "Body Beautiful" [*sic*] and "Mr. America". Our first male body beauty contest was organised in 1955 by Tagar Gymnastics House [which was] established in 1952 in İstanbul.... [These contests] were organised every year until 1959, [and after] having a break for seven years between 1960 and 1966, the sixth context was organised in 1967.

Contests took place in the gymnasium of the Tagar establishment in the presence of special invitation [*sic*] [guests] and the families of the young athletes. The participants in the contests were young men working at the Tagar Gymnastics House and men who devoted themselves to the sport of body building as amateurs. Some among them placed in the competition and were chosen for first place [for having] the most beautiful muscular body of the year and [being] male beauty kings by a selection committee that had full authority on the matter. Trophies were awarded to the first, second and third best in each contest [category]. Participation in the contests [required that the men be] naked except for a swimsuit.

The participants who rang in the [first place] bell in the initial five contests were as follows:
1955, Erdal Kaya, 25-year-old engineer
1956, Mahmud Mola, 22-year-old driver
1957, Mahmud Mola, 23-year-old driver
1958, Mahmud Mola, 24-year-old driver
1959, Yusuf Haleplioğlu, 24-year-old gymnastics teacher

The three young men out of twelve [participants] who placed in the competition organised in 1967 were as follows:

* Translated from the original Turkish in Reşad Ekrem Koçu, "Erkek Vücudu Güzellik Müsabakası," in *İstanbul Ansiklopedisi*, ed. Reşad Ekrem Koçu (İstanbul: Koçu Yayınları, 1971), 5192–93.

First place: Ahmed Enünlü, 19 years old, a student at Kabataş High School

Second place: Murad Sevim, 33 years old, married, a baker

Third place: Rafet Munla, 21 years old, a student at the Technical University

Ahmet Enünlü was born and raised on Büyükada, Murad Sevim was from Samsun, and Rafet Munla was from Syria.

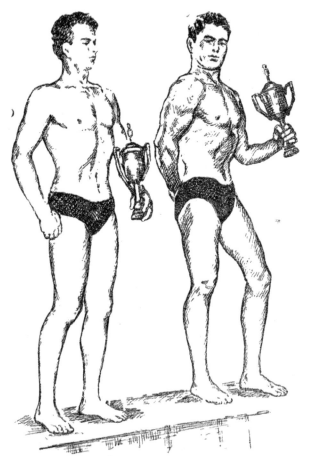

Yusuf Haleplioğlu (Sağda) ve o yarışmada ikinci olan delikanlı
(Resim: S. Bozcalı)

The entry on male body beauty contests provides information about a topic that would otherwise be difficult to track down. After presenting a brief discussion of similar contests held in Europe and the United States, it then provides details about the ages, occupations, education, and origin of the winners of the contests organised by the Tagar Gymnastic House in İstanbul from 1955 onward. Having a muscular body that was "cultured via various gymnastic activities and apparatuses" appears to have been the main criterion for the beauty of the male body. Moreover, having a "beautiful body" seems to have been closely related to being young, as almost all of the winners were in their early twenties. Like many of the other illustrations in the encyclopaedia, the illustration for this entry was drawn by Sabiha Rüştü Bozcalı (1904–1998); she was a major illustrator in the twentieth-century art scene of Turkey and influential as well. The drawing portrays Yusuf Haleplioğlu, the winner of the 1959 contest, along with the second-place winner as they received their trophies onstage. As the illustration depicts, the near-naked bodies on display were objectified in these contests and presented as such to spectators.

In addition to presenting such suggestive subject matter revolving around male bodies and the beauty therein, the entry also hints at a further political project of the newly established Turkish nation-state which prioritised the cultivation of robust, healthy bodies. In other words, the entry includes traces of how the state sought to control and use the bodies of its citizens as an ideological apparatus to create a stronger nation starting from the early years of the Republic of Turkey. The ways in which the *İstanbul Ansiklopedisi* reveals certain kinds of historical information and politics—in this case, biopolitics—at times merging it with entertaining content is not unique to this entry on male body beauty contests. Such a mingling of history, politics, and entertainment is, in fact, the most prominent feature of the encyclopaedia, enabling different modes of reading the content. Either way, whether one reads the entry merely as a source of information about male body beauty contests or as a source that remarks on state politics and its utilisation of the body for political purposes, Koçu provided specific information that is not easy to find in other sources on Turkish history. As such, this entry on male body beauty contests epitomises how Koçu looked at and wrote about the past from a vantage point which differed from that of his contemporaries.

***

These contests, which were organised to promote male body beauty, produced more than one outcome. In addition to publicising and consolidating the rhetoric of healthy citizens and a healthy nation, they constructed a new perception of beauty for male corporality. The regulation of the male body via physical training and the naked exhibition and objectification thereof brought together the politics of health created by the state and notions of male corporal beauty. In this way, Koçu's *İstanbul Ansiklopedisi* is a rich source of information about one way that this convergence occurred.

Koçu built up his encyclopaedia through his collection of materials, which ranged from newspaper clippings to photographs that he collected, materials that in those years conventional historiographies would not primarily have used. Moving beyond a conventional lexicography, Koçu's investment in material culture and use of ephemeral material in the creation of the encyclopaedia transformed it into a rather unique work. It offers an alternative version of Turkish historiography in the mid-twentieth century that differs from the state-shaped historiographies taught at schools. Koçu started to publish *İstanbul Ansiklopedisi* in 1944 but had to stop at the letter B in 1951 for seven years due to financial difficulties. He resumed work on the encyclopaedia in 1958, at which time he also revised the previously published sections. Koçu published thirty-four fascicles between 1944 and 1951 and 173 fascicles between 1958 and 1973, and those fascicles were then compiled as encyclopaedic volumes. In 1973, he ultimately reached the letter G, with an entry entitled "Gökçınar" in volume eleven, and he left behind drafts for the remaining volumes. While Koçu himself wrote the majority of the entries in *İstanbul Ansiklopedisi*, he also received help from his friends and colleagues, such as Semavi Eyice (1922–2018) and Kevork Pamukciyan (1923–1996).

The entry on male body beauty contests in *İstanbul Ansiklopedisi* demonstrates the ways in which discourses on politics, health, and beauty intersected in the 1950s. In addition to being a source for Ottoman and more recent Turkish history, the encyclopaedia itself is historical material that enables an observation of Koçu's history writing. Koçu added his own comments in places and personalised the entries in the encyclopaedia, which helped him convey his perceptions of the past. Moreover, it allows us to understand what a historian like Koçu, who had witnessed the political transition from empire to nation-state and the changing urban texture of İstanbul within that transition, found interesting or necessary enough to include in an encyclopaedia about the city. In brief, Koçu's work is simultaneously a historical source and historical material in and of itself. Thus, the *İstanbul Ansiklopedisi* contributes to the cultural memory of the Ottoman Empire and the early years of the Republic of Turkey regarding both the subject matters it covers and as an object of study.

The *İstanbul Ansiklopedisi* is currently out of print. Work is underway to digitise the published volumes of the encyclopaedia as well as certain unpublished materials, including the author's personal archive, through a collaboration between SALT, a contemporary art institution, and Kadir Has University in İstanbul. The digitised encyclopaedia will be accessible to the public.

Select Bibliography

Alemdaroğlu, Ayça. "Politics of the Body and Eugenic Discourse in Early Republican Turkey." *Body & Society* 11, no. 3 (2005): 61–76.

Altınay, Rüstem Ertuğ. "The Queer Archivist as Political Dissident: Rereading the Ottoman Empire in the Works of Reşad Ekrem Koçu." *Radical History Review* 122 (2015): 89–102.

Boone, Joseph Allen. "Creating a Queer Archive in the Public Eye: The Case of Reşad Ekrem Koçu." *GLQ: A Journal of Lesbian and Gay Studies* 23, no. 1 (2017): 51–81.

Boone, Joseph Allen. *The Homoerotics of Orientalism.* New York: Columbia University Press, 2014.

Krawietz, Birgit. "Sport and Nationalism in the Republic of Turkey." *The International Journal of the History of Sport* 31, no. 3 (2014): 336–46.

32
"Religion is Bound to the State": Ali Fuat Başgil's Critique of Secularism

Umut Azak

Religion and Secularism (*Din ve Laiklik*, 1954) was one of the first analytical assessments of the concept of secularism and the first scholarly critique of Kemalist secularist policies in Turkey. The work was penned by Ali Fuat Başgil (1893–1967), a professor of law who, like many other conservative intellectuals active in the 1940s and 1950s, cherished democracy above all as a means of doing away with state restrictions on citizens' freedom of religion. After the transition from the single-party regime to multi-party democracy in the mid-1940s, Kemalist policies, such as the requirement that the call to prayer be recited in Turkish and that institutions of Islamic education be closed down, were opened up to critique; and within the ranks of the Republican People's Party (*Cumhuriyet Halk Partisi*, CHP) and the emerging opposition, it became possible to openly assert that certain state policies were anti-democratic or unresponsive to the needs of the country's predominantly Muslim population. From May 1950 onwards, the government under the leadership of the Democrat Party (*Demokrat Parti*, DP) became a channel by means of which calls for reform could be voiced in the name of democracy. While DP leaders adopted a new position vis-à-vis Islam (such as removing the ban on the Arabic call to prayer, increasing the number of mosques in the country, changing the regulation on taking elective religion courses from "opt in" to "opt out," and opening state schools that trained preachers and prayer leaders), their intention was not to remove the constitutional principle of secularism, but rather to redefine it through public statements and policies. Instead of rejecting secularism per se, they reformulated and revised it in such a way that freedom of religion, i.e., freedom from state restrictions on worship, which Başgil saw as a violation of law and justice, became the new motto of secularism.

Başgil studied law in France and received his doctoral degree from the University of Paris. In 1930, he started teaching at faculties of law in İstanbul and Ankara as a professor of constitutional law, and he continued to do so until he was removed from his post along with 146 other academicians in the aftermath of the military coup of 1960. While in the 1930s he supported the statist policies of the CHP, from the mid-1940s onwards he began taking a different tack, championing democracy and taking a staunchly anti-communist position. In addition to engaging in anti-communist advocacy for democracy via the Society for Spreading Free Thought (*Hür Fikirleri Yayma Cemiyeti*), he also gave lectures on the subject of freedom of religion. Those lectures, which were published in the pro-government newspaper *Yeni Sabah* from May to June of 1950 during the first weeks of the rule of the new DP government, were compiled into a book that was published in 1954. The passage below is from the third and fourth sections of the book, which the author revised in 1962 and which became an essential point of reference for conservative critiques of early republican secularism as well as for a recasting of secularism with a fresh emphasis on the freedom of worship of the majority.

What Does Secularism Mean?[*]

Secularism in contemporary Western law entails the separation of religion and the state and the latter's non-interference in religious affairs, and similarly the non-interference of religion in the affairs of the state; the neutral position of the state regarding existing and recognised religions and sects in such a way that none are privileged by the state at the expense of another; and the simultaneous prevalence of religion as an order of ethical and spiritual life that is independent of the state, albeit relatively speaking. [...] Thus, secularism is neither the denial of, nor hostility against, religion; rather, it means abiding in governmental affairs and public relations only to the logic of the flow of life and expediencies while leaving religious rules and principles to the domain of the pious and the individual conscience.

[...] Today, it is impossible to reinforce old religious law. [...] [To insist on such a possibility] would perpetuate the struggles and clashes on the issue of religion, which would be detrimental for both religion and the public. In Islam, all actions which are detrimental to the public are deemed inappropriate and [hence] forbidden.

[...] Religion and the state, once separated from each other, should never be insignificant to or alienated from one another. [...] Both religion and the state exist for the sake of the welfare, security, peace, and comfort of the individual. Religion regulates individuals' inner worlds, while the state regulates external affairs. How happy are those countries in whose territories places of worship [*mabed*] and the government walk arm in arm like friends treading the same path.

[...] In addition, under secular regimes the non-interference of the state in religion means that the state does not intervene in religious affairs with regard to belief, worship, or educational activities, nor does it consider the provisions of any specific religion to be a guide for its own affairs.

This does not mean, however, that in a country such as Turkey where the great majority of the population is Muslim that the state should not engage in providing services to religious organisations and the religious needs of the people. The primary principle of a people's government is that it works for the people. Therefore, it is the duty of a people's government to take the people's religious needs into consideration and fulfil them.

---

[*] Translated from the Turkish original in Ali Fuad Başgil, *Din ve Laiklik* (İstanbul: Kubbealtı Neşriyâtı, 1998), 159–88.

[...] If speaking the truth shall not be deemed a crime, we can say without any doubts whatsoever that in Turkey today and in the last thirty years, there has been a system [in place] in which "religion [is] bound to the state". The Constitution of Turkey has been fully secularist since 1928 and on occasion our statesmen have expressed a sense of pride in the establishment of secularism in Turkey. Nevertheless, Turkey has not experienced secularism in the sense and form found in Western law. In the latter case, secularism is not a cover for veiling state interference in the affairs of religion and worship; rather, it is a strong guarantee for freedom of religion and of conscience. Nevertheless, here in our country, in opposition to [the notion of] secularism, religion with all its organisational aspects and personnel is under the command of the government and religion is firmly bound to the state.

***

Başgil's texts constituted the first Turkish work to systematically analyse the history of state-religion relations and secularism in both the Western context and in Turkey. His conceptual and historical survey of secularism was, as he elaborated on in his book, motivated by his opposition to atheism and his objective of proving the possibility of reconciling secularism and piousness. Inspired by the Western critique of materialism and the Enlightenment's approach to religion, Başgil pointed to an alternative West, i.e., a conservative philosophical tradition that approached religion as an essential individual and social need and the basis of moral and social order. Secularism, he believed, was necessary as a principle that protected such an essential need from all forms of government intervention. Specifically, Başgil's vindication of secularism originated in his commitment to the liberal principle of freedom of religion and hence his approach to secularism combined liberal democratic and conservative positions. According to Başgil, the existing secularist system in Turkey was similar to those that arose in the historical periods of ancient Rome, medieval Europe, the Russian Empire, and the Soviet Union, because, he argued, in all those periods, freedom of religion was restricted. The ban on the Arabic call to prayer, for instance, was argued to be an impingement on freedom of worship, which was incompatible with a secular system. Başgil's main inspiration was the tradition of Christian and conservative democracy in the West as well as what is called the "Anglo-Saxon model," which in his view proved the compatibility of secularism with religion on the condition that religious autonomy could be protected from state interference.

While Başgil advocated a complete separation between religion and the state, and hence the autonomy of the Directorate of Religious Affairs (*Diyanet İşleri Başkanlığı*, hereafter the Diyanet), he also envisioned a state where statesmen responded to the religious needs of the majority. In other words, although he criticised the existing system, in which religious matters were administered by the government via the Diyanet through a "flawed" system of religion that was "bound to" or "in the service" of the state, he did not see any problems with politicians' appeals to and promotion of the majority religion, namely Sunni Islam. Therefore, what was at stake in this new formulation of secularism was the principle of the neutrality of the state regarding different religions, a primary principle which Başgil himself promoted. This contradictory position concerning state neutrality while at the same time protecting the hegemony of Sunni Islam was also reflected in the policies of the DP government, which appealed to the religious demands of its mostly provincial electorate. Indeed, although the DP's leaders continued to promote secularism as an indispensable measure for countering the threat of Islamism (i.e., *irtica*, the Kemalist rhetoric about "religious reactionism"), they also exacerbated the state's existing bias towards Sunni Islam via the Diyanet.

***

Through his reinterpretations of secularism, Başgil came to be seen as a pioneering scholar for generations of conservative and Islamist intellectuals and politicians who rejected the Kemalist secularism of the single-party era on the grounds that it was authoritarian and instead proposed an "Anglo-Saxon" model of secularism in which state funding of religious services and the public visibility of religion were questioned to a far lesser degree. Başgil's book, which has been regularly reprinted since the mid-1950s, has been a crucial source which has inspired conservative nationalist and Islamist political elites who altered the meaning of secularism in such a way that it served the religious needs of the Sunni majority. Nevertheless, Başgil's call for the autonomy of the Diyanet did not find sympathy with the DP government nor with subsequent governments, none of which have relinquished their control over religion. However, his contradictory interpretation of secularism, which promoted Sunni Islam in the name of a majoritarian democracy, has been passed along and appropriated by several right-wing governments. Since the 1950s, Başgil's critique of the secularist policies of the single-party era and his reformulation of secularism "as it should be" provided the DP as well as later right-wing and conservative governments and their religious policies with a theoretical basis and justification. His perspective has also inspired Islamist politicians who, in their defence of "conservative democracy" in the early 2000s, defended the legacy of secularism as a principle that required state neutrality vis-à-vis existing religions and sects and as a guarantee for the existence of a pluralist democracy. However, once they obtained power, right-wing and conservative politicians have brushed aside Başgil's liberal calls for a neutral state, choosing instead to adopt his contradictory position concerning the idealisation of a "religion-friendly state".

Select Bibliography

Akan, Murat. *The Politics of Secularism: Religion, Diversity, and Institutional Change in France and Turkey.* New York: Columbia University Press, 2017.

Azak, Umut. "Dinle Dost Devlet: Ali Fuat Başgil'e Göre Laiklik." *İstanbul Siyasal Bilgiler Fakültesi Dergisi*, no. 51 (2014): 37–51.

Azak, Umut. *Islam and Secularism in Turkey: Kemalism, Religion and the Nation State.* London: I.B. Tauris, 2010.

Beriş, Hamit Emrah. *Ali Fuad Başgil'e Armağan.* Ankara: Kadim Yayınları, 2020.

Bora, Tanıl. *Türk Sağının Üç Hali: Milliyetçilik, Muhafazakârlık, İslâmcılık.* İstanbul: Birikim, 1998.

Önder, Tuncay. "Ali Fuad Başgil." In *Modern Türkiye'de Siyasî Düşünce: Muhafazakârlık*, edited by Ahmet Çiğdem, 291–301. İstanbul: İletişim, 2003.

33
Symbol of Turkish Modernity and Bastion of the West: The Hilton Hotel in İstanbul

Hans Theunissen

The Hilton Hotel in İstanbul is one of the city's most iconic twentieth-century buildings. It was built in the years 1952–55 in the so-called "international style" and is undoubtedly one of the prime examples of post-war modernism in Turkey. It was the first Hilton Hotel outside the USA and received financial support from the Marshall Plan. The İstanbul Hilton was the first 5-star hotel in the city and for several decades remained one of its most prestigious hotels. The construction of the Hilton Hotel was followed by drastic interventions in the urban fabric of İstanbul which aimed at renovating and modernising the dilapidated city. Although highway building had been a priority of Turkish governments since the late 1940s, in the second half of the 1950s the modernisation craze also reached the streets of İstanbul. Plans to "upgrade" the street network of İstanbul consciously took into account the location of the Hilton Hotel in the north of the European side of the city and that of the international airport in Yeşilköy to the south of the city. These new roads created a "corridor of modernity" between the airport and the hotel. Both the construction of the hotel and the interventions carried out in the urban fabric of İstanbul demonstrate the international and national ambitions of the governments of Prime Minister Adnan Menderes (1899–1961) in the 1950s. From the day it was opened (10 June 1955), the İstanbul Hilton played a multifaceted role in Turkish politics and society, both in practical and symbolic ways. Visual and textual sources dating from the 1950s show what the İstanbul Hilton expressed for different people in those times, in both national and international contexts.

First day of issue cover (FDC) with four stamps and the special stamp cancellation marks issued on the occasion of the Tenth Annual Meeting of the Board of Governors of the International Bank for Reconstruction and Development (IBRD) and the Board of Governors of the International Monetary Fund (IMF) on 12–16 September 1955 in İstanbul. From the collection of the author.

Early full-colour tourist postcard from 1956 showing the İstanbul Hilton with the İstanbul Hilton stamp and the special İstanbul Hilton cancellation mark. From the collection of the author.

The series of four stamps on the first day of issue cover was issued by the Turkish postal service on the occasion of the Tenth Annual Meeting of the Board of Governors of the International Bank for Reconstruction and Development (IBRD) and the Board of Governors of the International Monetary Fund (IMF) which took place on 12–16 September 1955 in İstanbul. This meeting was also commemorated with a special stamp cancellation mark which was also used on the envelope. The upper left stamp depicts the Hilton Hotel, the two other stamps below portray İstanbul University buildings, and the upper right stamp shows the *Kız Kulesi* (Maiden's or Leander's Tower) in the Bosporus. The depictions on three of the stamps are closely related to the IBRD-IMF meeting because the participants stayed at the Hilton Hotel, while the meeting itself was held in the building housing İstanbul University's Faculty of Economics and the stamp bearing the image of the Bosporus highlights the country's strategic position between the East and the West. As such, the envelope with the four stamps and special cancellation marks expresses the aspirations of the Demokrat Party (DP) governments in the 1950s to modernise Turkey and integrate the country into the international institutions of the West. In that way, the stamps embody the international and national political ambitions of the Menderes governments of the 1950s. Moreover, the full-colour postcard presents the İstanbul Hilton as a symbol of Turkish-American friendship (appropriately expressed by the flags of the two countries in front of the hotel) and as a beacon of Turkish modernity. The governor and mayor of İstanbul, Fahrettin Kerim Gökay (1900–1987), reformulated this image in a speech that he gave during the official inauguration of the hotel as follows: "Today the Turkish moon and sun stand together with the American stars. The old world embraces the new world."

Although the images emphasise Turkey's close relations with the West, Turkish sources usually do not explicitly point out the ideological role the hotel played for Conrad Hilton (1887–1979) and the US government. The Americans considered the İstanbul Hilton to be a forward bastion against Soviet Communism. The following quotes from Conrad Hilton's autobiography *Be My Guest* illustrate this ideological aspect of the İstanbul Hilton:

The Istanbul Hilton stands thirty miles from the Iron Curtain. (Hilton, *Be My Guest*, 326)

We humbly believe ... that our Hilton house flag is one small flag of freedom which is being waved defiantly against Communism.... (Ibid., 323)

"Each of our hotels," I said, "is a little America," not as a symbol of bristling power, but as a friendly center where men of many nations and of good will may speak the language of peace." (Ibid., 327–28)

Turkish politicians of the 1950s also used the phrase "a little America" in their political propaganda (i.e., "Türkiye'yi küçük bir Amerika yapacağız," "We will make Turkey a little America") in order to express their ambitions and promises to the electorate to create a modern and prosperous Turkey which could rival other modern nations in the West and where every neighbourhood had its own millionaire ("Her mahallede bir milyoner"). Although in Turkish the phrase "a little America" did not refer to the İstanbul Hilton but to Turkey, without a doubt for the urban segments of Turkish society the hotel became a symbol of the modern American-oriented lifestyle of Turkey in the 1950s.

The postcard of the İstanbul Hilton, bearing the Hilton stamp and the special Hilton cancellation mark (from 1956), is one of the many Turkish Hilton postcards produced in the 1950s and 1960s. This rare, early full-colour postcard also highlights the role the İstanbul Hilton played in the development of international tourism in Turkey, which was one of the other goals of the Menderes government in the 1950s. That goal was expressed by numerous Turkish government officials, for instance Finance Minister Hasan Polatkan (1915–1961) who, in a speech he gave at the hotel's opening ceremony, emphasised Turkey's rich history and heritage and the role the Hilton would play in the development of tourism in Turkey. As part of the government's efforts to stimulate tourism, shortly before the opening of the İstanbul Hilton, an English-language *Tourist's Guide to Istanbul* was published. In the introduction of the guide, Director-General of the Turkish Press, Broadcasting, and Tourist Department Halim Alyot (1909–1980) wrote, "Istanbul unrolls a panorama where [the] fabulous East meets [the] progressive West. Istanbul is the climax to every tourist's voyage. Turkey is making every effort to increase the number of visitors to this country and to ensure them a happy vacation. The construction in Istanbul of a modern hotel in cooperation with the Hilton Hotels International Inc. of America marks the first concrete stage in our endeavours."

The East-meets-West motif was also used in the interior decoration of the Hilton Hotel, which had some (Ottoman-) Turkish features (including tilework and carpets). In addition, a number of spaces in the hotel bore names referring to (Ottoman-) Turkish culture, while some hotel employees, such as female staff members who were known as "coffee beauties" (*kahveci güzelleri*), wore traditional outfits. Within the context of such references to an Ottoman past, the undulating roof of the entrance to the hotel, which was designed by the Turkish architect Sedat Hakkı Eldem (1908–1988), was often interpreted in an Orientalist way as signifying a "flying carpet from the Tales of the Thousand and One Nights." The Orientalist East-West contrast was also used in American advertisements, which juxtaposed the bright, sleek, and modern Hilton Hotel in the foreground with the dark, mysterious, and picturesque Blue Mosque in the background. For the American public, these references to an Ottoman past surely created an Orientalist image of Turkey, and in such an Orientalist view, Turkish modernity originated in the West and was like the Hilton Hotel brought to İstanbul by America.

***

The visual and textual sources from the 1950s related to the İstanbul Hilton reflect the international and national political ambitions of the Menderes governments directed towards Turkey's integration into the West, the upgrading of the country's infrastructure, and the modernisation of Turkish society. At the same time, for the Americans the Hilton Hotel and other infrastructure projects such as new highways embodied American modernity, which had to be brought to Turkey in order for the Cold War to be won. In their eyes, Turkey constituted an exemplary model of American modernisation in the 1950s. Turkish stamps, cancellation marks, and postcards contributed to the dissemination and popularisation of the idea of Turkish modernity and as such these sources offer alternative insights into the Turkish political and socio-cultural life of the 1950s.

Select Bibliography

Adalet, Begüm. *Hotels and Highways: The Construction of Modernization Theory in Cold War Turkey.* Stanford: Stanford University Press, 2018.

Bozdoğan, Sibel, and Esra Akcan. *Turkey (Modern Architectures in History).* London: Reaktion Books, 2012.

Gül, Murat. *The Emergence of Modern Istanbul. Transformation and Modernisation of a City.* London: I.B. Tauris, 2009.

Hilton, Conrad. *Be My Guest.* Englewood Cliffs: Prentice Hall, 1962 (ed. princ. 1957).

Wharton, Annabel. *Building the Cold War: Hilton International Hotels and Modern Architecture.* Chicago: The University of Chicago Press, 2001.

Ziyaoğlu, Rakım, Hayreddin Lokmanoğlu, and Emin Erer. *Tourist's Guide to Istanbul.* İstanbul: Halk Basımevi, 1953.

34
The Beginning of an End:
The Pogrom of 6-7 September 1955

Stefo Benlisoy

The Truman Doctrine and accompanying policy of containment targeting the Soviet Union laid the groundwork for a renewed rapprochement between Turkey and Greece after the Second World War. After the Turkish-Greek War of 1919–1922 and the population exchange of 1924, both countries had entertained the notion of establishing amicable relations throughout the 1930s since they both prioritised internal reconstruction and the continuation of the status quo in the Balkans. Naturally, this potential for Cold War rapprochement between the two countries had a positive impact on the Greek and Turkish minority populations living therein. Both governments placed a great deal of importance on making significant improvements to the living conditions of their minorities by way of cultivating better relations. At the same time, the new liberal political climate in Turkey created favourable conditions for the Greek minority. As a result, the Greek Orthodox minority of İstanbul, which for thirty years had been in a state of uncertainty with regard to its national and communal identity and had been trying to cope with discriminatory practices such as the Wealth Tax of 1942 and incessant threats to its economic and social existence, began to look to the future with greater confidence and optimism, leading to a multifaceted process of revival. When the charismatic Athenagoras I (Aristocles Matthaiou, 1886–1972) was appointed Ecumenical Patriarch of Constantinople in 1948, that sense of optimism was further bolstered. Athenagoras actively supported the full integration of the Greek minority into the Turkish Republic and society in Turkey and developed cordial relations with the government, a policy that culminated in the first and last visit by a Turkish prime minister to the patriarchal premises in 1952. This liberal climate led to a significant recovery and flourishing of the communal, cultural, and educational organisation of the community.

However, the emergence of a strong national movement led by Greek Cypriots in Cyprus who sought to end British colonial rule and achieve political union with Greece stoked existential anxieties among Turkish Cypriots, thereby dramatically altering the state of affairs in İstanbul. Due to the exacerbation of tensions over the Cyprus Question as Greece brought the issue to the UN in 1954 to demand self-determination for the island and also the partial decline in the sense of urgency regarding the Soviet "threat" in the mid-1950s, relations between the two countries began to deteriorate and the political atmosphere, which had led to positive changes in the lives of the Greek minority, changed radically. The government of Adnan Menderes (1899–1961), which was faced with a deteriorating domestic economic situation and a political crisis in the mid-1950s, presented the Cyprus conflict as a "national issue" as a means of redirecting public opinion. The United Kingdom also encouraged increased Turkish involvement in the issue, since that would make it possible to present the Cyprus Question to the international community not as another chapter of decolonisation but as a Greek-Turkish conflict and hence the UK could step in to take on the role of arbiter.

From 1955 onwards, a nationalistic campaign was carried out in Turkey around the Cyprus issue which targeted the Greek minority and the Patriarchate. Towards the end of August 1955, just before the start of the tripartite London Conference between the UK, Greece, and Turkey, the aim of which was to discuss the future of Cyprus, tensions in Turkey rapidly rose. The government was eager to demonstrate that the Turkish public was very concerned about the developments that were taking place on the island. By way of statements that were made by both the ruling Democrat Party (*Demokrat Parti*, DP) and members of the opposition from the Republican People's Party (*Cumhuriyet Halk Partisi*, CHP), as well as the activities of the government-supported Cyprus Is Turkish Association (*Kıbrıs Türktür Cemiyeti*, KTC) and the National Turkish Students' Union (*Millî Türk Talebe Birliği*, MTTB) and the enthusiasm of the press, the Greeks of İstanbul were portrayed as untrustworthy citizens who had betrayed the "national cause" or at best were indifferent about it and hence they were identified as "internal enemies". In the lead-up to September of 1955, the press had been actively engaged in a fierce campaign against the Greeks, especially the Patriarchate and Patriarch Athenagoras himself, which led to an increase in tensions on the streets. The press circulated rumours that the Greek Cypriots were planning to massacre the Turkish Cypriots, contributing to the anti-Greek climate in the city. The popular daily *Hürriyet* reacted to these rumours by asserting that there was a large number of Greeks in İstanbul on whom revenge could be obtained.

On 6 September 1955, the evening newspaper *İstanbul Ekspres* announced that the (supposed) birth home of Mustafa Kemal Atatürk (1881–1938) in Thessaloniki had been attacked. Indeed, on the night of 5 September a bomb had exploded in the garden of the house, which at the same time served as the Turkish Consulate. Years later it came to light that the attack had been orchestrated by Turkish security forces and the perpetrator of the attack was a member of the secret police.

Late in the evening of September 6, a demonstration that was being held in Taksim Square devolved into the looting of shops owned by non-Muslims on İstiklal Street, which since the late nineteenth century had been the most Westernised and cosmopolitan part of the city marked by the presence and visibility of non-Muslim minorities and foreigners. This constituted the spark which prompted masses of rioters to attack shops, houses, schools, churches, and even cemeteries in nearly all of the districts of İstanbul where Greeks and other non-Muslims resided. The pogroms continued throughout the night of 6-7 September 1955.

It has been estimated that around one hundred thousand rioters participated in the events. The simultaneity and organised manner of the attacks, the "target lists" of those who directed the rioters, the lack of action taken by security forces and the ways that they actually helped the rioters, and the transport of demonstrators to various districts in the city all point to the existence of a plan drawn up by the DP government. Local branches of the DP, student associations, and trade unions which were under the strict control of the Menderes government played a decisive role in mobilising the public on the night of 6-7 September. Approximately fifteen people were killed in the attacks, and 1,004 houses, 4,348 shops, 27 pharmacies, 21 factories, and 110 restaurants were looted and destroyed, along with a number of coffeehouses and hotels. Communal buildings came under attack as well, including 73 churches, 26 schools, and 5 sports clubs that were set on fire. It is thought that at least 200 women were raped by the attackers on the night of the pogrom. In districts that were far from the city centre along the Marmara and Bosporus shores, the attacks took the form of the raiding and looting of houses and the beating of people. Contrary to images that were later popularised, the pogrom was not restricted to the city centre, symbolised by İstiklal Street, but in fact it spread across the city wherever Greeks or other non-Muslim minorities resided.

In 1955, there were five daily Greek newspapers published in İstanbul that perpetuated the long tradition of Greek publishing in the city. The voices of Greek newspaper vendors still echoed in some districts of the city that had large numbers of Greek inhabitants. The newspaper *Embros*, which was launched in late 1954 at the time when living conditions for minority groups were improving, published an editorial on 15 September, its first issue after the pogrom, discussing the future of the Greeks of İstanbul.

*On Ruins**

We will stay here, in our places. We will rise from where we fell, we Greeks, to rebuild our churches, bury our dead, and piece back together our schools, workplaces, and homes. We will stay in this country where we were born and grew up, where our grandfathers and fathers' tombs, albeit now broken, still exist. We will create a new world from those broken tombs, from our ruined churches, schools, shops and homes. We should all have the courage to do this. [...] We, too, are the children of this country, and we strive in every field to prove this.

We have always been and we remain citizens who respect the laws of this country.

[...] We will raise our voices and shout that this disaster that befell us should not have happened. We will talk about guarantees and the safety of our lives. We are still Greek today.

We will shout that we are not hostages or captives in this country where we live and which is our homeland, and [we will shout] that we do not have to leave just because some people want to expel us. We will stay here. We will constantly tell the President, the Prime Minister, the Ministers, and the Members of Parliament that we have deep roots in this country, just like how a big plane tree digs into the soil with its roots. One can prune our branches, but no one can reach the roots of our old tree.

---

* Translated from the original Greek "Επί Ερειπίων," *Εμπρός*, 15 September 1955.

This cry of ours is not a rebellion or a revolt. We just want our right to live as humans. If the administrators of the state cannot digest this, they should openly say to us, "You have no right to live here." Then we will take care of ourselves.

We do not stay in this country through grace and arbitrary decisions. We are here because we have the right to stay. [...] And as long as this Turkish state exists, we will be here in it. God has wanted this to happen throughout history. From time to time, we may get caught up in fear and despair and say, "It's all over now." The state should have us say, "No, it's not over."

The state must help us regain the sense of trust we lost on the night of September the sixth. Undoubtedly, this sense of trust will not come back when they pat us on the back and say, "This too shall pass."

[...] Let our Prime Minister say to us, "We are very sorry for what happened. Let's heal our wounds together. Let's join hands and restore İstanbul. You are not captives or hostages here. You are equal citizens of our state and a part of our people. We want nothing more than for you to love this country and work for it with us. You are exemplary in your respect for the laws of the republic and the country you were born in, and no one has the right to disturb you." Then we will stay in our homeland without fear and continue our tradition of living together for 500 years. We will bury our dead who have been swept out of their graves. We will repair our churches, our homes, and our shops. People can replace everything they have lost financially by working with faith. We expect the government to fulfil a historic responsibility. If adequate assurances are given about our safety, we will stay here.

***

What is perhaps most striking about the article is its straightforwardness. The minority press in Turkey rarely expressed such a bold attitude towards the authorities. Together with lines that serve as a demonstration of loyalty, the article states clearly that the Greeks of İstanbul are neither captives nor hostages and they demand that they be treated as equal citizens. It openly states the meaning of the events for the Greeks of İstanbul and tries to describe to the authorities the policies and attitudes they should adopt to ensure the continued existence of the Greek minority. On the one hand, it expresses the strong will of the Greek community to remain in İstanbul on an equal standing with Turkish citizens but only on the condition that the state does not treat them as hostages or trump cards in Turkish-Greek relations and assures them that their equal rights as citizens will be protected. It also proclaims that the Greek minority must try to heal its wounds.

Despite the insufficient compensation offered by the government, most of the Greeks of İstanbul continued to support the DP and Menderes instead of the oppositional CHP. Ultimately, the pogrom would be considered a final reminder that the Greek minority would never be accepted as equal citizens. In contrast to the popular view, the pogroms of 6-7 September did not lead to a mass exodus from İstanbul but rather it resulted in the gradual decline of socioeconomically weaker Greek communities residing in suburban districts that were far from the city centre. After the pogrom, the Patriarchate, community leaders, and the Greek consular authorities tried to convince resident Greeks to stay in İstanbul. The increase in the number of students enrolled at Greek minority schools in İstanbul in subsequent years indicates that their efforts met with a certain amount of success.

***

The day after the pogrom, martial law was proclaimed in İstanbul, İzmir, and Ankara. The government denied any responsibility and described the events as a communist plot, and the police arrested 48 people, including some prominent leftist writers and intellectuals. Despite the prevailing Cold War mentality, however, the argument for a communist conspiracy was not very convincing. During the Trials of Yassıada (one of the Princes' Islands in the Marmara Sea) that took place after the coup of 27 May 1960, the pogrom of 6-7 September become the subject of a trial, by the end of which Menderes and Foreign Minister Fatin Rüştü Zorlu (1910–1961) were convicted.

As noted in the editorial published by *Embros*, the pogrom of 6-7 September was not a deathblow for the Greek minority living in İstanbul. In fact, the expulsions of 1964 which targeted the Greeks of İstanbul who held Greek passports constituted the last strike that led to the final mass exodus of the minority community from Turkey. Those expulsions were also the direct result of an increase in tensions between Greeks and Turks again because of the Cyprus issue. The fate of the Greek minority in İstanbul in the second half of the twentieth century was directly related to the state of Turkish-Greek relations, especially the course of the Cyprus issue. Successive Turkish governments tried to use the Greek community of İstanbul and the Patriarchate as a bargaining chip to obtain concessions from Greece. Ultimately, the Greek community and the Patriarchate itself more or less became a hostage in the dispute over Cyprus and the general course of Greek-Turkish relations. The anti-Greek attitudes and antipathy towards non-Muslims that culminated in the pogrom of 6-7 September 1955 were largely framed by and employed the strategies and lexicon of the politics of Turkification that predominated in the first half of the century. But rather than achieving internal Turkification or enabling the emergence of a Turkish-Muslim national bourgeoisie, it primarily constituted a means of putting pressure on Greece over the Cyprus issue.

The Greek minority of İstanbul was a prosperous community that enjoyed a relatively high standard of living but its politically and socially uncertain status and the constant attempts of the Turkish government to implicate it in Greek-Turkish relations and antagonisms nearly resulted in its eradication. Today, the Greek Orthodox community of İstanbul, which numbered around 120,000 after the signing of the Treaty of Lausanne, has plummeted to around 2,000 members, a figure that continues to dwindle.

Select Bibliography

Alexandris, Alexis. *The Greek Minority of Istanbul and Greek-Turkish Relations 1918–1974.* Second ed. Athens: Centre for Asia Minor Studies, 1992.

Benlisoy, Foti. "Anti-Greek Riots of September 1955 in Constantinople (Istanbul)." *Encyclopaedia of the Hellenic World, Asia Minor.* URL: http://www.ehw.gr/l.aspx?id=11464

Güven, Dilek. *Cumhuriyet Dönemi Azınlık Politikaları ve Stratejileri Bağlamında 6-7 Eylül Olayları.* Ninth ed. İstanbul: İletişim Yayınları, 2022.

Stamatopoulos, Costas M. *Η Τελευταία Αναλαμπή Η Κωνσταντινουπολίτικη Ρωμηοσύνη στα Χρόνια 1948–1955.* Athens: Domos, 1996.

35
Politicised Suffering:
On Being an Albanian Migrant in Turkey

Nathalie Clayer

In 2006, Isa Prekadini, a Kosovar Albanian living in Germany, published an Albanian-language memoir in Kosovo titled *Kujtime nga Stambolli* (Memories from İstanbul), an account of the five years he spent in his youth in Turkey after his father decided in late 1957 to migrate there with his family from Mitrovica (then in socialist Yugoslavia) and before his departure from Turkey in 1962 for Germany to continue his studies. Settling in Adapazarı, which is 150 kilometres east of İstanbul, the family joined tens of thousands of migrants, known in Turkish as *göçmen*, who at that time were primarily from socialist Yugoslavia, Bulgaria, and Romania. They also joined the descendants of other migrants/refugees mainly from the Balkans and Caucasus who had settled in the area in the nineteenth century, during the decade of wars (1912–1923), and during the interwar period. As Muslims, these migrants had left territories that were outside Ottoman/Turkish control because they were pushed, directly or indirectly, politically and/or economically, to seek refuge in the Ottoman Empire and later in the Republic of Turkey and also because the Ottoman Empire and later Turkey had a demographic and economic interest in welcoming this labour force. After the Communist takeover, new waves of departures from Yugoslavia occurred, since many Muslims—including Albanians, Turks, Slavs, and Romas—were against the Communist regime and its economic and religious policies. Sometimes, as in the case of Isa Prekadini's father, migration was driven by the possibility of economic advancement; here, the inheritance of goods in Adapazarı where a member of the family had already settled. A while after their arrival, a former teacher from their hometown of Mitrovica travelled there to visit local shop owners who were of the same background and origin.

*A Dispute about the Situation of Migrants**

We are in the shop of our friend's uncle. The man received us very well. After exchanging greetings, we started talking to him. He began to explain how all the *"göçmen"* [sic] in the city of Adapazarı are doing very well and have good jobs. They, according to him, work well and lead modest lives. At first, we did not know where he was going with this, but later, when he started talking, as they say, about Skopje and Shkodra [about anything and everything] and mentioned some people who were sending unpleasant

---

* Translated from the Albanian original in Isa Prekadini, *Kujtime nga Stambolli* (Mitrovicë: Lumi i bardhë, 2006), 56–8.

letters to Kosovo, criticising Turkey and exposing the reality in this Muslim state, thereby serving to hold back and restrain other people from coming here, everything emerged and was understood as a ray of sunshine. *"Here, gentlemen,"* he continued to preach, *"it is better than in any other country in the world! Work as much as you want, earn as much as you want. Nobody says anything. Those who speak and write badly about this country do not have problems surviving, but they play politics and try to turn this place into another Albania! But, you know, the Turkish police do not sleep! One day we will show the opponents of this country what their path is!"* This was a threat. According to him, everyone should lower their heads and agree with the situation, saying that it is good.

The truth is that many *"göçmen"* suffered for their livelihood. Every day, day and night, they are waiting in front of the municipality (*belediye*) looking for work. And they spend days and weeks not finding the opportunity to sell their labour. Neither the municipality nor the commune provides any assistance to these people. Sometimes only a few rich people help them, not every day of the week, but punctually on the occasion of the Greater Bayram or the Lesser Bayram.

The owner did not stop criticising some Albanians, Turks, and *Bosniaks* in Kosovo who continued to remain there under the "rule of the Serb" (*hyqmin e shkaut*). Apparently, the visitor was upset by this stale conversation, so he asked permission to leave. We walked along the road together for a while without saying a word. The man I accompanied seemed very upset and exhausted. I found a good opportunity to spruce up the conversation. I also tried to explain to him the many problems the country and *"göçmen"* were facing. My former teacher told me that in those days when he was in Turkey, he had a good impression of and opinion about this country and the *"göçmen"* who had come to live here. *"As long as a man is a guest and is invited from one table to another, it seems to be pleasant!"* I replied hot-temperedly, saying that when the time comes for them to earn their own living, they switch accounts. "Then, a man sees whether life in this country is easy or hard!... I have a friend from Prishtina who is a graduate, but he is forced to carry sacks of flour and bran to ensure his existence; another is a tailor and works day and night with all the members of his family in order to survive. Many families of *"göçmen,"* my dear teacher, work at various factories, especially in textiles and canning, and lots of women and children sew tags on shirts or perform various forms of physical work that are quite hard. They earn so little that it is unfortunate and that you shed tears for these people!" I explained many other things to my teacher, because I saw that during those days when he was in Turkey, no one had informed him [about them]. I explained many things, but I did not tell him who had written the letter that the owner's nephew had received and in which I asked him and others not to leave their most beloved and dearest country—Kosovo. Through that letter and many others that I had sent to relatives and friends, I wanted to persuade them to stay, because *"The heavy stone weighs only in its place!"*

For the *"göçmen"* who were willing to accept the peculiarities of the local people, there were no difficulties or problems in their lives, while for the others who did not agree to abandon or lose the best ethno-psychological qualities that had been planted in the soul and mind in their homeland, they faced different vicissitudes. Those who came here forty years ago, just like those who arrived from 1955 onwards, also faced all kinds of vicissitudes. The difference between the *"göçmen"* who had arrived in the last period and those who had arrived long ago is that the former settled where they wished, whether in İstanbul, Bursa, Manisa, Adapazarı and other places more suitable for living, while those who came before did not enjoy that privilege because the state settled them where it wanted, without taking into account their will at all. Something special that is common to both groups of *"göçmen"* is worth mentioning: marriage. They intermarry, but of course there are exceptions.

***

In this passage, the author refers not to migration per se, but to the less studied issue of the situation of migrants in Turkey. That situation appears here as it is perceived and explained in a contradictory and contested manner through an interaction between the author—the son of a merchant and small landowner who had just recently settled in Adapazarı—and another migrant who was an older merchant, as well as a visitor from their home region. Young Isa stands against discourses that praise the opportunities offered in Turkey and the generally "good" situation of migrants. Indeed, he refers to the very different economic situation of migrants, stressing the constraints imposed on them rather than opportunities. Some of the challenges he discussed included difficulties finding work, how some entrepreneurs saw them as a cheap labour force, the obligation placed on young students to work, the issue of underage labour, and women's working conditions.

The memoir also points to migrants' relationship with local and national institutions, and in this respect, the author refers to the important differences between migration flows, especially with regards to whether migrants had a choice about where they could settle and if they could benefit from financial support aid schemes. Moreover, it highlights relations between migrants forming strongly endogamous groups within which traditional forms of solidarity existed, where the wealthy would help the poorest and associations founded by migrants provided support. Finally, it should be noted that there are also several clues about circulations between Turkey and Kosovo, including the circulation of men and women (migrants, visitors) and the circulation of letters, to which must be added the circulation of goods as well. Isa Prekadini's father, who had once fought in the ranks of the Ottoman army, had actually emigrated to Turkey because an uncle had left him an inheritance in Adapazarı. Thus, the sending society and the host society were not disconnected; to the contrary, they formed a space that must be considered as one that was woven diachronically in an Ottoman and post-Ottoman fabric as well as synchronically.

The excerpt demonstrates that this space also bore tensions between individuals and generations that were partially politicised and ethnicised. In this case, tensions revolved around the issue of whether it was acceptable to encourage more Kosovo Muslims to migrate to Turkey. The argument, which was initially economic and individual, eventually turned political and strongly collective. A position considered pro-Turkish by the author stands in opposition to a position considered by the trader to be extremely pro-Albanian since it would supposedly promote Albanian sovereignty in Turkey, or in any case align with Albanian politics. In fact, as in the interwar period, Albania tried to slow down the departure of Albanian-speaking

Muslims from Yugoslavia to Turkey. In his personal political narrative construction, young Isa Prekadani, who suffers as a result of his father's decision to leave Mitrovica and dreams of studying in Austria or Germany, seems to offer a critique of Turkish society and Turkey through an affirmation of Albanianness, whereas those who try to integrate into Turkish society are automatically associated with Turkishness. Indeed, much of the book is devoted to his participation, in İstanbul, in a group of young Kosovars who were then eager to publicise the plight of Albanians in Kosovo under the Serbian/Yugoslav communist government and the tensions that existed due to the equally communist character of the Albanian state to which these young people were tempted to turn for assistance.

***

With, and despite, all their subjectivity and reinforced by the distance between the time of experience and the time of writing, Isa Prekadini's memoirs are among those narrative and personal sources that can be used to shed light on aspects of social developments in Turkey that have not yet been studied systematically. The question of populations and migrations is crucial for understanding the history of Republican Turkey, in particular policies of demographic engineering that lasted beyond the genocide of 1915, as well as the history of migration waves and policies, regardless of whether they were internal or external and more or less forced. These migratory dynamics have modified the "social fabric" of Turkey throughout the first 100 years of the Republic's existence. However, this type of source also encourages us to examine developments with a bottom-up perspective and consider Turkey's society as a complex entity in which the migration factor and mobilities, even up to the recent arrival of Syrian refugees, have contributed to the shaping of social, economic, and political relations. Yet, the social spaces in which the actors in Turkey's society interact have local, regional, national, and transnational dimensions, hence the need to broaden the focus beyond the Turkish state's borders.

Select Bibliography

Baklacıoğlu, Nurcan Özgür. *Dış Politika ve Göç Kitap: Yugoslavya'dan Türkiye'ye Göçlerde Arnavutlar 1920–1990.* İstanbul: Derin Yayınları, 2011.

Becan, Elif. "Structuring Migrants at the Local Level: Neighborhood and the Language Practices of Second-Generation Albanians in Post-Ottoman Turkey (1930–1960)." *Irish Slavonic Studies: Individuals and Institutions* 27 (2017): 1–24.

Kirişci, Kemal. "Post-Second World War Immigration from Balkan Countries to Turkey." *New Perspectives on Turkey* 12 (1995): 61–77.

Parla, Ayşe. *Precarious Hope: Migration and the Limits of Belonging in Turkey.* Stanford: Stanford University Press, 2019.

Trix, Frances. *Urban Muslim Migrants in Istanbul: Identity and Trauma Among Balkan Immigrants.* London: I.B. Tauris, 2017.

Ünal Serdar, "Sosyal-Mekânsal-Siyasal Kümelenme Biçimi Olarak İzmir Kentinde Balkan (Rumeli) Kimliği," *Çağdaş Yerel Yönetimler* 21, no. 3 (2012): 49–77.

36
"Actions in the Middle East Are Only a Beginning": Turkey and the Syrian Crisis of 1957

Onur İşçi

Shortly after the Yalta Conference in 1945, Moscow's demands for control of the Turkish Straits and borderlands in northeastern Anatolia drove Turkey to a take decisively pro-Western stance. The unremitting antagonism of Joseph Stalin (1878–1953) toward Turkey, which lasted until his death in 1953, compelled Turkish leaders to seek a stronger alliance with the United States. Turkey's quest for NATO membership ushered in a new era in 1952 amidst major transformations in the country's domestic politics and diplomacy. Heralding a policy of containment, which would remain the essence of the US approach during the Cold War, the Truman Doctrine launched in March of 1947 resulted in the delivery of military assistance to Greece and Turkey. Two months after Stalin's death in 1953, his successor, Nikita Khrushchev (1894–1971), admitted that Moscow's attempts to force Turkey to bend to its will had been a cardinal error and he withdrew earlier Soviet demands. At this point, Turkey's newly elected Democrat Party was heavily invested in the country's pro-Western alliance and the developmental aid that came with it. Proclaiming themselves the anchor of NATO in the Middle East, Ankara's new leaders, President Celal Bayar (1883–1986) and Prime Minister Adnan Menderes (1899–1961), took a proactive role in the establishment of the Baghdad Pact (CENTO) to prove their resourcefulness in the face of communist subversion.

Ankara's shift towards the West, as well as its proactive diplomacy in the Middle East, was connected to domestic changes that undermined the country's economic nationalism of the early republican period. Wartime neutrality had not shielded Turkey's markets, and in 1946 Ankara devalued the lira for the first time in the history of the Republic, instituted liberal trade policies, and shed its protectionist traditions. Under President Harry Truman (1884–1972), the extension of US assistance via the Marshall Plan strengthened Turkey's reorientation and encouraged political adjustments in Ankara. Menderes, who in 1950 became the country's first democratically elected prime minister, had a background that differed sharply from that of the older military-bureaucratic elite, as he was a landowner who hailed from the Aegean region of Turkey. Menderes's agricultural sympathies overlapped with some of the goals of the US officials who were involved in the distribution of aid, as the latter urged Ankara to reject the Soviet-style statist industrialisation model, which dated from the 1930s. Yet US advisers believed that Menderes's policies, despite their ostensible free-market basis, were characterised by unproductive subsidies designed to shore up his political base. When Turkey lapsed into a foreign payment crisis after international wheat and cotton prices fell in 1954, Menderes and his US advisers had a falling out, and public opinion in Turkey began to be tinged with doubt about whether the US alliance could address the country's economic concerns. Ultimately, Menderes started looking towards Moscow for a means to repair the economy.

Before truly opening up to the Soviet Union, Menderes tried one last time to shore up the Western alliance through the Baghdad Pact. With his economic policies failing, he sought an easy political victory in the 1957 elections by emphasising the instrumental role he could play in terms of the US policy of containment. With Arab nationalism on the rise and the Soviet Union backing Damascus, Turkey mobilised troops along the Syrian border and sought to draw Washington into the confrontation. Soviet Premier Khrushchev followed this move with a promise to retaliate against any Turkish aggression, and the Soviet Union and Turkey seemed to be on the brink of war. US President Dwight Eisenhower (1890–1969) was unconvinced by Ankara's maneuvers and suppressed tensions in Syria, and the simultaneous refusal of Turkish requests for aid further alienated Menderes. The Turkish prime minister expressed his frustration in a speech he gave at a NATO summit on 16 December 1957, an excerpt of which is given below, in terms that forecast a change in Ankara's foreign policy. Menderes argued that NATO had made a grave error and spoke more broadly about a sense of disillusionment regarding Turkey's isolation. The Syrian Crisis and US insistence that the Turkish government take the politically unpopular step of devaluing the lira yet again showed Ankara that carrying on an unqualified alliance with Washington entailed a number of dangers.

Turkish Prime Minister Adnan Menderes's Statement
*Presented at the NATO Summit Held on 16 December 1957**

After Stalin's death, there were certain hopes that the Soviet danger would recede. It was thought that the collective leadership which replaced Stalin's absolute dictatorship would govern Russia in a more moderate way. However, we now see that this collective leadership, in a roundabout way, resulted again in one man's domination over the fate of Russia. This occurrence in turn may increase the possibility of Soviet Russia to launch into dangerous adventures. This undoubtedly could create a just concern and anxiety. Khrushchev's attitude, after establishing his one-man rule and the open threats which he levied against the whole world in connection with the Syrian problem, clearly proves the above premise.

I think it would be appropriate to look back in order to appraise today's problems better. As it is known, after the Second World War, Soviet Russia brought many countries under its domination and these countries were placed behind the Iron Curtain as Soviet satellites. After the completion of this enterprise, Soviet Russia tried to impose a fait accompli in Berlin and, around the same period,

---

* Cited per the English original in the Prime Ministry Republican Archive (*Başbakanlık Cumhuriyet Arşivleri*) 030.01.00/16.85.4.1.

succeeded in communising China and later initiated an indirect armed aggression in Korea. Aggression in Indochina followed Korea. However, after a long period of time following the Berlin blockade, when the Soviet Union evacuated Austria and did not undertake any aggressive action in the vicinity of Europe; this created the false impression that it was Russia's intention to maintain the status quo around Europe. In reality, for the last two years, we have seen the Soviet Union concentrating its actions on the Middle East, after lengthy preparations. As a result of these actions, Soviet Russia took over Syria and established close cooperation with Egypt.

These actions in the Middle East are only a beginning... In point of fact, the conquest of the Middle East by Russia—even without an armed intervention—after establishing itself in Syria, would be extremely easy. With the fall of the Middle East, not only the position of North Africa would be endangered, but also the Mediterranean would become a Russian field of action... If today a communist regime has not been fully established in Syria and if this country has not been turned into a classical or typical satellite, if is only because of a definitive tactical purpose...What Soviet Russia really desires is to take over the Middle East with the least trouble and without the occurrence of any intervention. Last year's crisis in the Middle East has shown to all of us the worth of the very rich oil resources of that area... All these facts compel us to regard the Soviet actions in Syria as the beginning of an immense and extremely dangerous movement... The acceptance of the Syrian fait accompli, first of all, would bring about the encirclement of Turkey, which has a central and key position in the Middle East and on the other hand would endanger the situation of Iraq, Jordan, Lebanon, Saudi Arabia and even Iran.

It would be extremely erroneous to consider in its above scope and meaning the Syrian problem, and consequently the Middle East problem, as a question not directly interesting NATO... When we appraise the situation in this manner and recognise the conditions, the measures to be adopted become evident. First of all, it is necessary to recognise that we are faced with full-scale aggression... At this point, we have to confess that although the Syrian events, which cannot yet be considered as terminated, occurred following a long period of preparation, it is only at the ultimate stage of the crisis that NATO has shown an inclination towards dealing with the question which should have interested it very closely.

It is clear that rather than keeping the initiative, we have been acting only after the event, after all evil designs have been carried out and the accomplished fact consummated, and this confronts us with great dangers and results in losses... We think we commit a grave error, for instance, in condemning ourselves to inactivity in taking a short-term measure on the pretext that a necessary long term measure has not yet been adopted.

It seems that the Baghdad Pact is unfortunately the only institution at the present time which would serve as a base for the measures to be taken in the Middle East. We are convinced that one of the most important factors in the losses we sustained in the Middle East consist of the fact that the Baghdad Pact was not adequately reinforced up to now owing to various reasons.

***

Taken up within the context of the Eisenhower Doctrine, which assured US economic assistance and military aid to Middle Eastern countries if they were threatened by the Soviet Union, this archival document demonstrates Turkey's frustration with the West's unwillingness to support Ankara's attempts to contain communist subversion on its southern border with Syria. In the summer and early fall of 1957, Turkey, together with the Israeli government, mobilised troops, escalating tensions with regard to the Baghdad Pact and the Soviet-backed regime in Damascus. In that sense, the Syrian Crisis of 1957 constituted a turning point in Turkey's Middle East policy but also paved the way for a broader reorientation in the country's Cold War policy vis-à-vis the West and USSR. To this day, there is a widespread belief amongst Turkish intellectuals that the coup of May 1960, which removed the Menderes government from power, was the outcome of Ankara's rapprochement with Moscow following the 1957 crisis with Syria. Although recent historical scholarship points to the existence of more convincing factors to explain Menderes's fall from power, as far as the impact of the 1957 Syrian Crisis is concerned, Turkey did devise a new Cold War strategy which enabled Ankara to capitalise on the detente and cash in on both superpowers throughout the 1960s and 1970s.

***

Turkish foreign policy underwent numerous twists and turns throughout the Cold War, but the immediate post-war years were truly unusual. The remaking of Turkey as a pro-Western ally turned out to be unsustainable in the long run. Turkey's staunchly pro-Western and anti-Soviet orientation in the 1950s marked a radical departure from the grand strategy that had successfully guided the Republic through the interwar years and was to do so again in the latter half of the Cold War. In other words, this period of open tensions between Moscow and Ankara was an anomaly in the twentieth century, and ultimately it came to an end in the mid-1950s. That said, Soviet-Turkish relations were fundamentally transformed between 1945 and 1957. The sharp geopolitical differences against the backdrop of which Moscow and Ankara had to maintain economic cooperation after the First World War could no longer be ignored.

Select Bibliography

Abou-el-Fadl, Reem. *Foreign Policy as Nation Making: Turkey and Egypt in the Cold War*. Cambridge: Cambridge University Press, 2020.

Hirst, Samuel and Onur İşçi. "Smokestacks and Pipelines: Russian-Turkish Relations and the Persistence of Economic Development." *Diplomatic History* 44, no. 5 (November 2020): 834–59.

Little, Douglas. "Cold War and Covert Action: The United States and Syria, 1945–1958." *The Middle East Journal* 44, no. 1 (1990): 51–75.

Pearson, Ivan. "The Syrian Crisis of 1957, the Anglo-American 'Special Relationship,' and the 1958 Landings in Jordan and Lebanon." *Middle Eastern Studies* 43, no. 1 (2007): 45–64.

37

An Early Announcement of the 1961 Constitution: Calls for Reforms by the Opposition

Ahmet İnsel

When the Republican People's Party (*Cumhuriyet Halk Partisi*, CHP) became part of the opposition in the first free and democratic general elections in 1950 after having continuously ruled Turkey as an authoritarian regime since the proclamation of the Republic in 1923, it discovered the evils of the 1924 constitution in terms of the functioning of a pluralist democratic regime. Already on the eve of the 1950 elections, İsmet İnönü (1884–1973), president of the Republic and leader of the CHP, had expressed reservations about the 1924 constitution, especially about its ability to give the majority party, and thus the government, all of the power without a proper system of checks and balances. After losing to the Democrat Party (*Demokrat Parti*, DP), the CHP began to place more and more emphasis on the need to establish rule of law, secure fundamental freedoms, and further democratisation. The CHP's leaders started to protest the repressive practices that they themselves had practiced in the recent past. In order to win the electoral support of the working class, which had overwhelmingly voted for the DP in 1950, the CHP also started to lay claim to the issues of social justice, the right to strike, and rights to social security. Moreover, the need for a constitutional court was formulated. Its parliamentary group tabled a series of legislative proposals in 1952 to amend undemocratic laws that the DP leadership had promised to change while it was in the opposition. In the 1957 elections, the DP retained its parliamentary majority but received fewer votes than the three opposition parties combined. With the hope of winning the general elections scheduled for 1961, the CHP adopted at its Fourteenth Congress in 1959 a declaration containing its main proposals for constitutional change after the elections. At the same congress, politicians who had left the DP to found the Freedom Party (*Hürriyet Partisi*) in 1955 joined the CHP to "gather their forces" for the next elections. Like the rival DP before 1950, İnönü called for the constitution to be reformed along democratic lines by the newly elected parliament. In particular, he proposed the institution of a second assembly to oversee the constitutional conformity of enacted laws.

*The Declaration of First Aims**

1- All anti-democratic laws, procedures, mentalities, and practices that hinder and set back our democratic development shall be repealed.

2- Our constitution shall be amended to conform to a state order that is based on the principles of the people's sovereignty, the rule of law, social justice, and security in line with a modern conception of democracy and society.

a) The fundamental rights and freedoms which are the common property of all Turks shall be included in the constitution without discriminating on the basis of differences in race, religion, creed, political thought, social origin, birth, or property. The principles of the rule of law and human rights and freedoms accepted by the civilised world to which we belong, such as freedom of thought and speech, freedom of the press, artistic and scientific freedom, freedom of conscience and religion, personal freedom and freedom of residence, the security of trade and property, freedom of work and enterprise, the right to strike, the right to form trade unions and professional organisations, and the right to equality before the law and to the equal enjoyment of public services shall be acquired by Turkish citizens and these rights shall be guaranteed by their clear definition. These rights will be enshrined in the Constitution and their restriction and nullification by other laws will be prevented by the establishment of a Constitutional Court.

b) The Head of State, who represents the whole nation and the continuity of the state, shall be neutral in accordance with the needs of this representation and of national solidarity.

c) The oversight of the executive by the legislature shall become effective and efficient.

d) To ensure harmony and balance with regard to the law, a second assembly shall be constituted.

e) A High Council of Judges shall be established in order to create an institution of judges free from influence along with independent courts which shall be the foundation of state order and freedoms. All decisions concerning the guarantees of judges shall be dealt with in this council.

(f) All legal provisions shall be made to ensure that the administration is impartial, dependent on the law, and serving not one person, social stratum, or political organisation but the State and all the people.

(g) In order to create a developed and prosperous Turkey free from social imbalances and injustices, social rights shall be recognised which aim to free all individuals from the pressure of material needs, provide everyone with the means for physical, intellectual, and social development, and preserve the family as the central element of society.

The conduct of elections under free, equal, and fair conditions shall be subject to the sound provisions of jurisprudence and practice. [...]

---

* Translated from the original Turkish in *CHP 14. Kurultayı İlk Hedefler Beyannamesi* (Ankara: Kurtulmuş Matbaası, 1960).

***

"The Declaration of First Aims" of 1959 brings together all the proposals made by the CHP over the previous ten years for the democratisation of political and social life in Turkey. In this document, all the rights and principles relevant to the democratisation process are enumerated, including freedom of thought and expression, freedom of conscience and religion, freedom of the press, scientific and artistic freedom, personal freedom and freedom of residence, freedom of work and enterprise, and the right to strike. In addition, the declaration stresses that there was an imperative need for the Head of State to be impartial, and also that there was a need for the equal treatment of all citizens before the law so they could benefit from public services, the impartiality of the public media, the independence of the judiciary, and judicial reviews of the decisions of all administrative bodies. It also affirms a need to strengthen parliamentary control of the opposition over the work of the executive and a need to abandon the existing majority electoral system in favour of a proportional system. These statements implicitly contained a criticism of the practices of the single-party and party-state system established by the CHP in the past but never explicitly formulated by the CHP leadership.

At the Fourteenth CHP Congress, the Declaration, which was prepared by a committee consisting of Cevat Dursunoğlu (1892–1970), Halûk Faralyalı, Turan Güneş (1921–1982), Coşkun Kırca (1927–2005), and Mümin Küley (1920–1987), was read by Turan Güneş on 14 January 1959. It would be adopted by the entirety of the congress delegates with a standing ovation. The Declaration ends by affirming the CHP's confidence that the nation would "fully complete this struggle for democratic rule" and eliminate "by national will the spirit of repression and domination".

From January 1959 onwards, the CHP developed its electoral strategy around a promise to change the constitution—if it had the necessary qualified majority—in accordance with the principles proclaimed in the Declaration and to re-conduct the elections to apply the new electoral rules.

The DP's leaders reacted to the Declaration of First Aims by calling it a catalogue that could be found in all democracy textbooks, but they also encouraged their supporters to violently disrupt the meetings of CHP leaders in various Anatolian cities. Judicial and police pressure on CHP supporters increased significantly. Last but not least, the DP set up a Commission of Inquiry (*Tahkikat Komisyonu*) on 18 April 1960, bypassing the rules of procedure of the parliament. The commission, which was composed entirely of DP deputies, was created following a proposal tabled in the parliament by two DP deputies who requested a parliamentary inquiry into the "illegal, illegitimate, and destructive actions of the CHP throughout the country". The stated aim of the commission was to investigate the legality of "the activities of the CHP and a part of the press". The parliament enacted a law on 27 April 1960 which gave the commission wide-ranging and unappealable powers. The establishment of the Commission of Inquiry is generally considered to be the final step that led the officers' junta to decide to take action to overthrow the government.

***

The military coup of 27 May 1960, by proclaiming the dissolution of the constitution and parliament, prevented the holding of elections. The military junta (National Unity Committee, *Milli Birlik Komitesi*) appointed an Assembly of Representatives, forming, together with the junta, the Constituent Assembly. The presence of members of the dissolved DP was forbidden in the assembly, which was strongly marked by the presence of delegates close to the CHP. Immediately after the coup, professors from İstanbul and Ankara universities drafted two constitutions. The National Unity Committee appointed a sixteen-member committee, the vast majority of whom were university jurists. Drawing more on the Ankara draft, which granted a greater role to political parties, this committee prepared a draft of a new constitution that included all the principles expressed in the 1959 Declaration. Adopted by the Constituent Assembly, the new constitution was accepted with 61.4 per cent of the vote in a referendum held on 9 July 1961.

The Declaration of First Aims set out in detail the basic rules for a pluralist democratic system. However, its implementation was not the result of a normal electoral process but rather it occurred after a military coup that heavily repressed the DP leadership, which weakened its legitimacy in the eyes of the conservative segments of society in Turkey. The freedoms guaranteed by the 1961 constitution allowed for the creation of left-wing political groups such as the Workers' Party of Turkey (*Türkiye İşçi Partisi*, TİP), which present in the parliament in 1965, and the Confederation of Revolutionary Trade Unions (*Devrimci İşçi Sendikaları Konfederasyonu*, DİSK). However, these freedoms were quickly eroded by right-wing governments and deemed "a luxury for Turkey," and later they were partly abrogated by the military intervention of 1971. The military coup of 1980 established a new authoritarian regime. The authoritarian drift of the Justice and Development Party (*Adalet ve Kalkınma Partisi*, AKP) and the establishment of an autocratic presidential regime in the 2010s were partly inspired by a historical desire to seek out revenge on the 1960 coup and revive all the demands expressed in the 1959 Declaration to democratise Turkey once again in the early 2020s.

Select Bibliography

Demirel, Tanel. *Türkiye'nin Uzun On Yılı, Demokrat Parti İktidarı ve 27 Mayıs Darbesi*. İstanbul: Bilgi Üniversitesi Yayınları, 2011.

Kili, Suna. *1960–1975 Döneminde Cumhuriyet Halk Partisinde Gelişmeler, Siyaset Bilimi Açısından Bir İnceleme*. İstanbul: Boğaziçi Üniversitesi Yayınları, 1976.

Özbudun, Ergun. "Constitution Making and Democratic Consolidation in Turkey." In *Institutions and Democratic Statecraft*, edited by Metin Heper, Ali Kazancıgil, and Bert A. Rockman, 227–43. New York: Routledge, 1997.

Tuğluoğlu, Fatih. "CHP'nin 14. Kurultayı ve İlk Hedefler Beyannamesi." *Ankara Üniversitesi Türk İnkılâp Tarihi Enstitüsü Atatürk Yolu Dergisi* 60 (2017): 227–310.

38
Mobilising Youths for Political Change: Codeword 555K

Çimen Günay-Erkol

On 28 April 1960, upon the orders of Prime Minister Adnan Menderes (1899–1961), police opened fire on İstanbul University students at a demonstration, killing one of them, Turan Emeksiz (1940–1960), and wounding many others, including the professors who attempted to protect their students. The next day in Ankara, soldiers surrounded the buildings of Ankara University's Faculty of Political Science, and they were again told to open fire on protesting students in attempt to take control of a demonstration, but the soldiers decided to shoot at the walls of the university buildings instead. 555K was the codeword widely shared among university students to refer to a planned demonstration that was to be held on 5 May 1960 at 5 PM in Kızılay Square, which is in the heart of Ankara. Thousands of people, mostly university students, military students, and others, took part in the May 5 demonstration, chanting an altered version of the Plevna march, which is an Ottoman military march, beginning with the line "Do brothers fire at each other?" In this way, the students were calling on the government to put an end to the political pressure it forced on them. Poet Cemal Süreya (real name Cemalettin Seber, 1931–1990), a graduate of the Faculty of Political Science and a reserve officer doing his mandatory military service in Ankara at the time, wrote the poem "555K" and published it on the first page of the literary journal *Papirüs* in August 1960.

Cemal Süreya's Poem "555K"[*]

Now the girls spinning silk in Bursa
In a state of blind love are saying:
Many are the summers we have seen
That some away but some
Clove-moustached young lieutenants
White-haired professors, students
Are carving their names inside us right here
Ah cannot bear cannot bear to look eyes

[*] Translated by Victoria Holbrook and Çimen Günay-Erkol from the original Turkish in Cemal Süreya, "555K," in *Sevda Sözleri: Bütün Şiirleri* (İstanbul: Yapı Kredi Yayınları, 2017), 288–89.

In a state of blind love are saying
Now the girls spinning silk in bursa

Now the ones ploughing fields in Erzurum
Behind their eyebrows that allow none to pass
Their eyes deep, desolate, terrifying
As the iron of the morning cuts into the earth
It buries their rancour in the ground.
Because the traitors of the people in the Ankaras
Because in the İzmirs, because in the İstanbuls
Because in other parts of the country
They got under the skin of the blameless young
That is why their eyes are dark
Now those ploughing fields in Erzurum.

Now it's eight o'clock our night begins
They've shortened the day and lengthened the night
Now in the skies of pain and sadness
Hope's star yellow star blue star
At one edge of our sleep, bombs
At another edge faith in freedom till dawn
Between English-style foot soldiers with their rifles
And the honour of living like a human being
We the nation come and go
Now it's eight o'clock our night begins

Now the moon rises among the clouds
Pimp overlords heartless lords of Bolu
Thieves, bribe-takers, card sharks
The foul triangle taking our rights by force and trickery
Directing the tyranny and villainy
Did you know there is a forest growing now
Do you hear the songs countless deep
Of those with campfires lit in the mountains
Who catch one corner of the darkness aflame
And turn the night to day

Now you know how we talk in low voices
Silently unite silently break up you know
Our mothers steep tea for beautiful days
Our lovers put out flowers in a glass

We go to work in the mornings without a sound
This does not mean things will always be this way
We now gather side by side and we become many
But the day we all with one voice find the song of freedom
That is the day not even Gods can save you.

***

Cemal Süreya did not include this poem in his books during his lifetime but the poem reached a truly wide audience and emerged as an unwitting emblem of the student protests during the final year of the Democrat Party's rule. The poem begins with a lament for the victims of oppression, and it gives voice to a traumatised position of witnessing. However, despite the dark tone at the beginning, overall the poem signifies the resilience of people under political pressure. The youth kickstarted the demonstrations, but when those demonstrations gradually turned into bigger rallies for political freedoms, they had already been joined by crowds from all segments of society. The grief expressed in the initial parts of the poem embraces all of the dissidents who had been victimised by agents of the government. Prime Minister Adnan Menderes, who was at the centre of the state's despotic power, is targeted explicitly with spatial and geographical references such as Erzurum, which is an Anatolian city that was central to his political campaigns. This city is used as a symbol for the feudal-class background of Adnan Menderes, and it also reflects his high political ambitions and revanchism. Large cities such as İzmir, Ankara, and İstanbul are used to symbolise the city versus country divide and to express the political divisions in the public about the ongoing student protests. The play on metaphors such as night/day refers to the restrictions imposed at the time based on martial law. The 8 PM curfew that was declared at the time is thus reflected in the poem, as are the fluctuations of society under the despotic regime created by the Democrat Party. The allegations of corruption that were levelled against the Menderes government also find a place in the poem; here, the accusatory tone hints at a generalising attitude. The references to pimping, robbery, gambling, and so forth are anonymous, but bribery refers to the specific case of Fatin Rüştü Zorlu (1910–1961), the Minister of Foreign Affairs of the Menderes government, who is said to have cut a 10 per cent commission for himself from the American aid provided to Turkey at the time. "*Bolu beyi*," a folkloric despot who controlled the streets of the town of Bolu, is a reference to the attempts that were made to block the travels of İsmet İnönü (1884–1973), the political opponent of Adnan Menderes during his political campaign. For instance, on 2 April 1960, a train carrying İnönü to Kayseri was blocked by soldiers upon Menderes's orders. The poem is, in this way, a celebration of the dedicated struggle for freedom and the fight against political despotism, and it also contains a nod to revered poets such as Nâzım Hikmet (1902–1963) through the metaphor of the "growing forest". The end of the poem was inspired by a speech that İnönü made approximately a month before the military intervention, in which he appealed to members of the DP in Parliament on 18 April 1960, saying that "even he cannot save them" if they continued to nurture the despotic power to which they clung. Together with such historical references, the poem alludes to how the protests reflected the deep discontent of Turkish society with the despotism of the Menderes government, and it sheds light on their growth into a social explosion.

***

The poem "555K" points to how pioneering attempts to resist the religious and authoritarian turn of the DP's rule were transformed into a painfully bitter experience and how that shared experience united people, making them more resilient. The May 5 Demonstration not only became a huge protest against the anti-democratic measures instituted by the Adnan Menderes government, but it was also an act of remembrance for the students who suffered as a consequence of the government's reaction to their resistance. Such a collective act of mourning and civil disobedience was new for Turkish society in that era, and participants risked arrest and physical violence as they rallied in support of it. The crowds sang a modified version of the Plevna march to honour İsmet İnönü, as indicated by the fact that the original lyric "esteemed Osman Pasha" was replaced by "esteemed İsmet Pasha" in an allusion to the Kemalist revolutionary roots of the Republic and to show respect to Adnan Menderes's political opponent, whom they deemed to be the true inheritor of the Kemalist legacy in the Turkish state tradition. The motive underlying the demonstration was a desire to protest the authoritarian turn of the Democrat Party, which was attempting to increase its political control over the youth, and to push the government to return to democratisation. Approximately one month after the May 5 Demonstration, a military coup toppled the Menderes government and introduced a new constitution, which would be remembered as the most liberal constitution Turkey has ever had. It was not, however, top commanders but rather junior officers who carried out the coup d'état on 27 May 1960. In the meantime, university students' political awareness expanded beyond getting rid of social controls and political pressure, forming the basis for an anti-imperialist and class-informed politics within the context of the global movement of 1968 and its manifestations throughout Turkey. In that sense, the vibrant culture of revolt underpinning the demonstration and its memory still loom large over Turkish politics. Vedat Dalokay (1927–1991), one of the students who organised the May 5 Demonstration, was elected mayor of Ankara in 1973. As such, it is possible to say that the optimism that infuses the poem and its vision for a better future expressed through a "song of freedom" have kept several generations engaged in politics.

Select Bibliography

Alper, Emin. *Jakobenlerden Devrimcilere: Türkiye'de Öğrenci Hareketlerinin Dinamikleri (1960-1971).* İstanbul: Tarih Vakfı Yurt Yayınları, 2018.

Bali, Rıfat N. *Turkish Students' Movements and the Turkish Left in the 1950s-1960s.* New Jersey: Gorgias Press, 2010.

Neyzi, Leyla. "Object or Subject? The Paradox of 'Youth' in Turkey." *International Journal of Middle East Studies* 33, no. 3 (2001): 411–32.

Pelt, Mogens. *Military Intervention and a Crisis of Democracy in Turkey: The Menderes Era and Its Demise.* London and New York: I.B. Tauris, 2014.

Ulus, Bülent, and Hakan Güngör. *Parola 555K: Bir Başkaldırının Sıradışı Öyküsü.* İstanbul: Kor Kitap, 2019.

Ulus, Özgür Mutlu. *The Army and the Radical Left in Turkey: Military Coups, Socialist Revolution and Kemalism.* London and New York: I.B. Tauris, 2020.

39
Opening Pandora's Box:
The 1960 Military Coup d'État

Mogens Pelt

In the early morning of 27 May 1960, the Turkish Armed Forces toppled Turkey's democratically elected government. The plans for the coup dated back to the mid-1950s and sprang from the ranks of junior officers. A short while before the coup, the ambitious junior officers offered the position of leadership to a general, Cemal Gürsel (1895–1966), in the hope that his status as former Commander of the Army and as a war hero would prompt the other senior officers to follow his lead. Furthermore, he had recently been suspended for writing a letter demanding the resignation of president Celal Bayar (1883–1986). The conspirators were united by their dissatisfaction with, if not hatred of, the Democrat Party (*Demokrat Parti*, DP) government, which they held responsible for their loss of esteem and status and charged with undermining the principles of Atatürk. The coup was also a response to protests from the political opposition and the Kemalist establishment, which claimed that Prime Minister Adnan Menderes (1899–1961) was violating the rules of parliamentary politics and attempting to take the leader of the main opposition party, the Republican People's Party (*Cumhuriyet Halk Partisi*, CHP), out of the political running. The military decided to act at a juncture when tensions between the CHP and the DP had reached new hights and, in the wake of anti-government student demonstrations, the government had unleased a brutal clampdown on dissent. However, the coup against the DP government also had immediate consequences within the world order of the Cold War.

For the United States, Turkey was an ally of immense strategic importance. It shared borders with the Soviet Union and key countries in the Middle East such as Syria and Iraq. The US ambassador to Turkey, Fletcher Warren (1896–1992), had arrived in Ankara in March 1956 backed by five years of experience in Venezuela, and he would go on to serve in Turkey until November 1960. It was a period of significant ups and downs. Menderes had been following a proactive policy in the Middle East in order to promote the interests of the West and to enhance Turkey's role in the region. He did so to such a degree that he earned himself the nickname "Gendarme of the West," while the domestic opposition accused him of being Washington's lackey, a point that is particularly clear in relation to Syria. First, Menderes attempted to make Syria join the Baghdad Pact, a military alliance between Iran, Iraq, Pakistan, Turkey, and the United Kingdom. He then cooperated with the US to provoke a regime change in Damascus. Both attempts failed and further undermined Menderes' domestic position, which was already under fire because of increasing economic troubles. It was against this background that in

1960 Menderes stated that he would travel to Moscow to try to obtain Soviet economic support. That move must be seen within the context of the difficulties he was facing as he struggled to procure loans from the International Monetary Fund (IMF) and the US on agreeable terms, not as an attempt to switch sides in the Cold War. It is also clear that Washington's primary fear was that a confrontation between the government and the opposition could undermine the stability of its crucial ally, not that Turkey would join the Soviet Bloc. In a telegram sent from the US ambassador in Turkey to the Department of State, Warren informed Washington about his first meeting with the leader of the junta after the coup.

*The US Ambassador's First Meeting with the Junta Leader after the Coup**

Ankara, May 28, 1960, 11 p.m.

[Selim] Sarper [Turkish diplomat, 1899–1968] and I [Fletcher Warren] went in my car to General Gursel's office in General Staff Building. He received us alone. [...] General [*sic*] opened conversation and said he was pleased that I had come for informal talk. [...] Gursel then began longer explanation why revolutionary junta led by him had done what it did. It had felt Menderes Government had forgotten about rights of individual, freedom of press, constitutionality of its acts and in fact had embarked upon series of legislative acts (he never said those acts were unconstitutional) which had for their purposes further repression of people of Turkey. He said we in army were hurt, distressed, deeply concerned about course and goal toward which Menderes Government headed. [...] I said I believed I understood what had been thinking of military and I wanted to tell him something in that connection but, before making this statement, I must say certain other things. He nodded his head. I said I started my work out here with idea that it was relationship between Turk people and American people that was important. I felt Turkey had an importance to USA and free world difficult to overstate. It was equally important to Turkey maintain that relationship. Furthermore, I could not but have utmost respect for Turk military because of my association with American military here in Turkey. One big reason why Turkey was important to free world, particularly to US, was its stability and the Turk army tradition of not intervening in political affairs. By its coup yesterday Turkish military had broken with that tradition. It had opened Pandora's box. No one could foresee what would come out. I felt this morning that neither military nor people of Turkey had any conception of long-range importance of what had been done yesterday morning. [...] This brought me to statement I wanted make: I have served many years in Latin America. I have seen many coups d'etat. I said military in Latin America sits alongside and above other three government divisions. [...] This, I said, meant that army was balance wheel, or last court of resort in Latin American country. [...] Now [Turkey] was in exactly that position. I felt in future military would find it exceedingly difficult not to become involved any divisive political controversy that might involve Turk people. This idea worried me more than coup itself. [...] Earlier in conversation Gursel had said in passing that there had been no mistreatment of President, Menderes,

* Telegram from the US Embassy in Turkey to the Department of State, in *Foreign Relations of the United States, 1958–1960, Eastern Europe; Finland; Greece; Turkey,* Volume X, Part 2, No. 365.

Cabinet or other high officials. I now noted his statement was very important and that it would create fine impression abroad for his junta if there were no mistreatment Menderes government officials. He said, "I assure you that there has been no mistreatment and there will be no mistreatment. I am going to supply each of them with seashore cottage with bath where he can reside in comfort (with his family if he desires) until matters are cleared up."

***

The importance of the document lies in the ways in which Gürsel justifies the actions of the putschists and in the US ambassador's message to the new regime. Gürsel went to great pains to impress on the ambassador that the armed forces had toppled the government to protect the constitution and to prevent further repression, as the government had already infringed on the rights of the individual and freedom of press. Gürsel's invocation of the constitution and citizens' rights must be seen as an attempt to mitigate any possible negative US reactions to the coup against the Menderes government, which had acted as a loyal friend by serving American strategic interests well and which had been on good terms with Washington. It is less clear what Gürsel had in mind when he told Warren that the army was "hurt by and deeply concerned" about the goals of the Menderes government. But it is reasonable to assume that he had Menderes' alleged undermining of the principles of Atatürk in mind. This consisted of accusations that the prime minister had used religion for political purposes, allowed private religious institutions too much leeway, and left the gates wide open for all sorts of "reactionaries," a term used by Kemalists to denounce those who had not adopted the manners and mores of Atatürk's Turkey or who were dead set against it. It may also refer to the dissatisfaction among the officers brought on by their loss of social status as a result of Menderes' prioritisation of the private over the public sector and how his government had made the military subject to increased civilian control. As such grievances had led to a nurturing of a venomous hatred of the government, it is in this light that we should understand Gürsel's assurance that there had not been any mistreatment of Menderes or any other high officials, and that there would not be in the future. The gist of Warren's message to Gürsel was clear and simple: Turkey was an ally of immense strategic importance to the US and Washington was warning the new regime against the danger of the army not being able to extricate itself from politics in the future.

The junta established itself on the National Unity Committee, which was soon divided between senior and junior officers on the issue of handing power back to politicians. In the end, the senior officers won the day. After they had purged the junta of fourteen junior officers who wanted the military to stay in power in order to implement a comprehensive reform programme, the regime prepared the way for a return to parliamentary politics. In this process it agreed with the CHP and all the other political parties except one to prevent a resurrection of the DP and had a new constitution written. While the constitution established the conditions for pluralism in the political and social domain, it weakened the influence of voters and their elected representatives. It did so by creating a senate to which a certain number of its members were appointed, and it codified the right of the military to have a say in politics by setting up a national security council as a channel to influence the government. Furthermore, it established a court to try the members of the former government and in 1961 the court condemned Menderes and a number of his colleagues to death. The hanging of Menderes turned him into a powerful symbol which made it possible to use him both as the incarnation of a martyr of democracy and as a populist villain.

***

The Coup of 27 May did not bring stability. Rather, it marked the beginning of a long period in which the military would play a central role in politics and where coups would beget coups. The 1960 coup was followed by two attempted military interventions in 1962 and 1963, and three successful ones in 1971, 1980, and 1997. The instability of the 1960 junta was instigated by rifts among the military leaders themselves, which paralleled divisions in society and politics. The tensions within the military reappeared after the successor party to the DP, the Justice Party (*Adalet Partisi*, AP), came to power in 1965 and culminated during Turkey's 1968 movement when the traditional cleavage between state and society was transformed into a left-right battle. What now had become the left included among others a significant proportion of junior officers, the intelligentsia, and the CHP, while the right consisted of the AP, conservative officers, Islamists, and ultranationalists. The latter group was led by Alparslan Türkeş (1917–1997), a leading figure in the National Unity Committee until he was purged and exiled as a member of the group of fourteen. After his return to Turkey, he entered the political scene from the far-right as the leader of the Republican Peasants' Nation Party (*Cumhuriyetçi Köylü Millet Partisi*, CKMP) in 1965, which was later to be renamed the Nationalist Movement Party (*Milliyetçi Hareket Partisi*, MHP) in 1969. Protesting students celebrated the Coup of 27 May by hailing the actions of the soldiers involved and declaring that the "revolution" had to come from above through the leadership of a vanguard of intellectuals and officers. When it became clear that the AP could not suppress the social protests without the army, the conservative officers decided to act. But first, on 12 March 1971 they issued an ultimatum which forced the government to step down. Then they purged their own ranks of officers whom they suspected of supporting the students, and lastly they moved against the protest movements and the left. However, the social unrest and political violence continued, which ultimately paved the way for the 1980 coup. To gain control of the country, the new rulers implemented a series of brutal measures while intensifying their fight against the left, but at the same time they also placed a ban on existing political parties. In this way, the junta went further than any of the previous regimes that had been established by the military. In contrast to the conspirators of 1960 who saw "reactionaries"—in the Kemalist sense of the word—as the main threat, the 1980 regime attempted to combine Turkish nationalism and traditional Islamic values as an ideological platform from which to counteract leftist influence. In a symbolic expression of this move, the new regime abolished 27 May Freedom and Constitution Day, which the CHP government had established in 1963 as a national holiday.

Official appreciation of the symbolic value of Menderes underwent a rapid process of transformation culminating in 1990 when his name was rehabilitated and he was reburied and declared a martyr. The legal structures established by the constitution of 1961 and the practices that began with the 1960 coup meant that the military would remain an important factor. It emerged victorious for the last time in 1997 when the national security council forced prime minister Necmettin Erbakan (1926–2011), who was from the Islamist Welfare Party (*Refah Partisi*, RP), to resign. Ten years later in 2007, the military suffered a crippling defeat after the General Staff posted on its website a warning stating that the army might intervene if the candidate of the Justice and Development Party (*Adalet ve Kalkınma Partisi*, AKP) was elected president. In contrast to the situation in 1971 and 1997, when the government gave in to pressure from the military, this time the government resisted and decided to take the matter to the voters, who overwhelmingly supported the government in the elections held shortly afterwards. This also marked the end of the long-term impacts of the 1960 coup. In this way, Warren's warning to Gürsel that his coup had opened a Pandora's box and that the military would find it exceedingly difficult to not become involved in future divisive political controversies turned out to be prophetic. In the end, the coup of 1960 did in fact set Turkey on a course which resembled that of Latin America because of the central role that the army went on to play in politics for almost half a century.

Select Bibliography

Hale, William. *Turkish Politics and the Military.* London: Routledge, 1994.
Karpat, Kemal. *Turkish Politics: The Transition of a Multi-Party System.* Princeton: Princeton University Press, 1959.
Pelt, Mogens. *Military Intervention and a Crisis of Democracy in Turkey: The Menderes Era and Its Demise.* London: I.B. Tauris, 2014.
Pelt, Mogens. "The Colonels' Coup of 1967 and the Military Take-Overs in Turkey in 1960 and 1971." In *Revisiting the Greek Colonels: A Case Study of Southern European Dictatorships – The International Dimension*, edited by Antonis Klapsis, Constantine Arvanitopoulos, Evanthis Hatzivassiliou, and Effie G. H. Pedaliu, 167–78. London: Routledge, 2020.

40
"The Era of Planned Development": The Founding of the State Planning Organisation

Erwin Dekker

The Republic of Turkey first engaged in industrial planning in the 1930s on the initiative of the first president of the country, Mustafa Kemal Atatürk (1881–1938). After the Second World War, Turkey received significant amounts of financial support in the form of Marshall Aid from the United States for reconstruction and development, but the Americans favoured a trade policy that was focused on free international trade. During the early 1950s, there was an agricultural boom, which appeared to confirm the liberal development strategy. But a decrease in international food prices and subsequent poor harvests in Turkey resulted in an economic downturn and that situation, combined with the expansionary fiscal policies enacted by the government, led the country to the brink of defaulting on its foreign debts. By the late 1950s, the international consensus on development was quickly shifting and international organisations such as the International Monetary Fund and the International Bank for Reconstruction and Development now urged Turkey to return to practices of industrial, or rather developmental, planning and promised that in return it would receive financial support. However, under the leadership of Adnan Menderes (1899–1961), the ruling Democrat Party (*Demokrat Parti*, DP) was unwilling to shift back to such forms of planning because Menderes associated them with the dreaded single-party regime of the recent past. His government was overthrown in the coup of 27 May 1960, and shortly afterwards the National Unity Committee assembled an interim government under the guidance of General Cemal Gürsel (1895–1966). The Dutch international planning expert and later Nobel Prize winner Jan Tinbergen (1903–1994), who had reluctantly been allowed to enter the country earlier that year, managed to convince the military interim government to establish a State Planning Organisation (*Devlet Planlama Teşkilatı*, DPT) on 30 September 1960, even before a new constitution was adopted. Jan Tinbergen was a social democratic economist with a background in physics who had pioneered the development of planning models and procedures at the Central Planning Bureau (*Centraal Planbureau*) in the Netherlands, of which he was the founding director. The DPT became enshrined in the new constitution and would subsequently play an important role in the development of economic policies in the decades to come.

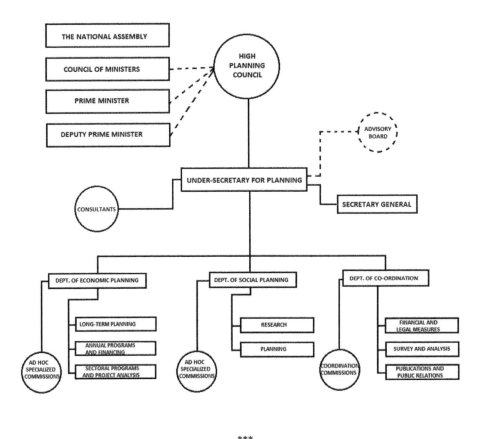

***

The first five-year plan for the period 1963 to 1967 proudly proclaimed that "Turkey has entered the era of planned development within a democratic order." But neither the origin nor the place of the DPT within the political structure of the country was democratic per se. Tinbergen's assistant had managed to convince the military interim government to establish the DPT by arguing that a civilian government was unlikely to be favourable to adopting such an approach to planning. After he succeeded in winning their support, two drafts for the organisation and political position of the DPT were worked out. The first draft, which was compiled by the Minister of State, Osman Şefik İnan (1913–1972), proposed the creation of a large General Planning Council to which appointments would be made by the prime minister.

* The illustration is from Erwin Dekker, *Jan Tinbergen (1903–1994) and the Rise of Economic Expertise* (Cambridge: Cambridge University Press, 2021), 316, which is adapted from Osman Nuri Torun, "The Establishment and Structure of the State Planning Organization," in *Planning in Turkey: Selected Papers*, ed. Selim İlkin and E. İnanç (Ankara: Middle East Technical University, 1967), 44–70.

He suggested that the DPT be placed under the auspices of the Ministry of State, meaning that the DPT's technical economic experts would be under direct political control and be further overseen by a council consisting of approximately thirty politicians and leading industrialists. The aim of İnan's draft was clearly to minimise the influence of the new agency. The second draft bill, which was developed by Colonel Şinasi Orel (1915–2004), respected Tinbergen's ideal of an autonomous DPT. However, it too involved the prime minister quite directly by placing the office under the prime ministry and proposing the assembly of a High Planning Council that would be chaired by the prime minister himself. In the draft bill, the schematic of which can be seen in the figure above, the High Planning Council would consist of fifteen members, eight of whom would be technical experts. In the final bill, that figure was reduced to eight members, four of whom were to be technical experts. The prime minister, who chaired the Planning Council, would make the final decision in cases where the vote was split between the eight members. In both drafts there was little to no parliamentary control over the DPT and the Planning Council, as it was expected that the DPT would work directly with the prime minister. At the time, planning was frequently presented as a technical economic matter. Tinbergen went to great lengths to promote that idea, suggesting that governments could set certain targets and planners could then calculate the most effective way to achieve those aims. In hindsight, we know that in order to implement plans, the state increasingly intervened in directing investments and the direction of particular industries. Even so, many of the targets were never met, and moreover the choice of instruments utilised to achieve policy targets frequently had significant political dimensions.

Cooperation between the prime minister and the other ministers in the Planning Council never proceeded as smoothly as imagined. Although Prime Minister İsmet İnönü (1884–1974), who returned to power in the elections of 1961, was a proponent of planning, there was still a great deal of resistance within his own party and among the other ministers. They opposed the more structural land reforms and further privatisation of the State-Economic Enterprises (İktisadi Devlet Teşekkülü) that the DPT had proposed, much to the disappointment of the ambitious planners in the DPT. When they announced that within the constraints of a balanced budget the maximum growth rate that could be achieved was 6.5% rather than the proposed 7%, the ministers put more pressure on the planners in the DPT to adjust their calculations. In response, three of the four department heads of the DPT, as well as Undersecretary Osman Nuri Torun (1923–2007), resigned even before the first five-year plan was presented. However, they were quickly replaced by others and the government ultimately won the battle over the (target) growth rate. Tinbergen had imagined the creation of a planning bureau model along the lines of the Central Planning Bureau, which he had founded in the Netherlands directly after the Second World War and which was positioned above politics so that it could function as a non-partisan institution. But the DPT never quite achieved that goal, and consequently development planning and economic expertise, which were supposed to be neutral, were politicised from the very start.

***

Nonetheless, the DPT proved to be a strong technocratic institution that provided a steady stream of future leaders in Turkish politics. It managed to do so despite the fact that it was frequently alleged to be a socialist stronghold. Over time, the DPT lost its special status and was "demoted" to a regular ministry. This meant that it became a "normal" element in Turkish politics, not an elite institution that was above politics as it was designed to be. Well into the 1980s, the DPT produced five-year plans, although planning was never as prominent in Turkish politics as it had been in the early 1960s. This state of affairs was in line with broader trends in Europe, in which planning lost most of its allure during the stagflation of the 1970s. Planning organisations such as the DPT and its sister institutions in other countries have mostly reinvented themselves as advisory bodies, but they remain a stronghold of economic experts. In 2011, the DPT was renamed the Ministry of Development (*Kalkınma Bakanlığı*).

Select Bibliography

Dekker, Erwin. "Tinbergen in Turkey: Exporting Institutions." *History of Political Economy* 54, no. 3 (2022): 505–25.
Milor, Vedat. "The Genesis of Planning in Turkey." *New Perspectives on Turkey* 4 (Fall 1990): 1–30.
Ünay, Sadik. *The Political Economy of Development Planning in Turkey: Neoliberal Globalization and Institutional Reform.* New York: Nova Science Publishers, 2006.

1963–1972

41

From Temporary Migration to the Struggle for Equal Social Rights: Turkish Workers in Germany

Ahmet Akgündüz

In 1960, some firms in Germany began recruiting workers from İstanbul through private bureaus to fill their job vacancies. Because recruitment from İstanbul continued—according to official German records the number of workers reached a total of 2,495, of whom 200 were female, by July 1960—and Germany signed a bilateral labour recruitment agreement with Greece in March 1960, the Turkish government demanded that the Germans conclude a similar agreement with Turkey.

The German government, however, initially refused Turkey's demand, invoking the racial argument that "Turkey is not a European country". This was not received well by the Turkish authorities at the time, given that Turkey was sensitive about being treated as a part of Europe and that it had applied for association with the European Economic Community (EEC), the progenitor of the European Union, in July 1959. The Turkish embassy in the German capital submitted its government's diplomatic note to the German Federal Ministry of Foreign Affairs in December 1960, stating that if Germany refused to sign an agreement, Turkey would consider it to be neglecting a NATO member in favour of Greece. Some ten months later, on 30 October 1961, the Federal Ministry of Foreign Affairs responded positively to the Turkish embassy, also with a note. Strangely enough, the labour recruitment agreement between the two countries appeared in the form of the response of the Turkish embassy to the German note and bore the same date, 30 October 1961, whereby labour migration acquired an official framework.

The Turkish Employment Service (*İş ve İşçi Bulma Kurumu*, İİBK), which was responsible for overseeing external labour migration, stated that the aim of Turkey's insistence on signing a bilateral labour recruitment agreement was to address multiple key concerns: to eliminate the involvement of unauthorised private bureaus in dispatching workers abroad; to ensure the provision of official protections and an orderly migration process for Turkish citizens in alignment with their qualifications and skills; to prevent the departure of skilled workers whose absence could have detrimental effects on Turkey's national economy; and, to safeguard the social security rights of workers throughout the duration of their time abroad.

The agreement, however, not only in terms of the way it was conducted and its form but also in terms of its content—especially as regards the social rights granted to migrants—was obviously lacking in comparison to the agreements Germany signed with Italy, Spain, Greece, and later with Portugal. But some two and a half years later, the issue of the discriminatory treatment of Turkish migrant workers with respect to social rights was resolved by the bilateral social security agreement of 30 April 1964 and the German-Turkish protocol of 20 May of the same year. The securing of the social rights in question had gotten underway, however, even before the official social security agreement by way of a reciprocal verbal agreement reached by the two governments in June 1963.

In the granting of social security rights in question before the signing of the official agreement, the protests of Turkish "guest workers" played an as-yet unknown but significant role. Dr Bekam Bilaloğlu, who held the position of the first Turkish labour attaché to Germany from 1963 to 1984, served as the intermediary between Turkish workers and the German federal government. As a negotiator and one of the three signatories of the 1964 Turkish-German Protocol, Dr Bilaloğlu shared his account of the verbal agreement reached in 1963, recounting the details as follows.

Gastarbeiter Diplomacy for Social Security*

In late January 1963, which was my first month in Germany, I attended an "entertainment day" for Turkish workers in Cologne, at their persistent request. I thought it would be a good opportunity to learn how things were going. Soon after entering the hall, which was full of relatively well-dressed young people, I realised that they had in fact organised a meeting to question me about their unequal social rights; entertainment was a façade to get me there. They had arranged everything among themselves beforehand. Two speakers took the floor, one after another. They were complaining about working and living conditions and unequal rights. The second one even spoke aggressively, gave concrete examples and shouted "all of you sold us out". Tension rose in the hall, some of them were seemingly drunk and had difficulty calming themselves down. I was seriously scared. I had no knowledge whatsoever of the issues that they were talking about. Before I came to Germany, I had been a judge at a court in Zonguldak. I knew the Minister of Labour [B. Ecevit] in person, he said to me: "You know the German law, you can be useful for workers there; I want you to accept the labour attaché post." I had accepted the offer only for two or three years. No Turkish official had briefed me before my departure or after my arrival in Germany. Thus, in my turn, I had nothing to tell to the tense crowd in the hall but the truth, and I took an oath on my dignity that I would do all that I could. I learned that indeed the workers were right regarding the social security matters. I immediately contacted the German Federal Ministry of Labour. The German authorities accepted the complaints and offered an even quicker solution (and also told of their willingness to lift the two-year limitation on the length of residence of Turkish workers). They said that making a written social security agreement covering the aforementioned issues would take time. Thus, if the Turkish government could provide a verbal

---

* From the author's personal interviews with Bekam Bilaloğlu, 29 April and 2 May 1993, in Berlin. Also quoted in Ahmet Akgündüz, *Labour Migration from Turkey to Western Europe, 1960–1974: A Multidisciplinary Analysis*, second edition (London: Routledge, 2018), 119–20, note 99.

agreement that Turkey would give the same rights to those Germans who were working, or would come to work in Turkey, they could start the implementation of social security matters immediately. This information prompted me to get in touch with the Turkish Minister of Labour via telephone. And a few days after my contact, the minister conveyed his government's approval via telephone. Thus, from 1 June 1963 onwards, Turkish migrants began to be paid child allowances and their spouses in Turkey were entitled to benefit from the hospitals belonging to the Turkish Social Security Organisation at the expense of the German side. Meanwhile, when I got a positive response on the social security issues from the German side, I asked the same workers to organise an even larger meeting to hear the good news, which took place in the early February 1963. I informed them about the impending solution of the social security problems and Germany's willingness and plan to lift the limitation on the length of residence. Now, I was a hero in the eyes of a huge crowd in the hall, and, as soon as I finished my speech, I was lifted on their shoulders.

***

After his initial tense meeting with Turkish workers in Cologne, the labour attaché from Turkey stationed in Bonn, Dr B. Bilaloğlu, indeed reached out to the German government with a request to improve the 1961 labour recruitment agreement, which diverged from those established with southern European nations. He wanted to put an end to the unjust treatment faced by Turkish workers concerning their social rights, including child benefit allowances and the entitlement of spouses residing in Turkey to access health insurance funded by the German health insurance organisation. The German government was quick to agree to the demands made by Bilaloğlu, leading to the conclusion of the verbal agreement and then both the 1964 social security agreement and the 1964 protocol between the two countries.

The German government's acceptance of the Turkish demands stemmed primarily from the following factors: Germany's discriminatory regulation in the field of social rights obviously contravened the International Labour Organisation's "Migration for Employment Recommendation, 1949" and the "Migration for Employment Convention, 1949," which Germany ratified in 1959; a dearth of labour influx from southern Europe, which intensified German reliance on Turkish workers; the performance exhibited by Turkish workers, which was more than satisfactory; and, mounting discontent among Turkish migrants due to disparities in social rights, which entailed the risk of disruptive incidents at the factories employing them. For example, in 1962 in the city of Essen, Turkish workers appealed unsuccessfully to German trade unions and the Turkish Consulate in Germany to help them secure the right to receive equal child benefit payments. Then, on April 30, 300 Turkish workers went on strike over the issue, and the police responded heavy-handedly and deported ten of the strikers. Meanwhile, Turkey was actively engaged in negotiating more advantageous bilateral labour recruitment agreements with other countries that were taking in migrant workers. Consequently, defending the existence of a "second-class" agreement signed with Turkey became increasingly arduous. Nonetheless, in one area discrimination remained. Germany granted residence and work permits to southern European workers who spontaneously showed up in the country in order to increase the volume of labour inflow from southern Europe but firmly denied the same to migrants from Turkey, including the wives of officially employed workers who entered the country in the same manner. The 20 May 1964 protocol included both a strong reiteration of the German government's stance and the Turkish delegation's opposing view on this point.

***

By the time labour recruitment with Germany was ameliorated, due to the Cold War division of Europe, the recruitment of workers from Turkey appeared to be the best available option to supplement southern European labour inflows, which were already insufficient to meet growing migrant labour demand of the German as well as other western European economies. There was simply no other alternative within the same geographical range. It is likely, however, that Turkey's membership in Western military, economic, and political organisations, apparent willingness to be a part of Europe, and its secular system eased the recruitment of Turkish workers when it became needed. The labour recruitment agreements that Turkey reached with Austria, Belgium, and the Netherlands in 1964, as well as with France in 1965, Sweden in 1967 and Australia in 1967, were carried out following official procedure. These agreements, which promised workers equal social rights, were initiated by the receiving countries themselves and concluded between the two states.

According to İİBK records, a total of 795,842 migrants went to eight European countries and 6,806 went to Australia through the İİBK between 1961 and 1974, of whom 145,848 were female. Of the total, 81 per cent (649,337 workers) went to Germany, while the rest moved to the other countries. Of the total female migrants, more than 95 percent were recruited by Germany. Aside from official channels, however, there was also a second exit channel for workers; namely, going to Europe on a tourist passport or traveling there spontaneously. Thousands of these workers—referred to at the time as "tourist workers"—regularised their status once they found a job in their countries of destination. The İİBK claimed that their number was included in the official figures. But thousands of others failed to do so and worked as irregular or "tourist workers". Migration, however, was not a one-way ticket, and it included a considerable amount of return migration as well.

The gender and skill composition and volume of the migration by the country of destination was determined by demand. The number of workers in each receiving country gradually increased because southern European countries were unable to meet the demand for labour. In Germany, for example, although the percentage of skilled workers among the migrants recruited from Turkey was higher than that of migrants from Greece, Italy, or Spain, the volume of Turkish migration remained limited and was less than that of Greek, Italian, or Spanish migration up to the end of 1967. The drawing in of workers from Turkey gained pace just after 1969, when Germany's demand for labour increased significantly and southern European, including Yugoslavian, labour reserves dissipated. Turkish workers became the largest migrant labour contingent in the last two years of the recruitment period (1972–73) but by a rather small margin, and the fact that there was a higher return rate among southern European workers was also a factor in that shift.

With the halt of the recruitment of labour by Germany in 1973 and by the other countries in 1974, migration did not end but continued mainly in the form of family reunification and marriage migration, especially in the following eight to ten years, a process that had already been underway in the last years of the recruitment period. Except for Germany, receiving countries acknowledged the transformation of guest worker migration into permanent settlement without excessive delay and provided migrants with access to citizenship and made the acquisition of dual citizenship possible. Thus, labour migration-based communities have become de jure, in some cases de facto, a part of society in western European countries. These communities have grown further and become more diversified by way of various forms of human mobility, such as return migration, highly skilled labour migration, and asylum migration, the most notable wave of which took place in the aftermath of the military coup d'état of 12 September 1980. In Germany, Turkish workers had acquired a place in and become a part of society even during the recruitment period through their struggle for equal social rights and their active and visible participation in working-class movements and trade-unions, especially in the iron-metal producing and processing industry. As they became a part of society in western European countries, Turkey-origin communities' connections with Turkey have not ended but continued to differing degrees. These connections encompass various aspects, including economic, social, political, legal, and emotional linkages, thereby creating a new dynamic that continues to influence relations between western Europe and Turkey.

Select Bibliography

Akgündüz, Ahmet. *Labour Migration from Turkey to Western Europe, 1960–1974: A Multidisciplinary Analysis.* second edition. London: Routledge, 2018.

Akgündüz, Ahmet. "Guest Worker Migration in Post-War Europe (1946–1974): An Analytical Appraisal." In *An Introduction to International Migration Studies: European Perspectives,* edited by Marco Martiniello and Jan Rath, 181–209. Amsterdam: Amsterdam University Press, 2012.

Miller, Jennifer. "Her Fight Is Your Fight: 'Guest Worker' Labor Activism in the Early 1970s West Germany." *International Labor and Working-Class History* 84 (2013): 226–47.

Penninx, Rinus, and Herman Van Renselaar. *A Fortune in Small Change: A Study of Migrant Workers' Attempts to Invest Savings Productively through Joint Stock Corporations and Village Development Co-operatives in Turkey.* The Hague: Remplod/Nuffic, 1978.

42

Dreams of Development:
Peasantism, Cadrism, and a Disciplined Society

Engin Kılıç

There is a tradition of utopian writing in Turkish literature. We see the earliest examples of this in the works of Young Ottomans such as Namık Kemal (1840–1888) and Ziya Pasha (1829–1880). The second wave came after the 1912–1913 Balkan Wars, when the Ottoman Empire was on the verge of collapse. During this period, many writers wrote utopian works that envisioned the country's rebirth and rise. The third wave was seen during the early Republican period, when the single-party regime was being established. Pro-government writers wrote utopias that glorified the regime's virtues in order to endear the regime to the people.

The novel *Toprak Uyanırsa: Ekmeksizköy Öğretmeninin Hatıraları* (If the Earth Awakens: Memoirs of a Teacher in Ekmeksizköy) was written at a later date, in 1963. Its author, Şevket Süreyya Aydemir (1897–1976), was a teacher, economist, historian, and bureaucrat. In his youth, Aydemir was a Turanist, meaning a Turkish nationalist who championed the union of all Turkic nations, from Turkey to Turkestan; he was such a dedicated Turanist that when the Surname Law was enacted in 1934, he chose the surname Aydemir, which was the name of the protagonist of the racist novelist Müfide Ferit Tek's novel *Aydemir* (1918). He later took an interest in communism. After joining the Turkish Communist Party, he studied at the Communist University of the Toilers of the East (KUTV) in Moscow and was later imprisoned in Turkey on charges of communist propaganda. Later, he began to delve into Kemalist ideas. Through the magazine *Kadro* (Cadre), which he published with Yakup Kadri Karaosmanoğlu (1889–1974) and some other friends of his, he tried to win Kemalism over towards a more left-wing policy, but the magazine was closed down two years later.

The novel *If the Earth Awakens* tells the story of a teacher who brings about a miraculous development in an Anatolian village called Ekmeksizköy, which literally means "Village without bread," implying that it is an unproductive, poor, barren place. The development of a single village is presented as a model for the development of the whole nation. The dynamics of that development will be discussed below.

If the Earth Awakens: Memoirs of a Teacher in Ekmeksizköy[*]

[Minister of Public Works] – But I was thinking that this country must have a way out anyway. The work that Mustafa Kemal started must continue. But how? Well, I still haven't untied that knot.

[Protagonist] – But, Minister, you are at the gate of an old town where a knot called the most impossible knot in world history, namely the Gordian knot, was untied in one stroke. Gordion is just behind those hills. That is to say, there are no knots that cannot be untied in this land.

The legend of Gordion seems to me like the struggle between the sword and the plough. Gordias was a man of the plough and Alexander a man of the sword. Alexander's empire crumbled. But the holy plough of Gordias always creates blessings.

[Minister] – So, you mean you put your hand on the plough here now?

[Protagonist] – Yes. But now we are not in the Gordion era. Our age also has a saying. Today, a lone farmer lives under the sword of Damocles under the pressure of needs, on the one hand, and the volatility of the market, on the other. So is the lone worker, so is the lone trader. So are the lone people today. If you do not unite the workers in the union, the farmers in the cooperative, and the merchants in the companies, this sword will come down on them sooner or later. Even a lone state cannot survive today... It will enter into alliances and provide aid. What we are doing here is reaching out to the farmers through the organisation. We already have a cooperative. But even they tried to re-establish the village.

[Minister] – Is that all?

[Protagonist] – No. We also have a small formula: "Mobilising the means." Here's your excavator that drained the swamp and now works in that stream. This is the mobilisation of a means. The establishment of the village grove, construction of the school, large-scale beet cultivation, equipment wells and underground water extraction, laying the foundation of the site and much more...

[Minister] – It's like a system. A peasantist system. This system may be simple and modest. But there is something to it. Instead of the top-down administration of the state, it's the people pulling the state into themselves. I congratulate you.

[*] Translated from the original Turkish in Şevket Süreyya Aydemir, *Toprak Uyanırsa: Ekmeksizköy Öğretmeninin Hatıraları* (İstanbul: Remzi Kitabevi, 1963), 344–45.

***

The book presents a utopian framework for the future of Turkey that would include a "middle ground" system. A "new order of life" will be created and that order will not abolish private property, but rather it will mobilise existing means and put the labour of society to good use within the framework of a planned economy that is tied to the land and the peasantry with cooperatives at its centre. And thus, "life will be more beautiful, more joyful".

The novel is set in an imaginary village in Anatolia at an unspecified period of time in early Cold War Turkey. The narrator, a retired teacher, decides to teach again. He is assigned to the village of Keltepe (Bald Hill) on the edge of a swamp. When he arrives in the village, he experiences complete disappointment. With its barren land, dilapidated houses, swampy smell, and scrawny people, this small village seems to have survived since antiquity without undergoing much progress. The narrator considers leaving the village immediately, but then decides to stay and fight.

First, he sets to work on the school, and with the financial and moral support of the gentry, the villagers, and the state, the school is quickly built, and everyone enthusiastically sends their children to school. That is followed by the draining of the swamp, which is then opened up to agriculture. By means of a system that is based on private property but maximises profits through cooperatives, great wealth begins to pour through those fertile lands. Vineyards, livestock, and milk production, as well as a new planned village, completely change the outlook of the villagers. It is emphasised in the novel that such success becomes possible on the basis of six premises.

The first condition of social development is working in good faith. Unlike most political and sociological theories, utopian thinking is based on the idea that human nature is malleable, if not good. This novel takes this assumption to its extreme. That is also the most important weakness of the novel in terms of its power of persuasion. The miraculous transformation that constitutes the storyline of the novel takes place thanks to the extremely good intentions of everyone involved. The teacher, who is the protagonist of the novel, seems to be quite charismatic. Everyone he meets, from the villagers to the governor, and from the engineer to the minister, accepts his leadership and does what he says. In the course of the novel, we do not come across anyone who has a conflict of interest or suggests another alternative. We understand that this solidarist and hegemonic social structure is an indispensable prerequisite for Aydemir's utopia.

Second, intellectuals should lead society and the peasantry. Aydemir emphasises and deals with the issues of leadership and guidance at great length. Members of two main social groups are seen in the novel: peasants and civil servants employed at various levels (teachers, engineers working at state institutions, the district governor, the governor, and so forth). Almost all of these civil servants define themselves as "we intellectuals". In other words, the intellectuals who should guide the public consist of civil servants. In that context, everyone in the book expresses a need to "herd" and "lead" the villagers. The implication here is also that a movement initiated from above can reach society only through a "cadre," namely the organised collective action of intellectuals who create and disseminate the ideology of the Turkish revolution.

Third, society must be disciplined. Another assumption that is accepted without discussion in parallel with the need for guidance is society's need for order. As one of the engineers who came to drain the swamp put it, it is essential to "keep the nation in line". This understanding of the need for order will lead the author to drop in frequent military connotations. And, according to Aydemir, to have a village like Keltepe—that unfortunate name was replaced with Keklikpınarı, (Partridge Spring) after it experienced such great progress—and a country made up of such villages, it is inevitable for society to be organised with military discipline and a militaristic hierarchy.

Fourth, the clergy must also contribute to progress. The approach to religion in the novel parallels the Kemalist understanding of religion. It is a prerequisite for progress that religious institutions and practices, though not directly rejected, be taken under control and that they are placed in the service of the regime. For instance, the old, paralysed, wise imam Hafız, who had initially moved to the village as an assistant imam so as to avoid going to jail for being a vagrant and gambling, provides a great deal of support to the teacher in terms of curbing people's reactions to innovations by way of his intellectual personality. In many respects he is more progressive than the teacher. Notably, he is against polygamy and respects women's rights.

Fifth, the state has to have sufficient means for the development of the entire country. Following the above premises, we can read into the author's assumptions about the economy. The most important and also the most questionable of these is the notion that the country's backwardness is not the result of a lack of resources. The state has the means and resources to spread the development experienced in Keltepe to the country as a whole. Therefore, what is missing is not resources, but guidance, as mentioned above. Development is inevitable when the land and the people are awakened and when such opportunities are activated under the leadership of intellectuals who guide the people.

Finally, Turkey's development can only be achieved through statist and peasantist policies. In the novel, Aydemir mostly deals with the idea that any development model suitable for Turkey's conditions will be based on a statist and planned economy. That model will also be largely centred on the land and the village. The protagonist's comrade Ayhan Bozkır, a young agricultural engineer who had the chance to put into practice his thesis titled "Unity in the Village" in Keltepe, establishes an equation along the lines of "village = nation = state" and claims that the development they achieved at the scale of the village can be adapted to the country at large. In parallel with this extremely reductionist approach, a concrete development plan is also included. The driver of development is cooperatives. The idea is that the miraculous transformation experienced in Keltepe will also lead to the transformation of Turkey as a whole into a huge cooperative.

***

In the Cold War context in which the novel was written, *If the Earth Awakens* echoes the planned economies and peasantist policies launched by the revolutionary regimes of the Global South. At the same time, within the context of utopian Turkish writing it envisions a society that, although it was written at a later date, bears many similarities to those of utopias that were written in the 1930s and 1940s. Such an understanding, which does not tolerate political pluralism and social differences, foresees the modernisation of society by way of a statist, Jacobinist, disciplined strategy and planning under the leadership of a revolutionary cadre organised under the auspices of the state. Thus, we indirectly get an answer to the question of how to integrate class conflicts into this system. The concrete projection of such an approach is a society placed under military discipline and administered per the principles of a corporatist economic model. Thus, the claim is made that Turkey will reach the level of development that France and Israel had already achieved.

Some of the ideologies featured in the novel, such as corporatism and peasantism, do not find much of a political following today. Such notions may even be ridiculed. The 2022 Netflix comedy series *The Life and Movies of Erşan Kuneri*, written and directed by popular Turkish comedian Cem Yılmaz, presents such an example. In an episode titled "Cooperative Kemal," we see the making of a fictional movie about a teacher who sees himself as the self-appointed leader and guide of ignorant villagers and imagines that he will unite and mobilise them under his leadership, showing them the way to progress. In the course of events, however, he is disgraced, mocked, and eventually forced to leave the village.

Nevertheless, Aydemir's novel demonstrates that certain inclinations, such as authoritarianism, sublimation of the state, militarism, and anti-pluralism, are part and parcel of popular utopic visions that go beyond ideological differences.

Select Bibliography

Karaömerlioğlu, M. Asım. "The People's Houses and the Cult of Peasant in Turkey." *Middle Eastern Studies* 34, no. 4 (1998): 67–91.

Kılıç, Engin. "Cumhuriyet Dönemi Ütopyalarında İdeal Toplum Tasavvurları." MA thesis, İstanbul Bilgi University, 2005.

Parla, Taha, and Andrew Davison. *Corporatist Ideology in Kemalist Turkey: Progress or Order?* Syracuse: Syracuse University Press, 2004.

43
Deviating from the National Narrative:
The Workers' Party of Turkey and Cyprus

Nikos Christofis

On 16 August 1960, Cyprus attained its independence from the British Empire. For a short period of time, it seemed that the Cypriot versions of competing Greek and Turkish nationalisms and the inter-ethnic conflict between the two largest communities of the island (Greek Orthodox and Turkish Muslims), which had been ongoing since the 1940s, had come to an end. Following the anti-British national struggle led by the Greek Cypriot EOKA (the National Organisation of Cypriot Fighters) from 1955 until 1959, the British were forced to accept the independence of the island by signing the London-Zurich Agreements in 1960. However, the new constitution of the Republic of Cyprus not only failed to guarantee the island's independence, it gave rise to a series of heated discussions among the political elites of the two communities. The tensions caused by paramilitary groups on both sides and the impasse that followed the talks that were held between the leaders of the two communities, Archbishop Makarios III (1913–1977) and Dr Fazıl Küçük (1906–1984), led Makarios to make a unilateral decision in November 1963 to amend the constitution in order to fulfil the goal of *enosis* (political union with Greece). Tensions culminated the following month after what had appeared to be a routine Greek Cypriot police patrol turned violent. When the Turkish Cypriots refused to show their credentials, the police opened fire, triggering the first Cyprus crisis in December 1963. The escalating crises that erupted in the following months affected every party involved, both in Cyprus and also in the so-called "motherlands," Greece and Turkey.

One of the groups involved was the Workers' Party of Turkey (*Türkiye İşçi Partisi*, TİP). The party was established in February 1961 against a backdrop of political liberalisation made possible under the terms of the 1961 constitution, which opened up a broad space for the establishment of left-wing parties and publications. In the first months after its founding, the party tried to maintain a moderate stance on foreign policy issues. On the one hand, it did so because the party was trying to consolidate its position in the political arena and avoid being labelled communist and anti-Kemalist by the Turkish authorities, as a consequence of which it could be closed down. On the other hand, the party was still, ideologically speaking, in the process of becoming established and it was undecided on a number of policy issues. Rather quickly, however, the TİP began to openly criticise the Turkish government for its pro-American and pro-NATO foreign policy stance. That criticism became increasingly vehement after the Cuban missile crisis broke out in 1962, during which Turkey's seemingly blind support for the Americans perpetuated a policy approach that had been in place since the end of the

Second World War. But it was the crisis of 1963–64 in Cyprus that provided the party with the perfect opportunity to elaborate on and popularise its own position on foreign policy issues, specifically regarding Cyprus, during the party's General Directory Council held in Bursa on 10 May 1964. The party chairman, Mehmet Ali Aybar (1908–1995), argued that imperialism lay at the heart of the so-called Cyprus Question, which prevented Turkey from pursuing an independent foreign policy.

*Aybar's Speech on Cyprus**

President Makarios had been complaining about the treaties and the constitution even before the recent violent events occurred. And most importantly, Turkish Cypriots never had an ideal such as [the Greek Cypriots have] to "become part of the motherland," which has been passed on from one generation to another. The absence of such an ideal can probably be explained by the fact that the island had been legally connected to the Ottoman state. But in any case, since 1878 when the island was ceded to England, whenever the Rums resisted and rebelled against England, the leaders of the Turkish community expressed their commitment to England and asked not to be considered the same as the rebellious Greeks. It is the Greeks who have nurtured the cause of Enosis [and passed it] from generation to generation. They have organised and armed themselves for this cause. They have been fighting against the English for years. The extreme nationalist, Enosist, and fascist terrorist organisation EOKA is once again active. And President Makarios met with the leader of this organisation in Athens.

When all these factors are taken into consideration, even if we also accept that some people from the Turkish community of Cyprus may have been following [their own] personal interests and ambitions, we cannot but accept that the most recent violent events were, in all probability, instigated by Greek Cypriots who support Enosis.

Another issue is equally important. With the Lausanne Treaty of 1923, we [Turkey] officially accepted the annexation of Cyprus by England. Until 1955, the Cyprus issue did not exist for Turkey. It was only following the Greek Cypriot uprising of April 1955 against the English colonial administration and the start of EOKA's terrorising acts that England called on Turkey to participate in the London Conference.

For England, which had just been obliged to surrender Suez, Cyprus had become an extremely important military base. British interests in the Middle East could be easily be controlled from Cyprus, and Britain's rights over the petroleum resources of the Middle East could be easily and effectively protected from there as well. However, the continuous rebellions of the Greek Cypriots in 1955 and Greece's appeal to the UN to acknowledge its self-determination put Britain in a difficult situation. If

* Translated from the Turkish original in "GYK'nun 10 Mayıs 1964 Bursa Toplantısında Genel Başkanın Açış Konuşması," Archive of the Social History Research Foundation of Turkey (Türkiye Sosyal Tarih Araştırma Vakfı Arşivi), Nebil Varuy Papers, box 4, folder 122; Archive of the International Institute of Social History, Kemal Sülker Papers, box 550.

Turkey appeared to assert its own rights over Cyprus, Britain would be spared isolation in the face of Greece's protests and international public opinion. Turkey was invited to the 1955 London Conference based on this calculation. In pursuit of easy successes, the adventurous government that had been overthrown zealously accepted the invitation. Since then, Cyprus has been turned into an issue that has created acute crises for Turkey. Today, we are experiencing the effects of the most vicious of those crises.

[...]

The bloody violence in Cyprus continues. The first thing to do is to stop it. The military forces of the UN on the island are there for that reason. We must ensure that they do not stand passively by. At the same time, the life and property of Cypriot Turks, the basic rights necessary to live as a human being, must be restored. And these necessary conditions must be further safeguarded.

However, all these tasks must be carried out in view of the "National Pact," the indispensable foundation of Turkey during the War of Independence.

We are a state that won a war of independence and purged an old inheritance. We have carved the borders of the motherland [in a manner that is] consistent with the existence of a homogenous nation. We lay no claim to any territory outside our current borders, and there must be no such claims. We have to develop and quickly reach [the level of] civilised societies. What is more, for a state born out of a war of national independence, attempting to seize other countries and peoples would be tantamount to self-denial. In any case, we also lack the means necessary to succeed in such an endeavour.

***

The Bursa speech set forth the party's first coherent and official policy on Cyprus. The importance of the speech is twofold. Firstly, the points raised by the party chairman, Mehmet Ali Aybar, show clear signs of maturation based on an internationalist, left-wing approach towards the issue of Cyprus. He noted, for example, that Cyprus did not appear on Turkey's national agenda until 1955, when EOKA emerged. Established in April 1955, EOKA was the Greek Cypriot nationalist liberation organisation whose struggle eventually led to the independence of Cyprus. Aybar also highlighted that Turkish Cypriots were quite satisfied with the London-Zurich Agreements of 1959–1960 and thus had never put forward a Turkish "ideal of annexation". At the same time, however, the speech was perceived as a "betrayal" of Turkish "national interests" (*milli menfaat*) not only by the governing and opposition parties and mainstream media, but also by some members of the party itself.

With regard to its anti-imperialist and internationalist stance, the party's criticism of the role played by Britain, and more generally of colonialism and imperialism, testify to its maturation. For example, Aybar highlighted how Turkey was running the risk of being dragged into the issue simply for the sake of bolstering British imperial interests in the Middle

East, especially after Britain's loss of the Suez Canal and in terms of its claims on Middle Eastern oil. This move was not, however, simply part of the party's attempt to consolidate its position in the political arena; rather, its members genuinely saw the party as the only staunch proponent of the Kemalist principles underpinning the National Pact *(Misak-ı Milli)*. Taken up in that context, if Turkey were to turn its attention to Cyprus and become actively involved, it would be violating the Kemalist foreign policy dictum "Peace at Home, Peace in the World". In other words, the Bursa speech can be seen as a call to revolution—namely, to pursue the enduring Kemalist mission to fulfil the socialist revolution that had been left unfinished in 1922 (the year the Anatolian nationalist movement won a decisive victory over the Greek troops, leading to the establishment of the Republic of Turkey the following year).

With respect to the general criticisms levelled against the party, the resignations of prominent members signalled in no uncertain terms that a socialist approach to issues with national ramifications was still inchoate. Arguably more important is how the party was put squarely on the defensive by the intense reactions and fierce attacks of the Kemalist establishment, which was staunchly nationalist and vehemently anti-communist. Aybar's assertions were taken entirely out of context by his critics and turned around on him, as when Aybar's reference to the National Pact in solving the crisis was presented as "the TİP's refusal of the Cyprus Question". The party tried several approaches in responding in a firm but principled manner, including the issuance of a joint statement in support of Aybar by party branch heads and the publication of a booklet containing Aybar's complete speech, in which Makarios is described as "the priest chief of fascist gangs". However, even those attempts by the TİP to rectify the situation were unable to change the tide, which forced the party to adopt a more nationalist and militarised approach to the issue that complied with the state's official narrative.

***

More than half a century after the Bursa speech, the Cyprus Question remains unresolved, and Turkey's recent stance regarding the issue is reminiscent of old Cold War approaches. Aybar's statements seem to have been forgotten among left-wing circles and likewise been relegated to occupying a marginal space in discussions on the topic today. Meanwhile, the "silence" of mainstream political groups on the issue is deafening, although prominent leftists like Bülent Ecevit (1925–2006), Mümtaz Soysal (1929–2019), and İsmail Cem (1940–2007) had kept the Cyprus issue alive over the decades. However, perhaps the most strikingly relevant aspect of the speech today is what followed afterwards—namely, the Turkish state's coercive attitude towards and eventual suppression of the party. It would appear that "silencing" the opposition and dissident voices rather than fostering dialogue has long been the preferred tactic of the Turkish state, not only during the Cold War but down to the present day as well under the Justice and Development Party *(Adalet ve Kalkınma Partisi, AKP)*.

Select Bibliography

Christofis, Nikos. "Encountering Imperialism and Colonialism: The Greek and Turkish Left in Cyprus." In *Cypriot Nationalisms in Context: History, Politics, and Identity*, edited by Thekla Kyritsi and Nikos Christofis, 283–305. Basingstoke: Palgrave, 2018.

Güvenç, Serpil Çelenk. *Solun Merceğinden Dış Politika: TİP Deneyimi, 1960-1970*. İstanbul: Daktylos Yayınevi, 2008.

Sargın, Nihat. *TİP'li Yıllar*. Vol. 1. İstanbul: Felis Yayınevi, 2001.

TİP'in Birinci Onyılı (1961-1971). Brussels: İNFO-TÜRK, 1982.

Ünsal, Artun. *Umuttan Yalnızlığa: Türkiye İşçi Partisi (1961-1971)*. İstanbul: Tarih Vakfı Yurt Yayınları, 2002.

Varuy, Nebil. *Türkiye İşçi Partisi. Olaylar-Belgeler-Yorumlar (1961-1971)*. İstanbul: TÜSTAV, 2010 [1975].

44
The Making of a National Symbol: Necip Fazıl Kısakürek and Hagia Sophia

Umut Azak

Hagia Sophia, a former Byzantine imperial church built in 360 CE which was later converted into an imperial mosque during the reign of Sultan Mehmed II, who conquered Constantinople in 1453, was closed to Muslim worship in 1934, whereupon it was transformed into a museum per the terms of a government decree. The official decision to secularise this grand monument on the basis of a scholarly perspective that kept an equal distance to both imperial and religious heritages was contested and critiqued, especially from the early 1950s onwards. Those critiques were largely made by conservative circles who, as pioneers of an Ottomanist nationalism, insisted on commemorating the conquest of İstanbul as a "national victory" and called for Mehmed II to be glorified as a "national hero". The fact that Hagia Sophia had been assigned the status of a museum was interpreted in the Ottomanist narrative as a mark of national humiliation and subservience. Islamist poet and activist Necip Fazıl Kısakürek (1904–1983) was a zealous proponent of such a view. He gave a speech about Hagia Sophia which became an iconic text for later generations of conservative nationalist as well as Islamist movements in Turkey, and it became one of the most circulated documents advocating the reconversion of Hagia Sophia Museum into a mosque. Kısakürek, who delivered that speech on 1 January 1966 at the İstanbul branch of the National Turkish Students' Union (*Millî Türk Talebe Birliği*), addressed the Union's young members, heralding the reinstatement of the monument as a mosque and stating that its transformation would be a key moment of national salvation and revival. That was just one of more than a hundred speeches given by Kısakürek, who travelled throughout the country with the aim of propagating his ideas, which centred around critiques of Westernisation, republican secularism, and communism, and which were also disseminated through the magazine *Büyük Doğu*, which he ran himself between 1943 and 1978. Kısakürek had a significant impact on the increasing number of educated youth with rural, conservative, and religious backgrounds who would go on to challenge the secular and socialist-oriented student movement and who from 1967 onwards dominated the aforementioned national student union. Those young students, as prospective readers of *Büyük Doğu* and similar Islamist publications such as *Sebilürreşad, İslam, Serdengeçti*, and *Tohum*, would have been familiar with the symbolism associated with Hagia Sophia, which had been a constant theme in such publications since the early 1950s.

Necip Fazıl Kısakürek's Speech about Hagia Sophia[*]

[...] Our soul and sacred room; the room in our conquered house closed to us by a 126-year-old current that brought us to this state, used our mothers' heaven-scented headscarves as mops for drunkards' vomit, lowered our morals to a lower level than Le Chabanais, that worldwide brothel in Paris, turned our national culture into garbage and our national economy into a casino, transformed our minds into those of monkeys, and made our hearts cancerous. This is Hagia Sophia!

For 126 years, this current, which is Turkish only in name, has been ruled over by blasphemers and cliques who act as the primary capital and voluntary henchmen of Western imperialism abroad and from within act as loyal agents of cosmopolites, Jews, *dönmes* [crypto-Jewish converts to Islam], and Freemasons, and who, by turning Hagia Sophia into a museum, have placed the very core of the Turkish spirit in a museum like the waxy syphilitic faces [displayed] in museums of health.

[...] When Fatih [Sultan Mehmed, the Conqueror], a ruler, chief, and man of action who was far too superior in terms of his cause and purpose to even accept [the likes of] Alexander the Great or Caesar as a chambermaid, conquered İstanbul, and as he was praying in Hagia Sophia, which is the heart of the city, he had with him the nail of the clamp of the Islamic offensive that was smashed in Southern France and would bite the West again in Vienna. Hagia Sophia is that tiny pin, that nail.

[...] It is an old Byzantine monument [that became] the new home for *tekbir* [the formula expressing the absolute superiority of the God, Allāh akbar]; it is a historical dome that unites the Western mind and the Eastern spirit, a dome which was freed from the weight of the cross and opened the way to the dome of the sky with the wings of the crescent, thus showing the world of the twentieth century world what real civilisation and eternal architecture are. Hagia Sophia is neither stone nor line, colour, matter, or a symphony of substance; it is pure meaning and meaning alone.

[...] In the home and homeland of the Turkish people, Hagia Sophia was torn from its spirit by the hands of so-called Turks. The sacred names of Allah and his prophet have been removed from its walls, the interior plaster has been scraped off to reveal heathen images [orthodox mosaics were covered during over during the reign of Ahmed I in the early seventeenth century], and [in the process] it was turned into a museum that hailed the "greatness" of the cross rather than the crescent. In other words, it has been turned into a sarcophagus where Islam is buried.

[...] Hagia Sophia is a bow-tied ribbon on the box of national values that was gifted to the Western world by spiritual, moral, social, economic, administrative, and political disasters caused by a certain administration and mentality. Nations that give such gifts which surrender their character to the enemy [...] are despicable and servile in the eyes of those who receive the gifts. Herein lies the Cyprus case! Do

[*] Translated from the original Turkish in Necip Fazıl Kısakürek, "Büyük Hitabe: Ayasofya," *Büyük Doğu*, no: 16 (1966). https://katalog.idp.org.tr/yazilar/140524/ayasofya-yi-cami-yapan-ruhtan-cizgiler

we not take notice of how the West—of which we claim to be a civilised, emancipated member—treats us? The West never counts us as part of itself, although we think of ourselves as such. It never embraces this imitative and malleable personage who is neither Eastern nor Western and thinks of nothing more than instant gratification and the preferential [treatment] of the miserable Greek, that spoiled child and bastardised limb of the Greco-Latin civilisation, the name of which it carried on. Our diplomats, who do not know that the great British poet Lord Byron died in the Greek wars of independence against the Turks and lays buried in Greek lands, still seek salvation not in the true character of the Turks, but in the aspiration to appear Western to the West. No! There is no protection or companionship that can be obtained from the Westerner by being a parasite. As we go on with such a mindset, it shall be seen what will befall us. And all these meanings depend on Hagia Sophia...

[...] Hagia Sophia should be opened [to Muslim prayers]. It should be opened with the closed fortune of the Turk. Keeping Hagia Sophia closed means keeping all mosques and the concept of the mosque closed because they are places, while Hagia Sophia is a soul. We said that to keep Hagia Sophia closed is no different than saying to the Greek, "I can't do it, [so] you come and open it [as a church]!"

[...] Keeping Hagia Sophia closed is a crime that is equivalent to cursing God, spitting on the Qur'an, throwing Turkish history into a toilet, polluting Turkish chastity, and enslaving the Turkish homeland. Why can't we reveal this burning, scorching, blasting truth? Here we are revealing [it]! Youth! Whether it be today or tomorrow, I don't know, but Hagia Sophia will be opened again [as a mosque]!

**

Necip Fazıl Kısakürek read the text quoted above during a speech he gave on the first of January in 1966 and then published a redacted version of it on the first page of *Büyük Doğu*. The speech reflected Kısakürek's nostalgic notions concerning the Ottoman past as the highest expression of Islamic civilisation and his aspirations for reviving that past through an authoritarian political program he envisioned and formulated as the "Great East". In this text, and more generally in Kısakürek's oeuvre, "religion" is equated with "civilisation" and "Turkish" coincides with all that is "Ottoman," and past Ottoman military successes are exalted as the apex of "Islamic Civilisation". The depiction of the latter as a "cradle of morality and spirituality" as well as a source of national authenticity that stood in contrast to "Western civilisation" went hand in hand with his rejection and abhorrence of the late Ottoman era of reforms (via the *Tanzimat* and political endeavours of the Young Turks), republican Westernism, materialism, Jews, the Freemasons, and communism, all of which are portrayed in his work as being united by the same anti-Islamic agenda. Hence this text does not just instrumentalise Hagia Sophia in the name of reclaiming the national memory of Turks' Ottoman past as a true source of national pride, it also reflects the racist, anti-Semitic, Islamist, sexist, and xenophobic dimensions of that nationalist narrative in a crystallised form that was not and still is not problematised by Kısakürek's followers. The spirit of "conquest" that Kısakürek aspired to revive has triggered feelings of hatred, vengeance, and resentment directed toward the "enemy," which has been variously portrayed as the West, the Byzantines, Christians, Greeks, Jews, communists, and Freemasons, as well as "cosmopolitanism" and/or local extensions of "foreign enemies".

This approach to Hagia Sophia stands in sharp contrast to early republican perspectives on the monument as "the common heritage of humanity," which resulted in efforts to protect the multiple and layered identities of the monument by turning it into a museum. Kısakürek contended that Hagia Sophia's status as a museum was the underlying reason for all the disruptive issues related to "the cause of Turkish spiritual salvation" and hence re-opening it as a mosque would be proof of Muslim-Turkish sovereignty. In his view, the decree of 1934 not only subjugated Hagia Sophia, which he saw as the greatest symbol of an Ottoman/Islamic/Turkish past (in a historical narrative that treats imperial, Islamic and ethnic trajectories as one and the same) steeped in glory and superiority, but also led to, in his words, "the museumification of the true spirit of the Turk". Only the re-opening of Hagia Sophia as a mosque could, as he claimed, rectify the "biggest betrayal of Turkish history, religion, and spirit."

Kısakürek's pejorative references to Greeks in the text reflect the dominant nationalist zeal of the period, which was further exacerbated by Greek-Turkish tensions arising as a consequence of the Cyprus crisis and public disappointment with how the US was handling the issue, which, according to Kısakürek, was proof of the failure of the project of Westernisation. This anti-Greek narrative and insults directed at the Greek Patriarchate and non-Muslim citizens based in İstanbul shaped the intellectual mindset of young activists such as the members of the National Turkish Students' Association and other right-wing groups who, in turn, organised rallies in support of the Cyprus cause and demanded the closure of minority schools as well as the shuttering of the Greek and Armenian patriarchates.

***

Kısakürek's speech about Hagia Sophia was well-known among his followers, and an unredacted full version of a voice recording of the speech, which includes the parts in which he said that the closure of the monument as a mosque amounted to nothing short of blasphemy, has long been available on the web pages of numerous online social media outlets. It has become even more popular since Hagia Sophia was reconverted into a mosque by the government of the ruling Justice and Development Party (*Adalet ve Kalkınma Partisi*, AKP) in July of 2020. Following five court decisions that were issued from 2008 to 2020, the "illegality" of the monument's status as a museum was confirmed and a presidential decree transferred control of the site from the Ministry of Cultural Affairs to the Presidency of Religious Affairs, which reopened it as a working mosque. On 10 July 2020, President Recep Tayyip Erdoğan (1954–) recited Kısakürek's Hagia Sophia speech during the (re)inauguration of the mosque. Erdoğan referred to Kısakürek as his "master" and presented himself as the figure heralded by Kısakürek back in 1966:

> Almost all of our intellectual and artistic citizens have depicted the destitute state of Hagia Sophia in their writings and speeches. The late Necip Fazıl Kısakürek revealed his belief in this matter by saying

"those who doubt whether Turks will remain in this country also doubt whether the Hagia Sophia will be opened [for Muslim prayers]." He even held a conference on the issue when we were young. Today, we are answering the call of the master, [who said], "Hagia Sophia should be opened [as a mosque]; it should be opened along with the blocked fortune of the Turks."

Not only for Erdoğan, but also for several generations of right-wing politicians who have been active in conservative, nationalist, and Islamist associations and political parties, Kısakürek's call to "liberate" Hagia Sophia by reconverting it into a mosque was perceived as a mission that needed to be accomplished to prove the sovereignty and superiority of the Turkish/Muslim nation vis-à-vis a Christian West that has been imagined to be the Turkey's archenemy. A number of literary and propagandist texts—including poems, essays, and songs—have reflected the same neo-Ottomanist nationalist obsession with the idea of Muslim/Turkish conquests as the salvation of national pride. For the last seven decades, Kısakürek's speech has been the most widely circulated and venerated source material used to inspire a commitment to "reconquer" Hagia Sophia, which has been a symbolic "cause" that united and still unites people under the banner of conservative nationalists and Islamists.

Select Bibliography

Azak, Umut. "'The Hagia Sophia Cause' and the Emergence of Ottomanism in the 1950s." *Turkish Historical Review* 13, no. 1 (2022): 1–22.

Eldem, Edhem. "The Reconversion of the Hagia Sophia into a Mosque: A Historian's Perspective." *Journal of the Ottoman and Turkish Studies Association* 8, no. 1 (2021): 243–60.

Ousterhout, Robert G. "From Hagia Sophia to Ayasofya: Architecture and the Persistence of Memory." *Annual of Istanbul Studies*, no. 2 (2013). https://blog.iae.org.tr/en/uncategorized-en/from-hagia-sophia-to-ayasofya-archi-tecture-and-the-persistence-of-memory

Uzer, Umut. "Conservative Narrative: Contemporary Neo-Ottomanist Approaches in Turkish Politics." *Middle East Critique* 29, no. 3 (2020): 275–90.

45

The Turkish Queen of the Hippies: Remembering Perihan Yücel

Yavuz Köse

After the Second World War, Turkey was quickly integrated into the Western block that was created under the leadership of the United States in opposition to the communist Soviet Union. This was achieved by means of considerable financial aid and membership in NATO, as well as by utilising Turkey's strategic position to secure the eastern borders of the alliance. In the 1950s, it seemed that Turkey was destined to become a "little America". Consequently, the period between 1946 and the late 1950s was marked by good relations between the two countries, and popular American culture spread throughout Turkey in those years. Turkey was integrated into the world market and (at least partially) opened its markets to imported goods. This, along with an unsteady and faltering economy, was the main reason for Turkey's growing payment deficits.

From the 1950s onwards, but especially in the 1960s, Turkey tried to develop its tourism sector. International tourism, it was hoped, would bring in money and thereby offset the payment deficits that had been accruing over the years. American tourists were quite willing to help out. From the 1950s until 1973, Americans comprised the largest group of international visitors to Turkey. The number of Americans entering Turkey stood at around 20,000 in 1953, but by 1973 that figure had soared to 230,000. After that time, Germans took the lead in terms of numbers of tourists. Certainly, Turkey had become an attractive holiday resort for US citizens because of the permanent presence of the US Army in the country, which by the late 1950s consisted of around 24,000 US officials and their dependents. Even when Turkish-American relations from the 1960s onwards began to be marred by tensions and public opinion became increasingly anti-American, US tourists continued to visit Turkey.

In the 1960s, the hippie movement first emerged in the United States and it quickly spread across the entirety of the Western world, as indicated by the fact that the movement had a powerful impact on the European youth movements of 1968. In the 1960s, İstanbul was the first stop along the so-called "hippie trail" to Kathmandu. Travelling along this route was part of the "ideology of dropping out," which challenged institutional hierarchy and materialist consumerism.

In the historic city centre near Sultanahmet Mosque and Hagia Sophia there was a small patisserie called Lâle Pastanesi, which became the first meeting point for hippies, who renamed it the "Pudding Shop." The patisserie provided basic touristic infrastructure and a noticeboard for travellers, helping them exchange information regarding their stay in Turkey and travel routes to South Asia. Sultanahmet, the old district, was also where hippies could find cheap hostels to stay at.

Hippies represented a specific type of tourism that was considerably different from the one that catered to middle- and upper-middle-class Westerners. Not only did the former travel through the entire country, they also spent very little money along the way. Nonetheless, they had a considerable impact on the public imagination.

Perihan Yücel (1952-1970) – "Queen of the Hippies"

"Here (Sirkeci) you meet like-minded people from all over the world. And here you can find everything a hippie needs: Hash, opium and heroin. [...] After the hash came the heroin. It sent a shock through her nerves. Perihan raved, 'Is it possible to have it better if you want ecstasy and detachment from the conventional, from the heaviness of the world?'" (*Quick* 8/23 (18 February 1970), 13).

"Death is not something you are happy about, but it is good (that she has died): We got rid of a microbe. [...] She was a girl with a terrible nature. She wouldn't listen. Perihan was the type of girl who wanted to be on her own. No one should interfere in her affairs, as she wanted to live the way she wanted. That was all that mattered to her. She would often run away from home. She was the child of an illegitimate relationship I had. I registered her so she wouldn't be homeless, but she never came back. I didn't look for her, because her mother took care of her. When I found out that she had gone astray, I broke off all contact with her. In fact, I also left her mother, with whom we had lived for fifteen years." (Aziz Yücel, a waste collector and Perihan's father, in an interview with the daily *Günaydın*, 9 January 1970).

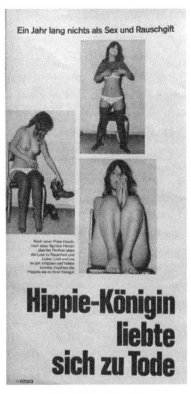

Ein Jahr lang nichts als Sex und Rauschgift

Nach einer Prise Hasch, nach einer Spritze Heroin überfiel Perihan stets die Lust zu Nacktheit und Liebe. Und weil sie so gut strippen und lieben konnte, machten die Hippies sie zu ihrer Königin

Hippie-Königin liebte sich zu Tode

*Perihan Yücel around 1969
(source: private)*

*Perihan Yücel, "Hippie Queen
Loved Herself to Death," Quick 8/23
(18 February 1970), 12.*

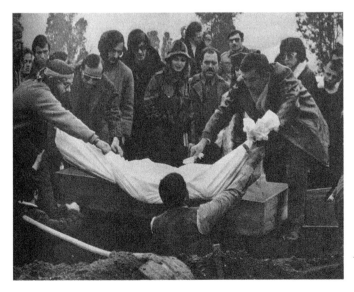

*Perihan Yücel's
funeral, Quick 8/23
(18 February 1970), 13.*

1963–1972

The photographs above, presumably taken in 1969, show Perihan Yücel (1952-1970), a young woman who left her parental home in İzmir for İstanbul when she was barely sixteen years old. Less than two years later, on 8/9 January 1970, she was found dead in a hotel room in İstanbul's district of Sirkeci, where she had spent the night with her German friend Horst Geiger. She had died of a heroin overdose. She was eighteen years old at the time.

Shortly after Perihan's death, the German magazine *Quick* published a sensationalist article that included photographs of her posing half-naked and pictures of her friend Horst Geiger, as well as a photo that captured the moment when, wrapped in a shroud, she was lifted from a coffin into her grave, accompanied by a group of tourist hippies. The supplementary text is full of hippie clichés and contains very little factual information. According to *Quick*, Perihan was not "crowned the queen of the hippies" because "she could handle more drugs than anyone else, but because she could love more fiercely, for longer periods of time and more orgiastically than anyone who lived with her in the drug centre of İstanbul". Supposedly, it was Horst Geiger, her German hippie friend, who introduced her to heroin and a sexually rambunctious lifestyle. The unnamed author sums up the situation in a degrading manner by saying, "After a dose of hash, after a shot of heroin, Perihan was always overcome by a desire for nudity and love. And because she was so good at stripping and making love, the hippies made her their queen." The article quotes from Perihan's alleged suicide note, which was found on the bed. Addressed to her mother, it implied that Perihan was tired of her life(style) and longed for a family life.

On 9 January 1970, the Turkish newspaper *Günaydın* also covered the death of Perihan from İzmir, where a reporter interviewed her father. The article included an identical picture of Perihan (holding a cigarette) and another, probably from the same set of pictures, that depicts her in a floral dress. The interview with her father is revealing, as he describes Perihan as a girl who was eager to lead a self-determined life. Perihan was an illegitimate child who apparently lived with her mother before leaving İzmir. Nevertheless, in the interview her father tried to keep up the façade of her "normal" and "moral" life, distancing himself in the harshest manner by stating that "death is not something you are happy about, but it is good (that she died): 'We got rid of a microbe'" ("Bir mikrop temizlendi").

In the 1960s and 1970s, numerous photographs of foreign and local hippies were taken by journalists or photographers who accompanied them on their forays through Sultanahmet, often in search of sensationalist scenes. Certainly, Perihan Yücel was by then the most famous local hippie. She dressed like a hippie, wearing attire similar to that of her idols, the Flower Children, and reflected a loose lifestyle through her choice of clothes. She soon gained local fame among the hippies on account of her dancing skills and open nature.

It seems that in general, however, hippies had a minimal impact on Turkish youth. Apart from a few exceptions like Perihan who belonged to the lower (middle) class, it was mostly students from well-to-do and liberal families or artists (such as Barış Manço) who followed hippie fashion trends. Certainly, some of them also adopted the hippie lifestyle with all its countercultural implications.

The few who did adopt aspects of the hippie lifestyle were often attacked (and mocked) by more conservative Turks and by the mainstream media. More than anybody else, hippies from the West attracted the attention of local youth and they were met with fierce opposition by traditional circles due to their appearance and behaviour. Turkish women who had contact with hippies, or even decided to become hippies themselves, faced even more resentment from society. As with foreign hippies and beatniks (the "beat generation," whose peak lasted from the 1950s to the mid-1960s), they were also perceived as a danger to and as having a negative influence on Turkish society; their immoral behaviour in public and their drug use were considered an additional problem.

The description of Perihan as a "microbe" by her father coincides with the pejorative labelling of hippies common in the Turkish press. In the daily *Milliyet* (October 4, 1969, 7) one writer asked, "What did dervishes and hippies bring to society?" and concluded that just like Sufi dervishes, who were often deemed to be responsible for the degeneration of the Ottoman Empire, hippies were responsible for the degradation of Turkish society.

Hippies were depicted as being dirty, having lice, being addicted to drugs, and threatening local morals and customs. Beside the press, the hippie motif was soon to be discovered by the film industry. In the same year that Perihan Yücels died (1970), Fehmi Tengiz made a film about her short life. "*Hippi Perihan – Korkunç Arzular*" [Hippie Perihan – Horrible Desire], a drama in which Feri Cansel played the lead role, portrays hippies in a derisive and stereotypical manner, depicting them as hedonistic drug addicts practicing free love and, interestingly, as members of a satanic cult. Several other (mainly erotic) movies from the 1970s included scenes with hippies.

Negative and stereotyped depictions of hippies were not restricted to the Turkish media. Soon, conservative parties discovered that they could be used as an election campaign issue. As mentioned earlier, Turkey had tried to develop the tourism sector as a source of desperately needed money in the 1960s. Every party brought the issue to the political agenda and included it in their party programs, promising to bolster the tourism sector in order to attract international tourists. However, Islamist parties like the National Order Party (*Milli Nizam Partisi*, MNP, 1970–1971) and the National Salvation Party (*Milli Selamet Partisi*, MSP, 1972–1980) were especially concerned about the dangers allegedly posed by international tourism with regard to the morality of Turkish society. The party program of the MNP in 1970 stressed that they would only encourage a policy of tourism that conformed to national morals and character. The MSP further sharpened its tone by promising its electorate that they would take measures to stop hippies from entering the country, and it blamed the governing Justice Party (*Adalet Partisi*, AP) for welcoming visitors to the country who were "hashish addicts who spend the night in (our) parks for free, penniless and lousy tourists, and shaggy drug dealing hippies."

***

Hippies were described in the manner that the public was accustomed to hearing and reading about in the media at the time. The American-based hippie/beatnik culture was embraced by some of the tourists visiting Turkey. Beside a few male Turkish artists who mimicked hippie fashions, for the most part the general public in Turkey frowned upon or even openly disparaged this counter-culture from "America". The position of the Turkish left-wing milieu vis-à-vis hippies was rather ambiguous, and the attitudes of radical leftist student groups regarding students whom they considered hippies became even more strident after 1969. Those groups were quick to take up a pejorative perspective on hippies.

Hippies and their lifestyles were met with attitudes that ranged from scepticism to outright rejection and, albeit rarely, fascination and admiration. The range of reactions to hippies points to the contradictions and dichotomies that were so characteristic of the modernising economy and society in Turkey in the 1960s and 1970s.

Select Bibliography

Alper, Emin. *Jakoblenen Devrimcilere: Türkiye'de Öğrenci Hareketlerinin Dinamikleri 1960-1971.* İstanbul: Tarih Vakfı Yurt Yayınları, 2019.

Güney, Aylin. "Anti-Americanism in Turkey: Past and Present." *Middle Eastern Studies* 44, no. 3 (2008): 471–87.

Köse, Yavuz. "'Coca Cola is Poison, Don't Drink It!' – From Enthusiasm to Hostility: American Consumer Goods, Tourists and Hippies in Cold War Turkey." In *Turkey in Turmoil: Social Change and Political Radicalization during the 1960s,* edited by Berna Pekesen, 63–94. Berlin: de Gruyter Oldenbourg, 2020.

Kozak, Nazmi. "Türkiye'de Hippiler (1965–1979)." In Vol. 10, *Dünden Bugüne Türkiye'de Turizm.Kurumlar, Kuruşlar, Turizm Bölgeleri ve Meslekler,* edited by Nazmi Kozak, 859–908. İstanbul: Yıkılmazlar Basın Yayın, 2018.

Uslu, Nasuh. *The Turkish-American Relationship between 1947 and 2003: The History of a Distinctive Alliance.* Hauppauge, NY: Nova Science Publishers, 2003.

46
A Fragile Liberal Democratic Moment: Demirel and the Turkish Centre-Right

Tanıl Bora
Translated by Salih Işık Bora

From 1965 to 1969, the liberal-conservative Justice Party (*Adalet Partisi*, AP), buoyed by the 50,8 per cent vote it garnered in the previous elections, ruled as a single-party government. Marked by a GDP growth rate of almost 6 per cent, this period was characterised by improved welfare and an increase in modernisation and urbanisation. Nonetheless, in parallel with global developments, a turbulent social movement was emerging, one that was marked by the contestations of May 1968. In Turkey, the workers' movement was becoming increasingly radicalised, while the student movement was shifting away from Kemalist progressivism towards socialism. Mass demonstrations and protests became more common as a sign of nascent societal unrest, taking on the role of political socialisation. Within the radical right, vigilance groups started to come into being among factions that associated such developments with a looming communist threat and a weakening of the state's security apparatus.

When he came face to face with negative reactions concerning this state of social upheaval at his party's provincial congress in Ankara in 1968, party chairman and prime minister Süleyman Demirel famously said that "roads are not worn down by marches". In fact, Demirel had explained his doctrine in greater depth at the opening of the Justice Party's İstanbul youth branch centre on 10 July 1967. The following excerpt exemplifies the rationale underlying Demirel's statement.

*Roads Are Not Worn Down by Marches**

We will not be afraid of the exercise of freedom. Hasn't the liberty to take part in [protest] marches been recognised? Let them march, why should we be afraid? Whoever wants to march, let them march... There is only one thing that we make sure of. We make sure that no pillaging, looting, or rioting takes place under the guise of marches. And law enforcement has the power to prevent [such actions].

We will get used to strikes so long as they don't jeopardise state security. After all, they are [part of] the institution of modernity. Recently there was a strike in Ankara. Garbagemen went on strike and the city

---

* Translated from the Turkish original in Süleyman Demirel, *Muhtelif Konuşmalar* (Ankara: AP Genel Merkezi Neşriyati, 1969), 34-9.

filled up with filth. There was trash all over the place. In that way, Ankara became like European cities. So, you give [people] the right to strike and expect that cities won't fill up with garbage. Well, that's not possible. Every right has a trade-off, regardless of how long the right to strike is deemed valid, whether that is three or four days, or ten days. If you want the rights of some people to be respected while at the same time you don't want cities to get filthy—well, good luck with that. No solution has been found for that yet. That is why there are strikes. So that the rights of some citizens in Ankara don't get violated, we will tolerate four to five days of filth. We will get used to it. If we don't get used to such things, we will not be able to establish a modern state. Just go to the free countries of the West, [and you'll see] everything there is a lot more complicated than here.

There will be some strange tumult stirred up by some folks. A country of 32 million people cannot remain quiet. So yes, there will be tumult that we are not used to. What will we do to deal with that strange tumult? We will, of course, stir up tumult ourselves wherever it is appropriate and necessary. Some voices will be raised with the aim of making us prevaricate, to confuse us and deflect us from our path. We will know how to respond to those voices. So why is there such tumult? Where does it come from? What is its origin? If such clamouring is against the law, if the law deems that it is illegal, then the law will deal with it accordingly.

If you're in government, you have to be tolerant. People will throw at you whatever they can get their hands on. There is no remedy for that. You cannot remain in government any other way. In a free country, in a country where there are 86,000 university students and 4,000 faculty members, you cannot simply wish such things away.

***

As noted above, the statement "roads are not worn down by marches," which served as the motto of Demirel's "liberal democratic moment," is exemplified by the quote given here. In subsequent decades, it would be repeated countless times in association with Demirel, thus becoming one of the most well-known phrases utilised in modern Turkish politics. Later, it would often be invoked as an illustration of Demirel's indifference, cynicism, and opportunism. From the perspective of the national-conservative right, it would be associated with his "carelessness" in the face of the emerging communist threat. On the other hand, Kemalists and leftists would see it as a demonstration of Demirel's contempt for social movements and more generally for extra-parliamentary politics. The perpetrators of the subsequent military coup of 12 March 1971 would repress left-wing social movements and portray their own actions as a harsh yet necessary response to be contrasted with Demirel's "softness". Somewhat paradoxically, they would also attempt to increase their legitimacy by cultivating an image of reformism that they held up in contradistinction to Demirel's lack of interest in societal grievances.

Within Demirel's doctrine, as typified by his statement "roads are not worn down by marches," it is possible to identify traces of right-wing populism, which tends to neglect social opposition and reduce democracy to the outcomes of elections, and also conclude that the leadership of the Justice Party was quite aware of the motives behind the coup of 27 May 1960. At the time, the military had used police brutality as a pretext to overthrow the democratically elected prime minister, Adnan Menderes. Lastly, it could be argued that in later years, Demirel would go on to tolerate and even support far-right vigilantism targeting social movements, thus underscoring the notion that "roads are not worn down by marches" is a claim that is at best ambiguous and at worst outright hypocrisy.

Nevertheless, the statement and its associated doctrine could also be interpreted as a genuine shift in the direction of liberal democracy. Indeed, Demirel gave the speech noted above in reaction to his own party's criticism of his lenient attitude towards left-wing social movements. The statement was, in fact, directed towards a party delegate who approached the podium at the AP's provincial congress in Ankara and proclaimed that the ongoing protests needed to be quelled. It should certainly not be forgotten that the AP's electoral base was vehemently anti-communist. A newly emergent radical nationalist movement regularly sought to stir up such reactionary tendencies. Within Demirel's party itself, the national-conservative faction was quite strong and challenged him in this regard. In the aftermath of a workers' uprising in June of 1970, those factions would accuse Demirel of having "capitulated," citing his allegedly ineffective and feeble use of state-of-emergency powers. In short, Demirel's suggestion that his own party should hold to a position of "tolerance" indicates that he was determined to remain faithful to his own political stance. In a way, Demirel almost appears to have been trying to "educate" his own electoral base about the virtues of civil rights and liberties.

In light of those developments, that debate can be characterised as a rare moment when ordinarily weak liberal democratic inclinations surfaced within the Turkish right. Similar instances had occurred in the past, notably when the Democrat Party (*Demokrat Parti*, DP) opposed the single-party regime (1946–1950) and, in an ironic twist, when the short-lived Freedom Party (*Hürriyet Partisi*, 1955–1958) was established as a means of denouncing the autocratic turn of the government, which hailed from the very same DP. Until the early 1970s, the Justice Party was clearly divided into liberal and democratic-conservative camps, with Demirel representing the former. That faction was a proponent of industrial development rather than a building up of commercial and agricultural activities. Consequently, it prioritised the interests of İstanbul-based big businesses over those of provincial small and medium-sized enterprises. That choice was balanced out, if not disguised by, Demirel's "peasant" image and populist discourses. Without a doubt, Demirel resorted to national-conservative agitation when it was deemed necessary. Nevertheless, he had developed a liberal or economistic conception of nationalism that was based on development, increased welfare, and "civilisation". As his speech indicates, he took the "free countries of the West" as an example that Turkey ought to follow. The liberal-democratic tolerance that he displayed through the statement "roads are not worn down by marches" can only be understood within the context of those broader tendencies.

***

In the early 1970s, the Islamist "National Outlook" (*Milli Görüş*) movement and right-wing Democratic Party (*Demokratik Parti*, not to be confused with the Democrat Party of 1946–1961) broke their ties with Demirel's AP, which would weaken them against the subsequent military coup of 12 March 1971. Both of the reasons underlying that schism were related to the dissatisfaction felt by small property owners. Firstly, the AP was criticised for implementing policies that catered solely to the interests of İstanbul-based big businesses. Secondly, they were seen as being excessively lenient towards left-wing movements and hence weak in the face of the "imminent" threat of communism. In the aftermath of rule under the military, socialist movements would gain momentum and an increasingly social-democratic CHP would score successive election victories. At the same time, anti-communist sentiment would spread to the electoral base of the right to a far greater extent than before. Consequently, Demirel would adopt an entirely new persona in the 1970s. His leadership of the Turkish right throughout the late 1970s would rest on his credentials as the prime minister of the "Nationalist Front" coalition government between April 1975 and June 1977. In that period, his liberal democratic tendencies would be entirely abandoned.

After the period of military rule in the early 1980s and with the advent of the Özal era, Demirel would once again embrace a liberal democratic rhetoric that was geared towards rights and freedom. He sought to appeal to popular resentment concerning the policies implemented by way of the coup and subsequently launched by Özal. More importantly, Demirel embraced liberal democracy as a means of protesting the fact that he had been banned from politics, a ban that would only be lifted through the referendum of September 1987. Towards the end of 1990, Demirel would once again advocate for people's right to demonstrate, citing the Prague and Leipzig uprisings in the Eastern Bloc. When confronted with the objection that such actions would "bring about a state of anarchy," Demirel retorted that "the people resorted to them to save them from the yoke of the government".

When Demirel once again became prime minister (1991–1993) and then president (1993–2000), he continued to defend rights and freedom "as a matter of principle," while at the same time warning about their "misuse". For instance, when Demirel met up with some Türk-İş labour union representatives before a gathering in January of 1997, he said to them, "We are not asking you to stop exercising your rights, just to avoid breaking things." In May of the same year, Demirel would defend an Islamist gathering in İstanbul by arguing that "public squares are a crucial organ of democracy". This is especially noteworthy given that the militantly secularist regime of the 28 February coup was still in power. Demirel would say, "Although we might hear some disturbing slogans at this gathering, we cannot ban it. We cannot forego the right to demonstrate. We cannot forbid many good ones simply because there happens to be a bad one." This example could be taken to mean that Demirel was, in fact, more supportive of right-wing movements' freedom to demonstrate.

The fragility of the liberal democratic moment of the Turkish right becomes readily apparent if we examine the historical context of the statement "roads are not worn down by marches" and the political trajectory of the man who coined it, Süleyman Demirel. The same pattern can be observed in the discourses of other prominent leaders. After expressing enthusiastic support for liberal democracy when he was in the opposition between 1946 and 1950, Democrat Party leader Adnan Menderes would quickly shrug off that commitment. By 1957, he went so far as to characterise democracy as an "exotic flower". Similarly, Turgut Özal ardently supported liberal democracy during the time he was president (1989–1993) and therefore did not directly wield governmental powers. As prime minister, however, Özal largely reduced rights and freedom to the question of living standards and material welfare. The notion of freedom of thought was thus conceptualised through free market metaphors such as the "competition of ideas". During the period when the Justice and Development Party (AKP) successfully presented itself as the new centre-right in Turkey (from 2002 to the early 2010s), Recep Tayyip Erdoğan held a relatively lenient attitude with regard to rights and freedom. However, he would subsequently become a hard-line representative of the authoritarian national-conservative tradition. That shift was backed by a renewed emphasis on the claim that the state represented the "national will". Social movements which opposed that "will" were labelled by Erdoğan as "putschist," an explicit reference to the 1960 coup against Adnan Menderes. He defended the notion that truly "democratic" politics meant "showing no weakness" and quelling "street movements". Erdoğan's supporters contrast his hard-line approach with Menderes' "softness" and Demirel's "indifference" in the face of the military coups of 1960 and 1971, thereby emphasising his historical "superiority" over his predecessors. As such, Erdoğan's approach and the adulation it has received illustrate the fragility and exceptional nature of the liberal democratic moments of the Turkish right.

Select Bibliography

Arcayürek, Cüneyt, *Uzakta Kalan Tarih.* Ankara: Bilgi Yayınevi, 2003.

Bora, Tanıl. *Demirel.* İstanbul: İletişim Yayınları, 2023.

Aslan, Murat. *Süleyman Demirel.* İstanbul: İletişim Yayınları, 2019.

Cizre Sakallıoğlu, Ümit. "Liberalism, Democracy and the Turkish Centre-Right: The Identity Crisis of the True Path Party." *Middle Eastern Studies* 32, no. 2 (1996): 142-61.

Demirel, Tanel. *Adalet Partisi.* 2004, 3rd edition. İstanbul: İletişim Yayınları, 2017.

Gevgilili, Ali. *Yükseliş ve Düşüş.* İstanbul: Bağlam Yayınları, 1987.

47
Contesting Family Planning: Birth Control as a Conspiracy

Heinrich Hartmann

On 7 April 1969, a group of young students stormed into an Ankara conference centre and raided a WHO conference on the topic of public health and human reproduction. They threw fireworks into the audience and chanted in protest against what they called the "sterilisation of the Turkish nation". Although left feeling intimidated, the conference participants were unhurt. Over the course of the following days, the seminar continued without further incident but under police protection. The leader of the far-right nationalist "Commando" group responsible for the assault, Yılmaz Yalçıner (1946–2021), was quickly arrested. This act of aggression, however, was not without precedent. In the months leading up to the event, a wave of nationalist anger had swept across Turkey. And Yalçıner himself was not unknown to the authorities and already had a history of turning to violence, especially as the leader of far-right nationalist student groups.

The action of Yalçıner's group has to be understood against the backdrop of extensive media coverage of the programs of family planning that Turkey had introduced as part of its first Five-year Plan starting in 1963. Especially in the later 1960s, plans to systematically promote contraceptives to the Turkish population provoked an outcry among nationalists. In the days before and after the Ankara events, a number of rather provocative articles and short notices were published by Turkish newspapers on the issue. The following newspaper clips from *Bugün*, *Akşam*, and *Bizim Anadolu* all express a sense of outrage about an alleged occidental conspiracy against the Turkish nation.

Birth Control as a Conspiracy?

Bugün, 2 April 1969

Scientists Warn Our People Against Birth Control Scandal

[...] Oestrogen, which is accumulated in the body, causes breast cancer. Birth control pills consist of oestrogen. Oestrogen does not cause cancer if the body only receives small amounts. But, if it is taken continuously and if it accumulates in the body to an excessive degree, it causes cancer. [...]

Oestrogen makes breast cancer worse and IUDs cause uterine cancer. At all cancer meetings these matters are being discussed but it is considered a crime for us to explain this.

Akşam, 8 April 1969

Birth Control Seminar Raided

Commando leader Yalçıner argued that imperialists are determined to sterilise the Turkish nation and said, "We are against birth control."

In a loud voice that rang throughout the hall, the commando leader said that the Russians and Americans had no place in Turkey, "If they want to leave, we will send them away."

Yalçıner argued that birth control would encourage the nation to engage in prostitution and immorality; addressing the foreign attendees, he said, "Remember that Kennedy had eleven children." The male and female foreign delegates, all professors, who attended the seminar, were puzzled and could not understand what had happened.

Bugün, 11 April 1969

Birth Control Will Bring Disaster

[...] Birth control is a trick which is being played by American capitalism and modern colonialism. Its aim is to abolish the communities of Moslems, Buddhists and others, except the Christians and Jews, by means of pills, IUDs, and propaganda.

Birth control is a big mistake for Turkey, whose neighbours are increasing rapidly. In the near future, Greek, Jewish, and Chinese immigrants will be settled in Turkey by force. Birth control pills and IUDs not only cause cancer, but also mental diseases.

It is sad that religious officials in Turkey keep silent, although the leaders of other major religions have expressed their feelings and opinions on the subject....

Bizim Anadolu, 11 April 1969

Birth Control is a Jewish Trick

The latest trick being played on us by the Christian community is birth control. Birth control, which causes many health complications and lays the groundwork for prostitution and immorality, is a trick being played on the Moslem Turkish Nation. To win its acceptance in our country, it is claimed that the increase of our population prevents development. A lot of money is being spent for propaganda purposes. The fact that birth control pills are being introduced into our country by American Jews is a subject which should be taken into consideration....

***

The violent protest against the WHO seminar has been understood as the result of growing tensions between Turkish nationalist politicians and those seen to represent the United States' interests in the Middle Eastern region. In particular, the developing conflict in Cyprus triggered Turkish nationalist resentment against all forms of multilateralism, especially the actions of international organisations on Turkish territory, in the 1960s. Shortly before the assault in Ankara, the establishment of the Nationalist Movement Party (*Millyetçi Harekt Partisi*, MHP), a continuation of the Republican Villagers Nation Party (*Cumhuriyetçi Köylü Millet Partisi*), had contributed to the growing self-confidence of the far right, whose adherents were willing to attack any symbol of what they considered to be Western imperialism. According to their world-view, the WHO conference represented a good opportunity for such violent protests. Unlike *Akşam's* rather neutral reporting style, the right-wing press joined the chorus of the anti-family planning movement, with newspapers like *Bugün* and *Bizim Anadolu* openly denouncing "population planning" as American capitalism and modern neo-colonialism. Opposition to US-driven international influences brought together not only right-wing nationalists and Islamists but also a radical left that was protesting capitalist imperialism. Dividing Turkey's political landscape in the 1960s into a purely left-right dichotomy does not do justice to the rising number of social movements in this decade, a trend which was the result of a multitude of social and economic shifts and was deeply influenced by transnational political movements.

On closer examination, however, the topic of family planning appears to be relatively distant from Cold War aggression. Moreover, the United States had little direct involvement in this field and by the 1960s, the US government had abandoned most of its interests in Turkey and was instead trying to scale down its engagement, encouraging European partners to take on more responsibilities in the country. The notion of birth control as a policy field had instead come from inside Turkey. Despite the warnings of the World Bank and other international organisations about Turkey's rapid population growth in the 1940s and 1950s, Turkish officials had not addressed the issue for quite a long time. Bound to a pro-natalist Kemalist tradition that originated from the shockingly low population figures presented in the first republican census of 1927, the government had consistently emphasised the need to increase the number of births. At the same time, improved care, especially for the rural population, was also a matter of concern in early republican politics, and this involved a clearer statistical understanding of population dynamics, which nurtured ideas about the acceleration of population growth. At the basis of those initiatives was an attempt to breathe life into Atatürk's idea of the hygienic conquest of the Turkish village. Early plans to bring basic healthcare services and midwives to every Turkish village had faltered due to a lack of qualified personnel. The Rockefeller Foundation had helped resolve this problem, contributing funding and expertise to the foundation of both the Ankara Institute of Public Health and the İstanbul-based School for Midwifery.

Population control made its way onto the domestic political agenda by the early 1960s. After the 1960 coup d'état, the Ministry of Health worked to quickly integrate a new population policy into its official programme and make it part of the new government's planned economy approach. In order to legitimise this new biopolitical strategy, the government asked religious authorities to issue a fatwa declaring the compatibility of Islam and family planning practices, a request to which the Directory of Religious Affairs (*Diyanet*) agreed in late 1960. The State Planning Organisation (*Devlet Planlama Teşkilatı*), Turkey's most powerful executive body, also adopted this new emphasis on population issues. By incorporating population policy and family planning into Turkey's first Five-year Plan and by abolishing the old legislation in 1964, which had prevented the distribution of contraceptives, the new government paved the way for an official family planning programme. But the government also asked foreign experts from New York's Population Council for advice on the implementation of such a programme.

The initiative to implement a family planning programme was strong on the Turkish side. Growing concerns about internal migration, the number of the urban poor in *gecekondu* (shantytowns), and the low productivity of Turkish agriculture made population growth a pressing issue on the political agenda. However, opposition to such a policy was also strong and debates about it became heated in the tumultuous political arena of the 1960s. The new focus on reproductive practices and on the female body provoked an outcry among conservative urbanites. Within the context of rising nationalism, family planning started to become the subject of conspiracy theories that supposedly embodied American imperialism in Turkey.

***

Turkey was not alone in contesting policies of family planning, which had provoked similar reactions in many countries of the postcolonial Cold War world. It was a field that made it possible to call into question American hegemony by denouncing the double moral standards of Western cultures and values. Much of this, however, was merely rhetorical, as most of the urgent demands for family planning policies arose in the "targeted" countries themselves, most of the time even supported by different political parties. This was true in the Turkish context with the transition from the İnönü to the Demirel government in 1965, And, of course, critics overestimated the role that such programmes played for the official US agenda. Most of the proponents of the population question found it difficult to bring their ideas onto the official agenda of international politics of the time.

The very fuzzy history of the idea of regulating the population has, instead, a very particular Turkish angle that explains the ideological conflicts of the period under scrutiny. It was profoundly revealing of the ambivalent attitude that Turkish nationalism held towards the poor segments of its rural population. Even though it was raised as a point of concern for the whole political spectrum, nationalists repeatedly opposed any real and direct politics in support of that part of the population.

In contrast to those nationalist elites, many rural residents as well as many public health officials in Ankara saw the family planning programme as a good opportunity to bring basic healthcare services to the people. In most parts of central Anatolia, the 1950s malaria eradication programme had been the only manifestation of healthcare policy that had been experienced first-hand by the local population. Other parts of the country, especially the majority-Kurdish southeastern regions, waited in vain for any medical support; indeed, this part of the country, with its relatively inaccessible villages, remained untouched by healthcare or other development policies until the 1970s or 1980s. The Ministry of Health's family planning campaign was the major exception to this rule. It addressed the villagers as representatives of a global class of increasingly impoverished peasants and confronted them with films, cartoons, and *Karagöz and Hacivat* puppet performances that emphasised the individual's responsibility for global development, avoiding any reference to the role of the government.

For many nationalists, however, villages and their culture should remain untouched as they allegedly represented the cradle of Turkish civilisation. This was more than just a nationalist reflex of the 1960s. Indeed, it was deeply rooted in the DNA of the Turkish Republic, and the ideology of a "Turkey of 100 million" is certainly proof of the continuation of such a discourse.

Select Bibliography

Erken, Ali. *America and the Making of Modern Turkey: Science, Culture and Political Alliances.* New York: I.B. Tauris, 2018.

Hale, William M. *Turkish Politics and the Military.* London: Routledge, 1994.

Halis Caliş, Şaban. *Turkey's Cold War: Foreign Policy and Western Alignment in the Modern Republic.* London: I.B. Tauris, 2017.

Hartmann, Heinrich, "A Twofold Discovery of Population: Assessing the Turkish Population by Its 'Knowledge, Attitudes, and Practices,' 1962–1980." In *A World of Populations: Transnational Perspectives on Demography in the Twentieth Century*, edited by Heinrich Hartmann and Corinna Unger, 178–200. New York: Berghahn, 2014.

Keyder, Çağlar. "Social Change and Political Mobilization in the 1960s." In *Turkey in Turmoil: Social Change and Political Radicalization During the 1960s*, edited by Berna Pekesen, 12–30. Berlin: De Gruyter Oldenbourg, 2020.

Uzer, Umut. *An Intellectual History of Turkish Nationalism: Between Turkish Ethnicity and Islamic Identity. Salt Lake City: University of Utah Press, 2016.*

48

Political Islam in the Turkish Parliament: The National Order Party

İlker Aytürk

The significance of the 1960 coup d'état as a turning point in modern Turkish history can hardly be exaggerated. Drawing a lesson from the authoritarianism of the Democrat Party (*Demokrat Parti*, DP), a new constitution and an electoral law were drafted by the constitutive assembly in 1961 in order to prevent the emergence of another autocratic executive branch in the future. The combined effect of Turkey's so-called "most liberal" constitution and the new electoral system, which was based on proportional representation, was unexpected, and the impacts were two-fold: first, starting with the general elections of 1961, the Turkish political centre fragmented, and this effectively ended the two-party system of the 1950s. Second, these developments paved the way for the founding of far-left and far-right parties as fixtures of Turkish politics. The Workers' Party of Turkey (*Türkiye İşçi Partisi*, TİP) took the lead in 1961 and four years later it was followed by the nationalist takeover of the Republican Peasants' Nation Party (*Cumhuriyetçi Köylü Millet Partisi*, CKMP), which was renamed the Nationalist Movement Party (*Milliyetçi Hareket Partisi*, MHP) in 1969.

Turkish political Islamists were the last among the other "far" movements in establishing a political party. Necmettin Erbakan (1926–2011), who was a successful academician and engineer (but a less successful businessman) as well as the scion of a branch of the Nakşibendi Sufi order in İstanbul, took the lead toward the end of the 1960s in the party-fication of Turkish political Islam. Erbakan rejected nationalist overtures for political mergers and entered parliament in 1969 as an independent candidate. He founded the National Order Party (*Milli Nizam Partisi*, MNP) in January 1970 and he was soon joined by two other parliamentary deputies. The MNP was shut down in May 1971 in the aftermath of a military intervention that took place in March of the same year and Erbakan fled Turkey. The MNP experiment is significant because it represented the first instance of a pattern that would emerge: successive Islamist parties in Turkey would repeatedly fall out with secular factions within the military and judiciary bureaucracy and be banned one after another.

Erbakan's greatest accomplishment during the brief lifespan of the MNP was that he predicted this danger and responded swiftly to neutralise the threat. His long-lasting solution was to organise his brand of political Islam as a civil society movement, parallel to but autonomous from political parties. As such, whenever an Islamist party was banned, the movement could immediately bounce back by founding another political party under a new name. Known over time as the National Outlook Movement (*Milli Görüş Hareketi*), Erbakan's political endeavour was partly inspired by the trials and tribulations of the Muslim Brotherhood in Egypt, and the following two points proved to be critical in its development: a) While its organisational model was hierarchical, there was an emphasis on local branches and grassroots efforts, b) Erbakan formulated the National Outlook ideology in bold but very simple language conveying clear populist messages. In the text that follows, Erbakan sketched out the contours of the ideology underlying the MNP program for the first time.

National Order Party: Program and By-laws*

Article 6: Our understanding of freedom of consciousness is [that it means] responding to the needs of the citizenry in terms of religious beliefs, worship, education, and spiritual education [*telkin ve terbiye*]. Although secularism [*laiklik*] is described as an assurance for the freedom of religion and consciousness, we oppose the instrumentalisation [of secularism] for oppressing religion and disrespecting the pious [...].

Article 7: Our understanding of nationalism is based on dedication to a common [Islamic] mission [*dâva*] and consciousness of a shared history; [we] regard communities that have coalesced and merged in a pot of shared culture, aims, and spiritual content as a monolithic union. We treasure the spirit more than the physical body. Our nationalism does not divide people as long as they conform to these criteria [...].

Article 19: [...] We aim to bring up the new generation as pious, hard-working, patriotic citizens who are dedicated to national morality, family order, and discipline, who share our national goal [*mefkûre*], culture, and consciousness of history, who are ethical, altruistic, and self-sacrificing, and who strive to contribute to all of humanity in the competition over science, technology, and civilisation [...].

Article 21: We will completely reorganise the National Education Policy and bureaucratic cadres in order to prevent foreign, cosmopolitan, Marxist, and destructive ideas, and the resulting moral rot, from seeping into our society [...].

Article 23: The second principal aim of our educational development [plan] is to disseminate in our country positive sciences which are actually the property of our civilisation but which the West co-opted from us and exploited for its own material development [...].

Article 24: Our party believes in the principle that men and women, everyone, has the right to study science [*ilim*] and we see it as absolutely necessary that relevant information concerning the household economy and the physical, spiritual, moral, and religious education of children be provided to our women, who will be future mothers and housewives [...].

* Translated from its Turkish original in *Millî Nizam Partisi: Program ve Tüzük* (İstanbul: Haktanır Matbaası, [1970]), 7, 12–14, 22.

Article 54: The rich natural resources of our country are sufficient to establish a powerful heavy industry. Heavy industry today ensures the political and economic independence of nations [...]. The empowerment of our nation in every respect and the birth of Great Turkey, which will play a dominant role in the global politics of tomorrow, is dependent on how successful we are in terms of industrialisation. Heavy industry is simultaneously the basis of the arms industry; today, it is very difficult for a nation to protect its independence and future if it does not rely on the heavy arms industry, and our party will approach this issue with all due gravity.

***

Similar to other "far" parties, the MNP also challenged the Kemalist foundations of the Turkish Republic as a secular, Westernising nation-state, and called for a radical overhaul of the system. In the eyes of the MNP's political Islamist founders, Turkey represented a "flawed republic." They believed that: a) Kemalist secularism oppressed Turkish Muslims and cut off the ties that once connected them with the global Muslim ummah; b) Kemalists pursued policies of cultural Westernisation and came close to destroying the traditional culture of the masses; and, c) Kemalist nationalism was ethnocentric and therefore less successful in integrating non-Turkish citizens into the nation than the Ottoman Empire had been. In short, the MNP openly promised cultural restoration but refrained from pronouncing in public its plans for political change. Since the threat of party closures hung over them like the proverbial sword of Damocles, Islamist parties became masters of double talk over the years. Starting with the MNP, they have exploited the multiple meanings of political terms to disguise their true intentions and they developed two political discourses, one for the general public and the other for internal consumption at closed meetings. The best example of this is the term *millet*, the adjective form (*milli*) of which we find in the party name. Until the twentieth century, Ottoman Turks employed this term to denote a religious community, as in the Greek Orthodox *millet* or the Jewish *millet*. As late as from the 1910s onward, the meaning of *millet* underwent a semantic change and it came to stand for the modern nation. As such, the MNP's party name can be translated as both the National Order Party and the Religious/Islamic Order Party.

Erbakan despised nationalism, claiming that it was a Western import. He regarded the Turkish nation-state as a flawed unit of analysis, because, as a political Islamist, he dreamed of a much broader Muslim context in which all Muslims lived under the rule of a single Muslim state. The definition of nationalism in the MNP program is completely devoid of ethnic references. The terms "Turk" and "Turkish" rarely appear in the text and never in reference to national identity. That was destined to put the National Outlook on a collision course not only with secular Kemalists, but also, and perhaps more importantly, with far-right nationalists as well. On the other hand, it is no surprise that approximately a third of the Islamist vote came from the Kurdish east in the 1970s.

According to Erbakan, Turkey's Muslims were destined to take the lead role in the rebirth of the global Muslim ummah, as that was deemed to be the natural outcome of their imperial past. Contemporary Turks, however, had to be re-educated to make up for the cultural losses and religious degeneration that allegedly took place in the Kemalist republic. Again, following the example of the Muslim Brotherhood, Erbakan intended to begin the education or, rather, the re-Islamisation, of society from the bottom up. Indeed, he made a concerted effort to create an extensive network of Islamist NGOs. He expected that Islamist civil society, together with the religious *imam-hatip* schools, would transform the new generation of Turkish voters and convince them that it was in their best interests to support the MNP as well as future National Outlook parties. In other words, the MNP was not a revolutionary party and Erbakan was no Khomeini; he hoped to come to power democratically. This should not be taken to mean that such Islamists were Muslim democrats, however. On the contrary, internal party discourses confirm that once securely in power, Erbakan had every intention to convert the Turkish political system into an Islamic regime and he would not have shied away from using state power to achieve the Islamisation of the nation. It is one of the ironies of political Islam that Turkish Islamists, as harsh critics of Western modernity, had no qualms about taking advantage of the penetrative capacity of the modern nation-state and its ability to pry into the private sphere.

Early on Erbakan and the National Outlook Movement recognised the benefits of establishing women's branches and involving women in grassroots development. However, this did not in any way mean granting women an equal role at home or in the public sphere. For instance, the female members of the MNP were not given any roles in the party's decision-making bodies. While the MNP program acknowledged women's right to education, it seemed to limit that right solely to the fields of housekeeping and child-rearing. The MNP program states that women are destined to be housewives and mothers, an obvious reference to the Islamic belief in the God-given nature of men and women.

Lastly, the MNP program's emphasis on economic policy and "heavy industry" is peculiar. In all probability, the discourse of industrialisation had a double function. On the one hand, it propped up Erbakan's image as a man of action who inhabited two worlds. He was both a pious, exemplary Muslim and an engineer, professor, inventor, and, above all, a self-acclaimed contributor to the material development and welfare of Turkey. When combined, those qualities made Erbakan a realistic competitor who could run against the centre-right leader, Süleyman Demirel (1924–2015), and it also made him more palatable for Turkey's secular elites. The second function of the "heavy industry" rhetoric was also related to image management. Evidence from memoirs and party publications reveals that Erbakan highlighted industrialisation to a greater extent in his public speeches and interviews given to newspapers than during closed meetings with grassroots party members, where he chose to emphasise Islamic restoration. His numerous references to "heavy industry" were therefore more likely a smokescreen that was used to conceal the MNP's Islamist-restorative agenda.

***

The NOP was the first in a long line of political Islamist parties in modern Turkish politics. Notwithstanding substantial variations in their policies and ideologies, the National Salvation Party (*Milli Selamet Partisi*, MSP, 1972–1980), the Welfare Party (*Refah Partisi*, RP, 1983–1998), the Virtue Party (*Fazilet Partisi*, FP, 1997–2001), the Felicity Party (*Saadet Partisi*, SP, 2001–), the Justice and Development Party (*Adalet ve Kalkınma Partisi*, AKP, 2001–), the Voice of the People Party (*Halkın Sesi Partisi*, HAS, 2010–2012), and the New Welfare Party (*Yeniden Refah Partisi*, YRP, 2018–) are all offshoots of the National Outlook. All—with the exception of HAS—were named by selecting terms from Articles 1-3 of the MNP program. The commonalities among these parties are many. To begin with, they have all addressed the same audience: people who have been marginalised, or even been harmed, by rapid modernisation, secularism, and Turkish nationalism. Potential supporters for National Outlook parties have included first- and second-generation rural immigrants in urban shantytowns, small business owners and shopkeepers in small towns, peasants, pious conservatives, and Sunni Kurds. Second, National Outlook parties have adhered to a right-wing populist strategy and claimed to speak in the name of the "true" people, namely the downtrodden and those who have allegedly been oppressed by privileged elites, foreign powers, and Jews. Third, the MNP initiated what is now a 50-year-old tradition of Islamic-leaning foreign policy. While Erbakan pledged to honour existing commitments (read NATO) and did not question Turkey's Western orientation, he nevertheless promised to pursue a foreign policy that was more in line with "our historical character". Furthermore, he singled out the defence of *hakk* and *adalet* (justice) as what he thought should be the guiding principle of Turkish foreign policy. As yet another example of double talk, "*hakk*" can be interpreted as meaning either "rights" or "God". Last but not least, his pledge to shift to a presidential system of government, which can be found in the MNP program of 1970, was fulfilled by the 2017 Referendum.

Select Bibliography

Landau, Jacob M. *Radical Politics in Modern Turkey*. Leiden: Brill, 1974.
Prof. Dr. Necmettin Erbakan Külliyatı. 5 vols. İstanbul: Milli Gençlik Vakfı Yayinlari, 2014.
Toprak, Binnaz. *Islam and Political Development in Turkey*. Leiden: Brill, 1981.

49
Appreciating Turmoil:
The Autonomy of Universities and
the Military Intervention

Funda Soysal

As the Cold War settled into a stalemate and Western democracies struggled to overcome economic difficulties, new social movements in the West and anti-colonial struggles in the Third World culminated in what came to be known as the failed revolutions of 1968. In Turkey, while the state reacted indecisively, labour unrest was on the rise, and student protests intensified, descending into revolutionary militancy and violence. The anti-Americanism of radical leftist students claiming to be upholding Atatürk's injunction to the youth to defend Turkish independence was put on full display during a visit by the American ambassador to the campus of Middle East Technical University in January of 1969 and when the US Sixth Fleet docked in İstanbul a month later. Under the terms of the 1961 Constitution, state security forces could not enter campuses without permission due to the administrative autonomy that had been granted to universities. By 1971, bank robberies, bombings, and shootings of police officers had become commonplace. While the right blamed the "dangerous" ideas propagated at universities for these disturbances, the fundamental problem of higher education in Turkey lay in the philosophical dilemma of mass versus quality education. With increasing numbers of students seeking post-secondary education, Parliament passed Law No. 625 concerning private higher educational institutions in 1965, thereby legalising for-profit education, which had long been desired by various hegemonic social circles. Yet neither the quantity nor the quality of instructors and students could sustain the rapid expansion that followed, and the pressure on public universities to expand their enrolment capacities was hardly alleviated. While university boards were often crippled with endless wrangling over budgets and jealousies among faculty members, the creation of private institutions of higher education threatened to drain away qualified instructors and the degrees they granted were deemed unacceptable by some professional associations.

In January 1971, the Constitutional Court repealed the 1965 law by a majority vote on the grounds that it contravened Article 120 of the 1961 constitution, which stated that universities, as public institutions granted scientific and administrative autonomy, were to be legally founded by the state. The ruling entailed the closing—or reform by way of integration with public universities—of forty-eight private higher education institutions that had opened since 1962, including a few that were opened by underground religious brotherhoods and also Robert

College in İstanbul, which had reopened in 1958. Before reaching its decision, the Constitutional Court had asked the seven existing universities to submit expert opinions regarding the 1965 Law, which the Ministry of National Education defended. The text of the minority opinion against the repeal personally named the four experts in favour of a repeal, including Mümtaz Soysal (1929–2019) and two of his colleagues from Ankara University. Soysal, who had been granted a professorship as the Chair of Constitutional Law at Ankara University's Faculty of Political Sciences in 1969, had served as the representative of the Republican People's Party (*Cumhuriyet Halk Partisi*, CHP) to the commission that drafted the 1961 Constitution, and he was also among the founders of *Yön* (Direction), a widely influential leftist periodical of the 1960s. On 1 March 1971, his colleagues had elected him dean, drawing on the hope that his well-known socialist sympathies and strict legalism would help quell rising student militancy.

On 12 March 1971, the paralyzed government of Prime Minister Süleyman Demirel (1924–2015) was handed a memorandum by the Chief of Staff of the Turkish Armed Forces, demanding the formation of a strong and credible government to put an end to the "anarchy and social and economic *huzursuzluk* [turmoil]" disturbing the peace of the country and to carry out reforms "in an Atatürkist spirit". On 26 March, a technocratic government led by Nihat Erim (1912–1980), a law professor who had been advised by the National Security Council to withdraw his CHP membership, received a parliamentary vote of confidence to form an interim government that was to be above party politics. Soysal penned an article discussing the implications of this development for university reforms, an excerpt of which is presented below, which was initially published in the second issue of the progressive weekly *Ortam* (Milieu) in November 1971.

*A Beautiful Turmoil**

The Erim government is built upon two founding programs which appear to be complimentary but are inherently contradictory: peace [*huzur*] and reform. [...]

Which of these two foundations is more important, urgent, and "vital"? The answer varies, depending on whose interests and concerns are taken into consideration. According to some segments of the military, the progressive press, professional associations, and youth platforms, the cabinet has been given the power to implement reforms and will hold onto that power so long as reforms are implemented but will lose it if it fails to do so. However, if you ask those who regard a couple of explosions, robberies, and kidnappings as "great turmoil" [*büyük huzursuzluk*] while forgetting how teachers were dragged across streets or simple folk were beaten for years at gendarmerie and police stations, they say, "peace comes first" and if this government does not ensure peace, it must fall.

[...]

* Translated from the original Turkish in Mümtaz Soysal, "Güzel Huzursuzluk," *Güzel Huzursuzluk* (Ankara: Bilgi Yayınevi, 1975), 56–59.

Let us ask: if serious reforms were undertaken, would we not hear cries echoing, "winds of insecurity in the country"? The force of the megaphones deployed by these circles is strong. [...]

If a true connection, a true unity is to be established between security and reform, it is necessary to first agree upon the concept of "peace".

It is necessary to first accept that boycotts, campus occupations, forums, and ideological conflicts are now ordinary, endemic forms of expression and protest. Most of the events that are called "youth events" are broader, tougher facets of the perennial conflict between generations. At the current level of "civilisation," when a single bomb can kill hundreds of thousands, incidents that are called "acts of violence" are hardly worse than firecracker fun. [...]

Calling such events "turmoil" and assuming they will all disappear through security measures or university reforms would be a great mistake. The true turmoil in the field of education existed during the years when society appeared to be completely peaceful and at ease. This was a quiet, unheard disturbance, that of the oppressed millions, uneducated, unable to form themselves, deprived of the mental tools needed to avoid being trampled over in a society of snatchers and yet unable to even utter a cry. Nobody considered this state of being to be disturbing. To the contrary, when measures were taken to alleviate the "poverty of education" in Turkey by opening Village Institutes, critics came forward saying, "The peace of Anatolia is being disturbed."

Now, once you take steps in education that would change the foundations of the social structure and implement deeply rooted measures that would open all the doors of education to the oppressed masses, then you will begin hearing cries of turmoil. No need to go too far: when significant changes will need to be made next autumn regarding universities due to the closing of private institutions, the most anxious people will not be the students piling up by the thousands outside the campus gates, but rather the conservatives inside them.

Inevitably, a reform, or rather, an "education revolution," will create surges of currents in society that some circles will call "turmoil". In that sense, "peace" and reform are not only irreconcilable, but they should also not reconcile. The disturbance of some is the necessary price to pay to bring about the peace of millions. And I suppose, in Turkey, one day, that price will have to be paid.

**

Born in the industrial port city of Zonguldak as one of seven children of a veteran naval officer who served in the War of Independence, Soysal had acquired an elite education at the French-language Galatasaray Lycée and the Ankara School of Public Administration (*Mülkiye*) thanks to state scholarships, which he pursued following in the footsteps of his elder sister, Selma Soysal (1924–2011), who later became the first female math professor in Turkey. After initially becoming an assistant at the Middle East Institute of Public Administration where he conducted research alongside Swedish political scientist Gunnar Heckscher (1909–1987) on the administrative issues of Van and Erzurum and publishing a book on state-owned enterprises, Soysal undertook graduate studies at the London School of Economics as a United Nations fellow and went on to receive the first PhD degree awarded in political science in Turkey from Ankara University in 1958. During his graduate work at the LSE, Soysal studied under William A. Robson, a scholar of administrative law and an early and active member of the Fabian Society, a British socialist organisation whose aim was to advance the principles of democratic socialism via gradualist and reformist efforts in democracies, rather than by overthrowing the government through revolutions. Soysal's dissertation, which served as the basis of the *Yön* Manifesto of 1961, called for economic planning under an effective but democratic political mechanism that reflected the interests of the majority—namely, the workers, peasants, and labourers—which he argued was the only way for the Turkish economy to develop rapidly. In his lucidly written textbook *Introduction to the Constitution* (1968), Soysal provided a historical materialist account of democratic, communist, and Third World constitutional systems and then focused on Turkish constitutional developments since the nineteenth century by ascribing a preponderant and largely progressive role to the military-bureaucratic class. Characterising the War of Independence as a constitutive alliance between that class and provincial notables, landowners, and men of religion, Soysal distanced himself from a romantic view of the early years of the Republic. In his work *Dynamic Constitutional Understanding* (1969), he elaborated on the concept of "the openness of constitutions" and argued for a broadening of acceptable political discourses. Soysal diverged from his old associates at *Yön*, who by then had gathered around the journal *Devrim* (Revolution), as they were seeking a shortcut by advocating a left-wing military junta.

In "A Beautiful Turmoil," Soysal was indeed stepping into the realm of politics as an educator. Although the article was primarily concerned with the impending university reforms, it also pointed out the ubiquity of student activism as a global phenomenon. However, the title, referring to the former, easily lent itself to being twisted in such a way that he could be framed as condoning the latter, namely "turmoil."

The original title used the word "*huzursuzluk*," the negative form of the highly evocative Turkish word *huzur*, which describes an omnipresent state of tranquillity. Soysal was conceptualising huzur dialectically, suggesting that the veneer of huzur had to be disturbed in order to attain true huzur. Perhaps, by invoking such a conservative term, Soysal was overstepping an invisible boundary; rehashing Kemalism for socialist goals was perhaps tolerable, but calling for a disturbance of the peace that Muslim theology considered to be an emanation of God in the hearts of the faithful was a step too far. In the aftermath of the 1980 coup d'état, "huzur is in Islam" would be the principal political slogan of the Islamist movement. Sociologist Ulus Baker (1960–2007) noted that this conservative discourse of huzur was Hobbesian, invoking security as a precondition for political life under a modern administration. Entailing a domestication of identity, it distinguished itself as a permanent state of exception, imposing a forced consensus over an all-encompassing consumption and media society.

***

The pace of events in the spring of 1971 soon overtook Soysal's article. On 22 April 1971, Prime Minister Erim declared that a "blow" would strike the heads of anyone who threatened the established order. Martial law was declared in major cities and Erim reiterated the rightist tenet that the 1961 constitution was a luxury for Turkey. On May 17, Israeli Ambassador Ephraim Elrom (1911–1971) was abducted by radical students waging urban guerrilla warfare. The next morning, the government launched Operation Sledgehammer, taking many leftist intellectuals and professors into custody, including Soysal. The same day, a memorandum of understanding, signed between the Board of Trustees and the Ministry of Education, resulted in the Bebek campus of Robert College being handed over to the Turkish state on the condition that a public university be opened in its stead. As Soysal's period of detention was about to come to an end, Turan Feyzioğlu (1922–1988), who had himself been suspended as dean of the Political Science Faculty by the Menderes government back in 1956 for a speech he gave at the opening of the new academic year, quoted from Soysal's article during a broadcasted parliamentary speech and asked rhetorically, "Is this not a crime?" implicitly accusing Soysal of condoning student violence. Soysal, who had already been asked to resign as dean by his colleagues, was duly arrested. On July 13, Soysal married author Sevgi Soysal (1936–1976), whose award-winning novel *Yürümek* (*Walking*) had just been banned for "offending the values of the Turkish nation," whilst he was still under arrest.

Late in the summer of 1971, Parliament passed two constitutional changes that curbed the administrative autonomy of universities, allowing security forces to directly enter campuses without having to wait for the administration to let them in. Soon after Soysal's trial began on 30 September, three student leaders who had been arrested back in March were sentenced to death, and they were to be executed the following May. On 3 December, Soysal was sentenced to six years and eight months imprisonment for ostensibly engaging in communist propaganda in his book *Introduction to the Constitution*. In the absence of any evidence to prove he had engaged in incitement to violence and given Soysal's incisive challenge to the prosecutor's case, his sentence shuttled back and forth between the court and the Military Court of Appeals until it was dropped with the 1974 Amnesty. Having spent a total of fourteen months in prison, Soysal was declared an international prisoner of conscience by Amnesty International, on whose behalf he delivered the Nobel Peace Prize Lecture in 1977 as the organisation's vice-chairman and the first ex-prisoner elected to the body's executive committee.

Just as Soysal had predicted, the 1973 University Reform passed under the Interim Regime abolished university autonomy but failed to bring an end to student activism, which descended into bloodier violence once the Twelfth of March interim regime came to an end by way of elections held in October of 1973. Nonetheless, the alliance forged during that period between conservative forces of order proved to be long-lasting and they were further consolidated with the coup d'état of 12 September 1980. A deep distrust of freedom of thought not only stifled political debates, it also resulted in the purging of such freedom from its natural habitat, the university. The Constitution of 1982 instituted a centralised Council of Higher

Education (*Yükseköğretim Kurulu*, YÖK) to oversee all higher education and it also allowed for the establishment of private universities. Although a relative degree of self-government was granted to universities with the democratisation reforms of the 1990s, university autonomy was almost completely abolished with the executive directives issued during the State of Emergency declared in 2016. These days, as we commemorate the centenary of the Republic, Boğaziçi University, the public university that replaced Robert College and went on to develop its own model of autonomy irrespective of constitutional constraints, is the only institution left in Turkey that still resists political interventions over university autonomy.

Select Bibliography

Alper, Emin. "Reconsidering Social Movements in Turkey: The Case of the 1968–71 Protest Cycle." *New Perspectives on Turkey* 43 (2010): 63–96.

Baker, Ulus. *Peace Discourse in Political Language: Peace, Discourse, and Opinion in Islam*. MA Thesis, Middle Eastern Technical University, 1993. (Later published as *Siyasal Dilde Huzur Söylemi: İslâm'da Huzur, Söylem ve Kanaat*. Translated by Onur Eylül Kara. İstanbul: İletişim Yayınları, 2020).

Christofis, Nikos. "Introduction." Special Issue on the '68 Moment in Turkey. Edited by Nikos Christofis, *Turkish Historical Review* 12 (2021): 108–30.

Soysal, Mümtaz, and İlter Ertuğrul. *Anayasa'ya Giriş: Mümtaz Soysal'ın ve Kitabın Yargılanışı*. Ankara: İmge Kitabevi Yayınları, 2011.

Ulus, Özgür Mutlu. *The Army and the Radical Left in Turkey: Military Coups, Socialist Revolution and Kemalism*. London: I.B. Tauris, 2011.

Weiker, Walter F. "Academic Freedom and Problems of Higher Education in Turkey." *The Middle East Journal* 16, no. 3 (1962): 279–94.

50

Imperialism, Colonialism, and Oligarchic Dictatorships: Mahir Çayan's Revolutionary Theory

Erol Ülker

Mahir Çayan (1946–1972) was one of the prominent leaders of the radical youth movement in Turkey's long 1960s. He was born in Samsun in 1946 but spent some of the early years of his childhood with his grandparents in Amasya, the hometown of his father. Later he started primary school in İstanbul, where his parents had settled. In 1964, Çayan enrolled in Ankara University's Political Science Faculty, where he was involved in radical politics and university student activism. On 30 March 1972, Çayan was killed in Kızıldere (a village in the province of Tokat in northern Anatolia) along with nine of his comrades. They had been engaged in an armed struggle against the military junta that had seized power a year earlier.

Çayan wrote the brochures *Uninterrupted Revolution I* (*Kesintisiz Devrim*) and *Uninterrupted Revolution II-III* in the context of the military intervention of 12 March 1971, which was followed by a harsh crackdown on radical political movements. He was one of the militant leaders of the Revolutionary Youth (*Devrimci Gençlik*, commonly known as *Dev-Genç*), the main organisation of the student opposition in Turkey at the time, and he had also been affiliated with the National Democratic Revolution (*Milli Demokratik Devrim*, MDD) movement. When the military intervention took place, Çayan and his friends had recently split away from that movement to establish a revolutionary organisation that would take the name the People's Liberation Party-Front (*Türkiye Halk Kurtuluş Partisi-Cephesi*, THKP-C). In the *Uninterrupted Revolution* brochures, the first of which was published in March 1971, Çayan came up with a number of new concepts, such as "artificial balance," "the third phase of the depression of imperialism," and "hidden fascism," which contributed to ongoing discussions about revolutionary strategies and tactics. He wrote the second part, *Uninterrupted Revolution II-III*, in the first months of 1972, while the country was under martial law. The following excerpt from *Uninterrupted Revolution II-III* brings to the fore Mahir Çayan's perspectives on imperialism, colonialism, and oligarchic dictatorships.

*Uninterrupted Revolution II-III**

I. THE THIRD PHASE OF THE DEPRESSION OF IMPERIALISM

American imperialism emerged from the second war of re-division as the least harmed imperialist country and the one that made the most profit. It brought the economies of other imperialist-capitalist countries under its hegemony through capital exports and transfers to an extent incomparable to previous periods. It assumed the role of the gendarme of the imperialist bloc against the people's wars and the socialist bloc. It would probably not be wrong to say that the world capitalist bloc turned into the American Empire in this period (2/5 of capitalist world production is produced by the USA).

In this period, which is called the third phase of the depression of imperialism, imperialist relations and contradictions have changed *in form* on two main fronts.
1) The possibility of inter-imperialist rivalry (irreconcilable contradictions) leading to an inter-imperialist war of redistribution has faded.
2) The form of imperialist occupation has changed. (Today, there are almost no fully colonised countries left in the world. Open occupation has been replaced by covert occupation).

[...]

In this period, imperialism in general and Yankee imperialism in particular resorted to two methods at home and abroad in the face of the extreme contraction of the domestic and foreign markets of imperialism and the inability to solve the problem through a war of re-distribution. Domestically it militarised its economy, and externally, in addition to [utilising] the old colonial methods, it started neo-colonialism.

[...]

The fact that neo-colonial methods are based on expanding the commodity market in colonised countries as a way to respond to imperialist monopolies' greedy policy of exploitation and that "top-down capitalism" is the dominant mode of production in these countries has resulted in the domination of strong centralised authority.

A "top-down democratic revolution" has been carried out to a certain extent; while feudal relations are generally maintained in the superstructure (as the feudal exploitation of labour and feudal ideologies are maintained), capitalism has become the dominant element at the base (production for the market).

This entails the establishment of light and medium industry in these countries and also the formation and development of a domestic-monopoly bourgeoisie (as the favourite ally of imperialism). However,

---

* Translated from the original Turkish in Mahir Çayan, *Toplu Yazılar* (İstanbul: Su Yayınevi, 2008), 281–90.

the domestic-monopoly bourgeoisie developed not through internal dynamics, but by being integrated with imperialism from the outset. Thus, imperialism, which was an external phenomenon for these countries during the first and second periods of general depression, has become an internal phenomenon at the same time (the principle of secret occupation).

II. OLIGARCHIC DICTATORSHIPS

Governments in both imperialist-capitalist countries that passed through the industrial revolution and countries that have been kept backward are oligarchic governments. However, capitalism in imperialist-capitalist countries has developed and become established not in a reactionary manner (not top-down), but in a revolutionary sense through its internal dynamics. Therefore, bourgeois democratic relations prevailed not only at the base but also in the superstructure, and feudal relations were eliminated. But in the monopoly period, capitalism discarded the principles of free competition, nationalism, and democratic rule and replaced them with monopolies, cosmopolitanism, and oligarchic dictatorships.

However, in the past, the proletariat and working masses acquired their democratic rights and freedoms through protracted and bloody struggles. The working classes are strong both in quality and quantity. That is why the oligarchies in these countries can limit classical bourgeois democracy and freedoms to a certain extent but can never touch their essence. The nature of oligarchies in these countries is that of the financial oligarchy.

Oligarchic dictatorships in countries like ours do not bear the stamp of finance capital alone. That's because capitalism developed in the country in a top-down manner, not through its own internal dynamics. Therefore, the domestic-monopoly bourgeoisie developed by integrating with imperialism from the very beginning, when it was a nucleus (since imperialism has become an internal phenomenon, it is within this oligarchy). However, the developing-monopoly bourgeoisie alone is not strong enough to maintain imperialist relations of production by maintaining its alliance with imperialism. Therefore, it shares power with the landed bourgeoisie and feudal remnants, which are necessarily dependent on foreign and domestic monopolies.

Within oligarchic rule, the comprador-monopoly bourgeoisie is not the only domestic class that maintains imperialist relations of production, although it is the mainstay of imperialism.

Oligarchic governments in countries like ours can easily rule the country through an absolute dictatorship where workers and the labouring masses have no democratic rights or freedoms. We can also call this a colonial type of fascism. This [form of] rule is either exercised through "representative democracy" (hidden fascism), which is not even remotely related to classical bourgeois democracy, or it is exercised openly, with no regard for electoral democracy. However, the open conduct of the colonial type of fascism is not permanent. It is a method that is usually resorted to when it [oligarchic government] loses control.

***

Çayan traces "imperialism's third depression" to the aftermath of the Second World War. American economic and political hegemony dominated the capitalist world during the initial phase of the post-Second World War period, but later that hegemony was challenged by European and Japanese imperialisms. The extreme concentration and centralisation of capital, on the one hand, and the exclusion of one-third of the world from capitalist exploitation with the formation of the socialist bloc, on the other, drove the imperialist system into a deep crisis, while at the same time shaking American hegemony.

In the third period of depression, according to Çayan, the changing character of the competition between imperialist powers no longer allowed for a general war of redistribution because of recent developments in the technologies of nuclear warfare. The older forms of direct colonialist domination were replaced by more subtle and hidden forms of imperialist exploitation that did not necessitate the formal occupation of Third World countries. Imperialism became an internal phenomenon through the penetration of new forms of colonial domination via the export of patent rights, technological know-how, equipment, and expertise. The rise of dependent industrialisation and the accompanying expansion of the market and social production led to the formation of a local class of monopolistic bourgeoisie. That class was completely dependent on imperialism and too weak to maintain imperialist relations by itself. Therefore, it shared power with the landed bourgeoisie and feudal remnants. The interests of this oligarchic bloc were represented by the central state apparatus.

For Çayan, in countries like Turkey, which were dominated by new colonialism, the oligarchic bloc was able to establish a "colonial type of fascism". Dependent industrialisation, urbanisation, and the development of communication and transportation infrastructures strengthened the central state apparatus to an unprecedented degree. In the face of the prospect of revolutionary civil wars, oligarchic states became heavily militarised by way of the army and police force. Oligarchic dictatorships can be imposed through "representative democracy," which has nothing to do with genuine bourgeois democracy, or they can be installed directly without formal democratic procedures.

Çayan argues, however, that the oligarchic state resorts to open fascism only temporarily, when matters get out of control. Otherwise, there is an "artificial balance" between the oligarchy and the popular masses. In the third phase of imperialism's period of depression, imperialist occupation is hidden, the central state apparatus becomes visible all across the country, and the growth of the market and production brings about a degree of relative welfare. Economic expansion mitigates the intensity of social contradictions, diminishing the reactions of the masses to the established order. Çayan's major concern was about presenting the right revolutionary strategy to break this artificial balance between the oligarchy and the people.

***

Mahir Çayan was engaged in revolutionary activism during one of the most crucial periods in the history of the Republic of Turkey. Politics were no longer confined to a narrow elite group or band of political parties in the 1960s, when broader segments of the population participated in grassroots organisations and new political movements associated with the radical left. University students in particular were at the forefront of revolutionary activism in the long 1960s. Along with many other youth leaders in this tumultuous period, including but not limited to Harun Karadeniz (1942–1975), Deniz Gezmiş (1947–1972), and İbrahim Kaypakkaya (1949–1973), Çayan and his comrades left behind a revolutionary legacy that inspired the next generations of activists involved in radical politics. He formulated his ideas at a time when anti-imperialism constituted a common ideological framework for all the factions of the radical left, and Çayan's insights were no exception. He presented his theory of uninterrupted revolution as a revision of the theory of national democratic revolution, which had a clear Third-Worldist orientation. Yet Çayan proved to be an innovative theorist by contributing a number of notably original concepts to the ongoing discussions on imperialism, colonialism, and fascism. Çayan's theories and analyses, which found their most systematic formulation in *Uninterrupted Revolution*, proved to be long-lived as crucial references for discussions concerning socialist strategies and revolutionary tactics in Turkey.

Select Bibliography

Aydınoğlu, Ergun. *Türkiye Solu (1960-1980): "Bir Amneziğin Anıları."* İstanbul: Versus Kitap, 2007.

Feyizoğlu, Turhan. *Mahir: On'ların Öyküsü.* İstanbul: Ozan Yayıncılık, 2007.

Şener, Mustafa. *Türkiye Solunda Üç Tarz-ı Siyaset: Yön, MDD ve TİP.* İstanbul: Yordam Kitap, 2015.

Ulus, Özgür Mutlu. *The Army and the Radical Left in Turkey: Military Coups, Socialist Revolution and Kemalism.* London: I.B. Tauris, 2011.

Ülker, Erol. "Anti-Imperialism and Kemalism in Turkey's Long Sixties: Mahir Çayan's Theory of Revolution in Context." *Turkish Historical Review* 12 (2021): 211–39.

Yıldırım, Barış. "Mahir Çayan ve 'Kesintisiz Devrim.'" In *Mühürler: Türkiye Sosyalist Hareketinden Eserler*, edited by Gökhan Atılgan, 367–417. İstanbul: Yordam Kitap, 2019.

1973–1982

51
A Growing İstanbul:
The Opening of the Bosphorus Bridge

Gözde Kırcıoğlu

Large festivities, timed to coincide with celebrations for the fiftieth anniversary of the proclamation of the Republic of Turkey, accompanied the opening of the first bridge over the Bosphorus Strait connecting the European and Asian sides of İstanbul on 30 October 1973. Starting at 11:00 AM at the Beylerbeyi entrance of the bridge on the Asian side, the ceremony was broadcast on national television, expressing sentiments filled with both national and international hopes and expectations. Reportedly more than ten thousand people were present, including President Fahri Korutürk (1903–1987) and Prime Minister Naim Talu (1919–1998), as well as state ministers, top army officials, the secretary of NATO, and foreign journalists. Speeches were made, celebrating fifty years of the successful modernisation and Westernisation of Turkey, in addition to lauding the positive impacts the bridge would have on international travel and commerce. As President Korutürk, followed by thousands of attendees, set out to walk across the bridge from Beylerbeyi to Ortaköy, each lamppost was adorned with Turkish flags, and the music of the tenth and fiftieth Republican anniversary marches rang out. Meanwhile, UNICEF ambassador Danny Kaye, a world-famous American actor, was accompanied by hundreds of children from around the world as he started walking across from the Ortaköy entrance of the bridge on the European side. The bridge started to swing due to the large number of people crossing it, causing a mild panic. According to the original plan, Kaye and Korutürk were to meet in the middle of the bridge, where Kaye would give flowers to Korutürk. However, the crowds were so large that the two were unable to meet and security staff cleared the bridge by 3:00 PM.

When completed it was the fourth-longest suspension bridge in the world and the longest outside the United States (US). The project to build the bridge also included Turkey's first ring highway, which was twenty-three kilometres long and known as the First Beltway (or O1). It started from Osmaniye in the Bakırköy district on the European side, traversed the city across the Golden Horn and the Bosphorus Bridge, and ended in the Söğütlüçeşme neighbourhood of the district of Kadıköy on the Asian side.

In addition to modernisation and Westernisation, the Bosphorus Bridge (*Boğaziçi Köprüsü*) symbolised the country's embracing of a car-centric infrastructure, as modelled by the US and Europe. It was built as part of efforts that had gotten underway in the 1970s to modernise İstanbul by building modern infrastructure projects through collaboration between the private sector and the state. As such, the bridge and highway were financed by a loan agreement struck between Turkey and the United Kingdom (UK) and involved a British consultation firm.

Before the bridge was built, the Bosphorus could only be crossed by boat. The earliest plans for a bridge over the Bosphorus date back to the year 1900 during the reign of Sultan Abdülhamid (1842–1918) but this project was never realised. Transportation in İstanbul had for centuries been primarily dependent on the sea and not much changed after the founding of the Republic in 1923. İstanbul continued as it had done for centuries until the mid-1950s. At the beginning of the twentieth century, the city was comprised of the old historic peninsula, the district of Pera (Beyoğlu) across the Golden Horn, and Üsküdar on the Asian side. Bridges that had been built in the nineteenth century across the Golden Horn had increased interactions between the peninsula, the old city centre, and Galata and Pera, which was the European face of the city with its increasing numbers of European traders and embassies. Üsküdar, on the Asian side across from Eminönü, remained a residential area accessed primarily by boat. In the 1930s, there was a plan to bridge the Bosphorus with a 20.72-meter-wide suspension bridge between Ahırkapı and Salacak. This project, proposed by established entrepreneur Nuri Demirağ (1886–1957), was never started, like most city plans for İstanbul until the 1950s. Between 1923 and 1950, the government followed conservative financial policies and limited borrowing to maintain a strong lira. Given the conservative budget, the development of Ankara, as the symbol of the new Republic, took priority over İstanbul. From the 1950s onward, İstanbul grew in importance with regard to investment projects. However, following through with plans for İstanbul suddenly became possible when the government of Prime Minister Adnan Menderes (1899–1961) loosened the state's financial policies as a result of increasing amounts of US aid coming in, which was meant to ensure that Turkey steered clear of Soviet influence. Adopting a car-based urban planning model seemed to have become an increasingly urgent issue for İstanbul as the 1960s drew near, and a "First Bridge" over the Bosphorus was included in the city plan of 1958.

The contract to build the bridge was signed on 25 January 1970 by Süleyman Demirel (1924–2015), the prime minister of the Justice Party (*Adalet Partisi*) government. It is still remembered as one of Demirel's greatest achievements. Demirel's economic policies emphasised private initiative and aimed to develop Turkey's economy as rapidly as possible. Between 1965 and 1969, Turkey saw unprecedented sustained economic growth and real income went up almost continually by an average of 20 per cent over a four-year period. When the first bridge was opened, most observers were optimistic about the country's prospects. But, despite the optimism, starting in the late 1960s the Union of Chambers of Turkish Engineers and Architects (*Türk Mühendis ve Mimar Odaları Birliği*) unsuccessfully fought against the decision to build the bridge. They argued that the bridge would harm the development of İstanbul. Below is an extract from an article about urbanisation around the Bosphorus that was written by a commission of architects, presented at a conference, and published in October 1973 in *Mimarlık Dergisi*, the bi-monthly magazine of the Chamber of Architects (*Mimarlar Odası*).

Settlement and Urbanisation and Its Problems on and around the Bosphorus[*]

Transportation and the Bosphorus Bridge

The report of the Master Plan [of the city of İstanbul], prepared under Prof. Piccinato's directive in 1958, states, "The route of the ring road, for which the Ministry of Public Works had a study done by an American company, was accepted with minor modifications, and the location of the Bosphorus Bridge [also contained in the study] was accepted as is into the Master Plan". In the discussion about the bridge held at the İstanbul Urban Planning Office in 1967, the head of the bureau, Mithat Yenen [1908–1987], said, "We have gathered here to realise the general policy of the government in the plan," making it clear that the bridge entered the master plan as a fait accompli as a political choice, not as a result of a scientific study.

The Chamber of Architects has clearly expressed publicly, and to interested parties as well, that the Bosphorus Bridge, the construction of which has now been completed, will be harmful for the planned development of İstanbul, rather than helping it.

The Bosphorus Bridge will not encourage "linear development," which was accepted as a principle in the Master Plan study. On the contrary, it will increase the [population] density in the existing city centre and encourage development to the north (in the direction of the Bosphorus). Due to the ease of contact with the western side, the development that will occur in the eastern side of İstanbul will not be self-sufficient, and the city will spread in the eastern part by maintaining its single centre.

It was possible to use the congestion at the Bosphorus crossing as a planning tool for a decentralised city layout. The fact that the bridge encourages development to the north will necessitate new bridges and ring roads in the very near future, and these developments will reveal important problems in the planning of recreational areas in İstanbul.

The intercity roads constructed right by the shore between İzmit and İstanbul and İstanbul and Tekirdağ [on the Marmara coasts] in the 1950–60s period caused coastal plundering in this 200-kilometre-long area by leaving it open to the most harmful land use and leaving the İstanbul metropolitan area deprived of the ability to meet the recreational needs of millions of people.

The Bosphorus Bridge, in a very short time, will cause great damage to the Bosphorus and its immediate surroundings, just like how the Marmara coasts [suffered harm].

[*] Translated from the original Turkish in Somer Ural, Şeref Yazıcıoğlu, Mete Göktuğ, Cihat Fındıkoğlu, Ersen Gürsel, and Niyazi Duranay, "Boğaziçi ve Çevresinde Yerleşme ve Kentleşme Olayları ve Sorunları," *Mimarlık Dergisi* (October 1973): 13–16.

***

Between 1950 and 1970, İstanbul's population tripled from one to three million, and the need for public transportation increased due to industrialisation and rapid urbanisation. The solutions of successive governments were criticised by the Chamber of Architects for constituting superficial urban planning and for profiting large international companies, rather than being in the interests of the public. For the government, cooperation with international companies was the only way to find loans for large construction projects.

The feasibility study for the Bosphorus Bridge was created almost in isolation and did not take into consideration the transportation of the city as a whole. The Chamber of Architects argued that the bridge would not solve the traffic problems of the city but only make them worse. They reasoned that the bridge would lead to an expansion of the city to the north on both sides of the Bosphorus and to the east on the Asian side as well as cause the growth of the city centre, which was easily accessible, to facilitate the not-yet-self-sufficient newly developed areas. The bridge would encourage car ownership, thereby increasing traffic and the duration of commutes, soon leading to a need to construct more bridges and highways. In fact, construction plans for a second bridge over the Bosphorus were announced by Demirel before the elections of 12 October 1975, only two years after the first bridge had been completed. However, it was not built until 1988.

The Chamber of Architect's other concern was that there was a need for new legislation to protect the Bosphorus from corrupt planning as it became exposed to urban development. Allowing the intensive construction of roads and housing would damage the beaches of the villages on the Bosphorus, which had already happened in the 1950s along the shores of the Marmara Sea. It was argued that such development would bring harm to the historical heritage and the architectural texture of the city and that the Bosphorus could be lost as a place to accommodate the recreational needs of İstanbul's growing population. The chamber recommended instead investments in public transport, a tunnel project, and a plan to situate the urbanisation of İstanbul within the larger context of its role in the immediate Marmara region and Turkey as a whole.

Construction of the bridge and the highway had already started before the necessary legal procedures were completed, which was also criticised by the architects. The municipality of İstanbul rejected the construction plans because the city master plan was not yet ready at the time. The General Directorate of Highways (*Karayolları Genel Müdürlüğü*) continued construction, however, even though it did not have the legal authorisation to do so without the consent of the municipal council. A draft bill granting the General Directorate of Highways the right of confiscation without municipal consent was presented to the National Assembly with the intention of establishing legal grounds after the fact.

***

Plans for a "First Bridge" (*ilk köprü*), as a symbol of modernisation and Westernisation, had been a part of government projects since the 1950s. The development of roads next to the

Bosphorus in the 1970s was the first significant road construction in İstanbul since the implementation of the Prost plan. The first bridge led to the development of the northern parts of the city on both sides of the Bosphorus, and in the 1980s it was calculated that if the city's population growth continued apace, an additional bridge would be needed every ten years to accommodate the growing amount of traffic. In 1988, a second bridge, named after Fatih Sultan Mehmet, the Ottoman sultan who conquered the city in 1453, was built sixteen kilometres to the north of the Bosphorus Bridge. In the 1970s and 1980s, after the construction of the bridges over the Bosphorus and peripheral highways was completed, (sub-)urbanisation continued at a rapid pace. By the 1990s, with the population of the city now standing at eight million, the focus on accommodating cars shifted to improving public transportation, which had been more or less completely neglected since the 1940s.

Policies instituted in the 1970s and 1980s to modernise İstanbul by building modern infrastructure with the private sector in the lead in close cooperation with the state were exploited to their fullest in the early 2000s under the government of the Justice and Development Party (*Adalet ve Kalkınma Partisi*, AKP) with considerably more investment in public transportation. Between 2004 and 2013, a rail tunnel (*Marmaray*) under the Bosphorus Strait was built between Kazlıçeşme on the European side and Ayrılıkçeşmesi on the Asian side. In 2015, a third bridge was opened to the north of the existing two bridges and it was named after Yavuz Sultan Selim, an Ottoman sultan who was known for his efforts to Sunnify the Ottoman Empire to the detriment of minority Muslim sects. The third bridge connects Garipçe in Sarıyer on the European side to Poyrazköy in Beykoz on the Asian side. The Eurasian tunnel (*Avrasya Tüneli*), a double-deck road tunnel was opened in late 2016 to connect Kumkapı on the European side with Kadıköy on the Asian side.

Transportation in İstanbul was and continues to be a major problem. A major cause of this is generally accepted to be the construction of infrastructure without following established plans or recommendations, as the Chamber of Architects had warned. The Bosphorus is the most important feature of İstanbul, which protected its identity as a waterfront city until the late 1960s. Starting in the early 1970s, the city grew in all directions with the construction of highways, gradually distancing itself from the water. As a result, water is no longer the most important means of transportation, and the sea is no longer as accessible for recreational purposes as it once was.

As one of the most iconic symbols of İstanbul, the Bosphorus Bridge was re-named the "15 July Martyrs Bridge" (*15 Temmuz Şehitler Köprüsü*) following the 2016 coup attempt, in reference to the 251 civilians who lost their lives on that night. Most of the clashes between the military and civilians took place on that very bridge.

Select Bibliography

Gül, Murat. *The Emergence of Modern Istanbul: Transformation and Modernisation of a City*. London: I.B. Tauris, 2009.
Mimarlar Odası. *Boğaz Köprüsü Üzerine Mimarlar Odasının Görüşü*. İstanbul: Mimarlar Odası Yayını, 1969.
Özus, Evren, Şevkiye Şence Türk and Vedia Dökmeci. "Urban Restructuring of Istanbul." *European Planning Studies* 19, no. 2 (2011): 331–56.

52
Cinematic Imagining of the Nationalist Soldier-to-be: Little Mujahid in Cyprus

Güldeniz Kıbrıs

Because it witnessed a tremendous increase in consumption and production, Turkish cinema from the 1950s to the 1970s is a significant source for grasping the nationalist and militarist popular culture that permeated everyday life in those times. Among many other examples, the film *Sezercik, Küçük Mücahit* (*Sezercik, Little Mujahid,* directed by Ertem Göreç), which was made in 1974 and released in 1975 during the heyday of the crisis over Cyprus, is one of the most intense representations of the militaristic values that dominated the nationalist state of mind in Turkey during the Cold War period.

The film's background was shaped by the anti-communist nationalist agitation that was prevalent in the Cold War era, which was reflected in the Cyprus issue. It provided a popular ground for the rise of militarist nationalism by reproducing the image of the enemy as Greek and reviving the trauma of Turkish-Greek encounters during the War of Independence (1919–1922).

Tensions between Greece and Turkey started to rise in the 1950s during the Greek Cypriot struggle for independence from British colonial rule. The National Organisation of Cypriot Fighters (*Etniki Organosis Kyprion Agoniston*, EOKA), an underground paramilitary organisation comprised of Greek Cypriots, fought initially against British colonial rule and then increasingly for *enosis* (the union of Cyprus with Greece) against the Turkish population of Cyprus, whose political leaders supported partition of the island. Over time, the nationalist aggressiveness of both sides increased. In 1960, the Republic of Cyprus was established after an agreement was reached between Britain, Turkey, and Greece, which gave the three countries guarantees for the independence and territorial integrity of the Republic. The constitution divided governmental powers between the Greek and Turkish sides. For the Greeks, these were controversial signs of a future partition of the island. The Turkish side thought that the constitution sought to limit its powers and identity. In November of 1963, the President of Cyprus, Archbishop Makarios III (Michael Christodoulou Mouskos, 1913–1977), proposed thirteen amendments to reduce the influence of the Turkish Cypriots. This prepared the basis for intense communal fighting, whereupon Ankara decided to intervene. Meanwhile, Britain utilised diplomatic tools to put an end to the internal strife in Cyprus. President Johnson, fearing an attack might lead to Soviet intervention, indicated in a letter to Turkey's Prime

Minister İnönü (1884–1973) that the US would not provide military assistance in the case of a Turkish attack on Cyprus and that no NATO materials were to be used in such an invasion. This letter effectively pushed Turkey into adopting a relatively passive policy and brought a brief interruption to the intercommunal violence, a pause which lasted until 1974.

The late 1960s and early 1970s witnessed increasing street violence and suppression of the left both in Greece and Turkey by military regimes. The Greek junta of 1974 orchestrated a coup led by Nikos Sampson (1935–2001) on 15 July to overthrow the government of Cyprus and revive *enosis*. Justifying its actions on the grounds of its guarantor status, Turkey launched a military attack on 20 July under the leadership of Prime Minister Bülent Ecevit (1925–2006), who adopted a proactive foreign policy. As a result of Turkey's two consecutive interventions, Turkish forces extended their control to 36 per cent of the island, leading to its de facto partition. In February 1975, the Turkish Federated State of Cyprus was proclaimed in the north.

*Sezercik, Küçük Mücahit (Sezercik, Little Mujahid)**

* https://www.imdb.com/title/tt5140650/

***

The Turkish film industry produced twenty-three films between 1959 and 1975 that addressed the Cyprus issue. *Sezercik, Küçük Mücahit (Sezercik, Little Mujahid)* is the only such film that reproduces nationalist militarist discourses by way of a male child as its protagonist. The film centres on Sezer's attempt to get revenge on EOKA in 1974. His mother is Lale, a primary school teacher, and his father, Murat, is a pilot officer, reaffirming conventional secular gender roles. In 1967, after Murat dies in a plane crash, Lale moves to Cyprus to live with her sister Aynur while she is pregnant, and she gives birth to a son. One day, she returns to Turkey to nurse her sick mother. During her absence, EOKA kills Aynur and her husband. Sezer, however, is saved by a couple who later adopts him as their foster child. In another attack in 1974, EOKA fighters murder this couple as well. Before they die, they tell Sezer, who is seven at the time, what happened in the past and reveal his real identity. He then sets off to get revenge for what happened and to find his mother. When his mother comes back to Cyprus, she finds out that her son is still alive and has joined the Turkish troops. While attending a military parade, she recognises her son and they are reunited.

The film focuses on Sezer's heroic actions despite his young age, revealing his nationalistic frame of mind and warrior identity. Sezer is a brave boy, aware of the animosity between the Greeks and the Turks. When Greek girls show an interest in him, he does not react; according to his foster mother, as only a Turkish girl would suit Sezer. This small example reveals Sezer's nationalist awareness and underscores his masculinity through the female other. Sezer is a proper and well-behaved child who follows his foster father's advice not to get involved with Greek children. One day some cruel children forcibly take Sezer and his friends' soccer ball and then try to make the Turkish children buy it back. Sezer argues they cannot sell a ball that is not theirs. They pretend to give the ball back and then beat Sezer up. This particular incident is enough for Sezer to call them "treacherous," which could refer to the 1974 revival of enosis despite the post-1963 settlement and the Turkish side's attempts at conciliation. In this regard, the film reproduces the official nationalist discourse and is devoid of a potentially irredentist approach that would defend the Turkishness of all of Cyprus.

The film represents Greek male children as being physically powerful, quarrelsome, and materialist bullies, in opposition to Sezer, who acted out of defence, similar to the Turkish Cypriots. However, after the EOKA murder his foster parents, Sezer takes revenge by revealing his innate militaristic characteristics, which stem from his Turkishness. He turns into a soldier who can defeat his enemies regardless of whether they are adults or children thanks to his will, determination, and intelligence, despite his physically smaller stature and young age. A scene in which he beats up four Greek children who attack him for the second time serves as an indication of his transition and reveals that the Greeks are perceived as being dishonourable. They do not fight in a manly way, ganging up to attack an innocent person, in parallel to the situation in Cyprus where the Turks were outnumbered by the Greeks.

After the murder of his foster parents, Sezer finds out that the Greeks plan to attack the village of Bayraklı. Since he is a naturally born and nationally conscious warrior, Sezer instinctively burdens himself with the mission of warning the villagers. A sergeant of the resistance forces, which are called *Mücahit* (from the Arabic-Islamic term mujahid, meaning "those who struggle") picks him up and when he gets mortally wounded on his way to head-quarters, he orders Sezer to deliver a letter to the commander of the Turkish army. Thanks to all his efforts, Sezer saves three villages from EOKA attacks. In addition, Sezer saves a woman who is about to be raped by a Greek. The scene exalts Sezer's masculinity over that of an adult enemy. It is the only scene in the film in which a Turk is depicted as killing the enemy, thereby reinforcing an image of Turks taking up a solely defensive position in favour of peace. As a result of his heroism, the commander rewards him first with the title of corporal and then lieutenant. This certification of Sezer's militaristic qualities and his warrior identity convey the message that even Turkish children are powerful enough to defeat the other.

In perhaps the most striking scene in the film, Sezer is portrayed wearing a military uni-form and pointing a gun, his eyes full of hatred, at some members of the EOKA, some of whom are the murderers of his foster parents. After thinking back on memories of the moment when they were killed, presented in dramatic flashbacks, Sezer decides not to kill the Greek men because they ask for mercy and because they may have children, as his parents had. The commander accompanying him remarks that "even the children of the Turkish nation do not pull the trigger on those who ask for mercy." Through Sezer, this scene depicts an ideal of Turkish soldiers being benevolent and virtuous. The civilised and humane Turkish soldiers never attack civilians, unlike the cruel, inhumane, and bandit-like Greeks who shoot everybody without distinction, even a baby in its cradle, as Sezer's foster father says. Thus, the film clearly depicts the Greeks as being a savage enemy. Strikingly, only EOKA guerrillas and male children represent the enemy in the film, so in this way it contributes to a homogeneous and totalising representation of the other as Greeks without distinguishing between Greeks and Greek Cypriots.

Likewise, the film hardly distinguishes between Anatolian Turks and Cypriot Turks; both communities are depicted as a single constituent. As such, the Turkish audience could inter-nalise Turkish-speaking Cypriots as fellow citizens. A tricky difference is that all of the Turks from Turkey in the film are middle-class professionals, such as military officers, a teacher (such as Sezer's mother), and Aynur's husband, who is a doctor. Cypriot Turks, on the other hand, appear to be from a lower class, as if they were conservative people from the rural peripheries. This form of representation marks a hierarchy between Turkey and Cyprus, depicting Cypriots as being less developed and therefore in need of Turks' help. In fact, Cyprus is regularly referred to as the *yavru vatan* (baby-homeland) in Turkey's political discourse and hence depicted as the offspring of the "motherland" (*anavatan*). For example, after noticing that his son has gotten beaten up by Greek Cypriot children, Sezer's father remarks that one day Turks' turn will come and that the mainland will never leave the baby-homeland's side, meaning that Cypriot Turks will get their revenge. In this way, Cyprus, similar to Sezer, is a little child in need of Turkey's protection, thereby legitimising Turkey's presence in Cyprus. This point contributes to the perception of Cyprus as an extension of Turkey, as a part of the unified national homeland, not a different country. Frequent travels between Cyprus and Turkey, as exemplified through Lale who visits her mother in İstanbul, also strengthen the idea of the connectedness and closeness of the two spaces—and hence the homeland is portrayed as a unified space. In fact, when the EOKA executes certain characters, they all shout "long live the motherland" before they die, indicating that they all feel loyalty towards the Turkish nation. This representation also reinforces the hierarchy and connection between the two lands, helping the audience imagine themselves as having a connection to Cyprus. Therefore, when Sezer fights with the children of the other, he is doing so not in a different space, but in fact in "our" neighbourhood. This representation marks off the idea that the enemy is in fact much closer than it was on the battlefield.

Furthermore, the film generously uses nationalist symbology including the Turkish national anthem, Turkish military academy march, and the Turkish flag. Some documentary scenes depicting the arrival of Turkish jets to intervene on the island are inserted at the end of the film. These are accompanied by images of weaponry, tanks, and real soldiers in military uniforms marching in an official parade. All of these symbols serve to bolster the militarist messages of the film.

Thus, *Sezercik, Küçük Mücahit* (*Sezercik, Little Mujahid*) depicts a heroic soldier-to-be fighting against the enemy during the heyday of the Cyprus issue. This representation surely contributed to the nationalist-militarist atmosphere that dominated Turkish politics at the time.

***

Nationalism and militarism are ideologies of hegemonic masculinity. Nationalism discursively constructs nationhood as a gender-based imagined community that assigns men the active role of defending honour, freedom, homeland, women, and children. It takes manhood as being connected with militarism; thus, men are perceived as protective soldiers, whereas women are the nation's mothers who are to be elevated and protected, confirming the gendered division of labour. In this context, female children are almost never depicted and male children are given the role of soldiers-to-be because they are men-to-be. Thus, they are laden with nationalist ideals so they can serve as miniature active agents of the nation. In addition to official instruments of the state such as schools, textbooks, museums, or the army, this particular discourse is reproduced through popular cultural products such as films. They represent the unofficial/informal/banal realm of everyday life, spread militaristic values, and constantly shape and are being shaped by the official/formal/state manifestations of national identity.

With a focus on the duties and responsibilities of a male Turkish child, *Sezercik Küçük Mücahit* (*Sezercik, Little Mujahid*) glorifies war, the military, and a warrior identity, and in doing so the film normalises violence and exalts killing and being killed for the nation during a period of time when the Cyprus issue was at its peak. In fact, this issue is still a significant foreign policy matter for Turkey. The Turkish Federated State of Cyprus has not been recognised by any other state except for Turkey. The 1974 intervention on Cyprus was never approached as a diplomatic success, but instead as an invasion that led to Turkey's uncertain disengagement from a Western alliance that has implications even today. Thus, *Sezercik, Küçük Mücahit (Sezercik, Little Mujahid)* serves the function of producing Gramscian consent to legitimise Turkey's national cause in Cyprus.

Select Bibliography

Aktar, Ayhan, Niyazi Kızılyürek, and Umut Özkırımlı, eds. *Nationalism in the Troubled Triangle: Cyprus, Greece and Turkey*. Basingstoke: Palgrave Macmillan, 2010.

Altınay, Ayşe Gül. *The Myth of the Military Nation: Militarism, Gender, and Education in Turkey*. New York: Palgrave Macmillan, 2004.

Canefe, Nergis. *Anavatandan Yavruvatana: Milliyetçilik, Bellek ve Aidiyet*. İstanbul: İstanbul Bilgi Üniversitesi Yayınları, 2007.

Fevzioğlu, Bülent, and Bilgi Fevzioğlu. *Sinema, Plak ve Bildirilerde Kıbrıs Türklerinin Direniş Yılları* (1), TMT 50. Yıl Anısı. Lefkoşa: Ajans Yayınları 2009.

Özkırımlı, Umut, and Spyros A. Sofos. *Tormented by History: Nationalism in Greece and Turkey*. New York: Columbia University Press, 2008.

53
Between Modernisation and Class Struggle: *Arabesk* Music

Kadir Dede

Arabesk (from French "arabesque") originally denoted a style of Arabic ornamentation employing intertwined foliate and geometrical figures which was used in Orientalist architecture and decoration in Europe starting in the sixteenth century. However, in the 1970s, the term came to signify a newly emerging musical genre in Turkey. Arabesk music was socially associated with *gecekondu* neighbourhoods, which were impoverished, dilapidated squatter settlements on the peripheries of cities. In subsequent decades, the cultural gap of these neighbourhoods, which was positioned between rural villages and urban areas, became the focus of discussions on a wide variety of issues such as modernisation, Westernisation, Orientalism, urbanisation, migration, class struggles and voting behaviour in Turkey. Although the lyrics of Arabesk songs usually centred on themes such as love, fate, injustice, hope, and melancholy, for listeners of lower socio-economic status, the tropes of Arabesk could be interpreted as addressing poverty, displacement, and deprivation, thus coding Arabesk as a form of oppositional and emotional protest music. The 1970s in Turkey were distinctive as the decade was marked by class struggles, strikes, student protests, a polarised political spectrum, unstable coalition governments, an economic crisis, political violence, a low-intensity civil war, and military coups that followed one after the other.

Arabesk as a musical genre is a permutation of the notion of an East-West synthesis, the roots of which extend back to the arguments of Turkey's "national" sociologist Ziya Gökalp (1876–1924), who laid the groundwork for the political discourses of the republican era. Arabesk music lays bare the inadequacy of policies shaped by the prohibition or disregard of certain musical genres and the promotion of others which were implemented by bureaucratic/artistic elites in a top-down manner. It represents a "spontaneous synthesis" that has gained the support of the masses. Shaped by middle and lower-class artists, that synthesis has been compatible with the dynamics of the music market and, despite state efforts aimed at suppression, it has often been successful. While the lyrics bound up with this musical synthesis have remained in contact with the streets, slums, and daily life, the music itself is a blend of East and West. Arabesk orchestras make use of Turkish and Arabic instruments as well as those with roots in the West such as strings, guitars, electro-guitars (and electro-*saz*), and polyphonic choruses, and they utilise Western-style musical notation.

Within this broader framework of Arabesk, the song "Batsın Bu Dünya" (Damn This World) by Orhan Gencebay (1944–) arguably best exemplifies the genre. As a traditionally educated musician who worked as a professional musician at the state radio station in the 1960s, Gencebay is an important figure not only as a pioneering Arabesk singer, but also as a musician and songwriter who has played a vital role in the theoretical and practical development of this type of music; additionally, he was an actor who contributed to the rise of Arabesk cinema, a genre of musical films that starred leading singers. The song, which was recorded in 1975 and featured in a film of the same name, is one of Gencebay's best-known and popular works. While the oppositional tone of the lyrics bears traces of the period, it also offers up a good impression of the daily life of the times and the "zeitgeist".

Damn this World*

What a shame, what a shame
Shame on such a fate.
Everything is dark, where is humanity?
Shame on those who serve as a slave of a slave.

Damn this world, may this dream end,
Shame on those who laugh after making others cry.
The ordeals are not over, the sorrows are not outlived,
Shall the longing heart be my own?

What did I do to you, Destiny?
You imprisoned me in myself.
A thousand complaints with every breath,
My complaint is to the Creator, my complaint is to the Creator.

Is it you or me who is baffled?
You inflicted such sorrow that I couldn't come back to myself
I am stuck in a blind alley, I cannot find my way out.
Ahh... Ahh... Ahh...

Am I the one who created it, am I the one who created it?
Am I the one who created sorrow and suffering?
If sin became fun, if fidelity grew fatigued,
If the order is corrupt, am I the one who created it all?

* Translated from the original Turkish lyrics of Orhan Gencebay, "Batsın Bu Dünya," track 1 on *Batsın Bu Dünya*, Kervan Plakçılık, 1975. http://www.orhangencebay.com.tr/albumler.php?id=44

Damn this world, may this dream end,

Shame on those who laugh after making others cry.

The ordeals are not over, the sorrows are not outlived,

Shall the longing heart be my own?

***

In the song's lyrics, the line referring to a "corrupt order" (*bozuk düzen*) encompasses both the general atmosphere of Turkey in the 1970s and the everyday language that prevailed in those years. Gencebay, who in subsequent years would describe the song as an oppositional "lament for my country," has emphasised that the song arose in an environment where forty to fifty people were getting injured or killed in conflicts each and every day. The song highlights the meaninglessness of a world where injustice leaves no room for goodness, decency, or righteousness. At this point, "the damned world" can put an end to the tension between a utopian realm and the real world, between spiritual and material satisfaction, between the inner and outer self—and to those ends, a damned world is sought out.

The lyrics' tone of protest, which draws attention to the injustices and exploitation experienced by Arabesk listeners, positions the song well for a class-based analysis. When he sang the song in later years, Gencebay would add the lines "For a fairer, happier world" and "For fraternity, for humanity, for the poor," which call for an analysis along similar lines. However, it is not only the topics of Gencebay's lyrics but also the audiences of his music who contribute to the song's societal relevance. The voice rising from Gencebay's song represents the troubles of the artist who himself had been unable to secure a footing in an acceptable musical field and hence it becomes the language of the intensified expectations, desires, and frustrations of the urbanising popular masses. Although the past patterns of rural-to-urban migration that originally drove the *gecekondu* phenomenon can be traced back further in Turkey, the function of art and literature mostly revolved around producing artwork "about" those migrants. In contrast, the Arabesk of the 1970s was a type of music made "for" such rural migrants. Despite the fact that it was described as vulgar, banal, and degenerate by the urban middle and upper classes and, from a self-Orientalising perspective, labelled as "Arab music"—ultimately being censored by the TRT (Turkish Radio and Television Agency), which monopolised broadcasting in that period—Arabesk rose in popularity and was loved by its fans for the sense of belonging it granted them, as it recognised and legitimised their existence and experiences.

However, even if the relationship between Arabesk music and its listeners has a representative function, it cannot be said to have a healing one. The troubles people faced and continue to face are expressed in the songs, and the emotive experiences conveyed through the music assure the listener that they are not alone; nevertheless, leftist critiques of Arabesk claimed that such musical expression is a kind of "opium for the people" rather than a means of striking upon solutions for the problems in question. Perhaps the most striking example of such a characteristic can, ironically, be found in "Batsın Bu Dünya," in which the oppositional and protestive elements of the lyrics are interwoven with fatalistic and defeatist references throughout. Despite its radical demands, the song does not address the oppressors, the exploiters, the rich, those who make people laugh and cry; rather, it speaks directly to God. Critical perspectives that can be associated with leftist/socialist discourses are steeped in references to religious notions of devotion, tolerance, and resignation.

At the same time, analyses that are framed solely around a class conflict perspective impede a full understanding of the importance of Arabesk music for republican Turkey. Arabesk music—"Batsın Bu Dünya" in particular—provides a rich agenda that intersects with Turkey's cultural policies, the relationship between the state and art, and discussions of modernisation, all within the scope of how the music is performed and its position in the public sphere and the market.

***

Over time, the evolution of society and Arabesk music came to place "Batsın Bu Dünya" in a more prominent position in the oeuvre of Gencebay's songs within the framework of Arabesk music, and the same holds true for Gencebay himself. In fact, Arabesk music, which is incapable of establishing equality and justice on its own, has been shifting its attention away from that goal since the 1980s. In the new neoliberal order, the focus has been on individual prosperity and salvation, and songs have made demands for an immediate response to the material interests of consumption rather than a desire for "the world to be damned or get better". That was also a period in which Arabesk music expanded its audience base like never before, especially following the abolition of bans on state television broadcast content and the launching of private television channels, and in the process it has become a product of popular culture, the class awareness and critical perspectives of which have gradually decreased.

Another dimension of the long-term and current effects of Arabesk music has come to light in terms of approaches to modernisation. Critics of Arabesk music claimed that it marked a deviation from the country's ongoing efforts at modernisation and declared that it was not indicative of the level of "civilisation" the country had achieved. It has become clear that such an approach is a reflection of the general acceptance of modernisation theory. Within the framework of the modernisation approach—which envisages a clear distinction between traditional and modern, rural and urban, religious and secular, agricultural and industrial—Arabesk music is considered an anomaly, just like the *gecekondu* neighbourhoods with which it has been associated. In a sense, it can be conceptualised as an attempt to perpetuate the village in the city and tradition in modern society. However, considering the fact that modernisation theory, which assumes that a transition within binary structures of modernity is essential, has been subjected to universal criticism over the decades, Arabesk music is arguably not an anomaly but a case that reveals the inadequacy of the theory itself. Likewise, Arabesk is neither simply a type of music that has moved from the village to the city, nor is it an anti-urban music genre. Rather, it is an urban product that emerged by way of the opportunities offered by the city, and it has become popular among urban dwellers, especially those who have recently migrated from villages.

Today, in the year marking the centennial anniversary of the Republic of Turkey, the term Arabesk remains polarising in evaluations of the country's successes and failures. Compared to the Western world, in the face of the problems that the Turkish example presents, Arabesk evokes the distinction prevalent in the 1930s between *alaturka* and *alafranga*. Just like how *alaturka* was utilised as a derogatory term to critically highlight differences from the Western world and contemporaneous similarities with the East, Arabesk is used as a disparaging adjective to describe the country's "degenerate" politics, economy, cities, literature, and infrastructure. On the other hand, Arabesk as a musical genre continues to be effective as a consequence of those features that have made it tangible in almost every type of music, especially Turkish pop, even though the status it held in the mid-1970s has dwindled and iconic figures such as Gencebay no longer hold the position they once were accorded. Today, the enduring popularity of "Batsın Bu Dünya" is not rooted in the social or religious messages it contains; instead, its privileged position reflects Arabesk's status as a signifying postmodern trademark, like that of hybridity, bricolage, and syncretism, designating a unique variety of kitsch. In fact, the modern dance club remix of the song is popular not in the *gecekondu* neighbourhoods in which it was first popularised but rather at high-end nightclubs along the Bosporus.

Select Bibliography

Gürbilek, Nurdan. *The New Cultural Climate in Turkey: Living in a Shop Window*. Translated by Victoria Holbrook. London and New York: Zed Books, 2011.

Özbek, Meral. "Arabesk Culture." In *Rethinking Modernity and National Identity in Turkey*, edited by Sibel Bozdoğan and Reşat Kasaba, 211–32. Seattle: University of Washington Press, 1997.

Özgür, İren. "Arabesk Music in Turkey in the 1990s and Changes in National Demography, Politics, and Identity." *Turkish Studies* 7, no. 2. (2006): 175–90.

Stokes, Martin. *The Arabesk Debate: Music and Musicians in Turkey*. Oxford: Clarendon Press, 1992.

Tekelioğlu, Orhan. "The Rise of a Spontaneous Synthesis: The Historical Background of Turkish Popular Music." *Middle Eastern Studies* 32, no. 2 (1996): 194–215.

Yarar, Betül. "Politics of/and Popular Music: An Analysis of the History of Arabesk Music from the 1960s to the 1990s in Turkey." *Cultural Studies* 21, no. 1 (2008): 35–79.

54

A Forgotten Wave:
Socialist Women's Activism and the Struggle
for Gender Equality

Sevgi Adak

The United Nations proclaimed the year 1975 as International Women's Year. That decision was made after years of mobilisation by women's rights organisations to bring the issue of gender equality onto the international agenda and to secure a UN declaration to launch a global campaign combatting discrimination against women. In the same year, the first UN World Conference on Women was held in Mexico City. At the conference, the years 1975–1985 were declared the UN Decade for Women, paving the way for the adoption of the Convention for the Elimination of All Forms of Discrimination against Women (CEDAW) in 1979. The convention came to serve as a monitoring mechanism on which women's rights organisations around the world still rely. It was at this global moment in the struggle for gender equality in 1975 that a group of women in Turkey who had been active in the socialist movement, which was on the rise at the time, decided to establish a mass-based women's organisation. The idea of creating such an organisation with the aim of seizing the opportunity to drive forward women's mobilisation was discussed within the ranks of the then-clandestine Communist Party of Turkey (*Türkiye Komünist Partisi*, TKP). Led by women who were members of the TKP but largely comprised of a wider circle of socialist women activists, the Progressive Women's Association (*İlerici Kadınlar Derneği*, İKD) was formally established on 3 June 1975. It was by no means the first socialist women's organisation in the country. Women active in the socialist left had already embraced the idea of building up a women's movement that was separate from the "mainstream" women's organisations of the time, which were dominated by a Kemalist discourse of women's rights and hence, in the eyes of socialists, were pro-state and bourgeois. The İKD nevertheless soon became the largest and most active socialist women's organisation in the country, thereby playing a key role in the expansion of socialist women's activism into a firmly established movement in the second half of the 1970s. For the founders of the İKD, it was crucial that they explain from the outset why there was a need for a broad-based woman's organisation and what differentiated their approach to the issue of women's oppression. To this end, they drafted a founding declaration entitled "Why a Women's Organisation?" together with a draft statute and an action plan, which were eventually finalised and adopted.

*Why a Women's Organisation?**

In essence the primary aim of the struggle for women's rights is to achieve equality between women and men in all areas of economic, political, and social life and to ensure that this equality does not just exist in a body of laws but becomes an actual lived experience. [...] Even in rich capitalist countries that have accepted equality between women and men, it remains out of reach. In those countries, too, inequality is ongoing. [...] Today, women are still exploited even more than men in this [capitalist] production system, employed as they are in the least desirable positions earning the lowest wages. At the same time, they take on secondary social functions such as motherhood, bear the arduous burden of housework on their own, and endure the pain of ongoing discrimination in education, in the family, and in society.

[...]

Forty years ago, women in Turkey obtained political rights and a rather high degree of economic and social equality in law. However, if we look at the extent to which this economic, political, and social equality has become a reality for the wider masses of women, the picture is far from being a bright one:

–   Illiteracy is twice as prevalent among women as it is among men. The number of women in secondary education is half that of men [...]. Only one out of every twenty students in higher education is a woman.

–   Due to the unfavourable and unequal situation experienced by women in vocational education and their inexperience as well as reluctance to engage in economic and social struggles, our women's professional skills and wages are lower than men's in general. The average hourly wages of female workers are 20 to 30 per cent lower than those of male workers.

–   Despite women's dual contributions to society through giving birth, on the one hand, and producing goods and services, on the other, our society does not pay its debt to women, neither as fully and equally paid workers nor as mothers. The availability, quality, and accessibility of maternity and child health services and social service institutions like nurseries and kindergartens are at shameful levels.

–   Our women, who are crushed under the double burden of work, motherhood, and housework and who are overwhelmed because they have to shoulder these burdens under difficult living conditions and economic hardship, cannot find the time or energy to use their legally bestowed economic and political rights.

* Translated from the Turkish original published in Muazzez Pervan, ed., *İlerici Kadınlar Derneği (1975-80): "Kırmızı Çatkılı Kadınlar"ın Tarihi* (İstanbul: Tarih Vakfı Yurt Yayınları, 2013), 18–21.

–   They cannot deal with the problems of the country or the world, and they are left behind in social and cultural life. The number of women who are actively involved in trade unions and professional and political organisations is extremely low.

Even just the facts listed above indicate that, despite existing legal rights and equality, the woman question is an ongoing vicious circle bearing enormous implications. Women must break and resolve this vicious circle, this loop that encircles them, with their own hands.

[...]

Progressive, democratic, and patriotic women in Turkey have to fight to solve their own problems, and they also must be vigilant against reactionary tendencies that would like to use those problems to break the unity of the struggle and solidarity among workers and deflect the class consciousness of women workers. The critical task that lays ahead of us involves working for the woman question, which until now has been a toy in the hands of high society and bourgeois women, so it can henceforth be tackled by its real proprietors through the establishment of a women's organisation in our country that is comprised of broad segments of women during the International Women's Year of 1975. The Progressive Women's Association was founded to fulfil that mission.

**

The declaration cited above demonstrates the vitality and determination of the struggle for women's rights in the 1970s. As such, it makes it possible for us to appreciate the longevity and diversity of women's activism in Turkey rather than seeing it as being composed of essentially two waves, the first being the women's movement of the late nineteenth and early twentieth centuries and the second being the post-1980 feminist movement with a blank space of "barren years" in between them, as has often been suggested in the literature.

In the declaration, the prominence of the idea that there was a need to go beyond legal gains and to aim instead for a broader socio-economic and political transformation to achieve equality for women attests to the difference in the positions taken by socialist women's activism and most of the Kemalist women's organisations of the time. The former sought to carry out a struggle for women's emancipation within the broader context of the struggle against capitalism. In that way they were different from their "bourgeois" counterparts, as they were the "real proprietors" of women's issues. As such, the declaration can be seen as being coloured by the dominant leftist rhetoric of the 1970s, categorically and heavily informed by classical Marxist theses on the "woman question" rather than feminist analyses. It is readily apparent how crucial it was for the women who penned the declaration to ensure in this founding text that establishing a women's organisation did not entail a deviation from leftist activism and that it would not harm workers' united struggle for socialism, accusations they frequently faced.

On the other hand, the declaration can also be read as a strongly feminist text, indeed as a determined and powerful call for gender equality, even though it neither mentions gender as a concept nor does it directly address feminism. Rather, it reflects a sophisticated analysis of patriarchy with a special emphasis on women's double burden within the specific dynamics of capitalist patriarchy and it also offers an examination of women's unpaid labour and the link between women's oppression within the family and in the public sphere. The emphasis on women's labour rights and domestic labour would come to mark the focus of the İKD and the wider socialist women's movement in subsequent years. The İKD's most effective campaigns, which were also broadly embraced by other socialist women's organisations, such as the "Equal Pay for Equal Work" and the "Nursery for Every Workplace" campaigns, reflected the founding vision articulated in the declaration. Thus, the declaration can be seen as a symbolic beginning for the women who were active in the socialist left as they started to raise their voices as women and to approach patriarchy, and hence not just capitalism, as a system of inequality. In addition, the reference to the 1975 International Women's Year at the end of the text signals not only attentiveness to the global mobilisation for gender equality but also how the İKD positioned itself as part of that movement. In this sense, too, the declaration shares the spirit of the global feminist current that began transforming the world from the 1970s onwards.

***

Until its dissolution in 1979 by a Martial Law Command, which was imposed in December of 1978 and used to crack down on left-wing groups and organisations, the İKD had opened 33 chapters and 35 representative offices across the county, gaining broad-based popularity with its fifteen thousand active members. It had a news agency and published its own monthly journal, *Kadınların Sesi* (Women's Voice), which attained a total circulation of thirty thousand copies per issue by the late 1970s. The İKD was joined by several other socialist women's organisations that came into being in the 1970s. An unprecedented mass mobilisation of women was taking place in Turkey, and arguably it marked a turning point in terms of the popularisation of an idea of gender equality which went beyond the women's rights organisations that had heretofore largely been confined to a circle of highly educated middle-class professional women who were based in the country's three largest cities. This expansion of the struggle for gender equality across a broader segment of the female population was the result of the collective efforts of the İKD's members and other socialist women activists as they worked to create a women's organisation that was as broad-based and independent as possible, and "Why a Women's Organisation?" articulated those aims. If we take into consideration the fact that this mobilisation also became a platform for articulating the shared demands of the wider women's movement, such as Civil Code amendments and the right to free and safe abortion, and thus enabled a reproachment between Kemalist and socialist women's activism towards the end of the 1970s, the importance of the momentum that got underway with this declaration can be better understood. That momentum, even though neither

Kemalist nor socialist women's activists of the 1970s referred to themselves as feminists, laid the groundwork for some of the demands and ideas that were later articulated by and came to be associated with the proudly feminist post-1980 women's movement in Turkey known as the "second wave". Years later when some İKD members looked back at the struggle they had undertaken, having broken the rigid ideological barriers that once spared no place for an openly feminist position in the political rhetoric of the left in Turkey at the time, they realised it was a feminist movement after all, a forgotten "wave" that ultimately contributed to the formation and popularisation of a feminist agenda in Turkey.

Select Bibliography

Adak, Sevgi. "Yetmişli Yıllarda Kadın Hareketi: Yeni Bir Feminizmin Ayak Sesleri." In *Türkiye'nin 1970'li Yılları*, edited by Mete Kaan Kaynar, 609–29. İstanbul: İletişim, 2020.

Akal, Emel. *Kızıl Feministler: Bir Sözlü Tarih Çalışması*. İstanbul: İletişim, 2011.

Çağatay, Selin. "The Politics of Gender and the Making of Kemalist Feminist Activism in Contemporary Turkey (1946–2011)." PhD thesis, Central European University, 2017.

Keşoğlu, Birsen Talay. "Socialist Women's Organizations in Turkey, 1975–1980." PhD thesis, Boğaziçi University, 2007.

Pervan, Muazzez, ed., *İlerici Kadınlar Derneği (1975-80): "Kırmızı Çatkılı Kadınlar"ın Tarihi*. İstanbul: Tarih Vakfı Yurt Yayınları, 2013.

Şahin, Yelda and Ezgi Sarıtaş. "Altmışlı Yıllarda Kadın Hareketi: Süreklilikler, Kopuşlar ve Çeşitlenme." In *Türkiye'nin 1960'lı Yılları*, edited by Mete Kaan Kaynar, 727–59. İstanbul: İletişim, 2017.

55
Mothers with Sons:
Sevgi Soysal's Critiques of Masculinity

Çimen Günay-Erkol

The late 1960s and the 1970s in Turkey were dominated by clashes between the right and the left that became so extreme they almost resulted in a civil war. University campuses, city districts, and streets were divided into camps, and opposing political groups targeted one another at marches and demonstrations. Both sides made attempts to gather intelligence as a means of securing targets. Physical attacks resulting in injuries as well as assassinations and murders were part of the daily routine. Aiming to halt the rise of violence in Turkey in 1968, the authorities used anti-communist youth as a weapon. While it attempted to display a nonpartisan attitude, the state supported right-wing paramilitary groups and overlooked the violence they unleashed. Following the military coup of 12 March 1971, an atmosphere of de-escalation was created after the brutal suppression of the radical Left, but it did not last long, and by the end of the 1970s, armed clashes resulting in casualties had resumed. Sevgi Soysal (1936–1976), a revolutionist writer who became well-known for her short stories and novels about the Turkish Conflict of 1968 and the "premature" aspects of Turkish modernism, was targeted by the authorities on charges of spreading communist propaganda. She not only witnessed but also documented those years, which were marked by Cold War anxieties. The clashes that took place between the revolutionary youth and the anti-communist Grey Wolves informed the work of several Turkish writers, but Sevgi Soysal was unique in the way that she blended her criticisms of the lack of freedoms in Turkey under militaristic rule and the acceptance of power abuses by society at large, together with a gender-conscious agenda. Her article "This Man, That Man: Real Men are Mothers," which was published on 31 May 1976 in the newspaper *Politika*, which at the time was managed by İsmail Cem (1940–2007), tackles the issue of mothers who are concerned about the rising tide of physical violence targeting their sons studying at university. Through the article, Soysal became a mouthpiece for families who were trying to protect their children and putting pressure on university authorities to investigate the crimes that were taking place.

*This Man, That Man: Real Men are Mothers**

[...] Our men are extraordinary. Whatever they do, they know that a legion of men and women are at their back, supporting and tolerating them, saying, "He is a man after all."

[...] Turkish delight first, Turkish men second. These days, every now and then we watch on television certain programs that are about Turkish masculinity from the past to the present. This approach to history, which evaluates Turkish and Ottoman history as a history of masculinity, will surely make our men more masculine.

[...] While horse, wife, and weapon masculinity extend through to karate masculinity, not a single Turkish man has stepped forward to make the Grey Wolves, which themselves try to prove that they are masculine by attacking revolutionaries, be held to account for the blood they have spilled. Ultimately, that falls to mothers. Mothers started to gather at the gates of universities to shield their sons, whom the very masculine guards failed to protect. They watched how masculinity gets proven with truncheons.

[...] They applied to the all-male Parliament, to members of Parliament. To the Senate, to the men of the men. To the Prime Minister and even to the President. And they got rejected in a masculine way. Never mind, mothers! Let masculinity stay with you. Let our grandiose men who are busy protecting the state, the nation, captive Turks, and the Turkic world turn their backs on you. Let those doors that are open to ambassadors, receptions, and the important men of the world swing shut when it is time to listen to your problems. Let a very masculine society, from the press to Parliament, from workers' syndicates to the government, avoid taking precautions for your children's safety; you on your own, taking risks, making a shield out of yourself, not only for your child but for all the children stuck in the violence. Courage belongs to you, bravery is yours. You know about giving birth. While some men fall ill because of a slightly bloodied nose, you know about giving birth and you know life as well. You go then and face those who turn masculinity into an act of destroying someone's family, taking someone's life, not having a family, annihilating anything beautiful that gives hope, those who attempt to take the lives of your loved ones; this is the most legitimate war of nature, confront them!

Now you are the realest men!

***

Men were at the forefront of the Turkish Conflict of 1968 and the civil war that broke out in the 1970s, both among revolutionary leftist and anti-communist groups. The armed clashes that grew more intense due to rivalries between men destroyed the option of dialogue and

---

* Translated from the Turkish original in Sevgi Soysal, "O Erkek, Bu Erkek: Asıl Erkek Anaları," in *Bakmak* (İstanbul: İletişim Yayınları, 2004), 103–106.

took hold of the entire country. Soysal shows in a very nuanced way that masculinity not only acts in one direction, from men's bodies to the outside world, but that society, with the special attention and applause it reserves for men, actually builds up the very masculinity that seeks to have an impact on its surroundings. It is notable that society, as a collectivity that consolidates gender roles, has been likened to "an army"; such a choice of words suggests how the oppressive conditions prevalent in Turkey in the 1970s, a period when street clashes forced militarised identities upon people, were exacerbated by the cultural atmosphere and patriarchal values that have always held masculinity in very high regard. Soysal treated the political violence and the powers that prevented investigations of its casualties as a show of masculinity. She used the term "Turkish delight" to point to cliché approaches to masculinity and then added a reference to show the ways in which the impact of popular television programmes is indicative of how the attitudes expected of men carry a historical burden that has been culturally projected onto every historical period. Soysal underscored the link between the Turkist movement and the anti-communist front by using the horse-wife-weapon trio (*at-avrat-silah*), and beside the ultranationalists, who had started gathering at karate dojos, and the paramilitary *komando* units of the Grey Wolf movement, namely the youth organisation of the Nationalist Movement Party (*Milliyetçi Hareket Partisi*, MHP) whose crimes were being whitewashed by state officials, she positioned the leftist youth who were being victimised by the ongoing violence at universities. Motherhood appears as a form of guardianship in the essay. Mothers seek justice in a self-sacrificing manner and display the courage needed to face those in power. By referring to this type of resistance as "real masculinity," Soysal attempted to shake up the supposedly direct relationship between men's bodies and masculinity. Mothers bravely appropriate the role of masculinity and replace toxic and destructive masculinity with their calls for justice. By rendering mothers' resistance to the authorities as legitimate and natural, she also connotatively says that it is not possible to escape the biological aspects of human nature. The essay concludes by praising women's nature through the concept of motherhood.

***

In 1978, two years after the publication of "This Man, That Man," Ali İhsan Özgür (1954–1978), the editor-in-chief of *Politika*, was kidnapped and murdered. Beyond its critique of violence, Soysal's essay is important as a gendered overview of the problem of power and also as a historicised approach to the period in terms of masculinity. The essay was written in the 1970s, a period when a widespread critical look at masculinity was lacking and feminism was not yet visible as a collective movement in Turkey. Given the ongoing political clashes, it was surely difficult to face and challenge the issue of hegemonic masculinity. For that reason, the essay was a pioneering work that transgressed the limits of the era in terms of its discussion of masculinity without the notion of a masculine essence, opting instead to examine the notion of the demonstration of power, the rivalries among men, and the monopoly men hold over masculinity. Soysal's comment about the link between popular television shows and the cultural circulation of masculinity was also an early intervention about the social reinforcement of gender roles. Soysal's take on the armed clashes of the time as a war of masculinities and the way she extended men's sphere of influence from the sidelines of the clashes to institutions such Parliament, syndicates, and the government demonstrate her lucid grasp of the deep connections between power and masculinity. The act of proving masculinity with truncheons reappears in Soysal's fictional works such as *Dawn* (*Şafak*) through phallic references and memorable scenes. Through such a perspective, referring to mothers as "men" emphasises the idea that it is possible to make one's voice heard only by imitating the powerful. Soysal refers to being strong, calling for justice, and fighting as "masculine" but she also defines mothers as the people who resist men's will to destroy. As such, the essay brings to the fore the idea of an alternative power that is built upon mothers' self-sacrificing guardianship, which is focused on furthering life instead of ending it.

Select Bibliography

Günay-Erkol, Çimen. *Broken Masculinities: Solitude, Alienation, and Frustration in Turkish Literature After 1970.* Budapest: Central European University Press, 2016.

Lüküslü, Demet. "Constructors and Constructed: Youth as a Political Actor in Modernising Turkey." In *Revisiting Youth Political Participation: Challenges for Research and Democratic Practice in Europe*, edited by Joerg Forbrig, 29–35. Strasbourg: Council of Europe Publishing, 2005.

Neyzi, Leyla. "Object or Subject? The Paradox of 'Youth' in Turkey." *International Journal of Middle East Studies* 33, no. 3 (2001): 411–32.

Pekesen, Berna, ed. *Turkey in Turmoil: Social Change and Political Radicalization During the 1960s.* Berlin: de Gruyter, 2020.

Soysal, Sevgi. *Dawn.* Translated by Maureen Freely. New York: Archipelago Books, 2022.

56
Revolutionary Martyrdom:
The Death of Haki Karer and the
Emergence of PKK

Joost Jongerden

The booklet *In Remembrance of the Proletarian and Internationalist Revolutionary Haki Karer* is a thirty-three-page text that was published one year after the killing of Haki Karer on 18 May 1977. Karer was one of the leading cadres of the *Kürdistan Devrimcileri* (Kurdistan Revolutionaries), a group that was carved out from the revolutionary student and youth culture in Turkey between the military coups of 1971 and 1980. Karer's violent death prompted a tighter organisation of the movement. On its way to becoming a party, the group organised a congress in 1978, in which it agreed on a party program and statute, and in 1979 it eventually assumed the name Kurdistan Workers' Party (*Partiya Karkerên Kurdistanê*, PKK).

Haki Karer (1950–1977) was a Turk from the Ulubey district of Ordu province. After completing high school, he went to Ankara in 1971 to study at the Faculty of Science at Ankara University. In Ankara, Karer shared an apartment in the district of Emek with Kemal Pir (1952–1982), a Turk from Gümüşhane district in the province of Trabzon, who studied at the Faculty of Language, History, and Geography at the University of Hacettepe. Like Karer, Pir would become one of the celebrated martyrs of the PKK after he died in the 1982 hunger strike of PKK prisoners protesting the torture and inhumane detention conditions at Diyarbakir Prison.

Haki Karer and Kemal Pir became acquainted with Abdullah Öcalan (1948–) at the end of 1972. Earlier that year, in April, Öcalan had been arrested and imprisoned for his involvement in the organisation of a university boycott to protest the killing of the leaders and cadres of the revolutionary leftist organisations the People's Liberation Party-Front of Turkey (*Türkiye Halk Kurtuluş Partisi-Cephesi*, THKP-C) and the People's Liberation Army of Turkey (*Türkiye Halk Kurtuluş Ordusu, THKO*). Öcalan was released at the end of October of the same year. Yet, because of his conviction, Öcalan was no longer allowed to stay in a student dormitory. *Doğan Fırtına (1949–), a* fellow student activist in the Faculty of Political Sciences, where Öcalan also studied, and with whom he was imprisoned and had befriended, referred Öcalan to Haki Karer, who was a THKO sympathiser, and Kemal Pir, a THKP-C sympathiser. Karer and Pir opened their doors to Öcalan and they became friends. They shared the apartment for about a year, until the end of 1973 or the beginning of 1974, after which time they moved to other apartments in different parts of Ankara.

The sharing of apartments emerged as the main means of bonding within the group and building bridges with others. In 1973, as the network around Öcalan, Karer, and Pir expanded, it mixed with other leftist circles in the Ankara Democratic Higher Education Association (*Ankara Demokratik Yüksek Öğrenim Derneği*, ADYÖD). ADYÖD facilitated a coming together of orphaned leftist groups. However, the association was closed down in December 1973 under the authority of the Ankara Martial Law Command (*Ankara Sıkıyönetim Komutanlığı*) after a confrontation with nationalist students and a police raid. Following its closure, a new association was established, the Association for Higher Education in Ankara (*Ankara Yüksek Öğrenim Derneği*, AYÖD).

Unlike ADYÖD, which had allowed for various factions and currents within the re-emerging left, AYÖD adopted a more sectarian character. The founders, mostly sympathisers of the THKP-C (who would later form the Revolutionary Path or *Devrimci Yol*, Dev-Yol), did not allow others to join, and Haki Karer, a former board member of ADYÖD, was not allowed into AYÖD meetings. The "flat-mate network" around Abdullah Öcalan, Haki Karer, and Kemal Pir, which started to include people who are part of the current leadership of the PKK such as Riza Altun (1956–), Cemil Bayık (1951–), Duran Kalkan (1954–), Mustafa Karasu (1950–), and Ali Haydar Kaytan (1952–), decided to develop their own network of kindred spirits. This group, which was composed of both ethnic Kurds and Turks, gradually developed into a coherent, independent organisation.

After a meeting in 1976, the group decided to develop its reach farther into Anatolian Kurdistan, and Haki Karer assumed group responsibilities in several cities there before moving to Adana and then to Antep, a hotbed of political activities. Karer worked in the construction industry to make a living and finance political group activities. In Antep, he ran into Alaattin Kapan (d. 1978), with whom he previously had heated discussions when they both lived in Adana. Kapan invited Karer to meet up at a coffeehouse in Düztepe on 18 May 1977. The meeting became chaotic, and when Karer was about to leave after a disagreement with Kapan, he was shot in the head. Although it was unclear in the midst of the chaos who had fired the shot, Haki's comrades pointed to Kapan as the perpetrator.

Alaattin Kapan had been active in other Kurdish organisations, including the Revolutionary Democratic Cultural Association (*Devrimci Demokratik Kültür Derneği*, DDKD), before becoming one of the leaders of Red Star (*Stêrka Sor*), a small Kurdish Maoist organisation that was mainly active in the Antep-Adana area. Following the killing of Haki Karer, the Kurdistan Revolutionaries declared *Stêrka Sor* a force of the counterrevolution and a satellite organisation of Turkey's intelligence services that needed to be eliminated. Now under attack, *Stêrka Sor* disintegrated. Kapan was killed at a May Day rally in İskenderun in 1978.

In Remembrance of Haki Karer*

Our comrade Haki Karer is one of the martyrs who fell in the struggle that aims to dispatch the final remains of the Capitalist-Imperialist colonial system to the museum of antique history. On 18 May 1977, Turkish colonialists and their local reactionary mercenary agents treacherously killed this great revolutionary, who had shaken off narrow nationalist ideas and dedicated his life to the Kurdistan Independence Struggle. To further counter-revolutionary violence, colonial forces and imperialists use various means to suppress the revolutionary resistance of oppressed peoples. They organise servitude, betrayal, and everything alien to peoples' national values; they intensify efforts to spread compromise and surrender. In order to divert and orient the patriotic revolutionary struggle of the people towards the wrong objectives, they make those who are in name struggling for "national liberation" dependent upon them and turn them into agent-provocateur organisations. An example of one of those organisations is "Istêrka Sor" or "Five Parts," as they are known among revolutionaries. That is to say, our comrade Haki Karer was killed by the bloody-handed murderers of this agent-provocateur group organised by Turkish colonialists and local reactionaries. (1)

The spirit that made comrade Haki Karer join the national independence struggle in a foreign country and the spirit that led to his death, in this case, is the spirit of internationalism, the spirit of great communism. [...] Comrade Haki Karer is like a flag in the proud struggle of the people of Kurdistan, a sacred symbol in the yet-to-be-established brotherhood and solidarity between peoples, a force against counter-revolutionaries and treacherous social-chauvinist Marxism, an example for revolutionaries who are prepared to risk death as the highest sacrifice possible and they will be held in high esteem in our history. (3)

It is not a surprise that treacherous Marxist social-chauvinism and bourgeois nationalism are, in their very being, against the legitimate demand of the people of Kurdistan for a life of independence and freedom. [...] In Turkey, higher cadres, up to the leadership of the "Communist Party," assumed all duties necessary, yet, in the case of Kurdistan, they avoid fulfilling even one such duty. For them, there is no Kurdistan, only Turkey. (4) The influence of Kemalist nationalism is widespread within the revolutionary movement in Turkey. [...] Yet, the Kemalist movement did not bring anything other than tyranny, oppression, and exploitation to the Kurdish people. [...] In Turkey, Kemalism does not recognise any other people and does not accept their existence. [...] We are proud that a revolutionary from Turkey joined the formation of a Communist Movement in our country and was martyred in his heroically fought struggle against colonialism. (25)

THE MEMORY OF HAKİ KARER IS IMMORTAL!
DOWN WITH COLONIALISM AND IMPERIALISM!
DOWN WITH THE COLONIAL AND FEUDAL-COMPRADOR ORDER!

* Translated from the original Turkish in Kurdistan Revolutionaries, *In Remembrance of the Proletarian and Internationalist Revolutionary Haki Karer*, 1978.

LONG LIVE OUR INDEPENDENCE STRUGGLE!
LONG LIVE PROLETARIAN INTERNATIONALISM!

***

Haki Karer was not the only member of the movement to be killed as a result of infighting within the revolutionary left. The list of members killed by rival movements is long; the PKK's "Album of Resistance Martyrs" (*Direniş Şehitleri Albümü*) contains the names of many militants who were killed by left-wing movements such as People's Liberation (*Halkın Kurtuluşu*), Revolutionary People's Unity (*Devrimci Halkın Birliği*, DHB), and the National Democratic United Forces (*Ulusal Demokratik Güçbirliği*, UDG), and Kurdish organisations such as the DDKD and Kurdistan National Liberationists *(Kürdistan Ulusal Kurtuluşçuları*, KUK). Within the context of infighting, the response of the Kurdistan Revolutionaries vis-à-vis other organisations was also to become more aggressive. The booklet *In Remembrance of the Proletarian and Internationalist Revolutionary Haki Karer* thus comprises a promise of retaliation. *Stêrka Sor* was declared a counterrevolutionary organisation and marked to be wiped out. Yet the text can also be read in at least three more ways:

First, there was a reckoning with the left and its perversion by Kemalism. Although the booklet denounces capitalism and bourgeois nationalism as well as Kurdish nationalism, what stands out is the fierce tone opposing the "social chauvinism" of the left. It would be wrong to conclude that the Kurdistan Revolutionaries were driven by animosity towards the left. On the contrary, it was the Kurdistan Revolutionaries' closeness to the left that fuelled its criticism, as the movement believed that the left's inability to emancipate itself from bourgeois and colonialist Kemalism was part of the reason for its failure to develop into a genuinely emancipatory force. Most of its cadres had worked in or with the revolutionary left for many years and become disappointed by the general attitude of leftist parties towards the Kurdish issue, either denying the existence of the Kurdish issue or rendering it irrelevant in the class struggle. For the Kemalist left, as the Kurdistan Revolutionaries argued, there was no Kurdistan, only Turkey. Thus, there was an analysis of class oppression but not of cultural oppression.

Second, there was a promise to fight capitalist exploitation and colonialism. Here, the fight against colonialism did not refer to the semi-colonial status which the left commonly attributed to Turkey, but rather it is a reference to the idea of Turkish colonialism in Kurdistan. In the booklet the Kurdistan Revolutionaries not only harshly criticised the failure within the left to recognise Turkey as a colonial state, they also presented a general analysis of the process of colonisation, distinguishing three phases within the Kemalist period: i) a military occupation, using rebellions as a pretext, starting with the Sheikh Said rebellion and coming to completion with the suppression of the 1938 Dersim rebellion; ii) a process of cultural assimilation, symbolised by boarding schools, which aimed at cultural genocide; and iii) from the 1960s onwards, a period of economic colonisation, symbolised by state-led agricultural modernisation, which functioned to break up the traditional and tribal structures of Kurdish society. The refusal to acknowledge this history of colonisation and the insistence on defining the revolutionary struggle in terms of class alone was equated with a denial of the colonial exploitation and cultural genocide in Kurdistan and of the suffering of many Kurds because of their cultural identity as well as class position. Relatedly, a brotherhood between Turks and Kurds could not be assumed and then concealed in the class struggle; rather, this brotherhood first had to be based on recognition of the colonial status of Kurdistan and, therefore, the articulation of an anti-colonial struggle along with the class struggle. The booklet claimed that Haki Karer's solidarity with the liberation of Kurdistan as a Turk made him a genuine revolutionary. He became the personification of a new post-Kemalist left, a genuine force of opposition symbolising the possibility of a common future that was 'to be established between the people".

Third, one can read a commitment to and expression of determination to continue the struggle. Abdullah Öcalan, the party's leader, reiterated on several occasions that the PKK had been established as an oath to the martyrdom of Haki Karer. Each of these bears consideration. Karer's martyrdom was declared the first milestone on the revolutionary road of the PKK, and it was claimed that the party program, discussed at its 1978 congress, was written in memory of Haki Karer. The brochure reads as a promise to the movement's determination to continue the struggle. In the historiography of the PKK, the decision to establish a party was directly related to the martyrdom of Haki Karer, who not only became an iconic figure in a culture of martyrdom, but whose death became associated with and also celebrated as a form of resistance. Therefore, Öcalan sternly criticised the thirty comrades who had attended Haki Karer's funeral for not explaining the importance of his martyrdom for the revolutionary struggle. Faithfulness to the memory of Haki Karer was expressed not by mourning his death but by explaining the importance of his martyrdom for the struggle, Öcalan argued. Öcalan turned Haki Karer's martyrdom into an icon of the movement's determination in the struggle against social chauvinism and the liberation of Kurdistan from colonialism. His death turned out to be decisive in the decision to turn the movement into a party named the "PKK," and his memory has been kept alive to this day, including outside of PKK circles.

***

This booklet shows how the PKK was a typical product of the 1970s, born from revolutionary struggles that sought fundamental change and addressed the intersecting systems of oppression and exploitation. It also points to another feature in the political history of this period, namely the rampant violence among the parties and movements of the left in Turkey. Yet, its primary relevance is the relationship between the martyrdom of Haki Karer and the decision to turn the network of kindred spirits into a party, which would organise an anti-colonial and anti-capitalist struggle for the independence of Kurdistan and for brotherhood in the Middle East. Now approaching their fiftieth year, the Kurdistan Revolutionaries and then the PKK have had a strong impact, shaping political struggles, both armed and unarmed, and fuelling debates about cultural and women's rights, citizenship, nation, and the state across a swathe of geography stretching from Turkey, Syria, Iraq, and Iran to Kurdistan and beyond. The name of Haki Karer, meanwhile, has been inscribed in the collective memory of generations of activists and revolutionaries. In Turkey today, Kurds, Turks, and others dedicated to radical societal change are among those who continue to celebrate in Haki Karer's name the memory of a martyr and a symbol in the struggle for freedom and equality.

Select Bibliography

Akkaya, Ahmet Hamdi. *The Kurdistan Workers' Party (PKK): National Liberation, Insurgency and Radical Democracy Beyond Borders.* Ghent: Ghent University, Faculty of Political and Social Sciences, 2016.

Houston, Christopher. *Istanbul, City of the Fearless: Urban Activism, Coup d'état, and Memory.* Oakland: University of California Press, 2020.

Jongerden, Joost. "A Spatial Perspective on Political Group Formation in Turkey after the 1971 Coup: The Kurdistan Workers' Party of Turkey (PKK)." *Kurdish Studies* 5, no. 2 (2017): 134–56.

Jongerden, Joost, and Ahmet Hamdi Akkaya. "The Kurdistan Workers Party and a New Left in Turkey: Analysis of the Revolutionary Movement in Turkey through the PKK's Memorial Text on Haki Karer." *European Journal of Turkish Studies* 14 (2012). https://journals.openedition.org/ejts/4613

Sayin, Mahir. *Erkeği Öldürmek: Abdullah Öcalan Ne Diyor?* Basel: Toprak Yayinevi, 1997.

Tanrıverdi, Burhan, Celal Polat, Doğan Fırtına, Haşim Bariş, and Süleyman Toklu. *Daha Dinmiş Değil Fırtına*, Ankara: Dipnot Yayınları, 2017.

57

Civil War Strategy of the Turkish Far-Right: The Maraş Massacre

Ahmet İnsel

1978 is a pivotal year in Turkey's political history. It was the year in which a series of assassinations, attacks, and pogroms took place, targeting figures known for their commitment to the left and Alevi and Kurdish populations. After the formation of Bülent Ecevit's (1925–2006) third government on 5 January 1978, the far-right ultranationalist militants of the Nationalist Movement Party (*Milliyetçi Hareket Partisi*, MHP) ramped up their strategy for taking power by accentuating political violence against perceived enemies of the state and nation, a methodology it had been employing since 1975 under the guise of confrontations between communists and anti-communists. All of the left-wing movements saw the MHP and the Grey Wolves as an expression of Turkish fascism. It was in this context that Ömer Laçiner (1946–), editor of the monthly magazine *Birikim*, published in May 1978 an initial analysis drawing attention to the MHP's civil war strategy. *Birikim* is a socialist journal of political analysis and culture which was started in 1975 under the editorship mainly of Ömer Laçiner and Murat Belge (1943–).

The MHP's strategy was to organise a series of provocative attacks in provincial cities, notably in Malatya in April 1978, where there were tensions fuelled by conservative Sunni right-wing groups targeting Alevi communities. The same strategy was implemented again in December of the same year in the city of Maraş, and the organised pogrom would cost the lives of more than hundred people. Following this latest provocation, the magazine *Birikim* published a brochure in March 1979 written by Ömer Laçiner titled "After Maraş..?" ("*Maraş'tan Sonra...?*"), which analysed the strategy of pushing for civil war, especially in the triangle formed between the cities of Çorum, Erzurum, and Gaziantep, an area with large Alevi and Kurdish minority communities. The aim of the drive was to provoke the proclamation of martial law and lay the groundwork for the military to take over the maintenance of law and order with more draconian measures targeting leftists and minorities. According to the MHP leadership, only a military coup would be capable of curbing the rise of left-wing movements, political parties, and trade unions. This was also the perception of a segment of the bourgeoisie, especially the Metal Industries Union. The booklet "*After Maraş...?*" is perhaps the most lucid analysis of the strategy of provocation unleashed by the Turkish far-right movement, which was bolstered in 1979 and led to the military coup of September 1980.

The Çorum-Erzurum-Gaziantep Triangle[*]

The triangle formed by the cities of Çorum, Erzurum, and Gaziantep is a region where Turks and Kurds live according to ethnic criteria and Sunnis and Alevis live according to religious denomination, in almost equal numbers and often in well-separated communities. The majority of these ethnic-religious groups also live in separate neighbourhoods in the major cities of this region.

The main reason for the importance of such an ethnic or religious divide is not the "strength of ideology," the attachment of the local population, especially Sunnis, to their religion, or other similar factors. The divide is essentially [based on the idea] that this ethno-religious distinction fuels a relationship of domination that determines and explains the differences in status between members of the communities. If the Sunni-Alevi and Turkish-Kurdish cleavages have come to the fore with such enmity in the 1970s, the reason is first of all the development of capitalism, which has begun to dominate in this region and manifests traumatic effects. This development challenges pre-capitalist relations of domination and creates a nostalgic reaction for the past among those who lose their former superior status. As their higher status begins to be invalidated, reactions sometimes turning into blind and unrestrained anger accumulate among them, turning against those who have lived in an inferior status for centuries and who are now, before their eyes, experiencing a social ascension, while their own "world" declines. Fascism in Turkey develops, organises itself, and recruits its militants on this terrain, the desperate and enraged darkness of the desire to "turn back the clock".

We want to emphasise this above all. The reason for the strengthening of the desire to "go back" among the Turkish Sunnis and some Kurdish Sunnis in the region is much more social-political than it is economic. The development of capitalism has not created a significant deterioration in their economic condition. What gives them the impression of a "deterioration" in their economic condition is the comparison they draw between their state of being and that of the Kurds and Alevis. The difference that was very much in favour of the former is starting to change because Alevis and Kurds, who used to live under very difficult economic conditions, have seized the work opportunities created by capitalism in the region or in the surrounding area and have been able to improve their economic condition significantly. [...] Sunnis who did not adapt to these new conditions, now faced with the rise of Alevis who had been inferior to them for centuries, began to feel that their own situation was deteriorating and, irritated by this feeling, they began to demand that the old "balance" be restored.

[...] These are the reasons for the rapid development of the fascist movement in Turkey in this triangle of Çorum-Erzurum-Gaziantep and the recruitment of most of its militants in this region, while elsewhere it has met with little development or even blockages despite all its efforts.

[*] Translated from the original Turkish in Ömer Laçiner, *Maraş'tan Sonra..?* (İstanbul: Birikim Yayınları, 1979), 21–22, 66.

***

Two months after the formation of the Ecevit government, a bomb attack killed seven students in front of İstanbul University on 16 March 1978. The bombing triggered a strong reaction from left-wing organisations and the Confederation of Revolutionary Trade Unions (*Devrimci İşçi Sendikaları Konfederasyonu*, DİSK), which organised actions in different cities around the slogan "Warning Against Fascism". Three days after the attack, the MHP's strategy of stoking tensions became clear with a call for a "large march" pronounced by the party's leader, Alpaslan Türkeş (1917–1997). In preparation for this march, planned for 15 April, in parallel with Mussolini's "march on Rome," the attacks and provocations multiplied. The most significant of these was a parcel bomb that killed, on 17 April, the mayor of Malatya, Hamit Fendoğlu (1919–1978), a member of the centre-right Justice Party (*Adalet Partisi*, AP) but who was known to be close to the MHP. Apparently, there was a delay in the delivery of the package because other parcel bombs targeting left-wing figures in the same region on the eve of 15 April march had failed.

Ömer Laçiner published his article in the May 1978 issue of *Birikim* analysing the possible strategy of the MHP in provoking a civil war in Malatya and rapidly spreading it to surrounding towns, especially Maraş. He drew attention to the triangle formed by the cities of Çorum, Erzurum, and Gaziantep, in which ethnic and religious tensions between the Sunni Turkish population on the one hand and Alevis and Kurds on the other were fanned by changes in socio-economic status brought about by the development of capitalism in the region. In the discourses of the MHP and its youth organisation and strike force *Ülkü Ocakları* (Idealist Hearths, commonly known as the Grey Wolves), the label "communist" was used to cover a broad swathe of people ranging from social democrats to socialists and Alevis to militant Kurds.

The assassination of the mayor of Malatya provoked, as was expected, the Sunnis in the region to attack the Alevis as well as more generally people known for their left-wing sympathies. Similar provocations were staged in the following months in several cities, most prominently in Sivas and Elazığ. An attack that cost the life of prosecutor Doğan Öz (1934–1978) on 24 March was among those initial attacks on known left-wing intellectuals, trade union leaders, and even non-political personalities aimed at accentuating an image of chaos in the country. The pogrom organised in December 1978 in the town of Maraş, following a blatant provocation, was the bloodiest of these "terror" actions organised by the MHP in that year.

In Malatya, attacks on Alevi businesses and homes continued between 19 and 26 December. According to the official toll, 120 people lost their lives and more than 200 houses and 100 shops and offices belonging to Alevis were destroyed by fire. On 26 December, martial law was declared in thirteen counties. Prime Minister Ecevit declared that "these events have been organised by counter-guerrillas," a reference to deep-state paramilitary organisations, to force him to declare martial law. Alevis left these cities en masse and migrated to larger cities in the west of Turkey.

***

With the Maraş pogrom, the first stage of the MHP's strategy was reached but the party failed to acquire hegemonic status within the Turkish right-wing spectrum, as many were frightened by the "blind terror" practices of MHP militants. This strategy also aimed at intimidating public opinion in large cities, stun the resistance of left-wing organisations, and allow the MHP to dominate with increasing influence in provincial cities.

The booklet *After Maraş..?* precisely analyses the implementation of this strategy and its partial failure to establish hegemony over right-wing movements (from the centrist right to the Islamist right). In doing so, the MHP leadership had more openly played the card of a military takeover. It transposed the strategy of chaos to the working-class districts of the large cities of western Turkey, reinforced violent actions, and widened the scope of the attacks in collaboration with the Special Warfare Directorate of the Turkish Army. In the absence of a military takeover, it was preparing for a general civil war of long duration.

Thus, the MHP actively participated in laying the groundwork for the military coup of 12 September 1980. But the military junta, once it had taken power without encountering any significant resistance, had the main political leaders, including those of the MHP, arrested and then launched an investigation into the extent of the responsibility of the MHP leadership for the strategy of chaos, attacks, and pogroms unleashed in the second half of 1970s. The requisition filed on 29 April 1981 by five military court prosecutors against the MHP leadership described in detail the implementation of their strategy of chaos, which fully confirmed the analyses in the booklet *After Maraş..?*. The most significant expression used among MHP activists during the reign of the military junta was "our ideas are in power, but we are in jail!"

Select Bibliography

Bora, Tanıl, and Kemal Can. *Devlet, Ocak, Dergâh.* İstanbul: İletişim Yayınları, 2019.

Gourisse, Benjamin. "Electoral Participation, Penetration of the State, and Armed Violence in the Turkish Political Crisis of the Second Half of the 1970s: Contribution to the Analysis of Long-Range Political Crisis." *Politix* 98, no. 2 (2012): 171–93.

Gümrükçü, Selin Bengi. "Ideology, Discourse, and Alliance Structures: Explaining Far-Right Political Violence in Turkey in the 1970s." *Terrorism and Political Violence* 35, no. 1 (2021): 210–24.

58

Capitalism after Military Intervention: Vehbi Koç and the Military-Industrial Complex

Kaya Akyıldız

On 12 September 1980, the Turkish military overthrew the civilian government and started to rule the country directly. The army stayed in power for three years and during that time Turkey was run as a typical military dictatorship. In 1983, competitive party politics were reinstated with political parties that had not been banned by the military, and after a referendum in 1987, party leaders that had been subjected to bans were able to return to politics. During the years of the military dictatorship, the Turkish Army introduced robust tutelary apparatuses and redesigned the state machine on the basis of a specific agenda. During the years of the military dictatorship from 1980 to 1983 and the years of the multi-party regime under Turgut Özal (1927–1993) in the remainder of the 1980s, the bourgeoisie, and their support for the coup and post-coup Turkey, played a decisive role. Three weeks after the coup of 1980, businessman Vehbi Koç (1901–1996) sent a letter of support to the leader of the coup, General Kenan Evren (1917–2015). Vehbi Koç is perhaps best known for the business empire he built in modern Turkey. He started his long career in the early years of the Republic of Turkey as a small shopkeeper, eventually transforming his small business into an empire through government contracts and international business partnerships that he built up over time. Given his background and business endeavours, he was considered a model businessman of the Republican establishment. Koç, who was a long-term member of the People's Republican Party (*Cumhuriyet Halk Partisi*, CHP) until the Democrat Party (DP) government forced him to resign prior to the coup of 1960, was a staunch supporter of centrist governments, and he had few reservations about such governments' economic policies and the CHP's leftist-inspired pursuits under Bülent Ecevit (1925–2006) in the 1970s. His public image was and still is that of an intelligent business magnate as well as a humble and down-to-earth person who believed in human decency and firmly supported the Turkish state. Moreover, he was lauded for creating employment in Turkey and working hard for the prosperity of his country. In left-wing and Islamist circles his image has been controversial, but in general Koç's reputation in contemporary Turkey was quite positive.

The letter that Koç sent to Evren makes more sense when scrutinised in the broader context of Cold War politics. Before the 1980 coup, leftist ideas were popular among the masses and there were powerful labour and student movements. Organisations dedicated to the working class, the urban poor, and leftist ideals made serious inroads in those years, and labour relations were becoming quite distressing for Turkish capitalists. For most of the

1970s, the country bore witness to civil war-like conditions, martial law, states of exception, political and sectarian violence, and mass killings. Compared to the preludes of the military interventions of 1960 and 1971, the conflict between leftists and right-wing groups in the late 1970s had escalated to levels never seen before. Coalition governments came and went one after the other, the political system was dysfunctional, and economic crises merely served to exacerbate the critically dangerous and bloody political crisis the country found itself in.

Throughout the history of the Republic of Turkey, relations between the capitalist class and the Turkish state have been at the heart of discussions when it comes to economic policies and strategies of industrialisation. The topics of economic growth, state capacity, and industrialisation are often discussed along the lines of the power of the capitalist class in Turkey. The creation of a Turkish, Sunni bourgeoisie during the years of the First World War when a "National Economic Policy" was introduced did not conclude as a success story even though it was accompanied by a massive wealth transfer program, favouritism in public procurements, and a policy of industrialisation. Again, the bourgeoisie was at the centre, despite its weakness and limited power, when statism came to the forefront in the 1930s and 1940s. Koç corporations operating as government contractors grew in those foundational years and initiated their first international partnerships. This weak capitalist class evolved in the liberal economic atmosphere of the 1950s, becoming an industrial bourgeoisie, and it was bolstered by an industrialisation policy of import substitution in the 1960s and 1970s. Seen in that light, Koç's letter to General Evren is revealing in terms of the nature of the relationship between the capitalist class and the state.

*Excerpts from Vehbi Koç's Letter to Kenan Evren, 3 October 1980**

It was impossible not to agree with the sincere words you spoke during the speech you made on Friday 12 September.

When matters fell into disarray in the country [during the coups of 1960 and 1971], the Turkish Army intervened and later withdrew to its barracks, leaving the state administration to civilian governments. After the elections of 1973, the country was [again in] a crisis because of the short-sightedness of politicians and the way that party interests were placed before everything else.

After the necessary steps are taken by the army [after a military intervention], the return of the army to its barracks is essential for the survival of our democracy. My fear is that if the army makes the wrong decisions and stays in power for too long, communists may take over. Turkey is a part of the West, and international agreements anchor Turkey to the free democratic world. If the return to democracy takes too long, Western countries will not fulfil their commitments.

---

* Translated from the Turkish original in Vehbi Koç, *Vehbi Koç Anlatıyor: Bir Derleme* (İstanbul: Yapı Kredi Yayınları, 2019), 283–88.

Laws that prevent anarchy, separatism, and smuggling must be enacted at once. The trials of anarchists and criminals should not be prolonged, and their punishment should be swift. Efforts to equip and strengthen the police should be undertaken with all due seriousness, and any laws needed to empower them should be drafted as soon as possible.

Propaganda is being spread nowadays, [saying that] a fascist army has come to power and that it is in the service of capitalists aiming to exploit Turkish workers. In the face of such slander, laws that will regulate labour relations should be carefully enacted. While making these arrangements, it would be wise to keep in mind how in the past the activities of certain unions crippled the Turkish economy. At the same time, some militant unionists seek to provoke workers and infiltrate the cadres of union management. Such matters should be addressed in the laws as well.

Provisions for severance pay should be collected in a fund. After the annual amounts allocated for workers are paid, the remaining money should be used for public and private investments at low interest rates and this fund should also be used to create a new workforce.

Tax laws should be prepared carefully and the tax burden should be distributed fairly. This time, we should have a system where everyone pays taxes in proportion to their earnings.

The TKP (*Türkiye Komünist Partisi*, TKP, Communist Party of Turkey), which was founded in East Berlin, has done much to destroy our country. It is certain that the TKP, leftist organisations, Kurds, Armenians, and certain politicians will continue their malicious attempts to provoke a working-class uprising. Law enforcement must be merciless in dealing with them, and the efforts of such groups to engage in terrorism must be brought to a halt.

In fact, there are rumours about the Minister of State and Deputy Prime Minister Turgut Özal. Özal is not a genius. He may have faults. But in these times, he is the one person who knows what is best. It would be good to trust him, regardless of the rumours.

Our points of contention with the Greeks, especially regarding Cyprus, the Aegean Continental Shelf, and the Flight Information Region line, must be resolved with our nation never losing confidence in our Armed Forces.

***

Without a doubt, Vehbi Koç wholeheartedly supported the coup, as indicated by how he listed his recommendations in the letter he sent to Kenan Evren after the coup had taken place. While he unreservedly praised the efforts of Evren and the military junta, he recommended that the army return to its barracks after finishing its work and hand power over to a civilian administration. He clearly stated that if the army decided to stay in power for a period of time that was longer than necessary, chaos could erupt, followed by a communist takeover.

In making that statement, Koç was pragmatically playing on the ever-present fear and hatred of communism in Turkey, which was also prevalent in military circles. His insistence on the military returning to its barracks was quite possibly related to his fear that Turkey would be excluded from the Western Bloc. Koç asserted that Turkey needed to remain in the Western Bloc and that returning to democracy as soon as possible was the most beneficial course of action. In its early years, the Koç Group relied heavily on government contracts to ensure its growth, but later it shifted its focus to international partnerships with Western corporations, thereby securing its position as a business empire. During the critical period following the 1980 coup, his companies distributed end products, assembling intermediate Western goods into final products in Turkey. His companies were extremely dependent on their Western counterparts, and the last thing he wanted was for Turkey to be excluded from the Western world. His insistence on the installation of a civilian government once the military junta restored order and keeping Turkey within the Western bloc was not really the outcome of a fondness for democracy and equal citizenship, but rather the reflection of the pragmatic, self-interested mindset of a successful capitalist. The growth of the Turkish economy and the accumulation of capital were genuine concerns for Koç, and it would seem that he was a firm believer in the notion that prolonged military dictatorships would not bring about prosperity. Still, he clearly had no problem with the military's involvement in politics, nor was he overly concerned about the nature of civil-military relations in Turkey.

He suggested that deputy prime minister Turgut Özal remain in office during the period of time in question. Özal was a firm believer in trickle-down economics, minimal state fiscal responsibility, and privatisation. Koç and the Turkish bourgeoisie wholeheartedly believed that Özal would be able to not only take the steps needed to overcome the problems of statism and policies of import-substitute industrialisation, but also dismantle the country's powerful trade unions. He also stated that banning the Confederation of Revolutionary Trade Unions (*Devrimci İşçi Sendikaları Konfederasyonu*, DİSK) would be the right move to make, and he thought that DİSK trade unionists might be secretly infiltrating more recently formed unions. In his view, that would have a devastating effect on the Turkish economy, as communists, leftist organisations, Kurds, and Armenians would resume their "subversive and destructive" activities in the country. Without any reservations whatsoever he claimed that Kurds, Armenians, and leftists were the foes of the Turkish state and nation, which, perhaps, should hardly be surprising. Koç did nothing to promote equal citizenship, he was never an advocate of real democracy, and he always carefully aligned himself with the state's ideology. He believed that justice needed to be meted out swiftly and unmercifully and that the activities of those groups and DİSK had to be brought to a halt at all costs. While Koç also emphasised the importance of religion, he argued that religious affairs should be regulated in such a way that political parties could not exploit them.

Koç also held to a strict position regarding state-owned enterprises (SOEs) and privatisation. He was opposed to the privatisation of unprofitable externalities (i.e., public goods/ services) such as railways and postal services, noting that the value of such public goods and services should not be measured by the merit of profit. He recommended that other

SOEs should become autonomous holdings and that they should obtain a legal status that would protect them from the interventions of politicians. Moreover, he contended that SOEs make indispensable contributions to Turkey's industrialisation, indicating that he was not an advocate of unlimited privatisation. He benefited a great deal from SOEs and understood the unprofitable nature of certain indispensable public services and goods like railways.

Koç's huge industrial companies such as Arçelik, Türk Demir Döküm, and Aygaz were founded in the 1950s, and he noted that the Koç Group had long been indebted to SOEs in terms of human capital, know-how, and the provision of cheap raw and semi-finished materials. Rather than portraying himself as a profit-seeking, rational, calculating entrepreneur, he preferred to be seen as a patriot performing noble acts at the risk and expense of losing money. First starting from a simple grocery store and then moving on to local commercial ventures, he moved his business to İstanbul and built lasting partnerships with foreign companies, and all the while he carried on with his business dealings as a sort of duty to the state. Up until the 1960s he did not consider himself an industrialist. His pragmatism clearly comes through in the letter he wrote to Evren when he made suggestions about increasing the productivity of SOEs and disapproved of the privatisation of public goods and services. He was well aware of what happened to workers when that happened and yet he kept quiet as a beneficiary of the state's policies. Koç stated that he favoured planned industrialisation strategies and a parliamentary democratic order in which the state and private sectors coexist, but in his view the interests of capital should come first and in that way strong governments would emerge.

***

In Turkey, a certain opinion about capitalism prevails: the Turkish capitalist class is far from being a real bourgeoisie like its Western European counterpart, which functions like an autonomous agent. Thus, Turkish capitalists are not independent of the state and do not act as rational calculating actors but rather as short-term rent-seeking puppets of the state. However, Koç's letter demonstrates that he was aware of class interests and that form of class interest was made readily apparent when Koç quite openly explained why he thought the 1980 coup was necessary and inevitable. He echoed the same sentiment expressed in the letter when he warned General Kenan Evren about the destructive effects of partisanship, nepotism, and lack of a plan for industrialisation. He repeatedly referred to the talks he gave and the efforts he made in the 1970s to overcome the existing political deadlock and encourage the establishment of a strong government. According to Koç, democracy is good as long as there is a strong government and radical demands are not made. He believed that while trade unions and workers' rights are a necessary component of democracy, militant organisations such as DİSK should not be allowed to exist and wage increases that would prevent businesses from being competitive should never be considered.

Almost everything Koç proposed in his letter was realised during the period of military rule and the subsequent Özal governments after 1983. Of course, the military and Özal governments were not taking direct orders from Koç or any other capitalist organisation in Turkey, but there was a great deal of overlap when it came to their worldviews and how to fix the Turkish economy and society as a whole. A neoliberal agenda was put into place in the 1980s, as a result of which the gains that had been made by the working class and urban poor were reversed and their real incomes and share of the GDP decreased drastically. In addition, the power of trade unions, civil society organisations, and left-wing grassroots movements diminished to a large extent. Institutional politics and governmental structures designed with the idea of bringing to power strong single-party governments emerged, and by means of new growth strategies, Koç and other capitalists made up for the losses they had incurred in the 1970s. In that sense, Koç's letter might seem like a blueprint for the policies that were later sought after by the Turkish capitalist class and his recommendations, policy suggestions, and to-do lists were all conveniently realised by the military junta and subsequent Özal governments.

Select Bibliography

Buğra, Ayşe. *State and Business in Modern Turkey: A Comparative Study*. Albany, NY: SUNY Press, 1994.

Keyder, Çağlar. *State and Class in Turkey: A Study in Capitalist Development*. London: Verso Books, 1987.

Koç, Vehbi. *Vehbi Koç Anlatıyor: Bir Derleme*. İstanbul: Yapı Kredi Yayınları, 2019.

59

Leftists from Turkey, Unite!
Behice Boran in Brussels

Oğul Tuna

The military coup of 12 September 1980 crushed left-wing political parties and activists in Turkey. Among the prominent social figures who had to leave the country was Behice Boran (1910–1987), the leader of the Workers' Party of Turkey (*Türkiye İşçi Partisi*, TİP). Boran was originally a renowned sociologist who, starting in the 1940s, was repeatedly persecuted by the Turkish authorities during crackdowns on socialists due to her involvement in left-wing politics. She was a member of the banned Communist Party of Turkey (*Türkiye Komünist Partisi*, TKP) since late 1942 and she was also involved in the founding of the pacifist Turkish Peace-Lovers Association (*Türk Barışseverler Cemiyeti*) in 1950, which was a crucial organisation in the protests against Turkish participation in the Korean War (1950–1953). She then joined the TİP in 1962. Founded by twelve unionists in 1961, the TİP was established as a pluralist socialist party which claimed to represent the masses. For instance, the TİP was the first political group to use the word "Kurdish" in Parliament and the first to pass a resolution on the "Kurdish Question" in Turkey. In the general elections of 1965, the TİP entered Parliament with nearly 3 per cent of the national vote. Party leader Mehmet Ali Aybar (1908–1995) developed an approach to socialism that was particular to Turkey, a model which he called "genial socialism" or "socialism with a human face," while Boran and her group favoured orthodox Marxism. The two groups fell into a dispute after the Prague Spring (1968), as Boran supported the Soviet occupation. Boran assumed the leadership of the TİP in 1971, but the party was banned following the military intervention that took place in the same year. After being imprisoned for three years, Boran re-established the TİP in 1975. However, the 1980 coup d'état was even harsher and more violent than the previous military interventions. Later denaturalised, Boran left Turkey and arrived in Brussels on 10 March 1981 as a refugee. As the leader of the TİP, Boran had launched an ambitious project in Europe through the founding of the Union for Democracy (*Demokrasi İçin Birlik*, DİB) a year before her exile on 15 June 1980. She later concentrated all of her efforts on the unification of left-wing organisations and associations in European exile in the 1980s. Now, herself an exile in Europe, Boran delivered a speech during the First European General Assembly of the DİB on 14 February 1981, calling on all of the exiled left-wing activists and organisations to establish a common platform as a means of defeating the military junta in Turkey.

*We Have a Duty—We Will Succeed**

The bourgeoisie and imperialism attempted to escalate oppression and terror to suppress the increasingly discontented and mobilised masses as well as progressive, democratic, left-wing, socialist developments. They adopted the strategy of using the right to crush the left. This policy was launched by Süleyman Demirel, [his] party, and his government before the 1970s. However, as a reaction to right-wing terrorism, gauchiste terrorism, or left-wing terrorism, emerged. [This] mutual terrorism escalated and increased over time. Terrorism could have been prevented had that been the desire before the junta came to power, if those who had the overall power had so desired. But the capitalists and imperialism realised that it was not possible to suppress and silence the masses [nor] progressive, left-wing, and socialist developments through the state oppression they use and the policy of using the right to crush the left. Despite all the difficulties, the militancy of the working class, far from declining, is rising up to a higher level. [...] Then, in their point of view, establishing "a strong government, a strong state" became a necessity. The junta of September 12 was thus a fascist military dictatorship aiming to establish such a powerful state.

The junta is at the service and in the control of the big bourgeoisie, monopolies, and imperialism in our foreign relations. [...] For imperialism, Turkey has become a significant country in the strategy and military organisation created by the USA and NATO against the Soviet Union and the world socialist system. Regarding the situation in the Middle East, Turkey is now considered a tool of the US [that it uses] to intervene in the Gulf due to its strategic location and the fact that it is the only NATO country in the region. However, as the Workers' Party of Turkey has repeatedly stated, Turkey has felt obliged to improve its relations with socialist countries, especially the Soviet Union, to expand its capitalist markets, reach out for favourable credit, [acquire] advanced technologies and energy, and develop certain heavy industry facilities. Now it seems that the junta feels obliged to improve these relations The Soviet Union and other socialist countries seem to be satisfied with the relations [they have]. This development is very important.

Turkey's working-class parties, trade unions, and progressive and democratic forces failed to build up a united force against fascism and prevent it. We must feel deeply responsible [for this] and never forget this duty. [...] Let's not forget that the roots of fascism lie in class [antagonism]. [...] Therefore, the antidote to fascism, the force that will defeat fascism, is again class [struggle] and the working class, [including] the toilers and all the other patriotic, democratic, progressive forces allied with them. For that reason, we have a duty.

I repeat: we have a duty. We have a duty to the working class of our country, we have a duty to the international working-class movement, and we have a duty to history. No power other than Turkey's

* Translated from the original Turkish in *Demokrasi İçin Birlik I. Avrupa Genel Kurulu Belgeleri: Ana Statü, Behice Boran'ın Konuşması* (Brussels: Demokrasi İçin Birlik Avrupa Komitesi, n.d.).

working class, workers, progressives, democrats, and patriots will defeat fascism in Turkey. And this struggle must be fought both within the country and abroad. We will succeed.

Long live the struggle for independence, democracy, and socialism!

Long live international solidarity!

***

Following the military coup of 1980, the new regime banned left-wing political organisations and then went on to persecute their militants and exile their leaders and activists. However, the left-wing political front in Turkey had already fragmented. The three major leftist political parties were the TKP, which was integrated into a broader international framework in Europe under the auspices of the Soviet Union, the Socialist Workers Party of Turkey (*Türkiye Sosyalist İşçi Partisi*, TSİP), and the TİP. Additionally, several Kurdish, Assyrian, and Armenian organisations had been mobilising workers who migrated to Western Europe. Boran's speech and her active role in unification efforts inaugurated a new period of negotiations, disputes, and compromises for the left in exile. Those efforts materialised through the announcement of a merger of the TKP and TİP into the United Communist Party of Turkey (*Türkiye Birleşik Komünist Partisi*, TBKP) in October 1987, just days before the death of Boran.

In her address, Boran analysed the quasi-civil war of the 1970s in Turkey and the roots of the military junta in terms of class. Accusing US imperialism and its partner, the Turkish bourgeoisie, of escalating instead of preventing bloodshed in the country, she pointed out the existence of what could be called a "deep state" that was executing political schemes behind the scenes. Perhaps even more striking than her *avant la lettre* concept of a Turkish deep state, Boran also denounced the Soviet Union and "other socialist states" for maintaining relations with the Turkish military junta. Nevertheless, she placed her belief in the struggle for a unified front, not only of socialists, but also of progressives, democrats, and patriots.

***

The fragmented structure and factionalism of left-wing politics in Turkey came to an end through Boran's efforts together with Nabi Yağcı (1944–) from the TKP and Nihat Sargın (1929–2010) from the TİP. They strove to forge a political structure that was new in the history of the working class in Turkey. After the announcement of unification, Yağcı and Sargın returned to Turkey but were arrested and imprisoned for two years. While the TBKP was finally officially founded in 1990, a year later it was banned. Despite this endeavour to unify all the factions of the left in Turkey, the TSİP, Kurdish organisations, and other factions that had Maoist or national-socialist leanings were not included in the TBKP.

Still, the majority of the current left-wing parties in Turkey are the progeny of the TBKP. Following the eruption of divisions within the modern TKP, which had been founded as the

Socialist Power Party (*Sosyalist İktidar Partisi*, SİP) in 1993 and re-baptised the TKP in 2001, a new TİP emerged in the late 2010s and claimed Boran's heritage. The experience of the efforts at unification also left an imprint on Turkish and Kurdish communities in Europe. Many of the activists who participated in the negotiations during the long decade of the 1980s still struggle against oppression and state persecution. Started as a movement in exile aiming for unification, it still generates tensions in contemporary Turkish politics. Since the Gezi protests of 2013, the Turkish left has constantly been trying to form a single platform for all leftist factions, including pro-Kurdish parties.

Select Bibliography

Atılgan, Gökhan. *Behice Boran: Öğretim Üyesi, Siyasetçi, Kuramcı*. İstanbul: Yordam Kitap, 2019.

Babalık, Naciye. *Türkiye Komünist Partisi'nin Sönümlenmesi*. İstanbul: İmge Kitabevi, 2005.

Çınar, Sercan. "Behice Boran (1910–1987): A Committed Communist Woman in Cold War Turkey." In *The Palgrave Handbook of Communist Women Activists Around the World*, edited by Francisca de Haan, 399–431. Cham: Springer International Publishing, 2023.

Lipovsky, Igor. *The Socialist Movement in Turkey 1960–1980*. Leiden: Brill, 1992.

Tuna, Oğul. *Resistance Everywhere: Politics of Turkey's Left-Wing Diaspora in France (1971-1988)*. İstanbul: Libra Kitap, 2021.

60

When Generals Do Etymology:
On the *Kart-Kurt* Myth of Kurdish

Deniz Tat

Among the deriving forces that strengthened the hand of the generals who planned and executed the coup d'état of 12 September 1980 was the rise of Kurdish separatism. It is therefore not surprising that the military junta addressed the issue in their subsequent policies. However, the military junta dealt with Kurdish separatism by overtly denying Kurdish identity rather than embracing discourses that at least presupposed it. Part of such denial involved the denial of the Kurdish language altogether. This deliberate attempt to deconstruct linguistic realities and spread pseudo-scientific knowledge was significantly successful in Turkey. The ways in which the Kurdish language was perceived by the masses was deeply affected by these policies, which were reinforced by men who did their military service in the 1980s and were taught such absurdities about the Kurdish language as part of their military training. It would be difficult to convince the masses otherwise, and the fact that the words *Kürt*—Turkish devoices word-final voiced sonorant consonants, hence, the final [t] instead of [d]—and *Türk* happen to share the same phonemes did not make it any easier.

The claim that Kurdish is a regional dialect of Turkish would be questioned by anyone who has a basic knowledge of the two languages, which are mutually unintelligible. The issue of whether one variety of a language is a dialect of another is always a socio-historical construct, not a linguistic reality. But even that view from linguistics is redundant here since Kurdish and Turkish are not genealogically related to one another, as has been shown by language typologists, and neither therefore qualifies to be a dialect of the other. Unlike many other instances of misguided beliefs about languages and their alleged origins, in this particular case the people who fabricated the "knowledge" also had an enormous amount of power to disseminate it. However, it should be noted that they were neither the first nor the last to offer up "scientific" explanations as to where the Kurdish language actually came from.

The early years of the Republic of Turkey were marked by reforms that placed Turkishness and the Turkish language at the heart of the nation-building project, while other ethnic and linguistic flavours of the Ottoman past were simply considered idiosyncrasies to be Turkified. The Latin script was adopted in 1928 to replace the Perso-Arabic script in a move that was intended to cut cultural ties with the Islamic world in the hope of bringing the new republic one step closer to becoming a Western state. The Turkish Language Institute (*Türk Dil Kurumu*), founded in 1932, launched a massive purification campaign that replaced words of Arabic and Persian origin with words that were derived from Turkic stems. Two years later, the introduction of the Surname Law of 1934 required that every citizen choose a Turkish surname. But perhaps the Sun Language Theory, which emerged in the same period, best exemplifies the extent to which the new state would go to reinforce a Turkish ethno-linguistic identity that would then be used to make the claim that Turks belonged to an ancient world civilisation. Developed by the linguists of the Turkish Language Institute in 1935 and 1936 and backed by the enthusiastic support of Atatürk, the "theory" was based on the premise that all languages in the world are derived from a proto-language which was most likely to be Turkish because of a few phonetic similarities. The aim was not only to construct cultural hegemony over ethnic minorities, but also to counter the Orientalist and racist theories developed in the West concerning which nation had inherited "true" civilisation.

Turkey witnessed three military coups (in 1960, 1971 and 1980), and with each coup, efforts targeting the Turkification of the Kurds proceeded apace. Kurdish intellectuals who resisted state policies were arrested; villages with Kurdish names were given Turkish names; political parties mentioning the Kurdish issue were banned; and numerous other measures that sought to assimilate the Kurdish identity were put into place. The words *Kürt* and *Kürtçe* were considered taboo and thus were typically not directly mentioned in state discourses. Of the three coups, the one that took place in 1980 was perhaps the most vicious; while military interventions successfully reduced the number of terrorist attacks, they also targeted anyone who expressed views that were even slightly leftist. A law that was passed in 1983 banned the use of any language other than those that were the primary official languages of countries that Turkey recognised. In practice, this meant that the use of Kurdish was banned since it was not the primary official language of any state at the time, and it did not acquire official status in Iraq until as late as 2005.

The Turkish Land Forces Command published a book about language in 1982 while the military junta was still ruling the country. Although the book was classified as "restricted (to military personnel)," it is now available at libraries and in bookstores. What is unique about this book is that the words *Kürt* and *Kürtçe* appear on thirty out of a total of eighty-eight pages. Perhaps it was permissible to use those words in "restricted" publications. Or perhaps, after decades of denial, the junta decided that it had to directly deal with the issue by overtly articulating those words while still denying their ethnic and linguistic validity. In any case, the authors cooked up an etymological explanation as to where the word *Kürt* came from: the Kurds were simply mountain Turks, to be called "eastern Turkmens" as instructed in the book, and the language they spoke was a regional variety of Turkish. The word *Kürt* was apparently derived from an onomatopoeic root, *"kirt-kurt,"* the sound you hear if you step on frozen snow, and thence it would later be referred to as the *"Kart-Kurt* Theory" of Kurdish. The following excerpt is drawn from that book; in the translation, the use of capitalisation as well as the grammar mistakes in the original text were deliberately maintained, as they proved to be significant in terms of understanding the mentality of the people who were behind such pseudo-scientific practices.

Destructive and Separatist Movements in Turkey[*]

KURDISM – SEPARATISM

Separatism: Activities carried out in order to divide society; the act of claiming that the unifying elements of society are separate races, separate religions, and separate sects is referred to as separatism.

[Engaging in] activities that are carried out with the claim that various peoples exist in TURKEY is separatism. Separatists always take advantage of the concept of *Millet* [the nation] and argue that the concept of *Halk* [the people] carries a different meaning. However, *Millet*, in its simplest definition, is a collection of people who share the same cultural values (Language-History-Custom-tradition). As for *Halk,* they are the living children of today. There is no sociological difference between *Halk* and *Millet.* The TURKISH *MILLET* is a concept that has been sustained from the depths of history up until today. And the TURKISH *HALK* are the living TURKS today who own the heritage of THAT *millet.* Our nation, who lives in TURKEY and differs from one another only in [their] regional dialects, is like the branches of a single tree.

As a matter of fact, ATATÜRK said, "The Turkish nation who has founded the Republic of TURKEY is called the TURKISH people," and he stated:

"Those from DİYARBAKIR, VAN, ERZURUM and THRACE ALL COMPRISE the CHILDREN of A SINGLE RACE and the VEINS OF A SINGLE ORE." (ATATÜRK in DİYARBAKIR, 1923, p. 4)

In our country, separatism is undertaken in every sphere. But of these, the most active one is separatism in the sphere of KURDISM. Is there, by any means, a separate Kurdish race? Where does the word KURD come from?

KURD:

On the higher sections of mountains, on the peaks, there is snow [both] in the summer and winter months. The surface of this snow melts slightly when the sun shines on it, and it freezes over, covering the surface with a glassy, shiny, hard layer. The top part is hard snow and the bottom part is soft.

When one is walking on this type of snow, the foot sinks where it is set down and makes a *Kırt-Kürt* sound. You see, snow that is compressed tightly is called *Kürt* snow or *Kürtün,* in attribution to that sound.

In many parts of Anatolia and in Azerbaijan, compressed snow, which storms and winds bring and fill in hollows, is still called *Kurtuk-Kürtük* today.

[*] Translated from the original Turkish in *Türkiye'de Yıkıcı ve Bölücü Akımlar* (Ankara: Kara Kuvvetleri Komutanlığı Yayınları, 1982), 43–48.

TURKS living on high plateaus and in snowy areas are called *Kürdak*.

As a matter of fact, SIBERIAN TURKS call their kin who live in the ALTAI Mountains *Kurdak* and *Kürdak*.

TURKISH clans that lived in the high mountains of Central Asia were identified as *Karluk-Karlık* in the saga of OGHUZ KHAN. Xenephon, in his writings titled *Anabasis*, which he wrote in 401-400 BC, [stated that] the people who lived in the basin of LAKE VAN are called *Karduk*. These people were *KARLUK* TURKS who migrated from Central Asia.

Hungarian TURKOLOGISTS and historians agree that the word Kurd means compressed snow. The word Kurd has in time been used to refer to resilient people with a tough nature who live in the mountains. In Zeki Velidi TOGAN's TURKISH History, it is stated that Kurd derives from Ekrad, and Ekrad is a clan of Oghuz.

[Section on the migration of Kurds to Anatolia that considers their possible relation to (i) Iranian ancestry, (ii) Arabic ancestry, (ii) and Georgian or Chaldean ancestry, rejecting all of them and strengthening the Turkish ancestry argument.]

While Kurd=Turk, because (the word) Kurd has been exploited by destructive movements, the term "EASTERN TURKMENS" will be used [henceforth] in accordance with the records of the General Staff.

THE TURKISHNESS OF EASTERN TURKMENS IN TERMS OF LANGUAGE:

Today, linguistics has advanced greatly and successfully identified languages together with their origins and patterns (structures). Today, language has become a great dependable tool in identifying Races.

The claim that Eastern Turkmens are a separate Race is most frequently made [by] toying with language. Separatism is undertaken by claiming that there is a Kurdish Race because there is a distinct Kurdish language.

Kurdish is not a distinct language; it is just a regional dialect. It has no alphabet, no linguistic rules. In order for a spoken language to be considered a language, it must have grammar rules, sentence rules.

The spoken Kurdish language consists of 7,000-7,500 words.

Of these:
3,500 – 4,000 Words are Original Turkish words brought from Cental Asia.
3,000 Words are Arabic and Persian (Turkified words).
300 Words hebrew
200 Words French
100 Words Armenian and other regional dialects.

As a matter of fact, Prof. Veber and Dr. Firiç have stated that Kurdish is not a language but (just) a pile of words; it does not suggest the existence of a separate people.

***

The excerpt quoted above uses four means to justify a Turkish origin for Kurdish: (i) an etymological fabrication to relate the word *Kürt* to snow-related onomatopoeia, (ii) an appeal to authority approach to convince the reader that the etymological account is a scientific one, (iii) a "historical" explanation as to why Kurdish could not have derived from other languages in the region, such as Arabic and Persian, leaving only Turkish as a possible origin, and (iv) falsely attributing certain features to Kurdish, such as a lack of grammar and a small lexicon mostly consisting of words of Turkish origin, as a means of claiming that it is not even a language.

The etymological fabrication is so absurd and unlikely that even Kenan Evren (1917–2015), the commander who led the military intervention of 1980 and served as president between 1980 and 1989, later denied he had anything to do with it. It is therefore not even necessary to provide a counterargument; suffice to say, linguists have considered various etymological explanations for the word *Kurd* and a snow-related sound is not one of them. The text also refers to Hungarian "scientists"—and the reason why Turkologists are all in uppercase and historians are in lowercase is also significant here—who also agree with the etymological fabrication. In the first place, we are not told who these researchers are. The writers clearly had no linguistic awareness, as *Ekrad* is simply the broken plural of *Kurd* in Arabic and does not prove any relationship to Turkishness.

Kurdish belongs to the Iranian language group, which is a branch of the Indo-European language family. The World Atlas of Languages online database hosted by the Max Planck Institute for Evolutionary Anthropology lists twenty-six Iranian languages, two of which are largely spoken in Turkey, Kurmanji (Northern Kurdish) and Zazaki (Dimli). While these two languages share certain grammatical features and lexical items, the level of mutual intelligibility is relatively low. Kurdish variants have been written in various alphabets depending on where they are spoken. But a lack of a standard writing system has nothing to do with the status of languages; of the ±7,000 languages spoken in the world, only a third have a tradition of writing. And the evolution of languages predates the invention of writing, which is about 6,000 years old, by at least a hundred thousand years. Given these facts, the arguments in the text denying Kurdish the status of a language have no validity. Moreover, any spoken or signed system that is in principle acquired by a child as a mother-tongue *is* a (living) language. Whether something is a language or not cannot be determined by powers external to language, such as that wielded by politicians or generals.

***

The text presented here shows that the military junta in the 1980s was willing to go to any lengths to deny the Kurdish identity and language even if it meant producing clearly invalid knowledge and disseminating it. State policy concerning the Kurdish language overall persists to this day, although some language rights have been granted in a piecemeal manner. For example, the law that banned the use of Kurdish in practice was repealed in 1991, though its use in education and broadcasting remained illegal. The Justice and Development Party (*Adalet ve Kalkınma Partisi*, AKP), which came to power in 2002 and has been led by Recep Tayyip Erdoğan (1954–), introduced various reforms as part of EU membership negotiations. Languages other than Turkish were thenceforth allowed to be broadcast so long as the integrity of the Turkish nation was not threatened, and parents were allowed to give their children Kurdish names so long as they did not include the letters Q, W, or X. Those letters were banned in every domain until they were finally permitted in 2013. The Turkish national broadcaster started a new TV channel, TRT 6, which has been broadcasting in Kurdish. These were positive advances within the socio-political context of Turkey. However, Turkey has seen a reversal of such policies under the AKP concerning their approach to Kurdish identity and language since 2016, and hopes for an improvement in language rights in Turkey have once again been postponed to an unknown future.

Select Bibliography

Baransel, Ali. *Bıçak Sırtında: Çankaya Köşkü Yılları.* İstanbul: Remzi Kitabevi, 2006.

Barkey, Henri J., and Graham E. Fuller. "Turkey's Kurdish Question: Critical Turning Points and Missed Opportunities." *The Middle East Journal* 51, no. 1 (1997): 59–79.

Belge, Murat. "Kart-Kurt Teorisi'nin Tarihçesi." *Taraf,* 13 September 2009.

Yeğen, Mesut. "The Kurdish Question in Turkish State Discourse." *Journal of Contemporary History* 34, no. 4 (1999): 555–68.

Zeydanlıoğlu, Welat. "Turkey's Kurdish Language Policy." *International Journal of the Sociology of Language* 217 (2012): 99–125.

Zürcher, Erik-Jan. "La théorie du 'langage-soleil' et sa place dans la reforme du langue turque." In *La linguistique fantastique*, edited by Sylvain Auroux, 83–91. Paris: Denoël, 1984.

1983–1992

61
Active State Participation in the Manufacture of Denialism: "The Armenian Issue"

Uğur Derin

According to documents that were left behind by Interior Minister and later Grand Vizier Talat Pasha (1874–1921), of the approximately 1.5 million Armenians living in the Ottoman Empire at the time, 924.158 were deported during the First World War between 1915 and 1916 under the pretence of security measures. Most of the officials who gave the orders for or organised the Armenian massacres were connected to the Committee of Union and Progress (*İttihat ve Terakki Cemiyeti*, CUP), which ruled the Ottoman Empire as a single-party government after 1913. The annihilation of the Armenians took place in several stages. On 24 April 1915, hundreds of Armenian intellectuals (including writers, doctors, lawyers, and politicians) were arrested and deported in a move that was widely described as a decapitation strike aimed at depriving the Armenian community of leadership and preventing possible plans for resistance. This was followed by large scale arrests of Armenians who were then deported to the Deir ez-Zor desert in Syria. Properties left by the Armenians were confiscated by the Muslims of Anatolia, and tens of thousands of Armenian orphanage children were later forced to convert to Islam, whereupon they were subjected to processes of Turkification. In the post-war tribunals of 1919-1920 following the defeat of the Ottoman Empire, the perpetrators were put on trial by the Entente powers, although all the leaders of the CUP had already left the country. Since the Turks were victorious in the National Struggle that ended in 1922, Westerners could not take much action in terms of imposing on the newly-founded Republic of Turkey responsibility for the deliberate massacres of the Armenians or demanding reparations, but the events of 1915 were perceived by the international community as the mass murder of a nation. The phrase "Armenian Genocide" has been used since 1948, when the term was legally coined, but international recognition of the event took place mostly after the end of the Cold War. Today, historians across the world consider it to be a prominent case of genocide.

Following the proclamation of the Republic of Turkey in 1923, whose leading cadre had been affiliated with the CUP, Turkish official policy regarding the Armenian Genocide of 1915 was first justification, then active silencing, and lastly voluntary oblivion. Save for a few publications, there was no mention of the Armenians, to the extent that they were removed from school curricula as if they had never lived in eastern Anatolia. Turkey's approach to the topic also determined its relations with foreign governments. Usage of the phrase "the Armenian

Issue" (*Ermeni Sorunu/Meselesi*) instead of "the Armenian Genocide" was seen by Turkey as a test of good relations. The silence in Turkey about what happened to the Armenians lasted until the beginning of the 1980s. The assassination of Turkey's Consul General and Vice Consul in Los Angeles in 1973 by 78-year-old Armenian genocide survivor Gourgen Yanikian (1895–1984) was soon followed by the emergence of two militant organisations: the pro-Soviet ASALA (Armenian Secret Army for the Liberation of Armenia) and the pro-Western JCAG (Justice Commandos of the Armenian Genocide). These two organisations carried out more than 100 terroristic attacks (mostly in Europe but in other parts of the world as well) in the next two decades, mostly targeting Turkish diplomats, killing dozens of people including non-Turks. Beyond revenge, the terroristic attacks aimed at reminding the international public about the forgotten and denied genocide of Armenians, the descendants of whom became part of a global diaspora spread across the Cold War's iron curtain.

For the general Turkish public, who was in a state of oblivion about the Armenian Genocide, these murders came out of the blue. Since the public was having difficulty understanding why Turkish diplomats were being brutally murdered abroad by Armenians despite having "done nothing wrong," the Turkish state felt compelled to explain what happened in 1915. And so was born the official historical narrative of "the Armenian Issue," which soon became known as "the Turkish thesis".

The state actively took part in disseminating the Turkish thesis and combatting Armenian genocide claims. The classic work on this subject, the 1950 book *The Armenians in History and the Armenian Issue* (*Tarihte Ermeniler ve Ermeni Meselesi*) by Esat Uras (1882–1957), was doubled in size and reprinted by the state. Himself an Ottoman officer and one of the perpetrators of the Armenian Genocide, Uras's book is widely accepted as constituting the foundation of denialist arguments. The military and several ministries also published books on the topic, most of them with titles bearing the phrase "the Armenian Issue," propagating the Turkish thesis. The fact that the victims of Armenian terrorism were Turkish diplomats and their families made the matter especially sensitive for the Turkish Ministry of Foreign Affairs. The Ministry's official think tank, the Foreign Policy Institute (*Dış Politika Enstitüsü*, founded in 1974), published a forty-two-page pamphlet titled *The Armenian Issue in Nine Questions and Answers* (*Dokuz Soru ve Cevapta Ermeni Sorunu*). Below are some excerpts from that pamphlet, which was published in 1983.

The Armenian Issue in Nine Questions and Answers[*]

Question 1: Is eastern Anatolia the original homeland of the Armenians?
Even Armenian historians disagree on the question of the roots of the Armenians. [...] It is understood that Armenians are not one of the indigenous peoples of eastern Anatolia and that they settled there from elsewhere.

---

[*] Translated from the original Turkish in *Dokuz Soru ve Cevapta Ermeni Sorunu* (Ankara: Dış Politika Enstitüsü, 1983).

Question 2: Starting with the Seljuks and the Ottomans, did the Turks take the lands of the Armenians by force?

Throughout history the Armenians [...] have never been able to maintain any sort of independent or unified Armenian state. [...] Most of these Armenian principalities were simply set up by foreign states that controlled the region.

Question 3: Have the Turks always persecuted and attacked the Armenians?

The Armenians were able to protect their existence as a society and their religion and churches thanks to the Turks. [...] Until the final phase of the empire, the freedom granted to and the great tolerance shown by the Ottomans towards non-Muslims made it a safe haven for those fleeing religious persecution.

Question 4: Did the Turks try to massacre the Armenians starting in the 1890s?

Armenian officers in the Russian army worked frantically to stir discontent among the Ottoman Armenians. [...] As Armenian writers themselves have freely admitted, the goal of their revolutionary societies was to stir up revolution and their method was terror. [...] In reaction to these revolts, the Ottomans did what any other state would do in such circumstances and sent armed forces against the rebels to restore order.

Question 5: Did the Turks undertake a planned and systematic massacre of the Armenians in 1915?

The Tashnak committee [Armenian Revolutionary Federation, founded in 1890] gave the following instruction to their organisation: "When the Russians cross the border and the Ottomans begin to retreat, rebellions should break out everywhere. [...] In case the Ottomans advance, the Armenian troops [...] will form gangs and merge with the Russians." Fleeing Armenians [...] undertook massacres in towns and cities... [and] stabbed the Ottomans in the back. [...] The deportations are the result of rebellions. [...] The Ottoman State ... because of the grave internal and external danger [...] took a measure no country would hesitate to take and deported the Armenians in the war zone to Syria. [...] What is in question is a world war, a rebellion, and a deportation as a result of that. [...] The damage caused by the difficult circumstances of the war, harsh climate conditions, and diseases like typhus should also be considered. Not just the Armenians but all Ottomans suffered because of these adversities.

Question 9: Do the Turks put pressure on Armenians living in Turkey today, too?

Most recently two statements made by Patriarchate Kalustyan ... upon the decision of the European Council in February 1982 that minorities in Turkey are put under pressure [...] Kalustyan stated, "Turkish Armenians live in Turkey peacefully as Turkish citizens ... [and] they can freely practice their religion."

***

According to this narrative, Armenians, who had co-existed side by side for hundreds of years with Muslim Turks, were tricked by the Great Powers after the nineteenth century. Siding with Russia, the enemy during the First World War, the Armenians stabbed the Ottomans in the back. The Ottoman government had no choice but to deport them, and on the road some Armenians died due to the wartime hazards of banditry, disease, and famine, which had also decimated the Muslim population of Anatolia in the same period. While not fabricated, this narrative exaggerated Armenian revolutionary separatism, relativised the extent of the massacres and suffering of the deportees, and fully denied any government intention and culpability in the organised destruction of the Ottoman Armenian population, thereby rejecting accusations of the crime of genocide.

The main arguments of the pamphlet can be summarised as follows: Armenians were not indigenous to eastern Anatolia; they were treated well by the Ottomans until the last phase of the Ottoman Empire; the reason for their deportation was their own fault (collaboration with the enemy and revolting against the state); approximately 300,000 Armenians died during these deportations; Muslim Turks also suffered during the First World War, and lastly, Armenians living in Turkey have no problems and are not subjected to pressure. To put it concisely: a) it never happened; b) it was their own fault; and c) it was not as bad as they say.

There are approximately fifty sources cited at the end of the pamphlet. Which sources were used and how they were utilised are important issues in terms of their contribution to the thesis of denial. The abovementioned book by Uras was cited throughout the pamphlet. However, non-Turkish sources were also used in an attempt to disprove the claims of genocide, including Russian eyewitness reports and the contradictory works of Western and Armenian historians. The common denominator of these sources is that only parts that document Armenians' collaboration with Westerners are cited and the most crucial parts are omitted, mainly the point that the Ottoman government deliberately massacred the Armenians and that Armenian casualties numbered between 800,000 and 1.5 million.

One issue that is conspicuous in the pamphlet is the blatant effort to cast the Armenians as tools of external powers, primarily Russia, completely ignoring the fact that it was not just those close to the Russian border, but almost all the Armenians of Anatolia were deported or murdered. This attempt to portray the Armenians as collaborating with external powers does not just concern the 1915 deportations, but the entire history of the Armenians. Accordingly, the Armenians have never been independent, have always needed the support of larger states, have been deported multiple times throughout their history, and they were provoked by the Great Powers and collaborated with them prior to the 1915 deportations. The Armenians are depicted not as the great enemy of the Turks, but as the insidious minions of great powers. This serves an important purpose, for once the reader "learns" that the Armenians were never a sovereign nation and have always been used by other nations, resorting to treason and terrorism, it is easier to portray "Armenian terrorists" (both in 1915 and the revenge killings of the late 1970s and the 1980s) as again "parasites" of the international order.

Of the abundance of books with the words "Armenian Issue" in their title that appeared in Turkey in the late 1970s and the 1980s, this pamphlet is by far the shortest. The whole topic is summarised in nine questions and in forty pages. It has been suggested that the pamphlet was given to Turkish students going abroad in those days to provide them with quick-and-easy answers for possible questions that they might encounter. In that sense, its content constitutes the foundation of the denialist argument—the Turkish thesis, namely that while Armenian losses were tragic, the deportations were a military necessity and that the events of 1915 cannot be referred to as genocide. These arguments (some of which are taken verbatim from this pamphlet) can be found today on the website of the Turkish Ministry of Foreign Affairs and in history coursebooks.

***

Both Turkey's approach to the Armenian Genocide and how those who were critical of it are treated have changed since the end of the Cold War. As a consequence of the relative democratisation of the early 2000s and especially in relation to Turkey's EU accession process, talking about 1915, including using the word "genocide" (*soykırım*), is not a taboo anymore in Turkey. Press releases made in 2014 and 2015 by the top of the Turkish state which, for the first time, described the events of 1915 as "inhumane," could be accepted as a watershed moment in describing the official stance of Turkey, though it does not seem realistic to expect the official adoption and usage of the word "genocide" or the acceptance of deliberate killings to occur in the near future.

Elements of "the Armenian Issue" narrative could be (and often are) applied to other non-Muslim or non-Turks in Turkey as well: Minorities came from outside, their roots are unknown, they do not have a long history, and, if they were persecuted, this was because they engaged in treason or collaborated with external powers. Such narratives are also utilised in discrimination against and the persecution of various other minorities including Kurds, Alevites, Jews, and Greeks. Minorities are often forced to state their allegiance to Turkey and to the Turkish nation to avoid being persecuted.

Select Bibliography

Dixon, Jennifer M. *Dark Pasts: Changing the State's Story in Turkey and Japan.* Ithaca and London: Cornell University Press, 2018.

Göçek, Fatma Müge. *Denial of Violence: Ottoman Past, Turkish Present and Collective Violence Against the Armenians, 1789-2009.* New York: Oxford University Press, 2014.

Gürpinar, Doğan. "The Manufacturing of Denial: The Making of the Turkish 'Official Thesis' on the Armenian Genocide Between 1974 and 1990." *Journal of Balkan and Near Eastern Studies* 18, no. 3 (2016): 217–40.

Kaligian, Dikran. "Anatomy of Denial: Manipulating Sources and Manufacturing a Rebellion." *Genocide Studies International* 8, no. 2 (2014): 208–23.

Suny, Ronald Grigor, Fatma Müge Göçek, and Norman Naimark, eds. *A Question of Genocide: Armenians and Turks at the End of the Ottoman Empire.* New York: Oxford University Press, 2011.

Turan, Ömer, and Güven Gürkan Öztan. *Devlet Aklı ve 1915: Türkiye'de "Ermeni Meselesi" Anlatısının İnşası.* İstanbul: İletişim Yayınları, 2018.

62

"My Body, My Choice!":
Conceptions of a Contemporary Feminist Slogan in Turkey

Sevil Çakır Kılınçoğlu

Given the strength and influence of the feminist movement in Turkey today, it is difficult to imagine that it was only 40 years ago, when a group of women first came forward and proclaimed themselves to be feminists. They did so after the military intervention on 12 September 1980, a time when all social and political opposition had been suppressed. For the most part it was women who had been active in the ranks of various leftist movements in the previous decades who formed the backbone of the emerging women's movement in Turkey. It all got started on the pages of the journal *Somut*, the weekly publication of *Yazko* (The Writers Cooperative), the fourth page (*4. Sayfa*) of which was dedicated to women's writing for the three months the journal was published in 1983. Nearly all of the prominent activist and intellectual women of the 1980s and afterwards either wrote essays for *4. Sayfa* or were immensely influenced by it. The essays published therein offer clues about the emergence of the modern feminist movement in Turkey right after the 1980 coup d'état, which suppressed leftist, revolutionary, and oppositional organisations by imprisoning their members or killing their leaders. In the repressive atmosphere created by the imposition of martial law and its aftermath, women who had been persecuted by the state and were disappointed by the behaviour their male comrades came together to mobilise as feminists. In addition to publishing, feminist activism in the 1980s revolved around a range of activities, including translating feminist literature, organising awareness-raising events, protesting domestic violence and other transgressions, and fighting for equality and legal rights. Most of the women who wrote in *4. Sayfa* continued their activities with various feminist organisations, established women's studies programmes, and shaped feminist literature in the following decades in Turkey, including such figures as Şirin Tekeli, Ayşe Durakbaşa, Şule Torun, Yaprak Zihnioğlu, Gülnur Savran, Ferai Tınç, and Stella Ovadia.

Abortion was one of the most common topics women wrote about in *4. Sayfa*, often in response to a newly drafted abortion bill and its subsequent legalisation on 24 May 1983 within the framework of the Population Planning Law (*Nüfus Planlaması Kanunu*). In their writings, women critically discussed the bill and its implications, opposed perceptions and practices of abortion as a form of contraception, and, more importantly, conceptualised abortion as an issue of women's bodily autonomy.

Abortion was and still is a highly contested issue in a wide range of geographies and cultures, just like many other issues related to women and their bodies. While the patriarchal state, religion, and related institutions, as well as men, have often seen abortion as a mechanism of exercising control over women, political authorities on the other hand have often considered it to be an issue related to the population, and they have occasionally attempted to employ it as a means of population control. Similarly, when the abortion bill was first proposed by the military regime in Turkey, it sought to both legalise a common practice in society and exercise population control—as the law's name indicated—rather than improve women's lives. In the face of the ongoing global economic crises, the increasing population of Turkey was seen by the military regime as a threat to economic growth and development. The excerpt of the article presented below, which deals with those issues in particular, was written by Şule Torun, who was the editor of *4. Sayfa*.

Women Should Be in Possession of Their Own Bodies*

Recently, there have been such important developments, especially concerning women, that it would be worthwhile to set aside the history of the feminist movement and focus on those issues. In that way, the new perspectives we raise can be a good example of the alternative [perspectives] offered by feminism.

The abortion bill, in the shape and form with which it was ratified by the Health and Social Help Commission, is a big step forward in the "legitimisation" of abortion under certain conditions. According to a statement issued by the Ministry of Health, "Abortion will be carried out at locations allocated by the state." The medical staff at state hospitals are to offer this service to all women for free (or for a small fee), so long as the baby is not older than ten weeks. The first question that should be asked is whether the infrastructure to provide this service has been properly established. [...] Another question, which might lead to a confrontation of doctors and women, concerns who is going to be accountable for making sure that the service is indeed carried out under appropriate hygienic conditions and free of charge. But what assurances will be made to ensure that women undergoing this procedure—both during the process and afterwards—are not treated badly, humiliated, and frowned upon? These issues also need to be considered.

Whose body is it?

Above all, women face another vital problem that is related to being human. It is indeed a problem women have with their bodies which surfaces in its most concrete form in the context of abortion. [...] A woman and her body are a unit that cannot be isolated from one another, that cannot be perceived separately. When we talk about a woman, we talk about an anatomical structure (her body). Therefore,

---

* Translated from the original Turkish in Şule Torun, "Kadın Bedeninin Sahibi olmalıdır," *Somut*, 11 February 1983, 4, in *Yazko-Somut 4. Sayfa: İlk Feminist Yazılar: 30. Yıl Kitabı* (Ankara: Kadın Kültür İletişim Vakfı, 2013), 115–16.

even the smallest intervention in a woman's body, and this could be anything from harassment to murder or abortion, is an intervention into herself, her personality, her identity. Now, what does the bill state? "To receive an abortion, a woman needs the permission of her husband." What we have here is a double intervention. First, the reference to a "husband" assumes that the status of being married is the norm and allows for the abortion of an unwanted child only in the case of wedlock. This is an outdated perspective which criminalises or disregards all forms of extramarital sexual intercourse and dismisses the problems that might result from such a relationship [...].

Another problem

The second issue is that women and women alone should possess all the rights to their body. (Actually, it is incorrect to phrase it as "should," because they already do, in light of the explanation above). This bill could trample on that principle by giving such rights to the husband. Birth has an indirect physiological and psychological impact only on the mother. It is only the woman who carries the baby in her belly for nine months, who undergoes all the subsequent biological and psychological changes, who may suffer and possibly get sick, and who eventually will give birth and suffer labour pains, with the possibility of death being ever present. How could it be left to the husband's discretion whether a woman wants to go through all that? Is this a humane perspective? Moreover, it is (traditionally) the woman who primarily takes care of the baby after giving birth. It should be completely up to the woman whether she wants to carry such a burden and responsibility, not her husband. [...]

***

Many women who took part in revolutionary leftist organisations had disappointing experiences as a result of the gender-based discriminatory practices that were prevalent in the revolutionary leftist organisations as well as the patriarchal behaviour of their male comrades and significant others, as they have repeatedly mentioned in their writings, memoirs, and oral histories. While such organisations either ignored women's problems in general or ideologically postponed them, saying they would be solved after the revolution had succeeded, men single-handedly made decisions, occupied positions of leadership, and in doing so took advantage of women's labour. Consequently, revolutionary women had to stick to their traditional gender roles not only in organisational activities but also in their romantic relations. Moreover, such women also had to undergo abortions, which were illegal at the time, taking sole responsibility for the procedure without the support of their organisations and families, whom they often left to engage in revolutionary activities.

At least eight articles dedicated to various aspects of abortion have been published during the three months this weekly has been in print. Taken up in light of women's previous experiences, the regular coverage of the topic of abortion in *4. Sayfa* should not simply be seen as a consequence of the ideological and political reactions of feminist women to the newly introduced abortion bill by the government, but also as a personal matter. The depth of these women's analyses, their ability to perceive and present abortion as a multifaceted phenomenon, and, more importantly, their conceptualisation of it as a matter of woman's bodily autonomy should perhaps serve as proof of their personal engagement with the subject; what is clear, however, is that they were ahead of their time when they adopted the now-popular feminist slogan, "My body, my choice."

Despite the fact that they welcomed legalisation, women have also been able to identify and critique the government's motivation and its authoritarian and patriarchal implications for women's bodies. Moreover, Torun and others have discussed abortion in a sophisticated manner without romanticising motherhood or shying away from opposing conventional convictions forbidding premarital or unmarried sex. Having dared to question social, religious, and cultural values, as well as the objectives of the political authorities on such a sensitive topic, Torun's piece, together with the other writings on abortion in *4. Sayfa*, showcase these women's courage and confidence despite the repressive military regime that was in power in the early years of their activism.

***

The feminist movement in Turkey has achieved numerous successes since the 1980s in terms of attaining greater legal, social, and cultural equality. These achievements have been the result of their regular publications, mobilisation, and organised activities, which gained momentum after the 1980 coup d'état and have increased ever since. At a time when political and social opposition in the form of demonstrations and protests on the streets was banned, the feminist movement was still able to organise a "March against Domestic Violence" in 1987, and by 1990, they opened the first of many women's shelters known as the Purple Roof (*Mor Çatı*). Various women's organisations and initiatives have lobbied and fought for legal and political measures to address pressing problems such as child marriage, domestic violence, and femicide. Despite everything and their years of activism, however, feminist and women's movements in Turkey are still far from achieving the majority of their goals, even as the Republic of Turkey marks the one-hundredth anniversary of its founding. Moreover, the threat of losing their rights and seeing their achievements taken away remains a real one, especially under the rule of the conservative and authoritarian government.

Torun's piece on abortion is important for a number of reasons. First, it is a testimony to the intellectual capacity and courage of feminist activists in the first years of their endeavours under the military regime. It is also symbolically significant at a time when attempts to curtail women's rights in general and the right to abortion in particular are more present than ever. Ever since then-prime minister Recep Tayyip Erdoğan (1954–) proclaimed that abortion is "murder" in 2012, women have had difficulty accessing free and safe abortions at public hospitals; the only reason that Erdoğan's government has to date been unable to ban abortions is that the feminist movement has relentlessly organised protests and voiced their opposition under the banner "abortion is a right and the decision belongs to women". This is an especially significant achievement given the unfortunate rise of anti-abortion politics and policies in a number of countries around the world.

Select Bibliography

Atay, Hazal. "Kürtaj Yasasının Arkeolojisi: Türkiye'de Kürtaj Düzenlemeleri, Edimleri, Kısıtları ve Mücadele Alanları." *Fe Dergi* 9, no. 2 (2017): 1–16.

Aytaç [Torun], Şule N. "Somut 4. Sayfa Fikriyatı: Türkiye'de Yeni Feminizmin Doğuşu." In *Modern Türkiye'de Siyasi Düşünce Cilt 10: Feminizm*, edited by Feryal Saygılıgil and Nacide Berber, 104–110. İstanbul: İletişim, 2020.

Berktay, Fatmagül. "Has Anything Changed in the Outlook of the Turkish Left on Women?" In *Women in Modern Turkish Society: A Reader*, edited by Şirin Tekeli, 250–62. London: Zed, 1995.

Çakır Kılınçoğlu, Sevil. "The Radicalization of the Left in Turkey and Iran in the 1970s and a Comparative Analysis of Activist Women's Experiences." PhD thesis, Leiden University, 2019.

Talay Keleşoğlu, Birsen. "Yalnızlıktan Meşruiyete… 1980 Sonrası Kadın Hareketi ve Kurumsallaşma." In *Modern Türkiye'de Siyasi Düşünce, Cilt 10: Feminizm*, edited by Feryal Saygılıgil and Nacide Berber, 148–57. İstanbul: İletişim, 2020.

Zihnioğlu, Yaprak. "Türkiye'de Solun Feminizme Yaklaşımı." In *Modern Türkiye'de Siyasi Düşünce. Cilt 8: Sol*, edited by Murat Gültekingil, 1108–45. İstanbul: İletisim Yayınları, 2007.

63
A Challenge to the Military Junta:
The Petition of Intellectuals

Cangül Örnek

On 12 September 1980, soldiers emerged from their barracks and took over city streets and squares, imposing an absolute silence on mass politics. Chief of Staff General Kenan Evren (1917–2015), who addressed the nation on state radio that morning, claimed that the armed forces had taken control of the country to protect the Republic of Turkey from "anarchy" and "chaos". In doing so, he was trying to present the military as a saviour that would end years of bloody political violence, which had in fact also been instigated by state security forces. Under the leadership of General Evren, the military junta remained in power for three years, during which time Turkey bore witness to intensive state repression. In the aftermath of the coup, Parliament was dissolved, political parties were suspended, and trade unions were banned. These undemocratic measures were carried out under a countrywide state of emergency. In the absence of Parliament and political parties, the National Security Council (*Milli Güvenlik Konseyi*, NSC), which consisted of the chief of the general staff and the commanders of the land, air, and naval forces, as well as the commander of the gendarmerie, held a monopoly over the governance of political life and state affairs.

Between 1980 and 1983, the junta purged dissidents from the bureaucracy and leftist professors from universities and put tens of thousands of political activists, unionists, and intellectuals behind bars. The press was placed under tight control as numerous newspapers and magazines were shut down for long periods of time, the news was censored, and many journalists were imprisoned. All public discussion of political matters was prohibited, and that went as far as forbidding retired politicians from discussing the past, present or future.

After nearly three years of military rule under the junta, a new constitution was promulgated in 1983 which placed severe limitations on the rights and liberties of citizens, although in the same year, the path was opened to civilian politics. All the same, military generals had the power to decide which parties could take part in general elections, and politicians had to obtain permission from the NSC to run for seats in Parliament. Soon after this partial relaxation of the ban on political activities, complaints started to pile up about the conditions at detention centres and prisons. It came to light that security forces were utilising systematic torture to such an extent that some people lost their lives due to the severe physical violence they were subjected to, and there were also cases of disappearances. Many dissidents, primarily leftists, sought exile in Europe, thereby escaping the terror unleashed by the state and the brutal punishments being meted out, which included the death penalty. The state also stripped many people of their Turkish citizenship. Given the circumstances, it was very difficult to openly criticise the policies of the junta regime, let alone openly resist them.

Once Turkey had succumbed to the pressure to comply with the military's edicts, few incidents ruptured the silence imposed on society, but there were a few. Probably one of the most remarkable such events involved the "Petition of Intellectuals". A group of intellectuals had decided to speak out by exercising their right to petition, which was guaranteed by the constitution. The resulting petition was signed by around 1,300 intellectuals including academicians, journalists, artists, writers, doctors, and lawyers. Two delegations composed of representatives of the signatories submitted the petition to the office of the presidency and Parliament on 15 May 1984. The six-page petition proclaimed that the ongoing crisis in Turkey and its repercussions, including political terror, could only be resolved by reinstating democratic norms and rules.

The Petition of Intellectual'

The Democratic System in Turkey: Observations and Requests

Turkey is experiencing one of the worst crises of its history. Of course, all segments and strata of society and officials are responsible for this crisis. As Turkish intellectuals, we are aware of the importance and precedence of our shortcomings and responsibilities. This awareness imposes upon us the duty as well as the right to state our opinions on the transition of our society to a safe and sound order. [...]

Democracy only lives by way of its institutions and principles. If the basic institutions, concepts, and institutions of democracy are destroyed, it will be very difficult to compensate for the damage incurred. [...]

Our people deserve all the principles of human rights that are recognised in modern societies and should have them all without exception. We think it is humiliating that the guarantees for human rights in our country are now being debated in foreign countries.

The right to live and the right to live humanely are the primary objectives of our organised and social existence, and they cannot be invalidated for any reason. These rights are natural and sacred. But they only make sense if people can freely express, develop, and organise their opinions. Unlike those people who hold them up as the reason for the [current] crisis, we are of the opinion that individuals who develop novel and different ideas are necessary for social vitality. [...]

Attempting to limit the rights of citizens without valid legal rulings, fabricating crimes through indisputable and unilateral administrative actions, depriving citizens of their political rights, and making

---

* Translated from the original Turkish petition in *Aydınlar Dilekçesi Davası* (İstanbul: Adam Yayınları, 1986), 27–31.

broad accusations against certain groups will only lead to social devastation. Making membership in associations, co-ops, foundations, chambers, unions, and political parties a crime is incompatible with the rule of law. According to the prevailing understanding, it is also unlawful to treat thoughts that were not considered a crime at the time of their disclosure as illegal acts. [...]

In light of all these issues, as [individuals who are] aware of our responsibilities towards Turkish society, we believe that despite the differences in how it is implemented given the particular circumstances of each country, modern democracy has an invariable essence. Our nation also embraces the institutions and principles that comprise this essence. Legal regulations and practices that contradict this essence must be abolished democratically. We sincerely believe that only in this manner can we get through this crisis safe and sound.

***

Following lengthy discussions, the petition was drafted by a group of intellectuals that included Aziz Nesin (1915–1995), Hüsnü Göksel (1919–2002), Uğur Mumcu (1942–1993), İlhan Selçuk (1925–2010), Bahri Savcı (1914–1997), Halit Çelenk (1922–2011), Haluk Gerger (1948–), Murat Belge (1943–), Emin Değer (1927–2018), Yakup Kepenek (1937–), Mahmut Tali Öngören (1931–1999), İlhan Tekeli (1937–), Şerafettin Turan (1925–2015), Mete Tunçay (1936–), Erbil Tuşalp (1945–2020), and Yalçın Küçük (1938–). It consisted of two parts, a prologue and the main body of the petition itself.

The petition primarily critiqued anti-democratic practices in Turkey such as anti-democratic laws, the destruction of democratic institutions, and the frequent infringement of fundamental human rights and civil liberties including the right to live, the right to freedom of expression, the right to association, and the [removal of] obstacles placed before political participation. It drew attention to the ongoing erosion of the sense of justice caused by the implementation of extraordinary measures and regulations that obstructed citizens' ability to pursue justice within the system. Moreover, the petition rejected approaches that blamed the democratic system for the existence of political terror, emphasising the importance of holding to legal norms while carrying out efforts to fight terrorism. It also drew attention to the importance of freedom of the press, the autonomy of universities, and the ability to live an intellectual and artistic life free from taboos and censorship. In the petition, the intellectuals called on the government to put an end to torture and lengthy incarcerations, abolish the death penalty, and cancel scheduled executions. They emphasised that even if a given case involved terrorism, there were complex social causes underlying every crime and everyone bore responsibility for such transgressions, meaning that solutions had to be sought out at the level of the system by applying the terms of democratic rule. In that sense, the text was more than a petition, as the entire process that was involved, from its submission to the testimony that the signatory intellectuals presented before the courts, constituted a political protest and a direct challenge to the anti-democratic rule imposed by the generals.

Before sharing the content of the petition with the public and submitting it to the authorities, the signatories waited for the Council of Europe to issue a ruling concerning human rights violations in Turkey. Such a move was deemed necessary to proactively shut down any attempts to associate the intellectuals' protest with a foreign intervention. That sensitivity and awareness was also articulated in the petition and clearly stated by the signatories during subsequent trials.

The "Petition of Intellectuals" caused a shockwave among the public, and General Evren, the serving head of state, was quick to lash out, accusing the signatories of engaging in treason and immorality. Shortly after Evren's verbal assault, a military prosecutor brought the signatories to court on allegations that the petition was a political leaflet and, as such, they had breached the protocols of Martial Law, which forbade the distribution of printed political materials. During the subsequent court sessions, 59 signatories were tried for breaking Martial Law no. 1402.

Even before the court handed down its verdict, several state institutions passed administrative mandates designed to punish the signatories. For instance, the Council of Higher Education (*Yükseköğretim Kurulu*, YÖK), which had been founded through precepts laid out by the constitution drawn up after 12 September as a means of imposing centralised control over universities, launched disciplinary proceedings against academicians who had signed the petition, as a result of which one academician was dismissed from the university where he worked. During the trials, Aziz Nesin made it known that the national public broadcaster, the Turkish Radio and Television Corporation, had issued an order to television and radio stations forbidding them from broadcasting works by the signatories.

During the lengthy trials that ensued, the signatories gave political testimony that critiqued the anti-democratic practices and policies of the regime. Using the public judicial proceedings as an opportunity to address the Turkish public and "leave a record for history," they articulated their ideas about certain political problems, mentioning numerous cases in which the state and its security forces had violated the constitution, broken laws, and infringed on the fundamental rights of the people. Their testimony was so powerful that they even urged the authorities to request a ban on publications concerning some of the infractions that had occurred. At the end of the trials, the signatories were acquitted of the charges levelled against them.

***

When they were asked why they had written such a petition, the signatories proudly declared that they were the most recent link in a chain of a 150-year history of Turkish intellectuals suffering under the rule of autocratic leaders yet still resisted and held out against tyranny. In their testimony, they made references to the struggles of the Young Ottomans and the Young Turks as they fought back against autocracy, citing that tradition as their inspiration for defending the rights of the Turkish people. They believed that it was their historical obligation to raise their voices against oppression and that by doing so they would be remembered with gratitude by future generations, and the connection they thus drew between the past, present, and future was strongly articulated. That temporal emphasis was important to them, as it was an indication of the ephemerality of the regime of 12 September with its executioners and guardians. Nevertheless, the intellectuals were alarmed by the fact that the regime was causing a great deal of harm to the country's democratic norms and institutions, which would have long-lasting effects.

In contrast to the left-wing politics of the pre-coup era, the petition made clear references to universal human rights. In the 1970s, human rights were at the top of the European political agenda, but they did not become a widespread political matter in Turkey until the 1980s. The "Petition of Intellectuals," by emphasising human rights violations and presenting a robust defence of the universal nature of rights and liberties, signalled that the issue would become an essential topic of political opposition starting in the 1980s. The fact that Turkey continued to be a country in which citizens faced numerous obstacles in terms of exercising their right to freedom of expression and the right to petition the government meant that human rights would go on being a pressing matter of concern. The most recent incident demonstrating that this is indeed the case was the petition of the Academics for Peace, which centred around the slogan, "We will not be a party to this crime." Originally signed by 1,128 academics and released in January of 2016, the petition and its signatories came under attack by government authorities, including President Recep Tayyip Erdoğan (1954–), who accused the academics who signed the petition of engaging in treasonous behaviour and terrorist propaganda. In the months that followed, a crackdown on the Academics for Peace led to the dismissal of numerous academicians from their university positions. Hundreds of academics faced judicial investigation, and some were even detained or arrested. This incident once again demonstrated that feeling a sense of responsibility towards society, even at great personal risk, continues to be a deep-rooted trait among Turkish intellectuals.

Select Bibliography

Ahmad, Feroz. "Military Intervention and the Crisis in Turkey." *MERIP Reports*, no. 93 (January 1981): 5–24.
Aydınlar Dilekçesi Davası, İstanbul: Adam Yayınları, 1986.
Baser, Bahar, Samim Akgönül, and Ahmet Erdi Öztürk. "'Academics for Peace' in Turkey: A Case of Criminalizing Dissent and Critical Thought via Counterterrorism Policy." *Critical Studies on Terrorism* 10, no. 2 (2017): 274–296.
Küçük, Yalçın. *Aydın Üzerine Tezler-4*. Ankara: Tekin Yayınları, 1986.
"1383 İmzanın Öyküsü." *Nokta* 2, no. 14 (May 1984).

64
The Intersection of State and Religion: National Unity and Religion on Television

Güldeniz Kıbrıs

The first issue of the *Diyanet Gazetesi* (*Gazette of the Directorate for Religious Affairs*), a biweekly publication, was released in 1968. With its sample khutbas, sermons, and articles about everyday politics, it was one of the means by which the state-established Directorate for Religious Affairs (*Diyanet İşleri Başkanlığı*, commonly referred to as the Diyanet) fulfilled its constitutional monopolistic role in regulating the production and reproduction of religious knowledge. In that sense, the Turkish state has never taken a neutral position with respect to religion. Instead, it has intervened and controlled religion in order to eliminate opposing voices that could potentially threaten national unity and integrity.

The early Republican elite attempted to minimise Islam's role in institutional and cultural life through a series of radical reforms such as the abolition of the Caliphate, the unification of education, and the closure of religious orders. In 1924, the Directorate for Religious Affairs was founded and authorised to oversee "all issues concerning the Exalted Islamic Faith which relate to beliefs and rituals of worship". The head of the Diyanet was appointed by the president upon the recommendation of the prime minister. Over time, Islamic elements became much more articulated in the political sphere as elites had to reconsider their radical policies due to a public backlash, in addition to fears of communism and the possible revival of religious orders that went underground. In the 1940s, elective courses about religion became part of elementary and secondary school curricula and seminaries were opened to educate preachers. Moreover, in order to maintain this monopoly on the production of knowledge, a Faculty of Divinity was established as part of Ankara University. In 1950, various subunits of the Diyanet were reorganised, to which the administration of places of prayer was assigned. Meanwhile, readings of the Qur'an started to be broadcast on state radio three times a week in the original Arabic, new mosques were constructed, and the sale of religious literature was made easier.

Both the 1960 and 1980 coup d'états enlarged the Diyanet's role in the political sphere by way of new roles that were assigned to it. After the military intervention of 27 May 1960, the Diyanet was inscribed in the constitution and was given the role of "enlightening the population with regards to religion" through sermons, khutbas, publications, and replying to questions about Islam, and the High Council for Religious Affairs and other new departments were established. The 1960s also witnessed the rise of explicitly Islamist political movements as the constitution of 1961 extended political rights, including freedom of expression. In the

1970s, Turkey was struggling with ethnic, sectarian, and ideological polarisations that were also magnified by a severe economic downturn caused by the 1973 oil crisis and migration from rural to urban areas. When the Turkish military again seized political power through the coup d'état of 1980, the opposition was silenced. In order to protect the unity and integrity of the nation, the military sought to adopt a policy of creating a "controlled" Islam in line with the "Turkish-Islamic synthesis," which considered the Sunni interpretation of Islam to be a means of unifying the Turkish nation against Kurdish and leftist movements. Within this framework, compulsory religious education was introduced at public schools and Qur'an courses were expanded. Since the constitution of 1982 tasked the Diyanet with the protection of national unity and solidarity, it was empowered to boldly engage in discourses pertaining to a wide array of matters about everyday life. The excerpts below are from an interview with Prof Talat Koçyiğit (1927-2011), who served as dean of the Faculty of Divinity at Ankara University. Published in the November 1984 issue of the *Diyanet Gazetesi*, the interview covers questions about the effects of television and television broadcasting in terms of raising a pious generation who would be ideal citizens conforming to the Turkish-Islamic Synthesis.

*Religious Broadcasts on Television**

TV ... has the greatest influence and power of indoctrination over audiences.... It is easily possible to educate societies in the desired direction through this medium. However, in our country, the broad influence and power of indoctrination of TV has not been properly utilised, and nothing has been achieved in [terms of] bringing a sense of national unity and solidarity to the people or bringing it to a superior moral level. No sane person could deny that religious and moral broadcasts will play the greatest role in achieving this. They ... were not given due importance and a fifteen or twenty-minute view of a mosque accompanied by a few words, squeezed in for show between weekly TV broadcasts, were deemed sufficient.

Our Constitution, by saying, "Everyone has freedom of conscience, religious belief and conviction" allows for the fulfilment of the requirements of religion regarding faith, worship, and morality; with the statement, "Religious and moral education and training is carried out under the supervision and control of the State," it has been pointed out that the necessary opportunities will be provided to those who want to receive this education and training, and ... this education and training depends on the will of the people.

Despite these clear and definite provisions of our constitution ... it should be noted with regret that people's consciences have been damaged by being pressured by various media organs as well as by TV, and people have been raised as if they do not need religious education and training; on the contrary, consider it a medieval remnant ... their conscience has not been set free... Until yesterday, beer advertisements by different companies were broadcast on TV numerous times ... and the Muslim

* Translated from the original Turkish in *Diyanet Gazetesi*, 30 November 1984, 3-4

people were encouraged to drink beer through various visual and sound games... On the other hand, only five or ten minutes a week ... [did] a TV speaker say that alcohol is forbidden in Islam. There are many programs ... such as TV series, movies, [and] provocative, half-naked images of dancing [...] that erase the sacredness of the family from the minds of the new generations and attract young people to the charms of sex life. In the face of these, religious and moral broadcasts remain weak, and the youth, who are tempted by a commercial they watched before that broadcast begins, do not even pay attention to religious and moral advice.

[...]

In order for religious broadcasts on TV to be useful, it is necessary to increase the influence of these broadcasts to at least the level of non-religious broadcasts. Only if that is the case will it be possible for consciences to freely incline to the belief and life they desire in the face of the equal level of indoctrination and influence of broadcasts containing the opposite beliefs and lives.

[...]

Religious and moral programs should be created under the full authority and responsibility of a committee that would be formed by the Presidency of Religious Affairs and the Faculty of Theology.

[...]

Films that teach Islam and inculcate Islamic faith and superior morality should be created and broadcast on TV. In order to make such films, financial support could be provided by a number of charitable institutions, especially the Diyanet Foundation.

***

According to Prof Talat Koçyiğit, television was the most effective medium of communication due to its ability to address many people at once. It also had the potential to educate and point audiences in a certain direction. Koçyiğit argued that television had a powerful ability to indoctrinate and shape public opinion. As such, television programs held significant potential for creating a pious Turkish generation that would work to ensure national unity and integrity. Koçyiğit criticised the state of television programming and its failure to effectively utilise its influence to promote national unity, moral values, and religious education. He stated that there was not much time set aside for programs on religion on television, even during religious holidays, and that the existing ones were usually very short and therefore never sufficient to effectively convey Islamic messages. The author then suggested that religious and moral broadcasts should be accorded more importance and that a committee should be formed by the Diyanet and the Faculty of Divinity to take full authority and responsibility for the preparation of such programs. Additionally, the author proposed the creation and broadcasting of films that teach Islam and promote the Islamic faith and superior morality by means of financial support from the Diyanet. In that way, it was argued, national unity and solidarity could be ensured.

Within the political context of 1980, in which the military junta reshuffled the entirety of society with the aim of creating social unity and obedience, the role assigned to the Diyanet involved controlling and enlightening society, which had the potential to be indoctrinated by radical elements, by teaching "true" Islam. The Diyanet more or less assumed the task of managing or governing religion in the name of national unity and solidarity. Through propagation and indoctrination, it reiterated the official ideology while eliminating different interpretations that had the potential to disturb the state of equilibrium. This is not, however, the simple utilisation of religion by the state to justify political aims. Instead, it implies a blurring of the boundaries between the political and religious, leading to an expansion of the role of Sunni Islam in the political sphere. In this regard, other articles and content in the *Diyanet Gazetesi* help complete the picture. Sample khutbahs emphasised national values and unity, creating an outline of the responsibilities of good citizens, such as "Paying Taxes is a Very Important Duty for the Citizenry," "Let's Hold to Our National and Religious Traditions," "Increase Production, Avoid Luxury and Waste," and the importance of "Savings and Energy." As such, the *Diyanet Gazetesi* was more than just a tool of the official ideology, it was a significant organ of the state that justified state policies and discourses within a religious framework. Secularism was thus sacrificed to create "ideal and acceptable citizens" who were loyal to the state ideology and would serve the ends of national unity and integrity. This represented a shift in the approach of the state away from an emphasis on religion as part of the private realm towards its increased presence in the public domain.

***

The French notion of *laïcite* is commonly taken to be the core model of Turkish secularism in terms of its emphasis on the complete separation of state and religious affairs. To this end, the constitutions of 1961 and 1982 did not officially endorse religion. However, despite the absence of an official state religion in the constitution, Islam has always been favoured as the de facto state religion. Therefore, on the one hand, the Turkish state engaged in imposing strict secular policies and limiting the role of religion in the public realm. On the other hand, religion was incorporated into the state to assist in the creation of national unity and to provide legitimacy to the regime. Given that situation, rather than endorsing a complete erasure of Islam from public life, political elites monopolised the production and spread of religious knowledge. Within that context, the Directorate of Religious Affairs played a crucial role in reproducing that specific form of Islam and adopting it to produce and reproduce the state ideology and suppress alternative voices with the goal of creating citizens who were loyal to the state. All of these issues paved the way for a strengthening of Islam as a key factor in Turkish politics as opposed to a pluralistic understanding of democracy. Over time, Islam has become much more visible in the political realm and eventually it captured the main avenues of politics in Turkey.

Starting in 2002, when the Justice and Development Party (*Adalet ve Kalkınma Partisi,* AKP) came to power in Turkey, the Diyanet underwent certain changes. First of all, it acquired more economic power, and as it took on an increasing number of employees, it grew in size, becoming a much larger institution than before. Bureaus of Religious Guidance for Families were established at muftis' offices in various towns and cities, and with the Religious Services Development Project, the Diyanet also started to work to make imams and other religious officials much more accessible so they could provide religious guidance to society. Thus, the Diyanet now plays a more active role in assisting in state politics and developing activities the aim of which is to make it more deeply embedded in everyday life. As such, it has become one of the major state institutions to adopt a new "national" understanding of Islam and at the same time it has been actively involved in reorganising relations between the state, religion, and the market in accordance with conservative neoliberal demands, as a consequence of which it has come to constitute a hindrance to the further democratisation of the country.

Select Bibliography

Azak, Umut. *Islam and Secularism in Turkey: Kemalism, Religion and the Nation State.* London: I. B. Tauris, 2000.

Bardakoğlu, Ali. "The Structure, Mission and Social Function of the Presidency of Religious Affairs (PRA)." *The Muslim World* 98, no. 2/3 (2008): 173–81.

Cizre, Ümit, ed. *Secular and Islamic Politics in Turkey: The Making of the Justice and Development Party.* New York: Routledge, 2008.

Davison, Andrew. "Turkey, a 'Secular' State? The Challenge of Description." *The South Atlantic Quarterly* 102, no. 2/3 (2003): 333–50.

Gözaydın, İştar. "A Religious Administration to Secure Secularism: The Presidency of Religious Affairs of the Republic of Turkey." *Marburg Journal of Religion* 11, no.1 (2006): 1–8.

Mardin, Şerif. "Religion and Secularism in Turkey." In *The Modern Middle East: A Reader,* edited by Albert Hourani, Philip S. Khoury, and Mary C. Wilson, 347–74. London: I.B. Tauris, 1993.

65

"The United States Will Be Buying
our Textile Exports!":
Özal, Reagan, and Neoliberalism

Howard Eissenstat

In the long period of time between Adnan Menderes (1899–1961), who was executed in the aftermath of the military intervention of 28 May 1960, and Recep Tayyip Erdoğan (1954–), whose party came to power in 2002, arguably no Turkish political leader has made as large an imprint on Turkish politics—or garnered as much controversy—as the short, stout, imperious Turgut Özal (1927–1993), who led Turkey first as prime minister from 1983 to 1989 and then as president from 1989 until his death in 1993. Özal's time in office represents a transition from the Cold War dynamics and preoccupations of Turkish politics to the tumultuous transitions of the post-Cold War era. Despite the clear Western orientation of Özal's own foreign policy, it should come as no surprise that the contemporary Justice and Development Party (*Adalet ve Kalkınma Partisi*, AKP) claims him as one of their own; in many ways, he presaged key components—such as the prominence of Islam in the public sphere, the embracing of markets, corruption, and international ambitions—that would become hallmarks of the AKP's rule after 2002.

Like most of the leading figures of Turkish politics in the second half of the twentieth century, particularly on the centre-right, Özal was a child of the provinces who made good. He was born to a middle-class family from the provinces; his mother was a primary school teacher and his father was a minor bank official. Özal excelled at school and earned a spot at İstanbul Technical University, where he studied electrical engineering, graduating in 1950. After a brief stint studying in the United States, Özal returned to Turkey, did his military service, and entered the state bureaucracy. Özal was part of a powerful consort of conservative politicians who graduated from the same university with engineering degrees and then went on to study abroad: His frequent political rival, Süleyman Demirel (1924–2015), graduated from the same university in 1949 and went to the US for post-graduate studies; the leader of political Islam at the time, Necmettin Erbakan (1926–2011), graduated in 1948 and went to Germany to pursue a PhD. After his return, Özal took up a position in the State Planning Organisation (*Devlet Planlama Teşkilatı*, DPT) and, in the following years, he spent most of his time in the upper echelons of the state bureaucracy, along with a stint at the World Bank from 1971–1973. An early sign of his political ambitions—and his rightward trajectory—was his campaign in 1977 to serve as a member of Parliament representing İzmir under the banner of Erbakan's National Salvation Party (*Milli Selamet Partisi*, MSP), a predecessor to today's AKP and other parties of the religious right. Özal's real success in politics, however, came through the 1980 military coup, which closed down the MSP and other major parties and banned their leadership. The general-turned-president, Kenan Evren (1917–2015), picked Özal to be deputy prime minister in charge of economic affairs from 1980 to 1982, when Özal resigned in order to seek office himself.

Taking advantage of the political vacuum created by the coup, Özal led the creation of a new political party, the Motherland Party (*Anavatan Partisi*, ANAP), which promised to unify the centre right and came to dominate politics for the next decade. In the 1983 election, with the major parties of the previous era still closed down and their leaders banned from politics, Özal was able to win a comfortable victory by positioning himself as being sufficiently safe for the military and sufficiently independent of the military for a public that had quickly grown tired of its excesses in power.

When Özal took office, Turkey's relations with the United States were its most important foreign relation and particularly fraught as well. After Turkey's invasion of Cyprus in 1974—a move that was wildly popular across the political spectrum in Turkey—the United States had imposed an arms embargo that lasted from 1975–1978. The period after the 1980 coup d'état provided a certain amount of warming for US-Turkish relations, in part because Ankara and Washington shared concerns regarding both the dangers of world communism and the recent Islamic Revolution in Iran. Still, distrust remained, particularly in the Turkish military, which had been stunned by what it saw as the disloyalty of the United States on the Cyprus issue and the calumny that it saw in US pressure to curb Turkey's opium trade. Özal evinced no such ambiguity. He saw the West as clearly ascendant and saw Turkey's own ascendency, particularly in those first years, as being contingent upon working with—and modelling itself after—the neoliberal wave that so fully shaped his time in office.

In the excerpt below, then-Prime Minister Özal reports to Parliament about his recent trip to the United States (in April 1985), where he was just beginning his eventually warm relationship with US President Ronald Reagan (1911–2004) and advocating for economic opportunities for Turkish manufacture abroad. The image is from a meeting he held with Reagan during that visit.

Özal reports to Parliament on his recent state visit the United States*

"Reagan and Ozal at the White House, April 1985." Provided by the Reagan Library.

If you will now permit, I'd like to present to you one or two parts of what President Reagan said in the Rose Garden.

In one part he said, "Mr. Prime Minister, you have every right to be proud of your success in restoring democracy and giving a new impetus to economic development. Taking control of a difficult international debt problem, you have opened your country to wide-ranging [opportunities] for trade and industrial development. Turkey's economic reform program reflects your courage and far-sightedness and shows the determination of the Turkish people. I understand and appreciate the sacrifices your citizens have made in this difficult but essential undertaking."

In another section he said, "Until recently, most Americans recognised Turkey as a NATO ally. But Mr. Prime Minister, thanks to your leadership and the forward-thinking policies you are following, we are now starting to get to know your country better as a trading partner and the great opportunities it offers in the fields of finance and investment." Later, [he said], "Turkey is a physical bridge between Europe and Asia and provides us with a special viewpoint. The Ottoman Empire handled Eastern and

* Translated from original Turkish in İrfan Neziroğlu and Tuncer Yılmaz, eds., *Başbakanlarımız ve Genel Kurul Konuşmaları*, vol. 8 (Ankara: Türkiye Büyük Millet Meclisi, 2014), 279–80.

Western affairs well, long before Europe recognised America. Today, as in the past, Turkey is a very important diplomatic and cultural bridge between the East and the West."

Distinguished Deputies, I will also quickly read part of the telegram we received today from the Washington Embassy: "US Department of Commerce officials report that, as of today (8 April), they are removing the compensatory tariff applied to our textiles and ready-made clothing..."

From now on the USA will be... (applause from the ANAP seats)

From now on the USA will be buying our textile exports....

***

The text above highlights three key elements of Özal's time in leadership: the embracing of neoliberalism as key to Turkey's resurgence; Özal's efforts to ensure that Turkey would play a larger role on the world stage; and, his reliance on warm relations with the West to do so. He prided himself on his personal relationship with Reagan and also with the British prime minister, Margaret Thatcher (1925–2013). For their part, the two seemed to think highly of him. Reagan, writing in his own diary on 2 April 1985 after the meeting, recalled, "We got along fine better [sic] than I could get along with the P.M. of Greece [Andreas Papandreou]."

In a sense, Özal was the right man for the right time. His time in office corresponded to the rise of neoliberalism in the world, and Özal oversaw Turkey's embracing of the moment. Özal's speech after his return from the US represents a core element of this transformation, which was defined by his warm reception in Washington. "Trade, not Aid" was the hallmark of Özal's policy, and textiles, the production of which allowed Turkey to leverage its relatively cheap labour costs, were an early driver for a more export-focused economy. Positioning Turkey as both a local power and a global player (and hoping to mollify European concerns about a Muslim majority country applying to the European Union), Turkey increasingly framed itself as "a bridge between East and West".

Economically and culturally, Turkey opened up to the world during this period, but the influence of the United States as a cultural model was particularly significant. He facilitated the establishment of private radio and television stations, and the DJs on some channels would announce Michael Jackson songs with exaggerated American accents. Turgut Özal's son, Ahmet, was one of the founders of the country's first television channel. Consumer culture and conspicuous consumption became woven into Turkish popular culture in ways that would have been anathema to an earlier generation. Credit cards were first introduced in 1988, a year before Özal took office as president, and they became popular to an unprecedented degree among the growing urban middle strata of society during his decade in office.

**

Özal saw himself as a peer to, and of common mind with, the dominant Western leaders of the era, Reagan and Thatcher. His embracing of those figures and the warm relationship he enjoyed with them was emblematic both of his era and the transformations that Turkey experienced in the late 1980s and in the 1990s, a period of time in which Turkey shifted from an economic policy that was dominated by an autarkist emphasis on self-reliance to a market-oriented economy that provided ample room for growth. In 1987, Turkey applied for full membership in the European Union. During the early years of Özal's first term in office, Turkish citizens still largely lived in a national economy; however, by the time he died in 1993, foreign goods, foreign music, and foreign ideas were evident everywhere, and Turkey was playing a much larger role, both economically and politically, in the region.

Özal has enjoyed a reputation, post hoc, as a liberal reformer, but, in fact, he was sometimes half-hearted in the political liberalisation that is often associated with him. He famously reminded audiences that he was "part Kurdish" (his mother, Hafize, reportedly had Kurdish roots) and spoke of a "Kurdish reality" in opposition to the state's denial of Kurdish language and ethnicity, but these nods to Kurdish identity did not extend far. He did not oppose the military's free reign to pursue perceived enemies, and torture and excessive violence against civilians were hallmarks of Turkey's campaign against leftists and the burgeoning Kurdish separatist movement of the era.

If Özal is sometimes remembered as a "Westerniser," that was largely because he saw the West as ascendant at a time when the Soviet Union lumbered from stagnancy to collapse. At home, he provided greater opportunities for expressions of religion and oversaw a dramatic expansion of mosques in the country. Özal worked closely with Western leaders and sought to place Turkey more fully in Western structures, but he was equally anxious to broaden Turkey's economic and political ties with the Middle East and, after the collapse of the Soviet Union, with former Soviet republics in the Caucasus and Central Asia, particularly those with cultural ties to Turkey. Özal, no less than Turkey's current leadership, expressed hope that Turkey would step forward as one of the world's great powers.

If the shifting global context has changed the tenor of Turkey's ambitions, the ambitions themselves—and the emphasis on manufacturing to achieve them, so much a part of Özal's term in office—remain central to Turkish national ambitions to this day.

Select Bibliography

Dağı, İhsan. "Human Rights, Democratization, and the European Community in Turkish Politics: The Özal Years, 1983–1987." *Middle Eastern Studies* 37, no. 1 (2001): 17–40.

Gümüş, Tezcan. *Turkey's Political Leaders: Authoritarian Tendencies in a Democratic State.* Edinburgh: Edinburgh University Press, 2023.

Önis, Ziya. "Turgut Özal and his Economic Legacy: Turkish Neo-Liberalism in Critical Perspective." *Middle Eastern Studies* 40, no. 4 (2004): 113–134.

Wuthrith, F. Michael. *National Elections in Turkey: People, Politics, and the Party System.* Syracuse: Syracuse University Press, 2016.

66

The Intellectuals' Hearth: A Republican Generation?

Zeynep Bursa-Millet

The Intellectuals' Hearth (*Aydınlar Ocağı*) was an influential right-wing political club that was active in the 1970s and 1980s in Turkey. Two themes often linked to the Intellectuals' Hearth are the coup d'état of 12 September 1980 and the ideology of what became known as the Turkish-Islamic Synthesis (*Türk-İslam Sentezi*). The coup of 1980, widely considered the most violent in Turkey's history of military interventions, came after a decade of tumultuous civil conflict, during which Turkish right-wing groups became considerably stronger through the support of the state. That ideological "synthesis," which defines Sunni Islam as an essential element of Turkish identity, has been defined as the official state ideology that the military regime adopted after the coup of 1980. Within that context, the members of the Intellectuals' Hearth are often presented as the ideologues or theorists of that new state doctrine. Although the most important members of the club were not active in politics, they maintained a privileged position as the "philosopher kings" of the Turkish Right and had a ubiquitous presence in politics, culture, and matters of the economy. The success of the association lay in its capacity to restore the authority of the Turkish state by reformulating its semi-official ideology and providing the intellectual impetus for a series of major reforms.

The emergence of the Intellectuals' Hearth can be explained by the extremely tense and polarised political context that existed at the time. The group presented itself within the framework of the reactions of conservative intellectuals to the movement of 1968 that arose in Turkey and elsewhere in the world. Turkey was not spared the turbulent global political climate of the 1960s and 1970s, which were marked by Cold War tensions and large-scale popular uprisings. It was within that political climate that the Intellectuals' Hearth was founded and held itself up as a solution to the perceived dangers of "anarchy," "cultural chaos," and "the threat of communism." The members of the club asserted that they were seeking out a programme of action and a nationalist-religious theory that would "save the country."

Comprised mainly of university professors, the Intellectuals' Hearth originally had 63 members who hailed from the various political factions of the Turkish Right. As an association, in the 1970s the Intellectuals' Hearth remained relatively small and essentially consisted of a close circle of right-wing intellectuals. It brought together activists and sympathisers from the three main currents in the Turkish Right: ultranationalism, Islamism, and the centre right. All of its members were known for being experts in their respective fields, e.g., history, economics, art, architecture, and medicine. They used their expertise to incorporate

"Turkish-Islamic values and ideas" into their respective political, intellectual, scientific, and economic areas of specialty. The political and intellectual activities of the Intellectuals' Hearth's spanned a period spanning more than two decades. In the 1970s, as its programme of action and networks expanded, members mobilised their cultural capital and interpersonal connections to act together in political life, and in the 1980s, the political ideas of the club became part of the official state ideology.

The Intellectuals' Hearth, comprised of individuals belonging to different generations, coalesced around a common collective memory and political mission. The letter presented below, which was written in 1988 by the members of the Intellectuals' Hearth, sheds light on the complex question of generations, common memory, and the political context of the 1970s and 1980s. The text was discussed during a closed meeting held by the Intellectuals' Hearth in 1988. Entitled "Analysis of the Situation," it also served as draft outline for a letter that was to be presented to Prime Minister Turgut Özal (1927–1993). While Özal was never an official member of the Intellectuals' Hearth, in the early 1970s he began participating regularly in its meetings and took part in the group's activities. Born in 1927, Özal had experienced patterns of socialisation and politicisation that were similar to those of many of the club's members, and the fact that he attended its meetings helped broaden its audience. Over time, the scope of the conferences and colloquiums put on by the Intellectuals' Hearth continued to grow, and they held gatherings at major hotels such as the Hilton, the Divan, the Intercontinental, and the Sheraton. When the Motherland Party came to power in 1983, the presence of Prime Minister Özal at Intellectuals' Hearth meetings bolstered media coverage of the club. The date of the drafting and discussion of the letter is also notable, as in 1988 several founding members of the Intellectuals' Hearth left the club, claiming it had fulfilled its mission, and from that date forward, the group began distancing itself from Özal's politics. The ostensible objective of the letter was to provide an overview of a unique era that was coming to a close.

*"One of Us": The Struggle of the Hegemony of a Generation**

We, who have gathered around an apparent and serious concern, are different representatives of the first generation of the Turkish Republic. Born in the decade after the foundation of the Republic and having been impacted by the educational policy of the Republic, we are now intellectuals who are over 50 years old. But why are we different? Because we occupy a singular place in this generation. Born as citizens of the Turkish Republic, we were able to absorb new policies and take quick action according to new precepts, while our fathers and grandfathers were born in [the era of] the Ottoman Empire. They all went to the front during the war to save the State and its order. They experienced both the melancholy and the euphoria of becoming citizens of the Republic.

* Translated from the original Turkish letter dated 1988 bearing the title "Bir Durum Muhakemesi" ("An Analysis of the Situation") from the private archive of Metin Eriş, who was the general secretary of the Intellectuals' Hearth from 1970 to 1988. He provided me with a copy of the letter during an interview I held with him on 17 July 2015 in İstanbul.

We had the opportunity to learn from our fathers, our grandfathers, and, even if there were not so many, from our teachers about the existence of another history of this country. This became our destiny and it set us apart within the first generation of the Republic. This particularity has accorded us a responsibility and a mission. We are different because we were convinced that there were other ideas and other truths than those that were taught at the Republic's schools. The Republic insisted that we turn our backs on the past and embrace "innovation" in all areas. But we were suspicious of them and our approach began to change in terms of both science and ideas.

Our generation had the strong conviction that everything had started [with the foundation of the Republic] after 1923. This generation didn't recognise or learn about the values of our past and even found them to be useless or harmful, so we were brought up as the hidden children of the Republic but thanks to God [we had] different emotions and ideas. Being different gave us a mission that came from our past and leads to our future. Our mission is still to hold onto and protect our national values. Our sensitivity to the protection of our values drove us to wade into the struggle and to militate against the other representatives of the Republican generation who chose to ignore and forget these values. We were in a difficult and complex situation. We were both excited young republicans and [members] of a pivotal generation that tried to build a bridge with the past in order to transmit our national and spiritual values to future generations. [...] This mission led [our generation] to transform our people according to a new and different model, "national culture," and to protect the identity and values of our people according to what is known as the Turkish-Islamic Synthesis.

***

The letter quoted above is the self-avowed political statement of the religious and nationalist members of the first "Republican generation," and although they were actually born decades apart from one another, the founding members of the Intellectuals' Hearth were convinced that they belonged to the same generation. The age range within the group was indeed quite broad, as indicated by the fact that forty-eight years separated the youngest member from the oldest. Osman F. Sertkaya, who was born in 1946, was an assistant at the Faculty of Arts at İstanbul University in 1970, the year when the Intellectuals' Hearth was founded; Ekrem Hakkı Ayverdi, an engineer and architect, was born in 1898. Eight older intellectuals, namely Ekrem Hakkı Ayverdi (1898–1984), Ziyaeddin Fahri Fındıkoğlu (1901–1974), Tahsin Banguoğlu (1904–1989), Nihat Sami Banarlı (1907–1974), İbrahim Kafesoğlu (1911–1984), Ekrem Kadri Unat (1914–1998), Oktay Aslanapa (1915–2013), and Mehmet Kaplan (1915–1986), were also invited to participate in the founding of the Intellectuals' Hearth, not only out of respect for their prestige, but also as a means of securing intellectual legitimacy. These "big brothers" or "masters," who adhered to different political and cultural currents of Turkish conservatism and had different fields of expertise, also symbolised a political, intellectual, and professional front in opposition to Kemalist and Marxist intellectuals. However, the vast majority of the members of the Intellectuals' Hearth were born two or three years before or five or six years after the founding of the Republic of Turkey in 1923. They constitute a generation of the Republic that was born, educated, and employed under the Republican regime. But beyond the question of age, what appears to have been decisive in their own definition of themselves as belonging to a singular generation is their shared view of Ottoman history and Kemalist projects. The text of the letter drafted by the Intellectuals' Hearth transcribes a generational understanding that was determined by notions concerning Turkish nationalism, Kemalism, and nostalgia for Islamic values, as well as the role of the youth in that history.

The question of "conflict" also emerges from such a definition of the "Republican generation," and the generation of the Intellectuals' Hearth was in obvious conflict with the Kemalist and leftist intellectuals of the time. The members of the Intellectuals' Hearth were very critical of the secularist policies that the Kemalist elite enacted in the 1930s and 1940s. Indeed, the members of the club described themselves as both the children and victims of the Republic. Like the Kemalists and leftists who were shaped by Western education and social- isation, the members of the Intellectuals' Hearth aspired to become the leading intellectuals of the Turkish nation, and at the same time they wanted to be the guarantors of national, religious, and moral values. Since they believed that intellectual and cultural life in Turkey was dominated by Kemalist and leftist intellectuals, they sought to stake out their demands for the recognition of right-wing intellectuals as well as assert their roles and legitimacy, as evidenced by the letter. Hence, within the context of that conflict, the letter indicates how the members of the club wanted to present themselves as belonging to a singular coherent generation that was laying claim to "true" Turkish culture and the Muslim faith. The historical context of the 1960s and 1970s provided the first opportunity for right-wing intellectuals to act together in an organised manner.

**

The longevity of the government of President Recep Tayyip Erdoğan (1954–), who has been in power for nearly twenty years in Turkey, has often been perceived as an enigma. However, it could be argued that Erdoğan owes his long hold on power to the Intellectuals' Hearth. Born in 1954, Erdoğan was shaped by the politics of the 1970s, a period that was marked by the Turkish-Islamic Synthesis. In order to understand the intellectual sources of the political ideology of the Justice and Development Party (*Adalet ve Kalkınma Partisi*, AKP), of which he was a founding member, it is necessary to analyse in detail the political context of the 1970s and its actors, among which the Intellectuals' Hearth played a prominent role. The funerals of the members of the Intellectuals' Hearth, which started in the 1990s and continue to the pres- ent day, are crucial for comprehending the Turkish political and intellectual heritage; while it is common knowledge that attending the funerals of members of the elite and committed intellectuals is a form of civility, it is also a political activity par excellence. In that sense, the funerals of the members of the Intellectuals' Hearth are part of a political and cultural context that facilitates the transmission of political values among the generations of the Turkish Right and also perpetuate its political legacy. Since the 1990s, Erdoğan has regularly attended the funerals of the members of the Intellectuals' Hearth successively as mayor of İstanbul, prime minister, and lastly as president of the Republic of Turkey, making sure that he always thanks its members for their contributions to his political and intellectual development.

Select Bibliography

Bora, Tanıl, and Kemal Can. *Devlet, Ocak, Dergah: 12 Eylül'den 1990'lara Ülkücü Hareket.* İstanbul: İletişim Yayınları, 1991.

Bursa-Millet, Zeynep. "Le Foyer des intellectuels. Sociohistoire d'un club d'influence de droite dans la Turquie du XXe siècle." PhD thesis, EHESS Paris, 2020.

Copeaux, Etienne. *Espaces et temps de la nation turque.* Paris: CNRS Éditions, 2020.

Fields, A. Belden. "Aperçus du problème des générations: Mentré, Ortega et Mannheim." Translated by Claudie Weill. *L'Homme et la société,* no. 111–112 (1994): 7–22.

Kurt, Ümit. "The Doctrine of 'Turkish-Islamic Synthesis' as Official Ideology of the September 12 and the 'Intellectuals' Hearth – Aydınlar Ocağı' as the Ideological Apparatus of the State." *European Journal of Economic and Political Studies* 3, no. 2 (2010): 111–25.

Taşkın, Yüksel. *Milliyetçi Muhafazakar Entelijansiya.* İstanbul: İletişim Yayınları, 2007.

67

Three Days in Bekaa Valley:
An Interview with Abdullah Öcalan

Serhun Al

If the *raison d'être* of the founding elites of the Republic was to establish a centralised nation-state based on a singular and secular Turkish national identity from the ruins of the multi-religious, multi-linguistic, and multi-ethnic Ottoman Empire, the single most and persistent challenge to this project was and has been Kurdish nationalism, which has been vibrant and ever-changing. As a counter-nation-building project with incentives for self-determination, Kurdish nationalism has survived as the antithesis of the Republican state and nation-building project steeped in ideals of Turkishness. Kurdish nationalism evolved into an anti-colonial form of nationalism with an agenda of socialist liberation during the Cold War period. The Kurdistan Workers' Party (*Partiya Karkerên Kurdistan*, PKK) was officially founded in 1978 and initiated its armed campaign in 1984 under the leadership of Abdullah Öcalan (1949–). Öcalan left Turkey in 1979 and was stationed in Syria before the heavy-handed Turkish military coup of 1980 suppressed almost all political movements in Turkey. As Öcalan found safe haven in Syria with the support of the Assad regime, he was able to prepare the PKK for armed insurgency, and its members received military training in Syria and in Lebanon's Bekaa Valley along with Palestinian liberation fighters. After this period of preparation, the PKK initiated its first armed attack in Turkey in Eruh in the province of Siirt as well as in Şemdinli in Hakkari province on 15 August 1984, in the course of which one Turkish soldier and two Turkish police officers were killed. As the PKK's militant and armed campaign expanded and gained ground in the late 1980s, investigative journalist Mehmet Ali Birand (1941–2013), who worked for the mainstream Turkish media, was one of the very few journalists to become intensely interested in understanding the Kurdish conflict, despite the state's strictly securitised policies regarding the PKK. His risky meeting with Abdullah Öcalan in 1988 in Bekaa Valley is considered to be the first one-on-one interview with Öcalan by the Turkish media. Birand's mother was from a Kurdish family (from the Palu region of Elazığ), which he interestingly found out later in his adult life. Birand was also the producer of one of the most influential and reputable television news programs in Turkey, *32. Gün* (1985–2016). Although he faced court trials because of his interview with Öcalan in 1988 for the newspaper *Milliyet*, Birand continued to investigate and seek to understand the PKK in particular and the Kurdish conflict in general until his death in 2013.

*When, Where, and How Was the PKK Founded**

We organised a demonstration in the spring of 1972 at the Political Sciences Faculty. It was the first demonstration after the 12 March [military memorandum of 1971]. We chanted "Damn Fascism". Then we were put in Mamak prison and spent around seven months there. [...] Prison was a school for me in terms of embarking on a political struggle. I met a lot of people. I witnessed their debates... In 1973, I brought around five or six people together near Çubuk Dam in Ankara. The initial steps of the PKK were taken there under a tree... Under that tree, I said that Kurdistan should be considered a colonised entity and it was a must that we approach this problem with a separate organisation and a separate group character. [...]

Unless Turkey changes its view of the Kurdish question, our armed activities will increase in the upcoming period and much blood will be shed. Our goal is not to carve out a territory from Turkey but to make Turkey gradually accept a reality. It all depends on Turkey. [...] The people who rule Turkey should discuss this issue [the Kurdish question] with a deep understanding. The state has politicians, soldiers, and civilians. They should recognise the historical facts and then place themselves in a bold and tolerant debate. If they have self-confidence, they can ready themselves for a political solution further ahead. In order to do this, freedom of association and organisation should be ensured and the suppression and use of force on the methods used in political struggles should be abandoned. We would make a truce if even limited progress could be made on these matters. Otherwise, it is clear that we will intensify our armed activities. Based on our experiences until today, whether I survive or not we have the capacity to improve these armed activities in terms of their scope and quantity due to the precautions that have been taken. We took precautions in the organisation in order to prevent any political games and plots. This is not about my personal situation. The ideological-political progress of the institution of leadership is the facilitator of this process. If one person leaves, forty others would easily come up. You see, five leave and fifty join [the organisation]. Yes, more blood would be shed. It has already begun; we will go into the cities more. Blood will be spilled on our side as well. We are ready for this too. So, I wanted to reflect this current circumstance at this moment. In a way, this is our responsibility. I must say that I am not very hopeful. We are talking in order to give such a message in this historical phase. If the situation does not change, the possibility increases that the war will expand. There will be some instances [that are] even out of our control. For instance, we could not control some of the armed attacks. We try at our full capacity not to lose control over [our] armed activities.

***

In his interview with Birand, Öcalan emphasises "the historical facts" with regard to the Kurdish question in reference to the exclusion of Kurdish identity and the suppression of Kurdish demands for self-determination that have been made since the founding of the Republic of Turkey in 1923. He invites the Turkish state and politicians to debate this issue

* Translated from the Turkish original in Mehmet Ali Birand, "İşte Apo İşte Öcalan," *Milliyet*, 16 June 1988.

by accepting this reality and coming up with democratic policies for a political rather than a military solution. In his argument, the PKK has been an outcome rather than the cause of this long-lasting problem. Before the PKK, many pro-Kurdish associations were established and Kurdish insurgencies occurred in the first half of the twentieth century, mostly organised and led by prominent members of notable Kurdish families such as the Bedirhans or Babanzades and tribal-religious figures such as Sheikh Said (1865–1925) or Pir Seyyid Rıza (1863–1937). Their ideas varied, shifting around the notions of independence, autonomy, and cultural revivalism without a strong ideological or organisational structure. In the 1950s and early 1960s, non-violent pro-Kurdish mobilisation still mostly centred around traditional elites such as Faik Bucak (1919–1966), the president of the Kurdistan Democratic Party of Turkey (*Partiya Demokrat a Kurdistanê-Tirkiye*, PDK-T), which was founded in 1965. Armed insurgencies in the early Republican era were put down by the Turkish military in a shorter span of time. In the interview, this is why Öcalan emphasises the organisational strength and mobilisation capacity of the PKK—namely, so that it can hold out against the strong Turkish military. He was planning for a long-lasting and continuous people's war rather than a single uprising. In other words, the PKK and Abdullah Öcalan represent a rupture in the long evolution of Kurdish national movements. First, the PKK emerged within the Cold War context, a period of time when a strong leftist and Marxist wave had been on the rise in Turkey, including among its Kurdish citizens, starting in the mid-1960s. In the interview, Öcalan discusses his political experiences among leftist circles in Ankara and how he arrived at the decision to found a separate organisation, one that was distinct from the Turkish left in particular. The PKK was a product of anti-colonial Kurdish nationalist discourses significantly juxtaposed with class consciousness and the idea of socialist liberation based on a long-lasting militant armed struggle. Strategically calculated political violence targeting similar rival organisations such as the National Liberationists of Kurdistan (*Rizgarîxwazen Neteweyî yen Kurdistane*, RNK) before 1980 helped the PKK gain ground in the post-1980 period. Second, Abdullah Öcalan came from a modest background as a member of a socially weak peasant family in Urfa. Öcalan's non-elite background, lacking significant tribal, sectarian, or large landowner ties, perhaps shaped his ideas not only about the socio-economic and political power hierarchies among Turkish and Kurdish communities but also within Kurdish society as well. As Öcalan discusses in the interview, instead of it being an elite-driven movement, the recruitment of peasants and ordinary citizens was important for the success of the PKK. The armed attacks that had been carried out against large Kurdish tribes, such as occurred in Siverek, had been driven by the notion that those tribes were collaborators of Turkish state repression and exploiters of landless Kurdish peasants. Öcalan and the PKK's critique and problematisation of patriarchal and tribal relations in Kurdistan later paved the way for the large-scale recruitment of peasants and women in the 1980s and 1990s. By the late 1980s, the PKK, now reinforced with thousands of militants, became a significant competitor for authority and sovereignty along the country's southeastern borders. In the interview, Öcalan states that he was not hopeful that the Turkish state would approach the problem with democratic policies and he was confident that the war would expand given the militaristic approach adopted by Turkey.

He was right about the spread of violence and war, as the 1990s became the bloodiest years of the conflict, and the PKK still exists today with a broader presence in the Middle East.

***

As the Cold War came to an end, many anti-colonial nationalist movements inspired by socialism started to vanish around the world. However, the PKK endured and expanded its influence across Iraq, Iran, and Syria with significant diaspora support in Europe as well. Öcalan's ideological flexibility and willingness to change according to new global and regional contexts perhaps helped the PKK endure. For instance, Öcalan gradually shifted the PKK's ideological position from a state-seeking socialist Kurdish movement in the 1980s and early 1990s towards a new vision of democratic confederalism that empowered the local autonomy of societies in opposition to centralised states, which became essential in the late 1990s and early 2000s. Despite the fact that he has been imprisoned on İmrali Island in Turkey since 1999, Abdullah Öcalan has remained a larger-than-life figure for many of his sympathisers as an elder wise man in prison. Today, Öcalan's PKK is no longer an organisation but more of a large network of armed organisations, NGOs, media outlets, political parties, and so forth. The peace process and dialogue that got underway between the PKK and the Turkish government under the rule of the Justice and Development Party (*Adalet ve Kalkınma Partisi*, AKP) between 2013 and 2015 was a time for hope but the process collapsed, leading to a new era of violence and war that spread to Syria and Iraq as well. Containing the PKK remains a significant challenge for Ankara, and the Turkish military continues to actively operate in Syria and Iraq to circumvent Kurdish autonomy in the region, which is perceived as a challenge to Turkey's sovereignty.

Select Bibliography

Al, Serhun. *Patterns of Nationhood and Saving the State in Turkey: Ottomanism, Nationalism and Multiculturalism*. New York: Routledge, 2019.

Connor, Francis. *Understanding Insurgency: Popular Support for the PKK in Turkey*. New York: Cambridge University Press, 2021.

Marcus, Aliza. *Blood and Belief: The PKK and the Kurdish Fight for Independence*. New York: NYU Press, 2007.

Romano, David. *The Kurdish Nationalist Movement: Opportunity, Mobilization and Identity*. New York: Cambridge University Press, 2006.

Yeğen, Mesut. *Devlet Söyleminde Kürt Sorunu*. İstanbul: İletişim Yayınları, 1999.

68
Turkish Pop:
The New Urban and Neoliberal Culture of Turkey

Kadir Dede

Turkey ushered in the 1990s in the shadow of neoliberal policies that were implemented after the coup d'état of 1980 and which are often identified with the economic strategies that were implemented by Prime Minister Turgut Özal (1927–1993). Those policies, which were consolidated in virtually all areas of life, transformed individual ideals, moral codes, and mindsets. While import-substitution industrialisation, strict foreign exchange policies, and high customs barriers were now a thing of the past, the new era presented itself as one of abundance, wealth, and diversity, even though its impacts were minimal for the lower-middle classes. Nonetheless, it was impossible for culture not to be affected by the *laissez-faire* principles that were shaping the economy. The new possibilities that arose as a consequence of the abolition of the state monopoly on radio and television broadcasting and the technological developments that occurred with the emergence of a free market enabled the rise of a form of popular culture that identified with abundance and ongoing diversification in Turkey. The pop music boom, which emerged in different ways and evolved throughout the 1990s, reinforced and became a distinctive symbol of this new cultural environment.

While music was among the fields targeted by efforts directed towards modernisation and cultural policies in the republican period, it was an exception in the sense that it remained independent of top-down practices to a certain extent. In the face of state attempts to create an East-West synthesis in music, other genres emerged that were shaped by the market, public opinion, and listeners' sense of pleasure. Those genres include Turkish Classical Music, which arose in night clubs in the 1950s, the Anatolian Pop movement of the 1960s and 1970s, and the Arabesk music movement of the 70s, all of which came into being through different types of "spontaneous synthesis". The pop music of the 1990s, on the other hand, was not only an original example of such a synthesis in terms of how quickly it drew in mass audiences, enjoyed widespread influence, and differed from the other genres because it had no connection to the rural, it also reflected an important transformation in definitions of "local" and "the people" through its lyrics, musical forms, and content.

Given the rich variety of songs and singers that were and still are a part of pop music, it is, of course, impossible to sum up the period with a single song. Nevertheless, the song "*Sakin Ol*" (Keep Calm) from 1992 was significant for a number of reasons, particularly with regard to its representation and the impacts it had on the music scene. First of all, the song was the result of a collaboration that brought together prominent figures that have constituted the cornerstone of Turkish pop from the 1990s to the present. While the lyrics were written by pop music legend Sezen Aksu (1954–) and the music was composed by the tragically deceased Uzay Heparı (1969–1994), the song was also the debut single of Sertab Erener (1964–). Moreover, unlike many singers who were one-hit wonders in the 90s, Erener has enjoyed a long and lasting career. In particular, Erener's individual story would directly intersect with processes of Westernisation that were set into motion approximately ten years later, and she would spark national excitement and pride when she won first place in the Eurovision Song Contest in 2003. Moreover, *Keep Calm* not only represents a form of music that synthesises Eastern and the Western influences, it also managed to interpret the content of the East and the West within the context of the developments and debates that arose in the 1990s.

*Sakin Ol**

Ah, what fury, what anger?!
Oh, a flurry, a hurry...
Everybody will strangle one another.
What will be our end in this way?

Some are bothered by Alaturka,
Some complain about the West,
So, what is there to get angry about?
This is just life, it goes on.

Whisht! Whisht! Keep down!
Keep your temper.
Whisht! whisht! Keep down!
Keep your temper.

Some are ashamed of lahmacun,
Some get irritated by what they come across,
Either everyone is far from one another,
Or the relationships are so conspicuous.

Some are hostile to intellectuals,
Some encourage ignorance,
What a nonsensical quarrel,
Nobody can teach anything to nobody, my dear.

* Translated from the original Turkish lyrics written by Sezen Aksu, "*Sakin Ol*," track 5 on *Sakin Ol!*, Tempa & Foneks, 1992. https://sertab.com/playlist/sakin-ol/

Whisht! Whisht! Keep down!
Keep your temper.
Whisht! Whisht! Keep down!
Keep your temper.

Oh!
Mortal life, mortal human.
Either you are learned or you are a tyrant...

Everyone's truth is the truest.
Everyone's word is wisdom.
Let's talk about ordinary things!
Is it worth it to devour each other?

It must be flawless,
We don't even have the right to make mistakes.
Everyone is in pain,
For anyone else, that's too much.

Whisht! Whisht! Keep down!
Keep your temper.
Whisht! Whisht! Keep down!
Keep your temper.

Oh!
Mortal life, mortal human.
Either you are learned or you are a tyrant.

***

An analysis of *Keep Calm*, which is a remarkable example of the rise of Turkish pop in the 90s, offers crucial insights into the connections between pop music and popular culture. Firstly, the 90s, which bore witness to a major shift in terms of political and cultural affairs in Turkey, enabled the emergence of a form of pop music that had particular political, social, and economic characteristics. The experience of those changes in Turkey, where an aristocratic culture was never disseminated to the general population in the course of the nation-building process, demonstrates the cultivation of a type of cultural content that zigzagged between imaginings of the West and the East yet failed to reach a state of equilibrium through the platforms of communication that were monopolised by the state. Given that situation, it could be argued that what was popular throughout the history of the republic mostly corresponded to the content that was broadcast by the Turkish Radio and Television Corporation (TRT) but never attracted a mass following; or, contrarily, the popularity of cultural productions that had strong mass support and generated a great deal of interest were limited by the fact that they were not represented on television or radio. However, the mobility of capital in the free market, especially in the fields of marketing and advertising, and the support provided by the Özal government made it possible for Turkish entrepreneurs to turn to private television and radio broadcasting as new areas of investment. Subsequently, the moulding of cultural life, particularly music, through state enterprises underwent major changes in processes that were shaped by the establishment of Magic Box-Star 1 as the first private television channel on 1 March, 1990 and the launch of Kent FM as the first private radio station on 4 June 1992. Only after those developments did it become possible to talk about a form of popular culture that was open to the effects of globalisation, which was part and parcel of processes of consumption influenced by commercial interests and competition that stood in sharp contrast to the constructed folk culture or official high culture that was set forth by the state. In relation to that cultural definition, pop became a kind of music that was created, disseminated, and consumed in a manner that was intertwined with new economic and technological practices.

For the first time in Turkish history, these new forms of musical production, of which *Keep Calm* is an example, coincided with an overlap between pop music and popular music. While other genres, especially Arabesk music, had enjoyed an increase in popularity, the traditions associated with the pop music of the 1990s only managed to garner a limited amount of attention under the overseership of the TRT with rather detailed yet artificial descriptions such as "light Western music with Turkish lyrics". In the 1990s, that situation would change dramatically, and with all its pros and cons, a kind of popular, up-to-date, and easily accessible pop music would take centre stage. It is clear that the genre in question developed by way of the opportunities offered by capitalist relations, reinforced one-dimensional superficiality, and was possessed of a timeless nature. However, for a period of time it had certain characteristics that reflected urban lifestyles and the cultural traits of city dwellers. In other words, it was marked by a lack of permanency, rapid consumption, and philosophical superficiality, which can be evaluated in a negative light as a way to describe the frameworks accompanying city life as well as the characteristics of the music itself.

One crucial aspect of *Keep Calm* that distinguishes the song from others of its era is how it echoed a dialectical process that occurred within the context of debates over the notion of synthesis, which had been on the country's agenda for more than a century. In the period of time leading up to the 90s, various types of "syntheses" had been enacted which drew attention in the West, such as the performance of folk songs with choirs, the playing of such folk songs with Western instruments, the use of instruments from various geographies to express local sentiments and feelings, and the use of Turkish for certain pieces. What *Keep Calm* achieved with exceptional success is an aspect that surpassed both the West and the East in terms of the point it reached and also reflected the influence and character of both imagined worlds through the lyrics and music. The lyrics in the second stanza of the song, which starts like a disco tune with rhythms created on a synthesiser, address the issue of the distinction between Turkish and Western musical styles, and from that point forward the lyrics delve into political and social matters that would normally not be expected of such enthusiastic musical render-ings in the context of the numerous topics of discussion related to issues that Turkey had been experiencing. By reflecting the pain of transition from collectivism to individualism, referring to social conflicts shaped by differences in lifestyles between the old and new residents of urban settings or reinforced by the educated-uneducated divide brought about by the new right-wing populism of the 1980s, and pointing to the state of in-betweenness created by the repressive policies of the recent past and the desire-provoking qualities of neoliberalism, the song offers a solution with its chorus. In the face of confusion and conflicts, the chorus creates a festive atmosphere drummed out in 9/8 time, in which local instruments such as the *kanun* and *darbuka* come to the fore and the lyrics emphasise the meaninglessness of conflict and the transience of the world, thereby conveying an apolitical message as well.

These qualities of *Keep Calm* are reminiscent of the unique aesthetic value and aura of products in this field, despite the criticisms that have directed at popular cultural production in general and pop music in particular. Even the term "pop music," which is often used in a pejorative sense on the basis of the claim that it is repetitive and disposable, can also show great dexterity in reflecting the behavioural patterns, sensitivities, social conflicts, and relations that predominate in a given time period. Moreover, although *Keep Calm* does not completely overcome the dichotomies shaped by the polyphonic-monophonic, local-univer-sal, artificial-natural, and dynamic-static pairings in Turkish music, it drives them into the background through a reference to the temporality of the world and mortal life.

***

The 80s were a period in which foreign exchange policies were transformed, the importation of goods was promoted, entrepreneurship and marketing were encouraged, and consumption, luxury, and vanity came into prominence as the result of the state's new economic program, and the 90s were marked by transformations in approaches to clothing styles, entertainment, holidays, transportation, and consumption in daily life—in short, the entire cultural climate underwent a major change. In addition to being a direct part of this transformation, the pop music of the era provided a unique soundtrack for these developments.

Keep Calm and the pop music of its time had a variety of impacts on the decades to come. The timing of the song's debut corresponded to the emergence of a threshold where it became possible to argue that the country was captivating and fascinating because of its geographical location between the East and the West. Turkey was approaching the West and becoming increasingly similar to Europe in the perceptions of many contemporaries. Moreover, that convergence not only applied to popular culture, as it could be observed in political develop-ments as well such as the Customs Union Agreement which was signed with the EU in 1995. Turkey's victory in the Eurovision Song Contest in 2003 with Sertab Erener's song *Everyway that I Can*, the lyrics of which were in English and the music of which was reminiscent of *Keep Calm*, especially in terms of the chorus, and the beginning of negotiations for full membership in the EU in 2005 all point to a similar, significant development in the cultural momentum of the 1990s. The repercussions of that momentum continued in the 2010s, but this time around it was in the opposite direction. Increasing authoritarianism in the political field, a notable shift away from the EU, and the diminishing of general interest in Turkish pop music took place simultaneously.

The pop movement that *Keep Calm* represents is a significant component of millennium-era nostalgia in today's Turkey. This is so much the case that in recollections of the 1990s, one of the most important reasons why issues such as the economic crisis, high inflation, corruption and nepotism, political instability, and the ongoing low-intensity war in Turkey, especially in the second half of the 1990s, can so readily be brushed aside is the music of the period and the feelings it stirs up in retrospect. The pop music of the era, which emphasised innovation, Westernisation, and dynamism in the period stretching from the 80s to the 90s, has become a major source of nostalgia given the state of oppression, authoritarianism, and anti-Westernism that has become so prominent today.

Select Bibliography

Gürbilek, Nurdan. *The New Cultural Climate in Turkey: Living in a Shop* Window. London & New York: Zed Books, 2011.

Kaptan, Yesim, and Ece Algan, eds., *Television in Turkey: Local Production, Transnational Expansion, and Political Aspirations.* Cham: Palgrave, 2020.

Karahasanoğlu, Songül, and Gabriel Skoog. "Synthesizing Identity: Gestures of Filiation and Affiliation in Turkish Popular Music." *Asian Music* 49, no. 2 (2009): 52–71.

Kozanoğlu, Can. *Pop Çağı Ateşi.* İstanbul: İletişim Yayınları, 1995.

Stokes, Martin. "Turkish Urban Popular Music." *Middle East Studies Association Bulletin* 33, no. 1 (1999): 10–15.

Ural, Haktan. "Turkishness on the Stage: Affective Nationalism in the Eurovision Song Contest." *International Journal of Cultural Studies* 22, no. 4 (2019): 519–35.

69
"Mafiacity Ümraniye":
Irregular Urbanisation and
the İstanbul *Gecekondu*

Jan-Markus Vömel

Rapid urbanisation in Turkey started in the 1950s but spiralled out of control in the 1980s post-coup era. While the first decades of the republic witnessed the slow recuperation of urban population losses caused by wars, expulsions, and genocide, steady growth from the 1950s onwards saw the urban population surpass that of rural areas by the beginning of the 1980s. The adoption of a neoliberal economic model placed the rural population under yet more strain and created conglomerations of capital in urban centres that attracted cheap labour and people seeking their fortunes in boomtowns. In the 1990s, an additional factor emerged through increasing displacements caused by the armed conflict in the predominantly Kurdish regions of the country. İstanbul's population grew from 4.7 million in 1980 to 7.3 million in 1990, and by the year 2000, that figure had reached 11 million. The authorities desperately tried to bring the growth of illegally constructed suburban shantytowns (the so-called *gecekondu*, literally meaning "put up overnight") under control, but for the most part was unable to do so. Local politicians and administrations often ended up legalising what had already been constructed as a fait accompli. On the ground, that process often took the form of lawless land grabbing along the outskirts of areas that had no developed infrastructure but were still close to established quarters. In 1992, journalist Oya Ayman Büber documented the urban sprawl in Ümraniye, a large district on the Asian side of İstanbul, for the popular weekly magazine *Tempo*.

Mafiacity Ümraniye*

Life in İstanbul's fastest-growing district is more difficult than in the Wild West...

Ümraniye was just a village until fifteen years ago. Since then, the people who came to Ümraniye settled here without regard for treasury land, forest land, or land without title deeds. Squatting and a population increase of 159 percent in five years turned Ümraniye into an illegal city. The real estate mafia sells not only land but neighbourhoods without paying heed to the land of others, the treasury,

---

* Translated from the original Turkish in Oya Ayman Büber, "Mafyakent Ümraniye," *Tempo* 5, no. 41 (14 October 1992), 32–36.

forests, title deeds, or zoning.... Almost every day a new street is added to Ümraniye. No one can put a halt to it. The only solution the mayor proposes to counter the mafias is to form gangs like them.

This is Ümraniye... It is the largest of İstanbul's suburbs and perhaps the fastest developing region in Turkey. Unfinished buildings rise up in areas that were woodlands until a few years ago. People who sell their fields in their villages buy any land they like here and start building their houses. If need be, they move into the forest and cut down trees... If need be, they erect an apartment building without stating that it is your land or his land... State lands are sold off, and even municipal buildings are rising up on treasury lands... A man comes to a neighbourhood, parcels it up, sells it, and then disappears. No one can say "stop" to this because they say "not so fast" to those who do. [...]

"I have been here for twenty-five years. We bought a place in Ihlamurkuyu. Later, I found out that it was a forest zone. The forest directorate took me to court. I dragged my feet in the courts for years and in the end, I had to pay a fine. It's always been like that in our neighbourhood."

Those words were uttered by a civil servant working for the municipality. He is also one of the victims of Sururi Yavuz, who parcelled up and sold off land in the Ihlamurkuyu neighbourhood. A few years ago, Sururi Yavuz built a hut in the forest and turned it into a real estate office, selling land to anyone who came by... But a few months ago, a ring road passing right next to the neighbourhood interrupted his business. He took their money and disappeared. The municipal official evaded our question about why they had not taken Sururi Yavuz to court: "Those are shady people, you can't touch them."

Şinasi Öktem, the mayor of Ümraniye, says the following about the land mafia: "The people who came here from the east and the Black Sea region couldn't find work. They realised that this land business was good. Those who tucked a gun into their waists became the mafia. After a while, those people became elected neighbourhood representatives, district governors, and regional governors, in short, everything. Now, if someone is going to get married or have a circumcision celebration [for their son], they ask them for help. They spare those with bloody hands [for themselves in the mafia] and send the young men off to the army.

Şinasi Öktem mentions that these people have their own sense of honour. "They do not engage in loansharking or anything like that. They are not purse snatchers either. They give money and take money. They respect the traditions and customs of the people in order to legitimise themselves."

Their work starts on Friday afternoon when the municipality's work slows down. On Saturday and Sunday, they can finish a *gecekondu* at night. On Monday the municipality may find a half-built *gecekondu* on a plot of land that was empty on Friday.

***

Büber's article emerges from straight out of the heart of the city's urban sprawl. In lively detail, it illustrates how the landgrab has been realised in practice and who is involved in carving up their slices of land—the migrants, the real estate mafia, and the local administration. Migrants, facing economic insecurity and living under the threat of eviction, are both exploited by the mafia and bound to them so they can protect the little they have from legal challenges or appeal to the mafia for charity when they lose it. Similarly, local politicians are torn between enforcing laws and regulations and their reliance on the votes of the migrant population. The scene above was followed by an interview with the godfather of the area, a man from the Black Sea region with ties to the far-right Nationalist Movement Party (*Milliyetçi Hareket Partisi*, MHP) who had served eighteen years for murder. Switching back to the mayor, the article then illustrates his struggle to keep irregular construction and mafia activities at bay. He complains about the toll this constant battle has taken on his health and, since the state is largely absent, he recommends forming an armed "counter-gang" on behalf of the municipality.

Pioneer migrants, mostly men trying their luck and seeking a modest income in the metropolis, settled in these new quarters, followed by the chain migration of families and later solidarity networks based on home regions (*hemşehri*)—all in need of cheap housing. The migrant population tended to keep one foot in their home regions, leading to a constant interchange between the metropolis and home regions and an outpouring of people during the holidays. Later on, migrants, too, were able to profit from the sprawl. As the quarters grew and developed into regular settlements, squatters from the early years were able to sell off their property to developers or build their own residential condos on top of former *gecekondu*s.

***

The 1980s and 1990s witnessed the making of contemporary urbanity in Turkey. During those two decades, a complete remake of Turkey's demographic, social, and economic structure took place. Irregular migration channelled through *hemşehri* networks brought about a stratification of quarters that emerged with the characteristic socio-demographic and even cultural profiles we see today: Black Sea people in Beykoz, Ümraniye, and many other districts; the mixed populations of old İstanbul; Kurds in several quarters in Beyoğlu, Esenyurt, Gaziosmanpaşa, and Sultangazi; Alevis in Gazi, Gülsuyu, and Okmeydanı; and other quarters with reputations for being conservative, secularist, leftist, or youth-oriented. Similarly, areas with residential, industrial, trade-based, service-focused, or entertainment- and culture-oriented profiles are often packed into specific quarters since the new districts lacked historically rooted structures catering to all of the needs of their inhabitants. Later, shopping malls popped up to substitute for that lack in the highly compartmentalised cityscape. Cheaply constructed housing, often built in blatant disregard of regulations and zoning laws, continues to be a danger for residents in this seismically active area. Another rather depressing effect of urbanisation without central planning or direction has been the emergence of densely settled districts entirely paved in concrete with few green areas in between.

From a nationwide perspective, the rampant urbanisation that has continued from the 1980s until today has meant that real estate and the construction industry have become the mainstays of the Turkish economy. Companies active in these fields have formed juggernaut holdings that branch out into other areas of the economy, forming a powerful web that included clientelist networks with politics. Construction thus became the motor of a development model that relies on unsustainable growth, feeding on ever-growing cityscapes. Such networks were made possible by a provision in the constitution of 1982, which permitted the creation of metropolitan municipalities (*büyükşehir belediyeleri*). A new political arena emerged with elected mayors who could distinguish themselves as contenders for power on the national stage. İstanbul, as the largest metropolis bearing the entire socio-cultural mosaic of the country and all kinds of cultural, social, and political cleavages, naturally came to represent the frontrunner in that regard. Islamists successfully integrated themselves into *hemşehri* networks, giving rise to conservative populism which campaigned against established urban elites, acquiring the support of migrant populations in the process. In contrast to the commonly held notion that metropolises tend to lean more towards liberal politics than the national average, Turkish metropolises have been dominated by populist Islamic conservatism. Only with the nationwide municipal elections of 2019 did this conservative sway over local politics show signs of wavering and new power dynamics surfaced.

Select Bibliography

Bora, Tanıl, ed. *İnşaat Ya Resulullah.* İstanbul: İletişim Yayınları, 2016.

Danielson, Michael N., and Ruşen Keleş. *The Politics of Rapid Urbanization: Government and Growth in Modern Turkey.* New York: Homes & Meier, 1985.

Ekinci, Oktay. *İstanbul'u Sarsan On Yıl.* İstanbul: A Kitaplar, 1994.

Erder, Sema. *İstanbul'a Bir Kent Kondu: Ümraniye.* İstanbul: İletişim Yayınları, 2013.

Erman, Tahire. "Urbanization and Urbanism." In *The Routledge Handbook of Modern Turkey*, edited by Metin Heper and Sabri Sayari, 293–302. London: Routledge, 2012.

70

On the Possibility of a Liberal Islam: The Resurrection of the Constitution of Medina in Turkey

İlker Aytürk and Anıl Kahvecioğlu

Representatives of the Muslim, polytheist, and Jewish communities of the city of Medina in the Hejaz drafted a contractual document, the so-called Constitution of Medina (*Medine Vesikası* in Turkish, meaning "the document of Medina"), in the year 1 AH/622 CE, thereby creating a city-state that had a certain amount of limited powers over the inhabitants of the town regardless of their religious beliefs. The Constitution of Medina's unusually egalitarian approach to interfaith relations and political membership was, however, soon to be replaced by the supremacist Muslim contract of *dhimma*. The dhimma contract (later, the *millet* system) allowed non-Muslims to coexist with Muslims under a Muslim government but subjected them to various limitations that corresponded to their second-class status. The Constitution of Medina was largely forgotten until it was resurrected in the 1940s by Muhammad Hamidullah (1908–2002), a French scholar of Indian-Muslim descent who was the first to refer to the contract as a constitution and who also made the claim that Muslims should be credited with having created the first constitution in history. A few decades later, a sociologist and Islamist public intellectual from Turkey, Ali Bulaç (1951–), set out in 1991 to publish a series of articles that focused on the liberating potential of the Constitution of Medina, and in doing so he jump-started a public debate which over the course of the next ten years generated literally hundreds of books, academic and journalistic articles, dissertations, interviews, panels, and conferences devoted to the topic, both for and against. Essentially, Bulaç based his argument on three very common tropes in the academic literature of the 1980s: the failure of modernity, the decline of the nation-state, and the weakening of the paradigm of secularisation. Faced with the downfall of the Eastern Bloc and the eruption of ethno-religious conflicts in the region, such as in former Yugoslavia, the Caucasus, Iraq, the West Bank and Gaza, and Algeria, Bulaç concluded that humanity needed a new social contract, specifically one that should be based on principles that could be extracted from the Constitution of Medina. The following extract appeared in an article Bulaç published in *Birikim*, the flagship journal of the Turkish liberal left.

*General Information about the Document of Medina**

The [...] important point is that, thanks to this project [a new contract] based on the Document of Medina, no one will attempt to put pressure on other people and there will be legal guarantees to ensure that everyone will accept others as a fact of nature and respect their way of life and thought. [...] The Document of Medina advocates a social project based not on "sovereignty," but on "participation" for all social blocs. [...]

Any model project which aims to establish real peace and stability [...] must come into being as a result of a contract. While drawing up this contract, the members or representatives of the social blocs must be present, and the basic principles of the contract must be determined in a free environment and by means of collective decision-making. [...]

Every religious and ethnic group [will have] total cultural and legal autonomy. No one will change [their previous lifestyles and practices] in terms of religion, legislation, systems of justice, education, trade, culture, arts, and daily life; all will express themselves in the way they define their own legal and cultural standards. [...]

In a pluralist society, not just one but many legal systems can be employed simultaneously. And, of course, if the social blocs have a disagreement because their different legal systems come into conflict—and they will—in such cases [...] higher courts must be founded which are to be comprised of the legal representatives of the constituent communities. [...] In the case of conflicting legal systems, the best solution is to allow the plaintiff to choose one of them; that is possible according to Islamic law. [...] If people can freely choose a religion, then their legal system and social life must be in accordance with their religion and beliefs. Under such circumstances, Islam as religion and as law is binding only for Muslims [...].

With its objective principles, the Document of Medina supersedes all of the constituent religious and social blocs. That is to say, Muslims, Jews, and polytheists [in the original document] may not transgress its general framework. This contract, which came into being as a result of a mutual agreement, is above the Quran, the Torah and local traditions. [...]

The political union [established by the Document] is referred to as the *umma* in the text. With this particular meaning, the *umma* is a political union in which Muslims, Jews, and polytheists participate. This union is a social project, blind to race, language, sect, and ethnicity, and it is based on the religious, cultural, and the legal autonomy [of every constituent bloc]. [...]

* Translated from the Turkish original in Ali Bulaç, "Medine Vesikası Hakkında Genel Bilgiler," *Birikim* no. 38-39 (June-July 1992): 108–110.

The Document of Medina assigns to the central authorities (state?) responsibility for the distribution of justice, defence, and declarations of war, but it relegates decision-making rights to civil society [comprised of the social blocs] in fields such as culture, science, the arts, the economy, education, healthcare, and particularly legislation. [...]

I personally believe that we can extrapolate from the Document of Medina—by way of generalisations—certain foundational principles for the contemporary world and that we can build upon those foundational principles to construct a pluralist social project. [...] We need voluntaristic, participatory, and pluralist projects that can bring together the religious, ethnic, and political groups in our region on the basis of a contract.

***

In essence, Bulaç was trying to carve out a living space for his fellow Islamists in which they could lead their lives free from the interference of the secular authorities in the name of liberal values or human rights. From the very beginning, his project was fraught with paradoxes. Bulaç needed to find an Islamic source of legitimacy for peaceful coexistence and multiculturalism in a utopian political system, which, in the way he described it, bore the trappings of anarcho-liberalism. Thinking he had struck upon such a source of legitimacy in the Constitution of Medina, he asserted that this ancient text could inspire a new social contract for the postmodern world. In short, Bulaç emphasised the notion that religions and religious communities were the building blocs of his utopia. He expected that every participating individual would join a religious community and hence select a religious law to which they would adhere, thus bringing into existence what he called "communities of law". Next, the representatives of those communities would enter into negotiations in the creation of a new Constitution of Medina. The new Constitution would primarily draw the boundaries of a minimal "central authority" the powers of which would be limited to carrying out very basic functions such as defending the communities of law against external aggression, providing internal security, adjudicating disagreements that arise between communities of law, and, lastly, collecting a minimum amount of taxes so it could fulfil those functions.

The most novel aspect of Bulaç's utopia is that his "central authority" is not a state. It lacks sovereignty and is less powerful than the communities of law which construct and control it. Each of the constituent communities of law would enjoy full autonomy in communal self-government, the drafting of their own (religiously sanctioned) laws, and the distribution of justice within the community via (religiously sanctioned) communal courts. By choosing to eliminate the modern state, which he regarded as an "evil" institution, Bulaç carefully and deliberately set himself apart from the political Islamist mainstream. While political Islamists want to capture the modern state and use its institutional and penetrative capacity to bring contemporary Muslims into harmony with the "true and original" form of Islam, Bulaç associated the modern state with totalitarianism and hence wanted nothing to do with it, regardless of who was in charge. Overall, Bulaç's proposal was a non-Western, Muslim rejoinder to what was until then a largely Western conversation on multiculturalism, communitarianism, and legal pluralism. Ultimately, Bulaç aimed to free his fellow Islamists from the shackles of what they perceived to be the secular Kemalist state.

Bulaç's two target audiences in the 1990s were the Turkish liberal left and Islamists. Starting with the first group, there is no doubt that Bulaç's insistence on making religion a central tenet of social organisation irritated the liberal left. They were also put off by the full autonomy that Bulaç wanted to grant to communities of law, because for all practical purposes that would hinder outside interventions in cases of serious violations of human rights within a given community. All of those concerns, however, did not prevent the liberal left from recognising the anarcho-liberal core of the Constitution of Medina project. They were also interested in collaborating with the numerically far superior Islamists in pushing back against the Kemalist state. It was for this reason that Bulaç was invited to publish his work in the leading liberal leftist journal *Birikim* in 1992, and in the course of the next two years *Birikim* ran ten articles about the Constitution of Medina, four of which Bulaç wrote. Major liberal-leftist writers such as Ahmet İnsel (1955–) and Taner Akçam (1953–) expressed serious reservations about the project but overall they contributed to the visibility and popularity of the debates surrounding the Constitution of Medina.

The second audience, Turkish Islamists, was united by a sense of empowerment in the 1990s and they expected that they would come to power in the foreseeable future. Indeed, a number of factors, such as state-sponsored anticommunism, the semi-official ideology of the Turkish-Islamic Synthesis, the inability of centre-right parties to deal with hyperinflation, and a growing network of Islamic NGOs and brotherhoods all overlapped in the 1980s and 1990s, ultimately helping to expand the electoral base of political Islam. The Islamist Welfare Party (*Refah Partisi*, RP) won mayoral elections in İstanbul and Ankara in 1994 and then won out against the centre-right parties in the 1995 General Elections. The party's leader, Necmettin Erbakan (1926–2011), became prime minister in 1996. Bulaç's Constitution of Medina project came into the spotlight precisely at the onset of this moment of euphoria and generated two very different responses among Islamists.

On the one hand, there were the so-called new Muslim intellectuals, including Mehmet Metiner (1960–), Ömer Çelik (1968–), and Şeref Malkoç (1960–) to name just a few, who would go on to collaborate with Recep Tayyip Erdoğan (1954–) as parliamentarians, advisors, or, as in the case of Malkoç, Turkey's public ombudsman starting in 2016. Those intellectuals defended Bulaç and championed the Constitution of Medina, if only for very pragmatic reasons. They welcomed the opportunity to join the anti-establishment coalition together with the liberal left and the Kurdish movement. They also hoped that the liberal language of rights and liberties, which Bulaç used to formulate his utopia, would diminish secular opposition to a future Islamist government. Setting aside that minority, the majority of Islamists, however, responded rather unfavourably to Bulaç's ideas. Islamist critics of Bulaç came from diverse backgrounds and their critiques were equally diverse; some questioned the textual authenticity of the Constitution of Medina, while others pointed out that an early version of the millet system replaced the Constitution of Medina even during Muhammad's lifetime. In general, those critics praised Islam as the only true message from God and thus refused to concede legal equality to the adherents of other religions or secular communities of law. More radical Islamist groups and intellectuals accused Bulaç of cosying up to old-school leftists, the losers of the bygone era of the Cold War. They considered such gestures to be not only un-Islamic, but also completely unnecessary as they believed that in those times Islamists were marching toward victory across the globe.

***

While the debates surrounding the Constitution of Medina slowly faded away under the impacts of the military intervention of 1997, it lingered in the public memory for years to come. Likewise, the Islamist-liberal coalition persevered and grew stronger when Recep Tayyip Erdoğan's Justice and Development Party (*Adalet ve Kalkınma Partisi*, AKP) came to power in 2002. Taking their cue in no small part from the debates about the Constitution of Medina, Islamist intellectuals were now able to couch party propaganda in liberal terms, and they were perceived both at home and internationally as pioneers of democratisation in Turkey. The Constitution of Medina project thus provided them with the opportunity to construct a new discourse of moderate Islam. Liberal-leftist intellectuals, however, had not closely followed the Islamist debates about the Constitution of Medina and hence were unaware of the extent to which illiberalism existed within those circles. Given that situation, they remained oblivious to the reasons why so many Islamists had opposed and even attacked Bulaç in the 1990s. Bulaç's utopian project and the debates surrounding it foreshadowed the future trajectory of political Islam in Turkey. This trajectory would eventually lead Turkey down an authoritarian path in the twenty-first century.

Select Bibliography

Guida, Michelangelo. "Ali Bulaç: Political Ideas of a Leading Turkish Islamist." *Oriente Moderno* 85 (2005): 483–501.
Karasipahi, Sena. *Muslims in Modern Turkey: Kemalism, Modernism, and the Revolt of the Islamic Intellectuals.* London: I.B. Tauris, 2009.
Uğur, Aydın. "L'ordalie de la democratie en Turquie: le projet 'communautarien islamique' d'Ali Bulaç et la laïcité." *Cahiers d'Études sur la Méditerranée Orientale et le Monde Turco-Iranien*, no. 19 (1995): 97–124.

1993–2002

71

In Between Invisibility and Recognition: The Sivas Massacre

Besim Can Zırh

The year 1993, another "pivotal year" in Turkey's political history, began with the assassination of Uğur Mumcu (1942–1993) on 24 January. Mumcu was an investigative journalist who was quite influential, particularly among the secular and republican segments of society. It then continued with the deaths of Adnan Kahveci (1949–1993), the minister of finance (in a car accident on 5 February); Eşref Bitlis (1933–1993), commander of the Gendarmerie (in a military plane crash on 17 February); and Turgut Özal (1954–1993), president of the Republic (of a heart attack on 17 April). The true causes of these deaths remain issues of public debate and some people still believe that conspiracies underlie the incidents. That year was also a turning point with regard to the Kurdish question, as the Kurdistan Workers' Party (*Partiya Karkerên Kurdistanê*, PKK) drastically transformed its strategy for conducting an intensified armed struggle by taking advantage of the situation that emerged in northern Iraq in the wake of the First Gulf War in 1991. In 1993, the PKK carried out 413 armed attacks in which 403 security officers, regardless of whether they were on duty or not, and 1,166 civilians, including teachers assigned to villages in the region as state employees as well as local residents, lost their lives. In the midst of those shocking developments, what happened on 2 July 1993 in Sivas deeply traumatised Alevis in Turkey and abroad.

It was the second day of a festival in Sivas named after Pir Sultan Abdal (a mythical rebellious bard believed to have lived in the sixteenth century in Sivas) but all of the scheduled events had been cancelled as, earlier in the day, it came to light that there was a possibility that the protests of a group of conservative Islamists who disapproved of the festival might turn violent. The participants who had been invited to the event took refuge in the Madimak Hotel, which was swiftly surrounded by a large mob shouting anti-republican Islamist slogans such as, "The Republic was founded in Sivas," a reference to a congress that had been held in the city in 1919 as the official beginning of the campaign for independence, "and it will be destroyed in Sivas". Law enforcement officers positioned in the city, including military units, were late in responding (and, according to some, rather unwilling) and in the end, thirty-seven people lost their lives when the Madimak Hotel was set on fire by the angry mob. Thirty-three of those victims were festival participants, most of whom had travelled from Ankara, including siblings Koray Kaya (12 years old) and Menekşe Kaya (15), siblings Asuman Sivri (16) and Yasemin Sivri (19), members of a *semah* dance group from Ankara, a promising young musician named Hasret Gültekin (22), a Dutch researcher working on Alevism named

Carina Thuys (23), Alevi folk musicians and husband and wife Muhlis Akarsu (45) and Muhibe Akarsu (44), physician and poet Behçet Aysan (44), and writer Asım Bezerci (62). Two hotel staff members and two others from among the crowd also died. The profile of the victims made the incident all the more traumatising for society.

Many books have been published in an attempt to contextualise what happened in Sivas that day, but one in particular, written by Muzaffer Erdost (1932–2020), was not discussed much at the time, probably due to his approach of contextualising the events as being part of a political conspiracy. Erdost was a leftist journalist who had established a publishing company (*Sol Yayınları*) in 1965 and began translating classical Marxist literature into Turkish. His brother, İlhan Erdost, was beaten to death in the Mamak Military Prison in the wake of the military coup of September 1980. In his book *Türkiye'nin Yeni Sevr'e Zorlanması Odağında Üç Sivas* (*Three Sivases within the Focus of Forcing Turkey to [Accept] a New Sèvres*), published in 1996, Erdost attempted to contextualise the incident in light of the changing geopolitical position of Turkey in the post-Soviet era by portraying Sivas as a "crossroads". The general framework of his contextualisation was based on an op-ed published in the *New York Times* on 2 January 1996, "Third American Empire with a Balkan Frontier," by Jacob Heilbrunn (1965–) and Michael Lind (1962–), and a series of articles written by Cengiz Çandar (1948–) on 6 and 7 January 1996 that brought the op-ed to the agenda in Turkey.

*Three Sivases**

The "heart" of the Third American Empire is, in the authors' own words, "the territories once ruled by the Ottoman Turks"—namely, the territories of the Ottoman Empire that later remained within the Soviet Union or became one of its socialist allies. Its "axis" lay in the Middle East and the Balkans; its "arc-boutant" and "balance point," according to Cengiz Çandar, was Turkey. If there was a country that acted as a "balance point," that country also had to have a balance point, and in *Three Sivases*, it was reiterated several times that Sivas was a focal point, a nodal point that connected Alevis in urban areas first in Sivas and in rural areas from Sivas to eastern Anatolia (from Tunceli to Erzurum) and again in the area from Sivas to the south (from Kahramanmaraş to Hatay). It would not be wrong to conclude that there was a close overlapping relationship between the design of the "Third American Empire" and social events, each resulting in a separate historical massacre that led to the cleansing of Alevis in these areas. [...] Sivas is geo-strategically important as a nodal point between Turkey's east and west, and secondly it is geo-politically important as a crossroads where people meet. [...] A shared characteristic of the 1978 Sivas, Kahramanmaraş, and Çorum Incidents and the 1993 Sivas Incident is that the ruling conserves had pitted the progressive and reactionary segments of the working class against each other. There were also differences, however, between the 1978 and the 1993 incidents. In the first, which took place in 1978, a fascist attack on revolutionary democratisation took advantage of the traditional Alevi-Sunni divide, and most of the people killed were Alevis. In the second, in 1993, an

* Translated from the original Turkish in Muzaffer Erdost, *Türkiye'nin Yeni Sevr'e Zorlanması Odağında Üç Sivas* (Ankara: Onur Yayınları, 1996), 12, 15, 17, 29 and 32.

attack on democratic and revolutionary intellectuals took the form of defending the honour of Islam, but here, too, the reason for the support of the Sunni community for the massacre must be sought in the Alevi-Sunni divide. [...] Politicised Islam became widespread and dominant in parallel with the suppression of Alevis' secular and democratic identities. This led Alevis to search for a political party as Alevis. That is why the statement that leftists "politicise" Alevis is false. [...] The aim of the 1993 Massacre was to demolish the context for the PKK, which sought to open a passage from Sivas to Samsun and hence settle in Sivas.

***

In the history of modern Turkey, Alevis had very limited opportunities to make themselves visible in public life. Moreover, even in cases of success, the visibility that Alevis acquired had developed in parallel with the political turmoil of the period and was not in their favour. For instance, most of the left-wing parties preferred to interpret what happened in Maraş in 1978 as an attack by ultra-rightists against the people, and they did not even mention Alevis. That situation triggered a deep sense of abandonment among Alevis and, as they faced the military coup of 12 September in 1980, they had a strong distrust of the left. Therefore, as Alevis went through a period of silent reconsideration in the early 1980s, they tried to preserve their culture within the new context of urbanisation though music, which plays a central role in their rituals. The silence was broken in 1987 when Turkey was preparing for a constitutional referendum on whether to remove certain provisional articles from the 1982 Constitution.

In this period, Alevis were discovered for their political potential when politicians from various parties attended the Hacı Bektaş Veli Commemoration Ceremonies (*Hacı Bektaş Veli Anma Şenlikleri*), which is the most important gathering for Alevis and has been organised ever since. As a result, Alevis acquired a new form of visibility by means of which they were now able to voice their demands by referring to their own identity. The titles of two special issues that were published by *Nokta* (an influential magazine at the time) three years apart are indicative of what occurred: "Alevism is Fading into History: A Story of Religious, Cultural and Political Extinction" (*"Alevilik Tarihe Karışıyor: Dinsel, Kültürel ve Politik bir Yok Oluşun Öyküsü"*), published on 27 September 1987, and "Alevis [Say], 'We Will Not Be Silent Anymore': Alevi Thought Has Witnessed a Great Revival in Recent Years" (*"Aleviler 'Artık Susmayacağız' – Alevi Düşüncesi Son Yıllarda Büyük bir Canlılık İçinde"*), published on 13 May 1990.

Also in May of 1990, an open letter signed by prominent left-leaning intellectuals and journalists was published in the newspaper *Cumhuriyet*. The letter, which became known as the "Declaration of Alevism" (*"Alevilik Bildirgesi"*), clearly framed the demands of Alevis for recognition for the first time. However, that visibility came at a cost. In response to the unexpected visibility that Alevism acquired, all of the major political factions engaged in a struggle about how to define Alevism. Secular republicanism, religious conservatism, and Turkish and Kurdish nationalisms have been struggling over definitions of national identity since the establishment of the Republic and they attempted to accommodate Alevism within their own political agendas.

The Sivas Massacre happened in that period of time when Alevism had gained greater visibility and it triggered a major reaction from Alevis in Turkey and abroad, resulting in an increase in the number of associations established by Alevis. On 12 March 1995, four coffeehouses and a pastry shop in the predominantly Alevi neighbourhood of Gazi in İstanbul were simultaneously attacked in the evening hours by unidentified gunmen firing automatic weapons from a stolen taxi. The attack caused an angry three-day uprising in various neighbourhoods of İstanbul primarily inhabited by Alevis. Nearly forty people lost their lives and hundreds more were injured during the brutal police crackdown that followed. These two tragic events in which Alevis were directly targeted, mirroring the events that had occurred at the end of the 1970s, were interpreted by Alevis within the framework of a republican-secular versus Islamic-conservative clash as an Islamist party was marching to power.

***

It is notable that Erdost's theory about Sivas came up again, but this time not in reference to his book, on the occasion of another constitutional referendum that was held in 2010 for a series of constitutional amendments proposed by the ruling Justice and Development Party (*Adalet ve Kalkınma Partisi*, AKP) following a process known as the "democratic opening" that aimed to resolve the decades-old human rights issues related to the Kurdish and Alevi questions. In this period, Alevis were hesitant to support the AKP's agenda and they were targeted by pro-AKP media circles for allegedly defending the old republican regime's tutelage, represented by the Republican's People Party (*Cumhuriyet Halk Partisi*, CHP), against this new period of political reformation.

On 24 June 2011, just one week before the eighteenth anniversary of the Sivas Massacre, a newscast titled "*Faili Meçhul*" ("Perpetrator Unknown") aired on TRT, the main public broadcasting network which is under the control of the government, explaining the events of 1993 as a provocation organised by the PKK to destabilise the country by exacerbating Alevi-Sunni tensions. That narrative was new even for Islamist circles, which had previously explained the Sivas Incident with implicit references to a conspiracy involving the military's desire to remove the Islamist Welfare Party (*Refah Partisi*, RP) from power. Alevis interpreted this new narrative as an attempt to whitewash the role of political Islam in stigmatising Alevi demands for recognition. In an interview published by *Özgür Gündem*, a newspaper affiliated with the Kurdish movement, an anonymous ex-member of the Department of Special Operations alleged that the Sivas Massacre in 1993 was actually a covert operation carried out by the military to counter the PKK's infiltration of the region. It was also said that a group of PKK guerrillas had raided the Sunni village of Başbağlar in Erzincan and killed 33 civilians in retaliation on 5 July 1993, just three days after the Sivas events. However, the leader of the PKK, Abdullah Öcalan (1949–), immediately announced that he had not ordered such an attack and that the leader of that specific guerrilla unit had made the decision to do so on his own.

In this politicised period, during which various political movements (including the AKP) attempted to rewrite history by way of "democratic initiatives," it was rather significant that debates about what really took place in Sivas in 1993 were ongoing, indicating that all of the major political currents in Turkey were still caught up in a struggle about how to accommodate Alevism within their agendas. None of them have been able or willing to contextualise the Sivas Massacre by recognising what Alevis have been demanding for over four decades since the late 1980s. In fact, the hotel, which operated as a kebab restaurant for many years after the massacre, was later converted into a science and culture centre in 2011 as part of an "Alevi initiative," despite calls from organisations representing the majority of Alevis in Turkey and abroad to open a museum of shame to commemorate in reference to a similar hate-crime incident in Solingen (Germany), in which five members of a Turkish immigrant family died when their house was set on fire by racists on 29 May 1993. On the memorial wall in the museum a statement says, "In the deplorable incident that took place on 2 July 1993, thirty-seven of our people lost their lives. We wish that such pain is never experienced again..." without referring to what really happened. If nothing really happened, then there is no one left to blame. Alevis, still lamenting the deaths that occurred in Sivas, continue to organise commemorations of mourning. What happened in Sivas has never been fully addressed within the scope of the law, and it still constitutes a powerful "chosen trauma" that defines Alevi identity at home and abroad.

Select Bibliography

Ata, Kelime. *Kızıldan Yeşile: Sol, Aleviler, Alibaba Mahallesi ve Sivas'ta Dönüşen Siyaset.* Ankara: Turan Yayınevi, 2021.

Çaylı, Eray. *Victims of Commemoration: The Architecture and Violence of Confronting the Past in Turkey.* New York: Syracuse University Press, 2022.

Ertan, Mehmet. *Aleviliğin Politikleşme Süreci: Kimlik Siyasetinin Kısıtlılıkları ve İmkanları.* İstanbul: İletişim Yayınları, 2021.

Van Bruinessen, Martin. "Kurds, Turks and the Alevi Revival in Turkey." *Middle East Report* 200 (1996): 7–10.

Yıldız, Ali Aslan, and Verkuyten, Maykel. "Inclusive Victimhood: Social Identity and the Politicization of Collective Trauma among Turkey's Alevis in Western Europe." *Peace and Conflict: Journal of Peace Psychology* 17, no. 4 (2011): 243–69.

Zırh, Besim Can. "Euro-Alevis: From Gastarbeiter to Transnational Community." In *The Making of World Society: Perspectives from Transnational Research*, edited by Remus Gabriel Anghel, Eva Gerharz, Gilberto Rescher, and Monika Salzbrunn, 103–32. Bielefeld: transcript Verlag, 2015.

72
The State's Informal Organisations: Paramilitaries in the Turkish-Kurdish Conflict

Ayhan Işık

During the conflict between the Turkish state and Kurdistan Workers' Party (*Partîya Karkerên Kurdistanê*. PKK), many irregular pro-state armed groups carried out violent acts that targeted Kurdish civilians. The 1990s were one of the most violent decades in the hundred-year history of violence in Northern Kurdistan (*Bakurê Kurdistanê*, or just "*Bakur*," the north), a region more often referred to in the literature and known popularly as "Turkish Kurdistan," or just "the east" or "the southeast". In 1984, the PKK initiated an armed struggle against the Turkish state, which responded by creating and making use of several paramilitary forces that became some of the most important actors in the conflict during the second half of the 1980s and throughout the 1990s. The largest and generally most important of those paramilitary groups were the Gendarmerie Intelligence and Counter-terrorism Organisation (*Jandarma İstihbarat ve Terörle Mücadele*, JİTEM), village guards (*Korucular*), Police Special Operation Teams (*Özel Harekat Timleri*), and Hizbullah, an illegal radical Kurdish Sunni-Islamist militant group in Turkey (not to be mistaken with the Shi'a-Islamist Hezbollah in Lebanon). In addition to those well-known groups, which had semi-formal and informal characteristics, other clandestine groups were also created by the state authorities, and they were used in conjunction with the abovementioned paramilitary forces.

On November 3, 1996, an event that came to be known as the Susurluk scandal occurred when a luxury car crashed into a truck near the town of Susurluk. There were four passengers in the car, three of whom died. Abdullah Çatlı (1956–1996) was one of them; he was the well-known leader of the militant radical-right Grey Wolves and a mafia kingpin who was wanted by Interpol for his involvement in a number of assassinations. The second was a model named Gonca Us, who was Çatlı's companion. The third victim was Hüseyin Kocadağ (1944–1996), who was director of the İstanbul School of Police at the time. The last passenger was a member of parliament, Sedat Bucak (1960–), who was injured in the accident. He was the head of a pro-state Kurdish tribe considered to be the most significant wing of the largest paramilitary organisation in Turkey, the village guards. This traffic accident revealed the existence of "deep state" (*derin devlet*) connections between politicians, security forces, and the mafia.

A month later on December 6, Turkish journalist and columnist İsmet Berkan (born in 1964) wrote an article titled "The MGK's Approval for Gladio" in *Radikal*, a liberal daily newspaper. Making reference to "Gladio," which was a NATO-led secret paramilitary organisation that operated in Italy during the Cold War, Berkan reported about a top-secret document that revealed the role of the Turkish state in paramilitary activities. The document that Berkan was alleged to have seen dealt with the issue of the creation of a special organisation by the Turkish National Security Council (*Milli Güvenlik Kurulu*, MGK) to eliminate pro-PKK Kurdish civilians and supporters. But how reliable was his claim? In a separate incident many years later, Berkan claimed that he had seen a video recording of an attack on a woman wearing a headscarf during the Gezi Park protests of 2013, which was subsequently used as government propaganda against the demonstrations, but he later withdrew the claim with an apology, saying that he had not actually seen such a recording. Berkan's credibility as a journalist was tarnished, his motivations began to be questioned, and his earlier claim was undermined. However, the Kurdish newspaper *Özgür Ülke* as well as some Turkish journalists, researchers, and state officials have made similar statements and written articles about the MGK's decision to establish and use a special organisation against the Kurdish population. Investigative journalist Uğur Mumcu (1942–1993) was killed in early 1993 and the office of *Özgür Ülke* was bombed in late 1994, which lent credence to Berkan's claims.

*The MGK's Approval for Gladio**

In fact, everything goes back to the beginning of 1992. At that time, the Turkish General Staff radically changed its strategy for fighting the PKK. From now on, the military, which had previously intervened and immediately retaliated after every attack, began to organise itself like a guerrilla force and take action without waiting for the PKK to act. This strategy shift would soon pay off. The initiative was no longer with the PKK, but with the military. The PKK was on the run, and the military was chasing after it. [...]

The inventor of the technique that was to be implemented was actually the British. This new tactic has two important pillars: The first is to capture terrorists before they act and kill them if necessary. The second is to treat people who provide moral and material support [to terrorists] in the same way that terrorists are treated.

This strategy shift came onto the agenda of the MGK in late 1992.

In an MGK document that was seen by the author of these lines, there was also an organisational chart [of a group] that was intended to be assembled and the names of the people who would take part in this organisation [were included]. Among the names was Abdullah Çatlı. Police officers from the Special Operations Team, several soldiers, and some of Çatlı's friends would also be involved in the organisation.

---

* Translated from the original Turkish in İsmet Berkan, "Gladio'ya MGK Onayı," *Radikal*, 6 December 1996.

This new tactic was initially rejected by the MGK. President [Turgut] Özal and the general commander of the Gendarmerie of the time, Eşref Bitlis, were opposed to the collaboration of the state with individuals who were not government officials.

This probably has nothing to do with the issue, but it is an interesting coincidence that first General Bitlis and then Turgut Özal died, one in an accident and the other from a heart attack.

Süleyman Demirel became president and Tansu Çiller became prime minister. [...]

Since those who had objected to the decision were no longer around, the issue could come onto the agenda of the MGK once again. It did so, and this new method of fighting was approved in autumn of 1993. What you call "Gladio" and I call a "special organisation" was established by way of a decision made by the MGK.

[...] We all remember Tansu Çiller's statement: "We will eradicate the PKK's sources of income."

Behçet Cantürk, Savaş Buldan, Yusuf Ekinci, Hacı Karay, Adnan Yıldırım, Medet Serhat and finally Ömer Lütfü Topal...

All these figures were involved in drug trafficking in one way or another. None of them are alive today. They either moved drugs for the PKK or they had to pay extortion fees to the PKK. Either way, the PKK was earning an income. And none of them are alive now.

Özgür Ülke [Free Country] was like the PKK's official publication. Abdullah Öcalan was writing articles for this newspaper under the pseudonym Ali Fırat. Its headquarters and offices were bombed. The İstanbul police allegedly caught the bombers, but because of an "order from above," they were released.

These lines were written based on a document that I could only skim quickly and which I was not allowed to make a copy of or take notes from while reading.

I wish that this "news," whose reliability I have been able to ascertain by looking into other matters, was actually a lie. Of course, I do not doubt that it will immediately be denied today. Indeed, it is my wish that those who deny it will be telling the truth.

***

Berkan begins by saying that the Turkish state's strategy for fighting the PKK changed in 1992. Indeed, the idea of formulating and establishing a new strategy had been debated by high-ranking soldiers, members of parliament, and journalists in Turkey starting in the late 1980s, and in fact a new strategy was implemented in the early 1990s through the concept of a "territorial army" (the aim of which was to hold positions outside urban centres) and the doctrine of low-intensity conflict (LIC) (essentially, a broad-based approach incorporating a counter-insurgency initiative). Berkan thus describes this new strategy as involving a military unit that is organised like a guerrilla movement. Although they are not mentioned here, there were internal as well as external factors that triggered this transformation. While inside Turkey support for the PKK in Kurdish society was increasing rapidly, outside the country other key events were unfolding, such as the Gulf War and the dissolution of the Soviet Union, which benefitted the Kurdish national struggle. Following these developments, the chief of general staff, Doğan Güreş, one of the founding actors involved in the application of the doctrine of LIC in Turkey, stated that in 1991 he had investigated the types of irregular warfare used by various countries (such as the US, UK and Spain) to see if they could be utilised in the fight against the PKK and he also noted that the Turkish army and the government subsequently began to implement the new doctrine. Berkan also says in his article that this idea/strategy originated with the British. The restructuring of the Turkish army on the basis of the doctrine of LIC played a determining role in the reorganisation and development of paramilitary forces, with members of this special organisation or "Gladio" consisting of far-right militants (including Abdullah Çatlı), soldiers, and special police teams.

The doctrine of LIC set forth crucial conditions in terms of the reorganisation and development of paramilitary groups during the period of its implementation. It was also as much a political concept as a military one. State institutions were administered by a particularly nationalist and radical secularist political and military elite during the first half of the 1990s, which created a political atmosphere that played an important role in the reorganisation of paramilitary forces. Thus, it can be said that the changing structure of paramilitary forces in Turkey was a result of a new war doctrine which combined with the political climate to produce dramatic increases in the membership figures for paramilitary organisations. As a consequence, the characteristics of paramilitary groups changed in terms of the types of violence they used. Specifically, while intelligence gathering had hitherto been their main task, they were granted new powers and began to focus on covert action and assault operations that did not exclude the killing of civilians, and a division of labour came into being among different paramilitary forces, which were now split up according to both geographical deployment (urban-rural) and operational functions (death squads-auxiliary forces). In short, the new strategy implemented by the state authorities after 1991 prompted a paramilitary war on civilians known or suspected to be supporting or sympathetic to Kurdish guerrillas, including pro-Kurdish political parties. There was a rapid increase in state violence against Kurds in the form of assassinations, forced disappearances, torture, and the burning and evacuation of villages and lands.

***

Berkan wrote that the state had established a secret organisation, one of the primary aims of which was the killing of pro-PKK Kurdish businessmen. Following the Susurluk incident, a new debate arose concerning the origins and functions of paramilitary organisations, particularly with regard to their role in the ongoing war against the PKK. By exposing the connections between and interlinkages of paramilitary organisations with formal politics, the Susurluk scandal came to hold a significant place in recent Turkish history. For the first time in the history of the republic, the complex network of relationships among state institutions and government authorities on the one hand, and paramilitary organisations and mafia leaders on the other, came to light. For their part, while refuting the existence of or claiming to have no knowledge about ties between some paramilitary forces and the mafia—in the political tradition of "plausible deniability"—officials did not deny that the state had a relationship with others. In an oft-quoted remark she made at the time, Prime Minister Tansu Çiller stated that "people who shoot bullets and those who suffer from bullets in the name of the state are both honourable."

The Susurluk incident and the public reactions it triggered were quite significant in terms of revelations concerning the state's paramilitary operations and its relations with paramilitary and criminal organisations. Following the car accident, parliament assembled a commission to investigate those relations. The Susurluk Research Commission prepared a report that reviewed the events that took place. The Susurluk Report revealed the existence of a network of organised crime and relationships between named members of paramilitary groups, right-wing parties, mafia leaders, members of the Turkish parliament, and military and administrative bureaucracies.

Years later in 2021, a series of video-based confessions made by Sedat Peker, which received millions of views and were interpreted by some commentators and the opposition as "the second Susurluk," shook up Turkey's political scene. The ultranationalist and eccentric mafia leader Peker, who has enjoyed relations with politicians, bureaucrats, the military, and intelligence bureaus, has allegedly participated in the war against the Kurds since the 1990s. In his videos, Peker has made numerous statements targeting both former and acting interior ministers, former intelligence officers, high-ranking army and police officials, businesspeople, journalists, and other politicians. In fact, given the history of the Turkish deep state, this continuity should not come as a surprise.

Select Bibliography

Bozarslan, Hamit. *Network-Building, Ethnicity and Violence in Turkey.* Abu Dhabi ECSSR, 1999.
Işık, Ayhan. "Pro-State Paramilitary Violence in Turkey Since the 1990s." *Southeast European and Black Sea Studies* (2021): 231–49. https://doi.org/10.1080/14683857.2021.1909285
Işık, Ayhan. "The Emergence, Transformation and Functions of Paramilitary Groups in Northern Kurdistan (Eastern Turkey) in the 1990s." PhD dissertation, Utrecht University, 2020.
"İsmet Berkan 'Kabataş' Suskunluğunu Bozdu: Çok Üzgünüm Ve Özür Diliyorum," *Diken.* 24 March 2015. https://www.diken.com.tr/ismet-berkan-kabatas-suskunlugunu-bozdu-cok-uzgunum-ve-ozur-diliyorum/
Savaş, Kutlu. *Susurluk Raporu.* 1997. https://tr.wikisource.org/wiki/Susurluk_Raporu_(Kutlu_Sava%C5%9F)

73

For the Liberation of Women:
Three Kurdish Women's Periodicals

Nicole A.N.M. van Os

Under the leadership of Turgut Özal (1927–1993), who was prime minister from November 1983 through November 1989 and president until his death in April 1993, Turkey gradually returned to a more democratic political system after the military intervention of 1980, yet with clear neoconservative and neoliberal features. Opening the way to an increase in the influence of Sunni Islam in the public sphere, he also created room for a different approach to the "Kurdish Question". While an increasing number of Turkish civilians felt a need to find a political rather than a military solution to the Kurdish conflict, the struggle between the Workers' Party of Kurdistan (*Partiya Karkerên Kurdistanê*, PKK) and the Turkish state intensified in southeast Anatolia from 1984 onwards. In 1991, Özal, who had Kurdish roots himself, unilaterally decided to allow the Kurdish language, which had been banned by the military junta in 1980, to be spoken, written, and sung again, even though the National Security Council wanted to leave little room for divergent voices.

The gradual process of liberalisation under Özal paved the way for a broader diversity of feminist voices as well. The dominant leftist feminism of urban, middle-class women of the 1980s started to be questioned by Islamist feminists, Kemalist feminists, women from the LGBT community, and feminists belonging to non-Turkish ethnic communities, such as the Kurds. The refusal of women's groups to let Kurdish women carry a banner in Kurdish or address attendees in their own language during a gathering on 8 March in 1989 led to the establishment of independent Kurdish women's groups in the 1990s, some of which would eventually start to publish their own women's periodicals.

Ji bo rizgarîya jinan (*For the Liberation of Women*), the bulletin of the National Democratic Women's Organisation (NDWO), published its first issue in September 1993 and as such was the first Kurdish women's periodical to appear in the country. The content of this first issue, which seems to have been the last issue as well, was completely in Turkish despite its Kurdish title. Rather than a proper periodical, it was more of a pamphlet put out by the NDWO in which its members laid out the reasons for the establishment of the organisation and its aims. However, the organisation was closed down soon after the publication was released.

Ji bo rizgarîya jinan was followed in suit by more Kurdish women's periodicals in the second half of the 1990s. The first was *Roza*, the title of which not only meant "pink diamond," but allegedly was also a reference to Rosa Luxemburg. Founded by a group of Kurdish activist women, the periodical was a vehicle to share their ideas, but ultimately their activism was more important to them than the publication. It was published more or less every two months from March 1996 until May 2000, resulting in the release of seventeen issues in total. The periodical *Jujin* (see below for an explanation of the meaning of the title), which was established by a group of women who separated from the circles of *Roza* after the latter's fourth issue had appeared, was published from January 1997 until March 2000. The third periodical appearing in those years was *Jin û Jiyan* (*Women and Life*, 1999–2001). The articles in all three periodicals were mainly in Turkish with an occasional article (translated) in Kurdish, as most of the authors could not write Kurdish.

*Three Kurdish Women's Periodicals**

"Hello, Dear Women"

What kind of *JUJIN*?

JUJIN has been born and says HELLO to you, [with the aim] to:
–   be independent and feminine,
–   contribute to the ethnic and gender struggles of Kurdish women and create an emotional bond between all women in general and more specifically between Kurdish women,
–   scrutinise everything, but first of all ourselves, through women's eyes,
–   be a place where we can share our experiences, where we can hear and see each other, and where we can have discussions,
–   be a means by which we can open our windows together, through which we can move from private to public spaces,
–   keep up with women's voices,
–   create a sense of togetherness where the love and interest which all Kurdish women need can grow,
–   contribute to the Kurdish women's movement and open the way to its organisation.

[The word] *JUJIN* is a contraction of [the words for] hedgehog and woman. *Juji* is hedgehog in Kurdish, *Jin* means woman. [...] We even included *Jîn* (life), bundled these words [together] and arrived at the word *Jujin*.

* Translated from the original Turkish in "Merhaba Sevgili Kadınlar," *Jujin* 1, no. 1 (December 1996): 1; Fatma Kayhan, "Roza Yayınına Ara Verdi!" *Roza* 4, no. 17 (May 2000): 3–6; "Bizleri Buluşturan 7. Sayımızla Yeniden Merhaba...," *Jin û Jiyan* 2, no. 7 (January-February 2000): 2.

"*Roza* Paused Publication"

Those who are closely following this periodical know that we have not published a new issue since our sixteenth issue in September [1999] and that we have basically paused publication. [...] We are sorry that we cannot give any clear information about how and when we will start up publication again. [...]

In contrast to all other women's periodicals, *Roza* pursues a policy that is against both gender as well as racial discrimination. And this was really the most difficult [part]. For one thing, there are very few people who ponder about this topic. Knowingly and unknowingly, racism has pervaded all the details of our lives, and it was more difficult than initially thought to fight, question, think about, and research it.

"Hello Again with Issue no. 7, which Brings Us Together Once More"

And this 8 March, women's groups, periodicals, and women from unions and political parties have started to work diligently. This year's 8 March is special compared to other years. Finally, women from countries all around the world who have universally experienced repression are coming together and continue with preparations for an international, long-lasting march.

The name of this march is "The 2000 World March of Women." The calendar of activities, which starts on 8 March 2000, will end on 17 October. On [International] Day for the Elimination of Poverty, i.e., 17 October, women from participating countries will gather in front of the UN after having marched in their own countries. The main themes of these activities are racism, poverty, war, and violence.

***

In the first text above, the editors of *Jujin* welcome their readers to the newly published periodical. They state their aims and explain their name: a contraction of "hedgehog" and "woman" with a touch of "life".

The second text is from *Roza*'s last issue. It shows how the editors of the periodical struggled not only with the intersectionality of their struggles and resistance against this intersectionality they experienced, but also how combining their activism with writing and publishing about it constituted a problem for them.

In the January-February 2000 issue of *Jin û Jiyan*, the editors expressed their hope for cooperation not only with Turkish women, but also with women on an international platform in the "2000 World March of Women," as will be seen below. Their hopes for local cooperation were dashed, however, during the 8 March gathering in İstanbul, as we learn in the next issue of *Jin û Jiyan*. The editors expressed their disappointment with other local women's groups because they had, to the dismay of the women involved in *Jin û Jiyan*, allowed a large group of men to be prominently present during the gathering.

The periodicals differed slightly in their content. *Roza* focused more on questions related to ethnicity and gender rather than class issues; within its pages, Turkish feminists were reproached for their lack of interest in the specific problems of Kurdish women, while Kurdish men, including activists, were condemned for their sexism and unwillingness to address the matter of patriarchy. The other two periodicals regularly published issues related to working-class women. While *Jujin* sought solidarity amongst women and aimed at cooperation with Turkish women as well, *Roza* focused more on the plight of Kurdish women and was less keen on soliciting support from Turkish feminists. All three periodicals, however, were critical of the war being waged by the Turkish government against the Kurds in southeast Anatolia and the atrocities being committed against Kurdish women. They also rejected, for example, Turkish "colonialism" of Kemalist-oriented women's groups who tried to assimilate the Kurdish community and its women through their activities directed at Kurdish women.

Although Kurdish women's periodicals could come into being and incidentally even published some articles in Kurdish, they could not escape the scrutiny of the National Security Council. The editors and writers of *Roza,* for instance, were tried and convicted for engaging in separatism more than once, while, on occasion, issues of the journals were seized by the authorities.

***

Kurdish women's periodicals constitute a clear example of several developments in the political landscape of Turkey in the 1990s, including a gradual return to a more democratic system of governance after the coup of 1980 and increased room for divergent voices within the political landscape, including those of women and minorities, and the possibility of expressing oneself in Kurdish. They comprise a fine example of Kurdish women's struggle with intersectionality and demonstrate the interconnectedness of issues related to race, gender, and class, as well as how these issues not only overlap, but also create interdependent systems of discrimination and oppression.

Select Bibliography

Açık, Necla. "Re-defining the Role of Women within the Kurdish National Movement in Turkey in the 1990s." In *The Kurdish Question in Turkey: New Perspectives on Violence, Representation and Reconciliation*, edited by Cengiz Güneş and Welat Zeydanlioglu, 114–136. Abingdon: Routledge, 2014.

Çaha, Ömer. "The Kurdish Women's Movement: A Third-Wave Feminism Within the Turkish Context." *Turkish Studies* 12, no. 3 (2011): 435–49.

Diner, Cağla, and Şule Toktaş. "Waves of Feminism in Turkey: Kemalist, Islamist and Kurdish Women's Movements in an Era of Globalization." *Journal of Balkan and Near Eastern Studies* 12, no. 1 (2010): 41–57.

Tahincioğlu, Nevin Yıldız, and Nalan Ova. "Counter Publicity of Kurdish Women Journals: ROZA as an Alternative Media Exam." *Review of Journalism and Mass Communication* 3, no. 1 (June 2015): 35–52.

74
Reckoning with a Life Lived Like a Storm: Repatriating Enver Pasha

Michael A. Reynolds

In August 1996, the Turkish government oversaw the return of the remains of the former Ottoman Minister of War Enver Pasha from Tajikistan to İstanbul for reburial. Enver had died in Central Asia seventy-four years earlier while leading rebels in battle against the Red Army. Unusually for a personage honoured by the state, the return of his remains generated considerable dissent and criticism in the media. The event highlighted the strides Turkish society had made in extending the boundaries of historical debate but also underscored the limits of that debate.

İsmail Enver (1881–1922) was arguably the most colourful and important figure of the Ottoman Empire in its final years. The son of a minor government functionary, Enver aspired to become a military officer while he was a child. He distinguished himself as a cadet in the Ottoman military education system and then as a junior officer fighting guerrillas in the Balkans. In 1906, he joined the underground "Young Turk" secret society, which would be renamed as the Committee of Union and Progress (*İttihad ve Terakki Cemiyeti*), in which a group of radical junior officers and civil servants advocated centralisation and accelerated administrative and social reforms to rejuvenate and preserve the flagging Ottoman state and its territories. Enver played a key role in the army mutiny of 1908 that compelled Sultan Abdülhamid II (1842–1918) to restore the Ottoman constitution. This event, known as the "Young Turk Revolution" or "Constitutional Revolution of 1908," catapulted Enver to fame throughout the Ottoman Empire and indeed around the globe as a "Hero of Liberty" (*Hürriyet Kahramanı*). The dashing twenty-six-year-old officer embodied the hope for a new constitutional era that would simultaneously revitalise the Ottoman state and preserve harmony among the tottering empire's diverse peoples.

Enver further burnished his reputation as a heroic figure when as a volunteer he led Muslim guerrillas in Ottoman Tripolitania (Libya) in resisting the invading Italians in 1911. In January 1913, fearing that the Ottoman government was about to sign an unfavourable peace treaty after its disastrous defeat in the First Balkan War of the previous year, Enver led a coup d'état and then, together with his "Unionist" colleagues Talat and Cemal, effectively established a dictatorship. Assuming the post of Minister of War and command of the army in 1914, he later that same year drew the Ottoman Empire first into an alliance with Germany and then into the First World War. In December 1914, the 33-year-old Enver took personal command of a grand offensive toward the Russian-held town of Sarıkamış in the Caucasus

Mountains. The operation concluded calamitously with the deaths of tens of thousands of Ottoman soldiers.

Upon the defeat of the Central Powers in 1918, Enver together with other leading Unionists fled the Ottoman Empire. In addition to escaping the ignominy of defeat, Enver and his colleagues were also trying to evade the Entente powers, who intended to charge them with "crimes against humanity" for the wholesale destruction of the Ottoman Armenian community through deportations and massacres during the war. Enver made his way to Berlin in 1919 and then to Moscow in 1920. Enver wanted to gain the support of Bolshevik Russia so that he might return to Anatolia and displace his former subordinate Mustafa Kemal (Atatürk, 1881–1938) as head of the Turkish nationalist forces and government. Kemal's supporters, however, worked to discredit Enver by reviving public memory of the debacle at Sarıkamış and painting him as a foolhardy adventurer leading a corrupt empire to its doom. When Mustafa Kemal defeated the Greeks in August 1921 and consolidated his control, Enver, at the behest of the Bolsheviks, gave up on his plan to return to Anatolia and instead headed for Bukhara to help pacify the local Muslim insurgents (the Basmachi) resisting Soviet Communism. Once in Central Asia, however, Enver switched sides to join the Basmachi and helped lead them until his battlefield death on 4 August 1922.

Even after Enver's death, supporters of Mustafa Kemal and Kemalism continued to use Enver as a foil in their presentation of history. Whereas they presented Mustafa Kemal as the embodiment of prudence with his slogan of "peace at home, peace abroad" and of secularism, the republic, success, and the future, they used the image of Enver to symbolise recklessness, fanaticism, the empire, failure, and the past. Enver and his legacy remained hotly contested in Turkey in the 1990s.

On 4 August 1996, Turkish Prime Minister Süleyman Demirel (1925–2015) oversaw the repatriation and reburial of Enver Pasha's remains. A funeral was held at İstanbul's Şişli Mosque and attended by Demirel, representatives of the parliament, government ministers, high-ranking military officers, and descendants of Enver. Afterwards, Enver's remains were brought for reburial to the Monument of Liberty (*Abide-i Hürriyet*), where the body of Talat Pasha had been interred in 1943. At the monument, Demirel delivered a brief speech. Enver and the nation's martyrs, Demirel declared, had never been forgotten and would never be forgotten.

*Demirel's Obituary at Enver Pasha's Funeral**

Enver Pasha with both his errors and achievements is an important figure from our recent history. We have no doubt that history will evaluate the events of the past and reach the correct judgement. The events that fit into a life that began in the mountains of Macedonia and ended in Tajikistan and was lived like a storm have rendered a general consensus that Enver was a true patriot, nationalist, idealist, and very honest soldier.

* Translated from the original Turkish TRT broadcast, 4 August 1996.

In the eyes of the Turkish people, Enver Pasha is a hero. As a token of our respect for our nation's sentiment, we have taken Enver Pasha, whose grave our friends in Tajikistan visited as a tomb of a saint, and brought him to this historical place, this hill [The Hill of Liberty], to be beside his friends. In this way, Enver Pasha's homesickness and exile comes to an end.

***

Demirel's remarks are notable for three reasons. The first is his acknowledgment that the record of an individual receiving state honours can be mixed and comprise errors as well as achievements. The second is the evasive manner in which he advances the claim that Enver merits a state reburial. Demirel never states directly that he or his government deem Enver worthy of admiration. Rather he assures his audience that history itself will issue a correct verdict on Enver. The notion that history pronounces judgments upon itself may be a reassuring idea insofar as it relieves people of the responsibility of passing judgment, but it is not a logically coherent one. Demirel next contradicts himself by declaring that the events of the past have already established that Enver was a true patriot and honest soldier. Third, he avers that the Turkish people regard Enver as a hero. By repatriating Enver's remains, he and his government are merely honouring that assessment.

An explanation for Demirel's multilayered evasiveness can be found in the press coverage of the return and reburial of Enver's remains. That coverage suggests that far from arriving at a consensus favourable to Enver, Turkish public opinion was highly polarised. Indeed, newspaper coverage overall was strongly negative toward both Enver's legacy and the repatriation of his remains. Notably, critics of Enver spanned the political spectrum from left to right. An analysis of eleven leading Turkish newspapers representing leftist, liberal, Islamist, and Turkist views identified seven newspapers as negative, two as neutral, and only two as positive in their coverage.

Liberal and leftist newspapers were uniformly critical of Enver, favouring words and phrases such as "Sarıkamış," "90,000 soldiers," and "Allahuekber Mountains" to remind readers of the Sarıkamış debacle, and "daydreamer," "adventurist," and "fantasiser" to paint Enver as heedless and irresponsible. These papers avoided words with positive connotations such as "patriot," "idealist," or "courageous." Liberal-leaning newspapers additionally castigated Enver as a rival of Mustafa Kemal and denigrated him as a "Germanophile," "German tool," and "German fanboy" (*Alman hayranı*). Two newspapers with centre-left leanings, the large circulation papers *Hürriyet* and *Milliyet*, highlighted the discrepancy in the government's treatment of Enver Pasha's remains and those of the poet Nazım Hikmet (1902–1963), a Turkish Communist whose body remains in the Moscow cemetery where he was buried in exile.

Turkish Islamists also voiced scepticism and disapproval. An Islamist opinion maker from the newspaper *Zaman* disparaged Enver as "a tornado" that whirled through history leaving everything behind "in ruins" and as someone who took "an empire as big as a curtain" and left it "a handkerchief." Other Islamists slammed Enver not only for his strategic blunders but also for his progressive and reformist political orientation, declaring of his role in the constitutional revolution of 1908, "Toppling Abdülhamid by engaging in banditry is unforgiveable." Another slammed Enver and the Unionists as "a group of mindless activists" who had lacked the maturity and prudence necessary to lead a state and had bequeathed a ruinous legacy to Turkey. Minister of State Abdullah Gül from the Islamist Welfare Party (*Refah Partisi*, RP) and future prime minister and president of Turkey conveyed only a tepid endorsement of Enver: "We have transferred the remains of Enver Pasha, who witnessed very important events and decisions throughout his life, from Tajikistan to İstanbul. He is a commander of ours who united all the Muslim and Turkish homelands in Asia and was martyred along with thousands of our brothers while fighting for this ideal." A small number of Islamists, however, did find Enver's efforts to promote Muslim unity admirable. The newspaper *Yeni Şafak*, for example, chose words with positive connotations such as "idealist," "courageous," and "martyr" to describe Enver.

Turks on the right with more ethno-nationalist leanings offered positive but qualified praise. News accounts of the reburial, however, mentioned a group of young men at Enver's funeral who boisterously chanted the slogans "Long live our great Turan ideal" and "Martyrs are immortal, the homeland is indivisible" while also shouting "God is Great" and using their hands to make the symbol of the wolf. These men identified themselves as the youth wing of the Idealist Hearths (*Ülkücü Ocakları*) which is affiliated with the Nationalist Movement Party (*Müliyetçi Hareket Partisi*, MHP). They are known more popularly as the "Grey Wolves," a reference to the Turkic myth of Ergenekon wherein a grey wolf rescued the ancient Turks by leading them to safety as they moved across Central Asia. Advocates of an aggressive pan-Turkism, the Grey Wolves were the one group who unabashedly hailed Enver's legacy and the return of his remains. They revere Enver as a legendary warrior figure who lived and died for the sake of Turan, the ideal of uniting the Turkic peoples of Eurasia. In essence, they embrace Enver for precisely those qualities that lead other Turks to reject him. Whereas the latter condemn Enver for being an impetuous dreamer, the Grey Wolves draw inspiration from what they see as Enver's pure and self-sacrificing spirit. Enver's personal piety also aligns with their embrace of both a Turkic ethnic consciousness and a militant Muslim identity, as symbolised by their utterance at the funeral of the *tekbir*, the declaration "God is Great," and their flashing of wolf symbols. The irony is that the Grey Wolves' image of Enver is as misinformed as those of his liberal and leftist critics. Enver as Minister of War never pursued and indeed explicitly disavowed the establishment of a greater Turkic state in the Caucasus, let alone Central Asia.

***

The repatriation and reburial of Enver revealed the fading of Kemalist orthodoxy in the 1990s and the nascent emergence of a wider spectrum of opinions in Turkish politics. At the same time, it also highlighted some of the conceptual and political difficulties cramping public debate in Turkey. By one measure, Demirel's decision to honour Enver challenged Kemalist orthodoxy, and his acknowledgement that Enver was a complex historical figure likewise tacitly legitimised disagreement and dissent. By another measure, however, Demirel's invocation of history as an autonomous and authoritative judge of itself was not merely incoherent logically but also revealed an inability to conceive of citizens as being responsible for making their own assessments. Similarly, Demirel's assertion that the Turkish people regarded Enver as a hero—an assertion not based on evidence and belied by media coverage—was an additional dodge of responsibility and an attempt to foreclose criticism or debate.

The Turkish media, insofar as it expressed a range of diverging opinions, revealed a more promising evolution. Notably, most of these opinions were critical of the government, although they were formed on the basis of the Kemalist myth of Enver. Paradoxically, in this instance the minority opinion that endorsed the government's decision to honour Enver demonstrated a finer ability to acknowledge historical complexity. Finally, it is worth observing that none of the discussions about Enver touched on the issue of the role he played in the mass destruction of the Ottoman Armenian community. Some historical issues in Turkey were clearly still not up for mention, let alone debate.

Select Bibliography

Aydemir, Şevket Süreyya. *Makedonya'dan Orta Asya'ya Enver Paşa*, 3 vols. İstanbul: Remzi Kitabevi, 1970-1972.

Koloğlu, Orhan. "Enver Paşa'yı Tartışırken: Tarihle Barışma ile Barışçı Tarih Arasında." *Tarih ve Toplum* 157 (January 1997): 43–49.

Reynolds, Michael A. "Buffers, not Brethren: Young Turk Military Policy in the First World War and the Myth of Panturanism." *Past and Present* 203 (May 2009): 137–79.

Rustow, Dankwart A. "Enwer Pasha." *Encyclopedia of Islam*, Second Edition. Brill Online, 2013.

Türk, Fahri. "Enver Paşa'nın Naaşının Tacikistan'dan Türkiye'ye Getirilişinin Türk Basınında Yansımaları." *Akademik Bakış* 9, no. 17 (2015): 71–89.

Yenen, Alp. "Enver Enigma." *The Lausanne Project Blog*. 4 August 2022. https://thelausanneproject.com/2022/08/04/enver-enigma/

Yılmaz, Şuhnaz. "An Ottoman Warrior Abroad: Enver Paşa as an Expatriate." *Middle Eastern Studies* 35, no. 4 (1999): 40–69.

75
Finding Nowhereland:
Totalitarian Nightmares as a Utopian Vision

Engin Kılıç

In 1997, İlhan Mimaroğlu (1926–2012) published a work entitled *Yokistan Tasarısı* (*A Plan for Nowhereland*). As the title suggests, the author proposes, albeit in plan form, a utopian vision, i.e., an ideal social order. The author is a notable figure in Turkish culture. His father, Kemalettin Bey (1870–1927), was a famous architect who designed buildings of major significance; he was so respected that today he appears on the back of twenty-lira banknotes. İlhan Mimaroğlu, on the other hand, was a renowned musician and an electronic music composer. When he was in his twenties, he received a Rockefeller scholarship and studied musicology at Columbia University in New York City. Afterwards, he worked as a producer for Atlantic Records, composed (with Nina Rota) the soundtrack of Federico Fellini's film *Satyricon*, and released several albums.

Although it is not a well-known fact, beginning in the mid-nineteenth century there emerged a tradition in Ottoman Turkish literature of writing utopian stories. The authors of these works (most of which were published in the late nineteenth and early twentieth centuries) share some similar characteristics. Many of them worked as teachers, bureaucrats, and parliamentarians, and most of the works they wrote were statist utopias. They identified with the state and sought to make the state stronger by giving it the highest priority. For this reason, utopias constructed around anarchist, feminist, and environmentalist themes were not very common in Turkish literature, and only more recently have such works been written. As such, earlier utopias tended to focus more around themes dealing with authoritarian and totalitarian states.

İlhan Mimaroğlu, however, does not fit the author profile described above. He had no organic ties to the state, lived in another country, and established connections with people from very different walks of life. Moreover, the work in question was published in 1997. Given that situation, it should perhaps come as no surprise that this work would reveal a utopian vision that was somewhat different from earlier ones.

*A Plan for Nowhereland**

The economic system of the country is communist capitalism. Capitalism, because any other economic system is like a non-existent dimension. Until now, it should have been understood that capitalism alone is an economic system that works and achieves its goals. However, for capitalism to function as a system working solely for the public good, changes are required, if not fundamentally, then in some of the features of existing form of capitalism. This capitalist system, which operates in a way that covers the whole country, all parts of which are governed by the state, seeks profits like conventional capitalism, but the profits are spent on public services, workers' wages, and new investments that will increase profits.

It is clear that we are talking about a form of state capitalism. The fact that other forms of state capitalism have not worked until now is not proof that they will not work from now on. Just as many of the companies that hold to traditional capitalism succeed because they are well-managed while those that are poorly managed suffer losses and go bankrupt, the failure of all state capitalisms to date due to mismanagement should not lead to examples of successful companies being ignored.

From where will the profit-seeking state, like every capitalist institution, get the profit that it seeks? Like any profit, it will derive it from the surplus value of labour. In the applied communist-capitalist system, workers are like the employees of a company. So where and how does communism take place? And how does it relate to capitalism? [...]

Although we have defined workers as the employees of a company, when we are talking about a communist-capitalist system, it is time to point out a very important difference with the worker's condition in traditional capitalism. This important difference occurs in the way that workers who work as company employees own not only the means of production, but the entire company, that is to say, the whole country. The identity card that certifies the citizenship of each worker is also a proof that he owns one share (and one share only) in the country. In this respect, the wage of the labourer is the share paid to him from the profit gained. This share is paid to the worker as a wage increase in proportion to the increase in profit. Just as the wages of each labourer are equal to the other, the wage increases are also equal.

***

The author presented his work in a way that was far from modest. He defined this tiny book as "the best utopia ever written". As can be seen above, the economic system of the country in the book is described as "communist capitalism". As for the other characteristics of the ideal country depicted in the text, it immediately becomes clear that the state is the most prioritised

* Translated from the original Turkish in İlhan Mimaroğlu, *Yokistan Tasarısı* (İstanbul: Pan Yayıncılık, 1997), 11-15.

and important organ. The country adopts the system of state capitalism. There is no private property. The only company in the country is the state, and the company is for-profit. In order to convince readers that communism and capitalism are compatible, the author puts forward the pretext that communism has never actually been implemented in any country before.

Everyone in the country gets an equal salary. Workers become civil servants. Since the state is a for-profit company, workers' wages are actually dividends. By the same logic, employees don't pay taxes either. Credit cards, which also serve as identity cards, are used instead of cash. Unemployment has disappeared. Also, there is no retirement. Everyone is given a job that they can do until they die. Since there is no private property, the goods people purchase are considered to be "rented". Since there is no institution of family, there is no inheritance, and people are "encouraged" to leave their valuable possessions to the state.

The author describes the system of electoral democracy as "crippled" and a "narcotic game". Since the utopian state is run like a corporation, administrators are appointed to office according to their skills, experience, and expertise, not votes. Therefore, in this text, we see that meritocracy is opposed to democracy, but we do not learn by whom and on what basis their skills and talents are determined. In response to this understanding of democracy as "crippled," politics is said to be raised to its "real" meaning in Nowhereland. In other words, the suggestions made by citizens are "carefully taken into account" and, according to the author, democracy in this way "takes place as constructive criticism".

Apart from this, the description of the country is carried out in the form of a series of prohibitions. Giving birth without permission is a felony, and the penalty is deportation. There are no private vehicles. It is forbidden to advertise products. It is forbidden to save money, as there will never be a need for such a thing. Everyone has to own a house with at least two rooms and at most four rooms. But there are no one-room houses in the country anyway. Still, there is freedom in some matters. For example, citizens are free to spend their holidays abroad so that they can have "different experiences" as well as see how backward foreign countries are compared to their own country.

The author also clarifies the issue of rule violations. In this country, the urge to commit crimes has been "quenched" by "a guided educational effort that nurtures the good by removing all evil from 'human nature'". However, we do not learn the details of this miraculous training method. Evaluating the possibility that bad tendencies might emerge, the author makes a "Big Brother" fantasy that has already been realised as part of his utopia, stating that anyone who attempts to commit economic crimes can be easily identified by computers. As for other crimes, there are two possibilities. The first possibility is that a crime was committed by mistake, and in that case, the mistake is corrected. If there was no mistake, there is only one possible explanation left, and that is that the perpetrator is mentally unstable. Such people are mentally treated.

***

Some aspects of *Nowhereland* distinguish it from mainstream Turkish utopias. First of all, it is interesting to note that communism was viewed positively in the book, but what is more interesting is its timing: the book was published in the 1990s, when the Soviet Union collapsed, the Cold War ended, and communism fell out of favour. Another difference is that the utopian vision in this work is not limited to Turkey but has a universal character. In connection with this, unlike many other Turkish utopias, this work is not based on any nationalist tendencies. Turkey is not even mentioned in the text. When describing Nowhereland, general concepts are used, such as "country" and "citizen". The last sentence of the work ("In the future world where Nowhereland is realised, there will always be the United Nations [albeit by another name]; and when it comes to hostility, the USA will not want to keep Nowhereland alive") may be key to understanding this issue. The only real country mentioned in the text, and in a very negative tone at that, is the USA. Therefore, it may be inferred that Mimaroğlu's dislike for the system in the USA motivated him to seek an alternative system and he tried to create a utopia consisting of the opposites of the main tenets (parliamentarism, capitalism, nationalism, etc.) that underpin the political and economic system in the USA.

On the other hand, in the Turkish context there are some striking similarities between *Nowhereland* and earlier mainstream Turkish utopias. With his global vision, experimental approach to art, and pioneering role in electronic music, it might be expected that Mimaroğlu would display an avant-garde utopian imagination unlike that of earlier pro-state, authoritarian-prone writers. However, what we see in his work is nothing but enmity towards democracy and sympathy for a Jacobinist, authoritarian regime, an outlook focused on the state rather than the individual, and a preference for centralism. In this sense, the continuity between the mindsets of the administrative cadres of the single-party regime of the thirties and Mimaroğlu is striking, and it shows that the centralist and totalitarian tendencies of the modernising late Ottoman era and the period before and after the establishment of the Republic continue to be predominant in the minds of utopia writers with Turkish backgrounds.

Select Bibliography

Kılıç, Engin. "Kemalist Perspectives in the Early Republican Literary Utopias." *New Perspectives on Turkey* 36 (2007): 53–70.

Kumar, Krishan. *Utopianism.* Buckingham: Open University Press, 1990.

Mimaroğlu, İlhan. *Yokistan Tasarısı.* İstanbul: Pan, 1997.

Tanyeli, Uğur. "Zihinsel Yapımız Ütopyaya Kapalı mı?" *İstanbul* 5 (1993): 22–25.

76
Of Minarets and Bayonets:
The Poem that Landed Erdoğan in Jail

Petra de Bruijn

On 6 December 1997, Recep Tayyip Erdoğan (1954–), mayor of İstanbul at the time, visited the southeastern Anatolian city of Siirt, which is the hometown of his wife Emine (1955–). He gave a speech in which he accused the Turkish state of not respecting intellectual freedom and discriminating against race and religion. As he often did, he embellished the speech he gave with poetry. Later, when he was on trial, he stated that the lines he recited that day were from a poem written by Ziya Gökalp (1876–1924), who was a poet, sociologist, and ideologue of Turkish nationalism.

At the time, Erdoğan was the rising star of Turkish political Islam. In the 1990s, the Welfare Party (*Refah Partisi*, RP, 1983–1998), of which he was a prominent member, had been gaining increasing popular support for its conservative Islamic agenda, and in the elections of December 1995, it won the majority of votes. The RP was the successor of several other Islamic parties, namely the National Order Party (*Milli Nizam Partisi*, MNP, 1970–1971) and the National Salvation Party (*Milli Selamet Partisi*, MSP, 1972–1980), which had been closed down by the Kemalist secular-orientated military-judiciary establishment as it had been trying to politically accommodate an emerging class of contemporary Turkish nationalist Sunni Muslims. The parties had succeeded in drawing in constituents in Anatolia from among Turkish and Kurdish Sunni Muslims and internal migrants to the country's larger cities who had obtained better educations, thereafter coming to constitute a new conservative Muslim middle class.

Under the leadership of Necmettin Erbakan (1926–2011), such political parties propagated their ideas through the National Outlook (*Milli Görüş*), a worldview in which Muslim culture and norms were seen as the shared heritage of Turkey's citizens. It was based on notions of high moral standing, just rule, fairness to different ethnic and religious groups, and fighting corruption. Adherents of the National Outlook embraced democracy and modernity but rejected the radical secular model of Westernisation adopted by Kemalists, stating that it ran contrary to Turkish/Ottoman culture. They sought a return to a nineteenth-century Ottoman combination of modernisation and Turkish-Islamic reinvigoration.

Sufi orders, which had been officially banned since 1925, played an important role in these developments, and over the years they were transformed into cultural and educational organisations. In particular, the İstanbul-based İskenderpaşa Mosque, which was led by the charismatic imam Mehmed Zahid Kotku (1897–1980) and later his son-in-law Esad Coşan

(1938–2001), provided spiritual schooling for leading politicians such as Erbakan and Erdoğan, as well as for Turgut Özal (1927–1993), who served as prime minister and president.

Secular Turkish Kemalists saw the emergence of these populist Islamic political movements as a threat. Since the founding of the Republic, secularists had tried to restrict Muslim beliefs to the private domain and subject it to the control of the state. While after the military intervention of 1980 a controlled form of Islamisation of society was deemed to be preferable to leftist ideologies, overtly religious political movements were relentlessly suppressed. However, as the RP gained increasing support, winning several municipalities in the 1994 elections, including, among other cities, İstanbul and Ankara, its members became more and more audacious. For instance, upon winning the mayoral elections, Erdoğan opened the first session of the municipal council with a prayer instead of paying the usual tribute to the Republic and Mustafa Kemal Atatürk (1881-1938).

In June 1996, Necmettin Erbakan (1926–2011), then-leader of the RP, became prime minister, whereupon the military tried to shore up Turkey's secular values by putting pressure on the government. In February 1997, the RP mayor of Sincan organised a rally in support of Hamas and Hizballah, during which the Iranian ambassador asked Turks to help their Muslim brothers on the basis of Islamic prescriptions. The military used the commotion stirred up by the event to justify the issuance of a declaration stating that Islamic movements were the most pressing threat to internal security and issued a memorandum consisting of eighteen points with the aim of securing the predominance of the secular Kemalist ideology. Muslim academics were fired and companies run by Muslims were persecuted. Moreover, newspapers and television and radio stations were closed down, as were İmam-Hatip schools, which were vocational institutions of education for aspiring Muslim religious leaders.

In May 1997, the prosecutor of a supreme court in Ankara demanded the closure of the RP, accusing the party of engaging in anti-secular and illegal activities. The party was banned on 16 January 1998, and several of its members were prohibited from taking part in politics for five years. In the aftermath of the ruling, in April of 1998 a court sentenced Erdoğan to ten months of imprisonment and banned him from taking part in active politics; basing its decision on the lines of poetry he had recited during his speech in Siirt, the court stated that he had been inciting the people to hatred and enmity. Erdoğan served four months of his sentence, and after his release, he became a founding member of the Justice and Development Party (*Adalet ve Kalkınma Partisi*, AKP).

However, the lines of poetry that Erdoğan recited that day were not from a poem by Gökalp, but rather a poem that had been written by a rather unknown graphic artist and poet, Cevat Örnek (1907–1980). In order to help untangle the content and structure of the lines Erdoğan recited, the two original poems are presented below in translation.

The Two Poems*

Cevat Örnek's "The Divine Army"   *Ziya Gökalp's "Soldiers Prayer"*

The minarets are bayonets, the domes helmets,   A rifle in my hand, faith in my heart,
The mosques are our barracks, the believers   I have two wishes: religion and the
our soldiers,   motherland...
This divine army protects my religion,   My hearth is the army, my greatness the Sultan
On their tongues the unity of Allah, Allah is   ...
great.   Oh my Lord, help the Sultan!
          Oh my Lord, make his life augmented!

The believers' army, with the help of God,   Our road is a holy military expedition, our end
Fights superstition for the sake of religion,   martyrdom,
From eternity to future times, guided by the   Our religion wants sincerity and service,
Koran,   Our mother is the homeland, our father the
Allah is great, Allah is great.   nation,
          Oh my Lord, make the homeland prosperous!
          Oh my Lord, make the nation happy!

The most Generous Messenger is the guide to   My banner is the unity of God, my flag the
righteous religion,   crescent,
Belief always inspires Tradition,   One of them is green, the other red,
There is nothing Concealed or secret in our   Feel compassion for Islam, take revenge on the
religion,   enemy,
To put it simply, Allah is Great.   Oh my Lord, make Islam flourish!
          Oh my Lord, ruin the enemy!

          The commander, the officer are our fathers,
          The sergeant, the corporal are our masters,
          Order and respect are our laws,
          Oh my Lord, make the army orderly!
          Oh my Lord, make the banner superior!

* Translated from the original Turkish in Haluk Seki, "Şairi Arayan Şiir...," *Milliyet Blog*, 14 March 2014, http://blog.milliyet.com.tr/sairini-arayan-siir-/Blog/?BlogNo=453676. The poem was originally published in Cevat Örnek, *7 Dağın Çiçeği* (Ankara: Ayyıldız Matbaası, 1966), 8, and Cevat Örnek, *Gülün Dikeni*, (Ankara: n.a., 1974), 12. Gökalp's poem was translated from the original Turkish in Muhammer Ferik, *Recep Tayyip Erdoğan'lı Yıllar* (İstanbul: E-kitap Projesi, 2015), 67–68.

On the battlefield, how many brave young
heroes
Did not become martyrs for religion and the
homeland,
Let the hearth smoke, let hope not be
extinguished,
Oh my Lord, do not make the martyrs grieve!
Oh my Lord, do not make your descendants
helpless!

***

During his speech in Siirt, Erdoğan only recited the following lines: "The minarets are *our* bayonets, the domes our helmets, and for the mosques, they are *our* barracks" (the italics indicating additions Erdoğan made to the lines). As this quote demonstrates, the lines were indeed not from Ziya Gökalp's poem, but they do closely resemble the lines penned by Cevat Örnek. The source of the confusion was a school textbook written by Ömer Naci Bozkurt, a retired governor, who ascribed the first stanza of Örnek's poem to Ziya Gökalp and added it to the original poem in a book entitled *Türk ve Türklük* ("Turks and Turkishness") published by the Turkish Standards Institute (*Türk Standartları Enstitüsü*, 1994). The Ministry of Education approved the text and recommended it for use at schools. When he was standing trial in court, Erdoğan stated that he had always known the poem as Bozkurt had presented it, asserting that he had recited the lines on numerous occasions during his speeches. In September 1998, after Erdoğan's conviction, RP chairman Recai Kutan distributed that version of the poem to the press, claiming that during the War of Independence (1919–1923), a member of parliament had suggested to Mustafa Kemal Atatürk (1881–1938) that mosques be used as barracks and that the lead of their rooves should be melted down into bullets. Apparently, the link to Mustafa Kemal was deemed a valid enough argument to justify the attribution of the lines to Ziya Gökalp. In 2015, Erdoğan once again started reciting the lines of the poem in his speeches, whereupon it acquired cult status.

Accounts state that Ziya Gökalp published "Soldier's Prayer" in 1913 as a reflection on the traumatic events of the Balkan Wars (1912–1913), in which Balkan states conquered almost all of the European territories of the Ottoman Empire. Those losses were a brutal blow for the Ottomans economically, demographically, and intellectually, as the Balkans had been the most prosperous and culturally most developed parts of the Empire. In addition, the war resulted in numerous atrocities carried out against soldiers and civilians alike. For a nationalist philosopher like Gökalp, the war underscored the need to develop a particularly Turkish type of nationalism. In the nineteenth century, the empire had struggled to formulate a response to newly emergent forms of Western nationalism, which gave rise to pressing questions. Should such nationalism focus on Ottoman citizenship or Ottoman Muslim citizenship, or should it emphasise Turkish identity? When Gökalp was formulating his ideas about nationalism, he focused on the empire's Turkish-speaking, Sunni Muslim Ottoman citizens. In "Soldier's Prayer," Gökalp placed love for the homeland on par with religiosity and called on the military to defend both. The enemies in the poem are the Balkan states that attacked the Ottoman Empire, and Gökalp linked Islam intrinsically with the (Ottoman) state. After the establishment of the Republic, Kemalists developed the idea of Turkish nationalism further into a form in which Turkey's main religion was still Sunni Islam but, under the control of the secular state, it was largely concealed from public life. Turkish secularists nonetheless respected Gökalp as one of the early ideologues of a form of nationalism based on Turkish identity. After the Second World War and the development of a multi-party system, religion gradually returned to public life, whereupon Islamist parties started to garner more and more support. A combination of Turkish nationalism and Islam, known as the Turkish-Islamic Synthesis (*Türk-İslam Sentezi*), emerged in the 1970s and became a semi-official state ideology after the military intervention of 1980. For Islamists like Erdoğan, a poem such as "Soldier's Prayer" illustrated the political ideals of a modern nation-state based on Sunni Islam.

Cevat Örnek wrote his poem "The Divine Army" in the 1960s, a period in which a space was opened up for religious expression in public life to a greater extent than ever before since the founding of the Republic. He self-published the poem two times in 1966 and 1974 but never received any recognition among literary circles in those years. "The Divine Army" speaks of the struggle for the right to religion, and in the verses, believers are compared to an army fighting superstition and protecting their true faith. In contrast to Gökalp's poem, absent are the soldiers that save their homeland and religion from ruin.

It is unlikely that Ziya Gökalp himself would have added the lines to the poem because the structures of the poems differ significantly. The stanzas in "The Divine Army" consist of four lines, while the stanzas in "The Soldier's Prayer" contain five. Moreover, Örnek wrote his poem in the syllabic Turkish folk metre of eleven syllables with a break after the sixth, but the poem by Gökalp uses a metre consisting of ten syllables with a break after the fifth.

***

The case of these two poems exemplifies the use of cultural products within a political context. A politician takes a few lines from an ostensibly well-known poet and, while changing them at his own discretion, shows no interest in the poem's origin and form. The political message of the lines and the symbolic value of the author's name is what matters. Ziya Gökalp is venerated by both secular as well as Muslim conservatives. By claiming that the poem was authored by Gökalp, Erdoğan thought he would be saved from persecution. Even after numerous journalists and scholars revealed the poem's true origins, Erdoğan continued reciting the lines, referring to them as having been written by Ziya Gökalp. It would seem that the link to the prominent poet Ziya Gökalp, who is respected in Islamist circles because he included Islam in Turkish nationalism, is more valuable to him than literary truth.

Select Bibliography

Bardakçı, Murat. "Erdoğan'ı Yakan Mısralar Örnek'in." *Hürriyet,* 23 September 2002. https://www.hurriyet.com.tr/gundem/erdogan-i-yakan-misralar-ornek-in-99286

Dressler, Markus. "Rereading Ziya Gökalp: Secularism and Reform of the Islamic State in the Late Young Turk Period." *International Journal of Middle East Studies* 47, no. 3 (2015): 511–31.

Ferik, Muhammer. *Recep Tayyip Erdoğan'lı Yıllar.* İstanbul: E-kitap Projesi, 2015.

Öztan, Ramazan Hakkı. "Point of No Return? Prospects of Empire after the Ottoman Defeat in the Balkan Wars (1912–13)." *International Journal of Middle East Studies* 50, no. 1 (2018): 65–84.

Seki, Haluk. "Şairi arayan şiir…" *Milliyet Blog,* 14 March 2014. http://blog.milliyet.com.tr/sairini-arayan-siir-/Blog/?-BlogNo=453676

Uzer, Umut. *An Intellectual History of Turkish Nationalism Between Turkish Ethnicity and Islamic Identity.* Salt Lake City: University of Utah Press, 2016.

77

"Turkey in our Hands":
Polemics and Protest against the Headscarf Ban

Jan-Markus Vömel

The Islamic headscarf has been a contentious issue ever since debates about reforms started taking place in the last decades of the Ottoman Empire. In the Kemalist Republic, an all-out ban on headscarves was never introduced but several anti-veiling campaigns were launched. Since then, the authorities have generally not interfered with female veiling in everyday life, but state institutions such as universities, schools, offices, and military facilities generally enforced a ban on the basis of Kemalist notions of civic secularism, stipulating their vision of the secular republic's ideal citizen and his or her outer appearance. Early pro-veiling activism started in the 1960s and 1970s, inspired by revivalist currents and the nascent Islamist movement. Even though the military coup of 1980 adopted a more conservative form of republicanism, it was also accompanied by the government's strictest attempts to ban the veil from state institutions. It was only in the 1990s that headscarf polemics grew to become a mainstream public issue with a ubiquitous presence in daily politics. The ascendant Islamist movement had turned veiling into its main tool of propaganda and the secularist establishment was challenged by unrelenting demands to grant women wearing headscarves full access to educational and state institutions. Secularist forces perceived a fundamental threat to the republican order when the Islamist Welfare Party (*Refah Partisi*, RP) led a coalition government in 1996 and 1997, and they staged the government's downfall in the so-called "post-modern" coup that took place in early 1997. Known in Turkey as the "28 February period," it acquired an important place in Islamist lore as an emblem of injustice and the victimisation of the religious segments of the population under the rule of Kemalist secular elites. During this period, conflicts surrounding the headscarf issue reached new heights since the headscarf represented the symbolic locus of the culture wars between the two camps and the different versions of Turkish modernity they represented. A series of protests and heated clashes erupted, particularly at universities. In the autumn of 1998, Islamist media outlets called for a nationwide protest on behalf of headscarf-wearing students who asked people to gather peacefully and form a human chain along predetermined routes. The following article, which was published in the conservative daily newspaper *Akit* (*Covenant*), appeared among those calls to action.

Turkey in Our "Hands"[*]

Three million people will join hands and form a chain to protest the oppression of faith and thought. Today at 11:00 a.m., citizens all around the country will join hands and form a single chain to silently protest violations of human rights. At the same time, people all around Turkey, Europe, America, Bosnia and Herzegovina, and Chechnya will also come together on roads. For the first time, a chain of people will symbolise freedom.

Starting from İstanbul and thence to Ankara, north to Hopa, and east to Siirt, Turkey's heart will beat for freedom. The students stated that today's hand-in-hand event will not be a political act, march, or rally and said, "This is civil disobedience. No slogans will be shouted and no flags or pennants will be carried to represent any group."

The headscarved students are calling on citizens to be ready at the designated routes at 10:30 a.m. at the latest to prevent congestion at certain points, and they are calling on all people of sensitivity, regardless of religion, language, or political preference, to stand up for friendship, hope, peace, and the dignity of living humanely.

[A detailed description of the assembly points appears here.]

There are no legal obstacles to prevent this protest of "civil disobedience" against the headscarf ban on university students, which, as has been noted, will be held today as part of the hand-in-hand [event] for "respect for beliefs and freedom of thought".

The "freedom chain," which will start in front of İstanbul University's Cerrahpaşa Faculty of Medicine, is a democratic right according to Article 34 of the Constitution, Law No. 2911 on meetings and demonstrations, Supreme Court decisions, the Universal Declaration of Human Rights, and the European Convention on Human Rights, and obstructing that right would be a crime according to all those laws and international conventions.

The public's reaction to the headscarf ban, [taking the form of] civil unrest that will extend to Hopa in the north and Siirt in the south, is a constitutional right. Legal experts point out that since the public's reaction is not in the form of a demonstration [and will not have] slogans, banners, speeches, or marches, there are no prohibitive articles in the law [preventing it]. [...]

Lawyer Zeyd Aslan stated that there are no legal obstacles to a reaction against the headscarf ban and that it is a democratic right. Pointing out that this reaction can also be considered a form of civil disobedience, Aslan noted that the Supreme Court has ruled that this is the only way to show social discontent in accordance with the spirit of the constitution. [...]

---

[*] Translated from the original Turkish original in "Türkiye 'el'imizde," *Akit Gazetesi*, 11 October 1998, 1 and 10.

Emphasising that communities will also contribute to democracy by ensuring that incorrect practices which cause unease are brought to the attention of the public, lawyer Aslan said, "When people, individually or collectively, protest against practices they find to be incorrect in order to influence public opinion, it should be accepted as an expression of their democratic reactions. Any other notion would be distant from democracy, [nothing less than] the acceptance of the dominant one-type-of-person and one-type-of-thought element typical of totalitarian regimes." [...]

A criminal complaint accompanied by a request for a sentence of up to three years in prison will be filed against any governors, police chiefs, or police officers who attempt to obstruct the protest on the grounds that they violated Article 240 of the Turkish Penal Code.

***

While it is unclear how many people participated and how long the human chain ended up being, the result was nonetheless one of the largest political demonstrations in Turkish history and in many ways represented the symbolic pinnacle of the headscarf controversy. It went mostly undisturbed, though the police and gendarmerie intervened at some locations and took some participants into custody. In the following days, several of the organisers were taken into custody as well. While the Islamist media called on their followers to take part in the human chain in support of a headscarved group of students at İstanbul University's faculty of medicine, the organisers and propagandists behind the event were a group of known Islamist activist-intellectuals, including journalist and writer Abdurrahman Dilipak (1949–), who was among those rounded up later.

Both the article's lengthy legitimising discourse as well as its recourse to the language of universal human rights were typical for Islamists in the post-Cold War period. While otherwise critical of universal rights as a Western product, Islamists still utilised these arguments in the realm of headscarf polemics. It allowed them to connect with liberal and leftist positions and paint the opposing secularist-Kemalist forces as backward, illiberal, and statist-authoritarian. Moreover, Turkish Islamists often took great pains to demonstrate their loyalty to the Turkish state and developed a broad legitimising discourse stating that all of their goals and activism were within the bounds of the laws and statutes outlined by the state and international norms. By way of a short reference, the article also linked the struggles of Turkish women wearing the headscarf to international struggles in the Muslim world such as the conflicts in Chechnya and Bosnia which played an important, emotionally charged role in the Islamist mindset.

***

The history of the Republic of Turkey witnessed the complete marginalisation of political Islam followed by its slow reestablishment from the 1950s onwards before it rose to become the most vigorous political, social, and cultural movement in the nation in the 1990s and 2000s.

During that time, campaigning for the right of women to wear the headscarf was arguably the most powerful propagandistic tool at the disposal of Islamist thinkers, activists, and politicians. Secularist-Kemalist rigidity and its siege mentality, which linked the headscarf to the survival of the republic itself, had left that door wide open. The issue thus became a trump card for Islamists, who could connect their own agenda to women's rights, human rights, liberalism, and democratic standards. Islamism and later Islamic populist conservatism were able to benefit from this framing for decades.

The article's headline played on the notion of people holding hands in a giant human chain as a symbol of them holding the entire country in their hands. At first, that might seem like a far cry from reality given that Islamist politicians only recently had been driven out of the government by state forces that actually did hold the country in their hands. But in this case, it was not only the unshakable Islamist self-confidence derived from its broad social base that became manifest, but also the characteristic ambivalence between victimhood narratives and grandiose ambitions voiced here. Islamists continuously fashioned themselves as righteous outcasts and also as the true "owners" of the country. Far from being a contradiction, claims of victimhood bolstered their claims to power. In the 1990s, the Islamist movement also discovered the potential of women's grassroots activism, which played a critical role in how the movement scored its biggest political triumphs in that decade. The importance of women's activism and the headscarf issue, however, did not translate into women's representation in the upper echelons of Islamist movements, and Islamist and Islamic populist conservatism remain an almost exclusively male domain to this day. Nevertheless, public visibility of women donning the headscarf in all walks of life and social settings increased over the following decades and is a normality in today's Turkey.

Select Bibliography

Adak, Sevgi. *Anti-Veiling Campaigns in Turkey: State, Society and Gender in the Early Republic.* London: I.B. Tauris, 2022.

Aksoy, Murat. *Başörtüsü-Türban: Batılılaşma-Modernleşme, Laiklik ve Örtünme.* İstanbul: Kitap Yayınevi, 2005.

Arat, Yeşim. *Rethinking Islam and Liberal Democracy: Islamist Women in Turkish Politics.* New York: SUNY Press, 2005.

İlyasoğlu, Aynur. *Örtülü Kimlik: İslamci Kadın Kimliğinin Oluşum Öğeleri,* İstanbul: Metis Yayınları, 1994.

Özdalga, Elisabeth. *The Veiling Issue, Official Secularism and Popular Islam in Modern Turkey.* Richmond: Curzon, 2013.

78
"Turkey's Birthright":
The Promises of Turkish EU Candidacy

Müge Kınacıoğlu

Turkey's relations with the European Union (EU) have had a long and at times quite strained history that dates back to the 1950s. In 1959, Turkey applied to join what was then the European Economic Community. Subsequently, an association agreement was signed as an interim stage towards accession. The Ankara Agreement of 1963, which established Turkey's associate membership, was later supplemented by an Additional Protocol in 1970. The main aim of the Agreement was to strengthen continuous trade and economic relations between the parties and gradually establish a customs union.

Through the Agreement, it was established that membership in the Customs Union would be the last stage on the road to full membership. The Additional Protocol of 1970 further detailed the timing and conditions of the transition phase preceding association with the Customs Union by progressively lifting customs duties and lifting quantitative barriers in the trade of industrial goods between the parties. In addition, the Additional Protocol set the stages that foresaw Turkey's alignment with the EU's Common Commercial Policy (CCP) and Common External Tariff (CET). According to the Protocol, while the European Communities (EC) was to gradually abolish all customs duties imposed on goods imported from Turkey except for certain goods such as textiles and oil products, Turkey would progressively lift customs duties on EC industrial products after twelve years. Subsequent to the Association Agreement and the following Protocol, Turkey's economic and political relations with the EC progressively developed, despite fluctuations in bilateral relations. In April 1987, Turkey submitted a formal request for full membership. However, the European Commission rejected Turkey's application and the opening of negotiations in December 1989 on the basis that Turkey had grave economic and political problems. Nonetheless, the Commission also noted that unlike Morocco, which had also applied for membership in 1987, Turkey was eligible for full membership.

Although Turkish politicians were profoundly disappointed and shocked by the rejection of their application, their hopes for the prospects of accession were raised when Turkey and the EU signed a Customs Union Agreement for industrial products in 1995 (it entered into force in 1996), which would lead to deeper economic integration. Turkey was the first associate member to have entered the Customs Union before full membership. Although the Customs Union represented an historical milestone in relations, in 1997 the Luxembourg European Council maintained the decision it had made in 1989 with regards to Turkish membership.

Finally, welcoming positive developments in Turkey under the coalition government led by Bülent Ecevit (1925–2006), in December 1999 the Helsinki European Council granted Turkey candidacy status although accession negotiations were not opened following that decision, in contrast to the case of other candidate countries, namely Central and Eastern European states as well as Malta and Cyprus. Before opening the negotiations, the EU asked Turkey to fulfil the Copenhagen political criteria as well as demonstrate progress in resolving the Cyprus issue and its tensions with Greece. Meanwhile, the European Commission was to increase its financial assistance to Turkey to support the domestic reform process in line with the Copenhagen criteria, and at the same time, the Commission was also to monitor progress in Turkey with regard to these matters. Candidate status was considered to be a very significant step towards Turkey's long-standing desire for EU membership and was thus welcomed enthusiastically both by the Ecevit government and the Turkish public. The talk that Prime Minister Bülent Ecevit gave in Helsinki on 11 December 1999 highlights the hopes and opportunities envisioned on the occasion of Turkey's EU candidacy.

*Statement of Prime Minister Bülent Ecevit in Helsinki**

The official recognition of Turkey's candidate status for full membership to the European Union is a landmark event not only for Europe, but for the world as well. This candidacy, and in due time, full membership to the European Union, is Turkey's birthright by virtue of Turkey's historical development, its geography, and its present-day attributes as well as the provisions of the 1963 Association Agreement.

Moreover, for the last four years, Turkey has been the only country to have effected [*sic*] a customs union with the European Union without becoming a full member.

The declaration of Turkey as a candidate country on an equal footing with other candidate countries in an unequivocal manner and with clarity is a positive development.

Thereby, the road to full membership for Turkey is opened.

Turkey through NATO has contributed to the security of Europe and the West as a whole throughout the decades of the Cold War. It carried the heavy economic burden of this responsible role with a great sense of duty. Following the end of the Cold War and the demise of the bi-polar world, the geostrategic importance of Turkey has further expanded and grown. And, Turkey became a pivotal country in the Eurasian process.

---

* Ecevit's statement is available in English translation on the website of the Ministry of Foreign Affairs of the Republic of Turkey: https://www.mfa.gov.tr/statement-of-prime-minister-bulent-ecevit-in-helsinki-on-turkey_s-candidacy-to-the-eu_br_december-11_-1999-.en.mfa.

The Bosphorus bridges do not only straddle the two sides of İstanbul but they also unite the continents of Europe and Asia. And this, not only in geographic terms, but in the political and cultural senses of the word as well.

The Turks have been Europeans for 600 years. But the Turks are not only Europeans. They are also Asian, Caucasian and Middle Eastern at once. Turkey is a power in the Eastern Mediterranean and the Black Sea basins and the Balkans. It is becoming the energy terminal where the gas and oil riches of the Caspian Basin and the Caucasus will be transported to world markets.

As such, it is living testimony to the interaction between Europe and Asia and the confluence of Christianity, Islam, and Judaism. Turkey is the leading country in democracy and secularism among the countries having a majority Muslim population. It epitomises vividly the fallacy of the thoughts that underline the thesis of Rudyard Kipling, who said that the East and the West would never meet and those who think like Mr. Samuel Huntington that the clash of civilisations is inevitable.

These are precisely [the reasons] why Turkey's membership to the European Union is not just to the benefit of Turkey, but to the Union as well.

[...]

Indeed, during the six and a half months that elapsed after our three-party coalition government took office, we took far-reaching strides in expanding human rights and democracy in Turkey and in improving our economic performance. By way of examples, I wish to cite the following:
- Through a constitutional amendment, the members of the State Security Courts are to be chosen solely from amongst civilian judges and prosecutors.
- Again, by amending the Constitution we have recognised international arbitration and facilitated privatisation. By the end of the year, we will complete the necessary legislation that these amendments entail.
- We have taken necessary measures to prevent every kind of mistreatment.
- We have adopted legislation rendering civil servants accountable before courts for any of their offences.
- We have taken effective measures to combat organised crime.
- We have freed on parole convicted writers and journalists.
- We have passed a repentance law for those involved in separatist terrorism.
- Through a new legislative arrangement, we have rendered more difficult the closure of political parties.
- We have enacted a comprehensive tax reform.
- We have adopted a new legislation reforming our social security system.
- We have introduced an extensive reform through a new customs law.
- We have taken legislative action to strengthen and streamline our response to natural disasters.
- We have prepared a new civil code that will further enhance gender equality.

These are only a few examples of what our government has achieved in the way of extensive reforms during the past six and a half months.

On the other hand, we have started to take necessary measures to dampen chronic high inflation and to decrease as fast as we can high interest rates. We already observe the positive results of these measures.

[...]

These important strides that we were able to achieve in a short span of time not only reflect the harmony and the determination that prevails in our government, but also the propensity and the quest of the Turkish people to change and modernisation.

Some members of the European Union may think that it will take many years for Turkey to become a full member. But I am convinced that given the dynamism of the Turkish people and their attachment to democracy, we will achieve this objective in a far shorter period.

This will of course require the bona fide and sustained efforts of the part of both Turkey and the EU regarding the responsibilities and obligations they have thus assumed.

I hope that the decision of the EU Council may serve the high interests of Turkey, the European Union, and indeed, humanity itself.

***

Turkish Prime Minister Ecevit's statement demonstrates the profound satisfaction Turkey felt with the EU's decision to grant Turkey candidate status. As accession to the EU has long been Turkey' political and strategic goal, recognition of its candidacy not only represented a watershed in EU-Turkey relations, it also set into motion a period of regular political and economic reforms under the Ecevit-led coalition government. The prospect of EU membership was thus instrumental in intensifying efforts towards democratisation in Turkey. In that sense, the EU impacted Turkish politics as the promise of accession initiated a process of political change driven by the aim of complying with EU standards of democracy and human rights. The acceleration of Turkey's reforms, especially after 2001, led the Copenhagen European Council to conclude in December 2002 that it would decide when to open accession talks with Turkey at the December 2004 meeting of the Brussels European Council. After the election of the Justice and Development Party (*Adalet ve Kalkınma Partisi*, AKP) in 2002, the momentum for reforms was maintained and Turkey adopted four democratic reform packages. The key constitutional amendments included the abolition of the death penalty, the right to broadcast and teach in languages other than Turkish, liberalisation of the freedoms of speech, association, and assembly, and recognition of religious minorities' property rights. Consequently, accession talks started in 2005, although full membership was by no means guaranteed. Nonetheless, for many at the time, the journey towards EU membership in and of itself would anchor Turkey in Europe and foster democratisation in Turkey, even if full membership was not eventually realised.

***

The Customs Union was one of the most tangible and concrete steps towards Turkey's integration into the EU. On the other hand, acquiring candidate status was a milestone with regard to the 200-year history of efforts dedicated to Westernisation under both the Ottomans and the leaders of the Republic of Turkey, a process that got underway with the Tanzimat reforms in the mid-nineteenth century, all of which was largely perceived as confirming Turkey's Europeanness. EU membership has also been identified as the ultimate realisation of the Republican goal set by the country's founder Mustafa Kemal Atatürk (1881–1938) to attain the same level of civilisation as countries in Western Europe. Currently, Turkey is the only candidate country to have negotiated to join the EU for almost two decades and been an associate partner for half a century. While all other candidate countries have achieved full membership after the accession process, in Turkey's case, negotiations have been marked by hurdles and roadblocks, thus making full membership seem uncertain, if not unlikely.

Ironically, the EU accession process and the EU's initial enthusiastic support for Recep Tayyip Erdoğan (1954–), the leader of the AKP, has served to legitimate and consolidate his illiberal and increasingly authoritarian rule. In particular, as part of the EU reform process Erdoğan eliminated the role played by the military as guardian of the secular Turkish Republic and changed economic balances through the privatisation of state-owned enterprises, which in turn created pro-AKP business holdings that have become the economic backbone of the AKP. In the meantime, however, the prospects for Turkey's EU membership have become ever dimmer.

Select Bibliography

Avcı, Gamze, and Ali Çarkoğlu, eds. *Turkey and the EU: Accession and Reform.* London: Taylor and Francis, 2014.
Aydın-Düzgit, Senem, and Nathalie Tocci. *Turkey and the European Union.* London: Palgrave, 2015.
Müftüler-Baç, Meltem. "The Impact of the European Union on Turkish Politics." *East European Quarterly* 34, no. 2 (2000): 159–79.
Nas, Çiğdem, and Yonca Özer. *Turkey and EU Integration: Achievements and Obstacles.* London: Taylor and Francis, 2017.

79
The Return to the Village:
Turkey's State-Building in Kurdistan

Joost Jongerden

As part of its counter-insurgency strategy to reclaim the countryside in southeast Anatolia from the Kurdistan Workers' Party (*Partiya Karkerên Kurdistanê*, PKK), the Turkish Armed Forces evacuated and destroyed rural settlements on a massive scale in the 1990s. According to official figures, 833 villages and 2,382 small rural settlements, totalling 3,215 settlements, were evacuated and destroyed in fourteen provinces in the east and southeast, namely in Adıyaman, Ağrı, Batman, Bingöl, Bitlis, Diyarbakır, Elazığ, Hakkari, Mardin, Muş, Siirt, Şırnak, Tunceli, and Van. Of the approximately 12,000 rural settlements that were in existence, that makes about 25% of the total. According to various estimates, the evacuations displaced between 1 and 4 million rural inhabitants.

Several plans for resettlement or the controlled rural return of Kurdish villagers had already been made and discussed when the evacuations took place. It took until 2001, however, for a comprehensive plan to be released, one that, as it turned out, was more concerned about the settlement structure than with the forced migrants. That was the East and Southeast Anatolia Region Village Return and Rehabilitation Project Sub-region Development Plan (*Doğu ve Güneydoğu Anadolu Bölgesi Köye Dönüş ve Rehabilitasyon Projesi Alt Bölge Gelişme Planı*) coordinated by the Regional Development Administration of the Southeast Anatolia Project (*Bölge Kalkınma İdaresi – Güneydoğu Anadolu Projesi*, BKI-GAP) and guided by a steering committee comprised of the Minister of Internal Affairs, the (twelve) governors of the war-affected provinces included in the study, the State Planning Organisation (*Devlet Planlama Teşkilatı*, DPT), and the General Directorate of Rural Services (*Köy Hizmetleri Genel Müdürlüğü*).

The research for the study was carried out under the auspices of Prof Dr Oğuz Oyan (1947–), then president of the Turkish Social Sciences Association (Türk Sosyal Bilimler Derneği, TSBD) and vice-president of the Republican People's Party (*Cumhuriyet Halk Partisi*, CHP), and Prof Dr Melih Ersoy (1948–), a professor in the Department of Urban and Regional Planning in the Faculty of Architecture at Middle East Technical University (Orta Doğu Teknik Üniversitesi, ODTÜ) in Ankara. Interviews were conducted with governors, deputy-governors, district officers, and mayors, and focus group interviews took place with villagers from 297 villages in eleven of the war-affected provinces (Batman, Bingöl, Diyarbakır, Elazığ, Hakkari, Mardin, Muş, Siirt, Şırnak, Tunceli, and Van) involving 1,097 people (most of them displaced villagers). The villages were selected from three different lists provided by national, regional, and provincial authorities (the government, the GAP, and governors) and nominated as potential locations either for concentrated settlements or for the provision of central functions for surrounding villages.

The resulting publication, *The East and Southeast Anatolia Region Village Return and Rehabilitation Project Sub-Region Development Plan*, consists of twelve volumes, one for each (war-affected) province (in alphabetical order Batman, Bingöl, Bitlis, Diyarbakir, Elaziğ, Hakkari, Mardın, Muş, Siirt, Şırnak, Tunceli, and Van). Each report consists of four parts. The first part, which is identical for each report, is entitled "Definition and Scope of the Return to Village and Rehabilitation Sub-Region Plan" and explicates the conceptual framework. The second part gives the results of the focus group interviews, which include quantitative information on pre- and post-migration work and income, and qualitative information about opinions concerning the process of returning to the villages, the support expected, and ideas about the post-return reality. The third part, which is the most extensive (covering almost half of each report, which varies between 100 and 120 pages in length), is called a "sub-region development plan" and includes a feasibility study assessing the socio-economic, agricultural, geological, and climatological variables. The fourth and final part is an investment action plan. In parallel with the twelve provincial volumes, twelve "summaries for administrators" were prepared, serving, in effect, as proposals for pilot projects. These pilots include an assessment of development potential, an action plan, and a budget.

*The Return to Village and Rehabilitation Project**

The aim of the "Eastern and Southeastern Anatolia Region Return to Village and Rehabilitation Project Sub-Regional Development Plan" is to bring the groups who were subjected to involuntary migration and experienced the most severe problems into a productive situation that will be much more ben-eficial both for themselves and the country; through the right planning of the return to the villages, the costs of involuntary migration for society and the economy will be turned into an opportunity, and, in this context, rather than leaving the process of their return to its natural flow, which, given the current structure of the scattered settlements which are difficult to reach, would come with high service delivery costs and be overly dependent on agricultural activities, a new settlement pattern will be developed that organises the damaged housing and rural service infrastructure around a new understanding and creates a more rational and liveable physical and social environment.

[...]

The main purpose of the project is to develop a model or models for the rehabilitation and sustainability of settlements where a return to the villages is possible and to develop a plan for the implementation

---

* Translated from the original Turkish in Oğuz Oyan. Melih Ersoy, H. Çağatay Keskinok, H. Tarık Sengül, Galip Yalman, Remzi Sönmez, and Erdal Kurttas, eds. *Doğu ve Güneydoğu Anadolu Bölgesi Köye Dönüs ve Rehabilitasyon Projesi Alt Bölge Gelisme Planı*, 12 vols. (Ankara: GAP Bölge Kalkınma İdaresi (BKI) ve Türk Sosyal Bilimler Derneği, 2001).

of this in selected rural settlements. Within this framework, specifications and suggestions have been developed about the rural settlements, which can be considered sub-regions.

[...]

It has been observed that despite the fact that the southeastern and eastern Anatolian regions have, on the one hand, an extremely dispersed settlement pattern and, on the other hand, a large number of villages and sub-village units, the second- and third-level centres are not developed.

[...]

One of the principal features of the geographically inaccessible settlement structure is the number of small villages and hamlets that are disconnected from one another. This scattered spatial pattern has been the source of considerable problems. The most important of these is the high cost of service delivery. Village communities typically demand the establishment of a school, health centre, post office, and similar service provision facilities in their own villages. However, that could only be realised at a very high cost, and in cases where such services were provided, the facility providing the service would inevitably work below its capacity.

[...]

When looked at on the regional scale, in particular at the level of villages, it has been observed that the ranking (stratification) between settlements is a serious problem. The existing second-category centres are more prominent as service provision centres, whereas, in terms of rural production, they do not have the characteristics of economic units that offer opportunities for the development of markets, trade, and urban production activities. As a result, the lowest settlement units tend to develop commercial relations with the upper tier centres by going beyond the centres to which they are affiliated in terms of service provision. On the other hand, the dispersed settlement structure prevents the articulation of sufficient demand for the development of intermediate level centres. Therefore, instead of intermediate level centres for the economic activities of lower centres, activities that should take place at this level are carried out at higher level centres. For example, in villages where detailed field studies were carried out within the scope of the Return to Village Project, it was observed that the basic activities and facilities that should be found in the first tier were not present. This situation was a characteristic feature of the southeastern and eastern Anatolian regions before the migration.

As a result of all of this, including limited accessibility due to seasonal conditions, the requirements and costs of access have increased more than expected. Moreover, the relative weakness of intermediate centres prevents the formation of horizontal relations between villages. An important feature in the social structure of the eastern and southeastern Anatolia regions, self-contained (inward looking) rural units will be affected positively by the strengthening of intermediate level centres.

In summary, in the planning efforts for the process of return, the aim is to develop an understanding that will promote a stratification of certain settlements in terms of a consolidation (concentration) of services, on the one hand, and economic functions on the other.

***

The master plan was essentially concerned with state-building in the countryside. The term "rehabilitation" in the title of the plan referred to the treatment of perceived structural handicaps in the settlement structure, the many small rural settlements, their dispersed distribution, and perceived lacks, especially of local level inter-settlement articulation. Therefore, the evacuation of small rural settlements was considered an opportunity for the design of an "improved" (i.e., integrated and more productive) settlement structure. To develop this new, integrated settlement structure, the plan introduced two concepts: sub-region (*alt-bölge*) and centre-village (*merkez-köy*). A sub-region is a virtual cluster of settlements, based on economic, cultural, geographic, and social characteristics. The centre-village is a settlement within a sub-region, which, on the basis of its characteristics—size, location, and infrastructure—could function as a centre, becoming the intermediate entity between a nearby district town and the sub-region of villages and hamlets, and therefore extend the span of control of the central bureaucracy into the countryside.

The East and Southeast Anatolia Region Village Return and Rehabilitation Project Sub-Region Development Plan builds upon a government publication dating from 1982 which provides a classification and ranking of settlements in Turkey. The plan developed a classification system of settlements based on the functions performed (administrative, economic, social, cultural, and political) and a ranking according to their spatial impact (local, sub-regional, regional, national, and international). Executed nationwide, the study concluded that more than 10,000 villages (not including hamlets) were considered to be disconnected from the administrative system. On the basis of its classification, the State Planning Organisation noted a perceived weakness in the state's bureaucracy in the countryside which, in the southeast in the 1980s and 1990s, had created a space for the PKK to develop its presence, and the apparent need to draw the rural grid more closely into the state system.

***

The Kemalist elite in Turkey has been preoccupied with the production of places and people as bearers of Turkish identity since the establishment of the Republic. People thought to be infringing on the new national order were subjected to physical erasure (the Armenian genocide), removal (population exchanges with neighbouring countries), and assimilation. In the context of the latter, the Kemalist nation-builders considered the small and dispersed settlement structure to be a barrier to bringing in "civilisation". To accomplish this mission, a reduction in the number of villages by means of a concentration of the population into larger units was considered necessary so the state could down-scale administration costs and increase central bureaucratic control over the population. In 1963, 1983, and 1987, costs were calculated for a complete overhaul of the settlement structure by means of "village unification," while in the 1970s, using the terms *"Merkez-Köy"* (Centre-Village), *"Tarım-Kent"* (Agriculture-City), and *"Köy-Kent"* (Village-City), models were developed for the purposes of administrative clustering and modular urbanisation. It was in this context of perceived tensions between, on the one hand, the extension of the state's bureaucratic network into the countryside and, on the other hand, the high number of villages and their dispersed make-up that the evacuation of villages in Turkey's southeast was considered an opportunity. The counter-insurgent clearing of the countryside there created an "opportunity" to redesign the countryside so that the state could more effectively penetrate the daily lives of the inhabitants of rebellious areas. As such, the East and Southeast Anatolia Region Village Return and Rehabilitation Project Sub Region Development Plan can be analysed not only as an extension of a military counterinsurgency through development planning, but also as the resuscitation of a Kemalist nation-building fantasy. In that fantasy, the Kurdish question is one of control and assimilation.

Select Bibliography

Bozdoğan, Sibel. *Modernism and Nation Building: Turkish Architectural Culture in the Early Republic.* Seattle: University of Washington Press, 2001.

Doğanay, Filiz. *Merkez Köyler.* Ankara: Devlet Planlama Teşkilatı Yayını, 1993.

Jongerden, Joost. *The Settlement Issue in Turkey and the Kurds: An Analysis of Spatial Policies, Modernity and War.* Leiden & Boston: Brill, 2007.

Kezer, Zeynep. *Building Modern Turkey: State, Space, and Ideology in the Early Republic.* Pittsburgh: University of Pittsburgh Press, 2015.

Nalbantoğlu, Gülsüm Baydar. "Silent Interruptions, Urban Encounters with Rural Turkey: Rethinking Modernity and National Identity in Turkey." In *Rethinking Modernity and National Identity in Turkey,* edited by Sibel Bozdoğan and Reşat Kasaba, 192–210. Seattle: University of Washington Press, 1997.

Öktem, Kerem. "Reconstructing Geographies of Nationalism: Nation, Space and Discourse in Twentieth Century Turkey." PhD thesis, University of Oxford, 2005.

80

The "Marlboro" Law:
A Turning Point in the Neoliberalisation
of Rural Turkey

Zeynep Ceren Eren Benlisoy

The neoliberalisation of rural Turkey has been deepening and accelerating for a long time now. This process, which began roughly in the 1980s, has followed a fluctuating course. The Tobacco Law of 2001 (Law no. 4733) has held a very important place in the setting of policies that impact the businesses run by small producers. The law, which can also be seen as a milestone on the road to the intensification of capitalist relations, was one of what were known as "The Fifteen Laws in Fifteen Days". The government had promised to enact the law within the scope of the Transition to a Strong Economy Program, which was agreed upon as a result of an agreement made with the International Monetary Fund (IMF) during the major economic crisis of 2001.

The "Marlboro Law," as it is popularly known in reference to the American tobacco company owned by Philip Morris USA, was presented to the Grand National Assembly in 2001. It changed the fate of hundreds of thousands of tobacco producers and their families. Tobacco, one of the leading products of Turkey's agricultural sector, was the main source of income for mountain villages with barren soil, especially in western Anatolia, the Black Sea region, the Marmara region, and in eastern Anatolia. Tobacco producers, the total number of which reached 600,000 at that time, generally grew their crops on small plots of land and relied on household labour, meaning the labour of women and children. The articles of the Law put an end to state purchases of such products (Article 6) as well as support for tobacco production (Article 10), which forced producers to contend with merciless free market relations in capitalist agriculture. The Law also excluded the state from the setting of prices, leaving it to "agreements reached between tobacco product manufacturers and/or traders and the producers and/or their representatives". It further stated that, except for tobacco produced under a written contract, "tobacco shall be bought and sold by auction at auction centres."

Tobacco production had been under state protection before the law went into effect. The state had protected tobacco production and producers from the effects of the free market through purchase guarantees and support provided by the Monopoly of Tobacco, Tobacco Products, Salt and Alcohol Enterprises (TEKEL, the literal meaning of which is "monopoly"), which was one of the largest state-owned enterprises. But the Marlboro Law brought about a major change: government support and purchase guarantees were abolished, production was capped, and small producers were confronted with the mechanisms of the free market. While the economically and socially destructive effects of the Malboro Law caused a great deal of upheaval in rural areas, it also triggered undeniable changes in gender relations, labour use patterns, and geographical and rural-urban relations. Tobacco was also an important export product, the production framework of which had been inherited from the late Ottoman Empire. As such, the law led to a historical break. In interviews conducted between 2013 and 2016, some former tobacco workers said the following:

*The Narratives of Tobacco Producers**

Süleyman, born in 1952, primary school education, ex-tobacco producer: "Why would I quit if I can make money? In the past, we had three different types of income. We used to make money from olives, tobacco, and cotton, one after another. You could not find anyone in the village in the summer, as everyone would go to the highlands and stay with the livestock for three months; [our] livestock was precious. They put a quota on tobacco production in 2002, and then it was over. Cotton was out too. You know those supermarkets they have in the city? Well, all that has come here. The state is going to finish off small producers. They used to chase after us for fresh cheese, now they buy whatever they find in supermarkets. [Agricultural] production has stopped, it's hard for us to do our work. I am telling you, so long as there are greenhouses [referring to large-scale agribusinesses], the small-scale shepherd or farmer is finished."

Sevim, born in 1961, primary school education, ex-tobacco producer: "In tobacco, you either need your own field, or your own workers. You need support from somewhere. We didn't have it, so we always worked for others. You work like a dog, ploughing the fields, working yourself to the bone. It's tough work. You work at night in the cold, get little sleep, and if you brought workers, you have to get up at three in the morning. We stopped producing tobacco in the 2000s after the quota was introduced. What we produced before was always much more than the amount set by the quota. First, we tried to find a way, such as registering our product in the name of another producer. Yet it did not work after a while, it was still too much, we still exceeded the production limits. [...] The men don't go to the fields alone. The women work a lot too. Maybe one per cent or something go to the fields alone and do their own work. My aunt's husband took her to the fields just so she could prepare food. He didn't want it prepared the night before. He wanted to eat it freshly cooked in the fields. That woman would prepare the entire meal from scratch there on the spot. Look, I worked as a farmer [unpaid family labourer] for so many years but I don't have any [social] security. [My husband] always did the insurance in his name. Back then we didn't know better, we were too young. And anyway, it's not like he'd have taken me to the bank if I'd asked him to. The women are stuck inside, work, work, work. [...] The youth are

* Translated from original Turkish-language interviews conducted with former tobacco producers during fieldwork carried out in the Bakırçay Basin in the Aegean region from 2013 to 2016 by Zeynep Ceren Eren Benlisoy, "Gendered Rural Transformation and Peasant-Workers: The Case of the Women Workers at the Greenhouse, Western Anatolia, Turkey" (PhD thesis, Middle East Technical University, 2020).

not willing to farm anymore. Almost everyone has given up on working in tobacco now. Everyone has moved to town. The youth want to be educated, to have a job with a regular salary and insurance."

Yakup, born in 1971, primary school dropout, ex-tobacco producer: "Now what we experience is in total contrast to what we once had as tobacco producers. Back then, everyone used to compare the price of tobacco with the price of *rakı* [a traditional alcohol drink flavored with anise] or gold; the purchasing power of the producers was quite high. TEKEL was around then, but now it is gone. You used to get [a quota of] two tons, so with one ton you'd pay off your debts, and with the other ton you'd buy yourself a tractor. Now four tons won't even buy you a motorbike. That was fifteen to twenty years ago."

Gülümser, born in 1969, primary school education, ex-tobacco producer: "Many workers from Kınık come to the greenhouses to work. Kınık is 100 kilometres away from the greenhouses. Those people get up at five to make it [on time] but they get the same wages. They are not natives of Kınık, but some of their mountain villagers have now also settled there. The workers come from the villages by getting on the worker shuttles. They come from many places, such as Soma, Cinge, and Dikili, to work in the greenhouses. They are tobacco producers. But since there are no jobs for them, they come to the greenhouses. If you ask them about their profession, they will say, 'I am a tobacco producer'. It's been four or five years since I got out of tobacco production too."

Behiye, born in 1982, primary school dropout, ex-tobacco producer: "My son turned one year old in 2004, and we used to go work the tobacco [fields] at two o'clock. We didn't have diapers, so we used rags. We used to build swings for them. We would breastfeed in the middle of doing tobacco work. We used to take care of our garden for kitchen goods [referring to subsistence production]. We lived in one room then, and there was no bathroom. I used to wash our clothes by hand and do all the housework. [...] Once, while we were working in the tobacco field, my son fell off the tractor. I asked, 'Is he dead?' and they said, 'He isn't dead.' I replied, 'Okay, nothing has happened then!' and continued working. [...] We were working for someone else in the morning [as agricultural labourers] and did our work in the evening [tobacco work]. I planted tobacco [for the last time] in 2010. There were seven acres on C. Plain. We put up a tent in the tobacco field; my husband [who was a mine worker at the same time] was travelling to and from the mine on a motorcycle. In the meantime, we hired workers for the harvest. There were scorpions, mice, turtles, snakes—you name it—out there in the fields. We earned little; the money we made from tobacco did not even cover our costs. My husband was very tired. We did not want to get back into it again. But back then, we used to plant tobacco and we also used to have tomatoes, cotton, and livestock. It would make a lot of money. Nobody would have thought of [social] insurance then. Not so now."

***

As can be surmised from the narratives of the producers presented above, the Marlboro Law had drastic effects on households that were engaged in small-scale tobacco production. The number of households involved in tobacco production fell dramatically. At the time the Law was signed into effect, tobacco was cultivated in 5,001 villages by a total of 575,796 families. Most tobacco-producing households had to abandon tobacco cultivation, and once the producers stopped cultivation, tobacco factory workers also lost their jobs. The number of tobacco-producing households fell from 583,400 in 2000 to 222,400 in 2006, while tobacco production dropped from 208 tons in 2000 to 82.3 tons in 2022. Production was restricted through the quota system and intermediaries started taking on more prominent roles. Along with the end of subsidies, contract-based production led to an even more drastic reduction in the areas used for tobacco cultivation. Transnational companies started to dominate the tobacco and cigarette market.

The shift in tobacco production, from being a traditional agricultural product to the current state of limited cultivation, further contributed to an intensification of the diversification of income and deepening forms of semi/full proletarianisation. The massive decrease in the number of unpaid family labourers in rural areas (the majority of whom were women) indicates that there were further changes in the use of women's labour. While rural women stopped being involved in tobacco production, it is clear that their participation in employment is still limited to rural markets, especially in terms of paid and formal jobs. However, as seen in the narratives of the women above, they had a heavy work burden because of their particular role in production and reproduction based on the gendered division of labour in tobacco production. In that sense, the Marlboro Law seems to have led to structural changes in gender relations for women living in rural areas, even though the potential was limited.

***

The neoliberal re-making of rural areas in Turkey, as crystallised in the Marlboro Law, was not only manifested in a decrease of national production and export rates as well as a reduction in the number of producers and their impoverishment, but also highlights the geographical, socio-cultural, and gendered implications of that shift. Mountain villages suffered more from outward migration, an aging population, and the end of tobacco production as the soil type generally does not allow producers to switch to an alternative agricultural product. The average age of tobacco producers in western Anatolia increased to forty-seven, indicating that the younger generations were leaving tobacco production. The loss of esteem for small-scale producers' identities associated with agricultural production now seems to have had a greater impact on younger generations in rural areas in terms of the separation from production and the devaluation of rural life.

Today in Anatolia, local strains are no longer produced but rather the strains are determined by capitalist motivations and demand in the global tobacco market. Tobacco production and marketing are dominated by international companies based on contract farming. Those contracts can be seen as concrete examples of the unequal relations between powerful international companies and poor, unorganised tobacco producers. Within that context, the Marlboro Law has played a pivotal role in the age of neoliberalism in the course of that drastic shift in rural Turkey.

Select Bibliography

Atasoy, Yıldız. *Commodification of Global Agrifood Systems and Agro- Ecology: Convergence, Divergence and Beyond in Turkey*. London: Routledge, 2017.

Aydın, Zülküf. "Neo-Liberal Transformation of Turkish Agriculture." *Journal of Agrarian Change* 10, no. 2 (2010): 149–87.

Aydın, Zülküf. "Yapısal Uyum Politikaları ve Kırsal Alanda Beka Stratejilerinin Özelleştirilmesi; Söke'nin Tuzburgazı ve Sivrihisar'ın Kınık Köyleri Örneği." *Toplum ve Bilim* 88 (2001): 11–31.

Aysu, Abdullah. "The Liberalization of Turkish Agriculture and the Dissolution of Small Peasantry." *Perspectives: Political Analysis and Commentary from Turkey* 6 (2013): 14–21.

Eren Benlisoy, Zeynep Ceren. "Women in Agribusiness Amid Crises of Social Reproduction: The Case of Women Workers at the Greenhouse, Turkey." *Journal of Peasant Studies* (2023). https://doi.org/10.1080/03066150.2023.2170790

Suzuki, Miki, and Ayşe Gündüz Hoşgör. "Challenging Geographical Disadvantages and Social Exclusion: A Case Study of Gendered Rural Transformation in Mountain Villages in the Western Black Sea Region of Turkey." *Sociologia Ruralis* 59, no. 3 (2019): 540–99.

2003–2012

81

Another Period of Hope and Disappointment: Yearning for Inclusivity and Diversity in Turkey

Ohannes Kılıçdağı

The Republic of Turkey was founded in 1923 and thereafter moulded into a Turkish nation-state. As a part of the nation-building project, political elites shaped the country's political, social, and cultural spheres in such a way that the ethnic Turkish and Sunni Muslim identity dominated over all others. The physical extermination of Christians (Armenians, Greeks, and Assyrians) during the First World War and in subsequent years and the exchange of the Anatolian Greek population with Muslims from Greece in 1923–1924 had already left the population much more homogeneous than it was in the pre-1914 period. According to the 1927 census, the number of Christians and Jews had dropped as low as 360,000, which is equal to approximately 2.5 per cent of the whole population, whereas that figure had stood at around 20 per cent in 1914. The remaining Christians and Jews have been discriminated against in overt and covert ways throughout the history of the Republic, and that has included discriminatory treatment by the state such as the levying of a Wealth Tax between 1942 and 1944, a pogrom in İstanbul in 1955, and the purge of Greeks in 1964 on the pretext of the Cyprus dispute. Additionally, as an extremely negative image of Christians and Jews has been created and spread through public education, the media, and popular culture, being visible in the public sphere has been very risky for them. Consequently, Christians and Jews have regularly left Turkey to settle in various other countries. Today, they constitute less than 0.1% of the whole population.

As for non-Turkish Muslims, especially Kurds, the state has followed an assimilationist approach. In official discourses, these groups were defined as "prospective Turks". As the goal is to Turkify those groups, educational, cultural, and linguistic policies have been shaped in accordance with that aim and the public representation of non-Turkish identities has been shown little tolerance. For example, although the severity of persecution has varied at times, usage of the Kurdish language in education, cultural activities, and in public spaces was suppressed. Similarly, recognition of Alevism as a legitimate faith or confession has been always a matter of debate and dispute in Turkey. Given this historical-political background, the public visibility and recognition of non-Sunni and non-Turkish identities has been an indispensable part of democratisation in Turkey. Every "democratisation package" prepared by the government has contained certain promises to improve the living conditions of minority groups. Their situation has been one of the headlines in every European Union (EU) progress report on Turkey since its application for membership in 1987.

Toward the end of the 1990s, it became relatively easier for non-Turks, especially non-Muslims, to articulate themselves publicly. There were various reasons for this shift, such as the arrival of postmodern modes of thought in Turkey and the collapse of the Soviet Union, as well as a concomitant relative easing of the political environment and increase in the legitimacy of identity politics. As for economic factors, years of hyper-inflation seemed to have been left behind, and from 2002 to 2007, the average annual rate of growth stood at around 7 per cent. On the political side, following a series of unstable cabinets in the 1990s, the Justice and Development Party (*Adalet ve Kalkınma Partisi*, AKP), which had been established by a group that split from the Islamist Felicity Party (*Saadet Partisi*, SP), won the majority in Parliament (363 of 550 seats) in the elections on 3 November 2002. Although the party only won 34.28 per cent of the vote, thanks to the 10 per cent threshold, it was able to form a single-party government. From 2002 until today, Turkey has been governed by cabinets formed by the AKP. The period 2002–2007 witnessed some reforms for democracy as Turkey's bid for membership in the European Union was revitalised. Indeed, the EU decided to start accession negotiations with Turkey on 17 December 2004, as the country was deemed to have sufficiently met the Copenhagen criteria as an indicator of democratic development. Negotiations officially started on 3 October 2005, and they were followed by a series of other reforms that expanded freedom of speech and association. In this way, the initial years of the 2000s were buoyed by a more optimistic mood.

The newspaper *Agos*, as the bilingual Turkish-Armenian voice of the Armenian community, was established in 1996. The aim of the founders was to create a space in which to respond to accusations and fabricated news about Armenians in the media, which associated Armenians with terrorism. From that point onward, *Agos* became a platform defending the rights of not only Armenians but all oppressed and marginalised groups in Turkey. The following excerpts are from two pieces published in *Agos*. They were written by Hrant Dink (1954–2007), a member of the Armenian community and one of the founders of *Agos* as well as the newspaper's chief editor. He wrote numerous articles in *Agos* in which he tried to establish a dialogue between Turks and Armenians as well as between Turkey and Armenia. After one article he wrote about Armenian identity was published, a hate campaign was launched against him on the grounds that he had "insulted Turkishness". A criminal lawsuit was also filed against him for the same reason in 2005. At the end of the trial, the court found him guilty but postponed his sentence. The Court of Cassation approved the sentence but sent it to the court of first instance to reassess the postponement. However, before the retrial concluded, Hrant Dink was assassinated on 17 January 2007 by a Turkist gunman. The following excerpts are from his articles *"Pariluys"* (which means "Good Morning" in Armenian) and *"Türkiyeli Olmak"* ("Being Turkeyite") which appeared in *Agos*. There is no established English equivalent for the term "Türkiyeli," which is used to denote all citizens of Turkey regardless of their ethnic or religious identities. "Turkeyite" is a possible translation, inspired by the terms İstanbulite and Cypriote.

Hrant Dink's Call for a Democratic Identity[*]

"Good Morning," *Agos*, 18 June 2004

We are living long overdue days.

Public television and radio are broadcasting in the languages of Anatolia, even if it is for the sake of appearances.

Zana and her friends are free... The local people of Diyarbakır, enjoying their cultural freedom, rejoice at festivals.

Master of the *duduk* [a traditional woodwind instrument] Jivan Gasparyan delivers songs of peace from the Armenian people to the Turkish people on a Turkish channel.

A movie about the agonies of the Armenian people is broadcast on a Turkish TV channel for the first time.

Good morning my beautiful country, good morning.

***

The joyful and promising events of the last weeks are like a bouquet of spring flowers.

Undoubtedly, they are not the ultimate solution to our problems, which have become unsolved taboos.

Surely, there are many shortfalls, piles of work waiting to be done.

But let it be so... Let it be.

Consider the beginning to be hopeful and welcome these small steps.

Say "good morning" to these tiny but huge steps...

***

This historical momentum is the most significant opportunity to end pains that have been lived through for years.

[...]

The intellectuals of Turkey, without any exceptions, have a very important duty now.

They should blow like a wind from the west and east. Peace lovers should not leave the room to warmongers. [...]

***

Our ship of democracy is [set] on an irreversible route.

Let the EU give a date for negotiations or not, there should be no return from this path.

[*] Translated from the original Turkish in Hrant Dink, "*Parıluys*," *Agos*, 18 June 2004, and Hrant Dink, "*Türkiyeli Olmak*," *Agos*, 18 September 2003. Also available in Hrant Dink, *Bu Köşedeki Adam* (İstanbul: Hrant Dink Vakfı Yayınları, 2009).

[...]

O Freedom, how magnificent you are.

"Being a Turkeyite," *Agos*, 18 September 2003

I believe that the concept of "Turkeyite," which has been brought up by the prime minister once again, is an important springboard for the democratisation of Turkey.

[...]

How can I so easily feel that I am Turkish after so many experiences in which our national unity is equated with Turkism?

[...]

Henceforth, there is a need for a new concept that makes us feel we are equal citizens of the Turkish Republic.

Turkeyiteness [*Türkiyelilik*], in Prime Minister Erdoğan's discourse, meets this need very well.

Terms such as Turkeyite Greek, Turkeyite Turk, Turkeyite Armenian, and Turkeyite Kurd are more realistic and plausible than the absurd and strained terms Turkish Greek, Turkish Turk, Turkish Armenian, and Turkish Kurd.

[...]

As far as I know, race, besides being a sociological term, is a biological term as well, and in both senses it serves to segregate creatures and human beings on the basis of their sociological and biological differences.

Not unite them.

Hence, speaking of race in the national anthem evokes not unification but discrimination, and what's more it is reminiscent of racism, which is the most violent [form of] discrimination.

***

These excerpts from pieces by Hrant Dink clearly reflect the optimistic and hopeful mood of the time. However, he also mentions a feeling of belatedness, as when these articles were written, 80 years had passed since the establishment of the Republic but the absolute equality of citizens had yet to be established. Still, the excerpts show he also believed that there was a significant amount of momentum for democratisation in Turkey in the early 2000s. Economic and political conditions, both domestic and global, seemed to be suitable for a new beginning and a new definition of citizenship, which started to become crystallised during discussions about writing a new constitution. In fact, the AKP formed a commission under the chairmanship of Prof. Ergun Özbudun (1937–) to draft a new constitution. This commission, in consultation with various segments of society, had prepared and submitted a draft in September 2007 which prioritised human rights and liberties and proposed a more de-centralised government. However, the AKP never adopted and declared the draft as its own proposal for a new constitution. Today, it has been almost completely forgotten.

It is not a coincidence that Dink referred to Kurdish and Armenian identities and how they are perceived and treated in public. A homogenising, centralist governmental mentality had criminalised both of them along with their representations. That is why Dink underscored the recognition of diversity and inclusiveness as ways to secure peace and social cohabitation. As an alternative to Turkishness, which denotes a specific ethnic identity, the concept "Turkeyite" (*Türkiyeli*) was seen by Dink, besides many others, as a notion that recognises diversity and the equality of citizens since it is an inclusive term encompassing Turks as well as non-Turks. However, there are proponents of another view that oppose the term. They, echoing the constitution of 1982, claim that anyone who is "tied to Turkey through citizenship shall be called Turkish". Indeed, that is the omnipresent formula of the official ideology in Turkey, which seems to reflect an understanding steeped in civic nationalism. Nevertheless, other policies, actions, and positions, such as constantly referring to the mythic narrative that Turks are a Central Asian people who immigrated to Anatolia, make this claim inconsistent and less credible. Similarly, suppressing languages other than Turkish in education and in public spaces conflicts with the civic nationalist assertion that the category of Turkishness includes all citizens equally. Underlining Turkish language and history as being particular to Turkishness, on the one hand, and claiming that everyone who has "ties to Turkey through citizenship is Turkish" on the other, is an inconsistency that still persists today. That is why Hrant Dink asked, "How can I so easily feel that I am Turkish after so many experiences in which our national unity is equated with Turkism?" He also rightfully pointed to the inconsistency of referring to race as a symbolic-descriptive element of Turkishness while claiming that the term "Turk" denotes all citizens of Turkey. Although Turkeyite is a more established term today compared to the early 2000s, it is still a matter of controversy and conflict.

In these writings, Dink was also aware that progress would not come easily and that there had to be a struggle for democratisation. That is why he made a call to intellectuals "from the west and east," meaning Turkish and Kurdish intellectuals, and to "peace lovers" to support the momentum of events against "warmongers," as nationalism was, and still is, a strong current in Turkish society and politics.

***

Dink was not able to witness the peace process and negotiations with the Workers' Party of Kurdistan (*Partiya Karkerên Kurdistanê*, PKK) that got underway in 2013 only to fail in less than two years and even pave the way for the opening of yet another bloody chapter. Even if the reasons for that failure are various, the vehement opposition expressed by nationalist circles who asserted that the peace process was "a concession to separatists" played a major role. Meanwhile, the AKP turned its back on its initial reforms.

Recep Tayyip Erdoğan's (1954–) AKP has been the ruling party in Turkey since 2002. However, even the party has become secondary, as one-man-rule dominates every process of decision-making in the presidential system that was accepted in the referendum held on 16 April 2017. Turkey has been experiencing a dramatic backsliding of democracy for the last decade, especially after the coup attempt on 15 July 2016. Accordingly, Turkish nationalist and statist discourses have regained momentum as President Erdoğan himself also spreads them.

Looking back, people tend to project the current state of authoritarianism onto the beginnings of the AKP's rule. They argue that the charged political atmosphere in Turkey has been the same for the last two decades. This perspective, however, glosses over the changes and fluctuations that have occurred. It is an ahistorical way of thinking and analysing. In order to avoid this fallacy, it is important to focus on the discussions that took place and the atmosphere of the early 2000s. In that sense, looking back at Hrant Dink's articles is a helpful way of remembering the debates and political atmosphere of the early 2000s as well as the discourses that Erdoğan put forward in those days. The fact that Dink belonged to a minority community that is typically more sensitive to changes, whether positive or negative, in the political atmosphere of the country in which they live makes his perceptions of those moments all the more important. Minorities in Turkey, or anywhere else for that matter, are like canaries in a cage carried into a mine or barometers of democracy. If they can "tweet" freely, then the political atmosphere is healthy enough for us to breathe and hope; if their voices are muted, it is the harbinger of an approaching storm. Indeed, the hate campaign that was launched against Dink and his assassination could have been seen as an omen of the years to come, but this had not been taken seriously enough.

Select Bibliography

Çandar, Tuba. *Hrant Dink: An Armenian Voice of the Voiceless in Turkey*. New Brunswick: Transaction Publishers, 2016.

Keyman, E. Fuat, and Ahmet İçduygu, eds. *Citizenship in a Global World: European Questions and Turkish Experiences*. London and New York: Routledge, 2005.

Kumbaracıbaşı, Arda Can. *Turkish Politics and the Rise of the AKP: Dilemmas of Institutionalisation and Leadership Strategy*. Abingdon: Routledge, 2009.

Suciyan, Talin. *The Armenians in Modern Turkey: Post-Genocide Society, Politics and History*. London: I.B. Tauris, 2016.

Tezcür, Güneş Murat. *Muslim Reformers in Iran and Turkey: The Paradox of Moderation*. Austin: University of Texas Press, 2010.

Turan. Ömer. "Yeni Bir Paradigmayı Beklemek ya da Tarihsel Sosyolojinin İlhamı." *Birikim*, no. 366 (2019): 67–80.

82

Towards New Ways:
Gendering the New Turkish Penal Code

Nicole A.N.M. van Os

During the period of rapprochement between Turkey and the European Union in the 2000s, the latter had been pushing for a revision of the Turkish penal code, which dated from 1926 and was based on the Italian Penal code of the 1920s. Such a revision would have the potential to make the code less discriminatory for women and, since it could provide women with better legal protection, a revised code offered the possibility to comply with the United Nations' Convention on the Elimination of All Forms of Discrimination against Women (CEDAW), which Turkey had ratified in December of 1985. During the process of revisions for another code—the civil code of 2001—a network of more than 120 women's organisations had joined forces under the auspices of the Women for Women's Human Rights – New Ways Association (*Kadının İnsan Hakları – Yeni Çözümler Derneği*) and succeeded in getting several points in the proposal amended to ensure a more equal gender balance. Their courage bolstered by that success, 27 women's organisations formed the Women's Platform on the Turkish Penal Code (*Türk Ceza Kanunu Kadın Platformu*) to critically assess the draft of the new penal code that would be released. While the EU was looking for changes such as the abolishment of the death penalty and improved guarantees for freedom of expression, the Women's Platform sought to make the penal code more gender equal and eliminate the underlying principle of the old code, which was based on the idea that women's bodies and sexuality were not theirs but belonged to society and their families, husbands, and fathers. The text below is an excerpt from their first analysis of the draft Turkish penal code and the Platform's proposed amendments.

Amendments Proposed by the Women's Platform on the Penal Code*

[4] Perpetuation of Gender Discrimination in the Draft Law Prepared by the Conservative Justice and Development Party
The underlying philosophy that women's bodies are commodities of men, family and society, and women's sexuality has to be suppressed and controlled is reflected in the provisions on sexual offenses both in the penal code in effect and in the draft law.

---

* Women for Women's Human Rights – New Ways Association, *Gender Discrimination in the Turkish Penal Code Draft Law: An Analysis of the Draft Law from a Gender Perspective and Proposed Amendments by the Women's*

[...]

[5] Unless Turkey is willing to accept being a State in which women can not exercise their basic human right to bodily integrity, the Penal Code Draft Law must be amended before it is approved. Otherwise, the Turkish judicial system will continue to be one which [...] legitimises killings in the name of "honor" [...] and classifies sexual assaults as crimes against society and public morality and assesses grievance of sexual crimes on constructs of "chastity" and "honor" rather than the individual's sexual and bodily integrity.

[...]

[6] The Penal Code Draft Law regulates sexual offenses under "Crimes against Society," instead of under "Crimes Against Persons"
Both the current Turkish Penal Code and the draft law classify sexual crimes under "Crimes Against Society." In the draft law, articles pertaining to sexual offenses (Articles 315-329) are listed under the sub-section entitled "Crimes Against Sexual Integrity and Traditions of Morality."

[...]

The emphasis on traditions, morality and chastity in the section's title further sanctions the notion that women's bodies and sexuality are to be controlled [and] suppressed as commodities of the society, family or men. Presenting these subjective values as criteria for legislation not only serves to manipulate the law as a tool for violating women's human rights, but also undermines the objective of legal authority in a social state.

[...]

[7] The so-called "honor killings" are premeditated murders that continue to infect all segments of Turkish society and threaten and violate the most basic human right of women: the right to life. The state holds a constitutional duty to protect this right and take the necessary measures to prevent and eradicate honor crimes. As the medium in which criminal law is regulated, the penal code has to be designed to recognise this violent crime and penalise it accordingly.
However, the provisions in the draft law do not propose preventive measures against honor killings. On the contrary, Article 31 (Unjust Provocation) implicitly offers license to perpetrators of honor killings and legitimises this violent tradition under the pretext of penal law. According to the current draft, with Article 31, honor killing perpetrators can benefit from "unjust provocation" and thereby receive up to three fourths reduction in their sentences.

Platform on the Penal Code, Summary Report, trans. Liz E. Amando (İstanbul: New Ways, 2003). https://www.zwang-sheirat.de/images/downloads/english/Gender_Discrimination_in_the_turkish_Penal_Code_Draft_Law.pdf

2003–2012

***

The excerpts above constitute only a small fragment of the Platform's analysis and proposed amendments to the draft penal code. In addition to honour killings, the Women's Platform raised issues concerning marital rape, the sanctioning of the forced marriage of rape victims to the perpetrators of the crime, and the drawing of a distinction between virgin and non-virgin and married and non-married women in the case of sexual assaults.

Crucial to their criticism was the argument that women's bodies continued to be objectified in the draft. Sexual offenses were not treated as offenses against the bodily integrity of an individual, but rather crimes against "honour/chastity" (*ırz*) or "morality," concepts which define a (female) body and what happens to it as relevant not to the (female) individual but to a larger community, such as, for example, the individual's family. The patriarchal concept of honour killing, the killing of, in general, women who are regarded to have dishonoured the family by way of the perceived transgression of social and sexual norms through their behaviour and its punishment, was pivotal to the Platform's critical review of the new TCP and its proposed amendments.

The work of the Women's Platform did not end with this analysis nor with its demands for amendments. Governments are required to officially report on a regular basis on the progress made towards the implementation of the Convention, the CEDAW, at the national level, such as in relation to the harmonisation of national laws with its tenets. Turkey is no exception. While the Turkish government did send in its regular official reports, women's groups joined forces to write alternative reports pointing out the shortcomings of the Turkish government and its reports. In the period of time between the acceptance of the new Turkish penal code in Parliament in September 2004 and its official implementation on 1 June 2005, the Platform submitted such an alternative report in January 2005. The report showed not only how the women's groups critically assessed the Turkish government and its implementation of the Convention, but also how the new Turkish penal code, despite the amendments that were made, still fell short of the expectations of women's groups, ultimately leading the CEDAW review committee to add further recommendations.

***

Through their campaign, the Women's Platform was able to get more than thirty articles amended to ensure the better protection of women's rights. The new penal code was published in the *Official Gazette* on 12 October 2004. While it was originally supposed to enter into force on 1 April 2005, that date was postponed until 1 June 2005.

Realising that cooperation had been a useful strategy for lobbying during the process of the revision of the Turkish penal code and, earlier, the civil code, more than 200 women's organisations established the Women's Platform for the Constitution (*Anayasa Kadın Platformu*) through which they demanded changes to twenty-six articles when the constitution was being revised by the conservative ruling Justice and Development Party (*Adalet ve Kalkınma Partisi*, AKP) in 2007.

The women's groups continued to lobby for further changes to the civil code and the penal code. While the Turkish government sent its official reports to the CEDAW, the Women's Platform wrote alternative reports pointing out the shortcomings of the Turkish government and its reports. These reports proved to be important means of leverage in the course of their struggle as a consequence of the pressure that the CEDAW applied.

In 2021, the Eighth Shadow Report was submitted to the CEDAW review committee. It demonstrated that despite the critical assessments of women's groups and the recommendations made by the CEDAW review committee over the years, the situation seemed to be deteriorating rather than improving. In March 2021, Turkey withdrew from the 2011 İstanbul Convention on Violence against Women. Moreover, also according to the Eighth Shadow Report, groups backed by the AKP were actively lobbying to withdraw from the CEDAW as well.

Select Bibliography

Altınay, Ayşe Gül, and Yeşim Arat. *Türkiye'de Kadına Yönelik Şiddet.* İstanbul: N.P., 2007. https://www.stgm.org.tr/sites/default/files/2020-09/turkiyede-kadina-yonelik-siddet.pdf

İlkkaracan, Pınar. "Re/forming Laws to Secure Women's Rights in Turkey: The Campaign on the Penal Code." In *Citizen Action and National Policy Reform: Making Change Happen*, edited by John Gaventa and Rosemary McGee, 195–216. London: Zed, 2010.

"Shadow Report on the 8th Periodic Review of Turkey, Submitted by the Executive Committee on NGO Forum for CEDAW to the United Nations Committee on the Elimination of All Forms of Discrimination Against Women for Submission to the 81st Session of CEDAW, July 2021." https://kadinininsanhaklari.org/wp-content/uploads/2022/02/CSO-Shadow-Report-for-8th-Periotic-Review-of-Turkey.1.pdf

Women for Women's Human Rights – New Ways Association. *Turkish Civil and Penal Codes from a Gender Perspective: The Success of Two Nationwide Campaigns*, third edition. İstanbul: Women for Women's Human Rights – New Ways, 2009. https://kadinininsanhaklari.org/wp-content/uploads/2018/06/LegalStatus.pdf.

83
Barbecues, Invaded Beaches, and White Turks: Cultural Wars in Turkey

Doğan Gürpınar

In 2002, the Justice and Development Party (*Adalet ve Kalkınma Partisi*, AKP) came to power. The breakthrough elections came as a shock for the secular middle classes alarmed by the new unbridled Islamist government. The party, however, was offering a reformist-Islamist platform at the time. Abandoning Islamist schemes that had long established a duality between believers and nonbelievers, the AKP formulated a new dichotomy that no longer ran along the lines of the "morally upright" pious and "rotten" secularists. Necmettin Erbakan, the historical chief of the Islamist movement (in the form of the political parties that preceded the AKP), had once declared that people who did not vote for them held to a "potato religion". The AKP's narrative was different in that it juxtaposed itself with authoritarian secularists. In that line of thinking, secularists were bad not because they were irreligious but because they leaned on an authoritarian political order and were fearful of a real democracy that would grant rights and liberties to all people who had been discriminated against, including Kurds, Alevis, and others. The AKP perceived itself as the very embodiment of the "real people" (as a monolithic entity) as opposed to the secular elite that had usurped political power from its legitimate bearers. Within this political, ideological, and cultural setting, "White Turks" became the emblematic term employed to marginalise the AKP's cultural and political others, implying that they were not Turkish and native enough. According to this account, "White Turks" held themselves aloof from the "real people," secluded as they were in their insulated posh milieus (of İstanbul, Ankara and İzmir) and hostile to the masses—and hence fearful of democratisation. Notwithstanding this rhetoric, liberals and liberal leftists supported the AKP's platform because of its defiance of the authoritarian national security establishment and its political order.

The White Turk cliché that was used to portray the urban elite who enjoyed a privileged lifestyle was first formulated in the early 1990s by Ufuk Güldemir (1956–2007), a liberal journalist. Over time, however, this catchy journalistic phrase acquired political meaning as it was an expedient means for Islamists to lampoon seculars. As Recai Kutan (1930–), then chairman of an Islamist party, once succinctly put it, "There are Whites and Blacks/Negroes (*zenciler*) in the country. Everything is permissible for the Whites but not for Blacks/Negroes." Thus, the term took on immense emotional power among Islamists who felt a profound sense of having been discriminated against.

Indeed, many public intellectuals and figures swaggeringly demonstrated the traits that had been attributed to them; they were proud of their "superwesternised" upbringing and self-styled elitism, and arrogantly dismissive of ordinary folk for being "miserably" traditional and slavishly religious. Such discourses were laden with coarse and blatant racist terminology and misanthropy. Mine Kırıkkanat (1951–), a Francophone intellectual and long-time Paris correspondent for newspapers, emerged as the foremost protagonist of this typology and thus well-suited to the Islamist schematisation. For her own column she once penned an article titled "Our People Enjoying Themselves" (2005), published in the (ironically) liberal-left newspaper *Radikal*, which was a showcase of this style of mingling cultural racism with unabashed elitism. The piece was long used by AKP propagandists, politicians, and journalists to betray the "brazen, shameless, and unmasked face" of Turkish seculars.

*Our People Enjoying Themselves**

Every Turk that wanders the world is proud of Atatürk Airport. Even more modern than many of its Western counterparts, it is the pride of Turkey's "non-Arab" face. So much so that a French friend of mine in transit from Cairo observed, "I can't describe to you the contrast. We were all happy to feel that we were back in civilisation after landing from Cairo Airport. Europe begins at İstanbul Airport!" She kept heaping on the praise. However, if anyone [a foreigner], after landing at Atatürk Airport in the summer on a Sunday, makes the mistake of taking the road along the shore, they will see neither the sea nor the sky, but only be exposed to a huge barbecue, where they will get smoked if not cooked. The municipality, in an effort to deliver services to the people, planted grass there, mistaken [in the thought that] that people would walk, play, and lie down on it. The hills of Çamlıca and Belgrade Forest [in the vicinity of İstanbul] had been already sacrificed to the Turks' passion for barbecues. The scenery of trees and grass drowned amid kebab smoke makes us wish they would rather eat the meat raw and be cannibals. The trees resemble smoked meat and the leaves grilled eggplant. All along the road on the shore, the commuters would only encounter barbecues because they line up at eye level. The grass that stretches for kilometres on the side of the road on the shore is invaded by these barbecues. Men, naked to their underpants, lie down comfortably, while women in black burkas or turbans, all of them clad in hijabs, are busy fanning barbecues, preparing tea, and rocking babies on their feet. Turning their asses to the sea, our black [dark-skinned] people [*kara halkımız*] are preoccupied with grilling meat. You can't come across one single family grilling fish. If they would love to eat fish and know how to grill it, they wouldn't keep up the habit of lying down in their dirty white underpants, constantly scratching, and they wouldn't go on being short-legged, long-armed, and hairy. On the weekends in the summer, from Atatürk Airport onwards carnivorous Ethiopia and Islamistan begins. The grass is occupied not by İstanbulites but by those who do not belong to İstanbul, proving this by every deed they undertake. They are the 4.5 million people added to the Turkish population, three million of whom have migrated to İstanbul [from the countryside].

* Translated from Turkish. Mine Kırıkkanat, "Halkımız Eğleniyor." *Radikal*, 27 June 2005.

Yes, they have the right to have fun and relax. But here and this way? The municipality created beaches [on the other side of İstanbul]. The aim was to resuscitate the nostalgic beach culture of the İstanbul of days gone by. It was a well-intended project. Once it was opened, from its beaches to its lawns and umbrellas it reminded one of Cote d'Azur. Because the scenery at the opening was so beautiful, both the metropolitan municipality and the Kadıköy local municipality took credit. Anyway, it was opened with a ceremony in which the local mayor dove into the sea accompanied by fashion models. Yet on the very next day after the opening, 2005 reality hijacked 1930s modernity. Ümraniye [a populous, relatively poor and conservative neighbourhood district distant to the shore] had made it to the beaches, making it impossible not only to swim with swimming suits but to walk without facing verbal assaults. While veiled mothers were fanning barbecues and fathers were lying down slothfully in their underpants, their bulky calves [sons] were playing raucously in the sea. The ban on barbecues didn't work and the wooden benches that had been installed for people to sit on were vandalised only two days later and indeed used as wood for barbecues. Now the crème de la crème of people from Kadıköy [a secular, wealthier and more prestigious neighbourhood along the coast] are sadly looking at their beaches and sea under Islamistan occupation while taking their morning walks. They curse the municipality for delivering beach services for only a very small fee. Yet, I would ask them, "What were you doing while these shantytowns were expanding and why didn't you take part in politics to voice your worldview? Did you think that these shantytowns would never make it to the sea and hijack you?"

***

Kırıkkanat's column was terminated after protests broke out and fury raged, especially among the newspaper's leftist and liberal columnists. Yet, this genre of writing that bashed the masses for being "uncouth and ignorant" was incessantly reiterated by many other columnists in articles published in mainstream newspapers with massive circulations. Kırıkkanat's piece also invokes anti-immigrationist polemic against people who relocated not from abroad but from provincial Turkey to İstanbul and its beaches. Her piece was merely one paragon of a prevalent genre. Indeed, many prided themselves on taking ownership of the label White Turk and gushed as they spoke as a "spokesperson of White Turks" as they deliberately artic- ulated in their pieces. The situation was exacerbated by other columnists, many of whom had come from the lifestyle magazines (fashion, sports, home decoration, and dining) that boomed in the 2000s. Picking up on this scheme, the AKP propaganda machine labelled all secularists as "White Turks". Associating them with these upper middle-class people living in their upscale milieus and enjoying their privileged lifestyles, even those secularists discriminated against and marginalised in the midst of conservative milieus throughout Anatolia turned elitist White Turks. This image was based on the presumption that there were two mutually exclusive cultural universes that were alien to each other, as if there was an impermeable boundary between the two. It was also deeply hierarchical. White Turks were a culturally and economically superior community, and thus oppressive. Yet this populist discourse could be possible, and persuasive, primarily thanks to Kırıkkanat and other self-styled "White Turks".

***

The Turkish media was dramatically transformed in the 1990s. Private television channels that began to air in that decade made the TV scene more colourful and showier than ever before. Notably, they were launched by newspapers. This trajectory made the Turkish media more affluent and glamorous, transforming it into an agent of influence with enormous political power. This made it possible for Turkish columnists to not only pocket huge amounts of money, but also become arbiters of power. These intersections were key to the creation of the image of the White Turk. Such journalists associated their own privileged lives at plazas and galas and the lives they portrayed in their lifestyle magazines with the daily routine of secularists *en masse*. This was populism in reverse. While the populist stratagem is universal, all national variants of it display cultural distinctiveness and benefit from a reservoir of exclusive and emotionally loaded cultural references. Islam and piety are the anchors of one Turkish populist discourse, yet it dexterously adapts to and mingles with contemporary global conservative tropes to reinforce an imagined cultural divide. However, one peculiarity in the Turkish case is the tendency of both sides to draw such sharp and impermeable lines with equal ardour. Dissociating oneself from average people (famously disparaged as "the man who scratches his—hairy—potbelly," following an expression first used in another newspaper column ridiculing AKP voters) is a strategy used to signal intellectual, cultural, and even moral superiority. People who embrace and articulate self-styled elitism presumed themselves to be the natural intellectual, cultural, and political elite (and therefore owners) of the country, regardless of the nature of transient governments. These snobberies, such as those of Kırıkkanat, have greatly facilitated populist appeal's popular outreach.

Select Bibliography

Bali, Rıfat. *Life Style'dan Yeni Türkiye'ye: Yeni Binyıl'ın Türkiyesi'nden Manzaralar. 2001–2021.* İstanbul: Libra, 2021.

Gürpınar, Doğan. *Kültür Savaşları: İslam, Sekülerizm ve Kimlik Siyasetinin Yükselişi.* İstanbul: Liberplus, 2017.

Özyürek, Esra. *Nostalgia for the Modern: State Secularism and Everyday Politics in Turkey.* Durham: Duke University Press, 2006.

Yashin-Navaro, Yael. *Faces of the State: Secularism and Public Life in Turkey.* Princeton: Princeton University Press, 2002.

84
A High-Rise on Cement:
The Turkish Construction Boom

Murat Gül

The elections of 2002 in Turkey saw the newly established Justice and Development Party (*Adalet ve Kalkınma Partisi*, AKP) come to power in a landslide victory. Led by Recep Tayyip Erdoğan (1954–), the AKP introduced economic policies aiming to improve social welfare, including targeted spending on public health and affordable housing. As such, the construction industry became the main impetus driving economic recovery. Growth in the industry was significantly higher than that of the GDP and the share of construction in the total value added reached as high as 8.5 per cent. Although this phenomenal growth brought prosperity, it also had several negative impacts, particularly in environmental and economic terms.

In the run-up to the 2002 elections, the AKP declared that construction would be one of the key sectors in its economic recovery programme. Erdoğan promised to construct 15,000 kilometres of dual carriageways within the scope of a comprehensive road-building programme. The total length of dual carriageways in Turkey in 2002 was around 6,000 kilometres, which increased to 21,000 kilometres and 28,000 kilometres by 2014 and 2021, respectively. New roads, with their associated tunnels, bridges, and viaducts, made many Anatolian cities and towns more easily accessible and supported improvements in living standards and economic prosperity in Turkey. The government also launched large-scale redevelopment projects such as new airports, suspension bridges, and improved motorway systems. These projects often drew criticism on the grounds of environmental concerns, as well as the economic models employed to finance such costly works. The real boom in the construction industry, however, occurred in the field of housing and commercial projects, particularly in the country's larger cities. The Housing Development Administration (*Toplu Konut İdaresi*, TOKİ) became the AKP's principal planning instrument for the construction industry.

Panoramas of the Construction Boom in İstanbul

TOKİ housing blocks, Kayabaşı, İstanbul (Murat Gül)

High-rise office towers, Levent, İstanbul (Murat Gül)

Public area in a TOKİ housing complex, Kayabaşı, İstanbul (Murat Gül)

***

Under the AKP government, the issuance of construction permits increased on an unprecedented scale, from 36 million m² to 280 million m² between 2002 and 2017. In the meantime, successful economic management measures saw inflation fall to less than 10 per cent. The passing of mortgage laws in 2007 allowed banks to offer long-term real estate loans at affordable interest rates, resulting in attractive homeownership opportunities for middle-income groups. Economic growth followed, as mortgage loans provided by banks increased from 48 million Turkish lira in 2001 to 15 billion lira in 2007, ultimately reaching over 50 billion lira by 2019. The total number of residence sales showed a corresponding level of growth, with the figure of 427,000 units for 2008 reaching around 1.5 million units in 2020.

Although it had been established years earlier in 1984, TOKİ quickly became a very powerful instrument in the building industry under the AKP government. Crucially, it was connected to the Office of the Prime Minister, and it provided generous financial support through the use of public funds for mass housing development projects. Empowered by a set of legislative arrangements, it also allowed for the transfer of public lands to private companies via either land sales or income-sharing schemes in exchange for land. Furthermore, it had the authority to administer city planning projects across Turkey, allowing for expropriation rights. And, even more importantly, TOKİ's activities were carried out independently of the central budget, which enabled it to receive foreign loans, issue stocks and bonds, and provide credit to banks that participated in housing development ventures.

These privileges made TOKİ more powerful than the other players in the real estate market, including metropolitan municipalities. Statistical data indicates that from 1984 to 2002 TOKİ constructed around 43,000 residential dwellings. In contrast, the total number of units built by TOKİ reached around 750,000 in 2016, and that figure climbed to over 1,000,000 by 2021, which made TOKİ one of the largest collective residential contractors in the world. Financed through long-term and low-yield mortgage loans, TOKİ's affordable housing projects made it possible for people with low incomes to experience a higher standard of living for the first time in their lives, as they could now enjoy the convenience of modern kitchens and bathrooms as well as access to pleasantly landscaped common areas. The housing programme thus became a popular policy initiative and an effective promotional tool for the AKP in elections.

Larger cities saw TOKİ play a different role. The agency developed residential projects for high-income groups in partnership with the private sector. Revenue from these high-end projects was used to finance social housing projects for low-income residents on the peripheries of these cities and also in medium and small-sized towns. Many high-value public areas in İstanbul and other major cities were assigned to TOKİ for joint-venture projects via real estate investment trusts (REITs) with large private development companies.

The projects constructed by REITs and other private enterprises offered residential lifestyles targeting the demands of the middle-class elite who, regardless of their political inclination, benefited the most from the AKP's economic recovery programme. This group transferred their prosperity and status into luxurious residential precincts. Encircled by secure walls and set in manicured gardens, these gated complexes incorporated high-rise residential towers with luxury shopping centres, upmarket restaurants, premium gyms, and swimming pools, becoming the preferred mode of living for the upper-middle class segment of the population. Gated complexes also became a development model for an even broader stratum of Turkish society, with modest gated compounds mushrooming in many cities. While they provide secure environments for residents, gated complexes have the negative effect of dividing and segregating communities, thereby moving people away from the idea of striving for the common good of all, and social analyses have shown that residents tend to become self-centred and exclusionary in such settings.

Many architects and academics have criticised TOKİ and the hyper-active construction boom on both environmental and aesthetic grounds. Apartment blocks are often based on similar plans and architectural modes of expression pay little heed to local conditions or the cultural context of particular localities. A large number of TOKİ projects have been designed on the basis of the cost-effective practice of producing copybook designs with little aesthetic quality. In particular, the high-rise TOKİ apartment blocks constructed on the outskirts of modest Anatolian towns and cities are devoid of architectural merit. Such critiques have led TOKİ to adopt a more sensitive approach in recent years, and it has begun to carry out projects that better correspond to local conditions, both environmentally and architecturally.

Luxurious housing developments targeting upper-income groups that are designed by leading architectural firms for the private construction industry have also drawn criticism for their lack of environmental awareness. The main difference between TOKİ apartment blocks and private sector housing projects is the latter's use of expensive finishing materials and luxurious accessories, such as kitchen and bathroom fittings, and private sector housing projects have been found to have far more adverse environmental impacts in terms of environmental performance and energy efficiency than is the case with TOKİ housing.

A critical point that should be taken into account is the fact that many of these projects have been built at the expense of appropriating high-value public land. The importance of open public spaces was brought into sharp focus during the Covid-19 pandemic. Millions of people living in the country's larger cities were confined in back-to-back apartment blocks during the lengthy lockdowns that occurred and they did not have access to open areas for leisure activities, as a consequence of which their well-being suffered.

Another rising star in the construction boom has been shopping centres. Often constructed as part of mixed-use developments containing office towers, lavish apartment blocks, and exclusive hotels, shopping centres offer profitable work opportunities for Turkish architects and lucrative prospects for international investors. The attractive architectural forms of shopping centres have made them alluring places for the retail-hungry middle class. Today, as is the case in many cities across the globe, shopping centres in Turkish cities are hubs that offer a wide range of facilities, including aquariums with exotic marine life, exhibition halls displaying artworks from prominent museums, sports amenities, theme parks, ice rinks, food courts, children's play areas, and prayer rooms. The multi-functional nature of shopping centres has transformed them into social centres catering to all segments of Turkish society, regardless of social, cultural, or economic status. With almost 450 such centres covering approximately

14 million square metres of floor space, Turkey has one of the most vibrant shopping centre markets in Europe. Despite their popularity, however, the negative impacts of shopping malls on small businesses and the community are common themes of discussion in academic circles.

***

Since 2018, hyper-activity in the construction sector has started to slow as the currency and debt crisis impacts all segments of Turkish society. Social and economic problems brought on by the Covid-19 pandemic and the recent military conflict in Ukraine have exacerbated an already unstable economic situation. A large number of public infrastructure projects, luxurious shopping precincts, and gated complexes were financed by cheap loans. Record-low interest rates in the United States and the abundance of liquidity in other leading world economies provided opportunities for Turkey to access low-cost credit, but in 2016 the situation began to change. Now the country can no longer utilise attractive foreign loans to finance such projects. The early 2020s saw the Turkish lira in freefall and as its value against all major currencies hit record lows, many economic indicators began sounding alarm bells. These dire financial conditions have raised the question of whether pouring local funds and international credit into construction was a logical choice. Many experts have argued that, in hindsight, financial resources could have been used more productively to support technological, industrial, and agricultural projects that would have contributed to sustainable social and economic development.

In addition to financial issues, Turkey's massive construction activities of the early twenty-first century have led to serious environmental problems. Planning control mechanisms were often expedited or minimised to allow for rapid development, as a result of which many large-scale projects have had negative impacts on local environments. That, in turn, has further contributed to a worsening of Turkey's already high natural disaster risk profile and aggravated the impacts of climate change. Many towns and cities are now experiencing major problems because of floods, landslides, and other natural disasters on an unprecedented scale. Almost all of the areas in Turkey that are seismically active have building stock that is far below contemporary engineering standards and it needs to be replaced. Despite the precarious state of the economy, however, housing market figures remain dynamic, since many still view investments in property as the only safe harbour for their savings. This means that the construction industry will retain its important position in the Turkish economy in the coming years, but future policies should be geared to deliver more sustainable environmental outcomes.

Select Bibliography

Bican, Nezih Burak. "Public Mass Housing Practices in Turkey: The Urgent Need for Research-Based Spatial Decision-Making." *Journal of Housing and the Built Environment* 35 (2020): 461–79.
Erkip, Feyzan. *Piyasa Yapmanın Yeni Yüzleri: AVM'ler, Sokaklar, Kentler*. İstanbul: İletişimYayınları, 2019.
Gül, Murat. *Architecture and the Turkish City: A History of Istanbul Since the Ottomans*. London: I.B. Tauris, 2017.
Özdemir Sarı, Ö. Burcu, Aksoy Khurami, Esma, Uzun, Nil (eds.). *Housing in Turkey: Policy, Planning, Practice*. New Yok: Routledge, 2022.

85

Darbukas against Dozers:
40 Days and 40 Nights to Save
the Sulukule NeighBourhood

Danielle V. Schoon

The Roma ("Gypsy") neighbourhood of Sulukule was located in the municipal district of Fatih in İstanbul on what is known as the Historic Peninsula. Sulukule was situated just inside the Theodosian Walls near Edirnekapı (the Gate of Edirne, where the Ottoman Sultan Mehmed the Conqueror made his triumphal entry into Constantinople in 1453). This would have been the periphery of the walled city, but as İstanbul grew far beyond the walls in the late twentieth century, Sulukule found itself at the centre of a massive metropolis. Sulukule was a local name for the area because of the presence of a historic water tower. It comprised the Neslişah and Hatice Sultan neighbourhoods and was the oldest continuously settled Roma neighbourhood in Europe. From at least the 1950s until the early 1990s, entertainment houses (*eğlence everli*, unlicensed nightclubs with live music, dancing, and food) run by Roma families provided nightlife entertainment to locals and tourists in Sulukule and sustained the local economy. Some of İstanbul's most famous Roma musicians and dancers were born and raised in the neighbourhood. It also gained international fame when it was depicted in a very orientalist fashion in the James Bond film *From Russia with Love* (1963). Sulukule was subjected to multiple redevelopment projects in the twentieth century. In 1958, residents of Sulukule were moved to make way for several large new streets, and two other small-scale demolitions occurred in 1966 and 1982. The entertainment houses that were the engine of the local economy were shut down by the municipality in the early 1990s and the neighbourhood experienced a swift decline.

Although Sulukule was located within a zone of the Historic Peninsula that was on UNESCO's World Heritage List, the Sulukule Renewal Project was approved in 2007 by the İstanbul Metropolitan Municipality. The Fatih Municipality claimed that the project would renew the area in harmony with the architectural heritage of the Historic Peninsula and involve the residents in planning the new development. The Housing Development Administration of Turkey (*Toplu Konut İdaresi Başkanlığı*, TOKİ) and a private Turkish architectural firm, *Aarti Planlama*, were responsible for implementing the housing project. The Mayor of Fatih used Law no. 5366, popularly known as the "Urban Transformation Law," which was enacted in 2005, as the legal basis for the project. The law grants expropriation powers to municipal mayors and allows them to implement renewal projects without permission from residents or property owners.

A coalition of academicians, artists, and activists that later came to be known as the Sulukule Platform was formed in 2005 to combat the demolition of Sulukule. They organised benefit concerts and street rallies, circulated petitions, and gave press conferences. Their aim was to convince city officials to rehabilitate the neighbourhood rather than demolish it, emphasising the historical importance of the area and the cultural heritage of the Roma. They proposed that the area's conservation should be a participatory process. The activist coalition successfully stalled the demolition process several times by filing lawsuits. The collective Autonomous Planners with No Frontiers (*Sınır Tanimayan Otonom Plancilar*, STOP) drafted an alternative plan for Sulukule that would provide a higher quality living environment and employment opportunities for the Roma residents. However, the demolitions went forward before the alternative plan could be approved. The last remaining house within the urban renewal zone was demolished on 12 November 2009. Only a few streets that had been part of the Sulukule neighbourhood, but were not included in the urban renewal zone, remain.

*"We will say it 40 times: Sulukule will live!"**

* "40 Kere söyleyeceğiz! Sulukule yaşayacak!," Myra Ajans, accessed December 12, 2020, http://40gun40gece-sulukule.blogspot.com/. Translated into English by Funda Oral.

***

The importance of Sulukule should be framed within larger issues such as neoliberalism, gentrification, and social movements to facilitate an exploration of the macro-economic and political processes that create the conditions for urban development and the displacement of marginalised citizens. Neoliberal policies were adopted in Turkey by then-Prime Minister Turgut Özal (1927–1993) in the early 1980s, as were plans to turn İstanbul into a "global city." Neoliberalism and urban gentrification have accelerated in the era of the Justice and Development Party (*Adalet ve Kalkınma Partisi*, AKP), which was elected to the government in 2002 and has since been under the leadership of Recep Tayyip Erdoğan (1954–). Their early policies were largely directed towards a two-pronged process of human rights reforms and urban development, both mainly targeting minorities, including the Roma. As poor inner-city neighbourhoods are often inhabited by minorities, they have been disproportionately impacted by urban renewal projects. However, these projects are rarely completed without significant opposition by activists.

In Sulukule, urban rights activists used local music and dance practices as a tool for mobilisation against the forced evictions. Their slogan was "*Darbukanı Susturma, Sulukule'yi Bırakma*" ("Do not silence your *darbuka*, do not leave Sulukule"). The *darbuka* is a goblet-shaped hand drum that features in Turkish classical and folk music and accompanies the performance of belly dance. The drum represents the expertise of the Sulukule Roma in music and dance and the contributions of Roma entertainers to Turkish culture. Sulukule residents and urban rights activists organised a festival as a part of which İstanbul residents were invited to Sulukule to see for themselves that it was not a dangerous place and that everyone was welcome. As activist Funda Oral recalled during an interview in 2011 with the author, "In March 2007, as we only had 40 days before the demolitions, we organised a '40 days and 40 nights' event in Sulukule with presentations, panel discussions, concerts, and press conferences to increase awareness about the culture and history of the neighbourhood. We had meetings about the rights of the inhabitants and exhibitions, as well as workshops for local people to inform them about their rights and the possible results of the demolitions, and to mobilise society about urban renewal plans." The poster shown above was used to promote the event, and the image of hands beating a *darbuka* appeared on the festival's materials. The hands are those of a child and illustrate the loss of heritage that Sulukule's children would experience with the demolition of their neighbourhood. The sound of the drum is a call to participate in the opposition movement, as the poster promises: "We will say it 40 times: Sulukule will live!" That sound echoed through the streets of Sulukule, competing with the sound of bulldozers.

Several international figures got involved in the 40 Days 40 Nights festival. The Spanish musician Manu Chao showed his solidarity with the movement by sharing a photograph of himself wearing a t-shirt that read "*Sulukule Susmayacak*" ("Sulukule will not be silent"). The American punk rock band Gogol Bordello showed up to play a concert with local Roma musicians and later released a song about Sulukule titled "Educate Thy Neighbor." The French Roma film director Tony Gatlif also made an appearance at the festival to show his solidarity.

"As a result," Ms. Oral explained, "Sulukule was proven to be part of 'the commons' and the demolitions were postponed for a few years, although in the end we couldn't prevent them."

***

Sulukule's demolition and the attempts to prevent it foreshadowed future events in İstanbul. The Occupy Gezi protests of the summer of 2013 were initially a series of peaceful demonstrations and sit-ins organised to contest an urban development plan for Taksim's Gezi Park in central İstanbul. However, the protests escalated into a full-blown social movement in cities across Turkey after the police violently evicted the protestors from the park with tear gas and the excessive use of force. The peaceful demonstrations were organised by Taksim Solidarity (*Taksim Dayanışması*), an umbrella group of Turkish civil society organisations and activists, many of which were also active in the Sulukule Platform. Just as music and dance had been used in the fight against Sulukule's demolition, they played an important role in the Gezi Park protests to bring people together and form the basis of peaceful protests. The Turkish hip hop group *Tahribad-ı İsyan*, which had formed in Sulukule with the support and mentorship of Sulukule Platform activist Funda Oral, contributed to that informal soundtrack during the Gezi Park protests. Their leading role in a short art film titled *Wonderland* (*Harikalar Diyarı*) by Halil Altındere (1971–), propelled them into the limelight when it was shown at the 2013 İstanbul Biennial. At the beginning of the film, Turkish rapper Fuat Ergin (1972–) instructs the members of rap group *Tahribad-ı İsyan*:

> They're at the gates to knock down our neighbourhood
> Today it's Sulukule, tomorrow Balat, Okmeydanı, Tarlabaşı, Gezi Parkı
> Time's running out
> They're taking from the poor and giving to the rich
> Knocked down the shanties to build expensive apartments
> Let art and music be your armaments
> Tahribad-ı İsyan
> Stop the demolitions!

Although the protests managed to postpone the larger plans for building a hotel and mall in Gezi Park, the area has been significantly altered by the municipality. If the protest movement in Sulukule represented the beginning of an era of hope for freedom of assembly and an active civil society in Turkey, the attack by the police on the country's own citizens at the Gezi Park protests marked the end of that era. Yet, music continues to be used as a tool to speak out. The 2019 Turkish rap epic "#Susamam" ("I cannot stay silent") included nineteen artists, including *Tahribad-ı İsyan*, rapping about various social issues in Turkey today, such as urban gentrification. The music video got twenty million hits on YouTube the first week it was released. Echoing the earlier refrain that "Sulukule will not be silent," the song insists, "I cannot stay silent."

Select Bibliography

Angell, Elizabeth, Timur Hammond, and Danielle van Dobben Schoon. "Assembling Istanbul: Buildings and Bodies in a World City." *City: Analysis of Urban Trends, Culture, Theory, Policy, Action* 18, no. 6 (2014): 644–54.

Foggo, Hacer. "The Sulukule Affair: Roma against Expropriation." In *Roma Rights Quarterly* 4 (2007): 41–47.

Marsh, Adrian: "The Gypsies of Sulukule." *City: Analysis of Urban Trends, Culture, Theory, Policy, Action* 14, no.6 (2010): 670–74.

Marushiakova, Elena, and Vesselin Popov. *Gypsies in the Ottoman Empire.* Hatfield: University of Hertfordshire Press, 2001.

Seeman, Sonia Tamar. "A Politics of Culture: Turkish Romani Music and Dance at the Dawn of European Union Accession." In *Voices of the Weak: Music and Minorities*, edited by Zuzana Jurková and Lee Bidgood, 206–15. Prague: Slovo21 + Faculty of Humanities of Charles University Prague, 2009.

Somersan, Semra, and Süheyla Kırca-Schroeder. "Resisting Eviction: Sulukule Roma in Search of Right to Space and Place." *Anthropology of East Europe Review* 25, no. 2 (2007): 96–107.

86

Tutelage's Terminus:
The E-Memorandum by the General Staff

Berk Esen

The so-called "e-memorandum" that was released on the website of the General Staff (*Genelkurmay Başkanlığı*) at midnight on 27 April 2007 probably represents the most important political document to have emerged during the first term that the Justice and Development Party (*Adalet ve Kalkınma Partisi*, AKP) was in office. The public posting of the digital document occurred against the backdrop of a contentious struggle between the secular military and the AKP government. Because of its Islamist roots, the AKP's rise to power after the elections of November 2002 was met with strong resistance and suspicion by the military's top brass. Despite its moderate electoral platform, the AKP was established by political leaders with strong Islamist backgrounds, and the fact that the wives of the leading party elites, such as Recep Tayyip Erdoğan (1954–), Abdullah Gül (1950–), and Bülent Arınç (1948–), all wore headscarves was seen as a direct challenge to the secular regime. Although it was, at the time, mostly a ceremonial position, the presidency still carried significant weight within the political system. Concerned that the election of one of those AKP leaders as president would undermine secularism in the country, the Chief of the General Staff, General Yaşar Büyükanıt (1940–2019), sought to block such an outcome by releasing that strongly-worded document.

However, the government's unyielding response, followed by the major victory it scored in the elections of July 2007, changed the dynamics of civil-military relations in Turkey. Even though it had formed a single-party government after the November 2002 elections, the AKP had met with strong and coordinated opposition from a secular bloc composed of President Ahmet Necdet Sezer (1941–), the military leadership, the Constitutional Court, and the main opposition, namely the Republican People's Party (*Cumhuriyet Halk Partisi*, CHP). As the CHP strove to block the AKP's legislative agenda in parliament and sent government-sponsored bills to the Constitutional Court to request their annulment, President Sezer used his constitutional powers to veto many of the government's appointments and legislative actions. Meanwhile, top military figures frequently pressured the AKP government to reverse its foreign and domestic policies on a variety of issues. Since clashes frequently broke out between the two, rumours circulated at the time that the military high command had plans to topple the AKP government. Aware of the fragility of the situation, then-Prime Minister Erdoğan was careful to not confront the military directly and instead he counteracted the resistance he faced by enacting reforms targeting democratisation that limited the military's powers, while in the meantime seeking out support from the public as well as from international actors.

Towards the end of the AKP's first term, the most contentious issue in the political arena was the election of a new president to replace Sezer, whose term was due to expire by summer 2007. While the opposition anticipated that the AKP caucus would be able to easily elect one of its own members as president due to the fact that the party held a sizable majority in parliament, it was strongly opposed to the election of an Islamist figure from the AKP such as Prime Minister Erdoğan or Foreign Minister Gül. For months there was a certain amount of ambiguity within the ranks of the AKP's leadership about who would be chosen as the party's presidential candidate. While Erdoğan decided not to contest the election and allegedly leaned towards supporting a moderate figure who would be acceptable to the military, conservative AKP elites such as the Speaker of Parliament, Bülent Arınç, supported the nomination of Abdullah Gül as the party's official candidate. Strong pressure from the AKP cadres eventually compelled Erdoğan to declare Gül's candidacy, thereby triggering a showdown between the government and the opposition.

The opposition led a vigorous campaign against Gül's candidacy. Months before Gül's name was even announced, retired Court of Cassation (*Yargıtay*) prosecutor Sabih Kanadoğlu (1938–) claimed that the election would be annulled if fewer than two-thirds of parliamentarians (367) attended the presidential rounds. Since the AKP did not have a two-thirds majority, Deniz Baykal (1938–2023), the leader of the CHP, stated that his party would boycott the presidential vote if the AKP did not consult the other parties and reach a compromise for a suitable candidate. During a press conference held on 12 April 2007, Chief of the General Staff Büyükanıt highlighted the importance of electing a president who would abide by the principles of the Republic of Turkey, i.e. secularism, not just in name but also in substance. Backed by strong media support, the AKP's opponents organised five "Republican Rallies" in major metropolitan centres in an attempt to shift public opinion on the issue. Against the backdrop of that public campaign, the e-memorandum was released on the day of the first round of the presidential election, in which Abdullah Gül emerged as the top contender with 357 (out of 361) votes. The CHP, which boycotted the first-round vote, had already appealed to the Constitutional Court to annul the results on the grounds of a lack of a two-thirds quorum in parliament.

E-Memorandum*

It has been observed that some circles who have been carrying out endless efforts to disturb the fundamental values of the Republic of Turkey, especially secularism, have recently escalated their efforts.

Those activities include requests for a redefinition of fundamental values and attempts to organise alternative celebrations instead of our national festivals symbolizing the unity and solidarity of our nation. Those who carry out the [afore]mentioned activities which have turned into an open challenge against the state do not refrain from exploiting the holy religious feelings of our people, and they try to hide their real aims under the guise of religion.

---

* Quoted from a BBC website that contains excerpts from the e-memorandum as reported by the Anatolia News Agency. "Excerpts of Turkish Army Statement," *BBC*, 28 April 2007. http://news.bbc.co.uk/2/hi/europe/6602775.stm

An important part of these activities occurred with the permission and within the knowledge of administrative authorities who were supposed to intervene and prevent such incidents, a fact which intensifies the gravity of the issue.

This fundamentalist understanding, which is anti-republican and harbours no aim other than eroding the basic characteristics of the state, finds courage in recent developments and discourses and extends the scope of its activities.

Developments in our region give numerous examples that playing on religion and manipulating faith into a political discourse can cause disasters. There are accounts in our country and abroad that a political discourse or an ideology can destroy faith itself and turn it into something else when it is imposed on faith... Doubtlessly, the sole condition for the Republic of Turkey to live in peace and stability as a contemporary democracy is through defending the basic characteristics of our state which are defined in the Constitution.

The problem that emerged in the presidential election process is focused on arguments over secularism. The Turkish Armed Forces are concerned about the recent situation. It should not be forgotten that the Turkish Armed Forces are a party in those arguments, and absolute defender of secularism. Also, the Turkish Armed Forces is definitely opposed to those arguments and negative comments. It will display its attitude and action openly and clearly whenever it is necessary.

Those who are opposed to our great leader Mustafa Kemal Atatürk's understanding "How happy is the one who says I am a Turk" are enemies of the Republic of Turkey and will remain so. The Turkish Armed Forces maintain their sound determination to carry out its duties stemming from laws to protect the unchangeable characteristics of the Republic of Turkey. Their loyalty in this determination is absolute.

***

In content, the e-memorandum reflects the notion of military tutelage that had characterised the general staff from the mid-1990s up to the presidential elections in 2007. Alarmed by the rise of political Islam, which had been ongoing since the local elections of 1994 when the Islamist Welfare Party (*Refah Partisi*, RP) unexpectedly won control of municipal governments in İstanbul, Ankara, and several other provincial capitals, the General Staff began to emphasise the military's "role as guardian" and its position as the "absolute defender of secularism". Upholding secularism became the primary justification for the military's increasingly frequent political interventions targeting the Islamist-led coalition government in 1997. For example, during a National Security Council (*Milli Güvenlik Kurulu*, MGK) meeting, top military brass compelled then-Prime Minister Necmettin Erbakan (1926–2011) to sign a protocol on 28 February 1997—later known as the "post-modern coup"—which required the government to fight against anti-secular activities in the country. Although the Turkish Armed Forces had been intensely involved in politics since the coup of 1960, the protocol provided the military authorities with the justification to monitor the government's agenda, influence policy-making for issues not pertaining to security, and keep civil society under surveillance. Under the rule of the AKP, the General Staff sought to preserve those tutelary powers, which led to frequent clashes between the government and the military on various issues dealing with foreign policy and domestic politics.

The e-memorandum linked the presidential election to an increase in attacks against the principle of secularism and emphasised the General Staff's strong preference for a president who would not challenge the nationalist and secularist principles of the Republic of Turkey. After highlighting the dangers of exploiting religion in the political arena, the document accused "the administrative authorities" of being complicit in, if not supportive of, such anti-secular activities. Furthermore, the document contained a clear warning to the AKP indicating that the military would take every possible measure to uphold the aforementioned principles. This represented a direct threat to the government since only a decade earlier the military had removed another Islamist party from power and expanded its own powers on the basis of the justification that it was protecting the regime against similar challenges.

Following the release of the e-memorandum, the AKP cabinet quickly convened to make a press statement that categorically rejected Büyükanıt's criticisms and voiced serious concerns about how the text would influence the Constitutional Court's impending decision about the legality of the presidential vote, thereby bringing harm to the democratic regime. Indeed, on 1 May the Constitutional Court annulled the first-round vote and ruled that two-thirds of parliamentarians (367) should secure a quorum so that the presidential rounds could take place. When 367 parliamentarians failed to attend the session for the second round of the presidential election on 6 May, the AKP cabinet called for early elections, which it won with a strong parliamentary majority (with 46.5 per cent of the vote and 341 seats). The ruling party used the obstruction of Gül's election as president to run a vigorous populist campaign against the opposition parties and in the end siphoned votes from centre-right parties. The new parliament, in which the AKP retained its majority, elected Gül as president, thereby ending the constitutional deadlock in favour of the AKP government. In order to prevent a reoccurrence of such a constitutional crisis, the ruling party amended the constitution to allow for the election of the president by a popular vote. Although President Sezer vetoed the constitutional package, the amendments were later upheld by the Constitutional Court and ratified via a public referendum in October 2007.

***

From a historical perspective, the e-memorandum can be evaluated in light of the 1971 memorandum and the 1997 MGK protocol, both of which were the result of clashes between the military leadership and the government. The military high command had sought and secured the resignation of the cabinet of Süleyman Demirel (1924–2015) by way of the 1971 memorandum, whereas the coalition government led by Necmettin Erbakan temporarily held onto its position in 1997 by endorsing the protocol that had been issued. In contrast, the AKP government decided not to appease the military, stood behind its presidential candidate, and appealed to the electorate at large for support. There are several reasons why the AKP struck a confrontational stance towards the military and ultimately succeeded. In contrast to the other two cases, the AKP enjoyed large-scale popular support, largely thanks to the favourable macro-economic conditions that existed at the time. The government's popularity played into the confrontational style of the AKP's charismatic leader Erdoğan, who successfully mobilised conservative voters across the country. Moreover, in those days the international climate favoured the AKP government. By 2007, the US administration no longer enjoyed close ties with the Turkish military due to the latter's criticisms of the 2003 Iraqi War, and European Union member states supported the AKP government as Turkey engaged in accession talks. Because of these factors, the military's threats were no longer a pressing concern for the AKP cabinet.

The AKP government's response to the e-memorandum is generally seen as a turning point in Turkish civil-military relations. Undeniably, the military's veto player status took a severe blow after the confrontation. Emboldened by its victory in the 2007 general elections, the AKP government—with help from prosecutors and police officers affiliated with the Gülen movement—used politicised cases like the Sledgehammer and Ergenekon trials to discredit and purge many of its opponents in the officer corps. The weakening of the military's veto power status enabled Erdoğan to consolidate his political authority and promote officers affiliated with the government or Gülenist circles. Erdoğan's power grab led to the rise of a "competitive authoritarian" regime that skewed the playing field against the opposition and placed the state apparatus under firm partisan control. After the interests of the AKP and the Gülen movement clashed, however, the latter joined the opposition camp and, in 2016, staged a putsch led by a number of Gülenist officers who had replaced those officers who had been purged or retired in the early 2010s. In the aftermath of the failed coup, the military fell under direct government control, albeit under the leadership of former Chief of Staff and later Minister of Defence Hulusi Akar (1952–). As a result, the civilianisation of Turkish politics has not been accompanied by democratisation but rather it left the military open to partisan influence by regime elites. Gül's election as president limited his role within the AKP since the presidency was largely relegated ceremonial roles at the time, thus allowing then-Prime Minister Erdoğan to expand his control over the ruling party. After the end of Gül's term in 2014, Erdoğan became the first popularly-elected president. The monopolisation of power in Erdoğan's hands ultimately culminated in the establishment of a hyper-presidential regime in 2017.

Select Bibliography

Akça, İsmet, and Evren Balta-Paker. "Beyond Military Tutelage? Turkish Military Politics and the AKP Government." *Debating Security in Turkey: Challenges and Changes in the Twenty-First Century* (2013): 77–92.

Arat, Yeşim, and Şevket Pamuk. *Turkey between Democracy and Authoritarianism*. Cambridge: Cambridge University Press, 2019.

Aydınlı, Ersel. "Ergenekon, New Pacts, and the Decline of the Turkish 'Inner State.'" *Turkish Studies* 12, no. 2 (2011): 227–39.

Eligür, Banu. *The Mobilization of Political Islam in Turkey*. Cambridge: Cambridge University Press, 2010.

87

Contested Power, Weaponised Memoirs: The "Diaries" of Admiral Özden Örnek

Fatma Müge Göçek

On 29 March 2007, the İstanbul-based weekly news magazine *Nokta* published some diaries that Admiral Özden Örnek had allegedly kept while serving as commander of the Turkish Naval Forces from 2003 to 2005. The admiral fervently challenged the veracity of the diaries, stating that he had not kept such notes in longhand and that the ciphered summaries of official daily events that he had kept were done so electronically. He went on to note that all of those were erased from his work computer upon his retirement from office. Nonetheless, the level of detail provided in the diaries was notable, especially his supposed discussion of three coup plans that had been drawn up in his first year in office in 2003, a year after the religiously conservative Justice and Development Party (*Adalet ve Kalkınma Partisi*, AKP) had come to power under the leadership of Recep Tayyip Erdoğan (1954–) in a landslide election victory. The discussion captured the attention of the public in Turkey because it empirically—albeit illegally—documented the power that the Turkish army had been wielding in politics for decades. Since 1950, for instance, there had been approximately ten attempts at military interventions in Turkey, four of which were successful. The fact that the diaries surfaced not in 2003 but four years later in 2007, a few weeks before presidential elections—when the Turkish armed forces may have opposed the candidate proposed by the AKP—led to speculation that the publication sought to undermine the public power of the Turkish military. As such, the AKP and the followers of the Islamic preacher Fetullah Gülen (1941–), who supported the AKP and gradually colonised the Turkish judiciary and security forces, were identified as the culprits. The argument was that they had not only accessed deleted computer files, but also doctored them so they would come across as more incendiary. It was rumoured at the time that the Gülenists had fully penetrated the judiciary, thereby adversely impacting the interests of the military, which had been privileged by the judiciary until that time.

Ultimately, it was legally difficult to establish any wrongdoing by the Turkish Armed Forces, especially since most of the documents presented as proof were doctored. Indeed, the additional spurious connection established between the diaries and the Ergenekon trials (2008–2016), the aim of which had been to hold high-level generals and admirals legally accountable for alleged coup plots, further undermined the Turkish military's public power, even though many of the documents used during the trials turned out to be forgeries. In addition, a number of high-level meetings were monitored by the National Intelligence Agency (*Milli İstihbarat Teşkilatı*, MİT), which was eventually separated from military intelligence in 2012, symbolising the rise of civilian control over the Turkish military. The following is an excerpt from Admiral Örnek's alleged diaries.

*The Alleged Diaries of Özden Örnek**

3 December 2003

A Supreme Military Council Preparatory Meeting at the [offices of the] Chief of General Staff [hereafter CGS]... First, the office of the CGS presented us with the exact report they had delivered on Monday and then the CGS himself let all the participants express their views in order, starting with the officer of lowest rank.

Faruk Cömert [commander of the Military Academies]: If the Justice and Development Party [hereafter the AKP] wins the local elections, it may make even more concessions to the West, leading us to lose even more of our rights...

Orhan Yöney [commander of the NATO Southeast Europe Joint Forces]: We must demonstrate to the populace that even though the AKP is in power [now], it is not competent. We must act in this direction. The mass [building up] against us is getting larger over time. ... Our actions should not be delayed until December 2004. Around that time, the European Union [hereafter the EU] will meet the AKP's demands and that will work against [our interests]... The judiciary is finished... Our natural allies are universities and the trade unions. These institutions await our signal. We have become alienated from the populace; we must get closer [to them] and be more transparent. One of the AKP's weak points is legislative immunity. We must keep working at this. Let us join voluntary associations without getting involved in their politics. By doing so, we can [both] promote ourselves and spread our ideas more successfully. We must keep pushing the opposition party [Republican People's Party, *Cumhuriyet Halk Partisi*, CHP]. Let's convey [to the CHP] the message that if we are forced to intervene one day, they too will have to account for their actions. They are taking us far too much for granted.

Fevzi Türkeri [commander of the Second Army]: Our homeland is swiftly becoming fragmented. We must take precautions now. Let's gather the press, TÜSİAD [the Turkish Industry and Business Association], and investors and tell them about what this government has done... A lot of difficulties await us in our course of action. Society [at large] views the actions of the government through rose-coloured glasses.

Deputy CGS (İlker Başbuğ): ... The single difficulty in our course of action is [this]: how much does society know about this matter? This is the most important point. How many people are aware of the gravity of the danger? The conjecture [about a military intervention] on 28 February [1997] was different. [This time], the populace is not yet ready.

---

* Translated by the author from its Turkish original in Ahmet Alper Görmüş. "Geçmiş Günler, Geçmemiş Gündemler," *Nokta*, no. 22 (29 March – 4 April 2007).

Oktar Ataman [commander of the Third Army]: A bad situation indeed, but no need to be pessimistic. In the [Kurdish] east and southeast, separatism and religious fundamentalism operate together hand in hand.

Hurşit Tolon [commander of the Fourth Army]: This government has revealed its true colours. Yet it constantly resorts to *takiyye* [i.e., publicly hiding religious beliefs]. The United States [hereafter the US] and the EU ... are trying to shape the Middle East like they did in 1915. The primary threat from the government is first separatism, then religious fundamentalism. This government is toying with our national honour. We are being humiliated. Is there an alternative to this government? It now looks like there is none. This must be communicated to the opposition.

Şener Eruygur [commander of the Gendarmerie]: ...I just want to add one or two topics. We are losing [control of] everything. For instance, the [civilian] police are competing with the gendarmerie, attempting to raise their status by badmouthing the latter. They have also started a webpage and are supporting the Prime Minister [Recep Tayyip Erdoğan].

Yaşar Büyükanıt [commander of the First Army]: ...Geopolitically, the US and the EU are trying to carve out a new role for our country. They are trying to fashion a new Turkey. When Prime Minister Recep Tayyip Erdoğan went to the US, he met with Fethullah Gülen. The acronym AK [the first two letters of the AKP, which means "justice" and "development" but also reads as "pure'"] was intentionally adopted from the written works of Bediüzzaman [Said-i Nursi (1878–1960), the spiritual forefather of Fethullah Gülen]. The most significant leverage for [gaining] the support of public opinion is the media. We must put that [leverage] to use.

İbrahim Fırtına [commander of the Air Forces]: The purpose of the action plan is to protect the constitution. ... We must act together with the president [Ahmet Necdet Sezer (1941–)]. Parliament should be shut down by the president. A new constitution must be drawn up and supported with all the legal elements necessary to defend itself...

Özden Örnek [commander of the Naval Forces]: ... After the Second Decree [a rejected legislative motion that would have authorised the government to send members of the armed forces to foreign countries and to invite foreign armed forces to Turkey] and especially after the promulgation of the August 2004 National Security Council law, the populace has started to lose its confidence in the military. It is not possible for Turkey to have moderate Islam... The most significant issue we must guard against from now on is propaganda against us as "atheists". If we encounter such an attitude, we need to respond swiftly and decisively. Our weapon is our deterrence. We should therefore not make official statements like, "I will not use my weapon." We must respond to every step the AKP takes with the same intensity and with great determination. I don't believe these people are going to become divided over time, and they will also win subsequent elections. Then it will be too late.

Aytaç Yalman [commander of the Land Forces]: All that needs to be said has been expressed. We have wasted so much time. I propose that we immediately start the course of action without delay. We must deliver a memorandum before the elections.

CGS Hilmi Özkök: Thank you, it is great that everyone agrees. I share about eighty percent of your opinions. But there are points I disagree on. I thank you all for speaking so openly. I have no intention to submit a memorandum. This government must go. [But] we should resolve this through democratic means. I also believe that there are many things we can do.

***

Based on information Örnek provided elsewhere, it seems apparent that these detailed minutes of the CGS to prepare for a future Supreme Military Council Meeting were not only top secret, but also solely and secretly audio recorded and archived by the CGS Chief of Operations. Their illegal removal and subsequent public disclosure as if they were part of Örnek's diaries undermine the admiral's authority to disclose official secrets, an act that would have been otherwise treated and tried as an act of espionage. It is evident from the level of detail in the summaries, some of which were later confirmed by certain participants, that this narrative does indeed capture the gist of the meeting.

The meeting itself was marked by the candour of top-level officers as they openly expressed their opinions. Almost all of them espoused some sort of political intervention, which was nothing new for the Turkish military, as it had carried them out multiple times since the beginning of the Cold War. They made the same three points repeatedly: first, the AKP government was making major concessions to the West; second, the government can and should be challenged by way of popular pressure applied by the military's coordination of the media and civil society; and third, if the AKP were to win the 2004 local elections, it would consolidate its authority at the expense of the military. Their repeated references to a need to mobilise public opinion against the AKP undermine a claim that was made when the alleged diaries were published—namely, that they pointed to preparatory meetings for a coup. Indeed, it appears that just about all of the allegations of coup plans were false. The military elite did indeed want to keep guarding the democratic secular regime in Turkey, not by way of a coup d'état but subtly through the media, universities, trade unions, and the political opposition.

Of course, one theme that immediately becomes apparent is the degree of political control that the Turkish military wielded over state and society, a degree of control that the military leadership took for granted. The military was not willing to listen to what society wanted at large, as the former assumed that the latter shared its priority of establishing national security at all costs. By doing so, it especially overlooked the need of civil society to prioritise economic prosperity through democratic governance without military control. It is notable, for instance, that in discussing civil society at large, all of the military officers in the text use the words "public" (*kamu*) and "public opinion" (*kamuoyu*) interchangeably, often meaning "the public" instead of "public opinion," as if the two were one and the same. Yet the military's monopoly on power was exactly what the civilian AKP and its allies, the Gülenists, were trying to publicly disclose with the aim of containing and eliminating it over time.

***

The publication of this text, which was likely doctored, marked an important turning point in Turkish politics. It emerged as three political actors collided with one another as they sought to influence the future trajectory of the Republic of Turkey at the beginning of the twenty-first century. The first actor was the Turkish military, which had been the lynchpin of the country until then, ruling indirectly behind a façade of civilian government. They openly declared to the public that they were in charge of sustaining democracy and that this responsibility had been bestowed upon them by Mustafa Kemal Atatürk (1881–1938), whom they regarded as the sole founder of the Republic. The second actor was the AKP, which started challenging the military's control once it established its own power base. It did so primarily by building up the police as a counterbalance against the military and the gendarmerie, but it also sought to do so by publicly releasing documents that "demonstrated" the high degree of political and economic control the military wielded over society at large. The third actor was the Islamist Gülen movement, which served as handmaiden to the AKP within the Turkish state by penetrating the ranks of the military, judiciary, and the police, thereby literally making it possible for the AKP to control the state. After these three actors laid out their challenges to existing claims to political legitimacy, it was the AKP that ultimately succeeded, at the expense of both the Turkish military and also the Gülen movement, leaving the AKP's leader, President Recep Tayyip Erdoğan, as the ultimate autocrat in power in Turkey. The process involved in the civilian takeover of the Turkish Armed Forces was completed with vicious purges of Gülenists following the failed coup attempt of 15 July 2016, when President Recep Tayyip Erdoğan and his AKP decimated the ranks of the military's officers.

Select Bibliography

Görmüş, Ahmet Alper. *İmaj ve Hakikat: Darbe Günlükleri – Tam Metin: Bir Kuvvet Komutanının Kaleminden Türk Ordusu.* İstanbul: Etkileşim, 2012.

Gürcan, Metin. *Opening the Black Box: The Turkish Military Before and After July 2016.* Havertown: Helion and Co., 2019.

Kadercan, Pelin, and Burak Kadercan. "The Turkish Military as a Political Actor: Its Rise and Fall." *Middle East Policy* 23, no. 3 (2016): 84–99.

Önen, Hakkı Göker. *Crossing Identities and the Turkish Military: Revolutionists, Guardians and Depoliticals: A Comparative Historical Analysis on Turkish Military Culture and Civil-Military Relations.* Berlin: Berliner Wissenschaftsverlag, 2020.

Örnek, Özden. *Sözde Darbe Günlükleri.* İstanbul: Nergiz, 2014.

Özpek, Burak Bilgehan, and Nil Satana. "Civil-Military Relations and the Demise of Turkish Democracy." In *The Oxford Handbook of Turkish Politics*, edited by Güneş Murat Tezcür, 97–116. Oxford: Oxford University Press, 2022.

88
Turkey's Moment in the World: Davutoğlu and Neo-Ottomanism in Turkey's Foreign Policy

Kerem Öktem

A speech that Ahmet Davutoğlu (1959–) made at a conference in Sarajevo on the future of Muslim communities in the Balkans marked the pinnacle of the proactive foreign policy of the Justice and Development Party (*Adalet ve Kalkınma Partisi*, AKP) in the 2000s. When Davutoğlu delivered his "Sarajevo Lecture," he had been Turkey's foreign minister for only a few months, but he had been shaping the AKP's foreign policy from the very beginning. Since 2003, he had been chief advisor to then-Prime Minister Recep Tayyip Erdoğan (1954–), holding the status of ambassador-at-large. In 2009, he became foreign minister and then he served as prime minister from 2014 to 2016. Davutoğlu was the key architect of Turkey's re-engagement with the post-Ottoman and Muslim worlds, a foreign policy doctrine for which he proposed several terms including "Strategic Depth," which was the title of a book he published in 2001, and later "Zero Problems with Neighbours". Some observers and academicians referred to this policy as "Neo-Ottomanism," a contested term popularised by US foreign policy think tanks. Others have referred to his brand of foreign policy as "pan-Islamist" because of his selective emphasis on the Islamic content of the Ottoman legacy as well as his personal commitment to political Islam, and he has also been called a "neo-imperialist" due to his revisionist disregard for established nation-state borders. As a former professor of international relations at the International Islamic University of Malaysia and at Marmara University, Davutoğlu mesmerised international observers as well as domestic audiences with his visionary discourses of Turkey as a global actor.

In May 2016, Davutoğlu resigned as prime minister as a consequence of disagreements with President Erdoğan over the government's increasingly aggressive course of foreign policy and leanings towards autocratisation. This conflict between the two most prolific leaders of Turkey's Islamist movement and Davutoğlu's subsequent fall from grace led to the disappearance of many of his speeches, which until then had been widely available on websites and the online archives of the Ministry of Foreign Affairs, as well as on news websites. That was also the case for the text presented below, which disappeared from the public domain and hence had to be reconstructed on the basis of several sources that contain fragments of the speech.

*Speech of Foreign Minister Ahmet Davutoğlu in Sarajevo on 16 October 2009**

It is often said that the Balkans are at the periphery of Europe. But is the Balkan region really a geographical periphery? No. Actually, the Balkan region is the centre of Afro-Euro-Asia. Where does this perception of the periphery originate? If you had asked Mehmed Pasha Sokolović, he would not have said that Sarajevo or Thessaloniki were outposts of the Ottoman Empire or Europe.

The Balkan region became the centre of world politics in the sixteenth century. This is the golden age of the Balkans. I am not saying this because we inherited the Ottoman legacy, but this is a historical fact. Who ran world politics in the sixteenth century? Your ancestors. They were not all Turks, some were of Slav origin, some were of Albanian origin, and some were even converted Greeks, but they ran world politics. So, Mehmet Pasha Sokolović is a good example. If there was no Ottoman state, Mehmet Pasha would be a poor Serb who lived just to have a small farm. But because of the Ottoman Empire, he became a leader in world politics.

Today, we want a new Balkan region based on political values, economic interdependence, cooperation, and cultural harmony. This was the case under the Ottomans. We will rebuild this. Some call us Neo-Ottomanist. That is why I do not see the Ottoman state as a foreign policy issue. What I emphasise is the Ottoman legacy. The Ottoman centuries of the Balkans are a success story. We now need to rebuild it.

Turkey is part Balkan, part Middle Eastern, and part Caucasian. We have more Bosnians living in Turkey than in Bosnia. More Albanians live in Turkey than in Albania, more Chechens live in Turkey than in Chechnya, and more Abkhaz live in Turkey than in Abkhazia! Why is this so? Because of the Ottoman legacy. For all these different nations in the Balkans, the Middle East, and the Caucasus, Turkey is a safe haven, it is their homeland. You are welcome! Anatolia belongs to you, our brothers and sisters! And we are sure that Sarajevo is ours! When I say it is your Anatolia, and you want to come, do come! But we want you to be safe here as owners of Sarajevo and of Bosnia and Herzegovina.

In short, our history is shared. Our destiny is shared. Our future is shared. Like in the sixteenth century, which saw the rise of the Ottoman Balkans as the centre of world politics, we will make the Balkans, the Caucasus, and the Middle East, together with Turkey, the centre of world politics in the future. This is the objective of Turkish foreign policy, and we will achieve this. We will reintegrate the Balkan region, the Middle East, and the Caucasus, based on the principle of regional and global peace, for the future, not only for all of us but for all of humanity.

---

* This excerpt is a reconstruction based on two main sources in English (the original language of the speech) and Bosnian, triangulated with personal notes: Gerald Knaus, "Multikulti and the future of Turkish Balkan Policy," *Rumeli Observer*, 4 December 2009, and Esad Hećimović, "Šta Turska hoće na Balkanu?" *Dani*, 23 October 2009.

***

Addressed to an audience of politicians, academicians, and Muslim leaders from the Balkans, the speech delineates two interlinked themes: the past and present of the Balkans as an "Ottoman success story" and the identity and global role of Turkey in the twenty-first century.

Davutoğlu offers a revisionist account of the history of the Balkans by re-drawing its spatial and temporal properties and dismissing Euro-centric, Kemalist, and Balkan national accounts of history. He places the Balkan region in the centre of a geopolitical continuum he calls "Afro-Euro-Asia" and posits the narrative of a thriving multi-cultural and multi-religious Balkans at the centre of world politics. In this section, he also briefly responds to the accusation of Neo-Ottomanism, which he perfunctorily rejects by emphasising the "Ottoman Legacy" as his key interest rather than efforts to reinstate an imperial body politic. This legacy is argued to be located primarily in the fifteenth and sixteenth centuries, as it refers to the expansion of the Ottoman state in the Balkans and the Middle East and the image of a just and powerful empire. Yet, his proclamation "Sarajevo is ours" clearly hints at a geopolitical imagining that dismisses existing nation-state borders and prioritises the bonds of empire and religious belonging. When Davutoğlu declares Turkey a "safe haven" and "homeland" for different nations in the Balkans, the Middle East, and the Caucasus, he means Muslims as "our brothers and sisters". When he declares, "We want you to be safe here as the owners of Sarajevo," he is referring primarily to Muslim Bosniaks.

Turkey's identity in Davutoğlu's imagining is defined in contradistinction to Kemalist nationalism and its project of a Western-oriented if inward-looking nation-state with clear boundaries with the Muslim and Arab worlds. Turkey here is defined by its geography—that is to say, by its location at the intersection of several geopolitical regions including the Balkans, the Middle East, and the Caucasus—as well as by ethnic and cultural diversity, which he sees as part of the Ottoman legacy. Davutoğlu frequently mentioned elsewhere that the Republic of Turkey, with its insistence on a secular and racially defined Turkish nation, was an aberration and a deviation from a more inclusive imperial history, an aberration that needed to be corrected. That correction, he argued, would be achieved by a reintegration of the Balkan region, the Middle East, and the Caucasus. Davutoğlu saw Turkey as the natural leader of this process of "re-integration" of the post-Ottoman and Muslim worlds. This project of correction and reintegration was also situated in a larger universalist claim to "regional and global peace … not only for us but for all of humanity" which a Turkey freed of its nationalist history and bolstered by a reintegrated post-Ottoman space would make possible.

The speech integrates several ideological and intellectual influences ranging from a celebration of the sixteenth-century Ottoman Empire as a golden age to a rejection of the Kemalist Turkish Republic as a desirable polity, tropes that are commonplace in mainstream political Islam in Turkey. Those notions are completed with a pan-Islamic concern for the well-being of Muslims in post-Ottoman regions and other spaces and the universalist claim of Turkish leadership of the Global South, which resounds with the subsequent mantra of Turkey's foreign policy in the early 2020s, "the world is bigger than five," a reference to the five permanent members of the Security Council of the United Nations: China, France, the Russian Federation, the United Kingdom, and the United States.

***

Ever since the age of Ottoman reforms, reflections on the future of the Ottoman and then the Turkish state, the form of its institutions, the demography of the people that inhabit its territories, and the relations it maintains with the rest of the world have been a primary concern of political elites and public debates. In the two centuries since then, various political projects have been advanced in the process of addressing those questions, beginning with the Tanzimat notions of equal Ottoman citizenship and constitutional governance to the pan-Islamist advances of the Abdülhamit era, as well as the nationalist forays of the Committee of Union and Progress. The Kemalist Republic was based on the ethnicised notion of an exclusive nation-state for Turkish-speaking Sunni Muslims in which intellectual, cultural, and political contact with the Muslim world and the post-Ottoman Muslim communities in the Balkans was discouraged. Ahmet Davutoğlu's Sarajevo lecture speaks to those concerns and the larger questions in which they are embedded. His answers concerning a reconstituted Ottoman space, even if the shape and form of that construct are left unclear, are suffused with a sense of disdain for the post-First World War territorial arrangements imposed by the Great Powers in the Balkans, the Middle East, and the Caucasus, a rejection of the secular-nationalist order of the Kemalist Republic, and notions of an imperial imagining that see Turkey as the leader of the Global South or at least of the Muslim world.

Questions about Turkey's place and role in the world are recognised by mainstream Islamist politics in Turkey, which welcomed the content of Davutoğlu's foreign policy outlook as discussed here, including his preference for actors and governments affiliated with the Muslim Brotherhood during the Arab Spring and Turkey's cooperation with Jihadist groups in Syria and Libya. While the opposition has been uniformly critical of this increasingly pan-Islamist type of foreign policy, for the AKP, Davutoğlu was only discredited when he fell from grace in 2016 due to an intra-party power struggle. Nonetheless, the larger questions resonate well beyond the Islamist constituency and remain largely unresolved in the first half of the twenty-first century.

Select Bibliography

Aras, Bülent. "Davutoğlu Era in Turkish Foreign Policy Revisited." *Journal of Balkan and Near Eastern Studies* 16, no. 4 (2014): 404–18.

Aydın, Cemil. *The Idea of the Muslim World: A Global Intellectual History*. Cambridge: Harvard University Press, 2017.

Benhaïm, Yohanan, and Kerem Öktem. "The Rise and Fall of Turkey's Soft Power Discourse: Discourse in Foreign Policy Under Davutoğlu and Erdoğan." *European Journal of Turkish Studies* 21 (2015). http://journals.openedition.org/ejts/5275

Davutoğlu, Ahmet. *Stratejik Derinlik: Türkiye'nin Uluslararası Konumu*. İstanbul: Küre Yayınları, 2001.

Oran, Baskın. *Turkish Foreign Policy, 1919-2006: Facts and Analyses with Documents*. Salt Lake City: University of Utah Press, 2010.

Yavuz, M. Hakan. "Turkish Identity and Foreign Policy in Flux: The Rise of Neo-Ottomanism." *Critique: Journal for Critical Studies of the Middle East* 7, no. 12 (1998): 19–41.

89
"Not Good Enough but Yes":
The Long Shadow of the 2010 Referendum

İlker Aytürk

On 12 September 2010, the thirtieth anniversary of the coup d'état of 1980, some 40 million Turkish voters went to polling stations on the occasion of a nationwide referendum. The ruling Justice and Development Party (*Adalet ve Kalkınma Partisi*, AKP) had proposed a total of 26 amendments to the post-coup constitution of 1982, ranging from eliminating provisional articles which provided immunity to the military regime of 1980–83 to limiting the privileges of military personnel and expanding the economic and social rights of Turkish citizens. At the heart of the amendment package, however, was judicial reform, which comprised an attempt to free the executive (i.e., the AKP government) from the shackles of judicial reviews and to put an end to what was known as military-bureaucratic tutelage over elected civilians. Then-Prime Minister Recep Tayyip Erdoğan (1954–) and a host of right-wing leaders before him had complained endlessly about the Turkish high courts, which they regarded as the protectors of bureaucratic interests and secularism. The referendum was held in an environment of unprecedented polarisation. The secular centre-left Republican People's Party (*Cumhuriyet Halk Partisi*, CHP), far-right Nationalist Movement Party (*Milliyetçi Hareket Partisi*, MHP), and a host of left-wing and secular civil society organisations opposed the amendment proposals, as they sought to prevent the executive from dominating the courts. Prime Minister Erdoğan, the AKP (of which Erdoğan was and is party chairman), and their erstwhile ally Fethullah Gülen (1941–), a Muslim preacher who headed a system of domestic and international networks, championed the amendments, as their ultimate aim was indeed to appoint loyalists to positions in the high courts, where they had always thought they had been underrepresented. In an unforgettable moment during the electoral campaign, Gülen even called on the dead to rise from their graves and vote "yes". In a critical move, the Kurdish Peace and Democracy Party (*Barış ve Demokrasi Partisi*, BDP) boycotted the referendum, although a number of Kurdish intellectuals came out in support of the proposed changes. Turkey's key allies at the time, including the European Union and specifically the governments of the USA, the UK, Germany, Italy, Spain, and Sweden, also supported Erdoğan and expressed their satisfaction when the amendment package was finally passed with a 58 per cent majority vote. Seen in hindsight, the 2010 Referendum is now widely recognised as a milestone in contemporary Turkish history, as it facilitated the AKP's turn towards authoritarianism.

An essential factor that contributed to Erdoğan's victory was the fragmentation of secular opinion leaders on the eve of the referendum. The Turkish liberal left, a numerically small but very vocal and influential group of intellectuals, journalists, academicians, and business elites, caused uncertainty and disorientation within the secular opposition by throwing their full weight behind Erdoğan's campaign. In fact, the liberal left never truly belonged in the secular opposition camp, and since 2002 they had been firm supporters of the AKP. However, their secular and Westernised lifestyles coupled with the prominent position they held in the media, academia, and the business world essentially left the opposition in a state of confusion. As a result, during the three summer months of campaigning, secular left-wing opinion leaders were split down the middle.

Although the liberal left had made calls for a completely revamped constitution and a much more radical overhaul of the Turkish political system, they considered the amendment package to be a positive step forward. The liberal left campaign slogan *"Yetmez Ama Evet"* ("Not Good Enough but Yes"), the most memorable relic of the referendum, continues to divide the Turkish intelligentsia to this day.

Why Do We Say, "Not Good Enough but Yes"?

[...] With the exception of the Constitution of 1921, no [Turkish] constitution has ever been drafted by the elected representatives of the people in this country. The Constitution of 1924 was drawn up by the single-party regime, which went on to rule the country by decree, and the Constitutions of 1961 and 1982 were drafted by juntas and their supporters and subsequently imposed on the people by force. We say "yes" to this constitutional amendment, because, for the first time since 1921, after nearly 90 years of republican history, [...] the people will accept or reject a constitutional amendment drawn up by their own elected representatives, and not by juntas or dictators.

We say "yes" because the constitutional amendments will shake up the military's tutelage and the high courts of justice, which have been the most important guarantors of a regime of coups. The Constitutional Court, established by the Coup of 27 May [1960], and the Supreme Council of Judges and Prosecutors, established by the generals of the Coup of 12 September, which have so far protected the juntas [...], will cease to be institutions of tutelage.

We say "yes" because Provisional Article No. 15, which protects juntas, torturers, and murderers, will be eliminated. The junta will be brought to justice.

We now say "Not Good Enough but Yes" so we can put pressure on the government to draw up a completely new constitution the first day after the referendum.

[This is] because, we, of course, realise that the constitution must be changed in its entirety; constitutional citizenship and freedom of association [must be included] and the electoral threshold, as well

* Documents related to the *"Yetmez Ama Evet"* campaign were originally maintained on the campaign website, which has since been removed from the internet. They are, however, accessible on other websites to which they were uploaded at the time. The quotes presented here were translated from the original Turkish text "Neden 'Yetmez Ama Evet' Diyoruz?" available at https://simurg.info/2010/07/

2003–2012

as racist, nationalist, and sexist discourses, must be completely eliminated. The proper way to achieve this goal is not to say "no" to this constitutional amendment package, because, however unsatisfactory it may be, it is in no way inferior to the existing constitution. The correct path today is to say "Not Good Enough but Yes" so that we can demand more on 13 September with a new spirit of self-respect [...]. As Cemal Süreyya [*sic*, "Süreya"] once stated, "One must not die of thirst while searching for pure water."

The greatest obstacle to Turkish democracy is the oligarchical judiciary. The constitutional amendment package that will be put to the vote on 12 September will shake that oligarchy to its core. That is why we say "Not Good Enough but Yes" to amending the constitution. It will be impossible to draft a civilian, democratic, and emancipatory constitution unless the oligarchy in the justice system is eliminated.

***

Hundreds of the signatories—and more would sign on later—of the press statement quoted above represented the liberal left, which was Turkey's counterpart to the global New Left. The rise of the liberal left as a distinct elite network in the 1980s was probably the most significant development in modern Turkish intellectual history. Former members of the Turkish far left, who were disillusioned with class politics in the aftermath of the coup of 12 September and, of course, the collapse of the Eastern Bloc, gradually embraced identity politics as the new frontier of social equality. After a failed attempt to establish a liberal-left political party, the New Democracy Movement (*Yeni Demokrasi Hareketi*, YDH) mainly acted as a pressure group through academia, the media, and civil society networks between 1994 and 1997. The top items on the liberal left's agenda included democratisation, pushing back against the military-bureaucratic establishment, the empowerment of ethnic and religious minority groups, and engaging in a thorough critique of Turkish nationalism, militarism, Kemalism, and secularism. From the beginning onwards, the liberal-left movement often regarded the Kurdish movement as well as Turkish Islamists as potential allies in their efforts to compensate for the historical weakness of liberalism and socialism in Turkey. In an attempt to connect with major identitarian mass movements that were opposed to the political establishment in Turkey, the liberal left sought to build up a broader, more inclusive, and hence stronger anti-establishment bloc.

Having given the Erdoğan-Gülen coalition their full support in the defamation and purging of the military establishment, which got underway in 2008, the liberal left welcomed the 2010 Referendum as an opportunity to push their other enemy, i.e., the justices of the high courts, back into the bottle and seal it shut forever. From the liberal-left perspective, the high courts embodied the last bastion of bureaucratic tutelage over Turkish democracy. Instead of protecting individual citizens, they argued, the justices gave precedence to state interests and colluded with generals to safeguard the Constitution of 1982, which had been drawn up by the military. Therefore, the referendum provided a welcome opportunity to draft the first civilian constitution of the Turkish Republic and to get rid of bureaucratic tutelage in one fell swoop. Furthermore, liberal-left critics also accused the Turkish justice system of being oligarchical. The notion that new justices had always been recruited from a small pool of leftist, secular, Alevi candidates was a common trope in Islamist condemnations of the system, and the liberal left started parroting the same line and called for a more inclusive and representative justice system.

In June of 2010, a loosely organised group of liberal-left activists launched an energetic campaign that lasted until the day of the referendum and in support of which they held public forums and rallies, funded an ad campaign, and created a website—now shut down and inaccessible—where they announced their activities and posted statements and e-brochures. Public intellectuals such as Orhan Pamuk (1952–), Sezen Aksu (1954–), Ahmet Altan (1950–), Lale Mansur (1956–), Can Paker (1942–), and numerous others spoke to the press in favour of the campaign. Although the campaigners purposely drew attention to the potential for the expansion of civil rights and settling scores with the junta of 1980, only a few acknowledged that a "yes" vote would grant the Islamist cadres of Erdoğan and Gülen broad powers to reshape the justice system. Those few dissenting voices, however, were hushed and, broadly speaking, the majority of leftist-liberal opinion leaders expected that they would join the club of movers and shakers and hence be recognised as partners in the remaking of a post-referendum, post-Kemalist Turkey if they lent their full support to the amendment package. Their critics, on the other hand, accused the campaigners of being either power-seeking opportunists or fools who were naively assisting an Islamist takeover of Turkey. Such critics spurned the carefully inserted "sweeteners" in the package because they argued that the referendum was essentially about Erdoğan and Gülen packing the courts with loyalists. During the three-month public debates that ensued, harsh words were exchanged between the groups involved. In response to their critics, the campaigners fervently defended the amendments but, as it soon became apparent, they did so with far too much confidence in how they thought the referendum would unfold.

***

In the end, it took Erdoğan—and Gülen—only a few months after the referendum to fill newly vacant seats on the Supreme Council of Judges and Prosecutors (SCJP) with partisan appointees. The new members of the council—membership of the SCJP had more than tripled, per the terms of the amendments—now played a leading role in the promotion and appointing of judges and prosecutors, the inevitable result of which was that the Turkish judiciary quickly came under the full control of the executive and of Gülen as well, a state of affairs that continued until the purge of the Gülenists in 2016. At the same time, as early as 2011 the AKP's leadership began to keep the liberal-left intelligentsia at arm's length and the Gezi Protests of 2013 made it clear that a complete rupture had taken place between the two sides.

In 2010, Turkey started sinking deeper and deeper into authoritarianism, and political polarisation increased exponentially. In that new environment, discouraged secularists, Kemalists, and leftists typically pinned the blame—perhaps not entirely but to a large extent— on the liberal left. They created the epithet "*Yetmez Ama Evetçi*" ("Sayers of 'Not Good Enough but Yes'"), which became a political swear word. In the eyes of the opposition, starting in

2010 *"Yetmez Ama Evet"* was transformed into, at best, a symbol of naïve optimism and, at worst, revanchist opportunism. The liberal-left campaigners of 2010, on the other hand, were shell-shocked and stunned by their fall from grace and the rapidity of the reversal of their fortunes. One referred to himself as a "useful idiot," some made public apologies, and many others expressed remorse. The majority, however, denied responsibility, opting instead to cling to the argument that what they had done in 2010 was the right thing to do at the time and that they could not have possibly predicted the AKP's authoritarian turn. In other words, if anyone was to be blamed, it was the AKP, not the liberal left.

After the dust had settled, the liberal-left campaigners who had supported the yes-vote found themselves on the receiving end of harsh criticisms, accusations, and even insults. That was not surprising, given what was at stake and how aggressively the campaigners had defended the AKP's arguments. That said, the role played by the liberal left in the 2010 Referendum is usually overstated. Numerically speaking, liberal-left voters never amounted to more than a tiny fraction of the overall vote and, as such, their contributions to the sweeping victory of the AKP at the ballot box were minimal. That, however, should not lead to underestimations of the otherwise critical role they played. Their decision to join the yes-camp influenced the outcome in three ways. First, liberal-left criticisms targeting the secular left-wing intelligentsia divided the opposition and prevented them from speaking as a united voice, which sowed doubt and confusion among opponents of the referendum with regard to what was at stake and thus numbed them to the painful consequences. Indeed, that numbness may have accounted for the relatively low voter turnout—by otherwise high Turkish standards—which stood at approximately 74 per cent. Second, and more significantly, liberal-left campaigners shifted the focus of public debates toward punishing the perpetrators of the coup of 12 September and away from the question of restructuring the judiciary. By making use of their networks in the national and international media, they sugar-coated measures that otherwise in their absence would have seemed more like a partisan attempt to take control of the judiciary. Third, and lastly, they acted as Erdoğan and Gülen's goodwill ambassadors to governments and media outlets abroad and thus garnered international sympathy for the yes-campaign with considerable success.

Select Bibliography

Budka, Alper. "Yetmez Ama Evet Diyenler Anlatıyor." https://www.gazeteduvar.com.tr/gundem/2020/08/18/yet-mez-ama-evet-diyenler-anlatiyor

Ersoy, Duygu and Fahriye Üstüner. "Liberal Intellectuals' Narration of the Justice and Development Party in Turkey." *Turkish Studies* 17, no. 3 (2016): 406–28.

Ertekin, Orhan Gazi. *Yargı Meselesi Hallolundu!* Ankara: Epos, 2011.

Gürpınar, Doğan. *Düne Veda: Türkiye'de Liberalizm ve Demokratlık (1980–2010).* İstanbul: Etkileşim, 2013.

Gürpınar, Doğan. "Left Revisionism and the Trajectory of Left-Liberalism in Turkey." *Insight Turkey* 14, no. 1 (2012): 147–68.

"2010 Anayasa Referandumu'nu Yeniden Düşünmek: 'Yetmez Ama Evet.'" *140journos*, 15 July 2016. https://140journos.com/2010-anayasa-referandumunu-yeniden-dusunmek-yetmez-ama-evet-b9f978e9444a.

90
Towards Peace or Further Troubles?
The People's Democratic Congress

Özgür Mutlu Ulus

The root of what is generally called "the Kurdish problem" lay with the founding of the Turkish Republic in 1923. The diverse Muslim ethnic groups that had populated the Ottoman Empire were considered "Turks" by the founders of the newly established secular Turkish state, which did not recognise an independent Kurdish or Islamic national identity. In the 1960s, many Kurdish intellectuals and youths blended socialism with the ethnic question and started to become active in leftist parties and organisations. Revolutionary Eastern Cultural Centres (*Devrimci Doğu Kültür Ocakları*, DDKO) were the first legal, autonomous Kurdish organisations to combine socialism with the ethnic question. The Kurdish revival was, however, suppressed by the military intervention of 1971, but many Kurdish activists continued their struggle through leftist parties and revolutionary organisations. It was only with the founding of the Kurdistan Workers' Party (*Partiya Karkerên Kurdistan*, PKK) in 1978 that the Kurdish revival gained renewed momentum. After the military coup of 1980, which strictly suppressed leftist and Kurdish organisations, the PKK started an armed struggle. That marked the beginning of a process that started to gradually win over the begrudging admiration of segments of the Kurdish population while brandmarking the PKK as a terrorist organisation in the eyes of the Turkish state, a designation that was also later recognised by the European Union, NATO, and many countries.

A legal, recognised pro-Kurdish party did not enter the political arena until 1990 with the establishment of the People's Labour Party (*Halkın Emek Partisi*, HEP), which was then banned in 1993—a fate that awaited many other subsequent pro-Kurdish parties. After the arrest of the PKK's leader, Abdullah Öcalan (1949–), in 1999, Turkey witnessed the emergence of a number of new alliances and coalitions between the Kurdish liberation movement and leftist and socialist political parties. Leaving behind the ideal of establishing an independent state, the Kurdish movement changed course and set its sights on a project of radical democracy and democratic autonomy in Turkey and the region at large. First articulated by Ernesto Laclau (1935–2014) and Chantal Mouffe (1943–), radical democracy is a type of democracy that advocates the radical extension of equality and liberty. For the sake of a democratic solution to the Kurdish problem, Öcalan proposed a model of "radical democracy" that drew upon an array of radical intellectual traditions including the ideas of libertarian social ecologist Murray Bookchin (1921–2006), Ernesto Laclau, Chantal Mouffe, feminist political theorists such as Judith Butler (1956–), leftist Foucauldians, and critical Marxists. The ecological, democratic, gender libertarian society paradigm that Ocalan proposed for the region has indeed been referred to as a type of "radical democracy". In 2005, democratic autonomy also entered the lexicon of the Kurdish movement. This particular form of democratic autonomy aims at realising Kurdish self-government in existing states with Kurdish populations. Instead of aiming to establish a central state, democratic autonomy seeks to empower local government as part of a general decentralisation and democratisation of state structures. The Turkish state, however, is a unitary and centralised state in which ideas concerning the federalism and/or democratic autonomy generally demanded by Kurdish politics are frowned upon.

This shift towards radical democracy instead of a national liberation movement made it possible for various alliances to be formed among leftist movements as a means of overcoming the 10 per cent national electoral threshold. In the elections of 2011, the Labour, Democracy, and Freedom Bloc (*Emek, Demokrasi, ve Özgürlük Bloğu*) secured thirty-six seats in Parliament, which would later play an important part in the founding of the People's Democratic Congress (*Halkların Demokratik Kongresi*, HDK) in Ankara on 15-16 October 2011 by 820 delegates from 81 cities across Turkey.

*The Opening Declaration of the People's Democratic Congress**

We call on those of you who support the people, the oppressed, the neglected, and those who stand for nature, labour, freedom, equality, peace, justice, and democracy to organise a common struggle for a humane life, a new society beyond the horizon of the two main political currents competing for the survival of the neoliberal and anti-democratic order imposed by rulers, a new society without exploitation where the servitude of human to human will come to an end.

We are taking a new step forward to nurture the spirit of the common struggle and draw strength from each other through solidarity, [standing] shoulder to shoulder with the ongoing struggles everywhere in the world, on Wall Street, in Santiago [de] Chile, in Cairo, Tunisia, Caracas, and Gaza, against the global domination of the capitalist system and all of its forms of exploitation and oppression which destroy social life and alienate the individual from his/her own labour, society, identity, and nature.

The People's Democratic Congress aims to end the war which has arisen from the deadlock over the Kurdish problem and cost the lives of more than 30,000 people in the last twenty years. The Congress aims to circulate an understanding of democratic autonomy as an important initiative and program of peace for a peaceful, democratic solution for the whole of society which is based on equal rights. Democratic autonomy will end the tutelage of the central administration over local administrations and ensure the broadest participation of local people in decision-making, processes of implementation, and the free expression of all identities.

* Translated from the original Turkish in "HDK Kuruluş Bildirgesi," *Halkların Demoratik Kongresi Bülteni*, no. 1 (15 April 2012): 5–6. Available at https://halklarindemokratikkongresi.net/

The People's Democratic Congress is the main opposition movement in Turkey. It is a true focal point of resistance against the AKP government, which has been the primary defender of the common interests of the Turkish right and the ruling classes as well as the regional fringe of world capitalism. All forms of struggle of all democratic and social forces are the common domain of the People's Democratic Congress. Our Congress, embodying the strength of the entirety of the opposition, aims to mobilise all oppressed, exploited, marginalised, and neglected forces, including labourers, immigrants, women, villagers, the youth, the retired, the disabled, LBGTQ individuals, and all faith communities.

***

As noted in the opening declaration, the main aim of the HDK was to provide an alternative to the social order of Turkey that departed not only from the foundations of the establishment of the Kemalist Republic but also from the contemporary neoliberal conservativism of the AKP government. Moreover, the Congress Declaration depicts a new trajectory for the Kurdish movement, not one that fights solely for Kurdish people's rights but for the rights of all of the people in Turkey, all of the oppressed and exploited, in a way that would later be defined as "developing a sense of belonging to Turkey" (*"Türkiyelileşme"*). Whether this was just a pragmatist turn or an actual change in the political paradigm is an issue that continues to be disputed. Nonetheless, the HDK declared that the Congress represented all oppressed and exploited forces, not just Kurds, and built up a new political discourse based on these ideas of pluralism and freedom. The delegates represented a broad range of diverse social actors, groups, and organisations, and some of these, such as LGBTQ communities, were part of new political movements (though with a rich history and an active social base). As was the case elsewhere in the world, identity politics came to fore in the 1980s and 1990s in Turkey. The Kurdish movement under the leadership of Öcalan had already developed a new discourse on gender equality, even to the point of declaring that the movement was a "Women's Revolution". The alliance with LGBTQ groups, however, was met with suspicion and reservations by more conservative members of the Kurdish movement such as Altan Tan (1958–). Such conservative politicians in the Kurdish movement set off on their own paths, as they saw the alliance as representing rather leftist and "marginal actors, mainly the LGBTQ," in a move that would eventually divide the Kurdish movement.

The declaration of the HDK clearly shows the internationalist vision of the new movement. At the end of the 1990s, the Kurdish movement adopted a radically critical stance concerning the nation-state and instead of insisting on the establishment of "Kurdistan" as a nation that would unite all Kurds in the region (in Turkey, Iraq, Syria, and Iran), as the leader of the PKK, Öcalan proposed the co-existence of a plurality of political communities at the local, municipal, provincial, regional, national, and transnational levels. Inspired by the work of Murray Bookchin, Öcalan suggested a new paradigm, radical democracy, in an attempt to go beyond what he referred to as the "classical Kurdish nationalist line". Under the leadership of Öcalan, the movement has developed a model of governance called "democratic confederalism," which aspires to establish a multi-layered system of political communities.

Democratic confederalism has been developed as a project of national self-determination for Kurds but does not involve the creation of a separate Kurdish state. This first declaration made by the HDK with its commentary on "democratic autonomy" lays bare the paradigm shift that occurred.

While the democratic republic is a project of state reform, the projects of democratic confederalism and democratic autonomy embody the idea of a politics that sets aside and transcends the nation-state. As was apparent in its first declaration, the Congress has taken up an internationalist perspective and focuses on establishing a sense of unity with all of the anti-capitalist, ecological, and democratic struggles occurring around the world.

***

The political success of the HDK is difficult to assess. It led to the creation of the Peoples' Democratic Party (*Halkların Demokrasisi Partisi*, HDP) with similar associations and more direct calls for "radical democracy" with the aim of achieving a peaceful, just, and more democratic transformation of Turkey. In 2015, the HDP managed to overcome the 10 per cent threshold and entered Parliament as a political party, not by way of independent deputies as had occurred in the past, which raised hopes for a peaceful solution to the Kurdish problem. However, after an escalation of violence in 2015 and 2016, including actions by the PKK and its militant offshoots, legal pro-Kurdish organisations such as the HDK and HDP were pushed into a difficult position, reducing hopes for the peaceful political change they advocated. Those events also drove the Turkish state to increase its security measures and discourses of securitisation in dealing with the Kurdish problem. Several members of the HDP (including its co-chairs) and the HDK have been imprisoned since then on charges of having ties to the PKK.

Beyond Turkey, the Kurdish radical democracy movement has been active in Syria since the outbreak of the civil war in 2013. The Autonomous Administration of North and East Syria (AANES), also known as "Rojava," has since expanded to include Arab-majority regions that were liberated from the Islamic State. Rojava's residents have developed political systems based on the principles of direct democracy and decentralisation, as shaped by the political thought of Abdullah Öcalan. In contrast to centralised representative systems, Rojava's democratic confederalism consists of decentralised institutions that empower local communities, particularly women and minorities, so they can directly participate in processes of decision-making. The smallest decision-making unit in this system is the commune, which brings together groups of several hundred people for the purposes of engaging in dialogue, decision-making, and resource sharing. Within communes, committees meet to address issues such as health, education, self-defence, and conflict resolution, in line with the issues most relevant to the local community. Although communes and councils are the primary structures utilised for bottom-up decision-making, other institutions also work towards that goal. Time will tell if "Rojava" will evolve and truly represent a new form of radical democracy.

Starting with early uprisings in the 1920s, the Republic of Turkey has long had to cope with the so-called "Kurdish problem". As it has escalated into a prolonged but low-intensity armed conflict with various Kurdish organisations, the prospects for a peaceful and political solution to the Kurdish problem remain unclear in Turkey. Through the HDK, the Kurdish movement has actively shifted away from the goal of a Kurdish nation-state towards a project involving the democratisation of Turkey's political and social order. However, the continued autonomous actions of the PKK in the region and its dominance in the Kurdish movement have complicated the political viability of legal pro-Kurdish movements. The situation in Syria has further complicated the problem by creating a geopolitical security concern for decision-makers in Ankara. Despite all the pressure and persecution, however, the HDK and HDP have managed to remain relevant in electoral politics in the centennial of the Republic of Turkey by representing a democratic alternative for a wide variety of people from different backgrounds.

Select Bibliography

Akkaya, Ahmet Hamdi, and Joost Jongerden. "Reassembling the Political: The PKK and the Project of Radical Democracy." *European Journal of Turkish Studies*, no. 14 (2013). https://biblio.ugent.be/publication/3101197.

Jongerden, Joost. "Looking Beyond the State: Transitional Justice and the Kurdish Issue." *Ethnic and Racial Studies* 41, no. 4 (2018): 721–38.

Kutan, Birgül, and Adnan Çelik. "Prefiguring Post-National Futures: The Case of the Peoples' Democratic Congress (HDK)." In *Turkey: Turkey Case Study: The People's Democratic Congress* (HDK). ESRC Grant No: ES/R00403X/1. Brighton: University of Sussex, 2021. Available at https://knowledge4struggle.org.

2013–2023

91

Solidarity and Diversity:
The Gezi Protests

Emre Erol

Towards the end of May 2013, news headlines in Turkey were dominated by developments occurring around a green space in İstanbul—Taksim Square's Gezi Park—and soon afterwards Turkey was shaken by waves of protests across 76 locations in the country, including in major international metropolitan centres, and also on social media platforms. Until that time, the Justice and Development Party (*Adalet ve Kalkınma Partisi*, AKP), headed by populist leader and then-Prime Minister Recep Tayyip Erdoğan (1954–), had been governing Turkey since 2002 after scoring back-to-back electoral victories, but its tenure was not without problems. In retrospect, it is clear that the year 2013 and the Gezi Protests were political turning points for the AKP and for Turkey. While the AKP remained in power for two more consecutive terms after the Gezi events and Erdoğan was elected president of the Republic of Turkey, widespread domestic and international criticism emerged about the AKP's democratic credentials. Many scholars, commentators, and observers have described the AKP's current approach to politics as authoritarian in one way or another. The AKP and Erdoğan started out in 2002 with high expectations, building up a generous—and apparently misleading—international reputation as harbingers of pluralism and democracy. For many, the party and its leader now conjure up a mirror image of their former selves. Some scholars have argued that authoritarianism has always been the primary ethos underlying the Islamist movement in Turkey, out of which the AKP initially emerged, while others assert that the AKP evolved into its current state as a result of both exogenous and endogenous political factors that arose along the way. Irrespective of those debates, the Gezi Protests undoubtedly constituted a crucial turn of events that reshaped the political and cultural landscape in Turkey by giving momentum to environmental awareness, shaping youth politics, and forcing conventional political parties to reinvent themselves. Many also take up the AKP's manifold reactions to the Gezi Protests as a crucial juncture in Turkey's democratic backsliding, the rate of which increased with subsequent events such as the June elections of 2015 and the failed coup attempt that took place in 2016.

The immediate cause of the Gezi Protests, if expressed through the symbolism of the first protesters, was a tree. However, what that symbolism really reflected was growing discontent with the AKP and its leader, as well as with the party's anti-democratic policies. More specifically, they were about the conversion of a public space in the heart of İstanbul into a profit-generating shopping mall. For the most part, protestors saw the demonstrations as a defence of the norms of representative democracy, which they thought were rapidly eroding at the time.

On the night of 27 May 2013 at around ten o'clock in the evening, following long debates about various aspects of the confluence of public spaces and politics, demolition operations got underway in a green space adjacent to İstanbul's famous Taksim Square: Gezi Park. The AKP government wanted to transform the park, one of the last remaining green spaces in İstanbul and also a place of historical and political significance, into a shopping mall despite overwhelming public opposition to the project. On that night, a tree in the park was uprooted by construction workers, who were accompanied by security forces. News of the demolition work appeared on social media and it was also reported on by conventional media outlets. Protesters organised a sit-in, and the violent crackdown by security forces that followed the protest triggered an even bigger public reaction. There had already been numerous political developments that year, and public opinion against the government was on the rise. The uprooting of the tree, the top-down decision-making process behind the project, the ensuing violence unleashed by the police, the symbolic and historical significance of Taksim Square, mounting criticism of the government's undertakings, attempts to crack down on the opposition, Erdoğan's uncompromising stance on polarising issues, and, in particular, government policies that disregarded environmental concerns transformed that moment into a wave of social upheaval that would basically last until the end of summer.

However, it should be emphasised that making generalisations about the Gezi Protests can be quite misleading since this predominantly middle-class movement meant something different for each individual involved. The diversity of demands, the lack of an organised hierarchy, and the multitude of voices raised during the demonstrations pointed to how the dissatisfaction of a broad swathe of people from various social backgrounds was becoming manifest during the protests, much like the other social movements of the decade that preceded and followed it. As was the case with the Arab Spring and the Occupy movement, the Gezi Protests were multifaceted, non-hierarchical, largely shaped by social media communications, and multi-vocal in their public expression. However, one group stood out in the initial days of the protests as an organised entity that attempted to provide the protesters with a framework for making their demands. Presented below are two visuals that illustrate both the diversity of the protesters' profiles and the slogans of Taksim Solidarity (*Taksim Dayanışması*), the latter of which became the most frequently used means of communicating the demands of activists in the first month of the protests.

The first image was hand-drawn by protesters, most probably during the early days of the Gezi Protests, while the second image is from a website that supported the demands raised by Taksim Solidarity. Those demands were readily visible in many of the visuals used at the time in the form of stickers, placards, and posters. Each was designed to represent one of the five main demands that Taksim Solidarity formulated as a reflection of the demands of the protesters. English translations of each of them, prepared by Taksim Solidarity, were provided along with the Turkish texts online.

*The Diversity of Demands During the Gezi Park Protests**

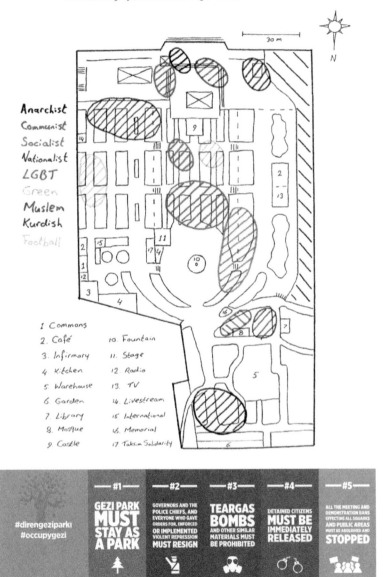

1 Commons
2. Café
3. Infirmary
4. Kitchen
5. Warehouse
6. Garden
7. Library
8. Mosque
9. Castle

10. Fountain
11. Stage
12. Radio
13. TV
14. Livestream
15. International
16. Memorial
17. Taksim Solidarity

* The hand-drawn map of the occupation of Gezi Park, which is available on Wikimedia Commons, was first published on 27 June 2013: https://commons.wikimedia.org/wiki/File:Gezi-park-encampment-map.jpg. The demands, which were released on 4 June 2013 by Taksim Solidarity, are available at the following address: https://file.ejatlas.org/img/Conflict/1042/taksim_demands.jpg

***

A digitised version of the hand-drawn "historical atlas of Gezi Park" was shared across multiple online platforms during the protests. A key detail about the map concerns the labels with which the protesters decided to designate each other in occupied Gezi Park. They initially included conventional political descriptors such as anarchist, communist, socialist, and nationalist but soon incorporated "LGBT" activists, "Greens," "Muslims," "Kurds," and "Football Fans," which encapsulated groups that were followers of İstanbul's well-known clubs. This broad spectrum is not only a testament to the diversity of protesters' profiles and motivations, but it also points to the increasing importance of identity politics at the time in Turkey.

Only by combining the image of the map with the many audio-visual recordings that were made of Gezi Park during the protests can the extent of the interactions of protesters from different backgrounds and hence driven by different motives truly be grasped. As such, the protests constituted a moment in which previously isolated or distanced proponents of particular political discourses and identity politics came into contact with each other. Today, the aftermath and effects of those encounters are issues that are open for debate, but the consensus is clear: the exchanges that took place between those diverse demands reshaped the political landscape, for better or for worse.

Contextualising the demands of Taksim Solidarity as presented above would require a discussion of the nature of the organisation that framed them and a basic chronological understanding of the events that took place. Doing so would make it possible to see that those demands were among the most significant and widely circulated in a social movement that was, in essence, non-hierarchical, partly digital, and multi-vocal. Taksim Solidarity (also known as the *Taksim Dayanışma Bileşenleri Platformu*, the Taksim Solidarity Platform) started out as a collective of neighbourhood associations, syndicates, occupational associations (such as those of architects, urban planners, and doctors), and certain political parties (representing a significant portion of the opposition) whose aim was to object to and amend an AKP-sponsored urban transformation project for the Taksim area (*Taksim Yayalaştırma Projesi*) which had been drawn up in 2012. By the time the protests broke out in 2013, Taksim Solidarity had already organised various protests and activities, but what brought them to the fore was the role they played during the sit-in and peaceful acts of resistance that were carried out when the demolition of Gezi Park got underway. Key to the central role played by the group during the early stages of the protests was the fact that they were involved in a dialogue that took place with then-Prime Minister Erdoğan in Ankara roughly two weeks after the initial wave of protests erupted in mid-June. Erdoğan received the representatives of Taksim Solidarity and others as well, but he angrily and abruptly left the meeting when disagreements ensued. Needless to say, no fruitful results were achieved and the protests continued to grow. Although Taksim Solidarity did not have a clear leader, Mücella Yapıcı (1951–), an activist, architect, and member of the Union of Chambers of Turkish Engineers and Architects (*Türk Mühendis ve Mimar Odaları Birliği*, TMMOB), was often the public face of the group. Yapıcı, together with around a dozen other individuals, later faced multiple legal charges and was tried in multiple court hearings in the decade that followed. In 2022, in the midst of worsening democratic backsliding and a devastating economic downturn in Turkey, Yapıcı was sentenced to eighteen years in prison. The court ruling and the integrity of the legal proceedings were harshly criticised both inside and outside Turkey. The organisation regularly emphasised that it had merely served as a medium of communication for a collective of concerned citizens and had firmly refrained from undertaking the role of a "revolutionary vanguard" or being represented as such.

The significance of each of the demands that were made must also be understood within the context of the times in which they were voiced. While the first demand is self-explanatory, addressing as it does the will of the protesters to counter the decision to convert a public green space into a shopping mall, it must also be noted that there were cultural and political issues at work that transcended the immediate environmental and urban concerns. Many saw the proposed shopping mall as a symbolic message reflecting the AKP's hegemony, since its design was inspired by an old building that had once stood where Gezi Park is located; the building in question was the Ottoman-era Taksim Military Barracks, which was the last stronghold of the counter-revolutionary movement of 1909 and as such is often nostalgically remembered in a positive light by Islamists in Turkey. In addition, there was growing discontent with the ruling government's approach to "development" which promoted the "commodification of everything" as well as the corruption brought on by crony capitalism and neoliberal policies of privatisation. The second and the fourth demands directly addressed the ongoing crackdowns on the opposition both before and during the protests. The third demand was slightly different, as it was raised in reference to a law (*Polis Vazife Salahiyetleri Kanunu,* Law on Police Powers) introduced under the AKP in 2007 that relaxed the limits of the legitimate use of violence by the police. During the Gezi Protests, the excessive use of violence by the police—especially tear gas—was often related to that legal development. The fifth demand addressed a general sentiment concerning the criminalisation of non-parliamentarian forms of expressing discontent, protesting, and voicing opposition, which, it was commonly argued, undermined norms of representative democracy. The protesters, by explicitly emphasising the peaceful and creative nature of their protests, called for a lifting of the legal and practical obstacles that the government placed before the holding of demonstrations and gatherings in public spaces, which activists claimed fell within the scope of the natural rights of all citizens in democratic societies.

***

What the Gezi Protests truly meant or achieved is still a matter of debate. To this day the AKP has continued to attempt to portray the protests as part of an illegitimate, dangerous, and anti-democratic insurrection by launching disputed legal procedures against the protesters and using its control over conventional media outlets and the state apparatus to persecute them. Many protesters were labelled as "terrorists, agents, or coup plotters," and the protests were followed by countless prosecutions, profiling, loss of jobs, and brain drain through emigration. For that reason, in today's age of post-truths, which is awash in a sea of misinformation and "alternative facts," being able to identify the most frequently circulated and communicated demands of the protesters is more important than ever as it will facilitate accurate assessments of the nature of the protests. As such, collecting and critically studying the predominantly digital sources that are related to the Gezi Protests remains the most productive way to grasp the authentic nature of this rather multi-vocal and non-hierarchical social movement.

Select Bibliography

Çakmaklı, Didem. "Active Citizenship in Turkey: Learning Citizenship in Civil Society Organizations." *Citizenship Studies* 19, nos. 3-4 (2015): 421–35.

Jenzen, Olu, Itir Erhart, Hande Eslen-Ziya, Umut Korkut, and Aidan McGarry. "The Symbol of Social Media in Contemporary Protests: Twitter and the Gezi Park Movement." *Convergence* 27, no. 2 (2021): 414–37.

Özkırımlı, Umut, ed. *The Making of a Protest Movement in Turkey: #occupygezi.* Basingstoke: Palgrave Macmillan, 2014.

Taksim Dayanışması Platformu. "Taksim Dayanışması." https://www.taksimdayanisma.org

Tuğal, Cihan. *The Fall of the Turkish Model: How the Arab Uprisings Brought Down Islamic Liberalism.* London: Verso, 2016.

Whitehead, Christopher, and Gönül Bozoğlu. "Protest, Bodies, and the Grounds of Memory: Taksim Square as a 'Heritage Site' and the 2013 Gezi Protests." *Heritage & Society* 9, no. 2 (2016): 111–36.

92

Puppies, Vegans, and Cheese:
Culture Wars in the Age of Populism

Doğan Gürpınar

As the Justice and Development Party (*Adalet ve Kalkınma Partisi*, AKP) gravitated towards authoritarianism, it used cultural politics and contentions arising therein as a pretext. A number of US culture war themes were imported and appropriated by Islamist intellectuals and the AKP leadership to demarcate, harden, and reinforce boundaries. Abortion, legal in Turkey since the early 1980s, had been a non-issue until anti-abortion rhetoric was introduced top-down by the AKP regime in 2012. To the disappointment of the AKP regime and intelligentsia, the heavy restrictions placed on abortion at state hospitals failed to transform the issue into a cultural controversy that could give them political leverage. The matters of Darwin and evolution, as well as feminism and LGBT+ activism, hitherto fringe issues, rose to become inflammatory themes avidly consumed in public debates. The teaching of evolution theory was removed from the high school curriculum during the AKP's rule as an extension of the ongoing culture wars.

While the AKP jettisoned its erstwhile liberal rhetoric, once it succeeded in eliminating the military and came to completely dominate Turkish politics, it doubled down on its populist "White Turks" discourse. During the AKP's reformist phase, the usual suspects had been Kemalists, who were depicted as epitomes of White Turk hubris and therefore represented obstacles to democratisation. This discourse rose over majoritarianism couched in democratic garb. As the AKP abandoned its pro-democratic parlance, however, the term "liberal" came to denote urbanites who were remote from and ignorant of deeply rooted traditions, moral order, and Islam. Thus, the dichotomy was shifted from the "political" clash between authoritarians (the Kemalist establishment) and "democrats" (the AKP government) to the "cultural," drawn between two immutable cultural communities.

Alcohol, hedonistic youth subculture, and sexual expressionism are all tropes readily exploited by the AKP from the playbook of populism. Anti-intellectualism is rampant. These are familiar themes consumed by populists from western Europe to Asia and Latin America. The 2010s not only brought about the rising public visibility of LGBT+, queer, and feminist activism, but also veganism and political correctness. Pride days, which were legally organised for the first time in 2003 (ironically the first June of the AKP government), grew both in terms of number of participants and public visibility with the milestone 2013 march, which drew in more than one hundred thousand participants. This ongoing trend had triggered the alt-right ideology in the West, particularly as organised by groups denouncing these trends as "woke". In Turkey, the same cultural agendas and penchants also swiftly caught appeal. The AKP readily used these tags on its culture war front. One striking piece written by then-head of the state news agency (Anatolian Agency/AA), Kemal Öztürk (1969–), using the pseudonym Ali Nur Kutlu, displayed this trope most lavishly with a ludicrous hatred for pet owners.

Letter to the White Turks*

I know that your mood is down. You faced yet another blunder in the elections [the 2014 municipal elections, as yet another AKP landslide victory since 2002, the year when the party came to power]... I can't remember the number of defeats you have encountered... I happened to come across Cihangir [a bohemian quarter in İstanbul] and saw all the folks in deep depression sitting on the sidewalks with empty [wine or beer] bottles. Don't be that frustrated, and ask yourself if it might be your fault... Is it because you are so alien to this country, my White Turk brother? Your intellectuals wrote pieces as if they were living in Swiss cantons. Why not walk out from your regular Nişantaşı [wealthy quarter where many İstanbul elite live] cafés and pubs and visit Ümraniye and Yenibosna [two poor and conservative neighbourhoods far from the city centre]. Then you would understand that the analyses developed in newspaper columns are relevant only for Anglo-Saxon countries. Our people, on the other hand, don't know who is Anglo and who is Saxon. Look at how our Anatolian folks live, my White Turk friend. Let me give a few examples. Our people are pious. They don't drink alcohol. They fast, follow the religious commandments, and are sensitive [about their moral values] Yet, your newspapers persistently ran headlines about an "Alcohol Prohibition". Your columnists at these newspapers wrote about wine brands whose taste we had no clue about. Only Abdüllatif Şener [an ex-minister and heavyweight in the AKP who had joined the opposition] supported you and he had famously maintained, "I know everything about wine except its taste." The families of this country are conservative and have strong family ties. Men are jealous [of their wives]. Yet, columnists who self-style themselves as the spokespersons of White Turks published their photos from their bedrooms like John Lennon and Yoko Ono. For you, this is freedom. For Anatolia, it is despicable. We call this alienation to society, my White Turk friend. You enter your apartments with your shoes on; we see such an act as outrageous. You speak about the taste and brands of wine; we speak of the elixir of the life of Rumi and Yunus Emre [two Islamic mystics]. You have your breakfast with croissants and coffee; we have it with bread, cheese, and tahini halwa. You prefer Roquefort cheese; we adore the blue cheese of Van. You keep cats and dogs and entice your children into adoring a hamster; we raise pious children and if we ever see a hamster in our flat, we hit it hard with broomstick as we see this animal as religiously impure. We utter the name of God and take pride with our Muslimness. You call yourself secular but even you yourself don't understand what you mean. As friendly advice, I could enumerate many other examples. To sum up, you suffer from not knowing your society. Every time, you ask why the AKP always wins. You should rather ask why you always lose and where you make mistakes. Before concluding, I also need to refer to a Twitter affair. You thought that once you ran a hashtag calling Erdoğan a dictator, everyone would

* Translated from the Turkish original in Ali Nur Kutlu [Kemal Öztürk], "Beyaz Türklere Mektup," *Yeni Şafak*, 23 April 2014.

be persuaded. For God's sake, go to Palu [a deeply conservative town] and say Erdoğan is a dictator to the locals and see how they respond, my White [Turk] friend. See, these hashtags look different in Palu than in cyberspace. You call Erdoğan the chief thief [as Erdoğan was dubbed after a corruption scandal run by Gülenist public attorneys and police chiefs] in Rize [the conservative hometown of Erdoğan] and see how they use their pistols against you. I know that your mood is down, but I can't stop reminding you that you have been alienated from your country, nation, and ummah. This is neither a matter of knowing a foreign language nor of carrying two passports. Please visit Anatolia. These people are not as you imagine them. If you visit Anatolia, please do so during Ramadan. They beat those who eat during fast time. If you speak the words "there is freedom," they beat you twice. The presidential elections are nearing. This time don't bet on the wrong side. This is because your body will not endure yet another mistake. As I am concluding my letter, I deferentially kiss the hands of those elders who don't keep dogs and greet children who don't keep hamsters."

***

In a sequel to this letter, Öztürk/Kutlu also maintained that; "We don't keep cats or dogs; we don't cry for seals; we don't campaign for the rights of homosexuals. Instead, we raise pious children at home; we cry for our deceased Syrian brethren, and campaign for the 528 innocents sentenced to death [in Egypt]." These pieces were blatant displays of the populist platform of the AKP delineating two cultural realms mutually alien to each other. Whereas one is authentic, pure, and homegrown, the other is artificial, rotten, and alienated from the national self. This trope significantly departs from the time-worn Islamic discourses of authenticity. It is heavily influenced by contemporary Western misogyny, homophobia, and woke-bashing, to the extent that it outlandishly blasts people who keep dogs and calls for the beating of hamsters. In fact, having cats around and feeding them, both indoors and outdoors, has for centuries been a prevailing practice in Turkey (and Prophet Mohammad loved cats and himself kept one named Muezza) and stray dogs have always been a curious facet of İstanbul and Turkish cities' landscapes, which in the past frightened Western travellers. The harmonious coexistence of dogs, cats, and humans was a constant texture of Ottoman urban spaces, so much so that modernising Young Turks were so embarrassed by this fact that they undertook the genocide of İstanbulite stray dogs in 1910 by sending them to a small nearby island where they killed and ate each other. In our contemporary world, however, placing dogs in an alien environment, keeping them at home with dry dog food, and taking them on morning walks distresses some modern-day conservatives and Islamists. Perhaps domesticated house dogs with their cute bowties are phony in contrast to the authenticity of the rugged stray dogs hardened by a life of surviving on the streets and in dumps and sewers. Or perhaps taking these "unclean" animals into the domesticity of the home is seen as a demonstration of their owners' disrespect for the sanctity of the home and its cleanliness. Dog-keeping is also associated with single young feminist women who prefer dogs as their companions. Back in the 1910s, Ömer Seyfettin (1884–1920), a famous pioneering Turkish nationalist man of letters, wrote a short story titled "Civilisation and the Dog," which was about an animal-loving woman who kept a dog for this pleasure. Seyfettin used this as a metaphor for the deviant nature of free European women and Turkish intellectuals who were alienated from their national mores. Thus, dog-keeping becomes incorporated into the misogynist arsenal. The rise of the protectionism (strikingly visible on social media) of stray dogs that threaten people and harass children, especially in the remoter parts of cities, became yet another line of demarcation drawn by those who ridicule these so-called "wannabe animal lovers who are insensitive to real human suffering". This animus is also a consequence of the rise of the visibility and prominence of social media and therefore youth subcultures in the realms of politics and political discourse.

***

These themes also came to play a role in intra-Turkish opposition debacles and ideological rifts. They serve as the arsenal of the (Kemalist but more outspokenly right-wing) nationalist opposition as they seek to portray the leftist and liberal opposition as feeble and thus as bogus opposition to the AKP's political, social, and cultural agenda, standing in contrast to the "vigour" of nationalists who pose the ultimate and real challenge to the AKP's policies. Indeed, stray dogs are a profound problem in Turkey. They terrorise, attack, and injure children and adults alike, especially in the outskirts of İstanbul and in cities where undeveloped urban facilities create an environment conducive to their livelihood. Dog keepers' affluent in-city quarters are safe from the stray dog scare which, in the eyes of their enemies, reveals animal-lovers' insensitivity to and even unawareness of the dangers posed by the stray dogs that are rampant in poor neighbourhoods and therefore their disconnect from the people, real problems, and suffering. Thus, common stray dog incidents constantly trigger polarised social media interactions.

For leftists and liberals, the AKP pursues authoritarian and xenophobic policies. The nationalist opposition, however, depicts the AKP's moral and cultural order as fraught with cosmopolitanism for a number of reasons; namely, its transnational form of Islam which forsakes nation-statist premises; its welcoming attitude and sympathy for immigrants from Syria, Pakistan, and Afghanistan; and, its animus against Atatürk's nation-statist premises and most notoriously its (now long-abandoned and overturned) efforts to resolve the Kurdish imbroglio by way of introducing some level of political recognition of Kurdishness. Therefore, against this commonality of multiculturalism shared by the AKP, leftists, and liberals, all of which "threaten" Turkishness, real opposition to the AKP is portrayed as being represented by the "nobody's fool" nationalist. Images of vegans, queers, and the woke are held up as showing how they are complicit in this cultural and moral order, as well as their "softness" on stray dogs and "extreme" animal protectionism. Accordingly, these wokes are easily cajoled by the wiles of the AKP because, for them, multicultural ornaments matter more than hard-bitten national interests and secularism, whereas nationalists never softened their rage, animus, and vigilance against the AKP order. Needless to say, associating the AKP's moral order and cultural politics with multiculturalism is outright nonsensical, yet imageries of the woke serve many political agendas in Turkey, as they do in the US. The cliché of vegan, feminist, and animal-loving woke became a fashionable political meme overconsumed not only by different strands of the political right from political Islam and secular right-wing nationalism but also by Kemalist nationalism and the nationalist left. The divide between the real people and the alienated liberal elites and hedonist urban youth constitutes the crux of populism, and not only for the ruling Islamist AKP.

Select Bibliography

Ayvazoğlu, Beşir. *Öteki Canlar*. İstanbul: Kapı Yayınları, 2022.

Bali, Rıfat. *Life Style'dan Yeni Türkiye'ye: Yeni Binyıl'ın Türkiyesi'nden Manzaralar, 2001–2021*. İstanbul: Libra, 2021.

Gürpınar, Doğan. *Kültür Savaşları: İslam, Sekülerizm ve Kimlik Siyasetinin Yükselişi*. İstanbul: Liberplus, 2017.

Kaya, Ayhan. "Islamisation of Turkey Under the AKP Rule: Empowering Family, Faith and Charity." *South European Society & Politics* 20, no. 1 (2015): 47–69.

93
The End of the Peace Process:
The Cizre Massacres

Gözde Kırcıoğlu

In mid-July 2015, a two-year ceasefire between the Turkish government and the Kurdistan Workers' Party (*Partîya Karkerên Kurdistanê*, PKK) collapsed. The so-called "peace process," or "solution process," marked a period of talks held from 2013 to 2015 between Abdullah Öcalan (1947–), the imprisoned founder of the PKK, and the Turkish National Intelligence Organisation (*Milli İstihbarat Teşkilatı*, MİT). The aim of the talks was to end the armed conflict between the Turkish state and the PKK, which has been ongoing since 1984 and claimed 40,000 lives so far.

One of the triggers for Turkey's renewed military response against the PKK was the growing international acceptance of the Kurdish People's Protection Units (*Yekîneyên Parastina Gel*, YPG) in the fight against the Islamic State (IS) and their success in establishing a *de facto* autonomous region in northern Syria by capturing the border towns of Kobane and Tel Abyad from the IS in 2015. Following a siege of YPG-held Tel Abyad on 15 June 2015, Turkey bombed the PKK's main base in Iraq (Kandil) for the first time since 2013. Ankara joined the US-led international coalition against the IS in mid-2014, but did not fully agree with its stated goals, particularly objecting to support of the Peshmerga (the military forces of the autonomous Kurdistan Region of Iraq) in their fight against IS. On 24-25 July 2015, the Turkish military conducted its first major operation against the IS with airstrikes against its positions in Syria, while simultaneously attacking PKK positions in northern Iraq. After 25 July, Turkey ceased airstrikes against the IS but continued attacks against the PKK both inside and outside Turkish borders. A series of curfews culminated in a permanent curfew in urban areas in the predominantly Kurdish region of southeastern Turkey and militarised security operations involving the use of heavy weaponry. Those operations were the response of the Turkish government against an urban guerrilla campaign led by the PKK's youth wing, the Patriotic Revolutionary Youth Movement (*Yurtsever Devrimci Gençlik Hareketi*, YDG-H). The group had declared "self-governance" in several places starting in August 2014 by erecting barricades and digging trenches, making those towns inaccessible to Turkish state officials. They claimed that the Turkish state was not taking the necessary steps following the PKK's withdrawal from Turkish soil, which began on 8 May 2013, and accused the Ankara government of supporting the IS and not letting PKK members cross the Syrian border to join the fight against the IS's siege of Kobane. That declaration of autonomy, which was also supported by some local politicians, and the riots of 6-8 October 2014 denouncing Ankara's position about the IS's siege of Kobane constituted major incidents signalling the failure of the peace process. Civilians paid the price for this breakdown in talks as neighbourhoods were razed to the ground, thousands fled, and hundreds were killed in 2015 and 2016.

The general public became aware of Erdoğan's position about the talks, especially when he took over the election campaign from then-Prime Minister Ahmet Davutoğlu (1959–) and started to lash out with fiercely anti-PKK rhetoric, denying the existence of a Kurdish problem in the final weeks before the elections to be held on 7 June 2015. The Justice and Development Party (*Adalet ve Kalkınma Partisi*, AKP) lost its majority in the parliament for the first time in the elections, winning 40.9 per cent of votes. The Pro-Kurdish Peoples' Democratic Party (*Halkların Demokrasi Partisi*, HDP) passed the 10 per cent election threshold for the first time in the history of pro-Kurdish parties in Turkey by garnering 13 per cent of votes, thereby forcing the creation of the first coalition government since 2002. The broad support for HDP members in the parliament was, to a large extent, motivated by expectations for an end to the conflict between the PKK and the Turkish armed forces. The assumed agreement between the Turkish state and Öcalan was intended to end the PKK's activities inside Turkey in return for a pro-Kurdish political party active in the parliament. However, the PKK and the Turkish government stopped supporting the plan and opted for violence in the summer of 2015.

The following are statements that were made by Kadir Kunur, the joint mayor of the city of Cizre between 2014 and 2016, The city is near the Syrian border, approximately 50 kilometres north of the Iraqi border entry point. Cizre was one of the places where large-scale militarised security operations were carried out starting in August 2015. Kunur spoke out after a fifth curfew was imposed on Cizre, which lasted 78 consecutive days between 14 December 2015 and 2 March 2016. The so-called "Cizre events" or "basement massacres" took place on 7 February 2016 when Turkish security forces raided and burned down three buildings where at least 177 people, some of them badly wounded, had taken shelter in basements.

*Kadir Kunur, the Joint Mayor of Cizre, Describes the Security Operations in Cizre**

Before the end of the "basement events," 85 people had lost their lives. These 85 people were all from Cizre; they are registered here, we know their addresses, and we know who they are. All the information about these people is registered with the Municipality of Cizre because their bodies were taken to the hospital with municipal vehicles. For example, there was a number of "112" [public] ambulances in the town, but they did not go into any neighbourhoods where gunfire was heard, only into those in the centre. During the armed clashes, our friends [municipality personnel] carried all the bodies. The circumstances were different back then. Providing a standard funeral service was impossible because we were treated similarly [like terrorists]. Our personnel were assaulted several times. We were stopped at four different checkpoints on the way to the hospital, even though the police accompanied the municipal vehicles. They were sometimes physically, sometimes verbally attacked. This is why our

* Translated from the original Turkish in MazlumDer, eds., *Cizre Olayları İnceleme ve Araştırma Raporu*, 4-6 March 2016. https://hakikatadalethafiza.org/wpcontent/uploads/2016/04/2016.04.02_MAZLUMDER_CizreRaporu_ENG.pdf

friends working in the ambulances could not do much. They could only do their duties minimally, and their main goal was to save the wounded but they had to do so quietly. There was no other way to live.

This is why I am sure everybody on this list of 85 people was originally from Cizre. [At first] we did not know about the people in the basements. Most were young university students who came to Cizre out of solidarity the day before the curfew started. Later we found out that they could not leave Cizre once the curfew had begun. We don't know their exact number, but we think it must be between 40 and 50. One of them was Cihan Kahraman; he could not be taken to the hospital when he got wounded, and he died in the basement. There was also Helin Öncü, whom we extracted in a wounded state. 176 people were massacred in three different basements. Neighbourhoods were attacked with tanks and heavy artillery. Before [the attack began], young people were getting arrested and subjected to verbal insults and torture. People did not want to leave their houses, but the state forced them out. People went to safer neighbourhoods and nearby places. The most brutal murders and deaths happened in these neighbourhoods that people left behind. People's attempts to enter the neighbourhoods and stop the clashes were constantly hindered by force. There are almost 270 dead. During the nineteen days following the end of the curfew, the buildings left standing were also demolished, and body parts mixed in with the rubble were thrown into the Tigris River.

***

The Human Rights Foundation of Turkey (HRFT) found that 381 curfews had been imposed in eleven provinces between August 2015 and January 2020, and 321 unarmed residents were killed, including 79 children, between August 2015 and August 2016. More than half a million people were displaced during the curfews, most of whom were dispossessed on the basis of an "emergency expropriation" order, allowing for the almost immediate (re)usage of expropriated properties, obstructing owners' right to object or demand compensation. The curfews continued after the security operations officially ended and more buildings were demolished, sometimes before an expropriation order was even issued. Gentrification projects, led by the state-run Housing Development Administration (*Toplu Konut İdaresi Başkanlığı*, TOKİ) got underway, blocking effective investigations and the return of residents. The scale of the expropriations in the region is extensive. In Sur, a UNESCO-protected historical district in Diyarbakır, almost all properties have been expropriated. That situation, combined with the damage to buildings and other infrastructure, prevents residents from returning.

Residents' witness accounts describe the events that took place during the curfews as follows: Teachers received SMS messages from the Ministry of Education calling on them to leave the towns a few days before the curfews were imposed so they could carry out their training elsewhere. In some towns, the police called on people to leave a few hours in advance. Once the curfews began, leaving or entering the cities was forbidden. Essential services were cut, including water, electricity, and telecommunications. City centres were battered by artillery fire, and snipers shot at houses and unarmed people. The operations were conducted by Police Special Operations Forces (*Polis Özel Harekat*, PÖH).

Most people fled to safety nearby. Cizre's population fell from around 130,000 before the operations to 90,000 at the beginning of the curfew, eventually dropping to 30,000 by February 2016. Many people had to move several times as the operations spread. Some sheltered with more than 40 other people in single houses. Not everyone, however, could or wanted to leave. Some remained out of fear of looting or damage to their homes. In particular, families now living in cities after having been driven out of their villages during the fighting in the 1980s and 1990s did not want to leave their homes. Some people remained because young family members were involved in the clashes.

Food and emergency medical care were almost impossible to obtain. Civilians were injured and killed in their houses and gardens (where homes' outhouses are often located) by snipers and artillery. The public ambulance operators and the police told people calling for help that they could not be helped due to safety concerns. The wounded and dead were left in houses and on the streets, in some cases for several days. Some witnesses reported that their houses were shelled after they called the police for help.

The Police Special Operations Forces made arrests at the entrances of hospitals. Wounded people were held in custody or taken to court before having seen a doctor, sometimes many kilometres away, including as far as İstanbul. Lawyers were barred from witnessing autopsies. Many families did not receive autopsy reports. Some bodies were spread in parts across multiple morgues, others were buried without identification. Some families were given only the bones of their loved ones, weighing just two or three kilograms. In January 2016, new regulations were passed to speed up burial procedures in cities under curfew, and provincial authorities would bury bodies not collected from hospitals within three days, even when relatives were not yet informed of what had happened. Many could not collect the bodies of their relatives due to the ongoing curfews and safety concerns. Public buildings, like schools and hospitals, were used by the special forces as operations bases. There was massive destruction of infrastructure and buildings, including places of worship.

Several human rights organisations reported "widespread human rights violations and accompanying impunity for the perpetrators." They concluded that the curfews were not supported by law and that "security forces were reckless in their use of firearms in curfew areas, and operations were conducted with the intention of killing—rather than detaining—armed individuals." Moreover, they reported that "the draconian restrictions imposed during indefinite curfews resembled collective punishment." Reported human rights violations included, but were not limited to, arbitrary and forced displacement and evictions, the arbitrary destruction of homes, and the obstruction of the return of displaced people. Although government-led systematic attempts at a cover-up were reported, sufficient evidence has been collected to reveal much of what happened. The situation further deteriorated under the two-year state of emergency imposed following the July 2016 coup attempt as the government closed down many Kurdish media outlets and NGOs, and also replaced elected mayors using a series of executive emergency decrees.

***

During the summer of 2015, both the Ankara government and the PKK were about to determine their positions in Syria in terms of the shifting power dynamics there. A new peace process and ceasefire could begin, some hoped, if Turkey was persuaded to coexist with the Syrian-Kurdish Democratic Union Party (*Partiya Yekîtiya Demokrat*, PYD). However, that did not fit with Erdoğan's ultra-nationalist campaign and ambitions to play a larger role in the region following the Arab Spring, nor did it coincide with the PKK's belief that its strengthened position could be used to persuade the public in the region to support a declaration of autonomy.

The end of the truce, as well as pressure on Kurdish organisations and individuals, played an important role in the AKP's antagonistic election campaign as it sought to regain support. The campaign succeeded in helping the AKP win 49.5 per cent of the vote in snap elections held in November 2015, but that was not enough to fulfil Erdoğan's ambition to change the constitution. The HDP still managed to pass the election threshold with 10.7 per cent of the vote, but the party still lost 2.4 points. The fuelling of violence in the summer of 2015 between the two elections remains a vivid memory, as the public fears it could possibly happen again in subsequent elections.

The events that Kadir Kunur described demonstrate how significant the "Kurdish problem" remains in Turkish politics, even 100 years after the birth of the Republic, and they are evidence of the limits of existing human rights protection mechanisms. In mid-2015, government pressure on Kurdish organisations and individuals increased. Selahattin Demirtaş (1973–), the leader of the HDP, was imprisoned in 2016. Helin Öncü (1996–), who was saved from a basement in Cizre, was sentenced to life and imprisoned in 2019. By February 2021, 49 out of the 58 elected mayors from the HDP had been removed from office, including the joint mayors of Cizre. Most have been imprisoned, while some are in exile. Hundreds of academicians were fired or suspended, stripped of their right to work in the public sector, while three were given a suspended jail sentence on terrorism charges for signing an open letter to the Turkish government in January 2016 calling for an end to state violence against Kurds. Now it is generally acknowledged, even by the PKK, that the campaign to declare autonomy was a grave political error which shut down an opportunity for peace, resulting in nothing but misery.

Select Bibliography

Allsopp, Harriet, and Wladimir Van Wilgenburg. *The Kurds of Northern Syria: Governance, Diversity and Conflicts*. London, New York: I.B. Tauris, 2019.

Amnesty International. *Displaced and Dispossessed Sur Residents' Right to Return Home*. London: 2016.

Gourlay, William. *The Kurds in Erdogan's Turkey: Balancing Identity, Resistance and Citizenship*. Edinburgh: Edinburgh University Press, 2021.

Human Rights Foundation of Turkey. "Cizre Field Report." https://en.tihv.org.tr/curfews/cizre-field-report/

Kurban, Dilek. *Limits of Supranational Justice: The European Court of Human Rights and Turkey's Kurdish Conflict*. Cambridge: Cambridge University Press, 2020.

TMMOB. Yıkılan Kentler Raporu 2019 Ankara Türk Mühendis ve Mimar Odaları Birliği. Ankara: TMMOB, 2019.

94

"An Insurrection Instigated by the Parallel Structure": The Night of the Attempted Coup

Berk Esen

Just after midnight on 15/16 July in 2016, President Recep Tayyip Erdoğan (1954–) made a live broadcast on the private news channel CNN Türk via a Facetime video call to deliver an unscheduled speech in which he called on the Turkish people to go out into public squares and go to airports to resist a coup attempt that was underway. He was interviewed by one of the station's anchorwomen, Hande Fırat (1974–), and a well-known pro-government journalist, Abdülkadir Selvi (1964–). By that time, the putschists had already cordoned off the Bosporus Bridge, occupied the offices of TRT (the Turkish Radio and Television Corporation), and broadcast a declaration on national television stating that a coup was being carried out. Erdoğan's speech, which ultimately contributed to the defeat of the coup, marked one of the most critical moments in his political career and raised popular support for the president to unprecedented levels.

Although Turkey has a long history of military interventions, the putsch of 2016 took analysts by surprise because the government, under the leadership of the Justice and Development Party (*Adalet ve Kalkınma Partisi*, AKP), had already succeeded to a large extent in bringing the military under its control. Owing to its Islamist background, the AKP government had initially met with strong opposition from the upper echelons of the armed forces, which had challenged the party's agenda on several key issues. There were even rumours that hardliners in the military had considered staging a coup against the government in 2003–2004 but were dissuaded by moderates who preferred to mobilise public opinion against Erdoğan with help from opposition parties, the media, and civil society. As a means of countering opposition within the military establishment, the ruling party tapped into its voter base to win elections and also obtained support from the US and the EU as well as various domestic groups, including an Islamist movement led by Fethullah Gülen (1941–), a political preacher based in the United States.

Through the strong backing it received from Gülenist circles, the AKP had managed to curb the powerful political sway held by the military and reshuffle its leadership not only through politicised trials based on forged evidence in the Sledgehammer and Ergenekon cases, but also via the support of the media. This cooperation allowed Gülenists to colonise the state apparatus and obtain a great deal of political influence within the judiciary, the police, and the military. As a result, when relations between the AKP and the Gülenists broke down, Erdoğan would go on to portray the Gülen movement as a "parallel structure"; in 2013, with their opponents now sidelined, the AKP leadership and the Gülenists began competing for power, and the intensification of their political rivalry and policy disagreements gave rise to increasing tensions. The Gülenists wanted to expand their political influence within the regime and clashed with the government over matters of foreign policy and the Kurdish question. More specifically, the Gülen movement opposed the AKP government's efforts to initiate a process of negotiations with Kurds and challenge the sway held by Israel as well as the United States over the region.

Although the Gülenists lacked a strong large-scale organisation that could rival the AKP and did not have a popular leader who could take on Erdoğan directly, they were well-organised within the state apparatus, the media, and academic circles. In the ensuing struggle for dominance, the Gülenists therefore relied on indirect attacks such as graft probes against Erdoğan loyalists and intensive media-based criticisms of the government. Erdoğan responded by targeting Gülenist media outlets and businesses, while also purging the judiciary and bureaucracy of individuals suspected of being affiliated with the Gülen movement. Among analysts there is broad consensus that the military was next in line and that Gülenist officers, many of whom had ironically been appointed to their posts by the AKP government, conspired to topple Erdoğan on July 15 before those purges could take place.

*Erdoğan's Live Speech on CNN Türk on the Night of the Attempted Coup**

President Tayyip Erdoğan: Of course, today's development is unfortunately the actions of a small minority within the Turkish armed forces. It is an insurrection instigated by the parallel structure. Those responsible for this attack on our nation's unity and solidarity will receive the necessary punishment and response by our people. Those responsible for using tanks, weapons, planes, and helicopters that belong to the nation [and] are being used to attack the nation will pay a heavy price. In this regard, be it the president, the prime minister or government, we will take the necessary steps and stand upright. We will not let them succeed. I believe that we will overcome this insurrection very quickly. I would like to underline that we are combatting this issue in a determined manner. No one has the strength to test our determination on this matter. Of course, I would like to call out to our people. I am inviting them to the squares and airports of our provinces. Let's gather as a nation at airports and squares. Let this minority come with their tanks and weapons and do whatever they may. Until today I have not seen a force greater than the people's will.

Hande Fırat: Mr. President, we are on [the] air with Abdülkadir Selvi. With your permission, Selvi, if you [would] like to go ahead and ask [your question] first.

Abdülkadir Selvi: Mr. President, today is the day to protect democracy. Are these developments [occurring] within the chain of command? Information regarding this is being spread. As the president of the country, what do you have to say?

---

* Taken from footage of Erdoğan's speech posted on the website of the news network TRT World and the English translation provided therein. "Here's How Erdogan Called on Turkey to Stop the 2016 Coup." *TRT World*, 11 July 2017. https://www.trtworld.com/turkey/erdogans-call-to-the-turkish-public-on-the-night-of-the-coup-398338.

President Tayyip Erdoğan: The chain of command is not in effect. Right now, the chain of command has been scrapped and rules are being broken. Those within the chain of command are currently, unfortunately, subjected to steps that are being taken from the bottom up. In accordance with the republic, I am the president and commander-in-chief of this nation. The judiciary gave a response to those who took such steps without my permission as the commander-in-chief and we will do what is necessary. Nobody should have any doubts, we are doing what is necessary and will continue to do so.

Hande Fırat: Mr. President, some are saying that the chief of general staff and some comrades are being held hostage. Anatolian Agency also shared this story. Do you have any information regarding this?

President Tayyip Erdoğan: I have also heard such stories. Right now, of course, we don't know if he is well or not. As you know, when such events occur, the air becomes rather murky. Right now, we are experiencing murky weather, and those who have caused this murkiness will pay a heavy price.

Abdülkadir Selvi: Mr. President, you are inviting people to protect democracy and take to the squares, and we are reiterating your call from here. Will this coup be repelled and will those behind it be able to be held to account in the eyes of the law?

President Tayyip Erdoğan: They are definitely going to pay a heavy price in front of the judiciary. This is going to make the job of those who believe in democracy even easier, but they will pay a very heavy price.

Hande Fırat: Mr. President, I would like to request a few more sentences. Everyone is...very uneasy. People are at home; their children are asking, "What do you mean a coup? What's a coup?" while we speak. I am talking about young children. There are many claims that some places have come under fire.

President Tayyip Erdoğan: Mrs. Hande, just as you came to your studio, just as Mr. Selvi [came] to his studio, I am now calling out to my people. Come to the squares, and let's give the necessary response from the squares. I am also coming to the squares.

Abdülkadir Selvi: Mr. President, our people have a request. Right now, this broadcast is being shared by all news channels across Turkey. Please, stay on our broadcast a little longer and call [out to] our people. Secondly, will the putschists be successful? This is what the public is asking. There is some apprehension regarding this.

President Tayyip Erdoğan: I definitely do not believe that these putschists will be successful. Throughout history, putschists have not been successful. Sooner or later, they disappear. You should know this.

Hande Fırat: Mr. President, will you be coming too? To Ankara?

President Tayyip Erdoğan: Of course, of course. Thank you very much.

Hande Fırat: We would like to thank you too.

***

Unlike Erdoğan's other national addresses, his impromptu speech on the night of the coup was neither carefully planned nor choreographed. The image of the president, who was sitting in front of a white curtain in an undisclosed location, was shown to the cameras via the anchorwoman's smart phone. Erdoğan's decision to appear on CNN Türk, whose owner, the Doğan Media group, had clashed with his government on numerous occasions in the past, arguably increased the credibility and accessibility of his address to the nation. During the call, Erdoğan took questions from two journalists, Hande Fırat and Abdülkadir Selvi, with whom he had close personal links.

In his speech, Erdoğan raised several important points. First, he confirmed the rumour that the coup had not been executed through the military chain of command but rather had been led by a small cabal comprised of officers affiliated with the Gülen movement. That may have helped mobilise the support of non-Gülenist officers, who may have otherwise stayed neutral so as not to clash with their fellow officers on the night of the coup. Second, Erdoğan pledged to bring everyone involved to justice, and he called on the citizenry to rally in public squares and at airports in open defiance against the perpetrators. His refusal to recognise any other power as being above the "national will" was taken directly out of a populist playbook. As a populist politician, mobilisation from above has long been a powerful tool for Erdoğan during his years in power. His decision to rely on popular mobilisation—as opposed to turning to military personnel loyal to the government for support—may have partly stemmed from Erdoğan's inability to determine whom he could trust in the armed forces that night. The fact that he could not confirm the whereabouts of the Chief of the General Staff is a testament to the prevailing uncertainty among political elites during the early hours of the coup. Naturally, Erdoğan decided to rely on his own base instead of leaving his fate in the hands of loyalist factions within the armed forces.

Even before Erdoğan made his public call to action, the AKP's provincial and district party organisations had already reached out to hundreds of thousands of party members and sympathisers by way of text messages and social media. Despite Erdoğan's frequent condemnations of social media in the past, his call was promptly disseminated to the public on various platforms, including Twitter, Facebook, and WhatsApp. As a result, many party supporters took to the streets after his address, thus paving the way for an unprecedented violent confrontation between civilians and putschist forces. Although military interventions have occurred repeatedly in Turkish history, never before had a coup attempt led to popular resistance and a massive number of casualties (over 200 dead and more than 2,000 injured). This popular mobilisation disrupted the coup by raising the cost of violence for the putschists and undermining their morale, as well as by shifting the momentum in the government's favour. Ultimately, however, it was anti-putschist military units that put down the attempted coup.

***

The putsch proved to be a "gift from God," in the words of Erdoğan. Most notably, the mass arrests that took place in the coup's aftermath changed the composition of the military: 151

generals and admirals (out of 358) as well as 1,656 colonels and about 3,500 junior officers were arrested in the first few weeks after the attempted coup. In addition, more than 100,000 public employees suspected of having links to the Gülen movement were either purged or suspended on short notice. Thousands of schools, newspapers, television and radio stations, businesses, civil society organisations, and publishing houses were swiftly closed down or taken over by government trustees for allegedly having ties to various "terrorist" organisations. A culture of fear permeated society and silenced many government critics, albeit temporarily.

Erdoğan's televised address on the night of the coup was arguably the most important speech of his long political career. The defiant stance he took towards the putschists, even as his presidency hung in the balance, became a tipping point for many AKP politicians and voters, leading them to declare their unwavering support for the government, and transformed him into a symbol of resistance. Even the main opposition Republican People's Party (*Cumhuriyet Halk Partisi*, CHP) sided with the government in defending the democratic system. Soon after the putsch was put down, Erdoğan turned the popular mobilisation that took place on the night of 15/16 July into a foundational event for the securing of a new regime. Rather than working together with opposition parties to strengthen democratic institutions, Erdoğan skilfully used the failed coup attempt as a pretext to target his opponents, purge tens of thousands of critics from the bureaucracy, and centralise his power. Through the support he obtained from the Nationalist Movement Party (*Milliyetçi Hareket Partisi*, MHP), Erdoğan was able to amend the constitution and establish a presidential system with limited checks and balances, thus sweeping away the last vestiges of the democratic regime in Turkey.

Although an atmosphere of euphoria dominated the country in the aftermath of the suppression of the coup, Erdoğan's speech garnered scant attention in academia. This is partly because even to this day little is known about the details of the failed coup, largely as a result of the government's efforts to propagate its own official narrative about the events that transpired. Nevertheless, Erdoğan's speech created a strong precedent of popular resistance against coups that may deter other interventionist officers from pursuing a similar course in the future. Unfortunately, however, the failure of the coup d'état did not pave the way for democratisation in Turkey, but rather further entrenched the authoritarian tendencies of the regime in power.

Select Bibliography

Baykan, Toygar Sinan, Yaprak Gürsoy, and Pierre Ostiguy. "Anti-Populist Coups d'état in the Twenty-First Century: Reasons, Dynamics and Consequences." *Third World Quarterly* 42, no. 4 (2021): 793–811.

Esen, Berk, and Sebnem Gümüşçü. "Turkey: How the Coup Failed." *Journal of Democracy* 28, no. 1 (2017): 59–73.

Gümüşçü, Sebnem. "The Clash of Islamists: The Crisis of the Turkish State and Democracy." *Contemporary Turkish Politics* (2016): 6–11. https://pomeps.org/the-clash-of-islamists-the-crisis-of-the-turkish-state-and-democracy.

95
"How'd I Transition?":
Turkish Queer Slang out of the Closet
and onto the Stage

Nicholas Kontovas

Relying on a mix of wordplay based on standard Turkish forms and a wealth of loans from minority languages such as Romani, Armenian, and Greek, *Lubunca* is a type of slang used predominantly among some gay men and trans women in Turkey. Romani contributes by far the largest number of unique *Lubunca* terms of any language after Turkish—nearly five times as many as any other. Though the scale of borrowing from Romani seems unparalleled among other European Queer slang varieties, borrowing from Romani occurs frequently among marginalised groups who romanticise Roma as the quintessential conscious Other. At the same time, speakers of *Lubunca* today seem only vaguely aware of its connection to Romani, and few if any are or have contact with fluent speakers of the language. What is more, much of the special vocabulary of *Lubunca* is derived from languages which are no longer widely spoken in İstanbul, where *Lubunca* seems to have originated. The number of Armenian speakers in İstanbul decreased dramatically after end of the First World War, while the number of Greek speakers has dwindled with successive waves of migration after the pogroms of September 1955 and the expulsions in 1963–1965. Some of the earliest recorded examples of modern *Lubunca* from the 1980s emphasise its intentional incomprehensibility to the police, which target these groups for vice crimes. Yet, for many gay and trans people in Turkey, *Lubunca* is a distinctly gay and trans mode of expression to be used wherever there are likeminded people, within the Queer community or—increasingly—outside of it.

As etymologies suggest, *Lubunca* is something of an unintended time capsule providing a glimpse into the history of Queer persecution and survival in Turkey. Several other elements of the *Lubunca* lexicon suggest an origin no later than the early twentieth century, among which are words based on Arabic numerical puns, requiring intimate knowledge of Ottoman. Examples include *ellisekiz*, "bottom"—i.e., the receptive partner in anal sex—literally "fifty-eight," which relies on the graphical similarity between the numerals ٥٨ and a penis and an anus, and *otuzbir*, "masturbation," from the numerological representation of the number "thirty-one" composed of the letters ڽل, which spell out the word *el*, "hand".

This older core of *Lubunca* vocabulary hearkens back to a change in the sociohistorical conditions surrounding non-traditional sex and gender roles which is inextricably linked to the birth of modern Turkish Queer identities. Works of Ottoman erotic literature make frequent mention of relations between what we might view as two men or a man and a boy, yet the vocabulary which they use is entirely different from that of *Lubunca*. Extensive use of Arabic and Persian words in this literature reflects the educated backgrounds of their authors: men, often from among the upper echelons of Ottoman society, who not only condoned these sex acts but participated in and even lauded them. Many works from the Ottoman period, such as the well-known seventeenth century *Dellāknāme-i Dilgüşā*, "The Heart-Gladdening Manual of the Masseur," describe in poetic language an industry of sex work organised around the hammam with its own set of rules and identity categories corresponding to this wholly un-*Lubunca*-like vocabulary.

The late nineteenth century saw the disappearance of this Ottoman courtly homosexuality largely as a result of a conscious reformation of sexual mores by the imperial administration. In correspondences with Sultan Abdülḥamiıd II (1842–1918), chief lawmaker Aḥmed Cevdet Paşa (1822–1895) boasted that his closing of hammams in the capital helped to redirect the male public's sexual appetites from boys to women. Such policies formed a part of a larger effort aimed at bringing certain aspects of Ottoman society into line with what were then perceived of as "modern" approaches to public morality encoded in legislation drafted by many European governments at the time. The crackdown on male sex work in the context of public bathhouses meant that individuals who, because of their sexuality and/or gender identity had no other avenues of economic integration, were now forced to ply their trade on the streets and out of their own homes.

Alongside top-down legislation, the swaying of public opinion against male homosexuality among the late Ottoman populace betrays an obsession with maintaining high reproduction rates among the Empire's Muslim population. As in the Turkish Republic, sex work among (cis) women was legal in the late Ottoman Empire within the framework of government-regulated brothels. In the Ottoman context, these were organised into Muslim and non-Muslim brothels; however, the overwhelming majority were run and staffed by non-Muslims, and contemporary observers speak of Muslim men's fetishisation of non-Muslim women. So widespread was this demand that some non-Muslim-majority areas of İstanbul had, since at least the mid-nineteenth century, boasted considerable numbers of unregistered non-Muslim sex workers, most of whom were Christian Romani women. This non-Muslim dominance of the sex trade posed a problem for ethno-nationalist lawmakers in the early Republic, who, fearing the dilution of pure Turkish blood through miscegenation, introduced stricter regulations on registered sex work. To avoid these restrictions, many Armenian-, Greek-, and Ladino-speaking sex workers went to work unregistered on the streets or in unlicenced brothels—precisely the spaces in which male and trans woman sex workers had begun operating. When we consider these factors simultaneously, a picture begins to emerge of a community with precisely the sort of linguistic "cocktail" from which the core vocabulary of *Lubunca* might have emerged.

A Cabaret of Cack (2017) is one trans person's loud and proud story of survival conveyed through humour and song, aimed in part at raising awareness about trans issues among the broader Turkish population. The play's author and only actor, Seyhan Arman, has peppered its script with *Lubunca*, attesting to its increasing visibility and accessibility. Yet, *Lubunca* has not always been meant for non-Queer ears, and this change of venue may signal the beginning of the end for *Lubunca* as we know it.

A Cabaret of Cack*

The curious and terrifying story of a tranny:

Pew-peeeewwwww

"HOW'D I TRANSITION?"

A CABARET OF CACK

One act, a bit of crack, a bit of palaver, and a smidge of love-charpering.

Author-Actor: Seyhan Arman

Director: Melisa İclal Yamanarda

* Poster obtained and reproduced with permission from the artist, Aslı Ersüzer.

Upon reading this poster for a theatrical production in İstanbul first staged in 2017, the average Turkish speaker might understand around 50 per cent of what was written there. Yet without understanding the words themselves, many will recognise them as belonging to the vocabulary of people who identify with particular sexualities or gender identities. Fewer still will know the name by which this vocabulary has come to be known: *Lubunca.*

The Turkish title of the play, *Küründen Kabare*, makes use of the *Lubunca* word *kür*, "cack, bullshit," of uncertain origin, but perhaps referring to the French-derived Turkish word for a popular pseudo-scientific remedy. According to interviews with Arman, it refers to the fact that so many trans individuals feel pressured to don "masks" to control interactions with the public by combatting dehumanising stereotypes.

The word *dönme*, rendered here with the offensive English "tranny," is a common and highly offensive Turkish slur which nevertheless has been reclaimed by many trans people. It is related to the verb *döndüm* used here in the phrase *"Ben nasıl döndüm?"* or "How did I transition?" referring both to the playwright's journey as a trans woman and her metaphorical return after immense personal setbacks.

The Turkish onomatopoeia *"Çiççuuuuuvvv,"* translated here as "Pew-peeewwwww," is most commonly a playful imitation of the sound of a gunshot, though it may also represent the snapping of a camera shutter. The former reading both evokes the rapid-fire wit of the play's stand-up-style comedy and conjures up images of the very real violence which many trans people in Turkey face, while the latter re-frames the unwanted attention of passers-by in the lens of the adoring paparazzi.

Several words in the translation are borrowed from England's Queer slang variety, Polari, which died out in the 1970s: "crack," from the Irish *craic*, "fun," and "palaver," meaning "nonsensical speech". They represent *Lubunca* words which, like their English counterparts, have made their way into general slang, though they are by no means universally understood. The first of these, *güllüm*, is a mutated form of Turkish *gül-*, "laugh," while the second, *madilik*, derives from the Armenian word մատը *madə*, "finger," through its metaphorical use in late Ottoman slang for "ruse, trick". The *Lubunca* word *tarizlik*, "yearning for love" (from the Romani *thar-*, "burn, spark") is less widespread, much like the Polari word "charper" for "search".

Since the early years of the Republic, *Lubunca* has, like all slang varieties, changed. Individual creativity is highly valued among its speakers, and some of its words come from Kurdish or English, which are widely accessible to Turkish speakers nowadays. Yet, *Lubunca* is a remarkable conservatory in terms of its elements that were derived from non-Muslim languages that are no longer widely spoken in Turkey. This conservation is no doubt a product of *Lubunca's* use as a semi-secret jargon, aimed at concealing unwelcome or illicit activities from outsiders, especially the authorities. While homosexuality and being transgender have never been illegal in Turkey, discrimination against trans and gay individuals has existed to varying degrees throughout its history. Like the theorised first users of *Lubunca*, individuals unwilling or unable to hide their identity continue to have trouble finding employment, and unregistered sex work and theft remain means of survival for some. It is precisely the inaccessibility of vocabulary from minority languages that has become a valuable element in the formation of *Lubunca* as a sort of Queer "cant" or criminal jargon, mirroring the incorporation of Romani and Yiddish words in the thieves' cant of other major European languages such as Dutch *Bargoens* or German *Rotwelsch*.

This cryptolectal aspect of *Lubunca* should not be overstated when explaining its overall function today, however. Many users of *Lubunca* employ only a few words at a time, enough that non-users could easily glean their meanings from the context, and *Lubunca* is also spoken in private amongst members of the "in-group," i.e., groups of Queer people with varying degrees of fluency in *Lubunca* from whom there is neither a need nor an ability to hide. While trans sex workers remain the *sine qua non* of the *Lubunca*-speaking community, gay and trans people who are more integrated into mainstream society may also maintain some degree of fluency concomitant with the time they spend interacting with them and one another. Since the early 2000s, *Lubunca* has even been used by Queer rights organisations and university clubs. This in-group use of *Lubunca* reflects its role as an integral part of the linguistic habitus of certain Queer spaces where *Lubunca* is a way of building rapport between members of the Queer community and of maintaining social hierarchies within it. A large part of *Lubunca*'s vocabulary is dedicated to insults based on gender identity, sex roles, and insufficient knowledge of the Queer world, affording trans sex workers a degree of power in their interactions with more "casual" speakers.

That *Lubunca* should appear on a poster for a stage play open to the public in the heart of İstanbul would have been unimaginable for its originators, but it is a testament to its transition from secret jargon to linguistic identity marker. *A Cabaret of Cack* is proof that the increased visibility of Queer people in Turkey has meant greater familiarity with *Lubunca* among non-Queer people. In the case of other Queer slang varieties, such as Polari in England, greater publicity has gone hand-in-hand with the gradual disappearance of a distinct Queer jargon altogether. Whether the same fate awaits *Lubunca* remains to be seen.

Select Bibliography

Kontovas, Nicholas. "Lubunca: The Historical Development of İstanbul's Queer Slang and a Social-Functional Approach to Diachronic Processes in Language." Master's thesis, Indiana University Bloomington, 2012.

Kyuchukov, Hristo, and Peter Bakker. "A Note on Romani Words in the Gay Slang of İstanbul." *Grazer Linguistische Studien* 51 (1999): 95–98.

Matras, Yaron. *Romani: A Linguistic Introduction*. Cambridge: Cambridge University Press, 2002.

Schick, İrvin Cemil. "Three Genders, Two Sexualities: The Evidence of Ottoman Erotic Terminology." In *Sex and Desire in Muslim Cultures: Beyond Norms and Transgression from the Abbasids to the Present Day*, edited by Aymon Kreil, Lucia Sorbera, and Serena Tolino, 87–110. London: Bloomsbury, 2020.

Wyers, Mark David. *"Wicked" Istanbul: The Regulation of Prostitution in the Early Turkish Republic*. İstanbul: Libra Kitapçılık ve Yayıncılık, 2011.

Yüzgün, Arslan. *Türkiye'de Eşcinsellik (Dün, Bugün)*. İstanbul: Hüryüz Yayıncılık, 1986.

96
The Return of Local Democracy: The CHP and the İstanbul Metropolitan Municipality

Kerem Öktem

The 2019 local elections constituted a critical juncture in Turkey's history of autocratisation and democratic pushbacks. Despite several instances of manipulations, the İstanbul mayoral candidate of the Republican People's Party (*Cumhuriyet Halk Partisi*, CHP) and other opposition parties, Ekrem İmamoğlu (1970–), won a narrow victory over Binali Yıldırım (1955–), the candidate of the Justice and Development Party (*Adalet ve Kalkınma Partisi*, AKP) and former prime minister, on 31 March 2019. The next morning, İstanbulites nevertheless woke up to a city that had been adorned with posters celebrating the victory of Binali Yılıdırm. Upon the prompting of the government, the Supreme Election Board decided to hold a rerun of the vote in İstanbul in June. This time, the CHP candidate won with a significantly larger margin, forcing the AKP to grudgingly admit defeat. Ekrem İmamoğlu was then sworn in as the Metropolitan Mayor of İstanbul.

In the ensuing years, the İstanbul Metropolitan Municipality (*İstanbul Büyükşehir Belediyesi*, İBB), a massive apparatus with approximately 50,000 employees, became the flagship for the opposition's political counterproject to the AKP's Islamist conservatism and Erdoğan's neo-patrimonial authoritarianism, creating niches of freedom under conditions of deepening autocratisation. İstanbul and the ten metropolitan municipalities run by the CHP constituted a power base from which the party was able to accrue expertise, experiment with novel social and cultural policies, create new cadres with government experience, and launch its challenge to the incumbent at the national level. The images presented below, which are from a publication put out by the Metropolitan Municipality, the *İstanbul Bülteni*, provide an empirical basis for an examination of the changes in ideology and policy that took place since the CHP's victory in the 2019 elections.

*December 2017 and September 2022 issues of the İstanbul Bülteni**

***

Published by the Metropolitan Municipality with a print run of 200,000, the *İstanbul Bülteni* is distributed for free in the city's public transport network. Its history dates back to 2007 when AKP mayor Kadir Topbaş (1945–2021) launched it as a means of informing citizens about the government's policies before the July 2007 national elections at a time when a significant segment of the national media was critical of the AKP government. Its publication continued after Topbaş's forced resignation in September 2017 and replacement with AKP appointee Mevlüt Uysal (1966–). After a brief hiatus following the election of Ekrem İmamoğlu in June 2019, the *Bülten* appeared again in September 2019 with a new editorial team. The journal has a major multiplying function: it provides content that is disseminated across a media network extending from websites to television stations whose programs are broadcast to more than 15,000 screens in public transport vehicles and reach around 3.6 million daily transport users in the greater metropolitan area of İstanbul.

The two issues shown here reflect the distinct worldviews of the country's two major political parties and current political traditions: the AKP with its roots in political Islam and neoliberal authoritarianism on the one side, and the CHP with its Kemalist background and

---

* İstanbul Metropolitan Municipality, İstanbul 2017 and 2019. Reprinted with permission from the İstanbul Metropolitan Municipality, 2021.

its attempts, under chairman Kemal Kılıçdaroğlu (1948–), to transform itself into an inclusive social democrat party on the other.

The cover of the July 2017 issue shows a photo from the opening ceremony of a metro line on the Anatolian side of İstanbul. At the centre stands President Recep Tayyip Erdoğan (1954–). On his left is Binali Yıldırım, former prime minister and the unsuccessful AKP candidate for the office of metropolitan mayor in the June 2019 elections. Situated to his right are Mevlüt Uysal, the interim mayor, and Berat Albayrak (1978–), who at the time was the minister of energy and natural resources, but more importantly, Erdoğan's son-in-law, who had been slated for higher office until he committed a number of severe policy blunders during his tenure as finance minister which led to his demotion and eventual departure from politics.

The photo summarises the workings of the AKP regime at the time. The men on the cover of the municipality's journal, with the exception of the appointed AKP mayor, are not local politicians but actors in national politics who do not have a constitutional role in the city's politics. They are depicted at the opening ceremony of a metro line, and hence a major construction project built by companies operating within the immediate circle of President Erdoğan's neo-patrimonial politics of economic favours. The stellar rise and fall of Erdoğan's son-in-in-law is the epitome of the personalised nature of AKP politics and the replacement of merit-based bureaucratic government with a system of obedience and reverence to the leader, who is often referred to as "*Reis*" (leader).

The themes and images used in the *Bülten* after the coup attempt of July 2016—a key rupture and an accelerator of the AKP's autocratisation—and then the resignation of the elected mayor, Kadir Topbaş, show a clear preference for authoritarian symbolism. In many of them, we see Erdoğan addressing large crowds waving Turkish flags, commemorating the "martyrs of 15 July," or images from construction sites and large infrastructure projects such as İstanbul Airport and the "*Kanal İstanbul*" project, representing the late AKP regime's reliance on the construction sector and rent-generation. One cover is devoted to Sultan Abdülhamit (1842–1918), a poster child of political Islam in Turkey.

On this cover, as was the case with most of the other cover pages of the *Bülten* in this period, women are largely absent. Conservative policies on gender have been part and parcel of the AKP's politics, and of political Islam, from its inception. However, it was particularly after the 2016 coup attempt that women in positions of authority disappeared from the pages of the *Bülten*.

The second cover, which is from September 2022, shows an image of one of the many flagship projects the CHP municipality developed after it came to power in 2019, City Eateries (*Kent Lokantaları*). These are low-priced restaurants which the İmamoğlu administration opened in low-income neighbourhoods and close to universities to provide students and residents with affordable, healthy food choices. As with many other social projects launched by the municipality—such as public kindergartens and women's support centres in the most disadvantaged neighbourhoods, and an app by means of which donors can pay the utility bills of people in need—City Eateries go beyond the provision of public services and aim to empower marginalised segments of society. As part of a chain of nine such venues, the restaurant's Bağcılar branch depicted here is run exclusively by women.

Women in positions of authority have been prominently placed on many of the cover pages of the *Bülten* published during İmamoğlu's administration. Several issues have presented news stories concerning the municipality's female decision-makers, such as the directors of the department of rail services and the department of sea transport. On other covers, the mayor is depicted together with female metro drivers and firefighters who have joined the workforce following changes that were made in the municipality's hiring policy, which under the AKP had excluded women from such jobs. Other issues include themes and actors that were missing from the cover pages created under earlier administrations, such as children at new city kindergartens, students moving into their new municipality-run dormitories, and, on national holidays, photos of Mustafa Kemal Atatürk.

***

The cover pages, as well as the content, of the *İstanbul Bülteni* provide insights into the ideological and political frameworks of the respective parties in power, while also hinting at the larger political framework and the transformations it has undergone. When the journal was launched in July 2007, its aim was to reach out directly to the public and circumvent the mainstream media and state apparatus, which eyed the AKP government with suspicion. Following the 2016 coup attempt and the subsequent resignation of the democratically elected AKP mayor, Kadir Topbaş, it became one of many government-funded propaganda outlets that disseminated the nationalist discourse of "one nation, one flag, one homeland, one state," often depicted against the backdrop of the "Rabia sign" of the Egyptian Muslim Brotherhood and against the "internal and external enemies" of the AKP regime. This framing was complemented with coverage of major building projects and advertorials for rent-generating urban transformation projects. Ironically, after the mayoral elections of 2019 the *Bülten* resumed its original role as an alternative to an unsympathetic mainstream media.

There are, however, some important differences. When the bulletin returned to İstanbul's metro stations and ferry piers in September 2019, it did so under conditions dominated by an intensifying autocratic regime under which more than 90 per cent of all media are owned by government cronies. Particularly in İstanbul, the *Bülten* has made a difference for millions of daily commuters thanks to the publication of its content on television screens in public transportation vehicles. It is one of the few widely broadcast channels of communication which the CHP has mobilised to present its counterproject to the AKP regime.

The Metropolitan Municipality under Ekrem İmamoğlu has been able to develop a wide range of policy initiatives with considerable societal impact and create the necessary funds for their realisation despite continuous interference and harassment by the central government and councillors representing AKP-run districts in the city parliament, where the opposition remains in the minority. These initiatives range from student loan programs to building and running student dormitories—not only with the aim of easing the student housing crisis, but also to create alternatives to government-connected religious foundations—and to the building of dozens of new libraries, cultural centres, and theatres, particularly in disadvantaged neighbourhoods with limited cultural infrastructure, which make it possible for residents to socialise in places other than mosques and shopping centres, the two preferred semi-public spaces of the AKP's Turkey. It is important to bear in mind that a significant segment of İstanbul's electorate, almost half of its voters, eyed this shift in approach with suspicion and continue to support the AKP.

The opportunity to create, run, and publicise a counterproposal to the authoritarian neoliberalism and Islamist politics of the incumbent is not usually available to opposition parties in competitive authoritarian regimes. There was already another such example of municipalities realising a political and cultural counterproposal to the governance model of the AKP that was brutally aborted. Kurdish-run municipalities in the country's southeast were overseen by the Peoples' Democracy Party (*Hakların Demokrasi Partisi*, HDP) and its predecessors starting in the late 1990s. In the 2010s, attempts were made to create a framework of local autonomy with a strong emphasis on Kurdish and minority rights, multiculturalism, and women's empowerment, which contributed to a more inclusive and democratic environment in those cities. However, in order to prevent the further entrenchment of these municipal projects aiming for local autonomy, the AKP regime eventually suspended the democratic process in almost all Kurdish majority-populated cities and replaced the elected mayors, many of whom were incarcerated, with government appointees loyal to Erdoğan.

The 2019 local elections were a major turning point in Turkey's recent history. They made possible a transfer of power and a return to democracy at the local level, both in terms of the electoral process as well as with regard to policies and politics. They functioned as a laboratory for coordination between opposition parties which allowed the CHP to win, and that would serve as a blueprint for the cooperation of opposition parties in the 2023 national and presidential elections. Opposition-run municipalities also empowered the CHP and its allies on several other fronts. In İstanbul, as well as in the other ten metropolitan municipalities governed by the CHP, tens of thousands of new positions were created for cadres that found the opportunity to gain expertise and thereby build government capacity mirroring the AKP in the mid-1990s, which turned the İstanbul Metropolitan Municipality into a cadre factory for its march to power in national politics. The availability of new positions turned opposition politics into a space of opportunity for aspiring young politicians and political activists, for whom employment at institutions controlled by the AKP-dominated state had become impossible, and all of those changes are reflected on the cover pages of and the articles in the *İstanbul Bülteni.*

Select Bibliography

Esen, Berk, and Şebnem Gümüşçü. "Building a Competitive Authoritarian Regime: State-business Relations in the AKP's Turkey." *Journal of Balkan and Near Eastern Studies* 20, no 4 (2018): 349–72.

Esen, Berk, and Şebnem Gümüşçü. "Killing Competitive Authoritarianism Softly: The 2019 Local Elections in Turkey." *South European Society and Politics* 24, no. 3 (2019): 317–42.

Öktem, Kerem. "Dilemmas of Subnational Democracy under Authoritarianism: Istanbul's Metropolitan Municipality." *Social Research: An International Quarterly* 88, no. 2 (2021): 501–37.

Tansel, Cemal Burak. "Reproducing Authoritarian Neoliberalism in Turkey: Urban Governance and State Restructuring in the Shadow of Executive Centralization." *Globalizations* 16, no. 3 (2019): 320–35.

Taşkın, Burcu. "The 2019 Provincial Elections in Turkey: AKP's Struggle to Retain Power vis-a-vis a Revitalized CHP." *Regional & Federal Studies* 31, no. 3 (2021): 461–74.

97

A Pandemic, a Curfew, and a Resignation: The Politics of COVID-19 in Turkey

Einar Wigen

For Turkey, the COVID-19 pandemic of 2020–2023 was the worst such outbreak since the establishment of the Republic after the devastating effects of the Spanish Flu of 1918–1920. According to official figures released by the Ministry of Health, COVID-19 killed some 100,000 people in Turkey, but there is reason to believe that the number may be as high as 270,000. While many citizens of Turkey had reason to complain about political and economic issues in 2020 and matters got progressively worse in the following three years, the situation paled in comparison to the problems faced by the collapsing Ottoman Empire in the aftermath of the First World War. When the Spanish Flu erupted, the Ottoman government was already struggling with the fact that millions of its subjects had died or been displaced in the war- which likely compounded the impacts of the epidemic. Although both the Ottoman Empire's last sultan, Mehmed VI Vahideddin (1861–1926), and the Republic's first president, Mustafa Kemal Atatürk (1881–1938), had probably contracted Spanish Flu, the pandemic has largely been passed over in the historiography of the transition from the Ottoman Empire to the Republic of Turkey. While reliable figures for the number of fatalities in the areas held by the Ottoman government and then the Turkish authorities may not exist, if the global number of total deaths was approximately 50 million and the areas hit the worst were those with displaced populations and high levels of malnutrition, it is fair to assume that at least tens of thousands of people perished in Anatolia in those years. Nevertheless, the significance of those deaths seems to have been overshadowed by the urgency of everything else that was going on at the time.

Like elsewhere around the world, in Turkey the COVID-19 pandemic interrupted social life, battered the economy, and took a severe psychological toll on the population at large. Moreover, the crisis fanned the flames of social polarisation across the globe. One might expect that the situation in Turkey would be no different, as Turkish politics tends towards the dramatic, the tabloid, and the spectacular, partly because the country has long been embroiled in a "culture war" not unlike the one underway in the United States and some European countries in which seemingly trivial issues become politicised as polarising symbols of political belonging. Ever since the Justice and Development Party (*Adalet ve Kalkınma Partisi*, AKP) rose to power in 2002, Recep Tayyip Erdoğan (1954–), the party's co-founder and leader, and his fellow party members have regularly used populist tropes to garner support. Given that situation, it might have been expected that a crisis as grave as the pandemic would have further exacerbated polarised political tensions, but that did not happen. Instead, people from across the political spectrum went about the pandemic with their usual trade-offs between individual health anxieties, begrudging acquiescence, and low-level resistance against government impositions.

When not taken up in the context of populism and mediatised crises, the longer-term history of the Turkish state is often talked about by characterising it as being technocratic. The pandemic illustrated that such approaches are not entirely wrong. The Ministry of Health was among the first ministries to be established in 1920, even before the proclamation of the Republic. In its 103 years of existence, the Turkish Ministry of Health has had a medical doctor as minister for all but eight years and two months and health policy is one of the areas of governance where the Turkish state still tends towards technocracy and a rare sentiment of "we're all in this together". This is not to idealise Turkish healthcare, but merely to note that the formulation of public health policy during the pandemic tended towards the application of expertise and for generalist politicians to quietly approve of the opinions of the experts rather than seek attention for themselves by voicing dubious theories about how to best prevent infections, treat the sick, or weigh in on the issue of whether vaccines are effective or safe. Instead of using the pandemic for political gain, President Erdoğan seemed to leave the handling of the pandemic to the Minister of Health, Fahrettin Koca (1965–). While far from being an expert in public health or epidemiology, in the political tradition of the Republic of Turkey, Koca is still a medical doctor. In late March 2020, the Turkish government announced that various restrictions would be imposed, much like the ones put into place in other parts of the world. Politics at the time focused on minute details and the restrictions placed on social and economic life, and as travel restrictions and fears of infection kept people at home, the economy suffered, a situation made all the worse by the fact that foreigners were prevented from travelling to Turkey, so tourism suffered immensely. The global supply crisis only served to worsen the situation, driving inflation up further.

Early on, public misgivings about the restrictions focused on then-Minister of the Interior Süleyman Soylu (1969–). On 10 April, Soylu announced that a curfew would be put into place in thirty-one provinces a mere two and a half hours later, causing a chaos. People thronged to grocery stores to stock up on supplies, creating the kinds of crowds that public health officials had been adamant about avoiding. After a wave of critiques erupted on social media, Soylu resigned from office, possibly as a bluff intended to increase his popularity, and his base of supporters did, in fact, issue calls for him to return to office. In the midst of this enacted political drama, President Erdoğan refused to accept Soylu's resignation, and the latter carried on as Minister of the Interior throughout the pandemic. The following text, which was written by Nebi Miş, an academic at Sakarya University, was published on the homepage of SETA, a think tank associated with the government.

*The Curfew and Soylu's Resignation**

The world is going through a difficult time due to the virus pandemic. Countries strive to overcome such challenges according to their capacities. While some of them have managed fairly well, some countries' governments have been crushed by the crisis. For example, the Western world's fragility has become ever more apparent.

Turkey is one of the countries that has managed to the fight against coronavirus well. [...] President Erdoğan's political leadership and experience, the rapid and effective decision-making mechanism of the Presidential System, the learning process of the tests and trials of crisis management, and the progress that has been made in infrastructure investments have all ensured that the fight against the virus has been managed well.

Which ministries carry the heaviest burdens varies with each crisis. In the fight against the pandemic, it has fallen more heavily on Minister of Health Fahrettin Koca, Minister of Treasury and Finance Berat Albayrak [Erdoğan's son-in-law] and Minister of the Interior Süleyman Soylu.

All three ministers have made great efforts to properly fulfil their responsibilities in the management of this crisis from its very beginning, and they continue to do so. [...]

In this context, the declaration of a weekend curfew in large cities was the correct decision. In hindsight, [matters] can be evaluated in different ways. [...] As Interior Minister Süleyman Soylu explained, the timing and announcement of the decision were carried out rationally, based on the experiences of Western countries.

In fact, the way that the curfew was publicly announced did not constitute a major problem. Situations similar to what happened on Friday night can occur in cities where millions of people live.

However, despite this being the case, Minister of the Interior Soylu unexpectedly resigned on Sunday night due to criticisms of the curfew, saying that responsibility lay with him [Soylu]. [He said he resigned] on the grounds that "the images that emerged, albeit for a limited time, did not harmonise with this perfectly managed process".

[...]

[Soylu] has gained the appreciation of the nation in many critical processes, especially in the fight against FETÖ and the PKK, and he has successfully ensured public security.

* Translated from the original Turkish in Nebi Miş, "Sokağa Çıkma Yasağı ve Soylu'nun İstifası," *SETA*, 14 April 2020, https://www.setav.org/sokaga-cikma-yasagi-ve-soylunun-istifasi/

Because of this, the people who were happiest about the announcement of his resignation were the supporters of terrorist organisations such as FETÖ and the PKK.[...] It is well-known that [President Erdoğan] does not look favourably upon the replacement of officials who hold important positions in such critical moments. Therefore, it was not difficult to predict that he would not accept Interior Minister Soylu's resignation in such a period.

That's what happened. President Erdoğan asked Interior Minister Soylu to continue with his duties.

[...]

***

Miş claimed that the Turkish presidential system, as well as Erdoğan's political experience and leadership style, had been sources of strength during the pandemic. The crisis called for quick and effective measures, and, as Miş argued, the system had been designed to provide exactly that. One of Recep Tayyip Erdoğan's main projects had been to transform the Turkish political system from that of a parliamentary republic, in which the president's role is largely symbolic and the prime minister runs the government, responsible primarily to the parliament, into a presidential republic in which the president is elected directly and appoints the cabinet which is answerable only to him. What the author of the above article did not mention, but which can be read between the lines, was how Erdoğan left such a major crisis for his ministers to handle, merely arbitrating on their performance. On the one hand, the episode of Soylu's resignation stands as a clear example of who bore responsibility for the management of policies directed towards dealing with the pandemic—which, in this case, were the ministers of health and the interior. On the other hand, this instance was revealing in terms of how it illustrated the inner workings of the Turkish presidential system. Ministers are responsible to the president, and it is up to the president, not the parliament as was the case before, to dismiss or appoint those ministers. As Erdoğan made clear, a minister may announce his resignation but, in the end, it is up to the president to accept or refuse that resignation.

Matters that are not deeply politicised or polarised do not lend themselves to easy tabloid exploitation. So, while the pandemic affected every aspect of life in Turkey and was placed at the centre of the mediatised political agenda, it nonetheless, remained largely unpoliticised, and the reasons for that are crucial for understanding Turkish politics. The text presented above is fairly typical in terms of how it combines the distinctly Turkish tendency of tying almost every political issue to matters of security and threats of terrorism, as was made evident by how the author interjected the issues of the PKK (*Partiya Karkerên Kurdistanê*, Kurdistan Workers' Party) and the FETÖ (*Fethullahçı Terör Örgütü*, Fethullah Terrorist Organisation) as well as the 15 July 2016 coup attempt into the discourse. Raising the subject of FETÖ is a distinctly partisan way of speaking about the followers of the Islamic preacher Fethullah Gülen (1941–). After Erdoğan and Gülen, who were erstwhile political allies, had a falling out in 2013, Erdoğan launched a massive campaign to purge Gülen's followers from the state bureaucracy, and some of those followers tried to seize power in a last-ditch attempt at a coup in the summer of 2016. Since the coup failed, 'FETÖ' is brought up whenever Erdoğan's supporters speak about threats to Turkish security, often in tandem with the long-standing separatist threat posed by the PKK. While 'FETÖ' is primarily the bugbear invoked by Erdoğan's supporters, Kurdish separatism, and the terrorist attacks that are irregularly perpetrated in its name, are seen as a threat across a much broader spectrum of the political landscape in Turkey.

Miş's text is also typical with regard to how it highlights Turkish successes, here lauding how well Turkey handled the pandemic and arguing that Soylu's measures were handled "in a rational manner taking into account the experiences of Western countries". In the context of the pandemic, it is crucial that Soylu's perceived mistake was not that he had mistreated the Turkish people or infringed on their rights as citizens, but that the decision had consequences which ran contrary to public health expertise. Whether or not Turkey actually handled the pandemic well is a debatable issue, but it is interesting to note that the people in power made almost no controversial statements regarding the pandemic worthy of appearing in the tabloids.

***

Unlike other populist leaders around the world, such as Donald Trump (1946–) in the United States, Jair Bolsonaro (1955–) in Brazil, Narendra Modi (1950–) in India, and Rodrigo Duterte (1945–) in the Philippines, who all used the pandemic to mobilise their supporters, Turkey's President Erdoğan was uncharacteristically toned down. Many people in Turkey were displeased and frustrated with the social restrictions that were imposed on them and the official figures that were announced about the spread of the coronavirus were met with criticism and a dose of scepticism, but for the most part those critiques did not result in vocal protests nor was the issue politicised on a broad scale.

Turkish politics in the twenty-first century have been marked by outrage upon outrage, bearing witness to an almost incessant string of crises, scandalous tabloid coverage, and populist interventions. There is more than enough material there to keep historians and social scientists busy for quite a while. But if we divert our attention solely towards controversies, we miss out on something crucial about how some issues are just regular, run-of-the-mill matters of decision-making pertaining to everyday concerns. This is not to say that it is not political, just that it is easy to miss that which is not controversial and there are instances where the Turkish state is non-exceptional. In hindsight, the statistics on cases and deaths during the pandemic indicate that Turkey as a country was somewhere in the middle in terms of how it was impacted by the pandemic. Moreover, the public health measures that were imposed were not out of the ordinary compared to those that were implemented in France, Italy, and Germany. Of course, this neither-great-nor-terrible situation still makes for an unpleasant narrative of a pandemic in which somewhere between 100,000 and 270,000 Turkish citizens died. However, focusing on points of controversy related to the pandemic would result in nothing more than dwelling on the non-representative, which runs the risk of giving the impression that Turkish politics are always and unavoidably tabloid-worthy and heavily contested.

Select Bibliography

Azak, A. Nalan, and Einar Wigen. "'Whatever They Say I Do the Opposite:' Vaccine Resistance in Turkey During the Covid-19 Pandemic." *Medical Anthropology* 41, no. 8 (2022): 778–93.

John Hopkins University Coronavirus Resource Center. "Mortality Analyses." Last updated 16 March 2023. https://coronavirus.jhu.edu/data/mortality.

Kim, D.G. "The Politicization of COVID-19 and Anti-Asian Racism in the United States: An Experimental Approach." *Journal of Experimental Political Science* (2023): 1–11. https://doi.org/10.1017/XPS.2023.16.

98
The Decade of Migration:
A Politics of Death or Life?

Sibel Karadağ

The 2010s coincide with a period in which Turkey opted to employ a construction-based investment and growth strategy with the intention of preventing an economic slowdown given the impending threat of mounting external debt and dwindling foreign investments in the country. While the Arab Spring of 2011 was turning into a civil war in neighbouring Syria, Turkey was witnessing the Gezi Park protests of 2013, which were in essence the culmination of social reactions against the government's increasing authoritarianism and rentier urban policies, and that moment was pregnant with dynamics that would shape the country's next decade. Due to Turkey's "open door policy," which was based on uncontrolled borders and a discourse of welcoming Muslim refugees, the number of Syrian refugees exceeded 1.5 million in 2014, while a year earlier that figure had been estimated to be around only 220,000. After initially being taken into camps located in border provinces as "guests," Syrian refugees scattered across the entire country and were registered on a provincial basis with "Temporary Protection" status, which started to be granted following the introduction of Turkey's first fully-fledged law on international protection in 2014 (LFIP). As a product of harmonisation with the European Union (EU) migration regime, the law hinges on temporary hierarchies in legal categorisations since it still applies geographical limitation to the 1951 Convention and accordingly provides refugee status only to arrivals from Europe. For non-Europeans, there are two main legal pillars: temporary protection status for Syrians and international protection status for non-Syrians who wait for third-country resettlement. The current magnitude corresponds to more than five million, including registered Syrians and people of other nationalities. Additionally, a third category includes a large spectrum of unregistered migrants whose number is unknown.

In 2015, when the number of Syrians rose to over 2.5 million, Turkey was holding one of the most critical elections in its history. In the aftermath of the June 2015 elections, the Justice and Development Party (*Adalet ve Kalkınma Partisi*, AKP) lost its parliamentary majority for the first time since it had come to office, while the pro-Kurdish Peoples' Democracy Party (*Halkların Demokrasi Partisi*, HDP) scored a record-high amount of electoral support. The following five months, from June until the repeat elections held in November, marked a historical and obscured period laden with suicide-bomb attacks, armed conflicts, and curfews in the south-eastern region of the country. Curiously enough, that five-month timespan concomitantly marked a climax in the mass movement of refugees from Turkey to Greece, referred to as a "refugee crisis" by the international community.

Accordingly, the EU put an urgent action plan into effect with the AKP government, which was re-elected in November 2015. In March 2016, the EU-Turkey Statement was proclaimed to stop unauthorised mobility into Europe. In fact, the Statement was not particular to Turkey but a part of the EU's broader migration and border governmentality scheme that had been in effect since the early 2000s, exercised by bilateral and multilateral agreements with neighbouring countries of origin, transit, and destination, and it was described by many as the externalisation or outsourcing of the EU's migration policies to its periphery. Turkey, having joined the EU's existing list of gatekeepers, was tasked with the mission of doing everything possible to protect the EU's borders in exchange for 6 billion euros. Over the past seven years, the Statement of 2016 has dramatically transformed the social and political landscape not only of Turkey and Greece but also the entire Aegean Sea and all EU countries.

Turkey's political regime was in a process of transition following the failed coup attempt of 2016 as thousands of people were being arrested and a series of military operations in northern Syria were taking place, and at the same time an export-based growth economy presented as the "Turkish model" was further entrenching the mechanisms of cheap labour and hyper-exploitation with an expanding informal labour market. In Turkey, as the world's largest refugee hosting country from 2015 onwards, millions of displaced people have become part and parcel of this cheap labour pool. Given the fact that the status of temporary protection for Syrians does not directly entail permission to work but is predicated on the mercy of employers, the fate of millions of refugees has been in the ruthless hands of the informal labour market. Nevertheless, the political economic reality of this model remained hidden and the whole process was packaged with Turkey's "humanitarian hospitality" approach, which was contrasted with "the cruelty of the West". However, the displaced population has become a trump-card in political and diplomatic negotiations between the two parties.

The Pazarkule event in 2020 marked a turning point in the trajectory of the Statement of 2016 and showcased the ways in which migrant bodies are instrumentalised by a wide range of governing techniques. In the evening on 28 February, following the death of thirty-four Turkish soldiers in Idlib in northwestern Syria, Erdoğan appeared on television screens and said that Turkey would no longer have to take care of and feed so many refugees, as "we opened up the gates".

Overnight, Turkey's rhetoric of welcoming refugees was put on ice and the Statement of 2016 was de facto abolished. Throughout the following days, thousands of migrants rushed to the Greek-Turkish border, driven by the promise of a free pass. Presented below is a photograph that was taken during the Pazarkule events that took place in March 2020.

Pazarkule border gate on the Greek-Turkish Border, Edirne, March 2020[*]

***

The photograph was taken in the buffer zone between Turkey and Greece, where thousands of migrants had gathered. As soon as news spread that Turkey had opened its borders, visuals of people embarking on a "journey to hope" from all corners of the country were broadcast live on screens. Images of people rushing to board the dozens of buses departing from various districts in İstanbul at the break of dawn began flooding in, and long queues of cars formed on the İstanbul-Edirne highway. Thousands of people who had left their homes and jobs to hit the road were directed to the Pazarkule border gate in Edirne. However, the scene they encountered at the border fell far short of their expectations, and those thousands of people buoyed by the hope of free passage into Europe came face to face with armed Greek police.

In the photograph, the sky is painted grey by the tear gas bombs shot from the Greek side beyond the buffer zone. The belongings left behind by the people who were caught between the tear gas bombs and plastic bullets during their struggle lay scattered around, including suitcases, backpacks, blankets, coats, shoes, and even baby carriages. According to reports, approximately 13,000 people had gathered at the Pazarkule border gate while many more tried to cross the border from different points of the Evros River. In the midst of the violence in the buffer zone, at least two men were killed and a woman remains missing after Greek

[*] Courtesy of photojournalist Murat Bay. The author would like to thank him for generously sharing the photo.

border forces reportedly fired live rounds and tear gas at the asylum-seekers and migrants. A few days later, the buffer zone was turned into a restricted humanitarian space, closed off to everyone except for authorised NGOs and governmental actors.

For weeks, people had fashioned their own makeshift shelters from the surrounding foliage, shrubbery, and blankets, setting up a camp in a bid to create a liveable habitat. Meanwhile, the Turkish authorities decried the situation as a "humanitarian crisis" at the doors of Europe, and initiated, albeit partial, humanitarian aid efforts. A field tent hospital was set up for those who had been beaten or otherwise wounded, mobile toilets were brought in; and food distribution began.

As the COVID-19 pandemic hit the country's agenda after March 11, the authorities launched efforts to persuade the thousands of migrants at the Pazarkule border gate to leave the area, offering them free transportation. In the last week of March, the most resilient group of nearly three thousand were forcibly removed from the area, the remaining tents were burned, and the space was completely evacuated overnight. The migrants, who were taken to and abandoned in various provinces, were the only people wandering the empty streets during quarantine.

***

The Pazarkule event put a complete damper on the humanitarian rhetoric, which had been invoked as a means of legitimacy since the 2015 migration movement. The body of two-year-old Alan Kurdi, whose lifeless body had washed up on the Turkish shore of the Aegean Sea and shocked the world, has now become as ordinary a phenomenon as what transpired in the Evros region. Since then, asylum applications in Greece have been frozen, systematic pushbacks in the Aegean Sea and Evros region have become a new routine, all civilian bodies in the area have been swept away, and search and rescue operations by NGOs on the Greek islands have been terminated.

While the devastating effects of the pandemic were still fresh, the ongoing economic downturn hit a new low, dealing a further blow to people's living conditions, which have been worsening since 2020. The inflation rate in Turkey has skyrocketed and become one of the highest worldwide, which in turn has led to the rapid impoverishment of citizens. Economic hardship has turned into social trauma, and society's collective anger has unfortunately been directed towards refugees. The untransparent and shifty migration and border policies implemented in the last decade have paved the way for the spread of misinformation about displaced populations. Consequently, the far-right Victory Party (*Zafer Partisi*), founded in 2021, has been actively promoting anti-refugee rhetoric and actions. Social media hashtags along the lines of "silent invasion" have gone hand in hand with an agenda of "send Syrians home" in a move that has been embraced by mainstream opposition parties. Consequently, the government has announced its "great return project," which foresees a new living space for one million Syrians in cities in northern Syria that are under Turkish control.

The Statement of 2016, which had initially aimed for the return of asylum-seekers to Turkey and the strengthening of Turkish borders with the EU, had first witnessed the de facto infringement of its objectives with the Pazarkule event, but it has now ended in plans to relocate Syrians in Turkey back to Syria with the support of EU aid and international funds. The project has been underway since January 2022 in the name of a "dilution and sweeping policy," aspiring for the "voluntary return" of Syrians and deporting undocumented migrants. In the meantime, the EU, which had promised visa liberalisation for Turkish citizens within the scope of the Statement of 2016, has now begun to systematically reject visa applications in line with figures showing that Turkish citizens constitute the third largest group of asylum applicants after Syrians and Afghans. On 6 February 2023, the Turkish-Syrian border region, which had hosted more than 1.5 million Syrians on the Turkish side alone, was hit by the devastating Kahramanmaraş earthquakes. Refugees have once again become homeless and started taking to the road again after ten years. Millions who were dispossessed overnight started to direct their anger and despair towards the refugees.

In today's age of migrations, the Pazarkule event is a manifestation of a striking example of how millions of bodies which are displaced, dispossessed, stuck in eternal waiting since they have permanently lost even the possibility of citizenship, and constitute one of the cheapest labour forces in the world under slavery-like conditions can be used as an apparatus in the game of politics. This is a period in which diplomatic negotiations and domestic policies are created over dehumanised and disposable bodies. While decades of conflict, war, and hunger in the Global South have driven a record number of people from their homes to an extent not seen since the Second World War, Turkey stands as a categorical case of this historical moment not only because it came to host the largest number of refugees in the world in just ten short years, but also because of the country's multilayered policies of instrumentalisation and arbitrary governing techniques that capitalise on displaced peoples.

Select Bibliography

Baban, Feyzi, Suzan İlcan, and Kim Rygiel. *The Precarious Lives of Syrians: Migration, Citizenship and Temporary Protection in Turkey*. Montreal: McGill-Queen's University Press, 2021.

İşleyen, Beste. "Transit Mobility Governance in Turkey." *Political Geography* 62 (2018): 23–32.

Karadağ, Sibel. "Extraterritoriality of European Borders to Turkey: An Implementation Perspective of Counteractive Strategies." *Comparative Migration Studies* 7, no. 12 (2019). https://doi.org/10.1186/s40878-019-0113-y

Kaşlı, Zeynep. "Migration Control Entangled with Local Histories: The Case of Greek-Turkish Regime of Bordering." *Environment and Planning D: Society and Space* 41, no. 1 (2022): 14–32.

Parla, Ayşe. *Precarious Hope: Migration and the Limits of Belonging in Turkey*. Stanford: Stanford University Press, 2019.

Saraçoğlu, Cenk, and Daniele Belanger. "The Governance of Syrian Refugees in Turkey: The State-Capital Nexus and its Discontents." *Mediterranean Politics* 25, no. 4 (2020): 413–32.

99
"Long ago, Enemies Raided Turkish Lands": Nationalism and Militarism in TV Series

Petra de Bruijn

Since the late 2000s, the military action series broadcast on Turkish television have become increasingly popular. These shows tend to be based on similar concepts, focusing on police or military special forces units carrying out secret missions usually against criminal or terrorist organisations. Often those organisations have Kurdish backgrounds, but American, British, Russian, "Zionist," and French agents sometimes also play a part. In some series, such international actors are depicted as working together with minority groups in order to re-establish the Treaty of Sèvres (1920), by means of which the Allied Powers divided up the Ottoman Empire into zones of influence after the First World War. As part of the treaty, Armenians and Kurds were promised independent states, and only part of Anatolia was left to the Ottoman Empire. Even in contemporary Turkish society there is a fear that international powers are ultimately seeking to destroy the Turkish state. In today's military action television series, which incorporate a great deal of special operations, fighting, hostage-taking, heroic rescues, and bloodshed, there are also storylines dealing with the private lives of soldiers and often there is a love story as well. Women, however, are not only depicted as taking on traditional roles; all of the squadrons in these shows have at least one female soldier, and villains can be female too. By combining tough masculine behaviour with female love and care for these brave soldiers, the shows appeal to male as well as female audiences.

The television channel Samanyolu, which was associated with the Gülen Movement, started off its broadcasts of military action series with the show *Tek Türkiye* (One Turkey), which ran from 2007 to 2011, and further developed the genre with series such as *Şefkat Tepe* (Compassion Peak 2010–2014) and *Sungurlar* (The Falcons, 2014–2015). Inspired by the box office success of the films *Nefes* (Breath, 2009), *Dağ* (Mountain, 2012), and *Dağ II* (Mountain II, 2016), mainstream television channels also started to produce and broadcast military action series. The most successful of these, in terms of scoring the highest ratings, were *Söz* (The Oath, 2017–2019) and *Savaşçı* (Warrior, 2017–2021). The show *Börü* (Wolf, 2018), produced by the same company as the *Dağ* film series, is aired on Netflix. The mafia series *Kurtlar Vadisi* (The Valley of the Wolves, 2003–2005, 2007–2016), which could be considered a predecessor for the genre, was the first show of its kind to directly refer to Turkish politics. *Kurtlar Vadisi* centred on a struggle with foreign enemies who sought to destroy Turkey's territorial integrity, and it advocated a religiously-inspired form of Turkish nationalism.

The focus on security forces and Turkish nationalism has found expression in these series on different levels, including their content, visuals, sound, characters, and props. All of them embrace the concept of Turkey as an indivisible nation-state that is the homeland of all Turkish citizens, regardless of the branch of Islamic faith to which they adhere or their ethnic background. As "good guys," Kurds are sometimes depicted as assimilated Turkish citizens. Although a universal type of Turkish nationalism comes to the fore in these series, there are still differences. The series that were broadcast by Samanyolu and *Söz* present a form of Turkish nationalism that is more clearly related to Muslim nationalism than *Börü* and *Savaşçı*, which depict a more secular brand of nationalism that places greater emphasis on the veneration of Atatürk. The dialogues, speeches, and action scenes in the series emphasise fighting and dying for the homeland, but the heroes are always Muslim, and most of the characters from other yet related ethnic backgrounds are depicted as being Turkmen, Azeri, or members of other Turkic groups; to date, non-Muslim characters have never been scripted as "good guys" and western-ers, Armenians, and Jews only feature as villains in the shows. The main symbols signifying nationalism are the Turkish flag and busts and portraits of Atatürk, and the more religiously-ori-ented series tend to focus on Ottoman sultans, especially Mehmet the Conqueror. All of these elements contribute to a broader agenda of nationalist propaganda in support of the Turkish state and its security forces. The first few minutes of the hundredth episode of *Savaşçı*, which was the first episode of the fifth and last season of the series and which aired in April 2021, are representative of how Turkic solidarity and nationhood are generally constructed in Turkish military television series. A translation of the transcript for that scene is presented below.

Warrior, Episode 100[*]

Long, long ago enemies raided Turkish lands and destroyed the tents that had been pitched there. Old men with beards that grew down to their chests were killed. One by one, the heroes, which were as wolves on the ground and eagles in the air, fell in action. Marriageable girls were enslaved. Babes suckling at their mothers' breasts were separated from their milk with knives and bayonets. All Turks were put to the sword. Only one child, one Turkish infant, was left alive as a warning [to others]. They cut his hands and feet and left him in the wilderness. God gives and takes life. A motherly she-wolf with a greyish-blue head saved the child, nursing him with her wolf's milk, and she protected and raised him. The blood of this last offspring of the Turks and the she-wolf became mixed. The Turks were reborn. They multiplied like wheat and grew as if sprouting from the soil; they rose as masters; they strained, shivered, and recovered. Forty generations later another Turkish child shouted, "You may hurt me, but you will not be able to kill me; you may spill my blood, but you will not be able to extinguish my life; you might take my soul, but you will not be able to stop me. I am the sword of the Turks. I am the revenge of the Turks. I am the warrior. You will not be able to kill this warrior."

[*] Translated from the original Turkish in *Savaşçı 100. Bölüm* (*Warrior*, Episode 100), which was produced by Limon Film. The producer and screenwriter was Süleyman Çobanoğlu, and the director was Eray Koçak. Broadcast by Fox TV on 10 April 2021. The timestamp for the section transcribed here runs from 00:02:06 to 00:03:47. https://www.fox.com.tr/Savasci/bolum/100

***

As retired Colonel Gündüz Göktürk, who is played by the well-known Turkish film star Ediz Hun, narrates this version of the fifth-century myth of the birth of the Turkic people in Central Asia, known as the Ergenekon epic, shots of him alternate with images depicting moments of Turkish heroism. His name, "Göktürk," which means "celestial" or "blue" Turk, is a reference to the first Turkic Khanates in Central Asia, which lasted from the sixth to the eighth century. When he mentions the raids that were carried out on Turkic lands, we see a map that is related to the Treaty of Sèvres showing how Anatolia would be divided up among the Allied Powers; when he narrates how the heroic Turkic warriors fell, we see footage from a battle that took place during the Turkish War of Independence; and when he talks about the suffering of women and children in ancient times, we are presented with scenes of displaced civilians and women sewing. The part of the story narrating how the wolf rescued the young boy is accompanied by footage of Atatürk surrounded by officers, and this scene ends with a shot of Atatürk, zooming in on his face, and then there is a flash, first of the eye of the wolf and later the whole face. When the story narrates how the ancient Turks were resurrected and went on to conquer the world, we see scenes of victorious Turks, first in the War of Independence and then more recent images from Turkish military operations, including a tank firing off rounds and civilians being rescued by and welcoming Turkish soldiers as liberators. The scene culminates with an image of a soldier planting the Turkish flag on a hilltop. Heroic music and realistic sound effects for the more recent footage accompany the fragment, as do the howling of wolves, horse hooves pounding the earth, and the roar of rockets.

The scene combines the veneration of Atatürk as the saviour of the Turkish nation with Turanism, a brand of Turkish nationalism that emphasises an imagined community of Turkic people living in Central Asia, ranging from the Uighurs in eastern Turkestan in today's China to the inhabitants of the post-Soviet republics of Kyrgyzstan, Kazakhstan, Uzbekistan, Turkmenistan and Azerbaijan and thence to the Republic of Turkey.

This fragment forms the start of a plotline that is set in Nagorno Karabagh, which in real life was "liberated" by Azerbaijan with the help of Turkish military experts, military equipment, and Islamist mercenaries during a short war that lasted from September to November 2020. Just as is the case in many military action series, *Savaşçı* integrates real-life events with its fictional narratives. The first seven episodes of the season (100–106) focus on Oktay, the son of Gündüz Göktürk, who is played by Tamer Karadağlı, another famous actor in Turkey. Oktay, a colonel, has been tasked with re-establishing the Turanian Army (*Turan Ordusu*), as it is called in the series and also as it is known by the general public in real life. It refers to the Organisation of Eurasian Law Enforcement Agencies with Military Status, an intergovernmental alliance of gendarmerie forces that was formed by Turkey, Azerbaijan, and Kyrgyzstan in 2013. Initially, Mongolia was a member as well, but withdrew at one point. The alliance aims to include more Central Asian Turkic nations as well.

While Colonel Göktürk is engaged in this secret mission, his twin brother Uzi, who had been kidnapped at birth and raised by the main villain, Mösyö (Monsieur or Pierre), as a professional assassin, murders his family. Monsieur is a spy who was hired by certain European and Central Asian secret organisations that seek to destroy the Turkish Republic. Monsieur seems to have a French background, although that is never mentioned explicitly. Hints are dropped suggesting that his female aide Yeva is of Central Asian or Russian descent, but her exact identity also remains unclear. Working together, they base their operations in Azerbaijan. Uzi and Oktay, in the meantime, are unaware of each other's existence. At one point, Göktürk is held hostage to make the Turks believe that he is the murderous traitor, but fortunately his old companion, the chief of the Kılıç (Sabre) Team, which is the main focus of the series, does not believe the allegations and comes to his rescue. The treason is revealed, the good brother shoots the bad one and, in the end, even the main villain gets killed.

***

The consumption of Turkish television series has grown exponentially over the years, and they take up more than half of broadcasters' programming time. It has been estimated that on average, Turkish viewers spent more than four hours a day watching television. As such, it can be surmised that episodes like this one reach a broad audience. These kinds of series reaffirm messages concerning the strength and sophistication of the Turkish military and make military operations in real life more palatable through fictional depictions of the life stories of soldiers and their families as they are pitted against traitors to the nation and international intrigues. In this case, Turkish audiences are "reminded" of their glorious Central Asian past and, through the juxtaposition of visual images of the heroic narrative of the War of Independence and the iconography of Atatürk with the wolf, they mark the recent resurrection of old symbols and ancient myths of Turkish nationalism that were emerging in the early twentieth century. In this way, the producers seek to make Turkish audiences feel proud of their military and the supposedly leading role it plays in uniting Turkic nations.

Select Bibliography

Bruijn, Petra de. "Deep State: Visual Socio-Political Communication in the Television Series and Serials of the Turkish Television Channel Samanyolu." *TV/Series*, no. 13 (2018): 1–22. https://journals.openedition.org/tvseries/2500

Çetin, Kumru, and Berfin Emre. "The 'Politicization' of Turkish Television Dramas." *International Journal of Communication* 8 (2014): 2462–83.

Öztürkmen, Arzu. *The Delight of Turkish Dizi: Memory, Genre and Politics of Television in Turkey*. London: Seagull Books, 2022.

Öztürkmen, Arzu. "'Turkish Content': The Historical Rise of the Dizi Genre." *TV/Series*, no. 13 (2018): 1–12. https://journals.openedition.org/tvseries/2406

Yanardağoğlu, Eylem, and Neval Turhallı. "From TRT to Netflix: Implications of Convergence for Television Dramas in Turkey." In *Television in Turkey: Local Productions, Transnational Expansion, and Political Aspirations*, edited by Yeşim Kaptan and Ece Algan, 189–204. Cham: Palgrave Macmillan, 2020.

100

That's Nobody's Business but the Turks': Rebranding "New Türkiye" for the New Century

Alp Yenen and Erik-Jan Zürcher

The year 2023 marks the centenary of the Republic of Turkey, not the centenary of "Turkey" as such. The term "Turkey" emerged from the Italian *Turchia* and Byzantine Greek *Tourkia*, which were used in reference to the realm of the Turks since the Seljuk conquest of Asia Minor in the eleventh century. It became widely used in major European languages throughout the history of the Ottoman Empire, with European contemporaries commonly referring to the "Turkish empire" as *la Turquie, die Türkei,* or *Turkey.* The use of "Ottoman Empire" was mostly restricted to academic circles. Arguably, the Ottomans only coined the term "Ottoman Empire" to describe the dynasty's governing polity in the nineteenth century to create a more European image of imperial sovereignty that legitimised the Sultan's rule over a multi-national population. Consequently, the Ottoman state had neither adopted the term "Turkey," nor was it opposed to being referred to as such in international politics. The only Ottomans to appropriate the term *"Türkiye"* (sometimes pronounced *"Türkiya"*) for their state and country were political exiles who were involved in constitutionalist opposition to the governance of the Sultan and his Grand Viziers. Both the "Young Ottoman" and later the "Young Turk" movements presented themselves in Europe as the champions of "Young Turkey," a name that echoed the liberal "young" movements that emerged in Europe after the founding of the Young Italy (*Giovine Italia*) movement in 1831.

When the centuries-old homelands of Turkish settlers in "European Turkey" were lost after the Ottoman defeats in the Balkan War of 1912–13, Turkish nationalists increasingly started to see the remaining territories in Thrace and Anatolia as the new homeland of the Turks. Nevertheless, contrary to common wisdom, the single-party regime of the "Young Turk" Committee of Union and Progress (*İttihad ve Terakki Cemiyeti,* CUP) that ruled the Ottoman Empire from the Balkan War to the end of the First World War remained committed to the Muslim-imperial sovereignty of the Ottoman Empire instead of following policies of Turkism. The same was true when defiant remnants of the CUP were mobilised under the Committees of the Defence of Rights (*Müdafaa-i Hukuk Cemiyetleri*) after the Ottoman defeat in the war. Their political vocabulary was focused on saving the Ottoman state and its Muslim nation, which were under threat of dissolution. However, as their political recognition grew in the years 1921–1922, Mustafa Kemal Pasha (Atatürk, 1881–1938) and his colleagues began referring to the counter-government of the Grand National Assembly in Ankara as the Grand National Assembly of Turkey (*Türkiye Büyük Millet Meclisi*). By 1923, this process was completed when the Treaty of Lausanne was signed, which effectively nullified international recognition of the Ottoman Sultan's government in İstanbul and recognised the independence of the new government in Ankara. On 29 October 1923, the "Republic of Turkey" (*Türkiye Cumhuriyeti*) was officially proclaimed.

The country's new official name was readily embraced by the international community, which saw in the Kemalist republic a bold experiment in Western-style modernisation. Numerous book titles from the 1920s and 1930s echoed the Kemalist message that a "new Turkey" had replaced the old one. For the first time in history, the way the country was referred to in the outside world and the name it officially used for itself coincided, although it was spelled differently in various languages.

For nearly a century, Turks took pride in the official name of their country. However, with the full-scale globalisation of the English language at the turn of the twenty-first century, certain Turkish nationalists became increasingly disturbed by the English word "Turkey". This discontent stemmed from the fact that several centuries ago, English merchants started calling large exotic birds (Meleagris) that originated from North America "turkeys," as they were similar to another bird that in earlier times they had imported through traders in (Ottoman) Turkey and hence referred to as "turkeys". However, turkeys are commonly depicted in comedic portrayals as unintelligent or clumsy birds, resulting in Orientalist and racist jokes about the country that dismayed Turkish nationalists. Turkish expatriates in North America lobbied in 1990 to change the English name of the country to "Türkiye" by way of a petition for which over 3,000 signatures were collected. The Turkish Language Association (*Türk Dil Kurumu*) gave its blessings for the name change at a congress that it held on 29 September 1990. Nevertheless, these initiatives did not gain significant diplomatic traction and were largely forgotten. However, with the introduction of internet search engines in the late 1990s, increased confusion over the names of the bird and the country contributed to a sense of dismay resulting from this lexical ambiguity.

In 2002, a discourse of a "new Turkey" emerged with the rise of the Justice and Development Party (*Adalet ve Kalkınma Partisi*, AKP) in opposition to Turkey's "old" Kemalist establishment. As the year 2023 drew near and along with it the centennial of the Republic, the AKP regime started to propagate its own vision of a new Turkey for a new century of the Republic. What few people expected was the return of the name issue. Hence, both the Turkish and international media reacted with astonishment when a declaration by President Recep Tayyip Erdoğan (1954–) was made public in the *Official Gazette* (*Resmi Gazete*) on 4 December 2021.

Using Türkiye as a Brand*

In light of its Millennia-year-old state tradition, the state of the Republic of Turkey has accepted as one of its fundamental duties the task of preserving and promoting the culture and values of our nation by carrying out distinguished and worthy endeavours befitting the ancient Turkish nation.

In the course of activities conducted at home and abroad on the basis of this understanding, great care has been taken with the values stemming from the deep-rooted history of the Turkish nation, and the brand "Türkiye" has been accepted as the flagship brand of our country in the national and international arena.

The term "Türkiye" represents and expresses the culture, civilisation, and values of the Turkish nation in the best possible way. In this regard, by adopting the phrase "Made in Türkiye" instead of "Made in Turkey" for our export products, which are a source of pride for our country in international trade, our products will be introduced with the "Türkiye" label and the entire world will be brought into contact with it. The aim is from now on to represent everything that our State [*sic*] and nation have accumulated over thousands of years under the "Türkiye" brand.

Within this framework, as part of efforts to strengthen the "Türkiye" brand, all necessary care will be taken with regard to using "Türkiye" instead of "Turkey," "Türkei," "Turquie," and the other versions therein for all activities and correspondences, particularly in official relations with other states and international institutions and organisations.

Please be informed accordingly and take the necessary actions.

3 December 2021

Recep Tayyip ERDOĞAN

PRESIDENT

* * *

The initial motivation behind the circular appears to have been a marketing ambition aimed at bolstering Turkey's growing achievements in the export sector. It calls for Turkish products to be rebranded and mandates the use of the Turkish name of the country for parties associated with or representing the state in their dealings with foreign institutions. In essence, it

---

* Translated from the original Turkish in Cumhurbaşkanlığı, "Genelge (2021/24; 03.12.2021): Marka Olarak Türkiye İbaresinin Kullanımı," *Resmi Gazete*, no. 31679, 4 December 2021. https://www.resmigazete.gov.tr/eskiler/2021/12/20211204-5.pdf

is an executive order intended to be implemented first and foremost within Turkey by the Turkish state. As a result, several ministries and state institutions have adopted the term "Türkiye" on their English-language internet pages.

In May 2022, the name-change campaign went global. Mevlut Çavuşoğlu (1968–), the Turkish minister of foreign affairs at the time, sent an official letter to the Secretary-General of the United Nations (UN), Antonio Guterrez (1949–), requesting "the use of Türkiye instead of Turkey for all affairs". The request was accepted, meaning that the name change went into effect at the UN starting from the day of the receipt of the letter, and the decision was then communicated to all member states. After the UN decision, the Presidency's Directorate of Communications (*Cumhurbaşkanlığı İletişim Başkanlığı*) launched a media campaign with the hashtag *#helloTürkiye*, promoting the "Türkiye" brand in multiple publicity campaigns on international media platforms and channels.

The circular is notable primarily because it sheds light on the nature of the Turkish state ideology in the early 2020s. The first part of the circular emphasises the ancient heritage of the Turkish nation and the longstanding state tradition among Turks. As such, Turkey is portrayed as the latest manifestation of a history of states that dates back thousands of years. This narrative establishes not only a continuity with the Ottoman past but also with numerous purported Turkic states that have risen and fallen since the fifth century AD. This portrayal has been characteristic of the way the AKP regime has presented the state since 2015, when Erdoğan appeared on the steps of his recently inaugurated grand presidential complex accompanied by sixteen soldiers wearing historical military costumes representing a chain of sixteen Turkic states. This construction of historical continuity serves the purpose of instilling national pride and positioning Erdoğan as a historical figure. This idea of the ancient and mythical origins of Turkey creates an ideological bridge between the neo-imperialist and Islamist nationalists of the AKP and the far-right, often pan-Turkist nationalists of the Nationalist Movement Party (*Milliyetçi Hareket Partisi*, MHP) at a time when Erdoğan is reliant on a coalition between these two currents to maintain his hold on power. Curiously, the emphasis on these mythical origins of Turkish statehood relegates the Republic of Turkey to a status of being just one among many. This is a remarkable shift because for a century, the "Republic" (*Cumhuriyet*) has been the central notion of the Turkish state ideology. The once-omnipresent official state acronym "T.C." (*"Türkiye Cumhuriyeti"*) that appeared on the records, registers, and documentation of all state institutions has been removed or replaced with "Türkiye" by the AKP in recent years. Hence, with the name change, Erdoğan has also distanced his ideological discourse from the Kemalist cult of "Republicanism".

The other remarkable aspect of the circular is its use of marketing terminology. The text introduces "Türkiye" as a brand (*marka*) and initially mandates its use on Turkish export products, only later extending its use to official communications. The introduction of "Türkiye" as a brand closely follows standard marketing principles, emphasising the "core values" that consumers are supposed to associate with the brand and then applying it to various product categories. The labelling of the brand ("Made in Türkiye") on a range of export products, which in the case of Turkey primarily consists of cars, spare parts, white goods, food products, textiles, ceramics, and more recently weapons technologies, aims to communicate to the consumers of these goods the inherent "greatness" of Turkish culture and history. The final paragraphs of the circular reflect the transformation of the country itself into a product that needs to be marketed. "Türkiye" as a single flagship brand (*çatı markası*) will thus be used to distinguish not only its consumer products, but also the activities of the Turkish state, thereby enriching all of them with positive associations. Reflecting the marketing mindset of the name-change campaign, Çavuşoğlu referred to the UN's approval of "Türkiye" as a *"tescil"* in a Twitter message, a term commonly used for registering industrial trademarks. The ease with which the circular draws an analogy between the value of consumer goods and the image of the nation-state, using marketing principles in the realm of international relations, highlights a significant aspect of contemporary Turkey. Not only has neoconservative nationalism become a hegemonic ideology, but neoliberal capitalism has also come to underscore Turkey's trajectory in the 2020s.

***

The renaming of towns, cities, or entire countries is not uncommon in international politics. Often, such moves have occurred within the context of decolonisation, where countries have rejected names that were imposed on them by European imperialists (e.g., Rhodesia to Zimbabwe) or normalised transcriptions that were imposed during the age of imperialism (e.g., Bombay to Mumbai, Peking to Beijing). Nationalism and nation-building have also driven name-changing campaigns, as in the change from Persia to Iran in 1935 and more recently in the Greek-Macedonian name dispute over "North Macedonia". Turkey was also keen on nationalising place names. During the years of the early Republic, thousands of villages that had Greek, Armenian, or Kurdish names were redesignated using Turkish names without drawing significant international attention. However, one name change that did garner international scrutiny occurred when the Turkish government made an announcement in March 1930 mandating the use of Turkish place names for telegrams and mail addressed to Turkey; from that point onward, "İzmir" had to be used instead of "Smyrna," and only "İstanbul" was deemed acceptable, although "Constantinople" was still widely used internationally. With the exception of Greece, however, the international community quickly accepted these name changes, as highlighted in the lyrics of the 1953 hit single "Istanbul Not Constantinople" by The Four Lads with the line, "That's nobody's business but the Turks.'"

Erdoğan's 2021 circular did not officially declare a name change but rather demanded the use of the Turkish name of the country in international trade and foreign relations. However, the request made through the United Nations for the exclusive use of the Turkish name in the international arena did result in a *de facto* name change, as none of Turkey's international partners were using that version at the time. This can be considered a significant and somewhat radical step that goes even further than name changes like the introduction of Czechia as an official shortened form in 2016. Many countries like Germany, Egypt, India, Japan, and China, for example, allow for the use of international descriptors that differ from the names of the countries in the local language (in these cases *Deutschland, Misr, Bharat, Nippon,* and *Zhōngguó,* respectively). The shift from Turkey to Türkiye is a political strategy, not a solution to a toponymical problem.

The insistence on the use of "Türkiye" in all languages seems to go beyond the lexical ambiguity of English but probably still stems from a perceived need to avoid associations of the country with the name of an ugly, ungainly bird. So far, the use of "Türkiye" has largely remained limited to interactions with Turkish state officials and has not yet permeated third party communications, international academia, or the vernacular of different countries. Since the name change from Turkey to Türkiye is part of the AKP's broader strategy to assert a revamped national identity and cultivate a positive image of the country during a period of economic and political crisis, the use of Türkiye in social media, journalism, and academia often indicates a favourable attitude towards the AKP's policies. Either way, the change marks one of the key moments in the unmaking of the old Turkey in favour of a new Türkiye in the country's new century.

Select Bibliography

Arat, Yeşim, and Şevket Pamuk. *Turkey Between Democracy and Authoritarianism.* Cambridge: Cambridge University Press, 2019.

Bozkürk, Batu. "30 Yıl Sonra Yeniden Hello Türkiye!" *Deutsche Welle,* 27 January 2022. https://www.dw.com/tr/30-y%C4%B1l-sonra-yeniden-hello-t%C3%BCrkiye/a-60564308.

Jäschke, Gotthard. "Vom Osmanischen Reich zur Türkischen Republik: Zur Geschichte eines Namenswechsels." *Die Welt des Islams* 21 (1939): 85–93.

Uluç, Doğan. "Hindi ile Adaşlığa Son Verelim." *Hürriyet,* 11 August 2009.